Handbook of Compliance & Integrity Management

Handbook of Compliance & Integrity Management

Theory and Practice

Edited by

Prof. S.C. Bleker-van Eyk

R.A.M. Houben

Wolters Kluwer

Published by:
Kluwer Law International B.V.
PO Box 316
2400 AH Alphen aan den Rijn
The Netherlands
Website: www.wolterskluwerlr.com

Sold and distributed in North, Central and South America by:
Wolters Kluwer Legal & Regulatory U.S.
7201 McKinney Circle
Frederick, MD 21704
United States of America
Email: customer.service@wolterskluwer.com

Sold and distributed in all other countries by:
Quadrant
Rockwood House
Haywards Heath
West Sussex
RH16 3DH
United Kingdom
Email: international-customerservice@wolterskluwer.com

ISBN 978-90-411-8818-2
e-Book: ISBN 978-90-411-8819-9
web-PDF: ISBN 978-90-411-8820-5

List of Contributors

Prof. S.C. Bleker-van Eyk

Sylvie Bleker-van Eyk (1960) is professor at the post-doctoral Executive Master's program in Compliance & Integrity Management of the VU University Amsterdam. Sylvie studied international law and Constitutional Law at the University of Tilburg (The Netherlands). She wrote her Ph.D. on the OECD Decisions & Guidelines for Multinational Enterprises (1995). She is also a Senior-Director at the Forensic Services department of PriceWaterhouseCoopers in the Netherlands. She has ample experience in both financial industry and manufacturing, as well as the energy sector. Her expertise lies with compliance and integrity management in general and is a renowned expert on Anti-bribery and corruption, export controls, crisis management, extraterritorial jurisdiction. Direct experience with negotiation with US authorities (OFAC, BIS, DDTC, DoJ).She served on the executive C-level as the Chief Risk and Compliance Officer at Stork (Stork Technical Services (oil) & Fokker Technologies (aviation)) and as the Chief Risk and Compliance Officer at Ballast Nedam (construction). Sylvie is founder of the Dutch Chapter of Transparency International in 1999 and has operated in various commissions such as vice-chairman of the Dutch Investigative Board on Governmental Integrity (until 2013); chairman of the Dutch Investigative Board on Corporate Integrity (until 2014) and Chairman of the Dutch NEN working group on the ISO 19600 Compliance norm.

R.A.M. Houben

Raf Houben (1960) is Coordinator of and Lecturer at the post-doctoral Executive Master's program in Compliance & Integrity Management of the VU University Amsterdam. Raf studied international and commercial law at the University of Leiden and began his career as lawyer at an Amsterdam law firm. He writes a doctoral thesis at the Faculty of Law of the University of Amsterdam as an external doctoral student. Raf is also Manager Compliance & Security at HDI Global SE, the Netherlands. He has ample experience in the financial services industry as specialist on the areas of compliance & integrity, (corporate) governance and financial supervisory law. He served as Compliance and Governance specialist at ASR Nederland, as Senior Manager at Deloitte Enterprise Risk Services, as Compliance Manager Benelux at Bank of America, as Head of Compliance at SNS REAAL and as international and senior supervisor at De Nederlandsche Bank NV and the Central Bank of Aruba. He has written several articles about compliance and integrity themes. He is editorial board member of the Jaarboek Compliance and was chief in editor and editorial board member of the Tijdschrift voor Compliance. Raf headed for several years the Dutch Association of Compliance Officers as chairman and is winner of the NCI Compliance Award 2005 and co-winner in 2008.

R. van Altena RA

Robert van Altena (1965) is Lecturer at the post-doctoral Executive Master's program in Compliance & Integrity Management of the VU University Amsterdam. Robert studied Economics and postgraduate Accountancy at the University of Amsterdam and is chartered accountant (Register Accountant, RA). Robert is partner with PricewaterhouseCoopers Accountants N.V. and acts within PwC in the field of Risk Assurance. His main focus is on advising financial institutes with regard to risk and compliance, taking into account governance frameworks, IT-systems, RegTech innovation, data analytics and human behavior.

F.R.P.M. van der Grint

Frans van der Grint (1962) is Strategy Director and advises businesses on a wide range of strategic communication challenges. Focusing on Financial and Corporate Changes and Crises, he is acting as a strategic communication consultant to Boards of Directors and Supervisory Boards in transaction, litigation, financial, campaigning and publicity issues. Frans van der Grint supervises Hill + Knowlton's Financial + M&A Practice in Europe, leading teams involved in national and cross border transactions. He handles campaigns in complex and influential cases, mobilizing a wide range of stakeholder groups. He is member of Hill + Knowlton's European Client Advisory Board. Frans is a renowned management coach and received highly acclaimed European and international awards for impactful campaigns. In 2016 he was elected 'Best PR Consultant in M&A' for the fifth consecutive year. Frans became CEO of Hill + Knowlton Nederland in 2000 and stepped back in 2007 to become Strategy Director. He previously held a board position at Nutricia Nederland and was Director Communications at multinational company Numico. He was Group Director Marketing Communication when he first joined Hill + Knowlton and Group Manager at the JRPM PR consultancy. Before his move into consultancy, he was a newspaper journalist for six years. Frans holds various board and other positions in associations and foundations, both professionally and privately. He is a regular speaker at seminars and universities.

Prof. W. Huisman

Wim Huisman (1970) is a professor of criminology and the head of the School of Criminology of the VU University Amsterdam, the Netherlands. The VU School of Criminology offers graduate and undergraduate programs in Criminology, which have about 700 students. Wim teaches criminology as well as course on white collar and corporate crime. The research focus of Wim Huisman is on the field of white collar crime, corporate crime, fraud, corruption and regulatory compliance. Recently funded research projects focus on criminal careers of white collar offenders, corporate complicity to gross human rights violations, causes of corruption, corporate environmental crime and the prevention of food fraud. Wim Huisman is founder and board member of the European Working Group on Organizational Crime (EUROC) of the European Society of Criminology. Currently, Wim is chair of the Netherlands Society of Criminology. He has been a visiting professor at Griffith University, Brisbane, Australia, Northeastern University, Boston, USA, and Mekelle University, Ethiopia.

T.A.H.M. van de Laar EMoC

Tom van de Laar (1982) is Lecturer and PhD student at the post-doctoral Executive Master's program in Compliance & Integrity Management of the VU University Amsterdam. The topic of his PhD dissertation is the interaction patterns in destructive leadership and to what governance these patterns causing destructive leadership can be prevented. Tom studied criminal law, European and international law at the University of Maastricht and completed the Executive Master in Compliance & Integrity Management at VU University Amsterdam. Tom is Senior Manager at Deloitte Risk advisory in the Netherlands. Before starting to work at Deloitte and VU University, he worked as an attorney at law specializing in corporate criminal defense, (internal) investigations and compliance related matters. Furthermore, he worked as a legal counsel and compliance officer for a Japanese bank. Tom has experience in both the financial industry and non-financial industry and has gained international work experience over the years (particularly Europe, the United States, Asia and Pacific). His expertise lies in fraud and white collar crime, anti-bribery and corruption, integrity management, customer integrity, sanctions and crisis management.

M.J. Osse

Marije Osse (1970) is lawyer and founding partner at Yieldlegal, a Dutch Law firm, located in Brussels, Belgium. She has over 18 years of experience in European and Dutch competition law and European Law, of which many years as partner at one of the largest Dutch law firms. Her extensive experience includes the representation of clients in EU and Dutch cartel investigations, the obtaining of merger clearances from the European Commission and Dutch regulators, and advising on cooperation agreements and various types of distribution networks. She also advises on and implements tailor-made compliance programs. She litigates before Dutch courts and the Court of Justice of the European Union. She is a member of the editorial staff of the Dutch healthcare magazine 'GZR-updates'. Her experience includes a wide range of sectors, such as life science & healthcare, the logistics sector, technology in the aviation and maritime sectors and the regulated postal sector. Her clients includes multinationals, medium sized companies and various trade organizations. Marije studied Law at the University of Utrecht, the Netherlands, and studied abroad at the University of Uppsala, Sweden and has previously worked at a law firm in Rome, Italy. She is a member of the Breda bar in the Netherlands and the Brussels bar (Belgium, EU-list).

Dr. M.M. Rietdijk

Marius Rietdijk (1964) is assistant professor Strategic Behavior Change at the VU University Amsterdam. Marius studied Clinical, Organizational and Social Psychology at the University of Amsterdam (UVA, The Netherlands). He wrote his PhD in Economics on Conditioning Organizations, examining the influence of reward and punishment on work performance (2009). He is European pioneer in Organizational Behavior Management (OBM), as both a scientific rigorous as practical relevant tool for increasing results and happiness, based on the theory of Ivan Pavlov. He is member of the Dutch Organization for Clinical Hypnosis and director of ADRIBA (Aubrey Daniels Research Institute for Behavior Analysis), a research and executive education center specialized in OBM. He has ample experience in leading behavioral change for measurable performance improvement within many sectors of the economy. In finance his interests are, apart from compliance and discretionary effort, changing investors' behavior and self-control. He is board member of diverse organizations, including an educational institute and a bank.

W. Seinen CIPP/E

Wouter Seinen (1973) is partner of the IP, IT & Commercial practice of Baker & McKenzie in Amsterdam. Wouter's practice focuses on data protection law and associated compliance matters, such as data security and data breaches. Wouter regularly assists national and international clients with respect to issues relating to the protection, compliant use and exploitation of data and digital assets. Internet related business, such as social media operators regularly seek his advice on compliance aspects of new services or business models prior to their commercial launch in the Netherlands. Wouter has worked in for IT, data driven and Internet companies for the past 18 years. He has a thorough knowledge of data protection law, and is often involved in research that touches on both the compliance side of the law as the fundamental rights that are the fundament of data protection laws and play a fundamental role in online legal issues including right to be forgotten, intermediary liability and IP infringement in on-line settings. Aside from advice to clients, Wouter also teaches on specialization courses of private institutions and he has contributed to tech law programs of various universities. Moreover Wouter works regularly on pro bono projects and projects for the legal community. Examples are the Citizen Lab study on reverse engineering and the revision of the IAPP textbook for the CIPP/E program after the GDPR was enacted. Wouter is also one of the founders and editors in chief of the leading tech law blog itenrecht.nl and the chairperson of the VIRA (the Dutch Computer Law Association).

Table of Contents

List of Abbreviations

ACM	Authority for Consumers & Markets.
AFM	Netherlands Authority for the Financial Markets.
Anti-Money Laundering Directive	Directive 2005/60/EC of the European Parliament and of the Council of October 26, 2005 on the prevention of the use of the financial system for the purpose of money laundering and terrorist financing 2005/60/EC, *OJEU* 2005, L309/15.
AP	Dutch Data Protection Authority.
Awb (Algemene wet bestuursrecht)	General Administrative Law Act.
Bgfo (Besluit gedragstoezicht financiële ondernemingen Wft)	Decree of October 12, 2006, containing rules relating to supervision of the conduct of financial undertakings (Decree on Supervision of Conduct of Financial Undertakings pursuant to the Financial Supervision Act), *Bulletin of Acts and Decrees* 2006, 520.
Bpr (Besluit prudentiële regels Wft)	Decree of October 12, 2006, containing prudential rules for financial undertakings that operate in the financial markets (Decree on Prudential Rules pursuant to the Financial Supervision Act), *Bulletin of Acts and Decrees* 2006, 519.
BW (Burgerlijk Wetboek)	Netherlands Civil Code.
CRD IV (Capital Requirements Directive IV)	Directive 2013/36/EU of the European Parliament and of the Council of June 26, 2013 on access to the activity of credit institutions and the prudential supervision of credit institutions and investment firms, amending Directive 2002/87/EC and repealing Directives 2006/48/EC and 2006/49/EC, *OJEU* 2013, L 176/338.

CRR (Capital Requirements Regulation)	Regulation (EU) No. 575/2013 of the European Parliament and of the Council of June 26, 2013 on prudential requirements for credit institutions and investment firms and amending Regulation (EU) No. 648/2012, *OJEU* 2013, L 176/1.
DDTC	Directorate of Defense Trade Controls.
DNB	De Nederlandsche Bank N.V.
DOJ	The US Department of Justice.
EBA	European Banking Authority.
EC	European Commission.
ECCN	Export Control Classification Numbers.
EIOPA	European Insurance and Occupational Pensions Authority.
ERM	Enterprise Risk Management.
ESMA	European Securities and Markets Authority.
EU	European Union.
FCA	(British) Financial Conduct Authority.
FCPA	(American) Foreign Corrupt Practices Act.
KSA	Dutch Gaming Authority.
KRI	Key Risk Indicator.
MAR	Regulation (EU) No. 596/2014 of the European Parliament and the Council of April 16, 2014 on market abuse (market abuse regulation) and repealing Directive 2003/6/EC of the European Parliament and of the Council and Commission Directives 2003/124/EC, 2003/125/EC and 2004/72/EC, *OJEU* 2014, L 173/1.
MAD	Directive 2003/6/EC of the European Parliament and of the Council of January 28, 2003 on insider dealing and market manipulation (market abuse), *OJEU* 2003, L 96/16.
MAD II	Directive 2014/57/EU of the European Parliament and of the Council of April 16, 2014 on criminal sanctions for market abuse (market abuse directive), *OJEU* 2014, L 173/179.
Mw (Mededingingswet)	Dutch Competition Act.

MiFID II (Second Markets in Financial Instruments Directive)	Directive 2014/65/EU of the European Parliament and of the Council of May 15, 2014 on markets in financial instruments and amending Directive 2002/92/EC and Directive 2011/61/EU, *OJEU* 2014, L 173/349.
MiFIR (Markets in Financial Instruments Regulation)	Regulation (EU) No. 600/2014 of the European Parliament and of the Council of May 15, 2014 on markets in financial instruments and amending Regulation (EU) No. 648/2012, *OJEU* 2014, L 173/84.
Nrgfo (Nadere Regeling gedragstoezicht financiële ondernemingen Wft)	Further Regulations on the Supervision of the Conduct of Financial Undertakings (Financial Supervision Act).
NVB	Netherlands Bankers' Association.
NZA	Dutch Healthcare Authority.
OECD	Organization for Economic Co-operation and Development.
OEE	Office of Export Enforcement.
OFAC	Office of Foreign Assets Control.
P+	Positive punishment.
P–	Negative punishment.
PDP Act	Personal Data Protection Act.
PEP	Politically Exposed Person.
Prospectus Directive	Directive 2010/73/EU of the European Parliament and of the Council of November 24, 2010 amending Directives 2003/71/EC on the prospectus to be published when securities are offered to the public or admitted to trading and 2004/109/EC on the harmonization of transparency requirements in relation to information about issuers whose securities are admitted to trading on a regulated market, *OJEU* 2010, L 327/1.
R+	Positive reinforcement.
R–	Negative reinforcement.
SEC	Securities Exchange Commission.
SIRA	Systematic Integrity Risk Analysis.
Solvency II Directive	Directive 2009/138/EC of the European Parliament and of the Council of November 25, 2009 on the taking-up and pursuit of the business of Insurance and Reinsurance, *OJEU* 2009, L 335/1.

SOX	Sarbanes-Oxley Act.
SSM	Single Supervisory Mechanism.
SSM Framework Regulation	Regulation of the European Central Bank of April 16, 2014 establishing the framework for cooperation within the Single Supervisory Mechanism between the European Central Bank and national competent authorities and with national designated authorities, *OJEU* 2014, L 141/1.
SSM Regulation	Council Regulation (EU) No. 1024/2013 of October 15, 2013 conferring specific tasks on the European Central Bank concerning policies relating to the prudential supervision of credit institutions, *OJEU* 2013, L 287/63.
STOR	Suspicious Transaction and Order Report.
TEU	Treaty on the European Union.
TFEU	Treaty on the Functioning of the European Union.
Transparency Directive	Directive 2004/109/EC of the European Parliament and of the Council of December 15, 2004 on the harmonization of transparency requirements in relation to information about issuers whose securities are admitted to trading on a regulated market and amending Directive 2001/34/EC, *OJEU* 2004, L390/38.
UCITS V Directive	Directive 2014/91/EU of the European Parliament and of the Council of July 23, 2014 amending Directive 2009/65/EC on the coordination of laws, regulations and administrative provisions relating to undertakings for collective investment in transferable securities (UCITS) as regards depositary functions, remuneration policies and sanctions, *OJEU* 2014, L 257/186.
UKBA	United Kingdom Bribery Act.
USFSG	US Federal Sentencing Guidelines.
USML	United States Munitions List.
VvV	Dutch Association of Insurers.
WED (Wet op de economische Delicten)	Economic Offenses Act.
Wft (Wet op het financieel toezicht)	Law of September 28, 2006, containing rules on financial markets and their supervision (Financial Supervision Act), *Bulletin of Acts and Decrees* 2006, 475.
WRR	Netherlands Scientific Council for Government Policy.

Foreword

Jean Frijns

The compliance discipline in companies and financial institutions has grown exponentially in recent years. A plethora of works on compliance have been published, the bulk of them concerned with 'flat' compliance (obeying rules) or the establishment of the compliance function. As an academic discipline, compliance is still in its infancy and, to put it kindly, is still developing.

Around 10 years ago the VU University Amsterdam took the initiative of introducing a post-doctoral program in Compliance & Integrity management to facilitate academic study of the subject and provide a scientific underpinning for the practice of compliance. The core aims of this program include conducting in-house research and bringing researchers together. This book is a result of these ambitions. Under the enthusiastic editorship of Sylvie Bleker and Raf Houben, the book provides a wealth of information on the expanding field of compliance as well as much yearned-for in-depth analysis.

This has proved most successful in Parts I and III of the work. Part I concerns human conduct and begins with a chapter by Sylvie Bleker in which she confronts us with the ethical dilemma whereby compliant behavior is not necessarily ethical. Think of Hannah Ahrendt's 'Banality of Evil,' for example. Bleker expressly distances herself from 'flat' compliance (defined as responsibility for obeying rules) and focuses her attention on the conduct dimension, thereby setting the tone for the ensuing chapters – a challenging but enriching assignment.

Part III concerns regulation and supervision and impresses with its analytical and hence critical approach to the existing practice of supervision. It continually asks why the current system prevails, particularly when alternatives such as greater trust in self-regulation or market discipline are possible. This is supported by a comprehensive study of the literature concerning the *raison d'être* of supervision and regulation, giving the reader access to important works of academic research.

In praising Parts I and III, I must not give the impression that Part II, concerning the Organization and Risk Management, and Part IV, with well-chosen chapters surveying the increasingly broad field of compliance, are any less worthy. They contain a wealth of information and provide an excellent overview of the field, making them an essential practical resource.

Alongside this commendation I would make one critical comment. I myself would have opted for a different chapter arrangement in some cases. Chapter 3 concerns the organization of compliance and would not have been out of place as the first chapter of Part II, while chapter 12 by Wim Huisman on regulatory compliance and enforcement would have fitted in well in Part I. Similarly I would have preferred to see chapter 6 on conflicts of interest in Part IV, under *Capita Selecta*. But these are minor observations that do not in any way detract from my great appreciation for this book. It meets a need for theoretical analysis of a discipline that is moving towards maturity.

Introduction

Prof. S.C. Bleker-van Eyk

In 2004, the first two-year post-doctoral Executive Master Program in Compliance & Integrity Management started at the VU University Amsterdam. Initially, the program was aimed at senior compliance officers from financial institutions. Thirteen years later, the program has flourished and hundreds of senior compliance officers from financial as well as non-financial and public organizations have received a thorough postgraduate education.

For years we have struggled with the same problem: the lack of a general handbook on compliance within financial, non-financial and public organizations. Literature on compliance exists, but it often focuses on specific elements of compliance or specific subjects. Finally, we decided to produce our own handbook and also to write it in English, in order to help compliance officers in countries other than the Netherlands. Parts of this book are based on existing publications by the authors and will refer to these publications. All authors have broad academic and practical experience in the field of compliance.

This book deals with compliance and integrity management in general and studies compliance from a risk perspective. Some *capita selecta* such as anti-bribery or export controls will be described because of their general importance to compliance. However, because this handbook is to be used in our own Post-doctoral Program, some minor parts will describe compliance issues from a European perspective, such as the part on the extraterritorial jurisdiction of USA legislation. This book follows the lines of the post-doctoral Executive Master Program in Compliance & Integrity Management at the VU University Amsterdam, but hopefully will be of assistance to all compliance officers worldwide in setting up the compliance function in their organization.

The definition of compliance used throughout this book is:

> *Observance of external (international and national) laws and regulations, as well as internal norms and procedures, to protect the integrity of the organization, its management and employees with the aim of preventing and controlling risks and the possible damage resulting from these compliance and integrity risks.*

In this book, compliance is viewed through the basic principles of the following knowledge areas: Ethics, Behavioral sciences, Change management, Risk management, Business administration, Accounting, and Law: Public law, Private law, European and International law. This book contains four specific parts:

Part I: Human Behavior (the relationship between human behavior and compliance)
Part II: Organizations and Risk Management
Part III: Regulation, Supervision and Enforcement
Part IV: Capita Selecta

The editors especially want to thank Ms. Robin Betten (work student at Deloitte) for the tremendous effort she put in managing the entire process. Publication of this book would not have been possible without her. She managed all the different versions of the chapters; was in constant contact with all contributors; managed the cooperation with the translation department for those contributors who needed translation. Robin, you're not a qualified publisher, but you could have fooled us! You deserve all our gratitude!

PART I – HUMAN BEHAVIOR

The tension between 'good' and 'temptation':
juggling conflicting interests

1. Why Humans Get Organized: From Cave-Dweller to Mars Explorer[1]

Prof. S.C. Bleker-van Eyk[2]

1.1 TERMINOLOGY

There is no generally accepted definition of 'compliance'. In theory, an organization can define the term any way it likes, in line with the maturity of its own internal awareness of the concept. Naturally, though, that definition should align with the organization's core objectives. After all, compliance refers to the way such objectives should be achieved, within the confines of the law and of the internal and external agreements made. The postgraduate program in Compliance and Integrity Management at Vrije Universiteit Amsterdam uses the following definition:

> 'Observance of external (international and national) laws and regulations, as well as internal norms and procedures, to protect the integrity of the organization, its management and employees with the aim of preventing and controlling risks and the possible damage resulting from these compliance and integrity risks.'

This definition can be summarized in one word: compliance is *behavior*. And it is inextricably linked with *integrity*. Unfortunately, that is a concept which has been seriously dented in the past two decades. Integrity has become a politically charged term, used mainly as a smear. Merely to have your integrity called into doubt has the potential to seriously damage your reputation. Repeated use of the word without conclusive evidence to support the accusations being leveled has eroded

1. This chapter is written in memory of my father Frank van Eyk (1920–1986), imprisoned by the Germans during the entirety of the Second World War and survivor of Buchenwald concentration camp.
2. The first chapter is based on an English translation of the Inaugural Lecture delivered upon accepting the office of Professor of Compliance and Integrity Management in the Faculty of Economics and Business Administration at VU University Amsterdam on June 23, 2015. In this chapter the inaugural lecture has been further elaborated upon.

its meaning. The threat now comes primarily from the use of the term itself, not from the underlying behavior. It is striking that it has become almost automatically associated with *personal* integrity. And in this case, personal means intangible. As the saying goes, nothing is more fickle than man. It would be more appropriate to describe integrity within the concept of compliance management as 'behavioral risk', thus being deprived of its negative connotations. Psychology is the science we usually call to mind when it comes to analyzing human behavior, whereas compliance and integrity management focuses upon behavior in the context of the organization, where it is bound by internal and external agreements. In other words, *organizational* integrity. Finally, there is a third form: system integrity, such as that of the financial system. In this domain, technical factors related to the system are also relevant, alongside behavior.

1.2 OUR PLACE IN THE ORGANIZATION

In biological taxonomy, man belongs to the *Animalia* and the class *Mammalia*, or mammals. In this book we begin our analysis of compliance and integrity management at the dawn of mankind, when our ancestors sheltered in caves. The problems the cave-dweller encountered in his everyday life were existential in the most primary sense of the term: staying alive, finding food and water, procreation and sleep. Conditions were tough. Man was an omnivore and so could not live on plants and berries alone. Mammoths had to be caught. But a sturdy club on its own was not enough to bring down the giant beast. To survive, the cave-dweller had to organize. Darwin calls this the 'struggle for life'. 'I should premise,' he writes, 'that I use the term Struggle for Existence in a large and metaphorical sense, including dependence of one being on another, and including (which is more important) not only the life of the individual, but success in leaving progeny.'[3]

In *The Descent of Man*, Darwin describes how primitive humans constantly adapted their survival techniques to suit their situation. They developed tools, and strategies, to feed and defend themselves. And they started working with other people. Tasks were shared out or, when they were too much for one person to complete successfully, performed collectively.[4]

According to Darwin, the tribes which developed the best weapons and tools grew in size and so were able to absorb or even exterminate competing groups.[5] He becomes more interesting, though, when he turns his attention to the *morality* of primitive man. People need other people in order to survive. And as they warn one another of danger and help each other to defend themselves, so feelings like sympathy, courage, trust and love can arise. Within the organization, the tribe, mutual support emerges in pursuit of the common goal.[6] Darwin goes on to state that cooperation requires a form of government, and hence obedience. This, he says, 'is of the highest value, for any form of government is better than none. Selfish and contentious people will not cohere, and without coherence nothing can be effected. A tribe possessing the

3. Darwin 1859, p. 62.
4. Darwin 1871, p. 158.
5. Ibid., p. 159.
6. Ibid., pp. 162, 164.

above qualities in a high degree would spread and be victorious over other tribes'.[7] Here, Darwin is actually describing an early form of *compliance*, as a prerequisite for a successful organization. Moreover, achieving that success demands that compliant behavior be praised because it is in the general interest and that actions to the contrary be condemned in the clearest terms.[8] Darwin also stresses the importance of exemplary conduct. Within a tribe, progress comes not from the group but from the one individual who develops new tools and methods. The organization moves forward by imitating the behavior of this pioneer. In other words, setting a good example strengthens the collective. Finally, in Darwin's analysis we can discern a hope that, as the tribe develops or learns new techniques and so advances as an organization, the morality of its members will also be enhanced. Unfortunately, if we are to believe Darwin, the evolution of the necessary 'good genes' is an agonizingly slow process. Those most inclined to self-sacrifice, those most prepared to do all they can for the group, are also those most likely to die trying, before they can pass on their selfless genes. In Darwinism, 'survival of the fittest' is not the same as 'survival of the finest'. Or, to put it another way, 'only the good die young'. The expression 'survival of the fittest' is wrongly credited to Darwin. In fact, Spencer was inspired by Darwin when he came to the conclusion that only the fittest survive. Spencer brings us some solace when he describes how species adapt their physiology to the circumstances under which they have to survive. When parts are no longer required under the existing circumstances, they will be rejected by the body. Cold comfort for those of us that do not care to be compared with a Neanderthal.[9]

From its original tribal form, human organization continued to develop down the ages, adapting continually as the world around it became more and more complex. The Industrial Revolution had a particularly massive impact. However, internal organizational morality has evolved more slowly than technology. The current digital revolution has seen exponential technological growth, but people remain people and unable to do everything by themselves. Division of labor is still the norm, so we have to work together to achieve each new goal we set ourselves.

The latest challenge is taking people to Mars. But without organization there can be no trip to Mars. And without coordination and agreement there can be no effective organization. The raw materials still need to be mined, the components manufactured and the spacecraft assembled. The data will have to be programmed and the astronauts trained in compliance with the protocols. And there will have to be a 'Houston' to deal with the problems. Everything has to be organized to protect the lives of the Mars explorers, to safeguard the interests of the organizations involved and to serve the greater goal, our ongoing quest to push back the boundaries of human achievement.

1.3 COMPLIANCE IS BEHAVIOR

If compliance is the same as behavior, then desirable behavior should be clearly flagged and the associated instructions followed. Even though a good example makes

7. Ibid., p. 163.
8. Ibid., p. 166.
9. Spencer, 1864, § 165, pp. 444–445.

for good imitation, exemplary behavior alone is not enough to guarantee that it will be followed in the long term. The key question here is why people behave as they do, and it is one various branches of science have addressed. Every person is different, but there is some degree of overlap between us all. Martine Delfos describes this at length in her book *De schoonheid van het verschil,*[10] or *The Beauty of Difference*, where she distinguishes between genotypes and phenotypes. That is, between genetic characteristics and the phenomena through which they manifest themselves. The behavior genotype reflects the hereditarily programmed aspects of behavior;[11] it determines predisposition and delineates the boundaries within which that can be expressed. But, as Delfos points out, 'what behavior looks like is not dependent only upon predisposition ... Predisposition – heredity – is not the sole determinant of behavior. Interaction with the environment is also crucially important.'[12] She thus believes that behavior is an interaction between predisposition and environment.[13] And so the environment is vital to inducing correct behavior. People are rational beings and hence are more inclined to act in a particular way if they can understand *why* that behavior benefits the organization or them personally. In its turn, the organization looks for people more or less similar in *predisposition* and then tries to create an *environment* in which the behavior it desires can flourish. It is in this way that countless organizations with different cultures develop, each adapted to the people working for it and the products and ideas it generates. However, finding the right mix of staff is an art in itself. Homogeneity is no guarantee of quality. Quite the opposite, in fact: sameness saps creativity, which is one of the prerequisites for any organization's continuing existence. When everyone agrees about everything, the saying 'no shine without friction' applies. Finding the right mix of the right people, with different kinds of predisposition, is essential if an organization is to achieve its objectives. But these also have to be met within a set legal framework, which is then translated into internal rules and regulations. And that requires a policy that restrains behavior in order to prevent the pursuit of the objectives being undermined by transgressive actions. In their enthusiasm to achieve their goals, employees must not stray off the right path. To prevent them doing so, barriers need to be erected. Moreover, the policy of restraint should not be undermined by the rigorous pursuit of overambitious objectives fueled by perverse incentives. Contradictory messages – telling people that they have to play by the rules, for example, whilst at the same time setting targets which can only be achieved by breaking them – inevitably result in the barriers being crossed. And that can cause accidents. Everything in life is a question of striking the right balance. That applies just as much to an organization as it does to people, because ultimately an organization is nothing more and nothing less than a collection of people.

Compliance is behavior and inextricably linked to obedience of 'external (international and national) laws and regulations, as well as internal norms and procedures' as described in our definition of compliance. However, stating that compliance and obedience are synonyms is incorrect. The 'moral' element should be

10. Delfos 2010.
11. Ibid., p. 68.
12. Ibid., p. 69.
13. Ibid., p. 71.

included in behavior. That is why our definition goes beyond sheer obedience and links compliance to the 'integrity of the organization, its management and employees'.

1.4 THE MORAL COMPONENT OF BEHAVIOR

Stanley Milgram observes that 'behavior that is unthinkable in an individual who is acting on his own may be executed without hesitation when carried out under orders.'[14] We do not have to go back to the horrors of Nazi Germany or other extreme life-threatening situations to see examples of collective behavior that would be unthinkable in the eyes of some of its offenders. For instance, before the financial crisis at the beginning of this century, many an employee of more or less renowned financial institutions carried out acts that created despair and desolation in many individual customers. People lost their life savings, their pensions, their livelihoods. The motives of the employees in taking these actions were partly for the greater good of the organization (profit, shareholder value etc.) and to obtain personal benefits for the employee such as bonuses. Many of the employees regarded these acts as normal business activity. They are part of the job. But would the individual - not in his capacity of employee - obtain personal benefits by destroying other people's lives? Most of them would probably say that they would never commit an act profitable to themselves knowing that the innocent counterparty would be unable to bear the consequences and would be left desolate. To counter the undesired behavior, organizations now draw up stringent internal procedures to ascertain that employees understand the ramifications of moral hazards. In addition to codes of conduct and bonus procedures, organizations set up dilemma training to create awareness. Further on in Part I of this book we will enter into more detail regarding ethical procedures and training. However, we should keep in mind that 'it is one thing to talk in abstract terms about the respective rights of the individual and of authority; it is quite another to examine a moral choice in a real situation.'[15]

The importance of compliance and integrity management lies in determining *why* and *how* people comply.

The first question to be raised is 'what' is the standard people are complying with. Is this a standard that is to be found in 'black and white' and that leaves no room for interpretation? Every individual interprets the words they read in his own way, influenced by their personal mix of predispositions and environmental influences. Is it a standard that the individual 'believes' to exist and that he needs to comply with?

At first sight, these two questions seem rather straightforward. However, they immediately raise considerable issues such as the legitimacy of the standards, the interpretation of the standard, the moral obligation to comply with (which can differ according to social context) or the possible coercion to comply.

A conscience requires certain characteristics. Descartes stated, '*Je pense, donc je suis il suivait très évidemment et très certainement que j'étais; au lieu que, si j'eusse seulement cessé de penser, encore tout le reste de ce que j'avais jamais imaginé eût été vrai, je n'avais aucune raison de croire que j'eusse été* ...'[16] ('I think, therefore I

14. Milgram 1974, preface, p. XIX.
15. Ibid., preface, p. XIX.
16. Descartes 1637, p. 34.

am ... it most clearly and certainly followed that I was; while, on the other hand, if I had only ceased to think, although all the other objects which I had ever imagined had been in reality existent, I would have had no reason to believe that I existed ...'). This is a line of reasoning we see reflected in Hannah Arendt's analysis of the trial of Adolf Eichmann. The former SS Commander concealed his own conscience behind the oath of loyalty he had taken, the rules imposed by the Nazi government and the orders he received from his own immediate superiors. Eichmann stated that from a legal point of view he could not be held responsible. He acted upon orders received by his commanding officer (Lieutenant-General Müller). Eichmann simply stated that:[17]

> *'Da dies damals eine politische Anordnung war, bin ich des Glaubens, daß Schuld im rechtlichen Sinne hier doch eigentlich derjenige empfinden kann, der die Verantwortung für diese politische Entscheidung trägt, beziehungsweise getragen hat. Wo keine Verantwortung ist, da ist ja keine Schuld und das Ergebnis meines Nachdenkens ist daher, daß hier die Verantwortung im Rechtssinne zu prüfen sei. ist Befehl und Gehorsam die Grundlage jeder Staatlichen Ordnung ... Bei einer guten Staatsführung hat der Untergebene Glück, bei einer schlechten Unglück. Ich hatte kein Glück.'*

Arendt seems to mirror Descartes' 'I think, therefore I am' by equating not thinking with not possessing a conscience.[18] She describes Eichmann's attitude as 'sheer thoughtlessness - something by no means identical to stupidity'.[19] Rather than thinking, he just hides behind the rules. In my view, this is the nub of the debate surrounding the ethical conscience of businesses. Or states, for that matter, or any other form of collaborative entity. In his defense Eichmann talks about *guilt* and quickly refers to this issue from the point of view of guilt in the legal sense of the concept (*'im rechtlichen Sinne'*). During the hearing it is obvious that Eichmann immediately switches from the moral concept of guilt to the legal concept. This is proof that he is aware of the possible moral implications of his actions. Therefore, Eichmann cannot hide behind amorality. He is aware of morality but he chose not to act according to moral standards that we may assume 'universal' and applicable within all cultures, such as the concept that it is forbidden to take a life, unless - in some legal systems - strict legal requirements are met. In this context Milgram states that 'the essence of obedience consists in the fact that a person comes to view himself as the instrument for carrying out another person's wishes, and therefore no longer regards himself as responsible for his actions.'[20] This brings us to the relationship between law and morality. Hans Kelsen introduced the theory of legal positivism. Kelsen separates the concept of law from morality. The law is the law and the concept of justice is an expectation colored through moral and social context. Kelsen's theory was highly appreciated in totalitarian states. Bearing this in mind, it is not unrealistic that Eichmann felt comfortable hiding behind the German concept of 'Befehl ist Befehl'. As long as the people involved do not think any further than the obligation they are confronted with, they are nothing more than amoral extensions of the

17. The Eichmann Trial: session 88, https://www.youtube.com/watch?v = YF2462I109A.
18. Arendt 2006, pp. 135–150.
19. Ibid., pp. 287–288.
20. Milgram 1974, p. XX.

organization. But from the moment they push aside the shield of amorality, there is no going back. From that moment on there are but two paths left which they can take: the path of morality or the path of immorality. Amorality is a neutral state, devoid and without thought. As long as the members of an organization remain unthinking, both the organization and its 'unthinking' members are amoral. As soon as they do start reflecting upon the actions of the organization and their own actions, they face only two options: morality or immorality. And in that choice lies the indispensability of compliance and its inseparable companion, ethics. This last conclusion leaves us with the question of whether the organization can be regarded as a moral entity, alongside its employees. Unfortunately, this question once again brings us back to the Second World War, during which German companies were closely involved in the horrors of the Nazi regime. Topf & Söhne was a company famous for its cooking ovens that built the incinerators for the concentration camps. IG Farben was a chemical company that contracted Nazi doctors such as the infamous doctor Josef Mengele to conduct inhumane experiments on living subjects and produced the Zyklon B gas used in the concentration camps. Also there was the Krupp company as well as the Flick company. The companies as such were not prosecuted, but the managers in charge of the companies were. 'I.G. Farben Industrie A.G. itself was not indicted in this trial, but it was alleged by the Prosecution that Carl Krauch and the other twenty-two accused acting through the instrumentality of Farben and otherwise.'[21] In fact, on May 3, 1947 the managers of IG Farben were confronted with the following indictments:[22]

1. Planning, preparation, initiation, and waging of wars of aggression and invasions of other countries.
2. War crimes and crimes against humanity through the plundering and spoliation of occupied territories, and the seizure of plants in Austria, Czechoslovakia, Poland, Norway, France, and Russia.
3. War crimes and crimes against humanity through participation in the enslavement and deportation to slave labor on a gigantic scale of concentration camp inmates and civilians in occupied countries, and of prisoners of war, and the mistreatment, terrorization, torture, and murder of enslaved persons.
4. Membership of a criminal organization, the SS.
5. Acting as leaders in a conspiracy to commit the crimes mentioned under counts 1, 2, and 3.

The companies as such did not have *locus standi* before the Court. As a result, the managers were prosecuted. None were found guilty on account of the third indictment. The sentences were mild, varying from acquittal to eight years. Flick was sentenced to seven years but released after four years. Krupp was ordered to sell all his property. His managers received sentences, some up to 12 years.

The Nuremberg trials demonstrate the difficulty of linking a legal person – not being a natural person – with morality. A legal entity can exist merely on paper. An active company can only develop its activities through human intervention. Morality is directly related to the individual and pertaining to the conscience, moral sense

21. The *IG Farben Trial* case no. 57, 1949, p. 1.
22. Ibid., pp. 1–2.

and general principles of right conduct. Enforceability of right conduct goes beyond mere positive law, because it results from belief or conviction and may even be independent in the mind from logical proof. Morality and conduct apply to humans. However, one may take the position that a group of individuals may transpose their moral conduct to the organization. In most countries the penal law opens up the possibility of an indictment on the basis of being a member of a criminal organization. The main purpose (at least in practice) of such an organization is to organize and commit criminal acts. Nevertheless, the individuals commit the offenses. An organization is the instrument to coordinate the individual actions. To put it more bluntly: an organization cannot be sentenced on the basis of criminal law. It can only be prohibited and dismantled. The penal consequences are to be imposed upon its members. An individual cannot hide behind an organization and thereby relinquish his responsibility for immoral acts perpetrated by the organization. The Nuremberg trial of IG Farben offers a rather balanced view of the criminality of the individual member of a criminal organization:[23]

> 'The Tribunal declared to be criminal those groups of said organizations [SS] which were composed of members who had become or remained such in the knowledge that such groups were being used for the commission of war crimes or crimes against humanity connected with the war, or who had been personally implicated as members of said organization in the commission of such crimes. Specifically excluded from the classes of members to which the Tribunal imputed criminality, however, were those persons who were drafted into membership by the State in such a way as to give them no choice in the matter and who had committed no such crimes and those persons who had ceased to belong to any of said organizations prior to September 1, 1939.'

Finally, the importance of combating organized crime such as the atrocities of the Second World War is described in the United Nations' proclamation of the Universal Declaration on Human Rights,[24] in which the General Assembly stated that 'this Universal Declaration of Human Rights as a common standard of achievement for all peoples and all nations, to the end that every individual and *every organ of society*, keeping this Declaration constantly in mind, shall strive … to promote respect for these rights and freedoms …' (emphasis added).

1.5 THE EXISTENTIAL QUESTION: 'WHY?'

An organization is made up of a group of people who pool their respective dispositions in pursuit of a common goal, one which no single individual can achieve alone. And the work they do has to be carried out within a set framework. As Darwin pointed out, some form of 'government' is needed. It is the external government which designs the barriers the internal government is expected to erect. The staff of the organization must be made aware of the behavior required of them, and kept aware of it. That is an ongoing process, which requires more than just training. Compliant

23. Ibid., p. 58.
24. Preamble of the United Nations General Assembly, Resolution 217 (III), Paris, December 10, 1948.

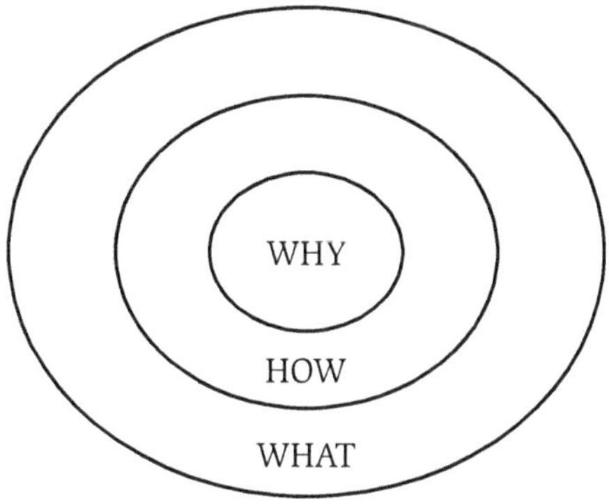

Figure 1: Simon Sinek's 'Golden Circle' concept

behavior is not simply a matter of learning by rote, like the times tables drummed into us at school; it is behavior in the service of a core objective which can only be achieved by the organization as a collective entity. It is in that collectivity that we should find the key to a heightened awareness of the importance of pursuing the objective in an appropriate manner, and hence a sustainable one. To this end, such behavior is best supported by incentives which rely more upon the 'carrot' than the 'stick'. Perhaps Simon Sinek's 'Golden Circle' concept can help here. This should enthuse the organization, and all its stakeholders with it, for the 'carrot' of the question *why* rather than the 'sticks' of *how* and *what*. The leader plays a crucial role in this. One which goes much further than setting the right example, because that only touches upon the *how*.

In the preface to his book *Start with Why*, Sinek sums up that role as follows. 'Whether individuals or organizations, we follow those who lead not because we have to, but because we want to. We follow those who lead not for them, but for ourselves.'[25]

If a leader wants to encourage their organization to act in a specific manner, they are most likely to be successful when they inspire the people under them in such a way that those individuals feel that adopting the desired behavior is the best course for them personally, rather than forcing it out of the group in a manipulative fashion. Behavior induced in that way is simply unsustainable; once the manipulation has been unmasked, resistance will follow. The focus in such cases is usually the product the organization wishes to generate, and following on from that the manner in which it can best be produced, including the behavior required. Here, the product is the objective and its production represents compliance. This is a highly pragmatic approach, which lacks inspiration. As tasks resulting in a finished product, the *what* and *how* are more or less tangible. But where is the passion? Say the organization is a brewery. Why do people start the process, collect the ingredients, brew up the right mix and follow a strict set of predefined rules to come out with the end product they want, beer? That *why* is a question at a more abstract level. The beer represents a

25. Sinek 2009, Preface.

mission, perhaps even a particular vision of a group of friends gathering at the end of a hard day's work to enjoy each other's company over a pint. That vision is not the beer itself, but the ability to create a product that generates conviviality. It is also a vision that gives the company the opportunity to devise other products which meet that same need. So if your mission is to improve the way people communicate, an open vision can allow a logging business with a paper mill that started over a hundred years ago to evolve into a television and Internet empire without deviating from that mission.

Sinek regards his Golden Circle as a mathematical aid to help develop practical solutions in the quest for the 'ability to inspire ..., a guide to vastly improving leadership, corporate culture, sales, and marketing ... [which] explains loyalty and how to create enough momentum to turn an idea into a social movement. But it all starts from the inside out. It all starts with Why.'[26]

What makes the Golden Circle concept interesting is the enthusiasm it engenders in the members of the organization, as a result of which the *why* becomes its driving force and the *how* and the *what* respectively merely the means to the end and one of the many possible results. As Sinek says in his preface, the leader inspires and the staff follow because they believe in what he is doing, including what it has to offer them as employees. The question is whether this approach can be made to work even in organizations which have been struggling for years with problems around the existential meaning of their work. Putting beer to one side, let us look at banks instead. What *why* can we distil from the banking process, and how can an industry in the midst of an identity crisis go in search of meaning? The Golden Circle approach would require far-reaching changes to its entire business model, which would first need to undergo a fundamental rethink. And that would be the hardest step of all. Returning to Sinek, it is the leaders who would have to instigate that about-face. Society's current search for the core objectives of our financial institutions perhaps presents their leaders with the ideal opportunity to design a robust new model that incorporates the *why*. In developing this more appropriate vision of their institutions, that *why* would be linked directly with the *who*. The social unease has arisen amongst their internal and external stakeholders: the institutions' employees, their customers and the wider community – sometimes as shareholders, but always as interested parties. The globalization of the financial economy means that these organizations' decisions affect not only their own staff and customers, but extend much further. With the fear engendered by an all-disrupting crisis still fresh in their memories, the stakeholders concerned have shown their displeasure with current policy. In this light, is the importance of instigating a quest for the *why* still merely a hypothetical question, or is it a fact the financial institutions are going to have to accept sooner or later?

In seeking out the success the Golden Circle can provide, a good place to start is with those smaller financial institutions which focus upon socially responsible banking. Since the crisis, we have seen that organizations that bring a clear ethical dimension to their activities are generally able to stand up to economic adversity reasonably well. At any rate, they have not had to deal with the demotivating demonization of the role played by the mainstream financial institutions. So perhaps

26. Ibid., pp. 38–39.

it is a good idea to look more closely at how much the *why* has helped those with an ethical or green business model to sustain their profitability and at how their approach influences their workforce and other stakeholders. It would also be interesting to look at the way the *why* has affected the *how* - by which I mean compliance, with internal standards as well as the letter of the law - and whether both together have strengthened the *what* - that is, the organization's products and financial objectives.

The quest for the *why* demands courage, insight and leadership, not to mention an excellent propensity for thinking 'outside the box'. The great thing about mankind is that circumstances can induce us to perform great deeds. Amongst our cave-dwelling ancestors, we saw that in those who put the collective interest before their own. Looking at the financial institutions, we also see a situation which could give their leaders the opportunity to excel themselves. To allay public discontent - which has the potential to ignite into social unrest - the political establishment should be prepared to seize its chance to turn things around and approach the traditional business model from a new perspective: that of the *why*. That would help forge new forms of loyalty, both internal and amongst customers and other external stakeholders, including shareholders. But it requires leadership on the part of the leaders, and thinking 'outside the box'.

None of this will be possible, though, unless the regulators also adjust their sights to focus more upon the *why*. Since the financial crisis we have indeed seen the regulators struggle in their quest to pay more attention to integrity, and hence behavior, so that a good first step could be made towards developing a *why*-based mindset in the spirit of the Golden Circle, with the *how* and the *what* being better attuned to that *why*. However, most of our financial institutions operate on the global stage. And there, unfortunately, regulators like those in the US still feel strongly attached to regulations. A straitjacket of innumerable and not always consistent rules has resulted in regulatory overkill and a 'box-ticking' approach which allows little or no time to consider the underlying thinking: the spirit of the law. A spirit which should be linked to the *why* guiding both the financial institutions and their regulators. We see the same problem looming at the European level, too. By strangling organizations with regulatory red tape, they are prevented from reaching the nub of the matter, the *why*. This is not to say there should be no rules, of course. They are absolutely essential, and so is their observance, but they and their enforcement should converge in the institutional *why* and that should be better synchronized with the regulatory one.

1.6 THE ROLE OF COMPLIANCE

The next question requiring an answer concerns the role of compliance within the organization. From what we have already seen, we can infer that human organization began with the use of forced acquiescence to elicit the requisite behavior, Darwin's 'obedience'. In recent decades compliance has been closely linked with so-called 'hard controls'. In other words, it specified how the objective should be reached. The regulators of this period wanted compliance enforced in order to counter undesirable behavior. In response, financial institutions were soon setting up ever larger compliance departments. But in the process it became a top-heavy function. Failing to keep pace with the organization's organic development, it began to resemble an alien body within – one being rejected slowly but surely by the host entity. Quite simply, compliance came to be ignored. For the leaders of the organization, it was merely a formality that only gained any importance once an issue had arisen and the regulators started insisting that the rules be observed. As soon as the crisis had passed, compliance once again retreated into the background. It withdrew back into its shell, returning to its previous status as an alien body in the second line of defense, a safety net in the face of increasing legislative controls, occasionally playing its old policing role. The financial crises in the early years of this century unleashed a flood of new rules, which compelled compliance to put all its effort into converting innumerable requirements into official policy so that all the right boxes were kept formally ticked. Life in the compliance department began to feel more and more like living in Charlie Chaplin's film *Modern Times*: entangled in the *how* and making no substantial contribution to the *what*, never mind having room for the *why*. Compliance had lost its focus.

In the end, it turned out that crises cannot be prevented through compliance alone. After all, it inevitably found itself caught in the cogs of the organizational machinery. But it did try to find a way out of the labyrinth, with some help from the regulators. Together they began to place an increasing emphasis upon behavior, as well as calling into question the compliance function's entrenched position in the second line of defense. From there it gradually began to move forward into the field of business consultancy, with compliance officers brought up to the front line as direct advisers. This transition is still under way, but we have already seen plenty of ill-considered steps taken along the path. In many cases, for example, the front is manned by compliance officers pulled straight out of the second line – often in order to save money. Here they remain in dialogue with the business side of the organization, but to a great extent miss the point. Much of their reasoning is complex, whereas the basic concept is very straightforward: everyone is responsible for their own behavior. Within the organization, each individual is accountable for their part of the process. And its management and leaders bear their own cumulative responsibility for the overall process under their command. The front line is production, in the broadest sense of the term, so compliance's role here should be to advise on and support the production process. But take note: this does not mean that it takes responsibility for compliant behavior in the front line! As stated *supra*, everyone is responsible for their own actions. Compliance is actually there to make sure that the front line knows how it is expected to behave and how best to incorporate that behavior into its activities, and also ultimately to monitor behavior. Final responsibility for the smooth running of the production process itself – including compliance's ability to do its job effectively – still rests with management and leaders. To return to Darwin's tribes, everyone has their own task to perform in pursuit of the common good. Only then is prosperity possible.

So should the entire compliance function be moved up from the second line to the first? No! That would create an undesirable situation. In fact, compliance has its place in both lines of defense. In the second it should maintain its position as adviser to the entire organization, as a partner in crisis management and – alongside the third line, internal audit – a guarantor of adequate compliance auditing of the front-line process. The compliance officer has a unique status within the organization, in that he monitors both its overall behavior as a corporate entity and that of all its individual employees. He is also the organization's integrity manager, charged with making sure that it sticks to the right path and that its personnel exhibit the behavior needed to ensure its prosperity.

In fact, we can compare the role of the compliance officer with Socrates' description of human motives in his dialogue with Phaedrus. In love, he says, we are guided by two ruling principles: the 'natural desire of pleasure' and 'an acquired opinion which aspires after the best'. These are 'sometimes in harmony and then again at war', the outcome of which may be either excess or temperance.[27] Socrates relates the allegory of a chariot drawn by two winged horses, one 'noble' and the other 'ignoble'. As a team, they are difficult to control; the noble horse flies up to the heavens whilst the other loses its wings and falls to earth.[28]

As far as behavior is concerned, the compliance officer is assigned by the leaders, management, to guide the organization, the chariot, down a track without knocking down the hurdles erected by legislators and regulators. The chariot has to keep to the right speed to avoid accidents, but also complete the course successfully to reach the future. Internal and external regulation are the reins the officer uses to keep the varied workforce of noble and not-so-noble characters pulling in the same direction. He has to make sure that they do not succumb to the forbidden fruit of selfish earthly temptations on the way, or cling to their own dreams, but instead realize that the organization has to produce so that everyone earns the oats they deserve. The track they are negotiating is not an even one, and in times of crisis it requires a driver with exceptional steering skills. Without that ability, sooner or later the chariot will overturn and the race will come to an abrupt end.

The role of the compliance officer is changing, due especially to the gradual realization that the organization has to be able to adapt to the rapidly changing circumstances of our age. The position requires maturity and the ability to help the organization implement the necessary behavioral adjustments. With the social tide turning, organizations today find themselves at a crossroads: the point at which habitual and desirable behavior diverge. How financial institutions have had to reconsider their objectives is a good example of the choices they face. Legislators and external regulators have been demanding higher standards of their leaders and internal regulators, for example ever stricter prerequisites for non-executive directors. And not just in the financial sector. The compliance officer is one of those internal regulators, responsible for overseeing the behavioral aspects of the organization. So this function needs to be further professionalized. We have just seen that the charioteer must possess specific qualities to be suited to his task. 'As well as warding off the risks posed by legal and regulatory transgressions, ideally the compliance officer should also be the organization's ethical conscience. The guardian of its internal standards and rules, including codes of conduct. If not the petty fraud officer, then certainly the serious fraud officer.'[29] Even with that kind of policing remit, however, the ethical responsibility should take priority. At the organization's ethical reins, the compliance officer must be in a position to indicate when it needs to change course – or even be brought to a standstill. But the final decision is not his to take.

27. Plato (translated by Benjamin Jowett), p. 54.
28. Ibid., p. 61.
29. S.C. Bleker-van Eyk 2013, p. 406.

That is up to the leaders. The compliance officer therefore needs direct access to the board of directors. And if it is unwilling to make a change he believes is 'mission critical', then the compliance officer must be able to refer the matter directly to the supervisory board.

This is a track that must be negotiated carefully to keep the chariot balanced and to keep hold of the reins in the relationship between compliance and the supervisory board. To do that, though, demands a readiness to emerge from your protective shell. To show courage. An ethical conscience should not be something you can silence, but a voice you hear when it really matters. In short, the compliance officer should be a 'countervailing power' within the organization. That is a concept introduced by Galbraith in the context of the power play between businesses and their customers. In his words, 'the existence of ... power creates an incentive to the organization of another position of power that neutralizes it.'[30]

Once we couple the notion of 'countervailing power' with the compliance officer's role as ethical conscience and the task of guiding the organizational chariot towards a sustainable future, we comprehend that he must be in a position to apply the figurative 'handbrake' in the event of possible irregularities.

1.7 SUMMARY AND CONCLUSION

The organization is a group of people jointly pursuing a goal no single individual can achieve alone, a goal which should serve the interests of all those who commit to the collective entity. Darwinism is not merely a biological trip through time, then, but a window into the complex world mankind has shaped in order to satisfy his needs as effectively as possible. The division of labor has allowed us to achieve great things, from successfully hunting much larger animals with the most primitive of means to interplanetary travel. When people join forces in an effort to reach a goal, leadership is needed in order to allocate the available resources in an appropriate and effective manner. But because the human journey began as an individual quest to satisfy personal needs, that collective – the organization – also needs a shared ethical conscience charged with ensuring that the totality of its behavior is directed towards its objective, and hence also that of the individual member. Uniting people under an organizational umbrella and allowing them to flourish in that associative context is an art in itself. One which requires leadership with an insightfulness that goes deeper than the intended product of the union. The leader has to be able to translate the *why*, that product, into tangible objectives which bind stakeholders, internal and external alike, to the organization. Only then does growth on all fronts become possible. And to ensure that it grows organically within bounds acceptable to society, it needs an ethical conscience with countervailing power for those moments of weakness all of us experience, even leaders. The compliance officer is that conscience.

30. Galbraith 1952, pp. 118–119.

BIBLIOGRAPHY

Arendt 2006
H. Arendt, *Eichmann in Jerusalem: A Report on the Banality of Evil (Penguin Classics)*, London: Penguin Books Ltd 2006.

Bleker-van Eyk 2013
S.C. Bleker-van Eyk, 'De Compliance Officer 2.0', *MAB* 2013-10.

Darwin 1859
C.R. Darwin, *On the origin of Species by Means of Natural Selection, or the Preservation of Favoured Races in the Struggle for Life*, New York: Appleton 1859.

Darwin 1871
C.R. Darwin, *The Descent of Man, and selection in relation to sex*, London: John Murray 1871

Delfos 2010
M.F. Delfos, *De schoonheid van het verschil: Waarom mannen en vrouwen verschillen én hetzelfde zijn*, Dan Diego: Harcourt Book Publisher 2004.

Descartes 1637
R. Descartes, *Discours de la Méthode, pour bien conduire sa raison et chercher la vérité dans les sciences*, Leyde (Leiden) : La Gaya Scienza 2012 (first published 1637).

Galbraith 1952
J.K. Galbraith, *American Capitalism: The Concept of Countervailing Power*, New Jersey: Transaction Publishers 1952.

Milgram 1974
S. Milgram, *Obedience to Authority: an experimental view*, New York: Harper & Row 1974.

Sinek 2009
S. Sinek, *Start with why: How great leaders inspire everyone to take action*, London: Penguin Books Ltd 2009.

Plato (translated by Benjamin Jowett)
Plato, *Symposium and Phaedrus*, New York: Dover Publications 1993.

Spencer 1864
H. Spencer, *The Principles of Biology*, Edinburgh: Williams and Norgate 1864.

Other references

The IG Farben Trial case no. 57 1949
Law Reports of the Trials of War Criminals, selected and prepared by the United Nations War Crimes Commission (Vol. X: The IG Faren and Krupp Trials), London: United Nationals War Crimes Commission by His Majesty's Stationary Office 1949.

2. Ethics and Integrity Management

Prof. S.C. Bleker-van Eyk

The subtitle of the last book by the philosopher René Gude, *The Agora model: the world is easier than you think*,[1] offers the link between the first chapter on human behavior and Darwin's theory where man is exposed as an ingenious and resourceful animal and this second chapter where a closer look is on integrity management within organizations. The jacket flap text is even more appropriate: 'Philosophy is man's natural need to integrate his different living environments and to create coherence between these environments. Philosophy offers an integrity check.' In fact, the organization is but one of the living environments within which we operate. Gude distinguishes the personal, private (organization), public and political environments.[2] In the following chapter the 'private' environment will be discussed and, willingly or not, the personal environment will intertwine with the private sphere.

The bottom line is simple and also extremely difficult to comprehend: organizations are conglomerates of individuals acting together to achieve both personal and organizational goals!

But note: there is a difference between ethics and integrity. Ethics is perceived as relating to moral action, conduct, motive or action. Ethics is not only about doing the right thing, but about doing the right thing when nobody is looking and nobody is judging, albeit that 'the right thing' is directly related to societally acceptable norms. Integrity reflects on the soundness or moral principle and character of an individual in his interaction with others. This is not the place to enter into the debate on whether a difference exists between integrity and ethics. In the United States of America, the terminology used to describe moral conduct is often referred to as 'ethics', while in Europe the term 'integrity' is more common. In this book integrity is used instead of ethics and this is based on the common use of the term 'integrity' in the Netherlands and other parts of Europe for that matter. Although – to some degree – the difference between 'ethics' and 'integrity' may be a semantic one, the core of the term 'integrity' may shed some light on the difficulty of grasping integrity

1. Gude 2015.
2. Ibid., p. 16.

from an organizational point of view. In Latin the word *integer* means 'whole' or 'untouched'. This concept of a whole or untouched entity – be it a human being or an organization – offers a different view of the concept of integrity. Finally, the term conduct may give rise to some confusion in relation to compliance and integrity. The definition of conduct is rather broad. It refers to the general behavior expressed in actions, reactions and interaction of an entity. Supervisory authorities may see conduct in relation to a culture of obedience to the law as well as obedience to the *spirit* of the law.

In this chapter organizational integrity will be at the center of the discussion, together with the risks the organization has to counter and the controls that it can put in place to mitigate these risks. The greatest risk that an organization can encounter – next to natural disasters – is the human behavioral risk. The principle is that the individual lies at the beginning of every risk not stemming from a natural disaster. And even in cases of, for instance, earthquakes, corruption may be the reason for the collapse of buildings – and as a result thereof the loss of lives – if building permits were issued by the authorities as a result of a bribe even though the building requirements were not met. The results of unethical behavior can be far-reaching: from corruption to program design errors due to lack of quality assurance.

2.1 ORGANIZATIONAL INTEGRITY

The subtitle of Part 1 states: the tension between 'good' and 'temptation': juggling conflicting interests. The organization is a group of individuals acting together to effectively achieve goals that they cannot achieve by themselves. As discussed in chapter 1 *supra*, the organization started while hunting mammoths and has evolved drastically over the centuries into vast conglomerates exercising complex tasks and creating extraordinarily sophisticated products or services that are in no way comparable with the initial loaf of bread. And yet, we are still human beings getting organized to achieve goals and we may consider ourselves far more evolved than the caveman, but in fact we are still driven by the weaknesses and strengths that are inextricably linked to our human nature. We constantly juggle the interest of the organizations and our own interest (retain our job, get a promotion, get a bonus). Hopefully, most of the time our interests are synchronized with the organizations, for instance through policies and controls. As soon as the individual's need is not 'in sync' with the organization's need, non-compliance risks may occur. Here two options are open:

- The integrity of the organization may be in danger due to non-compliance.
- The integrity of the individual may be in peril, because the individual has to stretch his actions beyond personal interests or, worse, personal moral parameters.

Compliance and integrity relate to behavior of individual employees, groups of employees and even the organization as such. In our definition, compliance and integrity relate to external law and regulations as well as other internal norms and procedures. Organizations and their employees are confronted with a broad range of laws and regulations. Due to some severe cases of corporate misconduct and more or less related financial crises and economic downturns, the amount of legislation has increased drastically as described in chapter 1 *supra*. Obviously, the more rules and regulations employees are confronted with, the bigger the risk that these rules and regulations are willingly or unintentionally infringed. When we look at willingly abusive actions, 'almost *nine out of ten employees* admitted to abusive conduct at some level'.[3]

2.2 FROM FRAUD TRIANGLE TO INTEGRITY TRIANGLE

The concept of the Fraud Triangle was first launched by Cressey.[4] According to Cressey, 'trusted persons become trust violators when they conceive of themselves as having a financial problem which is non-shareable, are aware that this problem can be secretly resolved by violation of the position of financial trust, and are able to apply to their own conduct in that situation verbalizations which enable them to adjust their conceptions of themselves as trusted persons with their conceptions as users of the entrusted funds or property.' The Fraud Triangle focuses on fraud opportunities within the organization. In fact, according to the Fraud Triangle perceived opportunity to defraud become dangerous when the potential fraudulent individual feels pressure to commit fraud (pressure from inside or outside the organization) and will rationalize the seizing of the perceived opportunity through arguments (often fueled by perceived culture) on why he should seize the opportunity. Behavior is influenced by three main factors: opportunity, pressure and rationalization. Fraud deterrence should aim at disenabling the Fraud Triangle by removing causal and enabling factors. The concept of the Fraud Triangle was further elaborated and still is regarded as a valid model to analyze abusive behavior. Steve Albrecht has renamed it the *Compromise Triangle* because in his opinion 'whether it is fraud or any other type of compromise, the same three elements of (1) perceived pressure, (2) perceived opportunity and (3) some way to rationalize the compromise as not being inconsistent with one's code of conduct are always present. For example, consider the student who cheats in school. The student might say (1) I need to cheat to get a good grade in order to keep my scholarship - a perceived pressure, (2) the professor left the room during the test - a perceived opportunity, and (3) everyone cheats a little - a rationalization'.[5] Albrecht translates the Fraud Triangle to the Fire triangle used in fire safety training: 'for a fire to occur, three elements are necessary: (1) heat, (2) fuel and (3) oxygen. When all three elements combine, there is a fire. If any one of the three elements is eliminated, the fire is extinguished.'[6]

Cressey, Albrecht and Wells all start from the point of view of the element of 'pressure' or 'nonsharable problem' in Cressey's terminology. Pressure is in fact the perceived pressure by the person considering abusive behavior. Both external and internal factors can contribute to the perceived pressure. Pressure can increase with, for instance, individuals with substance abuse or gambling debts. But in fact the 'pressure' factor cannot be objectified. What may be pressure to one may not be perceived as pressure by someone else. Also, the mere fact that pressure is felt

3. Wells 1997, p. 511.
4. Cressey 1953, p. 30.
5. Albrecht & Albrecht 2009, pp. 19–44.
6. Ibid., p. 20; Albrecht 2014.

will not automatically lead to abusive behavior. In fact, it is the combination of the three elements that may lead to abusive behavior.

Opportunity always exists. Opportunity is necessary to develop business. Without opportunity there is no commerce. From nails, hammers, wood to laptops, business activities open doors to abusive behavior such as stealing, embezzlement etc. It would be imprudent not to set up some kind of controls within the organization to protect the 'opportunity' against abusive behavior.

Rationalization is the most critical element of the Fraud Triangle. Rationalization is the argumentation by the perpetrator as to why he should abuse the opportunity. Even in cases in which little pressure is felt, the rationalization can easily lead to abusive behavior. For some individuals, rationalization such as 'because I want to' or 'because I can' may be enough. However, these are the more exceptional cases. On average, the rationalization is based on the perception of the opportunity or pressure encountered by the individual, reinforced by the perception of how others (peers or superiors) within the organization would act – or even worse *have acted* in similar circumstances. The rationalization is closely linked to the culture within the organization, or, even more intangibly, the culture as *perceived* by the individual. Here we find the major difficulty of adapting the Fraud Triangle or any other model that tries to grasp the essence of integrity for that matter: organizations focus on individual behavior. If an organization employs fifty individuals, it will already be difficult to manage the desired behavior of those fifty individuals. If an organization employs 100,000 individuals, integrity management seems to catch the stars in a faraway universe.

Organizational integrity management aims at achieving the *desired* behavior among the employees of the organization. This is partly overlapping with compliance management which *demands* compliance with external laws and regulations as well as internal norms and procedures. In order to be able to connect legal consequences with the obligation of employees to abide by the internal norms, these norms will, in some form, have to be concretized in contractual clauses with at least an explicit reference in the labor contract.

Organizational integrity management aims at creating an ethically compliant culture within the organization that aims at creating common ground to achieve the organization's objective, which is translated into individual targets through Key Performance Indicators (KPIs) or other means to indicate how the employee can contribute to the achievement of the overall objectives. People know intuitively that they may be more successful if they observe certain standards and values. Consequently, it would appear more obvious to comply with such rules than not to comply with them. However, there are circumstances in which the person involved prefers not to stick to certain rules, as will be discussed with regard to the Integrity Triangle *infra*. In addition to the objectives of the organization, the employee also has personal objectives such as remaining in employment to pay his bills, etc. The ultimate satisfaction for both the organization and the employee is to create a bond between the organization and the employee that stretches beyond the mere necessity to pay the bills, which is discussed in chapter 1 *supra* in Sinek's Golden Circle. The employee needs to feel a part of the organization. As Darwin would put it, the individual creates an emotional bond with the group which leads to loyalty and putting the group's needs above the individual's needs. Also, mutual respect is important. Mutual respect relates to individuals respecting each other. Where respect is concerned, behind the organization the employee will attribute given respect – or disrespect for that manner – to the group of individuals in the form of colleagues or management. A simple example will make this concept more tangible. A manager is not paid for overtime. He is required to do some overtime. He will be willing to do this for one or more of the following reason(s); out of his own necessity to achieve his personal targets and thereby sustaining his employment and benefits; out of loyalty to his colleagues; and/or out of loyalty to the organization. As overtime occurs more often, the employee may regard it as a form of disrespect for his privacy. In a perfect storm when opportunity and pressure come together, he may even rationalize why he is entitled to take the opportunity. If the organization respects his work and expresses gratitude, he may be driven to go the extra mile. The latter may also apply if he feels a strong sense of loyalty and pride through his bond with the organization's Golden Circle. However, loyalty is not an infinite source. It needs to be regularly replenished by respect.

The Fraud Triangle focuses on the elements that may translate behavior into fraudulent behavior. By dissecting the behavior into three elements, it becomes easier to manage. Each element can be managed through controls. In most organizations, opportunity is the best controlled element. The opportunity to commit fraud is often tackled by a wide variety of hard controls that are visible, such as entrance gates, access passes, internal procedures such as screening employees or third parties, use of communications, etc. In fact, the vast majority of all existing controls aim at preventing the misuse of means, funds or information. With regard to pressure, controls on external pressure exist such as screening of employees, procedures on substance abuse and similar procedures to mitigate pressure risks. Before the financial and economic crisis started in 2007, pressure controls mostly focused on external pressure. The crisis shifted the focus from external pressure to internal pressure. The bonus incentives given to employees and agents in the financial sector were one of the top issues leading up to the 2008 crisis. The incentive to sell products irrespective of possible risks to the consumer and/or the financial institution led to an increase in uncertain financial products regardless of the moral hazard, or any other hazard for that matter. The Dutch legislation is said to be the severest legislation on remuneration and bonuses in the EU. Public companies (NVs), cooperatives and private limited liability companies (BVs) qualifying as a bank, mutual insurance companies qualifying as an insurance company and financial institutions, regardless of their legal form, may revise and claw back directors' bonuses if they are excessive or wrongly awarded based on standards of reasonableness and fairness. For these entity types, the variable part (bonus) of the fee is limited to 20% of the fixed salary; an absolute/guaranteed right to a variable bonus does not exist; the severance payment is capped at 100% of the annual fixed salary; and the variable fee can be reclaimed in the event of misconduct.[7] This legislation has been introduced on top of self-regulation (Corporate Governance Code and the Banking Code allow for revision and clawback

7. Act on Remuneration policies of financial undertakings (Wet van 28 januari 2015 tot wijziging van de Wet op het financieel toezicht houdende regels met betrekking tot het beloningsbeleid van financiële ondernemingen (Wet beloningsbeleid financiële ondernemingen), *Stb.* 2015, 45).

of bonuses under certain circumstances) to give supervisory boards a stronger basis for exercising powers to claw back bonuses.

Dutch rules are thus more stringent than the bonus cap and clawback provisions in the Capital Requirements Directive IV (CRD IV). In summary, CRD IV prescribes that (1) variable remuneration cannot exceed fixed remuneration, or with the approval of shareholders twice the fixed remuneration, (2) guaranteed variable remuneration is not allowed, since it is not consistent with sound risk management or the pay-for-performance principle, (3) up to 100% of total variable remuneration is subject to clawback arrangements, and (4) the information to be disclosed in relation to remuneration will extend to the ratios set between fixed and variable remuneration, and the number of individuals receiving at least EUR 1 million in remuneration per year.[8] Furthermore, the EBA developed criteria as required under CRD IV to identify categories of staff whose professional activities have a material impact on the financial institution, and consequently to which the CRD IV requirements apply.[9]

Under the Sarbanes-Oxley Act (hereinafter: SOX) enacted in 2002 by the US Congress resulting from a rash of scandals of misrepresentations in public accounting, clawbacks are limited to the Chief Executive Officer (CEO) and the Chief Financial Officer (CFO) and apply to cases in which there is 'misconduct' resulting in 'material non-compliance of the issuer ... with any financial reporting requirement under the securities laws'.[10] However, personal misconduct by the CEO or CFO is not a precondition for triggering reimbursement obligations after an accounting restatement. *Sec v. Jenkins* was the first action in the US seeking reimbursement from an individual under Section 304 who is not alleged to be engaged in the fraudulent conduct. The District Court ruled that misconduct stemming from that of a corporate officer, agent or employee acting within the scope of their agency or employment is sufficient to trigger the reimbursement obligation of the CEO and the CFO.[11] Judge Sparks noted that the defendants 'should have been monitoring the various internal controls to guard against such misconduct; they signed the SEC filings in question, and represented they in fact were actively guarding against non-compliance. As such, they shouldered the risk of Section 304 reimbursement when non-compliance nevertheless occurred'.[12] Judge Sparks finally ruled that it is in the spirit of Section 304 SOX to hold the CEO and CFO accountable if they themselves do not engage in the misconduct in order to 'ensure ... corporate officers cannot simply keep their own hands clean, but must instead be vigilant in ensuring that there are adequate controls to prevent misdeeds by underlings'.[13]

Under SOX the clawback is for any incentive compensation paid during the 12 months following the date on which the original financial statement (giving rise to the restatement) was issued publicly or was filed with the SEC (whichever occurred first). In addition to the clawback, SOX requires a recovery from the CEO

8. Ibid., Arts 92–96.
9. Ibid., Art. 75 and 'Regulatory Technical Standards for the definition of material risk takers for remuneration purposes' of EBA.
10. Sarbanes-Oxley Act §304.
11. *Sec v. Jenkins*, Case No. A-12-CA-285-SS.
12. Ibid., p. 15
13. Ibid., p. 11

and the CFO of any gains realized upon sale of securities of the issuer during the same 12-month period.

In addition to the SOX legislation the Dodd-Frank Act also entails a clawback provision in Section 954. The Dodd-Frank provision in the US is to some extent broader than Section 304 SOX, as it extends to all current and former executives and reaches back three years and to all incentive-based compensation. The threshold to trigger a clawback is also somewhat lower, since a 'material non-compliance with applicable accounting principles' is sufficient, whereas under SOX a restatement resulting from misconduct is required. On the other hand it is more limitative in that not all incentive compensation received during the three-year period needs to be reimbursed, just the excess over what the compensation would have been in the absence of the misstatement. Another difference is that the Dodd-Frank provision is enforceable not only by SEC, but by plaintiffs' attorneys as well in derivative cases.

Following the bailout of the US financial system in response to the subprime mortgage crisis, the Emergency Economic Stabilization Act (EESA) of 2008 was enacted creating the USD 700 billion Troubled Asset Relief Program (TARP) to purchase failing bank assets. Financial institutions receiving TARP assistance must maintain certain standards for executive compensation and corporate governance and this includes 'a provision for the recovery by such TARP recipient of any bonus, retention award, or incentive compensation paid to a senior executive officer and any of the next 20 most highly-compensated employees of the TARP recipient based on statements of earnings, revenues, gains or other criteria that are later found to be materially inaccurate'.[14] This clawback provision is not limited to cases of misconduct. Furthermore it encompasses all bonuses, retention awards and incentive compensation and does not explicitly limit the clawback to the excess of such amounts over the amounts that would have been paid if the materially inaccurate statement had not occurred. The influence of EESA will lessen, since all TARP recipients repay their obligations to the Treasury and consequently will cease to be subject to EESA.

In 2016 Obama announced that rules were to be set up that 'would require the biggest financial firms to defer payment of at least half of executives' bonuses for four years, a year longer than the common industry practice. The plan also would require a minimum period of seven years for the biggest firms to "claw back" bonuses if it turns out an executive's actions hurt the institution or if a firm has to restate financial results.'[15] It seems, however, that US regulators face several hurdles in completing the measure by the end of President Obama's term. The question is whether these hurdles will be left intact during the Trump presidency. On 7 February 2017 Trump signed an executive order to review the Dodd-Frank Act, including the disclosure of the pay rate between the CEO and employees.

As the Fire Triangle was used to create the Fraud Triangle, the latter can simply be changed into the Integrity Triangle. While the Fraud Triangle focuses on misconduct, the Integrity Triangle focuses on desired behavior, applying the same elements of opportunity, pressure, and rationalization.

Opportunity is the oxygen of entrepreneurship; business opportunity is what makes it possible to survive in business. Pressure is comparable to the system of

14. Emergency Economic Stabilization Act §111(b)(3)(B).
15. Borak et al. 2016.

blood pressure: when the pressure is too low, the activities tend to stagnate and when the pressure is too high the danger lies in the mistakes made in order to keep up with the pressure. *Pressure* is good when it is a balanced pressure that enables activity but prevents overheating the processes and leaping over the protective measures. Pressure aims at fine-tuning the balance between desired behavior and demanded behavior while preventing misconduct, by means of regulations, procedures and norms within the business processes. The right incentives and the prevention of misconduct cannot be achieved by means of corrupt incentives such as bonuses based on targets that require circumventing ethical norms. Know Your Customer (KYC) procedures and the screening of employees, clients, and third business parties are also measures to prevent unwanted pressure that augment the possibility of undesired behavior. Finally, the *rationalization* lies at the heart of the vibrant organization where conduct is the right balance between the demanded (laws and regulations) and the desired (norms) behavior. With regard to rationalization, 'tone at the top' is often referred to as a crucial element to manage desired behavior. This is only party true. The executive management sets the tone and must always realize that their behavior must be typical for the behavior elsewhere within the organization. A strong example is the tone at the top of the Fédération Internationale de Football Association (FIFA). During the rule of Sep Blatter and his executive committee, corruption became a widespread phenomenon within the international, and all too often various national, football communities. In organizations with charismatic leaders demonstrating consistent desired behavior, the chance of creating the desired culture is highly feasible. One should bear in mind that only one issue of undesired behavior at the top can have serious effects. Unfair though true: one mistake is better remembered than a thousand examples of good behavior. The rationalization is 'he preaches decent behavior, but when he sets his mind to it, he goes beyond any decency whatsoever'. A moral culture can be compared with a glass of water. The desired culture is grown drop by drop and it takes years of consistent exemplary behavior to create such a culture. However, one mistake and the glass falls down, leaving the organization in splinters and disorder. The glass of culture will have to be refilled drop by drop. However, the 'tone at the top' is but one aspect of rationalization. Next to the tone at the top there is the rhythm of the middle management and the drumming of feet on the work floor. Every manager must be aware of the importance of his exemplary function and the 'tone of the peers' is also crucial in preserving a culture of integrity. One of the difficulties in creating a culture of integrity lies with the middle management that actually manages the performing employees. If the norms, virtuously and constantly preached by the executive management prevent middle management from achieving their targets, they will be more inclined to surpass integrity hurdles. Balanced integrity management requires a downward translation into achievable targets. The targets have to be verified against ethical norms.

2.3 THE TRIANGLE AS A MEANS TO MANAGE IN PRACTICE

By using the visualization of the Triangle, the compliance or ethics officer can overcome his anguish when confronted with the request to assist in creating a culture of desired behavior where misconduct belongs to the past.

An integrity management system consists of enforcement, prevention and detection. Enforcement is often associated with deterrence. Although deterrence forms part of enforcement, it usually relates to process-dependent measures that play a role in integrity management. Without rules there would be no enforcement. Enforcement is reflected in the consequences of the compliance or non-compliance with rules.

Prevention is better than cure. Prevention is often considered an important remedy for putting a stop to undesirable behavior. Total prevention, however, may impede the success of organizations. Modern organizations appear to be highly successful precisely because they take risks instead of avoiding them. A high degree of risk avoidance may hamper the organization.

Detective measures serve to identify in time whether certain adjustments should be made to a process, without disrupting the process that is being monitored. Proper detection does not simply focus on issues that are wrong or unacceptable, but also includes the monitoring of the proper implementation of the process. In this way, detection promotes the need for people to be accountable.

Organizations have almost always protected themselves against misconduct with a three-pronged approach: prevent, detect and respond. This traditional approach focused on prevention: controls, checks and balances, internal audit, policies and the internal control framework. The detection component is made up of internal and external audit, monitoring – of compliance, effectiveness and transactions – and reporting. When an incident was identified, the typical response was to understand what had gone wrong and implement more controls to pick off the newly identified risks one by one, after the event. This approach has its limitations in terms of cost and effectiveness. Too much control may backfire. The rationalization is that obviously, employees are not to be trusted as seems to be proven by the vast majority of controls and continuous audits.[16] Also, technology is increasing the risk to organizations, by placing powerful tools in the hands of miscreants. It is also allowing organizations to take action in advance to reduce the threat of misconduct and its impact on the business. In Part IV chapter 15 on Fraud *infra* will go into more detail with regard to the new challenges companies face due to new technologies and their impact on fraud management. In the current chapter we will only focus on the Integrity Triangle.

The ideal model for managing the risk of integrity breaches is to separately apply the three control components to each of the three components of the Integrity Triangle. The same elements as in the Fraud Triangle apply to the behavior in the Integrity Triangle. The difference lies in the approach of the behavior in the positive – and hence preventive – way instead of the negative – deterrence – method. For instance, in financial institutions opportunity may well be served by the involvement of compliance in the creative phase of product development. Pressure offers a wide variety of possibilities to protect employees against non-compliance due to undue exercising of pressure, for instance more attention for work-life balance, extremely tight targets, etc. We have already touched on the issue of good exemplary behavior with regard to rationalization. The way the controls are approached is of the utmost importance. The organization must find a balanced approach between mandatory compliance and the more voluntary approach.

16. Mendoza et al. 2016 and Mendoza et al. 2015, pp. 1–18.

Figure 1

The definition of compliance already entails business ethics and conduct. 'Observance of external (international and national) laws and regulations, as well as internal norms and procedures, to protect the integrity of the organization, its management and employees with the aim to prevent and control risks and the possible damage resulting from these compliance and integrity risks.' However, the approach has always been one of mandatory compliance where deterrence has to ensure that employees act in a compliant way. Every new infraction of the rule was countered by more legislation and therewith internal regulations. Here lies a 'fatal error' that leads to a very unsound compliance environment. The new fraud and risks are countered with legislative action which is translated into internal rules instead of using the business processes as a starting point and translating legislation into more effective business procedures. Employees are increasingly confronted with a legal environment with extra administrative actions. In the end the legal requirements pile up and mistakes happen, encouraging even more rules and legalized procedures, including administrative time and funds spent on an increase in internal and external audits. The point of departure creates a fatal error: the business process becomes unnecessarily complex and the chance of errors increases. What is missing is the element of *knowledge*. Employees active in the first line of defense – the business – should understand the root causes of non-compliance and together with the experts on the business process, these processes should be adapted to prevent non-compliance without excessive legal, administrative hassle coupled mainly with measures containing deterrence. Instead of translating into internal regulations, sometimes it may be more appropriate to convey knowledge to the business so as to *understand why* business can be affected by a certain type of business conduct/procedure, instead of simply translating law into legal administrative procedures focused on the *what* and the *how*. Scientific research now focuses more on the importance of transferring knowledge and explaining the 'why' and as a result comes to the conclusion that the transfer of knowledge to employees and more balanced management systems with both mandatory and voluntary compliance increases trust and thus decreases aversion/unwillingness to comply, which leads to more effective prevention.[17]

2.4 THE INTEGRITY MANAGEMENT ENVIRONMENT

In an environment where ethics are controlled one may expect to find a comprehensive system including:

- an explicit owner of integrity management;
- published and continuously communicated corporate business principles;
- a general code of conduct that fits seamlessly with the business principles;
- special-purpose codes of conduct, related to whistleblowing, conflict of interest situations, insider trading or sexual harassment;
- a balanced system of controls relating to risk situations, categorized according to the principles as described in the code of conduct, covering all three elements of the integrity triangle;
- a system of frequently testing the perceptions of employees on the effectiveness and acceptance of the controls;
- a system of centralized reporting on the quality of integrity/ethics control;
- a contingency procedure, when incidents occur.

These requirements are common requirements and will be dealt with in more detail in the appropriate chapters (Compliance Management and several chapters in Part IV Capital Selecta) *infra*. However, within the present chapter these requirements will be discussed briefly in the light of their importance to integrity management and obtaining and preserving a culture of integrity.

In order for integrity management to be effective, the CEO has to be the owner of integrity within the organization. The daily management of integrity can be delegated to an executive officer such as the Chief Compliance Officer, the Chief Ethics Officer or even the Chief Risk Officer (CRO). The ownership by the CEO is undisputed; integrity lies at the heart of the business activity and therefore is a responsibility of the business and its senior executive officer. Integrity is *not* the concern of the ethics officer or the compliance officer but of the entire organization and integrity management is a delegated responsibility to all levels of management within the organization. To ensure that within the Executive Board, important compliance issues are not set aside due to other priorities, the Chief (Risk &) Compliance Officer must have direct access to the Supervisory Board (in a two-tier system) or must be able to exercise a veto on mission-critical compliance issues (one-tier system).

17. Mendoza et al. 2016 and Mendoza et al. 2015, pp. 1–18.

Senior management must persistently refer to business principles in the decision-making process and make clear to all that decision-making and all actions resulting therefrom are in line with the underlying business principles.

The code of conduct is not a mere exercise on paper, but must be in line with the points of departure on normative force of norms as discussed in the following subparagraph on codes of conduct *infra*.

To stress the importance of certain norms or because of legal requirements of such a code, additional codes of conduct may be necessary. Also, this prevents the main code of conduct from becoming an excessive proclamation of mandatory rules and thus creating an effect of aversion, e.g. codes of conduct on bribery, competition or privacy.

With regard to the controls, we should keep in mind what was discussed on a balanced system of deterrent and positively formulated controls *infra*.

Monitoring of compliance should be construed as minimally intrusive and yet as effectively as possible, preventing administrative burdens resulting in aversion and non-compliance. Where possible, controls should be trust-based and use should be made of 'horizontal control' through rethinking vertical monitoring and auditing through the third line of defense by creating horizontal controls based on trust. Of course, at the beginning trustworthiness may need to be proven, but it must be rewarded by horizontal supervision as will be discussed in more detail in Part II.

The final auditing of the ethics program is part of the third line of defense. This should be centralized to ensure that the first line of defense – the business – and in the last resort the Executive Board, takes full responsibility for the effectiveness of compliance and integrity management.

Even in organizations with effective and balanced compliance and integrity management systems, accidents will occur. The importance is to have a structure in place that offers warning signals and copes with the accidents in a timely and appropriate manner. Some of these systems will be discussed in more detail *infra*, such as the whistleblower procedures and fraud management protocols.

2.5 SPECIAL FOCUS ON CODES OF CONDUCT[18]

The quest for codes of conduct started in the late 1960s due to conflicts between multinational enterprises and their host countries. One of the problems arose through the problem of 'extraterritorial' regulation by the home country and the possible loss of economic self-determination by the host country. The latter issue was of special relevance to developing countries. In the 1960s the presence of foreign corporations in the host society was characterized as constituting a form of cultural imperialism, or 'Coca-Cola-ization' of the society, through which the developing country loses control over its culture and its social development. Centralized decision-making, especially in respect of decisions affecting employment in the broad sense, the organization of work, the introduction of a central corporate culture which was often foreign and alien to local customs and consequently, in some cases, the lack of an 'interlocuteur valable' undoubtedly affected the balance of power between management and labor; multinationals thus escape the national social network and may become or seem to

18. Part of this paragraph is based on Bleker-van Eyk 1995, pp. 5–32, and pp. 67–75.

become inaccessible to the local partners. Nowadays, the problems with regard to labor mainly focus on exploitation, human rights and maybe still a matter of cultural dominance. The main problem connected with centralized decision-making is the lack of accessibility for the local representatives of employees to the centralized management at the headquarters in the home country, which often takes the important decisions affecting the subsidiary in the host country. These decisions may adversely affect the employees in the host country, but the trade unions seldom have the opportunity to effectively enter into contact with the central managers in the home country. Even for the local manager in the host country, the central managers may be difficult to reach. A number of international trade union organizations have created World Councils, where trade union representatives from subsidiaries of multinational enterprises (MNEs) can exchange information and experiences. However, most MNEs do not wish to hold consultations with such councils. They fear that these consultations might change into multinational bargaining, which would complicate the bargaining process by introducing a third level alongside the existing local and national levels. On the part of trade unions, too, it would create certain problems with regard to collective bargaining. For example, it would imply active participation by trade unions from different countries with different set-ups, backgrounds, and, most of all, different interests. Finally, a fourth and very important grievance relates to the negative political consequence that direct foreign investment may have on host countries, especially the lesser developed countries. It has been argued that MNEs prefer to establish subsidiaries in host countries that have a stable government which is sympathetic to the home country's economic system. MNEs, as well as their home country governments, sometimes intervene in the internal affairs of the host country. The bigger the MNE, the more influence it can exert. Giant MNEs can exert a great amount of political and economic pressure upon a host country. The power of an MNE sometimes goes as far as becoming involved in national politics.

As a result, international intergovernmental organizations started their quest to create codes of conduct for multinational enterprises. The International Chamber of Commerce (ICC) was already active with the codes of conduct and on November 29, 1972 the ICC adopted the ICC Guidelines for International Investment. In 1976 the OECD adopted one of the best-known guidelines. This is still referred to in numerous codes of conduct of multinationals: the 'OECD Declaration and Decisions concerning Multinational Enterprises'. The International Labour Organization (ILO) followed in 1977 with the 'Tripartite Declaration of Principles Concerning Multinational Enterprises and Social Policy'. Due to the lingering differences within the United Nations Conference of Tariffs and Trade (UNCTAD), the United Nations (UN) has been struggling with the code of conduct exercise. In 2011 the UN adopted the 'United Nations Guiding Principles on Business and Human Rights' and also started the UN Global Compact.

Companies themselves started to create their own codes of conduct. Due to the incidents with corporates at the beginning of this millennium, legislation started to raise the important question of conduct. An example is Section 406 of the Sarbanes-Oxley Act, which outlines code of ethics requirements for senior financial officers. Taken directly from the Act, a code of ethics comprises the standards necessary to promote 'honest and ethical conduct; full, fair, accurate, timely and understandable disclosure in periodic reports' and 'compliance with applicable governmental rules and regulations'. The United States Federal Sentencing Guidelines also referred to an Ethics program (codes of conduct) as one of the imperative measures to ensure honest conduct within companies: §8B2.1(a)(2).[19] At the beginning of this century, the codes of conduct became a common part of the internal mechanisms of companies to deal with issues of ethics and the prohibition of criminal conduct such as bribery and competition.

Having a code of conduct does not guarantee ethical behavior. Of course, a code of conduct is but a part of the ethical programs, but in practice too many companies feel that laying down values in the code of conduct is a relatively simple and effective means to make employees abide by the business principles and norms. On the contrary, creating an effective code of conduct is quite a puzzling problem. The code of conduct needs to be part of a comprehensive program and there are some challenges to overcome before the norms lead to effective compliant behavior. An important aspect of the effectiveness of norms is their normative force. Both legally binding norms and legally non-binding norms may have normative force. This leads us to the question of what is to be understood by the term normative force. Van Dijk defines normative force as 'the effect of a norm directed at influencing behavior'.[20] This normative force is not inherent in norms. One might say that the normative force brings about the norm rather than the other way around. Instruments which are legally non-binding may contain standards of behavior which have normative effect. The addressee may feel obligated to act accordingly. This, however, is not because of an *opinio iuris* of the addressee, but because he regards the norm as a moral obligation. Through its normative force, a standard of behavior turns into a norm.

Norms are not the same as business principles. Principles contain a set of values and they do not aim at an objective as such, but at the *quality* of behavior. A principle may contain a point of departure in the realization of a policy and may imply consequences for behavior. A principle can indicate means by which a policy must be realized. Consensus applies to the point of departure as well as to the values and the means but not, however, to the specific behavior required of the individual legal subjects. Principles are 'norms of aspiration' and their normative force lies predominantly in the sphere of prohibition.

Rules are precisely formulated and demand a specific behavior. A rule ideally lays down who is obligated to behave in a certain manner and who is the beneficiary of such behavior. On the one hand, States may not, in the first instance, intend to create rules, but only principles while, gradually, these principles may pave the way for the development of rules. On the other hand, what might initially be intended as a rule can be transformed into a principle.

The normative force, the willingness of the addressee to accept the norm as a guideline for his behavior, is influenced by internal as well as external factors. The legitimacy is conditioned by the way in which the norm has been created and formulated, by the internal consistency of the system of norms, by the consensus on values underlying the norms, but also by the authority or the power of the person or institution setting the norm, the self-interest involved in complying with the norm,

---

19. http://www.ucdmc.ucdavis.edu/compliance/pdf/ussg.pdf. The USSG will be dealt with in more detail in chapter 3 of Part I *infra*.
20. Van Dijk 1987, p. 113.

and the expectation of compliance with the norm. Norms in a code of conduct need to fulfill certain minimum requirements in order to increase their normative force:

- the norms have to be phrased in sufficiently clear terms and in a realistic way in order for the employee to be able to adapt his behavior to the requirements laid down in the norm;
- the objective of the norm should be clear, as must be the manner in which it should be achieved;
- the normative force of a standard increases through the importance given to the behavior described in the norm within the company;
- effective supervision is necessary to stress the importance given to abide by the norm;
- fear of repercussion may further increase the normative force of the norm.

Creating a code of conduct is only effective when the normative force of the norms clarifies the required behavior and offers a point of departure for compliant behavior.

BIBLIOGRAPHY

Albrecht & Albrecht 2009
W.S. Albrecht & Albrecht, *Fraud Examination & Prevention,* Independence KY: South-Western Cengage learning 2009

Albrecht 2014
W.S. Albrecht, 'The Compromise Triangle', *The Wheatley Institution* 2014-May.

Bleker-van Eyk 1995
S.C Bleker-van Eyk, *The OECD Declaration and Decisions concerning Multinational Enterprises,* Nijmegen: Ars Aequi Libri 1995.

Bleker-van Eyk 2013
S.C Bleker-van Eyk, 'De Compliance Officer 2.0', *MAB* 2013-10.

Borak et al. 2016
D. Borak et al., 'New Rules Curbing Wall Street Pay Proposed, *Wall Street Journal* 2016-April.

Cressey 1953
D.R. Cressey, *Other People's Money,* New York: The Free Press 1953.

Van Dijk 1987
P. van Dijk, 'Normative Force and effectiveness of International Norms', *GYIL* 1987-30.

Gude 2015
R. Gude, *Het Agoramodel: de wereld is eenvoudiger dan je denkt,* Leusden: ISVW uitgevers 2015.

Mendoza et al. 2016
J.P. Mendoza et al., 'Can too much Auditing Backfire: A cross-country analysis of Auditing and Tax Compliance', *Journal of Public Economics* 2016-June.

Mendoza et al. 2015
J.P. Mendoza et al., 'Only the Carrot, Not the Stick: Incorporation Trust into the Enforcement of Regulation', *PLOS ONE* 2015-february.

Wells 1997
J.T. Wells, *Occupational Fraud and Abuse: how to prevent and detect asset misappropriation, corruption and fraudulent statements,* London: Obsidian Publishing Company 1997.

3. Compliance Management[1]

Prof. S.C. Bleker-van Eyk

3.1 THE COMPLIANCE FUNCTION

During the 1990s, the importance of compliance increased. The amount of both national and international legislation grew rapidly. At the beginning of this century, after some important ethical breaches within corporate enterprises, the legislature followed by creating a deluge of laws and regulations, mostly aimed at governance risk and compliance. After 9/11, corporate enterprises were confronted with increased and complex regulations on sanctions and export controls. After Enron and WorldCom, the Sarbanes-Oxley Act was introduced. In 1977, the Foreign Corrupt Practices Act (FCPA) came into force. However, the prosecution of foreign multinationals has only truly been enforced since the beginning of this century, mostly due to the entry into force of the Anti-Bribery Convention of the OECD. In addition, the United Kingdom Bribery Act became effective in 2011.[2]

In this chapter, the requirements of the compliance framework will be discussed, as well as the skills necessary to become an accomplished compliance officer. Both national and international examples will be given of required or recommended compliance frameworks, from the United Nations Global Compact to the ISO 19600 guideline.

3.2 INSTITUTIONALIZATION OF COMPLIANCE

Since the mid-1990s, compliance has gradually carved out a place for itself in financial institutions, growing from a Friday afternoon role for managers on the verge of retirement to full-fledged departments, some of them with a staff of several hundred. Compliance was slower to establish itself in non-financial companies, at least under that name. It started with the companies that were heavily regulated, for example the

1. Parts of this chapter was previously published in Dutch in Bleker-van Eyk 2013, pp. 402–411.
2. Both the FCPA and the UKBA will be discussed in more detail in Part IV *infra*.

pharmaceutical industry and the aircraft industry, which had been subject to strict airworthiness rules since the 1950s. Only in the course of this current century have non-financial companies gradually become aware of the importance of creating a compliance role, mainly because of the increase in regulations and enforcement in the medical industry, the military industry and other industries increasingly faced with enforcement of all sorts of rules (e.g. on exports and imports, food safety and other types of safety). The extraterritorial application of the American export rules is still the driving force behind the creation of many compliance roles in the industrial world.[3]

In recent years, we have seen increasing attention to compliance in the non-financial sector, owing to growing awareness of the extraterritorial application of anti-corruption legislation. Since 1997, the OECD Anti-Bribery Convention has enabled the US to enforce its legislation more effectively in other countries, as the States Parties - not only the OECD Member States - meet the requirement of dual criminality once they have ratified it. However, true awareness in boardrooms of the extraterritorial application of foreign legislation only seems to have developed after the passing of the UKBA.[4] Undoubtedly, Great Britain is not so far away that directors can sleep at night. Most of them slept fine with the American Foreign Corrupt Practices Act, which presented - and still presents - a far greater danger. Competition cases have also created a good deal of turmoil in recent years, though they are rarely regarded as compliance matters, and are usually still dealt with by legal departments. The question is whether this is correct. Competition cases fall under national and international legislation and can entail substantial risks. The purpose of compliance is to promote the observance of national and international laws and regulations, as well as internal rules and standards, to protect the integrity of the organization and its directors and staff. The aim is to control the risks of non-compliance with laws, regulations and standards and to prevent the damage that could result.[5] In short, compliance in effect ensures desirable, agreed upon conduct, as laws and regulations can either be breached by action or omission. This does not by definition apply to all laws and regulations, but it does, particularly, to laws and regulations related to achieving the company's key objectives. One could say that compliance derives its *raison d'être* from a company's license to operate. Compliance risks are risks that can pull the proverbial rug from under the company, or at least cause major material and reputational damage.

3.3 THE COMPLIANCE LANDSCAPE

When setting up a compliance function it is important to take into account the necessary requirements from the point of view of both governance and requirements

3. *Cf.* the United States: Directorate of Defense and Trade Controls (DDTC) http://www.pmddtc.state.gov/compliance/index.html; Bureau of Industry and Security (BIS) http://www.bis.doc.gov/complianceandenforcement/emcp.htm; OFAC http://www.treasury.gov/about/organizational-structure/offices/Pages/Office-of-Foreign-Assets-Control.aspx.
4. Bleker 2012.
5. Sylvie C. Bleker-van Eyk's definition as used in the Postdoctoral Course in Compliance & Integrity Management at the VU.

set by the appropriate supervisory authorities that supervise the actions of a particular company.

The landscape of compliance is directly related to the scope of compliance. The scope of compliance cannot encompass 'the observance of external (international and national) laws and regulations' as such. This would lead to a tsunami of rules and regulations that would be better dealt with by other departments within the company that are directly linked to the behavior targeted by that particular field of legislation. The scope of compliance should be linked to the key objectives of the organization and hence to the laws and regulations that can affect the organizations' license to operate. Numerous supervisory authorities exist, including a wide area of laws and regulations that are not directly linked to key objectives and where compliance is better left to other departments. For instance, legislation with regard to food safety in canteens should fall outside of the scope of compliance. This might be taken care of by other departments, for example the facility department. However, if the organization is a consultancy company advising large organizations on how to set up canteens within their organization, from a point of view of possible reputational damage it would be wise to make food safety regulations an essential part of compliance.

Note that compliance can also require cooperation with other organizational departments such as legal or human resources. Within the institutionalization of compliance, cooperation with other departments may best be served through an interdepartmental body coordinating the efforts and preventing overlap, or worse, conflicting internal procedures.

3.3.1 Compliance Charter

Corporate governance is defined as an internal system encompassing policies, processes and people, which serves the needs of shareholders and other stakeholders by directing and controlling management activities with good business savvy, objectivity, accountability and integrity. Sound corporate governance is reliant on external marketplace commitment and legislation, as well as a healthy board culture that safeguards policies and processes.[6]

Corporate governance encompasses governance issues, risk management and compliance activities. Key elements of good corporate governance principles include honesty, trust and integrity, openness, performance orientation, responsibility and accountability, mutual respect, and commitment to the organization. Of importance is how directors and management develop a model of governance that aligns the various values of the corporate participants and evaluate this model periodically. In particular, senior executives should conduct themselves honestly and ethically, especially concerning actual or apparent conflicts of interest, and disclosure in financial reports.[7]

Good corporate governance practices, according to COSO,[8] will lead to an internal control system as a process, effected by an entity's board of directors, management and other personnel, designed to manage the 'key risks' and provide

6. Compliance Charter Fokker Technologies B.V.
7. Ibid.
8. See the Risk chapters Part II *infra*.

'reasonable assurance' regarding the achievement of objectives in the following categories:[9]

- achieving the strategic objectives and targets;
- effectiveness and efficiency of operations;
- reliability of financial reporting; and
- compliance with applicable laws and regulations.

Within an organization's governance structure, the Compliance Charter is the 'constitution' of compliance that directly links compliance to the key objectives of the organization and its license to operate. The Compliance Charter contains the basic principles of compliance and integrity management. It should entail the organization's vision on compliance, as well as the scope of compliance and the institutional set up of the compliance framework.

The Charter describes the activities of compliance, including the reporting lines and the goal of compliance and integrity management within the organization. The Charter is the main governance document linking compliance principles to the compliance framework.

A Compliance Charter should contain:

- the vision on compliance, in which the organization underlines the importance it attaches to conducting its business activities in compliance with existing laws and regulations;
- the definition of compliance;
- the scope of compliance;
- the objective of compliance: the main objectives of compliance should be determined from the point of view of:
  i. supporting the effective control environment,
  ii. creating a transparent compliance structure,
  iii. identifying, reporting and monitoring risks,
  iv. communicating on compliance issues,
  v. complying with all relevant laws and regulations;
- the importance of maintaining constant awareness of compliance;
- the compliance structure and functioning;
- the responsibilities for compliance throughout all levels of the organization;
- reporting on compliance;
- the budget for compliance.

3.3.2 Compliance Program

The Compliance Program contains a more extensive vision on compliance for a set period of time. In general, most compliance programs are set for a period of five years. While the Compliance Charter entails the more general principles, the Compliance Program contains a more specified program, including:

- the compliance cycle;

9. Compliance Charter Fokker Technologies B.V.

- the distribution of tasks between the different lines of defense against non-compliance;
- awareness programs;
- the distribution of tasks and responsibilities of the existing compliance officers within the organization;
- the implementation of compliance throughout the organization.

The primary responsibility for compliance lies within the business (the first line of defense) and, as a result, the final responsibility lies with the Chief Executive Officer (in a one-tier board) or the Chief Executive Officer together with the Chairman of the Supervisory Board (in a two-tier board). At first sight it may seem obvious that the business holds the primary responsibility for compliance. Compliance is directly related to the key objectives and business activities are the responsibility of the first line of defense. However, recent history has shown that this is not as obvious as it seems. Compliance is actually situated in the second line of defense and its function is to assist the business on matters of compliance. In practice, it has become a habit for business to 'outsource' compliance matters *and* the related decisions to the second line (compliance). In the decision-making process, the first line refers to the second line by stating that compliance has approved it, so the decision is in accordance with the requirements set by compliance. As a result, the business tries to shift its responsibilities away towards the second line. This is incorrect! The first line knows all the circumstances and the business requirements. It may ask for assistance, but it never tries to absolve itself of the responsibility for compliance. Also, shifting business decisions to compliance increases the burden on the compliance department, thereby creating an environment where compliance has to take decisions without an in-depth business perspective. Together with the existing excessive legislative burden, replacing compliance decision in the business by decision-making in the second line of defense creates an environment where the compliance function is increasingly pressed into a 'tick-the-box' mode, which will create more additional compliance risks. Also, relaying decision-making to the second line of defense is contrary to the 'Three Lines of Defense' model, according to which 'the board delegates to the CEO and senior management *primary ownership* and *responsibility* for *operating risk management and control* [including compliance risks]. It is management's job to provide leadership and direction to the employees in respect of risk management, and to control the organization's overall risk-taking activities in relation to the agreed level of risk appetite'.[10]

'To ensure the effectiveness of an organization's risk management framework, the board and senior management need to be able to rely on adequate line functions - including monitoring and assurance functions - within the organization.'[11] This model explains the relations between the three functions and serves as a guide to how responsibilities should be divided:

1. the first line *owns* and *manages* risk;
2. the second line oversees or specializes in risk (compliance); and
3. the third line provides independent assurance (internal audit).

10. https://www.iia.org.uk/threelines (emphasis added).
11. Ibid.

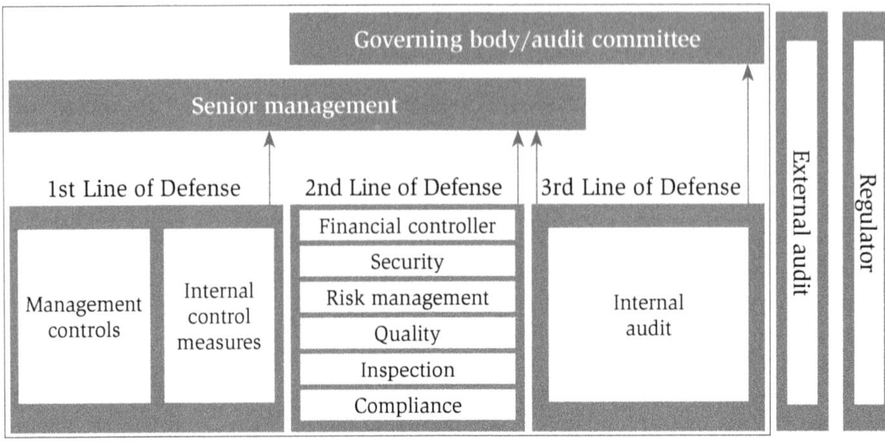

Figure 1: ECIIA/FERMA Guidance on the 8th EU Company Law Directive, Article 41

When assembling the 'Three Lines of Defense' model with the compliance structure discussed in the compliance program, the following compliance building arises.

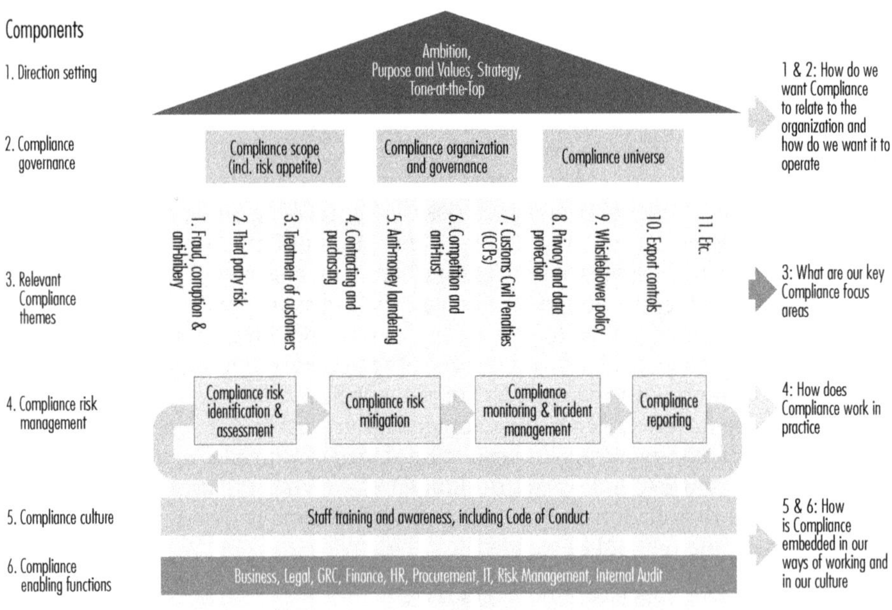

The compliance house is based on the COSO-ERM framework, relevant ISO-standards and leading market practices. To effectively manage Ethics and Compliance risks, it is essential to address Compliance at all levels of the 'Compliance House'.

Figure 2: The Compliance House PwC 2017

3.3.3 Structure of the compliance function

3.3.3.1 The final responsibility for compliance

In this chapter's paragraph on countervailing power *infra*, the issue concerning the independence of the compliance officer is discussed as it relates to skills. Within the compliance structure of an organization it is of particular importance to pay attention to the positioning of compliance within the chain of command of the organization and to ascertain that the highest ranking officer in direct command of the compliance function is sufficiently empowered to perform his duties and assure that compliance is regarded as the conscience of the organization.

As discussed *supra*, compliance is the responsibility of the business. As a result, the Executive Board bears the final responsibility for compliance. In practice, many flavors exist as to the chief ranking officer responsible for compliance. In some organizations, the Chief Executive Officer (CEO) bears the final responsibility for compliance. However, organizations often designate the Chief Financial Officer (CFO) as responsible for compliance. Also, sometime the Chief Operating Officer (COO) is in charge of compliance. Both the CFO and COO seem an appropriate choice, because the final responsibility rests within the Executive Board. However, their primary responsibility is not compliance, and compliance requirements may be set aside more easily because they conflict with the Officer's primary responsibility. CFOs or COOs may be more tempted to set aside compliance requirements. Recently, Executive Boards have been supplemented with a CRO. Compliance and integrity contain imminent risks for the organization, and the CRO seems to be well equipped to take on the task of Chief Compliance Officer (CCO). However, it is important that the CRO understands the importance of compliance and integrity risks and the effect they may have on the entire organization.

Yet, too often compliance is covered on a lower level instead of by the highest ranking executive officers. All too often, the CCO reports to the Chief Legal Officer, who in turn reports to the Company Secretary or the CFO. The sense of urgency on compliance and integrity risks may well become lost within the daily hassle of further legal risks waiting for better times, while the risk develops into a risk that may affect the license to operate. Finally, some organizations have bestowed the Human Resources (HR) department with the responsibility for integrity management. This must be regarded a highly undesirable situation. HR focuses on assisting the organization's management with employment-related matters. Their first aim is to assist management and some of the core tasks of integrity management should be in more neutral hands. For instance, receiving whistleblower information through Human Resources is a *contradictio in terminis*.

Understanding and assessing the potential impact of compliance and integrity risks within modern organizations and the intricate consequences of full-fledged incidents is a task that should not be accepted lightly and regarded as something to do on the side. The CRO on the Executive Board could easily become the Chief Risk and Compliance Officer (CRCO), giving compliance and integrity management (ethics) the proper place within the chain of command. However, compliance requires more than just a seat at the executive table. In those instances where compliance and integrity risks may adversely affect the organization and yet are set aside by the other members of the Executive Board – in a two-tier board – the CRCO must be able to step up the discussion on the risk level to the Supervisory Board, thereby ensuring that these risks are taken fully into consideration by all levels of governance within the organization. The decision to ask the Supervisory Board to make a final assessment of the compliance risk and the impact it may have upon the organization is not a step that should be taken lightly. It should be the joint decision of the Executive Board; otherwise it may poison internal management relations. Requesting the Supervisory Board to overrule the Executive Board will have serious consequences, but may be the ultimate way of trying to protect risks from exploding into a full-fledged compliance incident.

3.3.4 The Chief Compliance Officer

The description regarding the positioning of the CCO *supra* shows that the duties and authorizations can be regarded as a consequence of the CCO's position as the independent conscience of the organization. Consequently, the CCO:

- assists the Executive Board proactively in realizing the objectives of compliance. The CEO and CFO oversee the operations, and the CCO verifies compliance risks on decisions after having assessed these risks on a regular basis with the senior management and operational management;
- reports periodically (and when necessary independently) to the Supervisory Board (two-tier) and/or Audit Committee;
- is responsible for the organization's corporate compliance, integrity and fraud policies;
- supervises (where applicable) the country-specific compliance of the organization's subsidiaries;
- advises and supervises the divisional/local/business unit compliance officers of the subsidiaries; and
- executes the laws and regulations on insider trading with regard to the members of the Executive Board, the Supervisory Board and/or Audit Committee and all other relevant staff.

Resulting from this are the following tasks and responsibilities of the CCO:

- to develop, implement and monitor compliance activities and tools at corporate level for the organization;
- to review key compliance risks as reported by subsidiaries/divisions/business units, with the purpose of identifying material compliance risks organization-wide;
- to regularly adapt the compliance program in light of legal developments, developments in the businesses in which the organization is active, and developments and changes within the organization;
- to make recommendations to the Executive Board on ways and means to make business processes better geared to cater for compliance by the organization's divisional/local/business unit and staff with applicable regulations and codes of conduct.
- to perform and arrange *ad hoc* compliance reviews;

- to report *at regular intervals* to the Executive Board, the Supervisory Board (two-tier) and the Audit Committee on the implementation of the compliance program, progress made, issues, incidents and remedies, reports serious incidents *ad hoc* as may be appropriate.
- to coordinate the activities of the divisional/local/business unit compliance officers;
- to monitor that all relevant staff within the organization receive fit-for-purpose awareness and compliance training;
- to organize integrity workshops and other sessions to enhance the organization's compliance culture;
- to coordinate, draft and update the organization's codes/policies, and monitor the effective roll-out of and compliance with such codes/policies;
- to support internal and external auditors in preparing and conducting audits of the effectiveness of the program;
- to support directors and management in maintaining the 'right tone at the top';
- to act as the 'compliance face' for the organization both within and outside and at all levels of seniority;
- to be responsible within the organizations (including all subsidiaries/ divisions/business units/local) for all matters related to the development and implementation of the compliance program;
- to act as a sounding board for all within the organization on compliance and integrity-related matters.

3.3.5 The 'joint committee'

Compliance risks are inextricably interwoven with operations, and compliance is not the only department (partially) coping with a particular risk. Also, the tasks to be performed by compliance are sometimes quite similar to tasks performed by other departments of the organization. Consequently, from the point of view of efficiency, but also to prevent overlapping or even contradictory activities, it is advisable to establish some sort of 'joint committee', in which different departments synchronize activities. Departments such as Quality, Human Resources, Audit, Risk Management and Legal can divide or synchronize tasks. Looking at compliance risks from a broader perspective, it is far more efficient for all parties to agree on how best to mitigate the risk in a combined effort, than having every department doing its own part of the risk, thereby creating blind spots and/or inefficiencies. The CCO should chair such a joint committee.

The duties and tasks of such a joint committee are:

- to assist the CCO with the annual review of the compliance program on how to (i) monitor the effectiveness of the program; (ii) identify any compliance risk areas and weaknesses; and (iii) establish compliance objectives for the year;
- to coordinate activities between the different departments (compliance, internal audit, legal, human resources and quality management) necessary for the execution and administration of the compliance program;

- to provide solicited or unsolicited advice to the CCO;
- to advise on the development, implementation, maintenance, and administration of the compliance program;
- to advise on how to increase the awareness of all employees regarding the compliance program;
- to discuss and advise on investigations of reported violations of the compliance program or any other issues discovered through the annual compliance review or any other audit process;
- to advise on investigations into or studies of matters within the joint committee's scope of responsibilities;
- to advise the CCO as to the status of the compliance program and ongoing developments relating to compliance matters;
- to assess the adequacy of internal and external compliance auditing and controls.

3.3.5.1 *The divisional/business unit/local compliance officer*

In larger organizations consisting of various subsidiaries, divisions, business units or local entities, it is necessary, for the effective implementation of compliance, to create compliance departments with a divisional/business unit or subsidiary compliance officer. It should be borne in mind, however, that to prevent a compliance department becoming too large with respect to the compliance tasks that need to be performed, an organization may choose to have compliance officers at divisional or business unit level with no further compliance staff members within the division or business unit. For some organizations, it may be more effective to create a Compliance Shared Service Center at corporate level to support the divisional, business unit or local compliance officer with the performance of his tasks.

At subsidiary, division, business unit and/or local level, the compliance officer assists the general management in executing their responsibility for compliance. Compliance is the responsibility of the business and therefore management should be assisted on compliance matters. The ultimate responsibility for compliance nevertheless rests with the first line of defense.

The duties and responsibilities of the subsidiary, division and/or business unit compliance officer are:

- to perform and arrange *ad hoc* compliance reviews within the subsidiary, division and/or business unit;
- to make recommendations to the CCO on ways and means to make business processes better geared to cater for compliance by the staff of the organization's subsidiaries, divisions and/or business units with applicable regulations and codes of conduct;
- to report to the CCO on compliance-related matters and support the management of the subsidiary, division and/or business unit in maintaining the 'right tone at the top';
- to review the key compliance risks within the subsidiary, division and/or business unit with a view to identifying and reporting material compliance risks to the CCO;

- to monitor that all relevant staff in the business unit receive fit-for-purpose awareness and compliance training;
- to report *at regular intervals* to the management of the subsidiary, division and/or business unit and the CCO on the implementation of the compliance program, progress made, issues, incidents and remedies;
- to report serious incidents in the subsidiary, division and/or business unit on an *ad hoc* basis as may be appropriate to the management of the subsidiary, division and/or business unit and the CCO;
- to support internal and external auditors in preparing and conducting audits of the effectiveness of the compliance program in the subsidiary, division and/or business unit;
- to set up and maintain a compliance network in the subsidiary, division and/or business unit;
- to be responsible for the implementation of the compliance program in the subsidiary, division and/or business unit;
- to act as a sounding board for management and staff in the subsidiary, division and/or business unit on compliance and integrity-related matters.

Finally, the legal position of the CCO and the compliance officers in the subsidiaries, divisions and/or business units must not be harmed in any manner as a result of the execution of his compliance duties under the external and/or internal regulations. Their employment contracts should not be ended by management without a formal approval of the Supervisory Board or Audit Committee and a national court or other national labor authority. This is necessary to maintain the necessary independence of the compliance professionals.

3.3.6 Reporting

As discussed *supra*, the CCO should report to the Executive Board and be entitled to directly address the Chairman of the Supervisory Board (two-tier level) and/or the Chairman of the Audit Committee.

The CCO periodically submits reports to the Executive Board and the Audit Committee on the implementation of the compliance program, the progress made regarding the compliance process(es), training and the compliance environment, (ongoing) compliance issues, recent incidents and deployed remediation.

The CCO is the functional head of the compliance department. The structure and size (headcount) of the compliance department depends on the complexity and the size of the organization. Often, the CCO is situated at the headquarters of the organization and the different layers of the organization will have their own compliance department. For instance, every country in which the organization operates may have its own compliance department. Business units may also have their own compliance department. Thus, alongside the CCO, an organization may have divisional compliance officers and/or local compliance officers. These compliance officers are situated within the operations of the organization and have dual reporting lines. They have a functional reporting line to the CCO, as well as a reporting line to their general manager of the division/business unit, with a copy to the CCRO.

On a quarterly basis, the general management of the business units should also report on compliance to the Executive Board through a Letter of Representation (LoR).

3.4 VARIOUS EXAMPLES OF COMPLIANCE PROGRAM REQUIREMENTS

There are many examples of requirements set by local and international authorities regarding compliance programs. Within the financial system in particular, the requirements have become more and more explicit. For example, the Bank for International Settlements describes the responsibilities of the compliance function and how the compliance program should be implemented, including the review of policies and procedures. Already in 2005, the Bureau of Industry and Security (BIS) of the US Department of Commerce described the requirements of an effective compliance function and a compliance program. In Principle 1, BIS explicitly stated that 'the bank's board of directors is responsible for overseeing the management of the bank's compliance risk. The board should approve the bank's compliance policy, including a formal document establishing a permanent and effective compliance function. At least once a year, the board or a committee of the board should assess the extent to which the bank is managing its compliance risk effectively.' The responsibility of the first line of defense is stated clearly in Principle 2, which states that the bank's senior management is responsible for the effective management of compliance risks. In Principle 5, BIS explicitly states that the compliance function should be independent. In comment 21, BIS explains that the concept of independence does not mean that the compliance function cannot work closely with management and staff in the various business units. In fact, cooperation is required.[12]

The requirements for an effective compliance program will be discussed *infra* from the point of view of several authorities and institutions whose requirements are of guiding influence to many organizations that have set up their compliance function over the past decade.

3.4.1 ISO 19600 guidance and uniformity for the organization of compliance

Due to the increasing attention that is being devoted to compliance with laws and regulations and internal ethical and other standards and the notion that organizations must demonstrate that they promote compliance throughout the supply chain in our global economy, the International Organization for Standardization (ISO) has developed a guidance for all organizations on how to set up compliance.[13]

The compliance requirements in the financial sector have been expanded constantly, and since the credit crisis, further internationalization has taken place in the financial world with regard to compliance requirements. This is understandable at a time when global interdependence has steadily increased. The supervisory authorities make increasing demands in terms of compliance throughout the entire production process. As a result, compliance requirements are slowly but surely also being imposed on suppliers and customers in the industrial production process, services, etc. Compliance is no longer relevant only to financial institutions, which now have to include customers and affiliated banks in their compliance framework in addition

12. Basel Committee on Banking Supervision.
13. Compliance Management System Guidance 19600, 2014. http://www.iso.org/iso/home/store/catalogue_tc/catalogue_detail.htm?csnumber = 62342.

to their internal compliance. There is also a steady increase in attention devoted to compliance by supervisors of non-financial undertakings. The increase in fines and prosecutions of organizations in the Netherlands and abroad means they sense the need to be in control of compliance with laws, regulations and internal standards.

ISO 19600 provides structure for compliance within organizations. It is all about establishing the organization and assigning tasks in order to have visibility on compliant conduct by the organization and its employees. It is not so much about the personalities, but about what the organization has to do and what needs to be taken into account to be demonstrably compliant. The aim of ISO 19600 is to make compliance part of day-to-day business operations.

An additional advantage of ISO 19600 is that it is not a standard but a guideline. The Dutch representation was committed to this to prevent the guideline being applied to SMEs resulting in excessive costs. The organization must act in the spirit of the guideline and ensure that it is properly embedded in the organization. The ISO 19600 guideline enables organizations to see whether the organizations in their supply chain are fulfilling the compliance requirements. Certification is not really necessary. Compliance focuses on adherence to laws and regulations as well as internal standards. Compliance requires a certain conduct.

ISO 19600 is applicable to all types and sizes of organizations. It deals with a variety of compliance matters such as leadership, planning, support (resources, competence, awareness, training, behavior, culture, communication, documentation), operations (controls to manage obligations and desired behavior), performance evaluation (monitoring compliance performance, evaluation, compliance reporting, audit & management review), and improvement (management of non-compliance including escalation procedures). ISO 19600 is risk-based and fits within the existing ISO risk management framework.

Of particular note is the special focus of ISO 19600 on the role of leadership and its commitment to create a compliance culture within the organization. According to paragraph 5.3 of ISO 19600, leadership and commitment entail:

- upholding core values of the organization;
- ensuring establishment of procedures and provision of resources;
- ensuring integration of Client Management System in business processes;
- communicating importance of effective compliance management; and
- ensuring alignment between operational targets and compliance obligations.

In paragraph 7.3.2 attention is devoted to the necessity of a compliant culture. First, ISO 19600 emphasizes the role of top management in creating a compliant culture:

- creating an environment where reporting of non-compliance is encouraged and the reporting employee is safe from retaliation;
- identifying and acting promptly to correct and address non-compliance; and
- ensuring that operational targets do not compromise compliant behavior.

According to the guidance, a compliance culture requires:

- a clear set of published values;
- management to be actively seen abiding by values;
- leadership by example;
- visible recognition of achievements in compliance;

- prompt and proportionate disciplining in case of willful or negligent breaches of compliance obligations; and
- open and ongoing communication.

3.4.2 United States of America compliance requirements: principles of federal prosecution of business organizations[14]

Regarding the decrease in fines due to the existence of a dedicated compliance program by the organization, Competition Commissioner Almunia stated:[15] 'To those who ask us to lower our fines where companies have a compliance program, I say this: if we are discussing a fine, then you have been involved in a cartel; why should I reward a compliance program that has failed?'

It should be noted that on the basis of one infraction of the law, a compliance program should not be deemed to be ineffective. A good program will first of all prevent infractions. However, sometimes employees decide to (deliberately) act in contradiction with the internal requirements and a good compliance program will intercept wrongdoings and address them. Although intercepted, it may be likely that under certain circumstances the organization will voluntarily disclose the infraction to the appropriate governmental authorities.

With regard to the prosecution of companies and their employees, the US Department of Justice (DOJ) has developed quite an extensive view on what it regards as being a comprehensive and effective compliance program. According to the general principle on Corporate Compliance Programs stated in Chapter 9-28.800 of the US Attorneys' Manual – 'Principles of Federal Prosecution of Business Organizations':

> 'Compliance programs are established by corporate management to prevent and detect misconduct and to ensure that corporate activities are conducted in accordance with applicable criminal and civil laws, regulations, and rules. The Department encourages such corporate self-policing, including voluntary disclosures to the government of any problems that a corporation discovers on its own. However, the existence of a compliance program is not sufficient, in and of itself, to justify not charging a corporation for criminal misconduct undertaken by its officers, directors, employees, or agents. ... While the Department [DOJ] recognizes that no compliance program can ever prevent all criminal activity by a corporation's employees, the critical factors in evaluating any program are whether the program is adequately designed for maximum effectiveness in preventing and detecting wrongdoing by employees and whether corporate management is enforcing the program or is tacitly encouraging or pressuring employees to engage in misconduct to achieve business objectives.'[16]

As such, the DOJ has no formulaic requirements regarding corporate compliance programs. However, it describes the minimal requirements as well as the importance

---

14. United States Department of Justice, *US Attorneys' Manual*, Title 9, Chapter 9-28.000 'Principles of Federal Prosecution of Business Organizations', https://www.justice.gov/usam/usam-9-28000-principles-federal-prosecution-business-organizations.
15. Speech by Joaquin Almunia, at the US Chamber of Commerce, Speech/10/586, 2010.
16. 9-28.800 'General Principle on Corporate Compliance Programs'.

of effectiveness of the compliance program, which will be discussed in this sub-paragraph.

According to the DOJ, an organization's compliance program should be well designed and be applied earnestly and in good faith. In order to assess the good faith and effectiveness the prosecutor should assess the comprehensiveness and effectiveness of the compliance program. The Attorneys' Principles offer examples on the basis of which such an assessment can be made. The following examples are given:

- the organization's directors exercise independent review over proposed corporate actions rather than unquestioningly ratifying officers' recommendations;
- internal audit functions are conducted at a level sufficient to ensure their independence and accuracy; and
- the directors have established a reasonably designed information and reporting system to provide management and directors with timely and accurate information sufficient to allow them to reach an informed decision regarding the organization's compliance with the law.

According to the *Attorneys' Principles*, a compliance program should not be merely a program on paper, but should be 'designed, implemented, reviewed, and revised, as appropriate, in an effective manner. In addition, prosecutors should determine whether the corporation has provided for a staff sufficient to audit, document, analyze, and utilize the results of the corporation's compliance efforts.'

Another important source concerning the requirements of an effective compliance program is the US *Resource Guide.*[17] Although primarily focusing on anti-corruption, the *Resource Guide* offers insight into the requirements of compliance programs set by the DOJ.

According to the US *Resource Guide*, an effective compliance program promotes 'an organizational culture that encourages ethical conduct and a commitment to compliance with the law'. Such a program 'protects a company's reputation, ensures investor value and confidence, reduces uncertainty in business transactions, and secures a company's assets.'[18]

According to the *Resource Guide*, a company's failure to prevent every single violation does not necessarily mean that a particular company's compliance program was not generally effective. However, an effective compliance program should be designed, implemented and enforced in good faith. The *Resource Guide* uses a 'common-sense and pragmatic approach to evaluating compliance programs'.[19] The *Resource Guide* states the following so-called hallmarks of effective compliance:[20]

- Each organization has its own characteristics, and as a result there is no one-size-fits-all program.

---

17. *A Resource Guide to the* U.S. Foreign Corrupt Practices Act By the Criminal Division of the U.S. Department of Justice and the Enforcement Division of the U.S. Securities and Exchange Commission. https://www.justice.gov/sites/default/files/criminal-fraud/legacy/2015/01/16/guide.pdf
18. US *Resource Guide*, p. 56.
19. Ibid., p. 57.
20. Ibid., p. 58 et seq.

- A 'tick-the-box' compliance approach may be inefficient and as a result ineffective. A compliance program should be carefully designed and implemented and enforced in good faith.
- Compliance begins with the board of directors and senior executives setting the proper tone for the rest of the company. The tone at the top, the rhythm of the middle and the drumming of the feet. The *Resource Guide* emphasizes the importance of the right attitude of the executive level in order to create a culture of compliance. Commitment is necessary at the highest level and cascading throughout all levels. It is important to stress that a compliant culture requires an ethical culture.
- The foundation of an effective compliance program is a clear, concise and accessible code of conduct. The code should also be periodically reviewed and where necessary updated.
- Also, the organization needs to have the necessary policies and procedures in place that outline responsibilities for compliance, as well as proper internal controls, auditing practices, and documentation policies. According to the *Resource Guide*, 'effective policies and procedures require an in-depth understanding of the company's business model, including its products and services, third-party agents, customers, government interactions, and industry and geographic risks.'
- All policies and procedures should apply to personnel at all levels of the company.
- The responsibility for the oversight and implementation of a company's compliance program has to be attributed to one or more specific senior executives within an organization. Of particular importance is that the *Resource Guide* emphasizes that the compliance officers 'must have appropriate authority within the organization, adequate autonomy from management, and sufficient resources to ensure that the company's compliance program is implemented effectively. Adequate autonomy generally includes direct access to an organization's governing authority, such as the board of directors and committees of the board of directors (e.g. the audit committee).' Further on in this chapter we will discuss the importance of independence and autonomy with regard to the concept of 'countervailing power'.
- All relevant policies and procedures have been communicated throughout the organization, including through periodic training and certification for all directors, officers, relevant employees, and, where appropriate, agents and business partners.
- Finally, the *Resource Guide* states that 'assessment of risk is fundamental to developing a strong compliance program, and is another factor DOJ and SEC evaluate when assessing a company's compliance program.'

The most renowned list of requirements of an effective compliance program is presented in chapter 8 on the Sentencing of Organizations of the US Federal Sentencing Guidelines (USFSG).[21] The DOJ applies the USFSG's elements of an effective

21. U.S. Federal Sentencing Guidelines, Chapter 8, § 8B2.1. http://www.ussc.gov/guidelines/2015-guidelines-manual/2015-chapter-8

compliance program, as set forth in §8B2.1 of the Guidelines. Due to the importance of the USFSG for the interpretation of compliance programs of organizations with a US nexus, the USFSG §8B2.1 on an effective compliance and ethics program is inserted in full.

'*§8B2.1. Effective Compliance and Ethics Program*

(a) To have an effective compliance and ethics program, for purposes of subsection (f) of §8C2.5 (Culpability Score) and subsection (b)(1) of §8D1.4 (Recommended Conditions of Probation - Organizations), an organization shall -

(1) exercise due diligence to prevent and detect criminal conduct; and
(2) otherwise promote an organizational culture that encourages ethical conduct and a commitment to compliance with the law.

Such compliance and ethics program shall be reasonably designed, implemented, and enforced so that the program is generally effective in preventing and detecting criminal conduct. The failure to prevent or detect the instant offense does not necessarily mean that the program is not generally effective in preventing and detecting criminal conduct.

(b) Due diligence and the promotion of an organizational culture that encourages ethical conduct and a commitment to compliance with the law within the meaning of subsection (a) minimally require the following:

(1) The organization shall establish standards and procedures to prevent and detect criminal conduct.
(2)
   (A) The organization's governing authority shall be knowledgeable about the content and operation of the compliance and ethics program and shall exercise reasonable oversight with respect to the implementation and effectiveness of the compliance and ethics program.
   (B) High-level personnel of the organization shall ensure that the organization has an effective compliance and ethics program, as described in this guideline. Specific individual(s) within high-level personnel shall be assigned overall responsibility for the compliance and ethics program.
   (C) Specific individual(s) within the organization shall be delegated day-to-day operational responsibility for the compliance and ethics program. Individual(s) with operational responsibility shall report periodically to high-level personnel and, as appropriate, to the governing authority, or an appropriate subgroup of the governing authority, on the effectiveness of the compliance and ethics program. To carry out such operational responsibility, such individual(s) shall be given adequate resources, appropriate authority, and direct access to the governing authority or an appropriate subgroup of the governing authority.
(3) The organization shall use reasonable efforts not to include within the substantial authority personnel of the organization any individual whom the organization knew, or should have known through the exercise of due diligence, has engaged in illegal activities or other conduct inconsistent with an effective compliance and ethics program.
(4)
   (A) The organization shall take reasonable steps to communicate periodically and in a practical manner its standards and procedures, and

other aspects of the compliance and ethics program, to the individuals referred to in subparagraph (B) by conducting effective training programs and otherwise disseminating information appropriate to such individuals' respective roles and responsibilities.

(B) The individuals referred to in subparagraph (A) are the members of the governing authority, high-level personnel, substantial authority personnel, the organization's employees, and, as appropriate, the organization's agents.

(5) The organization shall take reasonable steps –

(A) to ensure that the organization's compliance and ethics program is followed, including monitoring and auditing to detect criminal conduct;

(B) to evaluate periodically the effectiveness of the organization's compliance and ethics program; and

(C) to have and publicize a system, which may include mechanisms that allow for anonymity or confidentiality, whereby the organization's employees and agents may report or seek guidance regarding potential or actual criminal conduct without fear of retaliation.

(6) The organization's compliance and ethics program shall be promoted and enforced consistently throughout the organization through (A) appropriate incentives to perform in accordance with the compliance and ethics program; and (B) appropriate disciplinary measures for engaging in criminal conduct and for failing to take reasonable steps to prevent or detect criminal conduct.

(7) After criminal conduct has been detected, the organization shall take reasonable steps to respond appropriately to the criminal conduct and to prevent further similar criminal conduct, including making any necessary modifications to the organization's compliance and ethics program.

(c) In implementing subsection (b), the organization shall periodically assess the risk of criminal conduct and shall take appropriate steps to design, implement, or modify each requirement set forth in subsection (b) to reduce the risk of criminal conduct identified through this process.'

The requirements as set by the Bureau of Industry and Security (BIS) of the US Department of Commerce will be discussed in more detail in Part IV Capita Selecta in chapter 18 on export controls and sanctions. The BIS requirements largely correspond to the requirements set *supra*.

3.4.3 Compliance management tools

Adherence by employees to the compliance requirements set by the organization, legislators and supervisory authorities has to be constantly monitored and regularly audited to prove the organization's compliance with laws and regulations.

It would be completely impossible to give an overview of existing monitoring tools. It is wise, however, to make some observations regarding the choice of monitoring tools. The first basic assumption is that buying tools 'off the shelf' may not prove to be effective enough to achieve compliance. No organization is the same. The core of the tool may be 'off the shelf' but some kind of transformation to the factual organization will be necessary. For example, in order for e-learning to be effective, the questions have to portray the actual business questions from the organization and business cases that are derived from actual business practice of the organizations. Photographs of people actually working within the organization enhance the effect. This does not refer solely to executive management.

E-learning is not enough. Face-to-face workshops where cases can be discussed and questions can be answered are key to enhance compliance. It should be emphasized that in order for employees to really grasp the essential requirements as to their conduct, the language used in policies, e-learning, training and other tools should be understandable and should definitely not be mainly a translation of legal requirements.

Numerous companies specialize in monitoring tools that can be bought. However, every tool needs to be adapted to the natural environment of the employee: the organization itself. Also, the tools should aim at making compliance easier instead of more difficult. The tools should not be descriptive and compelling, but should be construed as assisting employees in making it easier to achieve compliance. This will not always be possible, but the organization should always strive to apply tools that make it easier to comply or at least make clear why the employee needs to comply. Often, tools are built to monitor and prove compliant conduct, while the approach should be to support the employee with compliant conduct. The change of focus may lead to better tooling and consequently more compliant behavior. For instance, with regard to anti-corruption and bribery as well as conflict of interest and fair competition registration tools may be used. The back end of the tool may be complex, but the user end of the tool should be easy. Many organizations require permission for receiving or providing gifts, entertainment and hospitality. Permission can be granted through a tool with simple questions such as 'who is receiving what, offered/given by whom, on what occasion and representing what value?' The questions can be easily described and put forward through so-called drop-boxes. At the back end of the tool, connections are made to the Client Management System of the organization as well as the authorization matrix and where necessary screening tools. Screening tools can screen (future) employees, business partners, agents, customers, etc. against sanction lists or (criminal) reputation. Screening tools make highly difficult and time-consuming screening actions easier and can even be linked to the organization's management system, thereby preventing the organization from doing business with sanctioned parties or parties that may be detrimental to the organization's reputation.

Special attention should be paid to whistleblower policies and tools. Whistleblowers are important because employees may detect wrongdoing within the business process that may otherwise only be detected after the harm has been done or may even slip through the compliance net and never be detected at all. Ultimately, it could be stated that the use of a whistleblower system means that the organization's management has failed to create such a culture of compliance and integrity that the whistleblower does not dare to report a (possible) incident within the hierarchy of the organization itself and resorts to blowing the whistle internally through a secured system, or outside the organization, while seeking protection against possible internal retaliation (discrimination or even dismissal).

Section 922 of the Dodd-Frank Wall Street Reform and Consumer Protection Act (Dodd-Frank Act)[22] provides that the Commission shall pay awards to eligible

22. https://www.sec.gov/about/offices/owb/dodd-frank-sec-922.pdf.

whistleblowers who voluntarily provide the SEC with original information that leads to a successful enforcement action yielding monetary sanctions of over USD 1 million. The award amount is required to be between 10% and 30% of the total monetary sanctions collected in the Commission's action or any related action, such as in a criminal case. A whistleblower may be eligible to receive an award for original information provided to the Commission on or after July 22, 2010, but before the whistleblower rules become effective, so long as the whistleblower complies with all such rules once effective. The Dodd-Frank Act also expressly prohibits retaliation by employers against whistleblowers and provides them with a private course of action in the event that they are discharged or discriminated against by their employers in violation of the Act. The SEC has also opened a special Whistleblower website.[23]

Whistleblower protection focuses on the actual *protection* of the employee. Organizations with a comprehensive whistleblower policy offer the employee the choice between an internal and an external contact point. This dual system fits within the modern corporate governance structures and the organization remains in charge of the decision on whether or not to initiate an external investigation due to the fact that external investigations by national authorities may affect the reputation of the organizations. However, it has become customary to launch an internal investigation and at a later stage request prosecution of the culprits.

Where whistleblower policies are concerned, the same applies as stated *supra*. The regulation must be written in language understandable to all employees and communicated effectively and repeatedly to employees. The US legislation requires the possibility of anonymous whistleblowing. From the point of view of protection against retaliation, this is understandable. However, from the point of departure of an internal investigation and the necessity of contact with the whistleblower to obtain proof, this proves to be a difficulty in the process of gathering evidence. There are several web-based solutions available that create – together with a hotline – a single information system, generating a management report while assuring anonymity of the whistleblower. The personal data of the whistleblower must be protected to prevent retaliation. Sometimes this creates significant problems, because some national privacy legislators require the subject who is under investigation to be informed.

When an organization chooses to establish both an internal and external contact point, stringent procedures are necessary on the exchange of information vital to the investigation. However, it offers the whistleblower a choice between an internal and an external contact point.

Two internal contact points, in the event that one of the contact points is involved in the issue that is reported upon. Reporting to line management is the preferred option. Both the internal and external contact point should report at least once a year to the board and the Audit Committee. A general report should include the number of reported incidents, the nature of the incidents, the actions undertaken and the results. The reports must not go into detail concerning the incidents as such. Whistleblowing policies promote enforcement of the organization's code of conduct and all related policies and procedures, as well as the interest of the company, because whistleblowing is the most effective and efficient fraud detection method by far.

23. https://www.sec.gov/about/offices/owb.shtml.

3.5 REQUIRED SKILLS OF THE COMPLIANCE OFFICER

3.5.1 Training aspects

It is clear from the foregoing that today's compliance officer is no longer adequately equipped to meet the challenges facing him in the current climate. Different internal and external stakeholders, e.g. the organization, the regulators, the customers or other stakeholders, demand that the compliance officer is a highly professional person who performs his duties in accordance with the requirements as stated in the previous paragraph.

An accomplished compliance professional must nowadays be able to:

- apply a multidisciplinary approach to compliance and integrity issues (i.e. based on established academic disciplines such as ethics, law, risk management and auditing);
- chart an organization's compliance landscape, including the national and international regulatory mechanisms to which the organization is subject and the role and impact of the other stakeholders;
- understand the most important features of a compliance and integrity policy;
- formulate an organization's compliance and integrity policy;
- embed the compliance and integrity policy within the organization;
- make reliable, reasoned assessments of compliance and integrity risks;
- prioritize compliance and integrity risks in a reasoned manner; and
- link appropriate control measures to compliance and integrity risks.

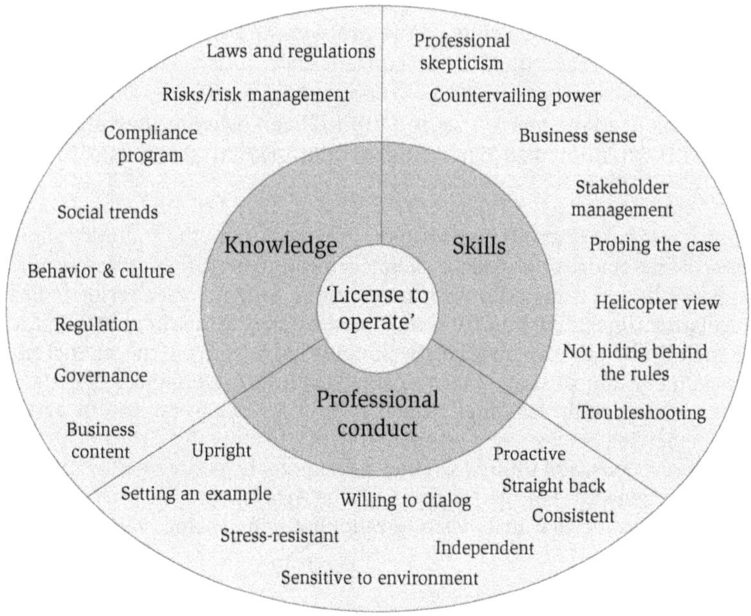

Figure 3: Requirements concerning skills, knowledge and professional conduct of an accomplished compliance officer

The post-doctoral Executive Master Program in Compliance & Integrity Management of the VU University Amsterdam developed an oversight of the requirements concerning skills, knowledge and professional conduct an accomplished compliance officer should possess (Figure 3).

3.5.2 Professional skepticism

Professional skepticism is cited as a skill but it is actually a state of mind without which one should not aspire to become a compliance officer. Professional skepticism should be embedded in the DNA of a compliance officer.

In 1952, J.K. Galbraith, the founding father of professional skepticism, stated that 'private economic power is held in check by the countervailing power of those who are subject to it'.[24] Even in 1993, Galbraith argued: 'The core thesis that an established answer to economic power is the building of a countervailing power is, indeed, still valid.'[25]

First, let us analyze the terminology of 'Countervailing power'. Countervailing can also be interpreted as 'compensating power'. Too much power on the one hand (for instance targets) may require a 'compensating' power exerted by compliance to prevent the goal being out-balanced through a lesser appreciation of the compliance risks. 'Counter' implies diverging interests and goals. 'Power' refers to individuality, independence, robustness. Also, the focus on another power requires an identity of its own, for example compliance. It implies that entity's 'own view' and critical faculties. But first and foremost, countervailing power and professional skepticism require a person to dare to be skeptical about himself. Do not decide at face value on the solution of a problem. The simplest explanation is often the right one, but look to discern the different layers of the problem and analyze each layer. Bear in mind that small risk may entail major consequences. Also, within an organization we should keep one another on our toes. Keep asking questions. Do not just listen to what employees or managers are saying; try to listen to what they are *not* saying.[26]

In the EU attention has been paid to professional skepticism in relation to auditing:

> 'when the statutory auditor or the audit firm carries out the statutory audit, he, she or it maintains professional skepticism throughout the audit, recognizing the possibility of a material misstatement due to facts or behavior indicating irregularities, including fraud or error, notwithstanding the statutory auditor's or the audit firm's past experience of the honesty and integrity of the audited entity's management and of the persons charged with its governance. The statutory auditor or the audit firm shall maintain professional skepticism in particular when reviewing management estimates relating to fair values, the impairment of assets, provisions, and future cash flow relevant to the entity's ability to continue as a going concern. For the purposes of this Article, "professional skepticism" means an attitude that includes a questioning mind, being alert to conditions

24. Galbraith 1952, pp. 118–119.
25. Galbraith 1993, p. 7.
26. Quadackers 2013, pp. 21–22.

> which may indicate possible misstatement due to error or fraud, and a critical assessment of audit evidence.'[27]

The International Auditing and Assurance Standards Board (IAASB) Staff Questions and Answers cites in A 18–20 the following requirements on professional skepticism:[28]

> '*Code of Ethics for Professional Accountants (IESBA Code) related to an audit of financial statements together with national requirements that are more restrictive.* A15. Part A of the IESBA Code establishes the fundamental principles of professional ethics relevant to the auditor when conducting an audit of financial statements and provides a conceptual framework for applying those principles. The fundamental principles with which the auditor is required to comply by the IESBA Code are:
> (a) Integrity
> (b) Objectivity
> (c) Professional Competence and Due Care
> (d) Confidentiality and
> (e) Professional Behavior'

The International Standard on Auditing (ISA) 200 defines 'professional skepticism' as 'an attitude that includes a questioning mind, being alert to conditions which may indicate possible misstatement due to error or fraud, and a critical assessment of audit evidence.'[29] As an attitude, professional skepticism is fundamentally a mindset. A skeptical mindset drives auditor behavior to adopt a questioning approach when considering information and forming conclusions. In this regard, professional skepticism is inseparably linked to the fundamental ethical principles of objectivity and auditor independence. Without a doubt, this notion also fully applies to the compliance officer.

3.6 THE COMPLIANCE OFFICER 3.0: THE VASCULAR SURGEON

Maturity of compliance seems to have been reached in the financial institutions, but as a result the tenability of compliance in that sector also seems to be increasingly up for discussion. In the industrial world, on the other hand, we see compliance growing apace. These two trends call for the overhaul of the compliance role, which should be more assertive and more robust. We need a fresh approach to compliance, the compliance officer and his relationship with the first and third lines. The question is whether today's compliance officer will survive the crisis, or whether there will only be room for the compliance officer 3.0. Compliance officer 1.0 did his job at the end of Friday afternoon. Compliance officer 2.0 became a professional, but despite all the efforts in the early years of this modern officer, it soon became obvious that

27. Art. 15 of Proposal for a regulation of the European Parliament and of the Council on specific requirements regarding statutory audit of public-interest entities, COM(2011) 779 final, 2011/0359 (COD), Brussels, 30/11/2011, pp. 39–40.
28. http://www.ifac.org/publications-resources/staff-questions-answers-professional-skepticism-audit-financial-statements
29. International Standard on Auditing (ISA) 200, Art. 13 Definitions (l), December 15, 2009.

compliance was suffering from hydrocephalus. Time for compliance officer 3.0 to take the stage.

In the financial institutions in particular, the incidents since 2001 and the financial and economic crisis have resulted in government bodies and other regulators unleashing a torrent of laws and regulations upon them: the term 'tsunami' may perhaps be appropriate here. On a European level, supervision already thrives. For example, the European System of Financial Supervision (ESFS), European Banking Authority (EBA), European Securities and Markets Authority (ESMA) and the European Insurance and Occupational Pension Authority (EIOPA).

More and more compliance is linked with so-called 'hard controls', specifying how the objective of the institution should be reached. The regulators enforce compliance in order to counter undesirable behavior. In response, financial institutions set up large compliance departments. Yet, in the process it became a top-heavy function. Failing to keep pace with the organization's organic development, it begins to resemble an alien body within – one being rejected slowly but surely by the host entity. Compliance gains importance when an issue arises and the regulators start insisting that the rules must be observed. As soon as the crisis has passed, compliance retreats to the background, leaving the conduct creating the problem in place. After the crisis has passed compliance is but a safety net in the face of increasing legislative controls.

Compliance's first priority is to safeguard the organization by channeling behavior within the framework of the legal requirements. Rethinking compliance will also require action on the part of national and international authorities. Through all the inextricable interdependencies it is not possible for an institution to go on a solo search for answers and solutions. Trust from the outside stakeholders is necessary to accomplish the why, how and what! Trust is also necessary to maintain internal stability. Employees need to have trust, and trust each other and the system in order to be stable enough to follow the institutions in change. Employees are part of society and we may and can no longer permit ourselves to close our eyes to the national and international movement of discontent. However, we should not adopt short-term solutions to ease the first signs of discontent: we should be transparent in our ambitions for the future and be ready to learn from our mistakes.

Compliance is a role that has gradually reached maturity. The incidents, many of them international but some national, have vastly increased the importance of compliance, but not without some question marks. Growth needs to be effective and go hand in hand with pragmatic understanding and a sense of balance between the various interests. The 'Three Lines of Defense' approach and the standard positioning of compliance in the second line, instead of dividing it up between the first line, which is primarily responsible for compliance, and the second line, have resulted in substantial compliance departments. Now that the fires have been extinguished, risk awareness is often carried away together with the water.

A quite challenging piece of research by Deloitte Australia in 2016 showed a tremendous loss of productivity due to ever increasing red tape and an associated constant increase in the combined cost of administering and complying with public and private sector bureaucracy at high costs.[30] This trend does only concerns Australia,

30. Deloitte Australia, 2014, p. 6.

but is a widespread phenomenon choking companies by strangulation with red tape. In total, self-imposed rules cost AUD 21 billion[31] a year to administer, and generate a stunning AUD 134 billion a year in compliance costs. When combined, the costs of administering and complying with public and private sector rules equate to a quarter of a trillion dollars a year: AUD 94 billion to administer and comply with public sector rules; AUD 155 billion to administer and comply with self-imposed rules and regulations, and, finally, unquantifiable losses from forgone incentives, enterprise and innovation. As a result: at least eight weeks of work just to cover the cost of administering and complying with rules.

According to this report 'the cost of our rules is much bigger than it needs to be because our rule-makers - both government and business - often try to achieve the unachievable. They set rules that are too prescriptive, overreact to momentary crises, let new rules overlap with existing rules, don't listen to those most affected, and don't go back later to check how well - or how badly - their rules are working.'[32]

As early as 2005, the former UK Prime Minister Tony Blair noted the pointlessness and cost of trying to 'eliminate risk in a way that is out of all proportion to the potential damage', and said the result was 'a plethora of rules, guidelines, responses to "scandals" of one nature or another that ends up having utterly perverse consequences'.[33]

The Australian report describes five steps (called the 5Cs) to encourage companies to:[34]

> '1. Cleanse: Slash the stupidity - ask staff to list the dumbest things they are required to do as a result of the business's own rules, then stop doing them.
>
> 2. Challenge: Businesses should stop asking 'What could go wrong?' and focus on 'What must go right?', then challenge their rules in that light. What are their rules really trying to achieve, could they be improved and are they cost-effective? If not, there may be more to dump.
>
> 3. Create: Foster a culture focused on performance rather than compliance, and ensure the organization's rule-makers are aligned to its business goals.
>
> 4. Change: Businesses and others should change the way they set new rules and audit old ones to better link rules with strategy and risk appetite.
>
> 5. Capitalize: Make the most of these changes to realize the business's full potential.
>
> Following these steps will allow your staff to generate extra profits while better controlling the risks that matter. In other words, we need to get out of our own way.'

Ever since the 1990s, compliance has grown, not only in importance but also in costs and headcount. The amount of national and international legislation is still growing. Most legislation used to be prudential. Know Your Customer (KYC) became an issue during the 1990s, as well as conflict of interest. At the beginning of this century, after

31. The Australian dollar in 2016 was 0.7 US dollar.
32. Deloitte Australia, 2014, p. 7.
33. Blair 2005.
34. Deloitte Australia, 2014, p. 8.

some important ethical breaches, legislation within large corporates gave rise to a deluge of laws and regulations, mostly aiming at Governance Risk and Compliance. After 9/11, corporates were confronted with increased and complex regulations on Sanctions and Export Controls. After Enron and WorldCom, the Sarbanes-Oxley Act was introduced. Also, anti-bribery and corruption legislation, sanctions and export controls have turned compliance and integrity management into an essential part of the sanitary condition of corporates and it has become increasingly complex and difficult to handle.

As always, a crisis is met with an inextricable clutter of national, European and foreign legislation. Compliance and integrity are thus essential risks that need to be tackled. After the crisis, the legislative clutter remains but the risk awareness decreases, making the top-heavy compliance department perfect prey for cutbacks. The Australian '5 Cs' as quoted *supra* may be helpful here. Simply cutting the clutter has no effect. First, before wise decisions can be made, the chaos has to be ordered and compliance needs to be reorganized without creating even more risks.

When an incident is identified, the typical response is to understand what has gone wrong and to implement more policies, procedures and controls to pick off the newly identified risks one by one; thereby creating an inextricable web of rules, procedures and audits. The results are threefold. First, employees find it more difficult to conduct their work and due to the complexity of the process mistakes occur more frequently. Secondly, the complex web offers the more creative employees possibilities to circumvent without being caught. Finally, more rules, procedures and audits have a negative impact on the rationalization of employees. The web indicates that the organization is full of unethical employees. This may push a law-abiding employee over the tipping point into becoming a fraudulent employee.

This approach has its limitations in terms of cost and effectiveness and not least because people intent on committing a financial crime will find ways around these controls or collude with someone operating within the control environment. It also creates more bureaucracy without adding value and lulls organizations into a false sense of security without increasing effectiveness. People within the organization assume that the existence of controls absolve them of the need to be alert to the risk of misconduct.[35]

Reorganizing compliance only makes sense when the focus lies on the key business objectives of the organization. The mere translation of legal requirements into policies requires employees in the first line of defense to become 'paralegals' ('legalizing' the business) is not enough. Instead, business requirements should be translated into policies within the limitations set by legal requirements. The focus should be on the business and creating the right conduct within the business instead of departing from law as the changing force. Organizations should be transparent towards the internal and external stakeholders on the conduct that is required from business. However, it often seems as if the legal framework rules the business. Employees in the first line just do not understand the requirements anymore and feel that they are left with the 'hassle' of compliance.

When looking at compliance and integrity management from a risk perspective, a similar sensation arises. Risk management does not analyze risks from a business

35. Bleker 2009.

perspective. Risks are dissected into manageable pieces. Each piece is analyzed separately and tackled by experts within expert departments and seldom from a primary business perspective. The analysis is intended to provide a 360 degree view on the issue/risk. This is a thorough exercise and necessary in our complex world. The results of this exercise have to be translated into norms, procedures and processes on how to tackle the risk. Here it becomes quite complicated and, therefore, in order to tackle the issue/risk, a complicated, inextricable web of procedures and processes is put in place. If, in the eyes of the expert, the result is complicated, the overall procedures and processes become even more complicated from the point of view of the employees who have to mitigate the risk through appropriate actions within their daily conduct. A different focus on risk may offer new perspectives and opportunities in mitigating the actual occurrence of the risk in daily practice. First, the realization that all activities start from the perspective of the key objectives. How often are we acting on risks that are no longer emerging from our key objective: business? Risks should be seen from the point of view of our *business.* As a result, the procedures and processes should be in the language used and understood by business. The main focus should be the risk and its effects on the business. Instead, every expert group looks at the risk and decides how to act to mitigate the risk from the point of view of their expertise. It would be more effective to have the different experts work together and coordinate actions with a primary focus on mitigating the risk in the language and activities of the business. This would lead to a better understanding of the risk in daily practice, and consequently better possibilities of mitigating the risk. Finally, the risk awareness of the first line would increase because of better understanding.

The financial crisis in the early years of this century unleashed a flood of new rules, which compelled compliance to put all its effort into converting innumerable requirements into official policy so that all the right boxes were kept formally ticked. The famous French expression: '*l'histoire se répète*' also applies to the reaction to financial crises. Every economic and financial crisis results in a considerable increase in laws and legislation from State legislators (e.g. Sarbanes-Oxley Act, Dodd-Frank Act), national supervisory authorities, and international authorities (e.g. European Union, European Central Bank).

The increase in legislation as such provokes new risks such as:

- compliance risks through conflicting legislative requirements;
- tick-the-box compliance due to the amount of legislation;
- conduct risk because not all rules and norms can be applied;
- conduct risks due to the quest for mazes;
- fraud risk;
- piling up of tasks due to lack of time;
- inefficiency and unnecessary costs.

The three pillars in Figure 4 are constructed out of building blocks such as risk management, compliance, supervision, remuneration, etc. In the past years after the financial crisis, organizations have worked on refilling the gaps in the liquidity and solvency pillars, and, yet, the structure is still unstable. Integrity is the key pillar. Not only the personal integrity of employees, managers and executives (Wells Fargo, Deutsche Bank), but also the integrity of the financial institutions as such, and, finally, the integrity of the financial system.

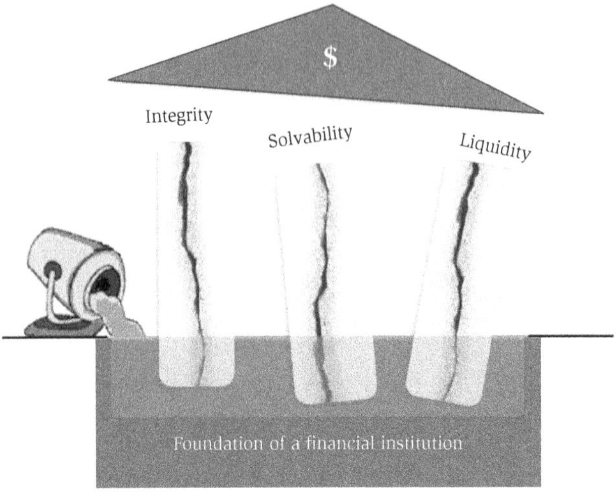

Figure 4: The three pillars of a financial institution

The long-lasting financial crisis has clearly demonstrated that integrity is a prominent risk. Liquidity is a problem that can be solved. Solvency is a bigger issue, but when a financial institution has the reputation of being an institution with integrity, it will be less hard to attract funds. However, if the institution has a reputation and a corresponding track record of being an institution without much integrity, trust in the institution will diminish and it is likely that the institution will default.

The first priority should be to stabilize the conduct & integrity pillar of the institution: organizations should focus on their key objectives and translate business into policies instead of translating legal requirements into business policies ('legalizing' the business). A focus on the business and conduct instead of law will create a changing force. Transparency towards internal and external actors (including all supervisory authorities) on conduct within the legal framework, instead of the legal framework ruling business: the first line simply does not understand anymore and leaves the 'hassle' to compliance.

The compliance department is vital to the organization. First, its task is to protect the organization from harm due to compliance and integrity risks. As a result, compliance is a major player in reassuring shareholders, regulators and other stakeholders concerning the extent to which the organization is 'in control' of its compliance and integrity risks. Compliance offers the outside world, as well as internal stakeholders, 'trust' and 'compliant conduct'. In those organizations where compliance has developed into an alien organ, it is impossible to slay the organ and replace it. The compliance officer 3.0 has to dissect the clutter and surgically remove the proliferation of compliance without affecting the notions of trust and 'in control'. This effort will take years and will depend not only on the surgical skills of the compliance officer, but also on the skills of the legislator and other supervisory authorities. The latter have to accept the translation of business conduct into policies and procedures instead of translating legislation into business.

BIBLIOGRAPHY

Blair 2005
T. Blair, 'Speech to the institute for Public Policy Research (reproduced by The Guardian)', *The Guardian* 2005-May.

Bleker-van Eyk 2009
S.C. Bleker-van Eyk, 'Reshaping the Financial Markets', Deloitte Netherlands 2009.

Bleker-van Eyk 2012
Dr. S.C. Bleker-van Eyk, 'Extraterritorialiteit: het meest onderschatte thema', in: C.A. Wielenga et al. (ed.), *Jaarboek Compliance* 2012, Capelle aan den IJssel: Nederlands Compliance Instituut 2012, pp. 51–67.

Bleker-van Eyk 2013
S. Bleker-van Eyk, 'De Compliance Officer 2.0', *MAB* 2013-10.

Galbraith 1952
J.K. Galbraith, *American Capitalism: The Concept of Countervailing Power*, New Jersey: Transaction Publishers 1952.

Galbraith 1993
J.K. Galbraith, *American Capitalism: The Concept of Countervailing Power*, New Jersey: Transaction Publishers 1993.

Quadackers 2013
L. Quadackers, 'Professionele scepsis: je weet ook wat je niet weet!', *Accountant* 2013-March.

Other references

Basel Committee on Banking Supervision
Basel Committee on Banking Supervision, 'Compliance and the compliance function in banks', *Bank for International Settlements* 2005-April.

Compliance Management System Guidance 19600, 2014
Compliance management system Guidance, ISO 19600:2014.

Deloitte Australia 2014
Deloitte Australia, Unleashing productivity, report 4, Building the Lucky Country, 2014.

A Resource Guide to the U.S. Foreign Corrupt Practices Act By the Criminal Division of the U.S. Department of Justice and the Enforcement Division of the U.S. Securities and Exchange Commission. https://www.justice.gov/sites/default/files/criminal-fraud/legacy/2015/01/16/guide.pdf

United States Department of Justice, U.S. Attorneys' Manual, Title 9, chapter 9-28.000 Principles of Federal Prosecution of Business Organizations, https://www.justice.gov/usam/usam-9-28000-principles-federal-prosecution-business-organizations.

Speech by Joaquin Almunia, at the US Chamber of Commerce, Speech/10/586, 2010.

4. Managing Organizational Integrity and Leadership

T.A.H.M. van de Laar EMoC

4.1 INTRODUCTION: PARADIGM SHIFT IN MANAGING ORGANIZATIONAL INTEGRITY IS NEEDED

Organizations have evolved dramatically over the centuries. Organizations started with mammoth hunting, but have evolved into vast conglomerates exercising complex tasks and creating extraordinarily sophisticated products or services that are in no way comparable with the initial loaf of bread. In order to prepare organizations to tackle the future challenges, however we need to search for radical new ways of organizing human abilities. The challenges organizations (and thus humans) are facing and the pace at which organizations need to keep up with these challenges are only increasing. Organizations are in a sort of continuous state of change; legislation, products and services, communication technologies and staffing are constantly changing. Digitalization allows for super-fast growth, but also causes faster obsolescence of products and can even threaten the survival of business models and organizations. More and more data is generated that has to be processed. Globalization causes cultural diversity within organizations with an increasing number of interrelationships and interdependencies in cross-border leadership. It also leads to further interdependence of economic activities, with the global economy shifting from the West and the North to the East and the South. Furthermore, new forms of finance are emerging: private equity, crowdfunding, crowdsourcing. And yet, we are still human beings getting organized to achieve goals.

Management is invented by us humans to organize and achieve these goals. It is unquestionably one of humankind's most important inventions. The development of management has helped to control economic growth. Modern management evolved in the second half of the 1900s, by people like Henry Ford and took a spurt in the early twentieth century by developments such as processes, structures and techniques to compound human effort.[1] Management solved two problems. First, it helped to organize semi-skilled employees to perform repetitive activities competently, conscientiously, and efficiently.[2] Secondly, it coordinates 'efforts in ways that enabled complex goods and services to be produced in large quantities'.[3] 'In a nutshell, the problems were efficiency of scale, and the solution was bureaucracy, with its hierarchical structure, cascading goals, precise role definitions, and elaborate rules and procedures'.[4] However, the problem with this bureaucratic way of managing an organization is that it does not tackle today's issues. We are living in a new reality that is asking for new imperatives. We live in a world of rapid change, products have become more volatile and the world has become less forgiving. The principles of 'standardization, specialization, hierarchy, control, and primacy of shareholder interest' dating from the industrial age are no longer equipping organizations with today's challenges.[5] The constructs of the bureaucracy-infused management practices therefore need to be reinvented. In the new reality we need an organization and management style that is more adaptable, efficient and still resilient.

This paradigm shift still needs to be made though, also when it comes to managing organizational integrity. In the wake of the financial crisis and economic downturns, budgets were dominated by change initiatives on risk and regulation, incident management, remedial efforts in order to adhere to rules and regulations, to manage audit findings and operational risk, updating the target operating models on roles and responsibilities, strengthening of controls, etc. Banks are still making remedial efforts driven by incidents, crisis losses and litigation. At the same time these remedial efforts are too often fragmented, tactical fixes, adding additional management layers and more compliance professionals, instead of combatting the root causes and making true strategic remedial efforts.

Pioneers in managing organizational integrity differently can only be found with a magnifying glass. Many organizations still do not seem to embrace ways of organizing human capabilities differently, while it is time to take this challenge to heart. An advantageous path in organizing human capabilities differently is having a good understanding of human nature. If we understand the strengths and weaknesses of human nature better, we can make organizations more human. Then management is not working against the grain of human nature, but with it.

The purpose of this chapter is threefold. First, a description will be given on how we can align conflicting interests in an organization in line with the grain of human nature (in section 4.2). Secondly, a framework will be provided to manage organizational integrity more humanly by compiling research and literature insights (in section 4.3). This framework provides the elements of a form of good government for the organization. Finally, an analysis will be made on what this means with regard to leadership (in section 4.4).

In doing so, this chapter makes several important contributions. First, it provides a new way of organizing human efforts. This provides a better understanding on

---

1. Hamel 2009, p. 1.
2. Ibid., p. 2.
3. Ibid., p. 2.
4. Ibid., p. 2.
5. Ibid., p. 2.

what needs to be done to create organizations that are fit for the future. Secondly, it will help (compliance) professionals to understand the key conceptual elements of the framework and the interrelationships between the elements within the framework. This will help to identify and remediate effectively and sustainably in case of shortcomings in organizational integrity. Thirdly, it provides a framework that works with the grain of human nature instead of against it – like the bureaucracy-infused management practices. It will spur initiative, creativity, passion, responsibility and innovation. This will make organizations more human and therefore more adaptable and efficient.

4.2 CONFLICTING INTERESTS MANAGED IN GRAIN WITH HUMAN NATURE

The subtitle of Part 1 states: the tension between 'good' and 'temptation': juggling conflicting interests. We constantly juggle the interest of the organization and our own interest (retain our job, get a promotion or a bonus, *see* Figure 1).

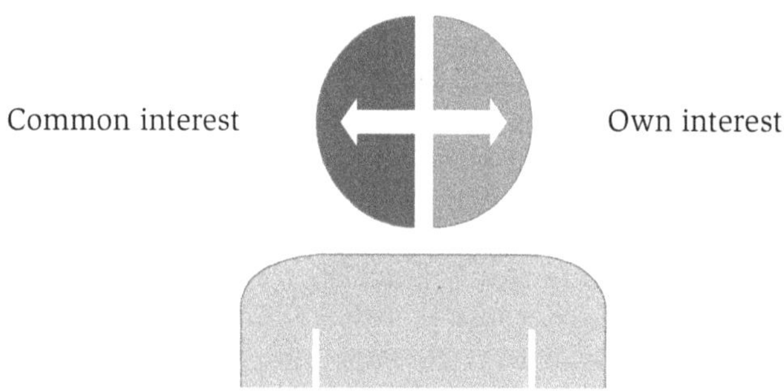

Figure 1: Juggling conflicting interests

Hopefully, most of the time our interests are synchronized with those of the organization, for instance through policies and controls. When the individual's need is not 'in sync' with the organization's need, non-compliance risks may occur. Here there are two options:

1. The integrity of the organization may be at risk through non-compliance.
2. The integrity of the individual may be at risk, because the individual has to stretch his actions beyond the personal interests, or worse, the personal moral parameters.

Severe cases of corporate misconduct and more or less related financial crises and economic downturns, have increased the amount of legislation dramatically as described earlier in chapter 1. The response of organizations to these failures of integrity are to a large extent still built on the constructs of the bureaucracy-infused management practices, adding additional management layers, more precise role definition, more procedures and more compliance professionals. These remedial efforts are often fragmented, tactical fixes that do not take sufficient account of other explanatory aspects of the problem. It often comes down to systematic failures in the organizational structures, systems and processes, culture, perverse incentives, lack of clarity about roles and responsibilities and so on.

In order to shift from a reactive to a more preventive approach, the influence of organizational factors should be acknowledged. Most important is a supportive environment. The perceived support or lack of support by others exerts pressure on people's decision-making. Influence by a social group can be instrumental. Social groups reward and punish people for certain conduct by awarding or withholding signs of group status and respect, or 'more directly by channeling material resources toward or away from particular members'.[6] But besides this instrumental component, individuals' behavior is strongly influenced by the normative climate created by a social group. The individual uses the group as a frame of reference, to convert appropriate conduct.

Sinek states that there are only two ways to influence human behavior, either by manipulating or by inspiring. As Sinek explains, people do not buy what you do, they buy *why* you do it.[7] Similarly, compliant behavior is not simply a matter of learning by rote. As explained in Part I, compliant behavior is behavior in the service of a core objective which can only be achieved by the organization as a collective entity. If you want people to follow you willingly in the pursuit of this objective in an appropriate and sustainable manner, you should inspire people in such a way that those individuals feel that adopting the desired behavior is the best course for them personally, rather than forcing it out of the group in a manipulative fashion. Behavior forced in a manipulative manner is simply unsustainable; once the manipulation has been unmasked, resistance will follow.

Very few organizations can clearly articulate *why* they do what they do. *Why* means the companies' purpose, cause or belief – *why* does your company exist and *why* should anyone care? Even more important, why should anyone want to become a part of it either as investor, employee, business partner or customer? For a compliance program to be truly effective, the infused values and guiding principles have to be like verbs. When articulating values as verbs, people have a good idea of how they should act in any situation.

4.3 LOOKING FOR A FORM OF GOVERNMENT

Compliance is a behavioral science in which we are looking for a form of government for the organization, similar to the claims of Darwin.[8] Good government is developed when structures, mechanisms and processes are well-balanced and supportive for decision-making. Far too often we see a top-down approach, a concentration of power in the hands of a few. In good government for the organization we see a wider distribution of decision-making power.

---

6. Tyler 2006, pp. 23–24.
7. Sinek 2009, Part 1, chapter 2 'Carrots and Sticks'.
8. Bleker-van Eyk 2017, p. 70: *'In mijn beleving is compliance eveneens een gedragswetenschap waarin – gelijk aan de bewering van Darwin – wij op zoek zijn naar een vorm van regering voor de organisatie'.*

Let us examine the hallmarks of good government for the organization and discuss how organizations can shape individuals' behavior. When crucial decisions need to be taken, for example when confronted with moral issues or anti-social, immoral or illegal behavior, the right set-up should help in identifying, acknowledging and understanding the dilemmas an organization is confronted with. It is important to have an understanding of values and norms, to respect and have an eye for the interests of others, to exhibit consistent and principled decision-making in the sense that values are kept upright and not disregarded if they are inconvenient. It should support the board, and other personnel for that matter, in taking a well-balanced decision.

There is of course no single correct government strategy. Elements such as coordination, reciprocity, leadership style, obedience, responsibility, cognition, diversity, independence, information-processing, sustainability, trust, accountability and cooperation should, however, be taken into account when constructing an organizational structure shaping individuals' behavior. All these elements of good government for the organization are shown in the framework (Figure 2) and will be discussed in more detail in the following sections.

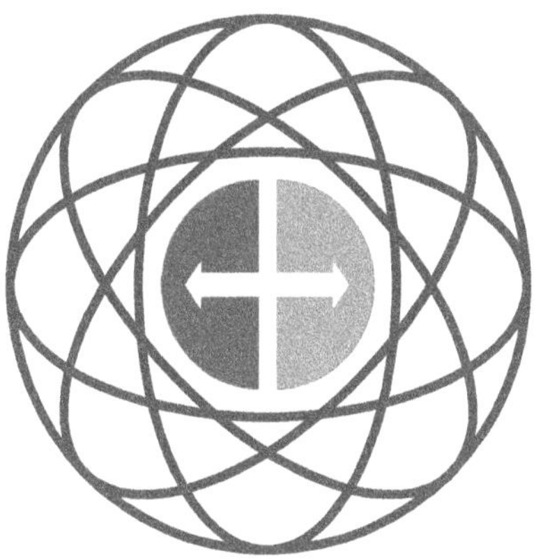

Figure 2: Elements of good government

4.3.1 Coordination

Coordination ensures that an organization functions as a unified whole.[9] We have organizations in order to achieve goals that we cannot achieve by ourselves. Organizations bring expertise, skills and resources together to perform (complex) tasks that are too large for an individual to undertake. As the size and complexity of the tasks grow, tasks and member dependencies come to be more numerous, diverse

9. De Mol et al. 2015, p. 245.

and complex.[10] The need for an organization to coordinate these tasks and member dependencies then becomes greater.

We coordinate tasks explicitly by making use of mechanisms such as schedules, plans, etc. or by communicating (e.g., orally, in writing, formally, informally, interpersonally, in groups).[11] Furthermore, often the law requires that organizations have adequate procedures, risk assessment and compliance standards in place. There is no doubt that organizations should have such a well-articulated program and mechanisms in place to comply with rules and regulations. Organizations need guidelines to maintain order and coherence. When such guidelines are missing or malfunctioning, the result is trouble. These procedures and compliance standards need to be communicated effectively through training and other forms of communication. Monitoring and audit processes should be in place. Furthermore, organizations need a whistleblowing procedure to report infringements of the law or company standards and employees should be able to report criminal misconduct without fear of retaliation. In the event of wrongdoing, appropriate (disciplinary) measures should be taken and reasonable steps should be taken to prevent the occurrence of similar wrongdoing in the future.

In a liberal society, though, authority through rules and regulations, policies and processes has only limited control over the behavior of individuals. Many coordination problems thus require a bottom-up and not a top-down approach. Members of a group therefore need to figure out how to coordinate their behavior with each other, knowing that everyone else is doing the same. Particularly interesting is the question of how people can coordinate their actions voluntarily in an efficient and orderly manner, without anyone telling them what to do.[12]

As the British economist D.H. Robertson explained, organizations are 'islands of conscious power in this ocean of un-conscious cooperation like lumps of butter coagulating in a pail of buttermilk'.[13] Robertson eloquently described how organizations make use of authority, many layers of management each responsible for the layer below, plans, forecasts and controls and other 'hard' aspects to accomplish their goals. Lynn S. Paine evocatively described how this legal compliance approach is built on the constructs of deterrence, 'which envisions people as rational maximizers of self-interest, responsive to the personal costs and benefits of their choices, yet indifferent to the moral legitimacy of those choices'.[14] But what does that really tell us about how an organization actually works? Not much. It does not explain which goals an organization should pursue, how to pursue them, how an organization can make sure that their employees work in a coordinated fashion, what value they are going to bring to the customer and how to deal with their suppliers.

Paine explains that organizations should provide their members with a 'common frame of reference' that can 'serve as a unifying force across different functions, lines of business, and employee groups'.[15] It defines what the organization stands for and

10. Espinosa et al. 2002, p. 107.
11. Ibid., p. 107.
12. Surowiecki 2004, p. 86.
13. Coase 1988, p. 35; *See also*, Surowiecki 2004, pp. 195–196.
14. Sharp Paine 1994, p. 110.
15. Ibid., p. 111.

gives life to a shared set of values and guiding principles that are deeply entrenched throughout the organization.[16] This is what Paine calls the 'integrity as a governing ethic', which 'is broader, deeper, and more demanding than a legal compliance initiative. Broader in that it seeks to enable responsible conduct. Deeper in that it cuts to the ethos and operating systems of the organization and its members, their guiding values and patterns of thought and action. And more demanding in that it requires an active effort to define the responsibilities and aspirations that constitute an organization's ethical compass. Above all, organizational ethics is seen as the work of management'.[17] Coordination of integrity management is distributed among all managers at all levels and across all business lines. This integrity strategy does not mean that there is no place for the (legal) compliance-based approach: 'a code of conduct, training in relevant areas of law, mechanisms for reporting and investigating potential misconduct, and audits and controls to ensure that laws and company standards are being met'.[18] They can go hand in hand, as some individuals do need the threat of disciplinary measures.

The values and guiding principles Paine is referring to will function as focal points for each member of the organization when confronted with a dilemma. The coordination experiments of Thomas C. Schelling illustrate the power of focal points. He demonstrated that in many situations there are landmarks or so-called focal points. As Schelling wrote: 'People can often concert their intentions or expectations with each other if each knows that the other is trying to do the same. Most situations ... provide some cue for coordinating behavior, some focal point for each person's explanation of what the other expects him to do.'[19] A focal point will help to whittle down the multitude of responses to the situation of conflict of interest the individual is confronted with. The stronger the cooperative focal point, the more closely the interests of agents are connected. If for example through cooperative interaction one individual becomes more reliant on another for his raw materials supply, cheating this individual might become more expensive since doing so jeopardizes his production process.[20] With reduced ambiguity about the behavior of others, exemplified by the repeated honest behavior of the other, people are willing to cooperate with others, moving away from the pure conflict extreme towards greater coordination. According to Schelling: 'Where there is no apparent focal point for agreement, he [the individual, the organization] can create one by his power to make a dramatic suggestion ... coordination requires the common acceptance of some source of suggestion.'[21]

The experiments of Schelling demonstrate that it is reasonable to expect that a certain level of cooperation between individuals is possible without centralized directions, because they can find their way to collectively beneficial results. Furthermore, the experiments demonstrate that people experience the world in a remarkably similar way, 'which makes successful coordination easier'.[22] As Paine explained,

16. Ibid., p. 109.
17. Ibid., p. 111.
18. Ibid., p. 111.
19. Schelling 1960, p. 57.
20. Leeson et al. 2006, p. 142.
21. Schelling 1960, p. 144.
22. Surowiecki 2004, p. 92.

organizations should provide their members with focal points by offering them a 'common frame of reference' that can 'serve as a unifying force across different functions, lines of business, and employee groups'.[23]

Organizations will then start to coordinate implicitly through a shared set of values which becomes a shared knowledge by the organization and as such they are not consciously employed for the purpose of coordinating. Such a shared set of values, focal points, will help to ensure that members of an organization interpret situations in a similar manner, make comparable decisions and actions.[24]

4.3.2 Reciprocity

Arguments about what is just either involve a conflict between reciprocity (only those who work hard should get the reward for hard work) or equality (everyone deserves a decent minimum income) or arguments about equal liberty and opportunity versus equal benefit.[25]

A good government structure should therefore coordinate institutionally the social needs of reciprocity and equality and allocate the 'benefits and burdens' within a community.[26]

Humans have a unique ability to reason, which inclines them to dominantly endow a more peaceful inclination. They can see the benefit of specialization, the division of work etc. If individuals start to realize that there is a commonality in their behavior, this could influence their ability to benefit from social interaction, which will then form the basis of their decisions. Participating in an effective government structure promotes healthy moral development and good decision-making. Social environments with well-organized structures facilitate role-taking opportunities more than poorly organized justice structures.

This evolution of a reciprocity trait leads individuals to repay kindness with kindness, while responding to defection or dishonesty with revenge.[27] Organizations thus need to take account of the social needs of reciprocity and equality, because they have their own motive component to rectify non-reciprocity or non-equality.[28] Hoffman refers in that respect to the 'eye-for-an-eye' mentality. In that sense reciprocity is not necessarily prosocial. It only becomes prosocial if it is associated with empathy. That explains why organizations need to bear in mind conventions or values and virtues emphasized in particular cultures and cannot maximize their profits regardless of history or unwritten (cultural) rules. They can have the force of law. This is why organizations rarely cut wages during a recession, but instead dismiss staff (although you could question whether this is a rational thing to do).

An example of the motive component to rectify non-reciprocity or non-equality is the ultimatum game. The ultimatum game is a game of economic experiments. The first player (the proposer) receives a sum of money and proposes how to divide

23. Sharp Paine 1994, p. 111.
24. Cannon-Bowers et al. 2001, p. 195.
25. Kohlberg 1981, p. 144; *See also*, Hoffman 2000, pp. 242–245.
26. Kohlberg 1981, p. 144.
27. Leeson et al. 2006, p. 140; *See also*, Hoffman 2000, pp. 242–245.
28. Hoffman 2000, p. 243.

the sum with a second player. The second player (the responder) chooses to either accept or reject this proposal. If the second player accepts, the money is split according to the proposal. If the second player rejects, neither player receives any money. A crucial point is that you do not play the game with the same person more than once. You could question why, then, responders still turned down offers, because that is not a rational thing to do, as you disadvantage yourself in doing so. Furthermore, since you are only playing the game once, there is no point in teaching the proposer a lesson. It is the evolution of the reciprocity trait, however, that leads individuals to respond to unfairness with revenge.[29] The social needs of reciprocity and equality thus have their own motive component to rectify non-reciprocity or non-equality.[30]

4.3.3 Leadership style

Plutarch discussed how leadership puts the issue of character to the test. In his famous *Parallel Lives* he says: 'It is an observation no less just than common, that there is no stronger test of a man's real character than power and authority, exciting, as they do, every passion, and discovering every latent vice.'[31] Every personality type has a brighter and a darker side. The darker personality traits are more common among managers and could lead to extreme leader behavior. Kaiser, LeBreton and Hogan documented in one of their sample tests that 98% of the senior executives developed a darker side of their personality that could potentially lead to management derailment.[32] It is therefore not an exaggeration to conclude that almost every senior executive is at risk as a result of their own darker side, since leadership can trigger extreme behavior. It seems that personality traits can predict such derailment to a certain extent.[33] Leaders therefore have to develop self-regulatory strategies to manage their darker side.[34]

Leadership has a considerable impact on an organization's performance. Leaders get things done by influencing other people, teams and organizational features.[35] Consequently, leadership behavior influences the behavior, attitudes and beliefs of individual employees. By facilitating communication and coordinating, by defining the policies, by setting targets, by rewarding a bonus or a disciplinary measure, by resolving a conflict, by assigning people to roles, by defining strategic direction and by deciding on the organizational structure they affect a team's dynamic.

The risk of management derailment seems to increase in the case of CEO duality (the CEO and Chair being one person), since such a CEO is more likely to assume power and increase personal wealth, which will fuel overconfidence.[36] There is no

29. Leeson et al. 2006, pp. 242–245.
30. Hoffman 2000, p. 243.
31. Plutarch's *Lives of the Noble Greeks and Romans*, commonly called *Parallel Lives* or *Plutarch's Lives*, is a series of biographies of famous men, arranged in tandem to illuminate their common moral virtues or failings, probably written at the beginning of the second century AD.
32. Kaiser et al. 2015, pp. 55–92.
33. Lombardo & Eichinger 1989.
34. Kaiser et al. 2015, p. 85.
35. Kaiser & Hogan 2007, pp. 173–193 (chapter 10).
36. De Haan & Kasozi 2014, pp. 256 and 279.

conclusive research, however, on whether CEO duality in a single-tier board shows a positive relationship with financial performance,[37] although overconfidence has a negative effect on board effectiveness. A good example is Deutsche Bank. Ullrich Fichtner, Hauke Goos and Martin Hesse describe how Deutsche Bank fell prey to failed leadership. They explain how the bank, once the embodiment of German values as reliable and safe, turned into an Anglo-American investment bank between 1994 and 2012.[38] This resulted in 7,800 lawsuits and caused it to rapidly lose value and become one of the largest systemic risks to the global financial world. On May 23, 2002 Josef Ackermann took over control of Deutsche Bank. He unified power in one single position, whereas the CEO of Deutsche Bank had hitherto sat on the board as one among many equals. Up until then all decisions had to be passed unanimously by the board. This change in the governance structure was revolutionary. As Fichtner et al. write: 'One hundred and thirty-two years after its founding, Deutsche Bank began imitating Anglo-American leadership structures'.[39] It deprived Deutsche Bank of its distinctive German character and the CEO assumed more power without organizing proper countervailing power.[40] Ackermann downsized the board from nine to four members and created a new body: the Group Executive Committee (GEC). This committee was made up of 12 members. The members of the management board also belonged to the new committee along with seven managers who led the bank's largest divisions and who reported directly to Ackermann. Allegedly, Ackermann became more and more pedantic and, ultimately, cruel.[41] Members of the management and the supervisory board stood aside, culminating in a loss of control by top managers of the bank during the period between 1994 and 2012.

Derailment behavior and ultimate failure correlate with the management discretion of the leader, the context they are operating in and the displayed behavior, personality characteristics or profiles of these leaders (whether or not in collaboration with each other).

Their leadership failures were not primarily the result of professional incompetence. They were well educated, with a significant amount of experience and proven professionalism. These smart executives failed due to too much management discretion, cultural factors and psychological dispositions. The first commandment of leadership – with a view to preventing leadership derailment – is for leaders to check their own dark impulses.

The example of Deutsche Bank demonstrates that in times of prosperity boards seem to neglect the importance of counterbalance to boardroom imperialism, the so-called 'performance fallacy'.[42] Derailment clearly seems to be the result of management discretion. If there is too much management discretion or a lack of counterbalance, our innate selfish tendencies have the opportunity to proliferate. They can send us

37. Galema et al. 2012, pp. 718–742; Crossland & Hambrick 2007, pp. 767–789; Joseph et al. 2014, pp. 1834–1858; Rechner & Dalton 1991, pp. 155–160.
38. Fichtner et al. 2016.
39. Fichtner et al. 2016.
40. Galbraith 1952, pp. 118–119. The notion 'countervailing power' was introduced by Galbraith.
41. Fichtner et al. 2016. The article describes that '[p]eople who witnessed the development speak of "psycho-terror"'.
42. Tuggle et al. 2010, pp. 946–968.

in a direction where we abuse power or derail. To concentrate power in the hands of one single person therefore does not make sense.[43] In fact, the more important a decision is, the more important it is that it not be left in the hands of one single person. The best CEOs recognize the limits of their own knowledge and of individual decision-making. The most important decisions need to be made by the board as a whole, which will even outsmart the smartest executive if the group is diverse enough and their independent judgments are aggregated. The decision-making process will be discussed later on. The second commandment of leadership is therefore to organize countervailing power and upward feedback.

The third commandment of leadership is to *support* the team (add resources, skills or enhance effectiveness), *inspire* the team (offer vision and strategy) and *protect* the team (offer encouragement, develop insight).[44] If the leader sets the right tone and provides the right cues, encouragement, (re)direction and protection, the team or organization will perform as effectively as possible. The effectiveness of the leader can thus be measured against the team efforts, and the extent to which the team members are able to achieve the right results and respond to new challenges. It is the team effort that is undermined when there is poor leadership. Those who notice failed leadership are primarily also those who are most dependent on that leadership, the direct subordinates. They are often not able to speak for fear of retribution. That is why whistleblowing procedures, designed to take away this fear of retribution, are key to any organization. In order to allow the team to perform at its best, the leader should voluntarily remain within the paths of management discretion and impose self-imposed restrictions in order to better enable the team to perform better.[45] As Goethe puts it: '*Wer Grosses will, muss sich zusammenraffen; In der Beschränkung zeigt sich erst der Meister, Und das Gesetz nur kann uns Freiheit geben*'.[46]

4.3.4 Obedience

As discussed, Darwin states that cooperation requires a form of government (leadership), and hence obedience. He says that this 'is of the highest value, for any form of government is better than none. Selfish and contentious people will not cohere, and without coherence nothing can be effected. A tribe possessing the above qualities in a high degree would spread and be victorious over other tribes'.[47] As explained, Darwin is describing here an early form of *compliance*, as a prerequisite for a successful organization.

Every coin has two sides, though. The bright side is compliance. As explained previously, compliance is behavior and inextricably linked to obedience of 'external

43. Feigelson et al. 2015. The International Corporate Governance Network consisting of over 200 of the leading institutional investors is opposed to the CEO and Chair being one person given the increased risk.
44. De Haan & Kasozi 2014, p. 69.
45. Ibid., p. 269.
46. Johann Wolfgang von Goethe, Sonnette – Kapitel 1 ('He who wants great things must pull himself together; In the limitation only the Master is shown, and the Law can only give us freedom').
47. Darwin 1871, p. 163 In: The Complete Work of Darwin Online.

(international and national) laws and regulations, as well as internal norms and procedures'. However, stating that compliance and obedience are synonyms is incorrect. The 'moral' element should be included in behavior. That is why our definition goes beyond sheer obedience and links compliance to the 'integrity of the organization, its management and employees'. As discussed, obedience to the external and internal norms and procedures is strongly influenced by its moral correctness,[48] and norms of reciprocity and equality that relate to the innate human preference for balance or harmony. Therefore it is very important that the 'why' of external and internal norms is explained, because otherwise employees may rebel against it.

There is, however, a dark side to obedience as well. As Milgram states, 'the essence of obedience consists in the fact that a person comes to view himself as the instrument for carrying out another person's wishes, and therefore no longer regards himself as responsible for his actions'.[49] Humans are social beings and are heavily influenced by the prevailing norms and values in society. For that reason most human beings are law-abiding citizens. Because we are heavily influenced by our social context, we often do what is expected and demanded of us, at home, at school and in the workplace. However, this abidance is also what makes humans susceptible to immoral or even criminal behavior; the situational context causes us to become involved in immoral behavior.[50] Features such as obedience, conformism and loyalty, which under 'normal' circumstances put us on the right path, also mean that we easily become involved in antisocial, immoral or even criminal behavior.[51] This explains why ordinary people can become involved in atrocious behavior (see also in chapter 1.4. *supra*).[52]

Milgram demonstrated how easily ordinary people within a laboratory context can be induced to administer an electric shock to others.[53] This experiment explained the dilemmas and the difficult choices individuals face when they receive antisocial, immoral or illegal orders. In this experiment, the subjects believe that they are going to participate in a learning experiment. In reality, however, the experiment is set up to see to what extent volunteers are willing to administer electric shocks to other persons. At the beginning of the experiment, the test person must administer an 'acceptable' shock of 15 volts, but with each new shock to be administered there is an increment of 15 volts up to a maximum of 450 volts. The test person did not know that the shocks were actually not administered. The person pretending to undergo the electric shocks was an actor. Milgram assumed that only a very small percentage of the subjects would be willing to eventually deliver a shock of 450 volts, but he was wrong. From the numerous experiments he conducted it was found that 65% of the subjects were prepared, at the request of another person, to give a (potentially deadly) electric shock of 450 volts. The person requesting the administration of these shocks was perceived to be a legitimate authority. This experiment clearly illustrated

48. Sharp Paine 1994, p. 111.
49. Milgram 1974, preface.
50. Smeulers 2012, p. 28.
51. Ibid., pp. 28–29; Grunfeld & Smeulers 1999.
52. Zimbardo 2008.
53. Milgram 1974.

how strong the social pressure of an authority figure can be and how many people can feel compelled to comply with a command.

The footage of the experiment clearly shows that many of the subjects were in distress. They showed signs of nervousness; sometimes they were very emotional and quite often clearly unhappy with the task they had to perform. Still, many of the subjects were not capable of disobeying the authority figure. If a subject indicated that he wanted to stop, the authority figure urged the subject to continue by using standard phrases indicating that it was important for the experiment that the subject continued. These seemingly slight pressure yields were sufficient for most subjects to continue administering the electric shocks.

A notable and significant finding following the Milgram experiment is that those who ultimately did not follow up orders from the authority figure and decided to stop voluntarily, felt guiltier than those who continued, most probably because they felt responsible for their actions.[54]

The Milgram experiment demonstrates unmistakably that it is very difficult to reject a command from what is considered to be a legitimate authority and to refuse to follow orders.[55] The subject has to break with the social context in which he is operating and all its prevailing values. According to the unwritten rules of our social intercourse, we have to uphold such values. This experiment shows that it is easier to put aside your own moral objections and follow orders. That is why the majority of the subjects in the experiment chose to follow the orders of the authority figure, sometimes with a little encouragement from the authority figure ('the shocks hurt, but they are not dangerous'). The subjects seemed to shift all responsibility for what they were doing to the authority figure, ridding themselves of any blame.

Likewise the influence of a social group or social pressure can make it difficult to attain the moral point of view in real life situations. The perceived support or lack of support from others exerts pressure on people's decision-making. The influence a social group has on individuals can be instrumental. Social groups reward and punish people for certain conduct by awarding or withholding signs of group status and respect, 'or more directly by channeling material resources toward or away from particular members'.[56] But besides this instrumental component, individuals' behavior is strongly influenced by the normative climate created by a social group. The individual uses the group as a frame of reference, to convert appropriate conduct.[57] Social influence can thus be described as the need to identify with or enhance one's image in the opinion of significant others, the willingness to conform to the expectations of others or the tendency to learn by observing others or seeking information from others.

The famous Asch experiments demonstrate the degree to which an individual's opinion is influenced by the opinion of a majority group.[58] Each participant was placed in a room with seven others. The other persons participating knew what the real purpose of the experiment was, but were introduced as 'true' participants. The

54. Schurz 1985, pp. 160–177; Smeulers 2012, p. 30.
55. Schurz 1985, pp. 160–177.
56. Tyler 2006, p. 23–24.
57. Ibid., p. 24.
58. Asch 1951, pp. 117–190.

participants were shown a card with a line on it, followed by a card with three lines on it (lines A, B and C). Participants were then asked to say aloud which of the three lines matched the line on the first card in length. On the face of it, this should be a very simple task. Prior to the experiment, though, all the conspiring participants, the accomplices in the experiment, were given specific instructions on how they should respond to each trial. In particular, they were told to unanimously give the correct answer or unanimously give the incorrect answer. The group sat in such a way that the real participant was always one of the last to respond. In the first two trials the accomplices gave the obvious correct answers and consequently the participant felt at ease. In the third trial, however, the accomplices all gave the same wrong answer. This placed the participant in a dilemma: would he give the correct answer or would he follow the group? There were 18 trials, 12 of which were the critical trials where the accomplices gave wrong answers. The Asch experiments also had a control condition where there were no accomplices, only one 'real participant'. In the control group there was no pressure to conform to other participants, and consequently the error rate was less than 1%. In the experimental group one-third of all responses in the critical trials were incorrect. These incorrect responses often matched the incorrect response of the majority group. In the experimental group, 75% of the participants gave an incorrect answer to at least one question.

Asch found that there were big individual differences in reaction to the experimental situation. Participants who did not conform to the majority group reacted sometimes with confidence. Although they did experience conflict between their own perception and experience and the wrong answer given by the group, they stuck with the answer that was based on their own perception. Other participants were withdrawn and did not experience the conflict between their own answer and the answer of the group. Some participants showed doubt, but nevertheless gave the correct responses because they felt a need to adequately take part in the task. Participants who did conform to the majority group in at least half of the trials sometimes reacted with a *distortion of judgment*. Most participants belonged to this category. At a certain point they perceived that they must be wrong and the majority must be right. Consequently they followed the group in their answers. These individuals were doubtful and lacked confidence. Some participants exhibited a *distortion of action*. They knew what the correct answer was, but despite that fact they conformed to the majority group simply because they did not want to seem inferior. On very few occasions participants reacted with a *distortion of perception*. They were never aware that the accomplices gave wrong answers and actually believed that the accomplices gave correct answers.

If group pressure is already so apparent in a fairly non-threatening context such as the Asch experiments, imagine the amount of distress group pressure might cause in more extreme circumstances. Moreover, the experiment shows the importance of personal traits as a determinant for (moral) action/behavior.

An extreme example of an immoral act as a result of group norms and processes is the massacre at My Lai during the Vietnam War.[59] The American army tried to cover up the massacre, but *LIFE* magazine brought the horror of My Lai to light. This led to the prosecution and conviction of Colonel Calley. After several revisions,

59. Bilton & Kim 1979; Peers 1979.

he eventually received only three years of house arrest.[60] In this tragedy, individual American soldiers murdered more than 500 non-combatant women, children and elderly men. In essence, this was a group action under extreme circumstances on the basis of group norms: 'The moral choice made by each individual soldier who pulled the trigger was embedded in the larger institutional context of the army and its decision-making procedures.'.[61] What happened in Vietnam also happened in Iraq and is still happening elsewhere today.[62] When the pictures of abuse and humiliation of Iraqi prisoners at Abu Ghraib were shown on the popular American TV show *60 Minutes* and caused horror, Bush condemned the perpetrators immediately and spoke of a few rotten apples in the barrel that had brought the army into disrepute and should be punished.[63] In the end, the Bush administration's 'rotten apple' theory turned out to be rotten itself. It was found that a large part of the humiliation and abuse to which the Iraqi prisoners were exposed had originated in the guidelines issued by the secret service of the Bush administration. White House Counsel Alberto Gonzales and the Defense Department's General Counsel Jim Haynes stood before the world's media and explained that the guidelines were implemented within the law and on the basis of careful legal advice. They proclaimed it produced useful and important results and it was essential in getting vital security information from men they considered 'the worst of the worst'. Water-boarding was not given blanket approval, but was allowed in individual cases. Donald Rumsfeld approved the memo and wrote next to his signature the following observation: 'However, I stand for 8–10 hours a day. Why is standing limited to 4 hours?'[64] The results of these guidelines, the group norms and group processes we all remember due to the photos of Charles Graner and Lyndie England among others: the photo of England holding a leash attached to a prisoner or the photo of England and Graner posing behind a pyramid of naked Iraqi prisoners giving a thumbs up sign. The memo signed by Rumsfeld might explain why the actions performed by Graner and his group were carried out without embarrassment and photographed without fear of any possible criminal prosecution.[65] Rumsfeld, Graner and England probably had a mature level of moral reasoning. Mainly because of the group processes and the social context in which they were operating, of which the guideline is a result, they did not act in line with this level of moral reasoning. Group processes are operative not only in the army, but of course also in business. Most incidents of non-compliance occur in the context of a group and they are the perception of the moral atmosphere. This perception reflects personal as well as environmental characteristics. The foregoing demonstrates that individuals do not always live up to their moral principles; under extreme circumstances, there is a risk of a significant downhill push.

60. Bilton & Kim 1979; Peers 1979.
61. Higgins et al. 1984, p. 75.
62. Greenberg & Dratel 2005.
63. In a nationally televised address on May 24, President George W. Bush spoke of 'disgraceful conduct by a few American troops who dishonored our country and disregarded our values'. Consult a transcript of this speech via: http://www.washingtonpost.com/wp-dyn/articles/A52723-2004May24_4.html. Full speech available at: http://www.americanrhetoric.com/speeches/wariniraq/gwbushiraq52404.htm.
64. Consult via: http://www.defense.gov/news/Jun2004/d20040622doc5.pdf.
65. Smeulers & van Niekerk 2009, pp. 327–349.

Social experiments have unmistakably demonstrated that it is very difficult for individuals to reject a command from what is considered to be a legitimate authority and to refuse to follow orders. The individual has to break with the social context in which he is operating and all its prevailing values. That is why many people will end up following orders from an authority figure. It is a human tendency to shift all responsibility to authority figures and to rid oneself of any blame.

4.3.5 Responsibility

The realization of the key role that the moral atmosphere, the social context and group norms play in individual moral action led Kohlberg, Power and Higgins to hypothesize 'that in many cases the best approach to moral education is one that attempts to reform the moral atmosphere in which individual decisions are made', which I presume must be understood as individual decisions of (personal) responsibility.[66]

Kohlberg et al. compared the moral atmosphere in schools and found that participatory democracy puts socio-moral decisions in the hands of the students. This gave them a greater sense of responsibility for actions concerning the school. Furthermore, they found 'that a positive moral atmosphere provides the context in which students feel it makes sense to think in terms of responsibility and to act morally toward their peers and teachers'.[67]

Let us now make a comparison with banks. In the wake of the financial crisis, banks have added endless layers of management, which has only made people less willing to take responsibility for their own work. Subordinates pass their work on to their managers and managers sign off on the advice submitted by their subordinates. The risk is that subordinates do not take real responsibility for the information passed on, since the manager is ultimately responsible for it. The manager, on the other hand, does not really check and does not feel responsible either, since he simply passes the information further up. In order to instigate a greater sense of responsibility, it is therefore important to delineate roles and responsibilities. It could be added that end-to-end responsibility should be felt throughout every process in business. Businesses do not always feel ownership and thus responsibility, especially when it comes to non-financial risk. There are banks that have shifted risk ownership from the second line to the first line, but most banks still fail to do so. To engender true responsibility, organizations should implement defined, end-to-end responsible business practices throughout their entire process chain. End-to-end transparency should also be present, and if issues arise in a given process, the relevant business line should focus on immediately remediating those issues, even when they are outside their remit (for example IT).

Another way to instigate a greater sense of responsibility is a wider distribution of power. Acknowledgment of responsibility is related to the perceived control over an act or decision.[68] Since there was little delegation of power, there was little encouragement for workers lower down the totem pole to show any initiative. The individual has to acknowledge that there is a choice, a decision to make.

---

66. Higgins et al. 1984, p. 75.
67. Ibid., p. 104.
68. Jones 1991, p. 386.

4.3.6 Cognition

Cognition problems are problems that define corporate strategy and tactics. They include decisions on all aspects from new products to setting prices, forecasting demand, building new factories and contemplating mergers. The important question is how to get the best answers. In order to answer that question, we should first have a better understanding of these cognition problems. I will discuss the phenomena of cognitive distortions, cognitive dissonance, cognitive bias and moral intensity.

Wrong behavior can 'stem from perceptions structured by schemas of self-serving cognitive distortions'.[69] Cognitive distortions are 'thinking errors', incorrect or biased non-truthful schemas for experiencing events.[70] 'Schemas refers to the mental codification of experience that includes a particular organized way of cognitively perceiving and responding to a complex set of stimuli'.[71] Gibbs introduced a four-category typological model of self-serving cognitive distortions: (1) self-centered, (2) blaming others, (3) assuming the worst, and (4) minimizing/mislabeling.[72] He divided self-serving cognitive distortions into two types of categories: the primary cognitive distortions that are characterized by self-centered attitudes, taking one's own perspective (the self-centered category), and secondary cognitive distortions that are protective rationalizations (blaming others, assuming the worst, minimizing/ mislabeling).[73]

Self-centered cognitive distortions are attitudes in which the individual centers on his own opinions and needs to such an extent that the opinions or needs of others are never or hardly ever thought about or respected.[74] Blaming others entails cognitive schemas in which one's own behavior is misattributed or externalized to sources outside the individual. Gibbs provides a sinister example. He refers to a man who fatally stabbed his wife after she and her children started to have dinner without him and told her as she died: 'You pushed me to the limits. You did this to yourself.'[75] Other examples of blaming others are, 'I was just following orders' or 'I was drunk'.[76] Blaming others displaces guilt, hurt or humiliation. It is done to neutralize effect and thus to protect oneself.[77]

Assuming the worst is defined as a cognitive distortion in which the individual considers the worst-case scenario as inevitable, attributes hostile intentions to others or assumes that an improvement in one's own or others' behavior is impossible.[78] It can be a protective rationalization for violence or other types of antisocial behavior. Extreme levels of exaggerated attributions can be diagnosed psychiatrically as delusional paranoid.[79]

69. Gibbs 1995, p. 137.
70. Ibid., p. 137.
71. De Mol et al., p. 245.
72. Gibbs 1995, pp. 137–149.
73. Ibid., p. 140.
74. Ibid., pp. 138–140.
75. Ibid., p. 141.
76. Ibid., p. 142.
77. Ibid., p. 142; Hoffman 2000, p. 291.
78. Gibbs 1995, p. 144.
79. Ibid., p. 144.

Gibbs refers to the situation of highly aggressive adolescents who make statements of overgeneralization, such as 'If you back down from a fight, everyone will think you are a coward'.[80] Not the event itself, but rather the overgeneralization accounts for the aggressive behavior.[81] Gibbs found that individuals who depict antisocial behavior do not only assume the worst of others, but often assume the worst about themselves, their capabilities and their future as well. He calls this 'self-debasing cognitive distortions'.[82] An example is 'I can never do anything right'.[83] Gibbs found that 'exaggerated other blaming is aggressogenic, whereas exaggerated self-blame is depressogenic'.[84]

Minimizing is described as distortions where the antisocial behavior is regarded as an acceptable or even necessary way to achieve certain goals.[85] Mislabeling is defined as a disparaging and dehumanizing way of referring to others.[86] An example is denigrating or minimizing the victimization. Gibbs cites the example of a purse-snatcher who took a purse from a supermarket cart and said it would teach the purse's owner a lesson to be more careful with her belongings in future.[87] Minimizing and mislabeling is also an attribute in crimes of obedience. It is common for gang members, soldiers, combatants and rebels to dehumanize their victims so that it is easier to inflict harm on them.[88] In the Rwandan genocide the Rwandan local radio incited the Hutus to use violence against the Tutsi by calling them 'cockroaches' that needed to be 'exterminated'. Another form of minimizing is the Nazi bureaucracy, in which certain actions were insulated from their enormity through routinization and procedural thinking.[89]

The abovementioned self-serving cognitive distortions contribute to behavior and can facilitate antisocial behavior. Gibbs also highlights the importance of social skills and makes the point that social skill deficiencies contribute to antisocial behavior. Gibbs explains that social skills should reduce self-centration and mutual respect, because 'the socially skilled individual also communicates awareness of the other person's viewpoint, feelings, and legitimate expectations', while asserting or explaining his own perspective.[90] Socially unskilled behavior can lead to destructive and unbalanced behavior, for example in deviant peer pressure situations this might lead to irresponsible submissive behavior or irresponsible aggressive behavior in anger provocation situations.[91]

In order to influence behavior durably, it is important to understand how people react to their own actions. Festinger's cognitive dissonance theory is of importance in this respect. Festinger found that human beings feel uncomfortable if cognitions,

80. Ibid., p. 145.
81. Ibid., p. 145.
82. Ibid., p. 146.
83. Ibid., p. 146.
84. Ibid., p. 146.
85. Ibid., pp. 146–147.
86. Ibid., pp. 146–147.
87. Ibid., p. 146.
88. Ibid., p. 147.
89. Ibid., p. 147.
90. Ibid., p. 149.
91. Ibid., p. 150.

ideas, attitudes and/or beliefs are not in conformity with each other or if cognitions are not in accordance with actions.[92] Human beings want to be good and like to do the right thing. It is therefore important that their ideas and views are in line with their actions. If that is not the case, the individual will then adjust one of the two in order to ensure that they are nevertheless aligned. If that turns out to be impossible, the individual will proceed by changing the meaning that is given to his actions. According to Festinger people thus either:

1. change their behavior or cognition ('I will not eat any more of this chocolate');
2. justify the behavior or cognition by changing the conflicting cognition ('I am allowed to cheat every once in a while');
3. justify behavior or cognition by adding new cognitions ('I will take the stairs instead of the elevator to work this off'); or
4. ignore or deny any information that conflicts with existing beliefs ('This chocolate is not high in fat').

People thus have a great ability to explain the world around themselves and their own actions in such a way that they play a good and positive role. Evidence of the opposite is ignored or considered unreliable, while unconscious protective mechanisms come into play.[93] Cognitive dissonance thus occurs when two opposing thoughts live in the same mind, producing inner conflicts and psychological distress. Cognitive dissonance is resolved by choosing one idea, belief or thought over the other.

Cognitive bias can be described as a mental shortcut or heuristics, which cause a glitch in our thinking and lead us to make questionable decisions and reach erroneous conclusions. It is a subconscious process that has to do with our limitations in mental processing. Examples are anchoring (the tendency to rely too heavily, or 'anchor', on one trait or piece of information when making decisions), availability bias (the tendency to overestimate the likelihood of events with greater 'availability' in memory, which can be influenced by how recent the memories are or how unusual or emotionally charged they may be), representativeness (judging probabilities on the basis of resemblance), status quo bias (the tendency to like things to stay relatively the same), optimism and overconfidence (the tendency to be over-optimistic, overestimating favorable and pleasing outcomes).[94] Cognitive bias may be guided by cognitive distortions.

Finally, moral dilemmas need to be recognized as such. Krebs and Denton found evidence that the structure of moral judgments tended to be inconsistent across different types of dilemmas.[95] Research indicates that the moral issue at hand thus provokes a certain type of reasoning, which means that people are not always inclined to use their highest level of moral reasoning. Jones argues that 'moral agents will economize on efforts devoted to moral reasoning when moral stakes are low'.[96] Moral agents will devote more time to their decision-making if the stakes are higher. They put more time and effort into social understanding and they most

92. Festinger 1957.
93. Smeulers 2012, p. 33.
94. Thaler 2008, pp. 33-48.
95. Krebs & Denton 2005, p. 637.
96. Jones 1991, p. 384.

probably think more accurately.[97] Jones refers to a study by Taylor that suggests that the 'magnitude of consequences' of acts and decisions has a paramount influence on the time and effort a person will invest in the cognitive processes: 'People may make use of external cues when stakes are low, but they will rely on self-perception processes more fully when the stakes are higher'.[98] Consequently, the moral cognitive process should be influenced by the moral intensity of the moral issue. Jones argued that in order to understand people's behavior towards certain moral issues, one should take into account moral intensity in decision-making. Moral intensity concentrates on the characteristics of the moral issue. Moral issues are present if the action or decision (1) has consequences for others and (2) must involve choice (volition) on the part of the moral agent.[99] The moral agent's actions are freely formed and may harm or benefit others.[100] Jones argues that 'moral issues vary in terms of their moral intensity'.[101] He derived these six components from social psychology: (1) magnitude of consequences; (2) social consensus; (3) probability of effect; (4) temporal immediacy; (5) proximity; and (6) concentration of effect. These six components are apparent in all moral issues.[102] (1) The magnitude of the consequences is defined as the sum of the harm or benefits caused to the victims or beneficiaries of the (im)moral act in question. Moral dilemmas facing serious consequences are more likely to bring about moral behavior.[103] (2) The social consensus of the moral issue is defined as the degree of social agreement that a proposed act is evil or good. A high degree of social consensus leaves less room for ambiguity and moves the moral agent to certain behavior.[104] (3) The probability of effect of the moral act in question is a twofold function of the probability that the act will take place and that it will actually cause the harm or benefit predicted.[105] (4) Temporal immediacy is the length of time between the present and the commencement of consequences of the moral act in question.[106] Impacts of events that occur sooner have a greater sense of immediacy and increase the moral urgency of the moral issue. (5) The proximity of the moral issue is the feeling of nearness that the individual has to either the victims or the beneficiaries of the evil or beneficial act in question.[107] The component of proximity has four variables that could be analyzed separately: social, cultural, psychological and/or physical nearness.[108] People are biologically programmed through evolution to care more about people who are close to them. Graner and England most probably did not have a guilty conscience, because their victims were strangers to them despite the fact that they were physically close. Milgram found out in his experiments, though, that increased physical proximity of the participant

97. Ibid., p. 384.
98. Ibid., p. 384.
99. Ibid., p. 367.
100. Ibid., p. 377.
101. Ibid., p. 367.
102. Ibid., p. 374.
103. Ibid., pp. 374–375.
104. Ibid., p. 375.
105. Ibid., p. 375.
106. Ibid., p. 376.
107. Ibid., p. 376.
108. Ibid., p. 377.

and the 'victim' considerably diminished the incidence of complete obedience. In the case of actual physical contact, complete obedience dropped from 62.5% in the baseline condition to 30%.[109] (6) The concentration of effect is a contrary function of the number of people affected by an act of given magnitude.[110] People with a sense of the vital significance of justice for the individual will be repulsed by immoral acts that result in (highly) concentrated effects. Individuals thus react differently to moral issues in a way that is systematically related to the characteristics of the issue involved.[111] The moral agent has to recognize the moral issue. If the moral agent does not apprehend the moral element of his decision, the moral agent will fail to employ the moral decision-making schemata and will make the decision-making in line with other schemata (cognitive distortion), for example economic rationality.[112] Moral issues with a high level of moral intensity will be easier to recognize as a moral issue and therefore the likelihood that moral decision-making schemas will be employed will increase.

Dealing with dilemmas requires time for reflection, different perspective-taking and stakeholder dialogue. But all too often there is not sufficient time to do so. The full agenda does not allow for such reflection and consequently a crucial decision is not identified as a dilemma and dealt with like any issue that is business as usual. Therefore there is a good reason to think of other means of decision-making as a solution to these cognition problems. Decision-making can be defined as '[t]he thought process of selecting a logical choice from the available options'.[113] The key decisions affecting the organization's ability to materialize opportunities and to survive over time, are made by a team and not by an individual. Knowledge diversity within such team contribute to team learning and therefore better decisions.[114]

4.3.7 Diversity

Diversity and independence are important because the best collective decisions are not the result of consensus or compromise, but the product of disagreement and contest. Independence will be discussed later on. Let us first focus on diversity. Diversity of thought in decision-making is very important, because each person has some private information. This information contributes to better decision-making if it is taken into account, even if it is a bizarre interpretation of the facts.

The presence of a minority point of view makes a group's decision more nuanced and rigorous.[115] Research by Charlan Nemeth demonstrated that the presence of a minority viewpoint, a dissenting opinion, challenges the group and requires that the majority re-question its own position more seriously.[116] Even when the minority point of view is ill-founded, it still makes the group's decision wiser. It stimulates

109. Ibid., p. 377.
110. Ibid., p. 377.
111. Ibid., p. 372.
112. Ibid., p. 380.
113. De Mol et al. 2015, p. 245.
114. West III 2007, p. 78.
115. Surowiecki 2004, p. 183.
116. Nemeth 2012, pp. 362–378.

divergent thinking and 'opens' the mind. It helps the group to recognize dilemmas, moral issues and solutions to these issues. Dissent helps people to consider more options, to search for information, to be more creative and balanced, which in the end helps with better decision-making.

Other research by Charlan Nemeth demonstrated the superiority of debate over brainstorming.[117] In brainstorm sessions the group is instructed not to criticize, in order to stimulate the flow of creativity. In the debate sessions the group was allowed to criticize if warranted. Surprisingly enough, this did not retard idea generation; it even led to significantly more total ideas than the brainstorm session. Speaking up is apparently deliberating. It helps people to say what they believe; it stimulates divergent thought.

It is very important, however, that these group discussions are well structured and managed. They should not be rushed (that can be aggravated by external or self-imposed deadlines), diversity of thinking should be ensured, a healthy debate should be facilitated and early consensus should be avoided. If there is no divergent opinion, there is a risk of 'group polarization', which has the potential of a more radicalized point of view that could make the outcome of the group discussion and the possible solution worse.[118]

In structuring and managing those group discussions it is important to appreciate the risk of talkativeness.[119] People who are more talkative are more influential. The more someone talks, the more he is talked to by others. Men tend to talk more than women and higher status people tend to speak more than lower status people. That does not mean that they are more right.[120] The order in which people speak is also important, since earlier comments are more influential, because 'they tend to provide a framework within which the discussion occurs'.[121]

Unsurprisingly, research indicated that diversity in the board has a positive effect on decision-making and performance. Women on the board have a positive effect, not because they are women but due to the balance between men and women in the board.[122] Different management cultures and interpersonal differences also increase board effectiveness. High demographic diversity among board members has a positive effect on financial performance and the quality of strategic decision-making.[123] Research conducted on diversity within family firms demonstrates that having a mix of family members and non-family members in the senior management team (top management team) has a positive effect on financial performance. This is strengthened when the CEO is a non-family member and when the board takes its countervailing power over the senior management team seriously.[124]

It is important that the organization exploits and expands on diversity, because it adds perspectives that would otherwise be absent. Besides increasing other

117. Nemeth et al. 2004, pp. 365–374.
118. Surowiecki 2004, p. 184.
119. Ibid.
120. Ibid.
121. Ibid.
122. Francoeur et al. 2008, pp. 83–95; Mallin et al. 2013, pp. 29–43; Campbell & Mínguez-Vera 2008, pp. 435–451.
123. Francoeur et al. 2013, pp. 85–101.
124. Patel & Cooper 2014, pp. 1624–1649.

perspective-taking it also makes it easier for individuals to say what they really think. Furthermore, it weakens some of the damaging characteristics of group decisions. Cognition diversity needs to be actively selected. It is even more important to do so in small groups, because in small groups it is easy for a few biased individuals to exert excessive influence and skew the group's collective decision-making. Finally, diversity also helps to preserve independence (as in the case of the Asch experiments).

4.3.8 Independence

In his inspiring book *The Wisdom of Crowds*, James Surowiecki states that 'independence does not mean isolation, but it does mean relative freedom from the influence of others'.[125] What he explains is that making own decisions, instead of following the herd, is crucial for good decision-making. It prevents mistakes being made because people are correlated and independent individuals rely on their own private information, rather than the information everyone else is also familiar with. This stimulates other perspective-taking that can lead to more nuanced and robust decision-making.

Most often, independence is regarded as the percentage of independent non-executives on the board, but independence is more than that. It relates to independence of thought. In many social and economic situations, individuals are influenced by the decisions of others. The most common examples are choosing a trendy restaurant or a popular movie. In normal social and economic life we see frequent imitation of behavior. There are two phenomena that are of particular interest: informational cascades and herd behavior. In a situational context these phenomena may cause the decisions and outcomes to be wrong despite individual rationality.

In the case of a herd, 'individuals choose the same action, but they may have acted differently from one another if the realization of their private signals had been different'.[126] The experiment by Milgram, Bickman and Berkowitz demonstrates the stimulus that emerges from crowds and especially larger crowds.[127] It is a simple though ingenious experiment. Milgram, Bickman and Berkowitz examined the reaction of passers-by to different sizes of groups standing on a busy city street looking up at a building. The stimulus group consisted of 1, 2, 3, 5, 10 and 15 men. First, a single person looked up for sixty seconds. Only a small fraction of the passers-by stopped to see what the man was looking at. Most just kept walking. When five men looked up, four times as many people stared at the empty sky. When 15 men looked up, 40% of all passers-by stopped and 86% actually tilted their heads and looked up. The assumption is that if everyone is looking, there must be a good reason why.

In the case of an information cascade, 'an individual considers it is optimal to follow the behavior of her predecessors without regard to her private signal since her belief is strongly held that no signal can outweigh it'.[128] An information cascade implies a herd, but a herd is not necessarily the result of an information cascade. In certain circumstances it may even be the norm. As discussed, groups can put considerable

125. Surowiecki 2004, p. 41.
126. Çelen & Kariv 2003, p. 3.
127. Milgram et al. 1969, pp. 79–82.
128. Çelen & Kariv 2003, p. 3.

pressure on their members. Following the group then seems to make sense from an emotional and professional point of view. When all your group members follow one direction, it is difficult to dissent and say what no one else says. Sticking to the group and maybe failing in a small way is then more risk-averse than speaking up and running the risk of failing big time. Pointing out the issues is very difficult. It is a necessary step, however, to see and acknowledge issues. Therefore whistleblowing is so important for organizations, even though it is rarely rewarded. Someone needs to feel the courage to point out the issue in order to fix it.

The problem with herding and information cascade is that if too many people adopt the same approach, it stops being smart. Although the group is right much of the time, sequential decision-making allows patterns of group behavior to be fragile and could cause a type of occasional instability that has the potential to harm the social and economic well-being of systems, organizations, teams, groups and individuals.[129] Although it makes sense to look at the crowds since in principle it makes you smarter if there is no situation of information cascade, paradoxically the best way for a group to be smart is to think and act as independently as possible. The more important the decision, the less likely it is that an information cascade will occur, since in principle more time and effort will be allocated to the decision-making.

Independence of thought of course increases with board independence. Research illustrates that board independence has a positive impact on a company's technical efficiency, measured by its ability to transform variables such as labor, capital and technology into increased output.[130] The effectiveness of the board is more robust when the number of independent members on the board is higher.[131] It will improve the board's objectivity and its ability to take multiple perspectives into account.[132]

Apart from independence in the board, organizations should think of ways to stimulate independence of thought in organizations. The ubiquity of the Internet and information technology provides possibilities to do so.

4.3.9 Information-processing

'Information processing refers to the gathering, interpreting, and synthesis of information in the context of organizational decision making'.[133] Many decision-makers in corporations face the difficulty of retrieving real information. All too often the IT infrastructure and systems do not allow a free float of real information. Furthermore, conventional corporations were set up as a hierarchical structure, characterized by bureaucracy. In many cases, in response to incidents, crisis management and litigation, layers of management were added, in an attempt to make the decision-making process as inclusive as possible. On the contrary, this deprived decision-makers at the top from the information they really need to make the right decisions. The more layers you add, the more diluted the information and thus the solution to the problem becomes. The top is isolated from the real opinions of anyone else.

---

129. Ibid.
130. Bozec et al. 2010, pp. 684–700.
131. Kock et al. 2012, pp. 492–514.
132. Mallin et al. 2013, pp. 29–43.
133. Tushman & Nadler 1978, p. 614; *See also* De Mol et al. 2015, p. 245.

By referring to *The Godfather*, James Surowiecki added another element, namely conflict of interest.[134] Since the messenger boys of Michael Corleone are pursuing their own interest, he has a difficult time retrieving the information he needs. Quite often it is not in the best interest of his messenger boys to disclose all the information they have. This becomes even more problematic when the business gets bigger, because when the business gets bigger you cannot stay on top of everything. Your reliance on others increases. 'Most important, the top-down nature of the organization means that Michael becomes more and more isolated from points of view other than his own. In a sense, although Michael has hundreds or thousands of men working for him, the organization doesn't just belong to him. It is him, which bodes ill for the family in the long run.'[135]

The most successful careerist – if you measure success by moving up the job ladder – tends not to disclose information about conflicts, budget problems and so on.[136] This has much to do with the reward and incentive system within organizations. Being honest about performance and expectations is not stimulated in the most prevalent performance management systems. This is caused by what Chris Argyris calls 'inauthentic behavior'.[137] Many managers dislike opposition from subordinates. Since people have a natural inclination to avoid conflict, 'inauthentic behavior', by pleasing the manager or holding back on information, is the norm within organizations. It gives the illusion of perfect decision-making by management, while everyone is just playing their role. In that sense, it is rather extraordinary that good information ever surfaces. Hierarchy will always be part of any form of organization, but there is a clear need to limit the shortcomings of a top-down authority structure.[138] The rigid hierarchical, multilayered corporation discourages the free flow of information.

Besides that, in the past there was an underappreciation of non-financial risk. A good example is Libor. This was not perceived to be a risk-bearing activity since it was not generating any profit or client-facing. Consequently, the risks related to Libor were not spotted by banks, although they were very critical.[139] For executives at the top it is therefore very difficult to know whether they have the full picture of the organization. Problems like these can partly be countered by taking a different lens to performance management. The most prevalent performance management systems pay insufficient attention to more adequate information sharing, since they overemphasize the achievement of some goals, most often profit targets, while undervaluing other objectives. Organizations should therefore look at their performance metrics and reorganize.

Furthermore, there is a paradigm shift in the flow of information. It becomes more and more important that the front line is informed and empowered so that it can add value to its customer by doing the right thing. This is what Gary Hamel calls 'democracy of information': 'Managerial power has traditionally depended on controlling information. Yet increasingly, value creation takes place at the interface

134. Surowiecki 2004, p. 199.
135. Ibid.
136. Ibid., p. 205.
137. Ibid.: Referred to by James Surowiecki.
138. Hamel 2009, p. 3.
139. Beck et al. 2016, p. 12.

between first-level employees and customer.'[140] It is important to have a common language as an organization, with aligned terminology, for example an integrated taxonomy over the three lines of defense to prevent confusion and distraction.

Organizations are set up to overcome coordination problems with efficiency and scale. Organizations today, however, face a new set of challenges, since the environment they are operating in is changing more rapidly, the economy and products being more volatile, the market being less forgiving. The challenge is therefore to make large organizations work as well as they would if they were small corporations. One way of doing this is to destructure and disaggregate the organization into smaller and more adaptable business units.[141] Another way of doing it is creating information systems that enable every employee to act in the interests of the entire organization, fully embracing the value creation required in the first line in the interface between the business and the customer.

4.3.10 Sustainability

Organizations should ask themselves the following existential question: Why are we designed as an organization? Darwin taught us that we organize in the pursuit of a common goal.[142] Darwin explained that we need a form of cooperation that requires a form of government. Modern organizations are thus a construct of human beings to organize. We do not organize solely out of self-interest, however, but to help make something bigger. In other words, there should be long-term value creation.

In the pursuit of long-term value creation, organizations need to take account of the social needs of reciprocity and equality. As discussed, these needs have their own motive component to rectify non-reciprocity or non-equality.[143] Darwin also stressed the importance of exemplary conduct. For long-term survival – in other words, a sustainable organization – robust compliance and integrity management is essential. It is your 'license to operate'.[144] Arguments about what is just either involve a conflict between reciprocity (only those who work hard should get the reward for hard work) or equality (everyone deserves a decent minimum income) or arguments about equal liberty and opportunity versus equal benefit.[145] A good government structure coordinates institutionally the social needs of reciprocity and equality and allocates the 'benefits and burdens' within a community.[146] By taking these principles into account, all parties can find their way to collectively beneficial results. This is also the rationale behind the concept of sustainability.

The concept of sustainability arose in the 1960s as the environment appeared on the global agenda as a world issue. There were concerns about environmental degradation as a result of poor resource management. In 1960 the Organization for Economic Corporation and Development (OECD) was created to promote policies

140. Hamel 2009, p. 6.
141. Ibid., p. 3.
142. Darwin 1871, p. 162 & 164.
143. Hoffman 2000, p. 243.
144. Bleker-van Eyk 2013.
145. Kohlberg 1981, p. 144; *See also*, Hoffman 2000, pp. 242–245.
146. Kohlberg 1981, p. 144.

that would achieve 'the highest sustainable economic growth and employment in member countries in order to stimulate employment and increase living standards'.[147]

The International Union for the Conservation of Nature released the *World Conservation Strategy* in 1980. The strategy describes the 'main agents of habitat destruction and environmental degradation as poverty, population pressure, social inequity and the terms of trade'.[148] It defines sustainable development as the maintenance of essential ecological processes and life support systems, including those of humans.[149]

In the same year, the World Commission on Environment and Development (WCED) was founded. WCED's report entitled *Our Common Future* provides a definition of sustainability that has widespread influence: 'Sustainable development is development that meets the needs of the present without compromising the ability of future generations to meet their own needs.'[150]

All these definitions refer to socially significant long-term goals. This means that organizations should look for alternatives to the traditional performance management system and implement a system that encourages long-term goals and stakeholders for short-term gains. This is also needed in light of the heightened expectations of the stakeholders.

Granting stock options to the CEO and management can provide useful incentives for long-term value creation. Research shows that CEO stock ownership and other performance-related compensation increase CEOs' tendency to seek external advice that results in better (financial) performance.[151] Environmental encouragement as part of board compensation or CEO long-term pay demonstrates a positive effect on environmental regulatory performance.[152] This effect is even stronger in predominantly polluting industry sectors.[153]

Furthermore, organizations should be looking for ways to give employees encouragement to uncover and act on private information. Many bonus systems are based on whether someone exceeds a financial target. The effect of this type of encouragement is that people become deceptive. People will do whatever they can to meet these targets, but this could be at the expense of the long-term goals. Then you are 'paying people to lie', instead of paying due regard to this long-term value creation.[154] Although a reward helps people to do their best, it is good to note that encouragements do not necessarily have to be financial. They just have to take into account the needs of reciprocity and equality.

---

147. Global Sustainability, Global sustainability: the history/time line of an idea, RMIT, Melbourne 2001, p. 4, at RMIT's Global Sustainability website: http://www.global.rmit.edu.au/resources/historyofanidea_25.07.01.pdf
148. IUCN/UNEP/WWF, World conservation strategy: living resource conservation for sustainable development, IUNCN/UNEP/WWF, Gland, Switzerland, 1980. Cited in RMIT, supra note 136, p. 8
149. Ibid.
150. World Commission on Environment and Development, *Our Common Future*, Oxford University Press, Oxford, 1987, cited in RMIT, note 136 supra, p. 9.
151. McDonald et al. 2008, pp. 453–475.
152. Rodrigue et al. 2013, pp. 107–129.
153. Beronne & Gomez-Mejia 2009, pp. 103–126.
154. Michael C. Jensen cited by James Surowiecki, *see* Surowiecki 2004, p. 209.

4.3.11 Trust

Darwin describes the competition between tribes that causes wars.[155] He then focuses on the morality within the tribe and states that people within that tribe need to be able to rely on each other, so that they can warn each other effectively when there is danger.[156] Today, the whole concept of trust is woven into the fabric of everyday business and it is in some sense impersonal.[157] In modern business times and with ongoing globalization we do not trust personal or intergroup relationships only, since we also do business with people with whom we have no ties whatsoever. Humans started to realize that they can benefit from impersonal ties as well. Trust has grown since strangers – in general – did not betray that trust. James Surowiecki explains that modern capitalism made the idea of trusting people with whom you 'had no prior personal ties' seem reasonable.[158] Businessmen have taken up the idea of individual responsibility for the enforcement of agreements. We invented the institutional and legal framework that underpins every modern capitalist economy to enforce agreements. In most cases, though, we do not need contract law to enforce it, since we have learned that there is mutual benefit in abiding by the contract voluntarily. Luckily I would say, because it would be unfeasible for any government to enforce all contracts. We do still need contract law, however, because there would be no trust if it did not exist.

As James Surowiecki eloquently puts it:

> 'trust begins there ... because of the shadow of the future'.[159] 'All you really trust is that the other person will recognize his self-interest. But over time, that reliance on his own attention to his self-interest becomes something more. It becomes a general sense of reliability, a willingness to cooperate (even in competition) because cooperation is the best way to get things done. ... Pro-sociality becomes stronger because pro-sociality works.'[160]

There is a downside to trust, though. In times of prosperity people become less attentive. Research has demonstrated that boards tend to forget or neglect to maintain oversight when times are good.[161] Then the organization runs the risk that too much management discretion is taken by the CEO. This risk is even more apparent when the CEO also holds the position of chairman. The more people trust, the easier it is to abuse that trust. 'If trust is the most valuable social product of market interactions, corruption is its most damaging. Over the centuries, market societies have developed mechanisms and institutions that are supposed to limit corruption, including auditors, rating agencies, third-party analysts, and, as we've seen, even Wall Street banks.'[162] However, we saw that these parties suffered from the same flaws.

155. Darwin 1871, p. 159.
156. Ibid.
157. Surowiecki 2004, p. 123.
158. Ibid.
159. Ibid., p. 124.
160. Ibid.
161. Tuggle 2010, pp. 946–968.
162. Surowiecki 2004, p. 126.

We know the detrimental impact if trust is lost. We only need to think of Arthur Anderson and the firm's handling of the auditing of Enron. We can overcome that broken trust by keeping the once responsible accountable, by having a countervailing power that neutralizes the power vested in others and by rebuilding or earning – to put it differently – the trust relationship by demonstrating exemplary behavior.[163]

4.3.12 Accountability

As Darwin explained, compliant behavior should be praised because it is in the general interest of the clan.[164] Actions to the contrary should be condemned in the clearest terms.[165] Modern capitalism is hale and hearty when people believe that the long-term benefits of honest and fair trade outweigh the short-term benefits of sharp dealing.

In the 1990s such understanding was not sufficiently entrenched in organizations. Dishonest behavior worked as a catalyst. This was the result of the evolution of reciprocity. Most people will do their fair share as long as they believe that everyone else is participating too. A good example is paying tax. In general people are willing to pay their taxes – not too much of course – as long as others do the same. If that is not the case, the wrongdoing needs to be restored. People will keep on paying their taxes as long as they believe that people who do not pay their taxes have a fair chance of being caught and punished. If that is not the case, others too will not pay their taxes. When people start to think that others are breaking the law and are getting away with it because the policeman is asleep, they start feeling as if they are being taken advantage of. People want to do the right thing, but no one wants to be a sucker. This evolution of a reciprocity trait thus requires that defection or dishonesty is punished.

In modern capitalism people thus need to understand that the benefits of honesty and fair trade outweigh short-term benefits. In the case of Enron there was no (sufficient) oversight by the board of directors, nor from other parties such as banks, underwriters, etc. The gains for short-term self-interest were enormous, which led to corrupt behavior. This worked as a catalyst for even more widespread corrupt behavior.

Corrupt behavior can be rectified by keeping the instigators, the ones responsible, accountable. We saw, however, that many top executives got away with their wrongdoing in the 1990s. An example is Wells Fargo. Senator Elizabeth Warren questioned Wells Fargo CEO John Stumpf before the Senate Banking Committee in September 2016 about accounts sold in the 1990s. Warren criticized Stumpf for the high-pressure sales culture that spurred employees to create 1.5 million checking accounts and issue almost 600,000 credit cards to customers who did not want them. She said: 'you squeezed employees to breaking point, so that they cheat customers.'[166]

163. Galbraith 1952, pp. 118–119.
164. Darwin 1871, p. 166.
165. Ibid.
166. Senator Elizabeth Warren question Wells Fargo CEO John Stumpf on September 20, 2016. The interview can be consulted via youtube. It is called 'Elizabeth Warren DESTROYS Wells Fargo CEO For Unauthorized Accounts "YOU SHOULD RESIGN" 9/20/16': https://www.youtube.com/watch?v = sOBmn0xU7wY

The Consumer Financial Protection Bureau, an agency Warren helped create, and once headed, led the investigation that punished Wells Fargo with USD 185 million in fines. Wells Fargo fired 5,300 employees responsible for cheating its customers, but this did not impress Warren. Senator Warren said that only low-level employees had been fired, but that senior management had got away with it. She stated that senior management should take their responsibility and keep themselves responsible and accountable. Warren told Stumpf: 'You should resign.'[167] Warren also said that the Department of Justice should prosecute the companies and individuals who triggered the financial crisis to keep them accountable.

What Warren expresses is that a market economy based on trust only works when the organizations and individuals that abuse that trust are held accountable. In the late 1990s all too often they were not. In most cases, neither these institutions nor their top executives had to pay the price (in the market) for their neglect of duty.

4.3.13 Cooperation

Cooperation is the process of two or more people working or acting together for a common goal or mutual benefit, as opposed to working in competition for self-interest. The work is divided or even jointly performed where one man would have insufficient strength to complete the work successfully. As explained *supra*, society, organizations, groups and teams only work if people cooperate. According to Darwin, humans are inclined to be altruistic, sympathetic and moral, because this is an advantage in the struggle for existence.[168] A society cannot rely on law alone to enforce responsible action by everyone. According to Darwin, people are prepared to cooperate if this adds value for the collective and hence for the individual, who can only survive in the protected environment of the collective.[169] Recent research seems to indicate that altruism may be hardwired in the human brain, which would mean that we are programmed to cooperate.[170] We at least know for sure that cooperation can emerge in a world of self-seeking individuals.

Axelrod states in *The Evolution of Cooperation* that 'the foundation of cooperation is not really trust, but the durability of the relationship .... Whether the players trust each other or not is of less importance in the long run than whether the conditions are ripe for them to build a stable pattern of cooperation with each other'.[171] Axelrod is explaining here that durability is built over time through 'trial-and-error learning about possibilities for mutual rewards' and imitation of past successful relationships.[172] It would be interesting to explore whether it is the durability of the relationship, trust or the interplay between the two that forms the basis of cooperation. In any event it seems that people who repeatedly deal with each other over time recognize the benefits of cooperation. In general they do not try to take advantage of each

167. Ibid.
168. Darwin 1871, p. 141.
169. Ibid., p. 159–164.
170. Christov-Moore & Iacoboni 2016, pp. 1544–1558.
171. Axelrod 1984, p. 182.
172. Ibid.

other, knowing that doing so could lead to punishment (accountability). The key to cooperation is what Axelrod called 'the shadow of the future'.[173]

But it is not only the durability of the relationship and trust; the social need for reciprocity should be upheld as well. I referred to the ultimatum game earlier. That clearly demonstrates that the evolution of a reciprocity trait leads individuals to respond to unfairness with revenge.[174] The social needs of reciprocity and equality thus have their own motive component to rectify non-reciprocity or non-equality.[175] Members of a group need to adopt a broader definition of self-interest than the narrow-minded short-term interest of maximizing profit. For that they need to be able to trust those around them. In the absence of trust, narrow-minded self-interest celebrates 'glory' days.

Now the question remains of how the work could be best divided. James Surowiecki explains very convincingly in *The Wisdom of Crowds* that decentralized ways of organizing human efforts are more often than not expected to yield better results than centralized ways. First of all - as discussed - decentralized working people feel more responsible for their own environment and work. Secondly, decentralization makes coordination easier. Organizations then rely on their employees to find new and more efficient ways of working, instead of having to opt for command and threats. That reduces the monitoring costs, cuts transaction costs and allows managers to focus on other things. Thirdly, very often the relevant knowledge to deal with a problem is in the head of the colleagues dealing with the issue on a daily basis and not their bosses. When solving the issue they should have the authority to do so. Decision-making should therefore be depoliticized.

The catch in all this is that decision-making is not depoliticized in corporations. Quite often corporate budgets do not echo the market's opinion on corporate divisions. Divisions have an incentive to ask for more resources from the organization than they deserve, even if that is not in the best interest of the organization as a whole. In organizations there is quite often internal rivalry, competition driven by self-interest. The beneficial effects of competition are undisputable, but severe internal competition defeats the purpose of having an organization, 'by diminishing economies of scale and actually increasing the costs of monitoring people's behavior'.[176] You should be able to trust your co-workers. In order to mitigate this, we should start by being honest about performance and revise the reward and incentive system within organizations. Being honest about performance and expectations is not stimulated in the most prevalent performance management systems.

4.4 ORGANIZATIONAL LEADERSHIP: CREATING ORGANIZATIONS THAT ARE GENUINELY HUMAN[177]

This contribution has not been written to underplay the importance of a more traditional strategy for legal compliance and formal hierarchy in an organization.

173. Ibid.
174. Leeson et al. 2006, p. 140; *See also*, Hoffman 2000, pp. 242–245.
175. Hoffman 2000, p. 243.
176. Surowiecki 2004, p. 214.
177. Hamel 2009, p. 8. The title is based on the concluding remarks in this article.

Without doubt it is necessary to have such a sound system of risk assessment, risk response, monitoring and control activities. However, strict controls are probably not the best way to foster integrity and responsible risk-taking in the long run. It can come 'at the cost of initiative, creativity and passion – the essential building blocks of organizational success'.[178] Furthermore, it is not sufficient for influencing human impulses for moral thought and action. As Paine describes it very eloquently, 'unethical business practice involves the tacit, if not explicit, cooperation of others and reflects the values, attitudes, beliefs, language, and behavioral patterns that define an organization's operating culture.'[179] Organizations therefore bear responsibility for fostering integrity. Organizations that fail to do so share responsibility with those who conceive, execute and knowingly benefit from organizational wrongdoing.

In modern society we should look at new solutions for long-term simmering problems. Management should embrace the responsibilities of citizenship and adopt a form of government that mobilizes and organizes human capabilities. Employees need incentives that require them to take a long-term view of success. They are responsible for safeguarding the interest of all those who put trust in them. Control has to come mainly from organizational norms, not review procedures. Organizations should motivate and inspire their people with a clear set of values and guiding principles deeply rooted throughout the organization. To foster a feeling of personal responsibility, decision-making authority has to be distributed. Trust is maintained when values and beliefs are actively managed. If organizations do not actively work to keep the guiding principles clear, to keep discipline and consistency in balance with sharing responsibility and keep those of wrongdoing accountable, trust starts to break down. As Sinek puts it, all organizations start with why, but only the great ones keep their why clear year after year. This is a continuous lifecycle of organizational integrity (see Figure 3).

The purpose of such an organizational integrity approach is 'to make every organization as genuinely human as the people who work there'.[180] The rigid approach of controlling organizational integrity that we see in most organizations deprives us to a significant extent of the very qualities that make us human. By balancing and maintaining the elements of good government and an integrity approach infused by a set of shared values and principles deeply rooted in the organization, we create organizations that have the capabilities of us humans: our vigor, inventiveness and sense of kinship.

This has a few implications for the way we look at leadership in the context of managing organizational integrity. This contribution will not solve the controversy around the appropriate definition of leadership, but there is one element that is especially interesting in relation to organizational integrity.[181] There are scholars that define leadership as a specialized role, and there are scholars that define leadership more as a shared influence process.[182]

178. Ibid.
179. Sharp Paine 1994, p. 106.
180. Hamel 2009, p. 8.
181. *See* for a discussion on the controversies, Yukl 2010.
182. Ibid., p. 22.

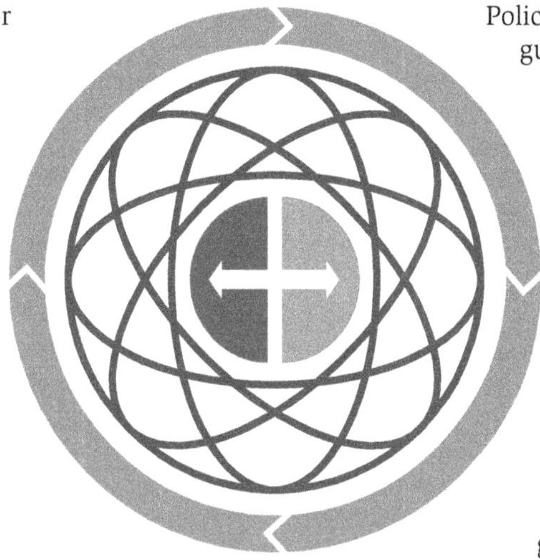

Figure 3: Continuous lifecycle of organizational integrity

In the classical idea of leadership, every group has role specializations, including a leadership role. Under these theories, the role of the leader cannot be shared too widely without jeopardizing the effectiveness of the group. Consequently, every group has a leader and followers. The leader might be a follower as well, because he needs to follow a higher ranking leader. Scholars who like to see leadership as a specialized role, like to study the attributes and typical behavior of those leaders and the effects of this behavior on the other members of the group. This means that in this classical way of thinking we tend to see leadership as a personal characteristic or difference of the leader itself, such as transactional leadership, authentic leadership, ethical leadership, servant or spiritual leadership. These ways of thinking about leadership fit the classical idea of hierarchical, vertical models typical for the bureaucracy-infused management practices common in many organizations.

The problem with defining leadership as a personality characteristic or difference is that it does not take sufficient regard of the wider social context, the role of followers, peers, supervisors and the purpose of leadership (e.g. goal realization, innovation, sense of ethics, trust and harmony). Furthermore, if we want to mobilize and organize human capabilities better, we should move away from this bureaucracy-infused style of management, because it hampers initiative, creativity, passion, responsibility and innovation, which are all critical success factors for organizations. Moreover, organizations are often too big to wait till the leader sends down his orders. Also, organizations are moving into a knowledge driven era, with a greater diversity of culture and further globalization. This means that individual based 'heroic' models of leadership are most likely not sustainable. Instead of central coordination, there should be more self-management. The time of leaders as all-wise decision-makers is therefore in the past. This means that we should rethink the way we look at leadership. Instead of putting the leader central, it is more beneficial to put the social context and interactive process central.

Defining leadership as a shared influence process does take into account all those factors. Leadership is then constructed as 'an influence process that occurs naturally within a social system and is diffused among the members'.[183] In more recent leadership literature, leadership is often depicted in various models as a shared, dyadic, relational, strategic, global and complex social dynamic and thereby focusing on these patterns and process.[184]

Leadership is then regarded a social process or pattern of relationship, instead of a specialized role. In this definition of leadership, there is no clear distinction between leaders and followers. Any member of the group may exhibit leadership at any time. This means that leadership can then be best defined as a form of shared leadership where leadership is distributed within the group or a team of individuals rather than localized in any one individual who serves the role of supervisor.[185]

As discussed, important decisions should not be made by one single person, but should be made by a group. Those decisions are made through the use of an interactive process involving (many) different people who influence each other. Decision-making benefits from diversity and independence of thought. That's why it is important to pay more attention to the complex influence processes that occur among members of a group, the context and conditions that determine when and how they occur and the consequences for the group or organization. When studying leadership or managing organizational integrity, it is therefore advantageous to look at the interaction patterns and process.

If leadership is defined as the process of influencing behavior to understand and agree about what needs to be done and how to do it, then leadership arises from people working together and interacting with each other.[186] Leadership then becomes a coordinating mechanism for the whole group to strive to common ambitions. This brings a whole new dynamic: everyone can be a leader.

This however also means that leadership needs to be earned and cannot be taken for granted. For old school leaders this can be difficult, because they might not be used to being part of a group. Rather they are used to putting themselves on top of that group. This mind shift is not easily made. We have trained and conditioned followers for decades or longer to follow the leader and not think for themselves. Likewise, we have often placed leaders on a pedestal in the past. There is however a new reality. We have seen many examples of people who say they are leaders, but rather they were driven by their own self-interest. This led to trust violations and for a new wave where people have become far more critical of those people who say that they are leaders. This new reality is characterized by the empowerment of the professional, reclaiming their authority on the work that they perform.

183. Ibid.

184. Avolio et al. 2009, pp. 421–449.

185. Spisak et al., p. 292; they define leadership as: 'initially ... an adaptive process where one or more individuals emerge as a focal point to influence and coordinate behavior for solving social challenges posed by dynamic physical and cultural environments'. Yukl 2010, p. 26; he defines leadership as 'the process of influencing others to understand and agree about what needs to be done and how to do it, and the process of facilitating individual and collective efforts to accomplish shared objectives'.

186. Ibid.

This however does not mean that we do not need leadership, because we do. Actually we are in need of far more leadership. We might however be able to do with much less management. As discussed, authority through control has only limited influence over the behavior of individuals and strict controls are not the best way to foster integrity and responsible risk-taking. It can come at the cost of initiative, creativity and passion. A bottom-up rather than a top-down approach is more beneficial. This implies that the means of control needs to be reinvented. Organizations should foster a strong control culture by leveraging the power of shared values and ambitions. More reliance must be placed on peer review and less on top-down supervision. This also requires a different mindset of the top and middle management. Rather than primarily focusing on track and control, management should focus on their added value. They should support, inspire and protect the team.

Organizations therefore need to move away from the bureaucratic structures, since it confines them. In the bureaucracy-infused management practices there is a separation of the thinking and the doing, while for organizations to flourish, uphold their moral standard and build upon the constructs of initiative, creativity, passion, responsibility and innovation, everybody in that organization is expected to do and think, act and reflect. It requires a redesigning of thinking and doing in an organization.

LITERATURE

Asch 1951
S. Asch, 'Effects of group pressure upon the modification and distortion of judgement', in: M.H. Guetzkow (ed.), *Groups, leadership and men*, Pittsburgh: Carnegie 1951.

Avolio et al. 2009
B.J. Avolio, F.O. Walumbwa & T.J. Weber, 'Leadership: current Theories, Research, and Future Directions', *Annual Review of Psychology*, 2009, Vol. 60.

Axelrod 1984
R. Axelrod, *The Evolution of Cooperation*, New York: Basic Books 1984, p. 182.

Beck et al. 2016
T. Beck, H. Heidegger, D. Mikkelsen, A. Raufuss, O. Salomon & O. Simula, *Managing non-financial risk in banking: Paradigm shifts in the making*, McKinsey & Company, April 2016.

Beronne & Gomez-Mejia 2009
P. Beronne & L. Gomez-Mejia, 'Environmental performance and executive compensation: an integrated agency-institutional perspective', *Academy of Management Journal*, 2009, Vol. 52.

Bilton & Sim 1979
M. Bilton & K. Sim, *Four hours in My Lai – a war crime and its aftermath*, London: Viking 1992.

Bleker-van Eyk 2013
S.C. Bleker-van Eyk, *Compliance officer 2.0*, publication part of the Free university (Amsterdam) Executive Master of Compliance & Integrity Management, on file with the author.

Bleker-van Eyk 2017
S.C. Bleker-van Eyk, 'Compliance is zo serieus nog niet. De rol van humor binnen compliance', in: C.A. Wielenga et al. (ed.), *Jaarboek Compliance 2017*, Cappelle aan den IJssel: Nederlands Compliance Instituut 2017.

Bozec et al. 2010
R. Bozec, M. Dia & Y. Bozec, 'Governance-Performance Relationship: A Re-examination Using Technical Efficiency Measures', *British Journal of Management Studies*, 2010, Vol. 21.

Campbell & Mínguez-Vera 2008
K. Campbell & A. Mínguez-Vera, 'Gender diversity in the Boardroom and Firm Financial Performance', *Journal of Business Ethics*, Vol. 83, 2008.

Cannon-Bowers & Salas 2001
J.A. Cannon-Bowers & E. Salas, 'Reflections on Shared Cognition', *Journal of Organizational Behavior, 2001*, Vol. 22, No. 2, Special Issue: Shared Cognition, March.

Çelen & Kariv 2003
B. Çelen & S. Kariv, 'Distinguishing Informational Cascades from Herd Behavior in the Laboratory', October 2003, to be consulted on: http://eml.berkeley.edu/~kariv/CK_II.pdf.

Christov-Moore & Iacoboni 2016
L. Christov-Moore & M. Iacoboni, 'Self-other resonance, its control and prosocial inclinations: Brain-behavior relationships', *Human Brain Mapping*, 2016, Vol. 37, Issue 4.

Coase 1988
Ronald Coase, *The Firm, the Market and the Law*, Chicago: University of Chicago Press 1988.

Crossland & Hambrick 2007
C. Crossland & D. Hambrick, 'How national systems differ in their constraints on corporate executives - a study of CEO effects in three countries', *Strategic Management Journal*, 2007, Vol. 28.

Darwin 1871
Charles Darwin MA, *The Descent of Man*, Vol 1, 1871, in: The Complete Work of Darwin Online. To be consulted on: http://darwin-online.org.uk/.

De Haan & Kasozi 2014
E. de Haan & A. Kasozi, *De Schaduwkant van Leiderschap. Herkennen en vermijden van hoogmoed, ontsporing en excessen*, Assen: Koninklijke van Gorcum B.V. 2014.

De Mol et al. 2015
Eva de Mol, Svetlana N. Khapova & Tom Elfring, 'Entrepreneurial Team Cognition: A Review', *International Journal of Management Reviews*, 2015, Vol. 17.

Espinosa et al. 2002
Alberto Espinosa, Javier Lerch & Robert Kraut, 'Explicit vs. Implicit Coordination Mechanisms and Task Dependencies: One Size Does Not Fit All', in: Eduardo Salas, Stephen M. Fiore, and Janis A. Cannon-Bowers, *Team Cognition: Process and Performance at the Inter- and Intra-individual Level*, Washington, DC: APA Books 2002.

Feigelson et al. 2015
J. Feigelson, L. Forsgårdh & P. Navarro Martínez., *Strengthening the role of Lead Independent Directors: an essential counterbalance to boardroom imperialism*, ICGN, 2015. Visited on 10/25/2016: https://www.icgn.org/strengthening-role-lead-independent-directors-essential-counterbalance-boardroom-imperialism.

Festinger 1957
L. Festinger, *A theory on cognitive dissonance*, Evanson: Row Peterson 1957.

Fichtner et al. 2016
U. Fichtner, H. Goos & M. Hesse, 'The Deutsche Bank Downfall: How a Pillar of German Banking Lost Its Way', *Der Spiegel*, 2016, October 28, to be consulted on: www.spiegel.de/international/business/the-story-of-the-self-destruction-of-deutsche-bank-a-1118157.html

Francoeur et al. 2008
C. Francoeur, R. Labelle & B. Sinclair-Desgagne, 'Gender Diversity in Corporate Governance and Top Management', *Journal of Business Ethics*, Vol. 81, 2008.

Francoeur et al. 2013
C. Francoeur, W. Ben-Amar, T. Hafsi & R. Labelle, 'What Makes Better Boards? A Closer Look at Diversity and Ownership', *British Journal of Management*, 2013, Vol. 24.

Galbraith 1952
J.K. Galbraith, *American Capitalism: The concept of countervailing power*, New Jersey: Transaction Publishers 1952.

Galema et al. 2012
R. Galema, R. Lensink & R. Mersland, 'Do Powerful CEOs Determine Microfinance Performance?', *Journal of Management Studies*, 2012, Vol. 49.

Gibbs 1995
J.C. Gibbs, 'The cognitive development perspective', in: W.M. Kurtines & J.L. Gewirtz (eds.), *Moral Development: An introduction*, Boston: Allyn & Bacon, 1995.

Greenberg & Dratel 2005
K.J. Greenberg & J.L. Dratel (eds.), *The torture papers – the road to Abu Ghraib*, Cambridge: University Press 2005.

Grunfeld & Smeulers 1999
F. Grunfeld & A. Smeulers, *The Role of the Perpetrator and the Bystander in Human Rights Violations*, October 12, 1999, afternoon session A 14:00–15:30.

Hamel 2009
G. Hamel, 'Moon Shots for Management', *Harvard Business Review*, 2009, February.

Higgins et al. 1984
A. Higgins, C. Power & L. Kohlberg, 'The relationship of moral atmosphere to judgments of responsibility', in: W.M. Kurtines and J.L. Gewirtz (eds.), *Moral behavior and moral development*, San Francisco: John Wiley & Sons 1984.

Hoffman 2000
M.L. Hoffman, *Empathy and Moral Development, Implications for Caring and Justice*, Cambridge: Cambridge University Press 2000.

Jones 1991
T.M. Jones, 'Ethical Decision Making by Individuals in Organizations: An Issue-Contingent Model', *Academy of Management Review*, 1991, Volume 16, No. 21.

Joseph et al. 2014
J. Joseph, W. Ocasio & M. McDonnell, 'The structural elaboration of board independence: Executive power, institutional logics, and the adoption of CEO-only board structures in U.S. Corporate Governance', *Academy of Management Journal*, 2014, Vol.57.

Kaiser & Hogan 2007
R.B. Kaiser & R. Hogan, 'The Dark Side of Discretion: Leader Personality and Organizational Decline', in: R. Hooijberg et al. (eds.), *Being There Even When You Are Not (Monographs in Leadership and Management, Volume 4)*, Bingley: Emerald Group Publishing Limited 2007.

Kaiser et al. 2015
R.B. Kaiser, J.M. LeBreton & J. Hogan, 'The Dark Side of Personality and Extreme Leader Behavior', *Applied Psychology: An International Review*, 2015, Vol. 64, No. 1.

Kock et al. 2012
C. Kock, J. Santaló & L. Diestre. 'Corporate Governance and the Environment: What type of Governance Creates Greener Companies?', *Journal of Management studies*, 2012, Vol. 49.

Kohlberg 1981
L. Kohlberg, *Essays on Moral Development, Volume I, The Philosophy of Moral Development. Moral Stages and the Idea of Justice*, San Francisco: Harper & Row, Publishers 1981.

Krebs & Denton 2005
D.L. Krebs & K. Denton, 'Toward a More Pragmatic Approach to Morality: A Critical Evaluation of Kohlberg's Model', *Psychological Review*, 2005, Vol. 112, No. 3.

Leeson et al. 2006
P.T. Leeson, C.J. Coyne & P.J. Boettle, 'Converting Social Conflicts: Focal Points and the Evolution of Cooperation', *Review of Austrian Economics*, 2006, Vol. 19.

Lombardo & Eichinger 1989
M.M. Lombardo & R.W. Eichinger, *Preventing Derailment. What to do before it's too late*, Greensboro, North Carolina: Center for Creative Leadership 1989.

Mallin et al. 2013
C. Mallin, G. Michelon & D. Raggi, 'Monitoring Intensity and Stakeholders' Orientation: How Does Governance Affect Social and Environmental Disclosure?', *Journal of Business Ethics*, 2013, Vol. 114.

McDonald et al. 2008
M. McDonald, P. Khanna & J. Westphal, 'Getting them to think outside the circle: Corporate Governance, CEO's External advice', *Academy of Management Journal*, 2008, Vol. 51.

Milgram et al. 1969
S. Milgram, L. Bickman & L. Berkowitz, 'Note on the drawing power of crowds of different size', *Journal of Personality and Social Psychology*, 1969, Vol. 13, No. 2.

Milgram 1974
S. Milgram, *Obedience to Authority: an experimental view*, New York: Harper Perennial Modern Thought 1974.

Nemeth et al. 2004
C. J. Nemeth, B. Personnaz, M. Personnaz & J.A. Goncalo, 'The liberating role of conflict in group creativity: A study in two countries', *European Journal of Psychology*, 2004, Vol. 34.

Nemeth 2012
C.J. Nemeth, 'Minority Influence Theory'. In: P. van Lange, A. Kruglanski & T. Higgins (eds.), *Handbook of Theories of Social Psychology*, Volume 2, London: Sage Publications Ltd 2012.

Patel & Cooper 2014
P. Patel & D. Cooper, 'Structural power equality between family and non-family TMT members and the performance of family firms', *Academy of Management Journal*, 2014, Vol. 57.

Peers 1979
W.R. Peers, *The My Lai inquiry*, New York: Norton & Company 1979.

Rechner & Dalton 1991
P.L. Rechner & D.R. Dalton, 'CEO duality and organizational performance: A longitudinal analysis', *Strategic Management Journal*, 1991, Vol. 12(2).

Rodrigue et al. 2013
M. Rodrigue, M. Magnan & C. Cho, 'Is Environmental Governance Substantive or Symbolic? An Empirical Investigation', 2013, *Journal of Business Ethics*, Vol. 114.

Schelling 1960
T.C. Schelling, *The Strategy of Conflict*, New York: Oxford University Press 1960.

Schurz 1985
G. Schurz, 'Experimentelle Überprüfung des Zusammenhangs zwischen Persönlichkeitsmerkmale und der Bereitschaft zum destruktiven Gehorsam gegenüber Autoritäten', *Zeitschrift für experimentelle und angewandte Psychologie*, 1985.

Sharp Paine 1994
Lynn Sharp Paine, 'Managing for Organizational Integrity', *Harvard Business Review*, 1994, March-April.

Sinek 2009
S. Sinek, *Start With Why: How great leaders inspire everyone to take action*, London: Portfolio Penguin 2009.

Smeulers & van Niekerk 2009
A. Smeulers & S. van Niekerk, 'Abu Ghraib and the War on Terror – a case against Donald Rumsfeld?', *Crime, Law and Social Change*, 2009, Vol. 51.

Smeulers 2012
A. Smeulers, In opdracht van de staat: gezagsgetrouwe criminelen en internationale misdrijven (oratie Tilburg) Tilburg: Tilburg University 2012.

Spisak et al. 2015
B.R. Spisak, M.J. O'Brien, N. Nicholson & M. van Vught, 'Niche construction and the evolution of leadership', *Academy of Management Review*, 2015, Vol. 40, No. 2.

Surowiecki 2004
J. Surowiecki, *The Wisdom of Crowds*, New York: Anchor Books 2004.

Thaler 2008
R.H. Thaler & C.R. Sanstein, *Nudge: Improving Decisions about Health, Wealth and Happiness*, Amsterdam/Antwerpen: Business Contact, 2008.

Tuggle et al. 2010
C. Tuggle, D. Sirmon, C. Reutzel & l. Bierman, 'Commanding board of director attention -investigating how organizational performance and CEO duality affect board members' attention to monitoring', *Strategic Management Journal*, 2010, Vol. 31.

Tushman & Nadler 1978
M.L. Tushman & D.A. Nadler, 'Information processing as an integrating concept in organizational design', *Academy of Management Review*, 1978. Volume 3.

Tyler 2006
Tyler, *Why People Obey the Law*, New Jersey: Princeton University Press 2006.

West III 2007
G. P. West III, 'Collective Cognition: When Entrepreneurial Teams, Not Individuals, Make Decisions', *Entrepreneurship Theory and Practice*, 2007, Volume 31.

Yukl 2010
G. Yukl, *Leadership in Organizations*, New Jersey: Pearson, seventh edition, 2010.

Zimbardo 2008
Ph. Zimbardo, *The Lucifer effect – understanding how good people turn evil*, New York: Random House trade paperbacks 2008.

Other references

RMIT Global Sustainability 2001
Global Sustainability, *Global sustainability: the history/time line of an idea*, RMIT, Melbourne 2001, at RMIT's Global Sustainability website: http://www.global.rmit.edu.au/resources/historyofanidea_25.07.01.pdf

IUCN/UNEP/WWF 1980
IUCN/UNEP/WWF, World conservation strategy: living resource conservation for sustainable development, IUNCN/UNEP/WWF, Gland, Switzerland, 1980.

World Commission on Environment and Development 1987
World Commission on Environment and Development, *Our Common Future*, Oxford University Press, Oxford, 1987.

Warren 2006
Senator Elizabeth Warren question Wells Fargo CEO John Stumpf on September 20, 2016. The interview can be consulted via YouTube. It is called 'Elizabeth Warren DESTROYS Wells Fargo CEO For Unauthorized Accounts "YOU SHOULD RESIGN" 9/20/16': https://www.youtube.com/watch?v = sOBmn0xU7wY

5. Conditioning Compliance

Dr. M.M. Rietdijk

5.1 INTRODUCTION

Compliance is a subject that can be analyzed from many different angles. It aims at compliance with rules in many different aspects of life. Sometimes we want our children to be compliant; the police want citizens to be compliant in traffic or after having attended a football game; supervisory bodies in finance, healthcare, safety and many other layers of society wish people to obey to the rules.[1] Supervisors take - sometimes elaborate - actions to achieve these goals, however, with mixed results.

This chapter explains compliance from a behavioral perspective and aims to offer concrete approaches on how to stimulate compliance and even behavior that goes beyond compliance. These approaches are embedded in scientific rules on behavior, discovered by the likes of physiologist Ivan Pavlov and behaviorist B.F. Skinner).[2] These scientific rules, especially those on behavior, are also known as 'conditioning'. These rules can assist supervisory bodies and others involved in upholding compliance in achieving their compliance goal.

These scientific rules explain why and when people comply, what the limitations of compliance are for both the supervisor and the compliant employee, and also how people can *enjoy* compliance, thereby obtaining maximum compliance through minimal requirements. Whether consciously or unconsciously, people comply with these rules of conditioning. These rules can assist in understanding behavior in general, and compliant behavior in particular.

The rules discussed in this chapter are derived from the conditioning theory. This theory has been build up from scratch by Ivan Pavlov[3] and B.F. Skinner.[4] Key to this theory is the influence of stimuli (Pavlov) and incentives (Skinner) on animal and human behavior. This scientific field has since exploded because of the enormous

1. Bleker 2009, pp. 14–22.
2. Skinner 1938.
3. Pavlov 1927.
4. Skinner 1938.

practical applications in areas such as education, raising children, sports, mental health (behavioral therapy)[5] This knowledge was made available for improving organizational performance by Daniels and Rietdijk.[6]

Life, as described by biology in chapter 1 *supra*,[7] is based on the rules discussed by Darwin. On an epigenetic scale, our species has been selected because we live and work together, cooperatively and efficiently in organizations, so that individual genes of the members are protected[8] and members of the species that deal with the organization benefit as well.

A specific fine-tuning of evolution is that organisms learn from experience[9] on an ontogenetic scale. If there were no learning mechanisms, we would be very inflexible and unable to adapt to changing circumstances. Therefore learning is a specific subdivision of biology.[10]

In this chapter the basic behavioral rules will be explained that clarify why people behave ethically or unethically, how we can stimulate compliance, and more promising methods for moving unethical behavior in the right direction.[11]

Learning theory has been studied most rigorously in psychology.[12] At the start of the twentieth century Pavlov discovered the rules of respondent conditioning, how reflexes and emotions are learned.[13] He taught dogs to salivate by ringing a bell after linking the bell to an unconditioned stimulus, like a piece of meat.

Later B.F. Skinner and colleagues[14] broadened the field of learning tremendously by discovering and applying the rules of operant conditioning. During operant conditioning 'voluntary' behavior, behavior operating on its environment, in contrast with the reflex behavior studied by Pavlov, is shaped by a combination of positive reinforcement, negative reinforcement, punishment and extinction. Reflex behavior and operant behavior are the two main behavioral classes that living organisms, including humans, show. The contributions of Pavlov and Skinner gave rise to behaviorism as a philosophy of science and behavior analysis as the science of learning. Experimental analysis of behavior studies the basic rules of change in laboratories. Applied behavior analysis is directed at the utilization of these rules for socially relevant purposes.

In nature the rules of Darwin shape species by variation, selection, and retention on an epigenetic scale. The rules of learning shape behavior during life by varying, selecting and retaining behavior on an ontogenetic scale.[15]

---

5. Martin & Pear 2015, pp. 12–21.
6. Daniels 2016; Daniels & Bailey 2014; Rietdijk 2009.
7. Inaugural speech Prof. S.C. Bleker-van Eyk: 'Why Humans get Organized: from Cave-Dweller to Mars Explorer', June 23, 2015.
8. Dawkins 1976, pp. 189–202.
9. Catania 2013.
10. Skinner 1966, pp. 1205–1213.
11. Mayer et al. 2014, pp. 39–51.
12. Gray & Bjorklund. 2014.
13. Pavlov 1927.
14. Fester & Skinner 1957; Skinner 1938; Skinner 1951, pp. 185, 26–29; Skinner 1953; Skinner 1957; Skinner 1966, pp. 1205–1213; Skinner 1968.
15. Skinner 1966, pp. 1205–1213; Moore 2007.

5.2 LEARNING RULES AND COMPLIANT BEHAVIOR

In chapter 1 *supra*,[16] compliance is defined as *behavior*. Behavior consists of two broad classes: reflexes and operants.[17]Reflexes consist of stimuli and responses. Examples are the knee, pupil and salivation reflex. Many inner body processes are reflexes. Because of their importance to survival, they have been 'automated' during evolution. The fact that they do not need to be learned extensively saves precious time. The second broad behavioral class is the operant. Operants are what we normally call 'voluntary' behavior, such as walking, talking, writing, typing and other movements that operate within the environment and have certain *consequences*.

The major distinction between respondents and operants is that respondents are caused by antecedent stimuli and operants are caused by consequences of similar behavior in the past. Compliance is an example of (unspecified) operant behavior.

5.3 FIVE WAYS FOR CHANGING BEHAVIOR

Behavior analysis describes the rules of respondent and operant conditioning. Central to the analysis of behavior is the ABC model. As Pavlov used dogs to discover the rules of classical conditioning, and Skinner used pigeons and rats to discover the rules of operant conditioning, I give you an example of the application of the rules of conditioning for the training of a *parakeet*. Before we can understand the complex behavior of *compliance*, we should first understand the simple behavior of a parakeet.

As a starter: Changing the behavior of a parakeet.

When I ask my audience how we can move a parakeet I first describe a situation that happened some years ago at a friend's house. I was invited to watch a football match. In the room there was a television set and a cage with a parakeet in it. This parakeet was sitting very quietly and I asked my friend what was wrong with it. He responded that it had been sick for two weeks. Since I had just read *How to Teach Animals*,[18] I asked my friend Jorge if he would allow me to cure the animal. To my surprise he accepted my offer. Within 20 minutes I had the bird actively flying around in its cage and my friend begged me to calm it down. And so I did.

When I tell this story to an audience I do not immediately give away the clue. Instead, I ask for suggestions. What would you do to make a parakeet move? If you know how to make a parakeet move, you are much better prepared to stimulate compliance or, even better, intrinsic change.

The suggestions I get from the audience are as follows and are put in columns:

Shuffling the cage

Opening the cage

Putting a cat into the cage

---

16. *See* note 7.
17. Holland & Skinner 1961; Skinner 1953.
18. Skinner 1951.

Putting another parakeet into the cage

Talking to the parakeet

Moving like the parakeet as an example

Putting a stick into the cage

Giving food

Heating the cage from beneath

On hearing these sometimes hilarious answers, I indicate that the right answer is not included. The audience is surprised and curious what I did do to move the parakeet. Then I explain the basic behavior analytical model of change.

Behavior is initiated in two ways: by antecedents and by consequences. Antecedents change the behavior *before* it occurs, consequences influence behavior *after* it occurs. All the suggestions for changing the parakeet's behavior were *antecedents*.

Antecedents	**B**ehavior	**C**onsequences
Shuffling the cage		
Opening the cage		
Putting a cat into the cage		
Putting another parakeet into the cage		
Talking to the parakeet		
Moving like the parakeet as an example		
Putting a stick into the cage		
Giving food		
Heating the cage from beneath		

Then I ask my audience to specify the observable behavior that we want from the parakeet. I ask the same of you. What is meant by *compliance*? The first step in stimulating compliance is *specifying* compliance. The observable behavior of the parakeet that I changed were *movement* and *making noises.*

Operant behavior, including compliance, is controlled by its consequences. Because consequences are so important in understanding and changing behavior. But first: the concept of *control.*

5.4 CONTROLLING BEHAVIOR

In changing behavior we have to address the concept of *control.* In a scientific account of behavior we must assume that every form of behavior – like any other natural phenomenon – has causes. We must therefore assume that behavior is controlled by causes. By natural causes. Like the law of gravity, and other consequences. That is the essence of behavior analysis. After describing current behavioral consequences of undesired and desired behavior, we can change the behavior in the desired direction by changing the consequences.

5.5 THE FOUR BEHAVIORAL CONSEQUENCES AND THEIR EFFECTS ON BEHAVIOR

All our behavior has consequences. Sometimes we get what we want, other times we don't get what we don't want, we get what we don't want or we don't get what we want. In the first two instances we will probably increase our behavior, after the other two consequences we will probably decrease the behavior. This is shown schematically in Figure 1.

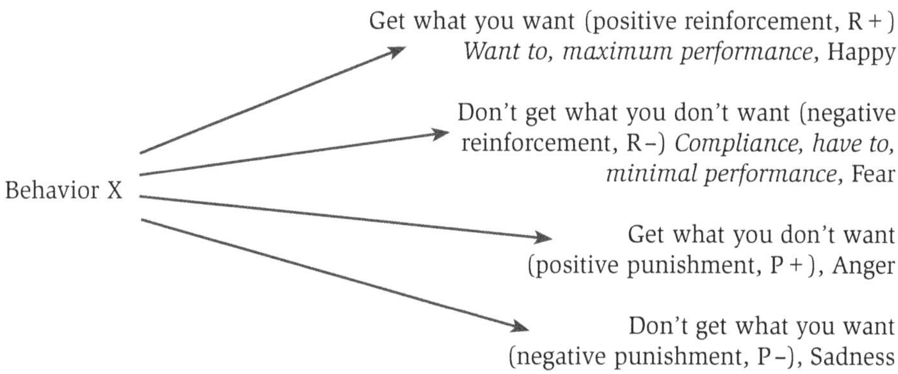

Figure 1: The four behavioral consequences

Compliance is classified as the second consequence category. During compliance people *have to* perform according to the rules of regulatory bodies. When people have to execute a task, they are less motivated than if they want to execute a task. When they want to execute a task, they do the maximum, when they have to execute a task they do the minimum necessary to avoid punishment or other adverse consequences. The four major emotions, happiness, fear, anger and sadness fit well within the four behavioral consequences. If you observe sadness in an organization you may assume that there is little reinforcement. If you observe anger, there probably exists extensive punishment. If there is a fear, the culture will probably entail excessive (threats of) punishment and in case of happiness, positive reinforcement will prevail. If we want people to perform to the maximum of their ability by not merely being compliant but by going the extra mile, positive reinforcement, R+, is the only practicable method.

We have to assess the culture of the organization, including leadership behavior and conduct change programs in order to obtain sustainable positive and ethical behavior.

5.6 CHANGING THE PARAKEETS BEHAVIOR, THE SOLUTION

If we want to encourage the parakeet to fly, we are inclined to use antecedents. As demonstrated again and again we use at least four times more antecedents than consequences. When it is assumed that consequences determine behavior and antecedents are only associated with consequences, a second mistake is made by choosing the wrong consequences. Four times more R–, P+ and P– than R+, when R+ is four times more effective than the other three. Here lies a third pitfall. When R+ is four times as effective as the other consequences, and sixteen times more effective than antecedents, the first association with R+ and rewards is money, whereas compliments and appreciation are much more effective than salaries and bonuses. The reason behind this phenomenon is that immediate and certain consequences are much more effective than future uncertain consequences. Salaries and bonuses are received a considerable time after the performance and are not directly connected to specified observable performance.

The specified performance of the parakeet is *moving* and *making sounds*. As a result, the best way to train the parakeet is by giving it attention as soon as it moves or makes sounds. When it started to make movements or sounds I immediately responded with a loud cry: 'YES!!!' At first, the bird was puzzled, but after a few pairings it started to understand that it was controlling my behavior as much as I was controlling its behavior. We could have some 'fun'. After 5–10 pairings of the R+ of mine, the bird moved more and more. In behavior analysis researchers also discovered the rules that preserve behavior.[19] Schedules of reinforcement have a profound influence on our behavior. Every relationship that we maintain has a certain order of reinforcement. Most of the time it is somewhat unpredictable. A classic example of a variable ratio schedule of reinforcement is to be found in the casino. This is the same schedule as I used for maintaining the parakeet's behavior. After continuous reinforcement during the first 5–10 responses I changed my schedule to 2, 3, 5, 8, 12 responses for the next reinforcement. Then the parakeet started to move faster and faster. When I changed to a variable schedule (such as 1, 6, 3, 12, 8, 8, 2 responses before reinforcement) there was a danger of it hurting its wings and neck when it tried to get out of the cage between the bars. My friend urged me to calm it down and I succeeded in doing so. Not by ignoring the moving animal, but by actively reinforcing quieter behavior. The conditioning of the parakeet took only 45 minutes, the time of the first half of the soccer match. An enlightening experience for me, the parakeet, and my friend.

5.7 CHANGING TO COMPLIANT BEHAVIOR

In order to change behavior for the better, including compliant behavior, the same rules of behavior should be applied in a certain order.

19. Fester & Skinner 1957.

The following protocol may prove to be useful in this endeavor:

1. specify the behavior;
2. measure the behavior;
3. analyze the behavior in terms of A's and C's (ABC analysis high to low);
4. feed the data back to the performers;
5. set (sub)goals with the performers;
6. reinforce when a group has succeeded in reaching the goals.

1. We should specify in a certain context what we mean by compliance. Every situation is different, but governed by the same rules of change.
2. We should measure the number of times or occasions that people behave in a compliant way as specified in step 1.
3. We should analyze the antecedents and consequences of current non-compliant as well as compliant behavior.
4. When people see how much they behave correctly it helps them to change for the better. Feedback alone however is not sufficient for a sustainable behavioral change. We need to take two more steps:
5. Based on the baseline measure in step 2, the goals we set in the more distant future may be ambitious, but not attainable. Therefore subgoals should be set, beginning with a subgoal just above baseline standard.
6. As a result of the previous subgoals, ample opportunity will exist regarding R+ desirable behavior. A prerequisite for change. Without using enough R+, the change simply will not take place. Plans for sustaining the behavior should entail more elaborate reinforcement schedules, that not only include money, but also other - softer - reinforcers, such as compliments, appreciations and celebrations. This requires a change in corporate culture and leadership from antecedents, R–, P+ and P– towards positive reinforcement as change philosophy and competence.

5.8 LESSONS AND CONCLUSIONS

Compliance is learned behavior and susceptible to the same rules of conditioning as other operant behavior. In order to change behavior into compliant behavior, awareness of the rules regarding the changes that govern our behavior is essential. These basic rules of change were first discovered by Pavlov (respondent conditioning) and Skinner (operant conditioning). Since their discoveries more than 50,000 replicable laboratory and field experiments have been executed. We stand at the beginning of a scientific revolution in understanding and changing human behavior. Compliance officers and others such as regulators should remember these rules, so that they can promote not only compliance, but bring out the best in people, and themselves as well.

BIBLIOGRAPHY

Bleker-van Eyk 2009
S.C. Bleker-van Eyk, 'Integrity Management after the credit crunch', in: J.H.M. van Grinsven, *Risk management in financial institutions*, Amsterdam: IOS Press 2009.

Cantania 2013
C. Cantania, *Learning (Cambridge Center)*, Cornwall-on-Hudson: Sloan Publishing 2013.

Daniels 2016
A.C. Daniels, *Bringing out the best in people. How to apply the astonishing power of positive reinforcement*, New York: McGraw-Hill 2016.

Daniels & Bailey 2014
A.C. Daniels & J.S. Bailey, *Performance Management*, Atlanta: Performance Management Publications 2014.

Dawkins 1976
R. Dawkins, *The selfish gene*, New York: Oxford University Press 1976.

Fester & Skinner 1957
C.B. Fester & B.F. Skinner, *Schedules of reinforcement*, New York: Appleton 1957.

Gray & Bjorklund 2014
P.O Gray & D.F. Bjorklund, *Psychology*, New York: Worth 2014.

Holland & Skinner 1961
J.G. Holland & B.F. Skinner, *The analysis of behavior: A program for self-instruction*, New York: McGraw Hill 1961.

Martin & Pear 2015
G.L. Martin & J. Pear, *Behavior Modification. What it is and how to do it*, New York: Prentice-Hall 2015.

Mayer et al. 2014
G.R. Mayer et al., *Behavior analysis for lasting change (Cambridge Center)*, Cornwall-on-Hudson: Sloan Publishing 2014.

Moore 2007
J. Moore, *Conceptual foundations of radical behaviorism*, Cornwall-on-Hudson: Sloan Publishing 2007.

Nijhof & Rietdijk 1999
A.H.J Nijhof & M.M. Rietdijk, 'An ABC-analysis of ethical organizational behavior', *Journal of Business Ethics* 1999-20.

Pavlov 1927
I.P Pavlov, *Conditioned reflexes*, New York: Oxford University Press 1927.

Rietdijk 2009
M.M. Rietdijk, *Conditioning Companies, The influence of reward and punishment on work performance*, Amsterdam: VU University Press 2009.

Skinner 1938
B.F Skinner, *The behavior of organisms: An experimental analyses*, New York: Appleton 1938.

Skinner 1951
B.F. Skinner, 'How to teach animals', *Scientific American* 1951-185.

Skinner 1953
B.F. Skinner, *Science and human behavior,* New York: MacMillan 1953.

Skinner 1957
B.F. Skinner, *Verbal behavior.* New York: Appleton 1957.

Skinner 1966
B.F. Skinner, 'The phylogeny and ontogeny of behavior', *Science* 1966 vol. 153 no. 3741.

Skinner 1968
B.F. Skinner, *The technology of teaching,* New York: Appleton 1968.

6. Conflicts of Interest

R.A.M. Houben

6.1 INTRODUCTION

Dealing with intertwined or conflicting interests is a universal theme in compliance and integrity management. It is the basis for regulation and supervision in *inter alia* the financial markets, financial companies, listed companies and institutions in the public/semi-public sector.[1] A large number of the laws and regulations are based on prevention or control of various interests, including social, personal or private interests, and the field is consequently very wide.[2]

If intertwined or conflicting interests lead to an undesirable (or even prohibited) situation, the company concerned can suffer serious reputational damage or losses. Such a situation also jeopardizes the integrity of the sector in which the company operates and the players within it. There are countless examples in which, for example, directors' personal interests have led to companies' insolvency[3] and consequent tighter regulation of entire sectors.[4]

A report by the Ethics & Compliance Initiative (ECI)[5] expresses this concisely as follows:

> 'Conflicts of Interest ("COIs") are among the thorniest issues that organizations and ethics and compliance ("E&C") professionals face. There are a virtually

1. Some of the many national and international examples concern the banning of intermediary commissions and the regulation of pay and bonuses in the financial and semi-public/public sector.
2. Moreover, the prevention or control of actual or potential conflicts of interest is not only regulated by means of laws and regulations; 'best market practices' also indicate how they should be dealt with.
3. Examples range from the Enron affair in 2001 to the Madoff and Libor affairs. In this connection reference is also made to chapter 17 on anti-bribery and corruption *infra*.
4. Examples are intermediaries, credit rating agencies and institutions in the semi-public sector, such as housing associations.
5. ECI 2016, p. 4.

infinite variety of situations that might create a conflict, existing as they do at the intersection of personal, family, financial and organizational interests. Additionally, because appearances are so important in this area, it is often difficult to draw bright lines. Moreover, actual, apparent, and potential conflicts very often involve family and other personal relationships, triggering various sensitivities, both individual and cultural. Unlike many other E&C-related risks, conflicts of interest are a real possibility for a large number of employees in most organizations.

Managing these risks requires hard work and thoughtful approaches. Organizations must clearly define the issues and ensure employee understanding. This necessitates comprehensive code of conduct and/or standalone policy provisions, periodic training and communication that explains conflict risks and targets the conflict of interest situations employees are most likely to confront. Because potential conflicts arise so frequently, and in so many contexts, organizations also must establish workable mechanisms for their identification and disclosure. Finally, an effective COI program requires procedures for investigating, managing and otherwise resolving conflicts, including corrective action where appropriate.'

From this perspective the compliance function has an important role in controlling or preventing conflicts of interest or situations involving unauthorized intertwining of interests.[6] This takes up a large part of the compliance officer's day-to-day work.[7]

When we refer to interests, intertwining of interests, conflicts of interest, apparent intertwining of interests and opposing interests, what do these terms mean? What, for example, is the customer interest?[8] What interests are actually at stake in a company? According to Broekhuizen, there is evidently no clear, unequivocal definition or framework. Many definitions and descriptions have been formulated so broadly that they cover almost all situations in which interests can conflict, so they provide an inadequate basis for informed, specific application in practice.[9] Another question is what can be done to avoid or control conflicts. Finally, it is legitimate to ask whether it is actually possible to eliminate undesirable intertwining or conflicts of interest.[10]

This chapter addresses this matter in more detail from the perspective of laws and regulations, ethics[11] and risk management. It does so on the basis of the interests

---

6. In this book 'compliance' is deemed to mean: 'observance of external (international and national) laws and regulations, as well as internal norms and procedures, to protect the integrity of the organization, its management and employees with the aim of preventing and controlling risks and the possible damage resulting from these compliance and integrity risks.' *See* in the Introduction *supra*. This naturally also includes preventing conflicts of interest.
7. In this connection it would therefore be better to speak of a 'conflicts of interest officer' or 'ethics officer'. In the Anglo-Saxon sphere, for example, the term 'compliance and ethics officer' is used.
8. In consumer protection in the financial sector, there is an inclination to adopt a 'mono' approach to regulation of interests, summed up in the expression 'customer's interests first'.
9. Broekhuizen 2016, p. 181.
10. Broekhuizen 2009, p. 380.
11. Ethics or moral science is a branch of philosophy that deals with critical reflection on correct action. In a general sense ethics attempts to define the criteria required to assess whether

at stake within companies in business (including financial) services, i.e. not interests relating, for example, to the citizen and the state[12] or in the private sphere. Section 6.2 deals with various terms used, section 6.3 with the terms 'customer interest' and 'customer's interest first'. Section 6.4 deals with conflicts of interest and the loyalty obligation and section 6.5 with conflicting interests in other situations. In section 6.6 the previous sections are briefly summarized. Section 6.7 deals with the regulation of interests in laws and regulations, and finally section 6.8 considers the day-to-day handling of conflicts of interest, including from the perspective of risk management.

6.2 CORPORATE INTEREST, CONFLICTS OF INTEREST AND INTERTWINING OF INTERESTS

As described in section 6.1, there are many interests at stake in society, institutions and companies and among customers.[13] Every legal relationship between a (private) customer and a (financial) company involves various interests, as does every commercial transaction. A vendor and a purchaser of a house, for example, have different interests. One wishes to sell at the highest possible price, while the other wishes to buy at the lowest possible price. According to Broekhuizen, however, this does not immediately lead to a conflict of interest in the legal sense; rather there is a situation with conflicting interests in which a real estate agent, for example, can play a mediating role.[14]

In a company, the so-called corporate interest plays an important role. This interest is pluralistic, which means that it encompasses multiple interests.[15] In performing their duties, executive and supervisory directors of a public limited company must focus on the interests of the company and the enterprise associated with it.[16] The same applies to the private limited company.[17]

Broekhuizen states that other terms are used in common parlance, day-to-day practice and literature that actually amount to the same thing.[18] Examples are opposition of interests, conflicting interests and opposed interests. He proposes that these terms be reserved for general situations in which parties have different interests.

---

an action can be deemed right or wrong, and to evaluate the motives and consequences of that action. In ethics the philosopher questions what the ultimate standard is for human action. Although 'ethical' is used in everyday language with the meaning of 'moral', these are two different fields: 'moral' refers to the moral action itself, whereas ethics is the study of it. The handling of conflicts of interest must certainly be analysed more closely in this light.

12. *See* chapter 11 *infra* on Regulation and Supervision on Financial Markets that deals with the relationship between the citizen and the state. It therefore deals with the associated interests that arise.
13. This refers to both private and business customers (such as companies).
14. Broekhuizen 2016, pp. 182–183.
15. Ibid., pp. 195–203. Broekhuizen discusses in detail what is understood by the corporate interest. For the purposes of this chapter, this matter is only dealt with briefly. Examples of multiple interests include those of shareholders and customers. This chapter is based on the so-called 'stakeholders model' in contrast to the 'shareholders model'.
16. Arts 2:129 paragraph 5 and 2:140 paragraph 2 BW.
17. Arts 2: 239 paragraph 5 and 2:250 paragraph 2 BW.
18. Broekhuizen 2016, p. 190.

That situation can arise when there is a conflict of interest, but an opposition of interests, conflicting interests and opposed interests may equally arise if the so-called 'loyalty obligation'[19] plays no role, as in the case of a normal purchase agreement. A conflict of interest is evidently a subset of the set comprising oppositions of interests, conflicting interests and opposed interests.

A term frequently used in both day-to-day practice and in laws and regulations is 'intertwining of interests'. Broekhuizen proposes using this term in situations where someone occupies more than one position in a company. For example in a situation in which a person is an executive director of company A and of company B, and A and B do business with each other. Such an intertwining of interests can lead to a conflict of interest, but a conflict of interest does not necessarily arise as a result of an intertwining of interests.[20]

Although this is certainly useful in day-to-day (compliance) practice, it is a (strictly) legal approach. As already noted *supra*, there are many interests at stake in a company. All these interests are in a sense intertwined, but will not necessarily lead to an undesirable situation or a conflict. Intertwining of interests could even be characterized as 'normal'. It is therefore striking that laws and regulations focus both on the prevention or control of intertwined interests and on conflicts of interest, whereas in fact they mean the same thing.[21] It would be better to speak of a conflict of intertwined interests. After all, this can lead to an undesirable situation. On the other hand, a semantic discussion on different terms should be avoided. The focus should be on finding an appropriate (prudent) method of dealing with them.[22]

It is further noted that the frequently used expression 'appearance of' intertwining of interests or conflict of interest is regularly used in practice, in the literature and in laws and regulations.[23] In practice it is often completely unclear what this means, since a possible situation of conflicts of different interests, let alone their intertwining, may arise at any time. The desire to control or prevent these therefore always leads in principle to a 'better safe than sorry' assessment, a culture of fear and a box-ticking mentality instead of considered decisions.[24] A case is made for the

19. Section 6.4 *infra* deals with the loyalty obligation.
20. Broekhuizen 2016, pp. 190–191.
21. Section 6.7 *infra* deals with examples in laws and regulations.
22. A good example of the interchangeable use of various terms is the DNB Booklet 2015. This states (p. 6) that there is an intertwining of interests if personal or professional interests, other than those of the pension fund, are taken into account (consciously or unconsciously) in the decision-making. Such a strict separation is almost unachievable in practice, however. Interests are always intertwined; otherwise, so to speak, it would be impossible to operate effectively. The booklet then deals with the notion of incorrect or impure decision-making, which again is another concept. A third example of intertwining of interests in the booklet is financial gain through personal enrichment. This is not sufficiently concrete. It would be better to speak of a conflict between the corporate interest and a director's own (or personal) interest with a (possible) undesirable or fraudulent situation that leads to an offense included in the Penal Code or tax legislation.
23. Often as a means of pressure applied by supervisors, but also by compliance officers.
24. This appears to be at odds with the principles of good market supervision. *See also* chapter 11 *infra*.

use of consistent terminology in which, for example, the term 'conflicts of interest' can have a clear meaning.[25]

6.3 CUSTOMER INTEREST AND CUSTOMER'S INTEREST FIRST

The terms 'customer interest', 'customer first' and 'customer's interest first' in the financial sector merit a more precise explanation. The terms have become commonly used expressions in financial companies (such as banks, insurers and investment companies) and are used as catch-all terms.[26] These terms started to take on a life of their own following the publication of the report of the Maas Committee.[27] This Committee was established in 2009 on behalf of the NVB under the chairmanship of Cees Maas to investigate the causes of the financial crisis and the lessons that could be drawn from it for the future.[28] One of the published recommendations was the issuance of the Banking Code 2010, which was replaced in 2014 by the Banking Code 2014.[29] This latter version included disciplinary law for bank employees (in addition to the oath/promise).

An important conclusion that can be drawn is that the Maas Committee did not intend the expression 'customer's interest first' to be used in the way it is currently used. The expression 'customer first' also does not arise as such in the aforementioned report. It was used, however, in the presentation of the report. In the report, the 'interest of the customer' is interpreted as follows:

> 'The common thread in the report is that when weighing up the interests of the customers, shareholders, employees and the society in which they operate, banks must give primacy to the interests of the customer. The banks will thus fulfill their social role better. This will also benefit the interests of the employees and the shareholders. In future it must not be the case that profits benefit the shareholders and bonuses and that the bill is picked up by the taxpayer, the customer and the employee. In this regard a fundamental change of mindset and reorientation in banking is required. The recommendations of this report are intended to contribute to this. The ultimate aim is that the banks' customers

25. Also according to Broekhuizen 2016, pp. 181–183.
26. A good example is the difference between 'customer's interest first and 'customer first'. These are different concepts. In a financial company the customer cannot always be the first. That would render normal operational management impossible. It is important, of course, that the customer is the first as far as possible and that the interests of the customer take precedence as far as possible. This is completely different from the expression often used in day-to-day practice: 'that must be done as part of putting the customer's interest first'.
27. Report of the Maas Committee, entitled '*Naar herstel van vertrouwen*' ('Towards a restoration of trust').
28. *See* for a more detailed description of the formation of the Maas Committee and its report, Dieben & 't Hart 2012, pp. 14–25 and Broekhuizen 2016, pp. 115–122.
29. Banking Code of October 2014, which was introduced in the banking sector together with the Social Charter and the Rules of Conduct under the title of 'Future Oriented Banking'. *See also Parliamentary Papers II* 2014/15, 32013, p. 88.

> and hence society as a whole will once again receive optimum service and that broken trust will be restored.'[30]

A debate subsequently arose in the general and legal literature as to whether the Maas Committee had thereby introduced a new corporate standard.[31] After all, as part of the corporate interest directors must take into account the interests of all 'stakeholders' and give appropriate consideration to them depending on the situation and the decision. The Maas Committee stated that in that assessment of interests, the interest of the customer must be central. This would be at odds with the established doctrine before April 2009 of the corporate interest that must be interpreted as being pluralistic.[32] After all, this appears to mean that no further interests can then be taken into account in a company's decision-making. In Dutch company law there is no rule stating that within the framework of the corporate interest priority must – or can – be given at all times to one of the interests or partial interests concerned. The position of the Maas Committee did not therefore appear consistent with Dutch law.[33]

The debate appears to be settled with the Banking Code 2010 and the Banking Code 2014. The Banking Code 2010 does not put the customer first in the balanced assessment of interests, but states that the customer must always be treated with care.[34] This arises again in the rules of conduct of the Social Charter. It can be concluded, however, that more attention must be devoted to the customer's interest than was the case in the past.[35] But that this must happen in the framework of an assessment of interests of all stakeholders of a financial company.

6.4 CONFLICTS OF INTEREST AND THE LOYALTY OBLIGATION

Broekhuizen states that a conflict of interest can arise (actually only) when there is a legal relationship in which one person has a loyalty obligation towards another.[36] A loyalty obligation is deemed to mean a situation in which a person (A) has to act in

30. Maas Committee, p. 7.
31. Broekhuizen 2016, pp. 96–98; Dieben & 't Hart 2012, pp. 14–17; Raaijmakers 2010, section 2.
32. For the term 'corporate interest' *see* section 6.2 *supra*.
33. Broekhuizen 2016, p. 206.
34. Dieben & 't Hart, p, 16. Principles 3.2.1 and 3.2.2 of the Banking Code 2010. The explanatory notes state the following with regard to these principles: '3.2.1 … In the governance model that is prescribed by law in the Netherlands, the interests of all *stakeholders* must be taken into account. Principle 3.2.1 expresses this in a balanced way. 3.2.2 The Banking Code states not only that the interests of the different parties involved must be considered in full, but also that customers must at all times be treated with care and that the duty of care towards the customer must be embedded in the culture of the bank (Maas Committee 1.11). This is in line with the Maas Committee's views on a more prominent place for the customer in the assessment of interests between the various parties concerned, without compromising the interests of the other stakeholders.'
35. This has now been widely complied with by the financial sector (particularly banks and insurance companies). This is evident from the research conducted primarily by the AFM, which after all has primacy with regard to putting the customer's interest first.
36. Broekhuizen 2016, p. 183.

the interest of another person (B) and A, in the interest of B, has to take one or more decisions for which A has a certain room for maneuver and (therefore) discretion.[37]

If a bank acts for example as a representative of the customer's interest, there is a principal-agent relationship.[38] The bank (the agent) must in that case act in the interest of the customer (the principal) and has a loyalty obligation.[39] That is the case if the bank acts as an adviser or intermediary or if an investment company provides those investment services.[40] Acting in the interest of the customer implies that the bank must not allow other interests to prevail over the interest of the respective customer. Loyalty, however, is not sufficient; careful fulfillment of the loyalty obligation is also required.[41]

Broekhuizen also believes that the loyalty obligation does not apply in a principal-to-principal relationship. That is the case when a bank offers a financial product without advice, or sells a product (without advice). The absence of a loyalty obligation, however, in no way means that the customer's interests no longer play a role. On the contrary, banks are obligated under the Wft, but also under civil law, to treat customers with care.[42] As already noted, precisely what that care standard involves in practice depends on the circumstances, such as the type of product, the associated risks and the type of customer. Those circumstances, as it were, define the interest of the customer to be respected. The basic standard here, however, is not that the bank must put the customer's interest first in all respects, but that the bank must take account of the justified interests of the customer, according to Broekhuizen.[43]

Broekhuizen also states that the loyalty obligation must be distinguished from the legal rule that the creditor and the debtor are obligated to take account of each other's interests. That obligation has a fundamentally different effect than the loyalty obligation. The loyalty obligation arises in legal relationships in which person A takes care of the interests of person B with the consequence that B has or may have confidence that A will be guided in his actions primarily by the interests of B. The loyalty obligation can also mean that A takes an independent and objective stance with regard to B. This can be the case, for example, if A gives advice to B.[44]

According to Broekhuizen the phenomenon of the conflict of interest lies in (or is a consequence of) the loyalty obligation. The nature of the loyalty obligation does not tolerate other interests prevailing over the interests of the principal. There is a conflict of interest if the loyalty obligation which the agent has towards the principal 'comes under pressure' because the agent, when he has to take a decision on how to act, does not take into account, or does not only take into account, the interests of the principal, but also takes into account other interests, whereby that decision can be influenced in such a way that it is not taken exclusively in the interest of

37. Ibid.
38. For a more detailed explanation of the principal-agent theory, *see* Part II *infra* of this book.
39. Broekhuizen 2016, pp. 138–139.
40. Within the meaning of the Wft.
41. Broekhuizen 2016, pp. 138–139.
42. See chapter 20 *infra* that deals with the duty of care in both private law and public law.
43. Broekhuizen 2016, pp. 138–139.
44. Ibid., pp. 183–184.

the principal. The 'other interests' may be the agent's own interests, but also the interests of other principals of the agent.[45]

As stated at the beginning of this section, according to Broekhuizen conflicts of interest can only arise in the framework of the loyalty obligations in which A, in the interest of B, has to take one or more decisions on a matter for which for A has certain room for maneuver and discretion. After all, if A does not have to take such decisions, there is also no danger that his actions for B will be influenced by other interests. The existence of a degree of discretion for A in taking his decisions is just as important. Situations in which it is established in advance which decision the agent must take ('bound decisions') similarly do not have to be considered as a conflict of interest, even if it is possible that the agent will not take the (bound) decision in connection with the aforementioned 'other interests'.[46]

6.5 CONFLICTING INTERESTS IN OTHER SITUATIONS

Elaborating on issues *supra*, the question is how conflicting interests in a company should be distinguished in legal relationships in which there is no loyalty obligation. Careful and consistent use of language is required here because the field is very wide. As stated *supra*, there are many interests at stake in a company that may be opposed or in conflict with each other. Personal interests, for example, can play an important role in decision-making in a company and are very relevant because their prioritization may lead to undesirable or prohibited situations.[47] An employee, for example, will always have a personal interest (or even self-interest) with regard to an employer, which must be dealt with prudently. Both the employee and the employer each have an (contractual and legal) obligation to act as a good employer and as a good employee.[48]

Illustrative in this regard are various incidents in the public/semi-public sector in which the personal interests (or self-interest) of directors have played too much of a leading role.[49] Directors wearing different hats have taken decisions that have gone awry.[50] As noted earlier, Broekhuizen considers that in these situations it would be possible to refer to an intertwining of interests.[51]

---

45. Ibid., pp. 184–185.
46. Ibid.
47. Particularly in the case of personal interests or self-interest, the reference framework is somewhat more difficult to determine. Usually it amounts to conduct that is prohibited in the Penal Code (such as corruption, discrimination, intimidation and unofficial bribery) or acts that are (currently) considered socially undesirable. The latter is a gray area, however.
48. Art. 7:611 of the BW.
49. There have been high-profile occurrences, such as the scandals in the housing association sector at Vestia in 2012 and Rochdale in 2009. At Vestia the director Eric Staal conducted fatal derivatives transactions leading to losses of over EUR 2 billion. The case at Rochdale included fraud committed by the director Hubert Möllenkamp, who ultimately appeared before a criminal court and was convicted.
50. This is difficult to dissociate from maladministration or mismanagement under company law. On the other hand such situations always involve different interests that appear not to be transparent or which in any event have not been well handled.
51. Broekhuizen 2016, pp. 190–191.

A study[52] of such cases concludes that 30% of (investigated) semi-public senior officers proved unsuitable to become 'entrepreneurial directors', 50% were suitable and 20% pushed the boundaries, of whom 5% ultimately 'derailed'. One of the causes identified for this is that the governance of public/semi-public institutions has been copied too much from the private sector. The role of directors and internal supervisors was also underestimated. Finally, it can be stated that indignation about scandals in this sector is leading to intervention through a growing body of rules. This leads to a box-ticking mentality at the expense of individual responsibility.[53]

Even in situations in which a financial company has no advisory or mediation role, there may still be different or conflicting interests. An entirely different approach is necessary in situations in which a financial company has different roles, as in investment banking.[54]

6.6 SUMMARY

It can be seen from the foregoing that the range of situations in a company in which conflicting interests can arise or in which interests become intertwined in an undesirable way is very broad. Distinguishing such situations also depends on the perspective from which the situation is approached. This could be from the perspective of the:

- shareholders;
- the Supervisory Board;
- the Executive Board or management;
- the company itself;
- employees;
- intermediaries;
- suppliers;
- customers;
- supervisors/regulators and other competent authorities;
- society.

In line with the foregoing sections, Broekhuizen considers that in situations where there is no loyalty obligation (in the framework of a principal-agent relationship), it would be better to speak of 'situations in which there is or may be conflicting or opposed interests'.[55]

For purely practical reasons, however, it can be stated that in order to distinguish situations in a company in which interests are intertwined in an undesirable way or conflicts of interest arise, it is preferable to use the term conflicts of interest in

52. Goodijk 2015.
53. Ibid., p. 4.
54. This could include a situation in which a business bank provides various services for businesses and high-net-worth individuals and as a result of these services for the business the bank has access to information that it is not permitted to share with other departments or the private customer. Such 'information walls' are also known as 'Chinese walls'. This is dealt with in greater detail in chapter 21 on Market Abuse *infra*.
55. Broekhuizen 2016, p. 190.

the broader sense. In this chapter the term is therefore interpreted in the sense that conflicts can also arise in situations in which there is no loyalty obligation and in which interests may be in conflict or opposed or intertwined with each other.

6.7 REGULATION OF CONFLICTS OF INTEREST IN LAWS AND REGULATIONS

A brief examination of examples of laws and regulations governing interests, intertwining of interests and conflicts of interest is discussed *infra*. It is striking that in laws and regulations relating to the financial sector[56] the terms conflict of interest and intertwining of interests are used interchangeably.[57] This appears to contradict section 6.2, but it can be assumed that in principle the same is meant.[58]

In general it can be said that in the laws and regulations of financial companies it is possible to distinguish three methods for dealing with conflicts of interest, namely prohibition, control and/or disclosure.[59]

For example, banks and insurance companies (based in the Netherlands) must conduct an appropriate policy that guarantees sound operation of the business.[60] This is deemed to mean among other things that measures are taken to counter any intertwining of interests.[61] The same applies to investment companies and investment institutions.[62] In the case of non-financial companies, such requirements are not explicitly stated in laws and regulations.[63]

56. This refers to the Wft and all derived laws and regulations as well as all laws and regulations at European level (such as Directives and Regulations), i.e. public law as distinct from private law. Public law specifically governs the relationship between the institution/ company and the state, whereas private law governs the relationships among (all) the parties.
57. In the Wft, for example, the term 'conflict of interest' occurs 26 times, while the term 'intertwining of interests' occurs five times.
58. Broekhuizen has a different opinion. *See* Broekhuizen 2016, pp. 190–191.
59. Also according to Broekhuizen 2009, pp. 401–403 and Broekhuizen 2016, p. 189. Strictly speaking there is a tension here between control on the one hand and transparency on the other. Some conflicts of interest cannot be resolved, in which case they must in any case be made transparent.
60. Art. 3:10 paragraph 1a of the Wft. In short, this is covered by the term 'sound operational management'. This also applies to a settlement company, payment institution, clearing institution, electronic funds institution, risk acceptance entity, credit union, premium pension institution or foreign exchange institution. Art. 3:17 of the Wft then states that the operational management must be organized appropriately, which is summarized as 'controlled operational management'.
61. Broekhuizen wishes to reserve the term 'intertwining of interests' solely for the situation in which a person occupies more than one position, *see* Broekhuizen 2016, pp. 190–191. The legislator thus gives the term a much broader range.
62. Art. 4:11 paragraph 1a of the Wft and Art. 115q of the Bgfo (for investment institutions). Art. 4:14 of the Wft then states that the operational management must be organized appropriately, which is summarized as 'controlled operational management'.
63. With the result that integrity codes and codes of conduct are more akin to 'best market practice' than 'firm' legal measures. Listed companies are governed *inter alia* by the Corporate Governance Code 2016.

The scope of the term intertwining of interest has also been set down in subordinate legislation, regulations and guidance issued by DNB and the AFM.[64] For example, Article 11 paragraphs 1 and 2 of the Bpr states that banks and insurance companies must have procedures and measures in place to counter any intertwining of private interests of group and company directors, members of the Supervisory Board and other employees or other persons who work on a regular basis for the company, with the interests of the company or of its customers. Banks and insurance companies must also have procedures and measures in place with regard to the provision of financial services on personnel terms for group and company directors.[65]

The Wft contains countless other examples. Article 3:10 of the Wft can be seen as a catch-all term (or an open standard) by which the legislator and supervisors are given scope for more precise interpretation depending on the social requirement.[66] According to the parliamentary history, in the case of banks this would include, for example, occupying additional positions, the granting of loans to executive and supervisory directors and private investment transactions.[67]

An example of conflicts of interest concerns companies that offer investment services or perform investment activities, i.e. investment companies. These must have an appropriate policy to prevent and control conflicts of interest between the company and their customers and among their customers.[68] The aim of such a policy must in any case be that the investment company recognizes situations in which it:

- can achieve a financial gain or avoid a financial loss at the expense of the customer;
- has an interest in the result of a service performed for the customer or a transaction conducted on behalf of the customer, which differs from the customer's interest in this result;
- has a financial or other motive to allow the interest of another customer or group to prevail over the customer's interest;
- exercises the same activity as the customer;
- receives or will receive a commission from a person other than the customer for an investment activity, investment service or ancillary service performed for the client in the form of money, goods or services that differs from the usual commission or remuneration for such activity or service.[69]

Furthermore, an investment company must ensure that its customers are treated fairly in the event that a conflict of interest proves to be unavoidable. In that case

64. Such as orders in council, ministerial regulations and interpretations by DNB and the AFM. European regulations are not included.
65. Art. 11 paragraph 2 of the Bpr, further elaborated in paragraphs 3-5. Comparable articles for other types of financial companies are included *inter alia* in the Bgfo.
66. This approach has given rise to criticism in the legal literature, mainly due to excessive leeway given to the legislator and supervisor and the resulting lack of legal certainty (*lex certa* principle). *See also* chapter 13 *infra* on the legal basis for the supervision of conduct and culture.
67. *Parliamentary papers II* 2004/05, 29708, 10, p. 240. *See also* Van der Eerden & Silverentand 2015, p. 74.
68. Art. 4:88 paragraph 1 of the Wft.
69. Art. 167 of the Bgfo.

the investment company must inform its customers of the conflict of interest – before starting to do business.[70] The investment company states that it has sufficient particulars to enable the customers to take an informed decision on the investment service, investment activity or ancillary service in relation to which the conflict of interest arises.[71]

A more recent example of a prohibition that must be mentioned concerns the ban on commission for financial service providers such as insurance and other intermediaries.[72] This prohibition has been imposed as part of putting the customer's interest first.[73] It means that the interests of the provider, the intermediary and the customer are clearly separated.[74]

In the case of listed companies the Corporate Governance Code 2016 can be cited as an example that includes various principles to prevent or control conflicts of interest or situations with conflicting interests.[75]

6.8 DEALING WITH INTERESTS AND CONFLICTS OF INTEREST IN DAY-TO-DAY PRACTICE

Taking the above into account, the question is how to deal with conflicts of interest in day-to-day practice. What it amounts to is developing and implementing an action plan to control and/or prevent conflicts of interest in the broad sense. The situation is not helped by the fact that – as stated *supra* – some of these activities have been legally regulated, while others are covered more by 'best market practices'. Moreover, those that are legally prescribed represent open standards that provide more scope for own interpretation but on the other hand can also be interpreted by supervisors.[76]

According to the parliamentary history a bank must draw up and implement its integrity policy on the basis of an analysis of the integrity risks of relevance to it.[77] This policy must then be introduced and assessed and where necessary adjusted.[78] Equivalent provisions are included in the Wft for other types of institution supervised

70. Art. 4:88 paragraph 2 of the Wft.
71. Art. 167 paragraph 2 of the Bgfo.
72. Art. 86c of the Bgfo. A similar prohibition for investment companies is included in Art. 168a of the Bgfo.
73. *See* section 6.3 *supra*.
74. Also referred to as the '*het zuivere marktmodel*' (pure market model).
75. Corporate Governance Code 2016. *See* for example principle 2.7 on preventing intertwining of interests between the company and the executive and supervisory directors.
76. A good example concerns internal rules for employees on conducting private investment transactions (known as insider rules). In the past this was dealt with in a more rules-based way in the Decree on the Sound Operational Management of Credit Institutions and Insurers, but it became a more open standard with the entry into force of the Wft on January 1, 2007. An employment contract (including the personnel guide) will usually include information on the rules of conduct a company. The rules of conduct then mostly concern a framework for conflicts of interest that the employee must adhere to. In the case of banks, investment companies and insurers, prudent compliance with these is also linked to the oath or promise which must be given (also known as the banker's oath). In the case of bank employees, there is also disciplinary law.
77. *Parliamentary papers II* 2004/05, 29708, 10, p. 240.
78. Art. 10 of the Bpr.

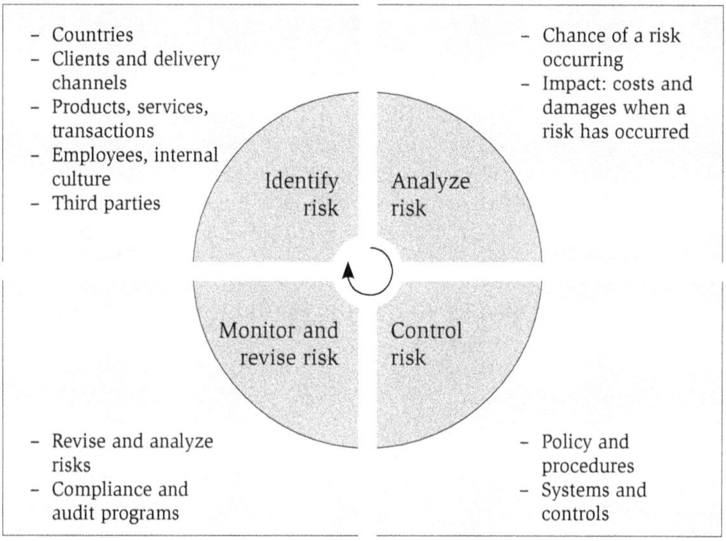

Figure 1: Risk cycle from the DNB Booklet August 2015

by DNB and the AFM (such as insurers, investment companies, investment institutions and pension funds). This provision dates from the time of introduction of the Wft, but also predates it.[79]

For the financial sector DNB issued guidance in 2015 on the so-called Systematic Integrity Risk Analysis, because it believed this compulsory analysis was not being conducted.[80] Part of this concerns the analysis and control of situations in which conflicts of interest may arise (including undesirable intertwining of interests). Scenarios must first be identified, which must then be analyzed and assessed and measures must then be drawn up and introduced to control the risk.[81] Particularly when identifying conflicts of interest the challenge will lie in conducting an overall analysis of the company concerned and the perspective from which scenarios are examined.

Typical examples of the control of possible conflicts between the interest that a supplier has in a company and the company itself are giving and receiving business

79. Decree of October 10, 2003 containing rules to promote sound operational management by credit institutions and insurers and amending a number of royal decrees in connection with the law on the updating and harmonization of financial supervision acts (Decree on the sound operational management of credit institutions and insurers), *Bulletin of Acts and Decrees* 2003, 396. Repealed on January 1, 2007.
80. DNB Booklet August 2015
81. Typical measures include, for example, instruction, training, codes of conduct, confidentiality declarations, integrity declarations, conflict of interest certifications (COICs), the appointment of a Monitoring Compliance Officer, audits, awareness sessions, technical measures, permanent or temporary 'Chinese (information) walls' and the use of a restricted list (for example for trading in shares of the own company).

gifts. A code of conduct concerning business gifts is usually the result checked by the HRM or compliance departments. Another example is the interest of maintaining a good, neutral or objective reputation as a company, as a result of which ancillary functions, personal relationships and private investments must be reviewed. Another example of themes with potential conflicts of interest are financial and other investments, including by the company itself, personnel discounts, bonuses and pay.

In the analysis and assessment of possible risks the following can be used as frameworks:

- laws and regulations;[82]
- internal standards or rules of conduct (including with regard to objectivity and neutrality);[83]
- is a particular act explainable and transparent?;[84]
- is a particular act media-proof?[85]

In conclusion it can be stated that identifying and dealing with conflicts of interest is a complex subject. In laws and regulations it is far from always clear what is meant by conflict of interest (or intertwining of interests). It is usually up to the company itself to make a proper assessment and strike a balance in such situations. The same applies to non-financial companies where less has been regulated by law, and control will depend more on 'best market practices'. In practice the risk approach appears to work best in combination with a solid plan of action for training, awareness and monitoring.[86]

---

82. *See* section 6.7 *supra*.
83. In other words: 'Will participation in the activity or transaction affect your ability to be objective with regard to any decision concerning customers, an associate or a product of service provider? If an outside activity, will the time required interfere with your ability to effectively carry out your responsibilities to the corporation, its shareholders and customers?'
84. In other words: 'Is the activity or transaction being offered in an attempt to influence your judgment?'
85. In other words: 'Could the activity or transaction be perceived as a potential conflict by others? If all the related facts were made public, would you or the corporation be embarrassed? Will the corporation, shareholders or its customers be disadvantaged without legitimate reason if you participate in the activity or transaction?'
86. *See* ECI 2016.

BIBLIOGRAPHY

Broekhuizen 2016
K.W.H. Broekhuizen, *Klantbelang, belangenconflict en zorgplicht* (diss. Amsterdam UvA), The Hague: Boom Juridisch 2016.

Broekhuizen 2009
K.W.H. Broekhuizen, 'Regulering van belangenconflicten', in D. Busch & C.M. Grundmann-van de Krol (eds.), *Handboek Beleggingsondernemingen* (Serie Onderneming en Recht deel 51), Deventer: Kluwer 2009, pp. 379-455.

Dieben & 't Hart 2012
E.M. Dieben & F.M.A. 't Hart (eds.), *Klantbelang Centraal*, Amsterdam: NIBE-SVV 2012.

Goodijk 2015
R. Goodijk, *Van afvinken naar aanspreekbaarheid. Over deugdelijke governance in de semipublieke sector'* (oratie Amsterdam VU), Amsterdam: VU Amsterdam 2015.

Raaijmakers 2010
G.T.M.J. Raaijmakers, 'Corporate governance 2.0 voor banken en beursondernemingen: meer aandacht voor cultuur en gedrag', *Ondernemingsrecht* 2010/62.

Van der Eerden & Silverentand 2015
F.W.J. van der Eerden & L.J. Silverentand (eds.), *Hoofdlijnen Wft*, Deventer: Wolters Kluwer 2015.

Other references

Banking Code 2010
Banking Code of September 9, 2010 under the auspices of the NVB.

Banking Code 2014
Banking Code of October 2014 under the auspices of the NVB.

Corporate Governance Code 2016
Corporate Governance Code of December 8, 2016.

DNB Booklet August 2015
DNB Booklet, 'De integriteitrisicoanalyse; meer waar dat moet, minder waar dat kan', August 17, 2015.

DNB Booklet January 2015
DNB Booklet, 'Risicobeheersing belangenverstrengeling bij pensioenfondsen', January 2015.

ECI 2016
Report of the Ethics & Compliance Initiative (ECI), *Conflicts of Interest*, 2016, published by the Ethics Research Center (ERC), the research arm of the ECI.

Maas Committee
Report of the Advisory Committee on the Future of the Banking Industry (Commissie Maas), *Naar herstel van vertrouwen*, April 7, 2009.

PART II – ORGANIZATIONS AND RISK MANAGEMENT

Trust is good, but control is better (*Lenin*)

Control is good, but trust is cheaper (*Forbes*)

Control is good, trust even better (*Kees Cools*)

7. Corporate Governance

Prof. S.C. Bleker-van Eyk[1]

7.1 INTRODUCTION

In the previous chapters, several issues have been discussed concerning the way compliance should interact with the board and in a two-tier system also the Supervisory Board as well as the Audit Committee. In this chapter the bits and pieces from the previous chapter will be put together to give a clear vision on the role of compliance within the governance of an organization.

Compliance and integrity are now indispensable matters at management level. Both executive and supervisory directors are slowly becoming used to these new pawns on the chess board, but working with them is still a somewhat unfamiliar process. For example, the compliance officer must be able to escalate the situation if the organization is threatened by – usually non-financial – risks. The board may perceive this as a threat. Compliance and integrity are matters of growing relevance to the top tier of the governance structure. Should compliance be on the agenda every quarter at meetings of the Board of Directors and even the Supervisory Board? Should the compliance officer have a direct line to the Audit Committee?

Both executive and supervisory directors can be tackled directly about non-compliant conduct in the organization. For example, in the Netherlands the chairman and a number of former members of the Supervisory Board of Housing Corporation Vestia reached a settlement with Vestia worth EUR 4.8 million, in exchange for Vestia's withdrawal of a lawsuit.[2] The Public Prosecution Service sees the chairman of the Supervisory Board in a two-tier system as the person who ultimately has the power to intervene if the organization commits criminal offenses. In such cases the Public

1. Part of this chapter was published in *Jaarboek Corporate Governance 2016–2017*. *See* S.C. Bleker-van Eyk, 'Compliance en integriteit kloppen aan de hoogste deur van de governancestructuur', in: B. Bier et al. (eds), *Jaarboek Corporate Governance 2016–2017*, Deventer: Wolters Kluwer 2016, pp. 107–121.
2. C. Vis, 'Oud-bestuurder Staal betaalt 1 miljoen aan Vestia, rechtszaak ingetrokken, *NRC* January 6, 2016.

Prosecution Service expects robust intervention by the Board of Directors and – if the Board of Directors fails to intervene – the Supervisory Board. Failing that the Public Prosecution Service also considers the Supervisory Board responsible for continuing criminal practices (with the chairman having primary accountability).

The role of the executive and supervisory (non-executive) directors is undergoing fundamental changes. Following a long series of compliance-related and integrity-related incidents in various sectors, demands are increasingly being made on the expertise and integrity of the executive and supervisory (non-executive) directors. These demands are coming from the supervisor or industry associations. In the Dutch Corporate Governance Code of December 8, 2016, the subject of specific expertise also arises in Principle 2.1.4.[3] The supervisory (non-executive) director is expected to have expertise and be honest. Expertise can be assessed and the Supervisory Board (non-executive) members can be brought up to speed. Integrity, on the other hand, is inherent in a person. Knowledge of standards can be instilled through training. The same applies, for example, to the desired procedures, but translating words into deeds remains a question of personal action 'at the time'.

This example of the discussion on corporate governance in the Netherlands demonstrates a more fundamental discussion worldwide on the need for understanding of compliance and integrity management by senior management in general and the Board of Directors and the Supervisory Board (two-tier) in particular, for the latter bear the final responsibility for compliance and integrity management and may well be held accountable in case of wrongdoing.

7.2 THE USE OF THE TERMS 'COMPLIANCE' AND 'INTEGRITY' WITHIN CORPORATE GOVERNANCE CODES

The new Dutch Corporate Governance Code contains no definition of what is meant by compliance.[4] It is clear, however, that the control of compliance risks has acquired a permanent place. Principle 1.2.3 states that the board should monitor the operation of the internal risk management and control systems and should carry out a systematic assessment of their design and effectiveness at least once a year. This monitoring should cover *all* material control measures relating to financial, operational and *compliance* aspects. Attention should be given to observed weaknesses and lessons learned, indications from whistleblowers, and findings from the internal audit function and the external auditor. Where necessary, improvements should be made to internal risk management and control systems.

Principle 1.4.2 states that the board should render account in the management report on:

3. 'Each Supervisory Board member and each Board of Directors member should have the specific expertise required for the fulfillment of his duties. Each Supervisory Board member should be capable of assessing the broad outline of the overall management.' Dutch Corporate Governance Code, p. 19.
4. Dutch Corporate Governance Code pp. 12 and 16.

> 'i. the execution of the risk assessment, with a description of the principal risks facing the company in relation to its risk appetite. These risks may include strategic, operational, financial, compliance and non-financial risks.'

Finally, Principle 1.2.3 states that the board should carry out a systematic assessment of the design and effectiveness of the internal risk management and control systems at least once a year. This monitoring should cover all material control measures relating to financial, operational and compliance.

Compliance and integrity are matters of growing relevance to the top tier of the governance structure aspects. Here compliance is obviously much more firmly established; it belongs there, whereas in Principle 1.4.2.i *supra* it is stated more as an option.

Unfortunately, the Dutch revision of the Corporate Governance Code provides no clarity with regard to what is meant by compliance. The established position of compliance in the governance of an organization needs to be embedded more clearly in the Corporate Governance Code. After all, compliance concerns the way in which the core objectives of the organization are to be achieved within the limits of the law and internal and external agreements. An example may be illustrative here. Laws and regulations give rise to obligations which, if there is a risk of non-compliance, can have a direct relationship with the organization's license to operate. Take for example financial institutions. They must be compliant with a complex network of laws and regulations, or they run the risk of losing their license. They must also comply with the 1998 Occupational Health & Safety Act, but compliance with this will be assigned to human resources and not to compliance. In a consultancy firm in the field of occupational health and safety, however, compliance with the 1998 Occupational Health & Safety Act will be a crucial component and may be assigned to compliance. After all, the credibility of the firm and hence its license to operate will be in danger if it flouts the laws on occupational health and safety. Compliance risks are risks which can pull the proverbial rug from under the company, or in any case lead to major material and reputational damage.

As discussed in the first chapter of this book *supra*, compliance and integrity are difficult terms to define. The term compliance may be defined in some specific laws related to specific subject-matters such as banking, but in general corporate governance codes will refer to compliance and integrity – or for instance 'honesty' as in the OECD/G-20 Principles[5] – without further elaborating on the exact definition. It lies open to interpretation. This might be considered a dangerous flaw within the principles of corporate governance, but in fact it is a blessing in disguise, because no organization is the same and interpretation may be the tool towards adaptation to particular circumstances of the organization, its trade and specific laws and regulations. Due to the lack of definitions, in this chapter the definitions as described in chapter 1 of this book will apply. The definition can be summarized as: compliance is about conduct. The task is to complete the picture. The black line around the color picture represents laws and regulations. These must not be violated. The internal processes and procedures, including internal conduct standards, make up the color

5. G-20/OECD Principles of Corporate Governance, The Responsibility of the Board, OECD Publications 2015.

palette from which each organization forms its own color picture. It is therefore not sensible to copy and paste internal conduct standards from the Internet, because the core of the organization consists of conduct appropriate to it and that cannot be copied; after all, it is a question of individual identity.

The definition *supra* shows that integrity is inextricably linked to compliance. After all, non-compliance with internal standards and guidelines can also entail risks and in the worst case even jeopardize the license to operate.

Anyone looking for references concerning the integrity of the organization, its directors and employees in the proposed revision of the Corporate Governance Code will get no further than the references concerning the integrity of the financial reporting and the 'in control statement'. Once again there is no description of an important component: 'integrity'. Corporate Governance Codes often have a very limited view of integrity and focus primarily on the correct presentation of financial reporting. Imtech Germany is an excellent example of the risks of this limited perspective. Imtech Germany consistently posted excellent results. For many years there was no doubt about the integrity of the reporting, until it turned out that there were basically hardly any internal risk control systems. There was even no internal audit or control function. Liquidity was generated, for example, by obtaining an advance through bribery. The holding company Royal Imtech was the jewel in the crown of the Dutch Stock Exchange. Imtech was active in several European countries. At its height Royal Imtech was worth EUR 5.4 billion. The Holding consisted of approximately 20 employees, there was no compliance and even an internal control department did not exist. And incredible but true: the CEO only wanted to hear great news, the local management was to solve all problems and not to bother the CEO with problematic situations. When it became obvious that the German subsidiary of Imtech – worth over EUR 2 billion – embellished the facts through fraudulent behavior, the walls of Imtech came tumbling down.

Integrity is not a term that can easily be summed up in a few core elements, but it does appear to be a kind of burning ember that is thrown back and forth. No one wants to get their hands burned if something looks difficult to grasp but can actually cause serious injury. It is notable that the term integrity is generally linked to personal integrity. Integrity is key when selecting members of the board and Supervisory Board, because their actions affect the organization as a whole. Using various terms such as 'unimpeachable', 'honest', 'sincere', incorruptible' or 'reliable', efforts are made to state the characteristics which a person of integrity must have. These are people and we therefore find it difficult to engage with them directly about their character traits. Integrity has everything to do with 'acting in the moment'. It is the circumstances of the moment that can sometimes lead to significant unexpected actions. A quiet, introverted person for example, can turn into a real hero under extreme circumstances. Sometimes, however, people who are generally believed to meet all the standards of integrity *supra* fall hopelessly short. The question that should then be asked is: was that person a wolf in sheep's clothing or was it understandable in those circumstances that the person acted contrary to everything he stood for? A good example is an executive director of a large financial institution who was asked by a customs officer of an African country to show his vaccination booklet. He had his passport, but not his vaccination booklet. He faced the following dilemma: pay up or be injected with a dirty needle which the officer pulled out. Here the choice was simple. No one will call his integrity into doubt, even if he bribed the official. But what about the case in which a Supervisory Board suddenly has to pull out all the stops during a long period to refinance a company in difficult conditions – weekly meetings that last well into the night. Then suddenly the chairman of the Supervisory Board receives a letter from the compliance officer revealing a problem calling into question the integrity of the CFO. The passing on of the letter to the other members of the Supervisory Board could have major consequences for the entire company. What should be done? This is a major dilemma to which widely differing responses are possible. Various gradations are also possible in the actions that can be taken. Personal integrity is a glowing ember; you do not know what you will do until you are placed in those circumstances. It is advisable to give executive and supervisory directors regular dilemma training. Not gratuitous dilemmas but decisions that have to be taken at the cutting edge. Simulation training may be a good option here.

Compliance and integrity management is focused on the conduct of people in an organization, which is limited by external and internal agreements, i.e. organizational integrity. Here the emphasis is on the internally agreed standards to which all participants in the organization must adhere. The standards apply within the organization and deviating behavior is generally not accepted and can even constitute grounds for terminating an employment contract. The standards characterize the nature of the organization and organizational integrity applies within the frameworks of the specified standards. The Mafia, for example, could be seen as an extremely honest organization from the perspective of organizational integrity. A clear penalty applies in the event of a breach of the organization's core values – *omertà*. Fortunately, organizational integrity is based on an assumption that organizations will not perform their activities outside the framework of national criminal law.

Generally, when searching for the integrity of an organization, we come to general standards set out in the code of conduct which largely agree with the conduct standards that apply in the country – or rather the continent – in which the parent company is established. In multinational companies the trick is therefore to find the right tone that interconnects cultures rather than separates them. An excellent example of this is the Dutch standard that applied at the end of the 1960s in a Netherlands-based multinational company with regard to healthcare. In the Netherlands healthcare for employees and their families was provided free of charge by the company. The young manager had his first directorship in Africa. He had to set up a factory. At that time there were still quite a few problems in various African countries and the parent company had experienced some problems in the past. The manager asked the director how healthcare should be dealt with locally. The director answered the question simply by saying that he wanted to apply the same standard as in the Netherlands: free healthcare for all employees and their families. The manager explained that in this African country the 'family' actually included the entire village. The young director did not grasp the problem and generously applied the Dutch rule in full. It subsequently turned out to be one of the factories that had few problems, due to the prevailing peaceful industrial relations. A stroke of luck? No, a translation of a national standard into a universally recognized principle of equality. Two apparently conflicting principles proved to share a common core feature: healthcare in the employee's social environment provides for peace and promotes his abilities. The definition of the 'social environment' is culturally determined.

7.3 THE PLACE OF COMPLIANCE IN THE ORGANIZATION

As discussed in chapter 3 *supra*, financial institutions have gradually become familiar with compliance since the end of the 1990s. Following the scandals at the beginning of this century and the subsequent economic and financial crisis, the importance of compliance to financial institutions is now beyond doubt. The term 'compliance' is also gradually becoming known in other sectors. Before consideration is given to the possible establishment of compliance in a non-financial organization, it is not unusual for an assessment to be made of how the financial institutions have tackled it: 'better to steal something good than invent something bad'. Unfortunately, this idea does not hold true. First, it is a tightly regulated market with specific national, international and foreign legislation and regulators. It is also the case that compliance has arisen in financial institutions in reaction to changing regulations and not on the basis of a well-considered strategic intervention in the structure. A critical approach is recommended when establishing a compliance structure. This is illustrated by a practical example from some years ago in which a director decided in consultation with a supervisor – still in its infancy at that time – that the non-financial undertaking must set up a compliance function. They had jointly requested assistance from a financial institution and worked with a compliance structure that suited a bank but not this organization.

From the definition of compliance used in this book, it must be directly related to the fulfillment of the core objectives. Compliance must 'fit in' with the type of activity and must tie in with the requirements set by the applicable supervisors in the fulfillment of those objectives. The extent to which the market is regulated will have a considerable influence on the nature and scope of the compliance function to be achieved.

In recent times DNB has focused increasingly on what happens in the boardroom. An important subject for DNB is organizing 'cross-examinations' in an organization. In 2013 DNB said it was striking 'that only a few organizations had consciously taken measures to organize cross-examinations at the top of the organization in a structured way'.[6] This will be discussed in more detail in chapter 13 on Supervision of Conduct and Culture *infra*. The most important task of the compliance officer is that of exercising countervailing power – as discussed in chapter 3 *supra* – with regard to the business. Compliance must let its voice be heard right through to the boardroom. Even during the Supervisory Board's Audit Committee meetings. After all, it is the duty of compliance to act as a mediator and restorer of balance between the interests of the company and the interests of society that are articulated in laws and regulations and internal integrity standards. According to DNB, even internal integrity standards must be viewed in the light of socially acceptable standards. In its response to the Panama Papers, DNB states that it is no longer sufficient for an organization to adhere to the law and its own internal integrity standards. According to DNB, the conduct of the organization must also correspond to the prevailing social standards.[7] Here we see once again the important link between compliance

6. DNB booklet, 'Leading by example', March 2013.
7. DNB Persbericht May 19, 2016: 'Lage rente uitdaging voor gehele financiële sector; integriteit blijft zorgpunt'.

and integrity, with DNB offering a broad interpretation of the prevailing integrity standards by stating that what is legally permitted can be 'overruled' by 'socially appropriate conduct', with an assessment being made of what the socially accepted standard is 'at the time'.

The potential for external 'cross-examination' is becoming increasingly important for organizations as a result of modern developments such as social media. It is important, however, to also institutionalize internal 'cross-examination'. That means the possibility must be created within the organization for other voices to penetrate through to the Board of Directors and the Supervisory Board, so that they can take a decision on the basis of the fullest consideration possible. The discussion of both sides of each coin actually needs to be institutionalized.

The question is, however, where the countervailing power should lie; with the Works Council? However, the Works Council has a limited range of tasks for fundamental matters that materially affect the company (opinion) or matters which directly affect the employees (consent).[8] The Works Council acts in the interest of the employees and not so much in the general interest. The aim is to find the 'Jiminy Cricket' of the company who knows the frameworks, engages in the debate on the implementation of the frameworks and clearly pulls out a red card as soon as the boundaries are exceeded or conflict with what is socially appropriate. This warning does not necessarily have to lead to discontinuation of an activity. That depends on the risk appetite determined by the Board of Directors.

If the compliance officer actually wants to be able to exercise his role as a countervailing power, in addition to the periodic consultation with the Board of Directors and the Supervisory Board, there must also be a direct line between the compliance officer and the chairman of the Supervisory Board or the Audit Committee. After all, it is important that if the compliance officer identifies an acute problem for the organization and the Board of Directors incorrectly assesses the seriousness of the risk in the opinion of the compliance officer, he can refer directly to the Supervisory Board. It goes without saying that this will be an exceptional case. The same applies when the compliance officer sees that the Board of Directors or its members are knowingly engaging in unauthorized practices. In that case he must have direct access to the Supervisory Board and if he receives a negative response to his request, he must refer to the supervisor.

As well as guarding against the risks of violations of laws and regulations, the compliance officer must therefore also be the ethical conscience of the organization, because the compliance officer is the guardian of the internal standards and rules, including the conduct standards.

If the compliance officer also wishes to be the conscience of the organization, strict standards must be set for the expertise and integrity of the compliance officer, as well as more personal characteristics such as determination, firmness, incorruptibility, reasoning skills, etc. as discussed in chapter 3 *supra*. It is striking that increasingly strict requirements are placed on executive and supervisory directors in terms of their expertise and integrity, but that similar requirements do not apply to compliance officers. Organizations now specify their own requirements for

8. Art. 25 (right to express an opinion) and Art. 27 (right of consent) of the Dutch Works Councils Act.

compliance professional such as in the Netherlands the so-called DSI registration, or a Certificate of Good Conduct (VoG) given by the Dutch government (to the extent that the VoG has any real value when it comes to a compliance officer's mandate) and minimum training requirements. However, fewer requirements are placed on those who are supposed to make dissenting voices heard and who are required to stand firm against their superiors (the executive director). It may be worth providing greater insight into the skills and characteristics that can be expected of a compliance officer. As in everything in life, in the case of the compliance officer too, the various characteristics must be in balance. After all, a notoriously headstrong thinker or a yes-man will impede a good and effective dialogue.

7.4 COMPLIANCE STRUCTURE

Alongside financial institutions, compliance is increasingly becoming a topic in large and medium-sized non-financial organizations in which the size of the function depends on market conditions. We also see the subject of compliance increasingly coming to the fore in the larger national and multinational companies outside the financial sector. There may be all kinds of reasons for this. For example because the market is tightly regulated, as is the case with telecom companies or the energy sector. In fact, almost all sectors worldwide are facing some form of regulation. In the Netherlands alone, hundreds of supervisors exist, of which only the largest are well known. Many smaller supervisors operate in a specific niche.

The compliance structure has been discussed at length in chapter 3 *supra*. However, in the context of corporate governance it is important to emphasize that compliance (chief compliance officer) should report directly to the board. If placed under another department e.g. the legal department, compliance will be one of many issues and may not have the attention it should have. The Chief Legal Officer will be triggered to discuss the important legal issues with the board instead of the compliance issues, unless they might raise important legal issues. Also, in case of a serious concern, the Chief Compliance Officer should be able to reach out to the Supervisory Board. Compliance issues may be mission critical and are therefore '*Chef-sache*' and the national supervisory authorities will hold the board and Supervisory Board responsible for not having acted on serious compliance matters and this may even lead to criminal prosecution.

7.5 RISK-BASED COMPLIANCE

Compliance must set up an annual program determining the priorities for the forthcoming year as well as the budget. Compliance cannot tackle everything. Practice shows that there is a constantly changing hotchpotch of laws and regulations and demands from supervisors. Compliance must therefore be tackled on the basis of prioritization. The prioritization is directly linked to the organization's risk appetite. The Board of Directors periodically determines the risk appetite of the organization, in close consultation with the Supervisory Board. Attention must also be devoted to the compliance risks and the extent to which these must be covered at any cost. In practice we often see that as soon as an organization falls within the crosshairs of the authorities due to prosecution in the Netherlands or – even worse – abroad (the United States of America), the risk appetite switches to risk aversion, which in certain areas results in a zero-tolerance policy with regard to specific compliance risks.

It is unwise to lump all compliance risks together in the periodic – at least annual – risk analysis of the organization. That is what often happens in practice, however. The compliance risk is often assessed during the session with the Board of Directors. In fact, there are many compliance risks and it is important to assess these in advance within the organization and then to present them to the Board of Directors so that they can be prioritized – after an analysis of probability and impact. The substantiation of the main compliance risks must also be discussed with the Supervisory Board, which is after all the ultimate internal supervisory body. The Supervisory Board must realize that it also has to devote attention to compliance and internal mitigation of compliance risks.

7.6 CONCLUSION

Over the past few years it has become clear that a marked change is occurring in the role of supervisory directors with regard to the supervision of compliance and integrity in the organization. It is true that the members of the Board of Directors are directly responsible for their own conduct, but they are increasingly held liable for serious compliance and integrity incidents in the organization as the party with ultimate responsibility.

The Board of Directors and the Supervisory Board must be increasingly aware of the importance of compliance and integrity management in their organization. The associated risks are of such a nature that they have a direct effect on the license to operate.

If the Board of Directors and the Supervisory Board have visibility on the compliance and integrity risks, they will have to give compliance and integrity a clear position in the organization. Please note: compliance is customized work. A copy-and-paste approach will let the organization down, because then it is not only a dead letter but it actually poses an additional risk. They will then have to sit around the table with the compliance officer regularly to engage in the discussion and tackle risks in good time. The door of the Board of Directors and the Supervisory Board must also be open to the compliance officer. It should be noted in this regard, however, that higher requirements are set for the expertise and integrity of the compliance officer, because he exerts influence on the highest level of governance. In short: it is still very much work in progress!

8. Risk Management

R. van Altena RA

This chapter addresses the Why, How, What and Who of risk management in general and in relation to compliance. The theory used in this chapter consists of the internationally generally accepted framework for enterprise risk management, i.e. COSO's Enterprise Risk Management (ERM) Framework, and thought concepts by reputed scholars such as Robert Kaplan and Robert Simons.

8.1 WHY RISK MANAGEMENT?

8.1.1 Business value and license to operate

Organizations aim to turn their mission and future vision into strategy and business goals and hence into business value for their stakeholders. Organizations face uncertainty in creating and protecting their business value and they have the challenge of allocating scarce resources.

An organization gets to its business value through performance and compliance. Performance is about continuous delivery of goods and services, return on capital, contribution to staff and community and those connected to the organization and finally the societally beneficial objectives with regard to people and planet. Compliance generates confidence and trust. Compliance relates to the rule set applied to the organization through laws and regulation (outside in) and the rule set applied by the organization based on explicit self-regulation and the code of conduct flowing from its mission, vision and behavioral and cultural core values (inside out).

Performance and compliance come together in the reputation of the organization, promoted by satisfied customers and stakeholders. Reputation in turn forms the basis for the organization's license to operate.

Risk management is about the challenge faced by managers of an organization in balancing uncertainty against positive or negative reward from business opportunities, investment initiatives and dealing with threats in relation to its license to operate, in both strategy-setting and day-to-day business operations.

True entrepreneurs realize that it is ultimately about risk-taking and that opportunities and gains entail risks. An example of this lies in the following quotation ascribed to Mark Zuckerberg, the founder and CEO of Facebook: 'The biggest risk is not taking any risk.' And this quotation on the importance of risk-taking may become even more meaningful when taking into account a quotation from the scholar Karl Weick:[1] 'Organizations are defined by what they ignore.'

8.1.2 Revealing Hand concept

The concept of looking at risk management as the Revealing Hand for the organization was introduced by Robert Kaplan and Anette Mikes.[2]

They observe that many people believe that the global financial crisis demonstrated the failure of sophisticated quantitative risk models, as used by banks. And that many believe that top-down risk management hampers innovation and entrepreneurial activities and that risk managers are regarded as representatives of the 'business prevention department'.

In recent years scholars like Nassim Taleb have provided a forceful critique on a quantitative approach to risk management. They note that almost all financial risk models failed during the global financial crisis – and in other recent bouts of market volatility – to signal the huge losses (labeled by Taleb as 'Black Swan' events[3]) that occurred with far greater frequency than expected.

Kaplan and Mikes also refer to Albert Hirschman,[4] who believes that too much concern about future threats can discourage people and organizations from undertaking bold new ventures. According to Hirschman there is a dual fallacy that necessitates the Hiding Hand (in contradiction to a Revealing Hand): first, business planners tend to underestimate challenges and risks, and at the same time they also underestimate their organization's creative capacity to deal with those challenges.

Kaplan and Mikes disagree with Hirschmann and argue that risk management should function as a Revealing Hand to identify, assess and mitigate risks in a cost-efficient manner. And they advocate that the Revealing Hand of risk management adds value to firms by allowing them to take on riskier projects and strategies. But at the same time they stress the need to keep in mind that risk management must overcome severe individual and organizational biases that prevent managers and employees from thinking deeply and analytically about their risk exposure. They refer to a quote by a veteran NASA systems engineer, who states that risk management is 'not a natural act for humans to perform'. One can add to this quotation: '... so people and organizations have to be aware of the effect of their human nature and arrange their own help'.

Perhaps risk management is primarily about behavior, helping business people to understand the psychology of risk more than the mathematics of risk. This is in line with the ideas of Kahneman et al.,[5] who argue that psychological and

1. Weick 1998, pp. 72–75.
2. Kaplan et al. 2016.
3. Taleb 2008.
4. Hirschman 1967.
5. Kahneman et al. 2011.

sociological biases within organizations lead them to overlook important risks and to systematically underestimate and undermanage those they do identify.

A Revealing Hand concept for risk management is aware of human behavior and enables risks to be identified and then mitigated in a cost-effective manner and is thus an important element of business planning.

8.1.3 Benefits of Enterprise Risk Management

According to COSO's Enterprise Risk Management (ERM) Framework[6] an organization needs to be able to identify challenges that lie ahead and adapt to meet those challenges. It must engage in decision-making with an awareness of both the opportunities for creating value and the risks that challenge the achievement of value.

Benefits of ERM include the ability to:

Increase the range of opportunities

By considering all reasonable possibilities – both positive and negative aspects of risk – management can identify opportunities for the entity and unique challenges associated with current opportunities. These could include anticipating upcoming regulation that impacts a company's access to client groups or forces them to change product features.

Identify and manage entity-wide risks

Every entity faces risks that can affect many parts of the entity. Sometimes a risk can originate in one part of the entity but impact a different part. Management must identify and manage these entity-wide risks to sustain and improve performance. This applies both to integrated businesses operating under the same brand name (e.g. product incidents) and to conglomerates with a portfolio of diversified business activities (e.g. bribery and corruption by management).

Reduce surprises and losses

Enterprise risk management allows organizations to improve their ability to identify potential risks and establish appropriate responses, reducing surprises and related costs or losses. Being able to detect events and related risks at an early stage offers the company time to react before a wider group of stakeholders gets involved. Time between the first 'red flag' and the proper response is an important critical success factor for the quality of risk management within a company.

Reduce performance variability

For some entities, the challenge is less about surprises and losses and more about performance variability. Performing ahead of schedule or beyond expectations may cause as much concern as performing below expectations. This is the case, for example, with power plants and other general utilities.

Improve resource deployment

Obtaining robust information on risk allows management to assess overall resource needs and enhance resource allocation. Knowing what is going on in the outside world by being able to envision risks such as cyberattacks can help companies

6. COSO 2016.

to implement protective and preventive measures in terms of firewalls, recovery capacity, hiring specialists and implementing emergency protocols.

The benefits will come to the organization by integrating enterprise risk management practices with strategy-setting, performance management and compliance risk management. These benefits will help the organization to achieve business value and maintain its license to operate.

8.2 RISK IS ABOUT BALANCING UNCERTAINTY AGAINST REWARD ('HOW AND WHAT')

Risk management should be seen as a dynamic managerial process aligned with the business processes. It turns mission, vision, core values and strategic priorities into processes safeguarded by risk appetite-setting and related reporting and monitoring. Risk management is formed and influenced by the organization in terms of internal governance, business structure and infrastructure, in terms of data and information systems. In the framework in Figure 1 the elements of risk management are brought together. This framework is an interpretation by the author based on various generally used risk management framework models.

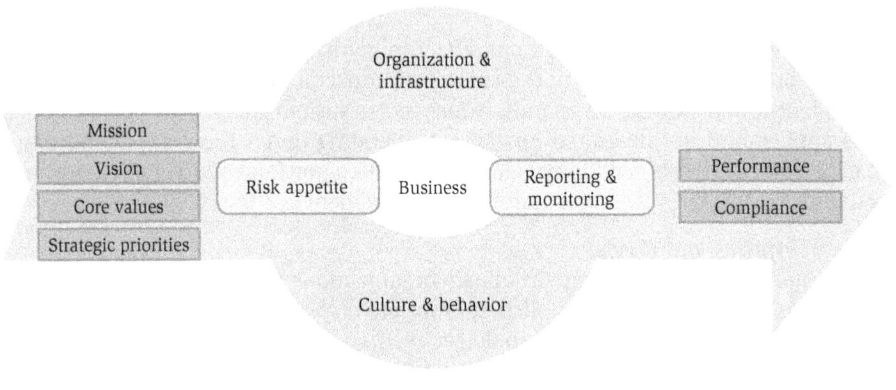

Figure 1: Risk Management Framework[7]

The framework shows that performance and compliance are the outcome of a sound risk management process that turns 'mission, vision, core values and related strategic priorities' into 'performance and compliance'. This forms the basis for the reputation of the organization, promoted by satisfied customers and stakeholders. Reputation in turn forms the basis for the organization's license to operate, which brings us back to the goal of risk management.

---

7. Figure 1 has been retrieved from the lecture documentation by Robert van Altena – Vrije Universiteit – FEWEB Compliance & Integrity Management.

8.2.1 Mission, vision, core values and strategic priorities

The first step in designing an effective risk management framework is coming to an agreement with regard to the mission, vision and core values of the organization and translating this into the strategic priorities. This is perhaps the most important phase of risk management. It makes it necessary to capture the objectives of the organization taking into account the business value for its stakeholders and getting to the 'Why' of the organization.

The core questions in this phase are: 'Why do we exist as a business?' and 'Are we doing the right things?' These questions can be answered by having dialogues with internal and external stakeholders. They are the ones that allow the organization its license to operate.

In his global bestseller *Start with Why*, Simon Sinek[8] states:

> 'WHY: Very few people or companies can clearly articulate WHY they do WHAT they do. When I say WHY I don't mean to make money – that's a result. By WHY I mean what is your purpose, cause or belief? WHY does your company exist? Why do you get out of bed every morning? And WHY should anyone care?'

Why is about the mission, vision and core values of the company and its stakeholders and community and will materialize through the related strategic priorities into organizational structures and business processes.

A great example of a company that stipulates its Why and translates its Why into strategic priorities is ING,[9] a globally active financial institution with Dutch roots.

ING's purpose is:

> 'We believe all sustainable progress is driven by people with the imagination and determination to improve their future and the futures of those around them. We empower people and organisations to realise their own vision for a better future – however modest or grand. Our purpose therefore is: Empowering people to stay a step ahead in life and in business.'

ING's three core values can be summarized as follows: 'We are honest. We are prudent. We are responsible.'

ING has brought together its purpose and its core values into four so-called 'customer promises' that form the basis for the strategic priorities:

> *'Clear and easy*
>
> Banking doesn't have to be difficult and time consuming. Less is more. It's all about clear products, plain language, fair prices and simple processes. That saves both time and money.
>
> *Anytime, anywhere*
>
> We work to get our services where our customers are. Banking should be possible anytime and anywhere.

8. Sinek 2009, p. 39.
9. ING Bank – www.ing.com.

> *Empower*
>
> The best financial decisions are informed decisions. Customers want relevant, up-to-date information at their fingertips. They need to understand their choices, and the implications, both today and for the future.
>
> *Keep getting better*
>
> Life and business are about moving forward. We will keep looking for new ways to make things better with new ideas, new solutions and new approaches to make things easier for our customers. That way, we can all stay a step ahead.'

The customer promises are the input for the key strategic risk indicators for the company that will be addressed in the following phases of the risk management framework.

ING's strategic priorities are:

> 'We are a global financial institution with a strong European base, offering banking services. We draw on our experience and expertise, our commitment to excellent service and our global scale to meet the needs of a broad customer base, comprising individuals, families, small businesses, large corporations, institutions and governments. Our customers are at the heart of what we do.
>
> Our more than 52,000 employees offer retail and commercial banking services to customers in over 40 countries. Our strengths include our well-known, strong brand with positive recognition from customers in many countries, strong financial position, omnichannel distribution strategy and international network. Moreover, ING is currently among leaders in the Dow Jones Sustainability Index "Banks industry" group.
>
> Our strategy aims to create a differentiating customer experience, enabled by simplifying and streamlining our organisation, further striving for operational excellence, enhancing the performance culture within our company and expanding our lending capabilities. ....'

Getting from the mission, vision and core values to strategic priorities requires the implementation of interactive controls. The term 'interactive controls' was introduced by Robert Simons.[10]

Interactive controls are defined by Simons as follows: 'Interactive control systems track the strategic uncertainties that keep senior managers awake at night – the shocks to the business that could undermine their assumptions about the future and the way they have chosen to compete. Depending on the business, these uncertainties might relate to changes in technology, customers' tastes, government regulation, and industry competition.'

According to Simons interactive control systems have four characteristics:

- *Focus on constantly changing information that top-level managers have identified as potentially strategic;* we often see this in the form of analysis of multiple scenarios.
- *Information is significant enough to demand frequent and regular attention from operating managers at all levels of the organization*; this is about bringing

10. Simons 1995.

all managerial levels 'on the same page', which requires the board of the company to determine specific areas of attention, with the utmost focus on a 'handful' of topics that are driven by individual members of the board or senior managers and are considered as 'Chefsachen'.
- *Data generated by the interactive system are best interpreted and discussed in face-to-face meetings of superiors, subordinates, and peers*; this fits in very well with modern trends such as agile working that bring various specialists together in a dynamic manner. This is also in line with the trend of companies being closer to their stakeholder communities, including involvement of staff on demand and third parties (e.g. open source programming).
- *The interactive control system is a catalyst for an ongoing debate about underlying data, assumptions, and action plans*; this debate can take place using modern technologies in the field of data analytics and social engineering, collaborative working methods, new media and use of machine learning.

Interactive controls are highly oriented towards people's vision and insights, their interaction and handling of information and are thus greatly influenced by the other elements of the framework, i.e. culture and behavior, organization and infrastructure.

8.2.2 Culture and behavior

The company's culture and behavior and its internal and external stakeholders form the basis for risk management. In chapters 2, 3 and 4 *infra* of this book culture and behavior are described and explained in more detail and looked at from the perspective of desired culture and integrity as such.

When looking at culture and behavior from the perspective of risk management it is very wise also to consider the term 'belief system' as introduced by Robert Simons.[11]

Robert Simons states that 'beliefs systems empower individuals and encourage them to search for new opportunities. They communicate core values and inspire all participants to commit to the organization's purpose. ... Managers who use their missions as living documents - as part of a system to guide patterns of acceptable behavior - have discovered a powerful lever of control.'

In fact, coming to an agreement about the company's belief system, about its objectives, values and priorities, is the first - and in some ways the most important - part of developing an effective risk management system.

From a risk management perspective, belief systems act in two ways. On the one hand meeting desired organizational behavior is a goal for the organization in achieving its purpose and mission. On the other hand the way the people in the organization treat risk management is an important feature for risk management as a whole. In this regard questions such as 'are we aware of risks or not?' and 'are we able to identify control measures that capture risk awareness?' can be raised.

Risk awareness and related control measures can vary throughout the organization. Some staff will look at risk in an optimistic, entrepreneurial way and tend to seek a certain level of risk, typically to be found in sales staff. Back office staff who

11. Ibid.

record sales may tend to focus on strict accuracy and regulatory compliance when looking at desired risk for the organization. Both tendencies are part of the total belief system of the organization as a whole and both staff groups should understand that working together, and understanding each other's role, is very important.

How can a company manage risk awareness?[12]

Leadership

Maintaining strong leadership that focuses on the right risk awareness within the company. The company's leaders stimulate a culture of risk awareness and interact with staff to discuss risks. Management is supported in this by compliance and risk officers. These officers will contribute their professional understanding of behavioral concepts around risk awareness.

Accountability

Management documents policies of accountability and demonstrates to staff and business partners that a lack of accountability is not tolerated and that practicing proper accountability is rewarded. Management itself is also aware of its role in accounting for risk awareness to external stakeholders such as shareholders and regulators.

Risks as part of decision-making

Management is aware of risks when making key business decisions and explicitly addresses risks in its decision-making. This includes discussing and reviewing risk scenarios that can help management and staff understand the interrelationship and impacts of risks. It is about open and honest discussions about risks and not considering risks as negative, but as critical to achieving the strategy and business objectives.

Awareness

Management continually sends messages to staff that managing risk is a part of their day-to-day business operations and that risk-taking is not only valued but also critical to the entity's success and survival.

Transparency

Management communicates to staff and business partners about its attitude towards risk-taking and reports on risk to all stakeholders involved in a transparent manner.

8.2.3 Organization and infrastructure

Organization consists of the governance arrangements of the organization, from corporate governance (such as the role of shareholders, mandates of board members, checks and balances within the boardroom in terms of internal and external supervision) to the set-up of the organization in group companies, divisions and business units and the related various internal roles (e.g. reporting lines to head office).

Organization and governance arrangements are described in more detail in chapter 7 *supra* of this book.

12. As indicated by Coso 2016.

Infrastructure concerns both the physical infrastructure and the information infrastructure of the organization.

The physical infrastructure of the organization can be looked at from various perspectives:

- people arrangements, using concepts such as staff on demand, open sourcing, flexible workforce;
- geographical spread, including applicable local jurisdictions with their own laws, rules and (unwritten) codes;
- markets organization, taking into account diversification to industries and sectors and the use of alliance partners;
- production methods, also considering the outsourcing of primary and secondary business processes.

The information infrastructure concerns the process of obtaining and sharing information throughout the organization. It also concerns the way things are communicated within the organization; for instance whether communication is 'top down' from head office to business units or whether there is a 'network of business units' that connects with and is supported by the central 'help office'.

A very good example can be found in some globally active companies that maintain a central 'policy house' to capture the policies that are applicable to all business units throughout the world. These policies are based on a central mandate, but are created by head office departments and management and staff of all business units together in the form of an iterative approach comparable to the 'Wikipedia approach'.

8.2.3.1 Exponential organization

A very interesting phenomenon from an organization and infrastructure point of view is that of the 'exponential organization' as described by Salim Ismail.[13] He defines these organizations as follows: 'An Exponential Organization (ExO) is one whose impact (or output) is disproportionally large – at least 10x larger – compared to its peers because of the use of new organizational techniques that leverage accelerating technologies.' In his book he captures and discusses the features of ExOs such as Google, Uber and Airbnb.

The features of ExOs have a very strong influence on the organization and the infrastructure of the organization and hence on risk management.

Let us look at a couple of elements from the perspective of risk management.

The Massive Transformative Purpose leads the way for the company in its entrepreneurial and innovative spirit to get to the company's mission, vision, core values and strategic priorities.

The 'SCALE' elements are important for the company's creativity and growth and carry an intrinsic uncertainty connected to entrepreneurial and innovative goals. Staff on demand influences the scope of the effect of behavior and risk awareness. Community and crowd form stakeholders that are very close to the company,

13. Ismail et al. 2014.

comprising clients, business partners and suppliers that also determine the risk profile of the company. Using algorithms brings new risks in terms of accuracy, completeness and continuity of the systems involved, including concepts of artificial intelligence and machine learning. The use of leveraged assets – assets used but not owned by the company – brings new risks such as continuity in use and the quality of the assets. Engagement with society and the environment can make a company vulnerable to reputation risk.

The 'IDEAS' elements focus on order and control and hence create stability for the company. The company captures order and control through interfaces, for instance between the company and its community and crowd. Dashboards are based on an 'Objective and Key Results (OKR) approach' answering two questions: 'What do we want to achieve?' and 'How do we know that we are going to achieve things?' The experimentation, autonomy and social elements are about the way professionals within the company deal with innovation, learning and interconnection. These are important as a basis for risk management; from risk awareness through to communication.

8.2.4 Risk appetite

An important initial step in the risk management 'plan do check act' cycle is expressing the company's 'risk appetite' with regard to how much and what kind of risk can be tolerated, based on the strategy and business objectives of the company.

Risk appetite clarifies what risks can be accepted and left unattended, and what risks need immediate attention and action. Risk appetite can be captured in both qualitative and quantitative terms.

The most important terms in relation to risk appetite are defined *infra*. These definitions are partly derived from the COSO ERM framework:[14]

First start with the definitions around the term 'event', being an occurrence or set of occurrences that (can) happen to the company. The state of not knowing how potential events may or may not manifest themselves is defined as 'uncertainty'. 'Severity' is the measurement of considerations such as the likelihood and impacts of events or the time it takes to recover from events.

Afterwards the definitions of risks in relation to internal controls are of importance. 'Inherent Risk' (IR) is the possibility that events will occur and affect the achievement of strategy and business objectives *not* taking into account the quality of internal control measures, also referred to as 'gross risks'. The possibility that events will occur and affect the quality of the internal control activities is called 'Internal Control Risk' (ICR).

Next we turn to the outcome of the aforementioned terms. 'Residual Risk' refers to the possibility that events will occur and affect the achievement of strategy and business objectives *after* taking into account the quality of internal control measures ('net risk'). Finally, for risk appetite, setting the 'Desired Risk' definition is key. Desired Risk is defined as the level of Residual Risk acceptable to the management of the organization. This risk is not zero because resources are limited and because of future uncertainty and limitations.

14. COSO 2016.

An organization identifies and assesses risks that may affect an entity's ability to achieve its strategy and business objectives. It prioritizes risks according to their severity and considering the entity's risk appetite. The organization then selects risk responses and monitors performance for change. In this way it develops a portfolio view of the amount of risk the entity has assumed in the pursuit of its strategy and business objectives.

Figure 2 demonstrates the mechanism that connects Inherent Risk (gross) to Residual Risk (net) and Desired Risk (risk appetite), making use of the quality of internal controls.

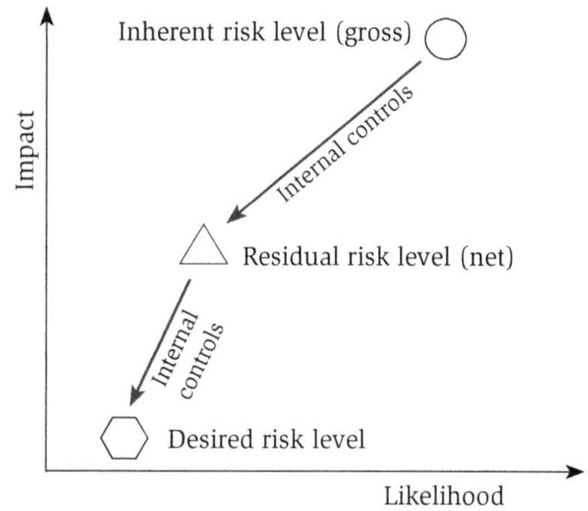

Figure 2: Risk model[15]

8.2.4.1 Strategic risks

Strategic risk appetite starts with the company leadership team reaffirming its mission and values.

> 'Consider the situation faced by the Merck executive team when the first clinical-trial evidence emerged that its blockbuster drug Vioxx was associated with an increase in cardiac incidents for patients who used it for more than 18 months. Merck decided immediately to withdraw the drug from the market, following the mandate of its core value, "Merck puts patients first." Every decision and action Merck took, before and during the event, was consistent with this core belief that elevated a standard of patient safety above short-term profits as the corporate pre-eminent goal. Merck's CEO Raymond Gilmartin subsequently decided to litigate, not settle, every single private law suit brought against the company. He was confident – based on Merck's strong culture and value

15. Graphic has been retrieved from lecture documentation by Robert van Altena – Vrije Universiteit – FEWEB Compliance & Integrity Management.

> system – that even under the extraordinarily intrusive discovery rules during litigation, no Merck employee would be found to have ignored or suppressed scientific information suggesting that Vioxx put its patients at risk. Merck ended up winning all of the litigation, either at trial or upon appeal. The FDA regulatory agency subsequently judged that Vioxx could be returned to the marketplace, reflecting the ambiguous nature of the evidence and the ability of consumers to make personal judgments between immediate and sustainable pain relief versus a modest increase in cardiac risk. But Merck refused to reissue the drug because putting patients first was such a core value.'[16]

A company voluntarily accepts strategic risks in order to generate superior returns from its strategy ('reward versus risks'). Strategy risks are therefore desired by the company, with the urge to manage those risks.

8.2.4.2 *Operational, (financial) reporting and compliance risks*

Whereas strategic risks are often about unquantifiable reputational risks, these three risk categories can be quantified. The non-strategic risks have a preventable character in the sense that the organization does not have an entrepreneurially strategic, comparative strength to make use of a positive 'reward versus risk' balance. Operational risks can be quantified in terms of critical success factors, such as time to market (innovative product development), production costs and human resource development. Financial reporting risks are often connected to requirements of external stakeholders, such as financial reporting to shareholders and external financiers. Reporting risks are measured in terms of relevance and reliability, using timelines and materiality based on the information needed for stakeholders to take well-informed investment decisions.

As stated in chapter 3 *supra*, compliance risks are risks that can pull the proverbial rug from under the company, or at least cause major material and reputational damage.

Of great interest from a strategic and compliance risk perspective is the following definition of the Basel Committee on Banking Supervision:

> 'Compliance risk is defined as the risk of legal or regulatory sanctions, material financial loss, or loss to reputation a financial institution may suffer as a result of its failure to comply with laws, regulations, rules, related self-regulatory organisation standards, and codes of conduct applicable to its activities.'[17]

Besides the fact that compliance risks can pull the rug from under the company, compliance risks can also be quantified in terms of costs of preventive, detective and repressive actions. These costs can consist of time spent by staff, hiring external advisors and lawyers, remedial compensation, claims and fines.

Compliance risks are covered in more detail in chapter 3 *supra*.

16. Simons 1995.
17. Basel Committee on Banking Supervision – Compliance and the compliance function in banks (April 2005).

8.2.5 Business (risk execution)

Day-to-day risk execution is part of the business processes of the organization and includes risk identification (events and their likelihood), risk assessment (impact on business objectives), risk response and control activities.

The identification of events and their likelihood can be carried out on the basis of ongoing managerial monitoring (see section 8.2.6 Reporting and Monitoring) and in specific sessions with managers and staff involved, using relevant and quality information from both internal and external sources.

Risk assessment focuses on measuring the severity of the risk identified and prioritizing the risks to select the response. Risk response itself has four alternative dimensions that offer response scenarios to board and senior management:

- reducing risks, by adapting the governance, people, operations and related internal controls of the organization;
- transferring risks, by means of insurance, sharing with and/or outsourcing to business partners, portfolio diversification or entering hedging arrangements;
- terminating risks, by stopping business activities, withdrawing from the market, divesting or reducing scale;
- accepting, by 'letting things happen' and 'hoping' that the consequences can be cushioned by the (financial) buffers of the organization.

Control activities are put in place to ensure that aforementioned risk responses are executed as intended. Examples of (internal) control activities are analytical top-level reviews, direct functional or activity oversight, management information processing, physical controls, performance indicators and segregation of duties. For information systems we distinguish two types of specific internal controls: general controls (IT management, IT infrastructure, security management, development and maintenance) and application controls (e.g. check digits, reasonableness tests).

8.2.6 Reporting and monitoring

By monitoring enterprise risk management performance, an organization can consider how well the enterprise risk management components are functioning over time and in light of substantial changes. So monitoring is related to the organization's risk management (including controls) for strategy, operations, (financial) reporting and compliance.

According to COSO's Monitoring Guidance,[18] monitoring builds on two fundamental principles. First, ongoing and/or separate evaluations enable management to determine whether the other components of internal control continue to function over time. Secondly, internal control deficiencies are identified and communicated in a timely manner to those parties responsible for taking corrective action and to management and the board as appropriate.

18. COSO's 2006 Guidance: 2.

In order to have effective and efficient monitoring, personnel with appropriate skills, authority and resources should be charged by management with addressing four fundamental questions:[19]

1. Have we *identified the meaningful risks to our objectives*? This concerns the objectives of the company at strategic, operational, compliance and reporting level. Examples of operational objectives are client intimacy, innovation, personnel satisfaction and business continuity. In the case of reporting, for example, the risk may concern risks to the production of accurate, timely and complete financial statements.
2. Which controls are '*key controls*'? These are the controls that will best support a conclusion regarding the effectiveness of internal control in those risk areas. If these controls fail, it is highly improbable that other controls could detect the control absence. These controls are usually part of entity-level controls or high-level analytic controls. An example of a key control in the field of risk reporting is management's assessment of the impairment of assets and receivables based on historical analysis and market information.
3. What *information* will be persuasive in telling us whether the controls continue to operate effectively? Getting to the conclusion that controls are effectively in place will be based on verifying that the controls are designed by means of policies and procedures that are translated into controls. Verification will be carried out by desktop review of available documents, interviews with staff involved, direct observations within the organization and gathering evidence of controls being performed.
4. Are we currently performing effective monitoring that is not well utilized in the evaluation of internal control, resulting in *unnecessary and costly further testing*? Often lots of internal administrative actions and registrations are performed by staff on the basis of their role in the primary business processes of the company. For example, the head of the sales department who observes by 'walking around' and performs end-of-day analysis of daily sales. Is there any monitoring of the administrative activity of this head of the sales department that is used as part of internal control?

The four questions *supra* form the basis for reports on the outcome of monitoring in terms of Key Risk Indicators (KRIs), related key controls and underlying evidence for the controls. These reports are also the basis for setting scenarios to trigger discussions among managers and staff about the risks the organization faces and the possible responses.

Monitoring and reporting is described in more detail in chapter 10 *infra* of this book.

8.3 ROLES IN RISK MANAGEMENT ('WHO')

In this section the various roles of risk managers are described, including in relation to the roles of other officers in the company, such as internal auditors. The roles

19. COSO – Guidance on Monitoring Internal Control Systems – Introduction (2009).

described for risk managers also apply to compliance officers in their role of 'compliance risk managers' and are also described in chapter 3 of this book.

8.3.1 'Three Lines of Defense' model

The 'Three Lines of Defense' (3LoD)[20] approach to risk management is generally accepted and described in many ways 'from COSO to standards of individual regulators'.

The 3LoD model clarifies roles within risk management and control and their interaction, mandated and overseen by senior management and the board of directors. Three separate groups (or lines of defense) within the organization are necessary for effective risk management. The 3LoD is most powerful when attention is also devoted to aligning the activities of the professionals in the various lines of defense. The alignment concerns the information used and the scope, frequency and timing of activities. This is often quite a challenge and is generally referred to as the risk of having 'siloes' within the organization; both siloes between the lines of defense themselves and siloes in domains such as operational, compliance and reporting by risk professionals.

What are the three lines of defense?

8.3.1.1 First line: core business[21]

Management is responsible for identifying and managing the performance and risks resulting from practices and systems for which they are accountable. The first line is also responsible for the risks inherent in the strategy and business objectives. As the principal owners of risk, they set business objectives, establish acceptable variations in performance, train personnel and reinforce risk responses. In short, the first line implements and executes the day-to-day tasks to manage performance and risks taken to achieve strategy and business objectives.

8.3.1.2 Second line: support functions

Support functions (also referred to as business-enabling functions) include the management and personnel responsible for overseeing performance and enterprise risk management. They provide guidance on performance and enterprise risk management requirements, and evaluate adherence to defined standards. Each of these functions has some degree of independence from the first lines of accountability, and they challenge the first line to manage performance and take prudent risks to achieve strategy and business objectives. In some entities, independent teams without separate and distinct reporting lines may provide some degree of challenge. These organizational functions or operating units support the entity through specialized skills, such as technical risk management expertise, finance, product/service quality management, technology, compliance, legal, human resources, and others.

20. Since 2016 COSO has used the term 'Three Lines of Accountability' ('3LoA') instead of 3LoD.
21. COSO 2016.

As management functions they may intervene directly in modifying and supporting the first line in appropriate risk response.

8.3.1.3 *Third line: assurance functions*

Assurance functions, most commonly internal audit, often provide the last line of accountability by performing audits or reviews of enterprise risk management practices, identifying issues and improvement opportunities, making recommendations and keeping the board and executive management up to date on matters requiring resolution. Two factors distinguish the last line of accountability from the others: the high level of independence and objectivity (enabled by direct reporting to the board) and the authority to evaluate and make recommendations to management on the design and operating effectiveness of the entity overall.

8.3.2 Second line of defense roles

In this section we will look more closely at fulfilling the second line of defense roles. In practice four roles can generally be found to describe the characteristics and challenges of the second line of defense. These roles are also described by Kaplan and Mikes in getting to what they define as a new framework for managing risks.[22]

8.3.2.1 *Embedded expert 'gatekeeper per transaction'*

A generally known form of 'embedded expertise' concerns 'embedded journalism'. This refers to news reporters being attached to military units involved in armed conflicts, being part of the units without carrying weapons and maintaining their 'journalistic' approach and responsibility. It first came to be used in the media coverage of the 2003 invasion of Iraq by the United States military. The effectiveness in this role lies in the closeness to day-to-day operations and truly understanding what is going on and at the same time observing and recording ('gatekeeping') on the basis of a specific individual mandate and responsibility.

The main activity of the embedded expert within the organization is to continuously monitor and influence the business's risk profile, working side by side with the line managers. The officer in this role reports both to line executives and to a centralized independent (compliance) risk management function. The embedded expert can be effective when the risk profile of the company can change dramatically with a single transaction.

There is, however, a danger in 'going native', when the officer gets personally too closely connected to the management of the business unit and 'becomes a deal maker rather than a deal questioner'. This is taken care of by means of functional oversight, culture and awareness sessions, peer review and rotating the embedded experts periodically.

22. Kaplan et al. 2012.

8.3.2.2 *Facilitator – 'gatekeeper by helping business professionals signal red flags for risks'*

A facilitator is an individual who enables groups and organizations to work more effectively; to collaborate and achieve synergy. He is a 'content-neutral' party who, by not taking sides or expressing or advocating a point of view during the meeting, can advocate for fair, open and inclusive procedures to accomplish the group's work.[23]

The facilitator focuses on increasing line managers' awareness of the (compliance) risks that have been taken on across the organization and provides decision makers with a full picture of the company's risk profile. The facilitator also provide line managers with information and tools to detect possible events at an early stage and to address mitigating controls measures. The facilitator role is most effective when the organization operates in stable product, market and regulatory environments, with relatively predictable demands.

The danger is that the facilitative risk manager is too far away from understanding the details of the daily operations and does not focus on signaling red flags himself. Risk management therefore relies basically on the signaling quality of the business managers in the first line of defense. This is taken care of by investing in risk awareness and training programs for business managers and providing adequate administrative tools to support them. The facilitative role must also be explicitly combined with one of the other roles in terms of focus on specific events and topics.

Independent challenger – 'gatekeeper at crucial (strategic) moments at a distance'

The independent challenger acts at arm's length with an independent mindset. He shares his knowledge from an 'outside in' perspective. This officer acts as devil's advocate, counterbalances the business managers' natural overconfidence, helping to avoid escalation of commitment to projects with unacceptable levels of risk. The independent challenger is most effective when the company faces high intrinsic risks in pursuing long, complex and expensive product (market, new law) development projects. The danger is that the independent challenger does not fully understand the circumstances of the risks facing the business due to his distance. This is offset by selecting professionals who act as independent challengers based on their business background (comparable to the business under review) and their deep specialism in the legal or technical field. Often this role is supported or played by specialized third-party consultants.

8.3.2.3 *Independent monitor 'gatekeeper by signaling red flags'*

The independent monitor acts at arm's length with an independent mindset with a focus on separate, fresh-look monitoring. This officer provides insight into how well the organization has implemented (compliance) risk management. This role is most closely connected to the third line: assurance functions and focus on alignment (not integration) with the third line.[24]

23. Wikipedia on the search term 'facilitator' – Michael Doyle, quoted in Kaner, et al., 2007, p. xiii.
24. See chapter 9 *infra*.

BIBLIOGRAPHY

Hirschman 1967
A.O. Hirschman, *Development Projects Observed*, Washington D.C.: The Brookings Institution Press 1967.

Ismail et al. 2014
Salim Ismail et al., *Exponential Organizations*, New York: Diversion Books 2014.

Kahneman et al. 2011
Kahneman, D., Lovallo, D. & O. Sibony, 'Before you make that big decision', *Harvard Business Review*, June 2011, pp. 51–60.

Kaplan & Mikes 2012
R.S. Kaplan & A. Mikes, 'Managing Risks: A New Framework', *Harvard Business Review*, June 2012.

Kaplan & Mikes 2016
R.S. Kaplan & A. Mikes, 'Risk Management – the Revealing Hand, Working Paper 16-102', *Harvard Business School*, March 10, 2016.

Simons 1995
R. Simons, 'Control in an Age of Empowerment', *Harvard Business Review*, April 1995.

Sinek 2009
S. Sinek, *Start with Why*, New York: Penguin Group 2009.

Taleb 2008
N.N. Taleb, *The Black Swan: The Impact of the Highly Improbable*, New York: Random House 2007.

Weick 1998
K.E. Weick, 'Foresights of Failure: An Appreciation of Barry Turner', *Journal of Contingencies and crisis Management*, Vol. 6, No. 2, 1998, pp. 72–75.

Other references

COSO 2016
Committee of Sponsoring Organizations of the Treadway Commission (COSO), Risk Management – Aligning Risk with Strategy and Performance, Public Exposure, June 2016

9. Monitoring Risk Compliance and Integrity

R. van Altena RA & Prof. S.C. Bleker-van Eyk

This chapter addresses the Why, How, What and Who of monitoring in general and in relation to compliance. The theory used in this chapter mainly consists of the internationally generally accepted framework for enterprise risk management, which is the COSO's Enterprise Risk Management (ERM) Framework and the related COSO Internal Control Framework.

9.1 INTRODUCTION TO COSO

The Committee of Sponsoring Organizations (COSO) of the Treadway Commission is a private sector initiative that is sponsored by organizations in the field of accounting and auditing, such as the American Institute of Certified Public Accountants (AICPA) and The Institute of Internal Auditors (IIA). Although it is a US-driven initiative, its impact is global due to the extraterritorial effect of US laws such as the Sarbanes-Oxley Act on financial reporting (2002) and due to its adoption by the globally active Big Four auditing firms, PwC, Deloitte, EY and KPMG, by means of their 'standardized approaches to audit'.

The Treadway Commission itself was founded in the US in 1985 and is dedicated to providing thought leadership and guidance on internal control, enterprise risk management, and fraud deterrence designed to improve organizational performance and oversight and to reduce the extent of fraud in organizations.[1] Over time COSO has

1. Due to questionable corporate political campaign finance practices and foreign corrupt practices in the mid-1970s, the US Securities and Exchange Commission (SEC) and the US Congress enacted campaign finance law reforms and the 1977 Foreign Corrupt Practices Act (FCPA) which criminalized transnational bribery and required companies to implement internal control programs. In response, the Treadway Commission, a private-sector initiative, was formed in 1985 to inspect, analyze and make recommendations on fraudulent corporate financial reporting. The Treadway Commission studied the financial information reporting system over the period from October 1985 to September 1987 and issued a report

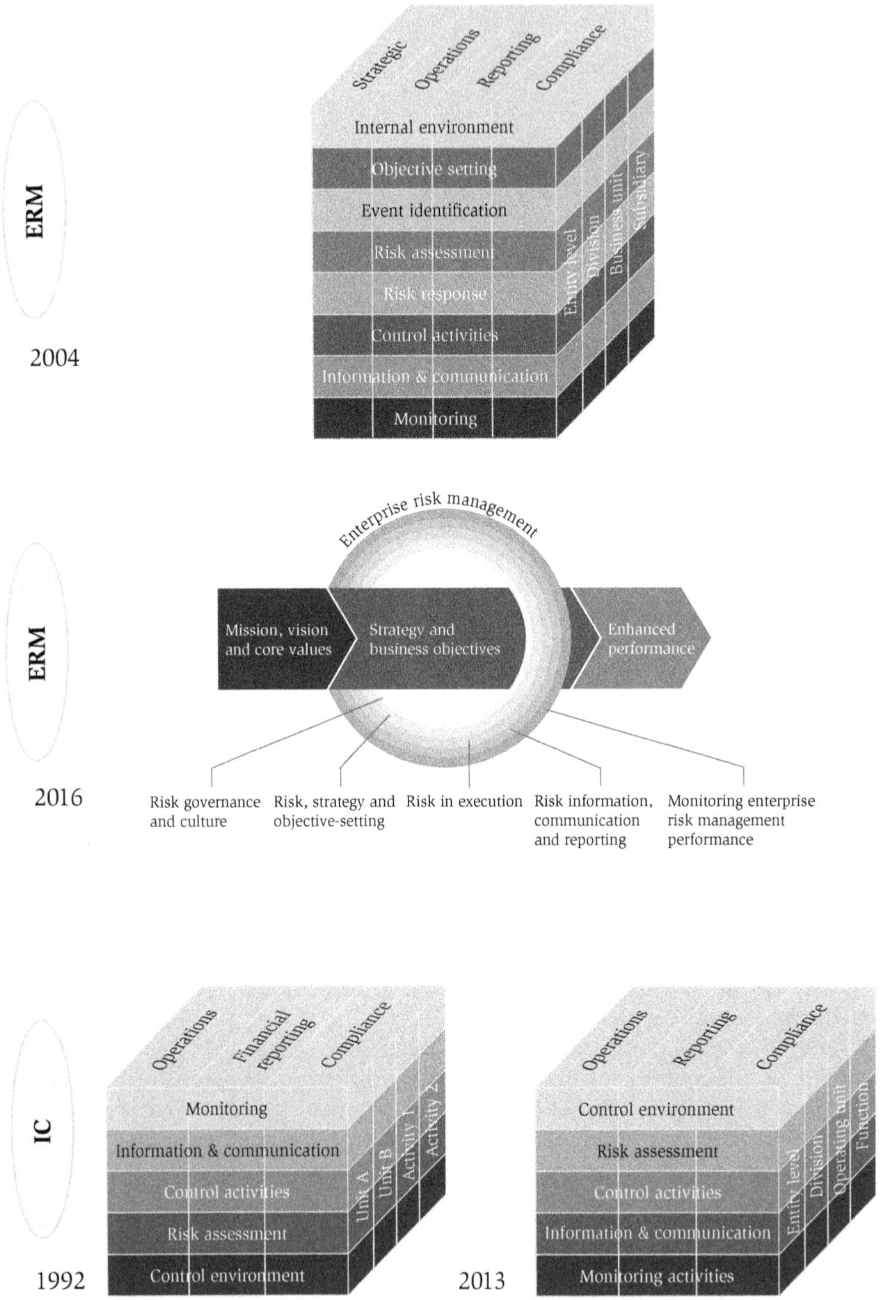

Figure 1: The COSO Cube(s)

used various models to communicate its thoughts on ERM and on Internal Control (IC) and the mechanisms of the frameworks and their components. Hereafter, we will show the various symbolic depictions used up to now. The years in which the models were published are also shown.

On the top layer you will find the models on ERM frameworks and at the bottom you will find the IC frameworks, in accordance with the idea that ERM and IC are interrelated, that ERM is about the organizational goals in a broad sense and that IC is at the heart of this. IC is the means of measuring and 'proving' the quality of risk management as a whole.

The first IC framework was published in 1992 following all kinds of financial reporting incidents, such as the so-called Junk Bond frauds. This first IC framework introduced a guided approach to the use of the components of internal control and introduced the term 'Control Environment'. This component focuses on the risk management culture within organizations. Relevant questions include: are people throughout the organization aware of the importance of risk management and do they understand the risk profile of the organization? Do management and the board of directors set the tone at the top? Is risk awareness and mitigation embedded in the values of the organization, the integrity and competence of staff? Is risk management part of management's philosophy and operating style and the way management assigns authority and responsibility? COSO thus introduced what we nowadays refer to as 'soft controls'.

The use of the 1992 IC Framework was catalyzed by the enactment in 2002 of the Sarbanes-Oxley Act. This law extends the long-standing requirement for public companies to maintain systems of internal control, requiring management to certify and the independent auditor to attest to the effectiveness of those systems.[2]

In 2004 COSO initiated a project and engaged PriceWaterhouseCoopers to develop a framework that would be readily usable by managements to evaluate and improve their organizations' enterprise risk management. High-profile business scandals and failures (e.g. Enron, Tyco International and WorldCom) led to calls for enhanced corporate governance and risk management, with a broader focus than internal control only.

In 2013 COSO published a new IC Framework. The changes made to update the 1992 Framework are evolutionary, not revolutionary. The 2013 Framework takes into account changes in the business environment and operations over the last 20 years. The 2013 Framework retains the definition of internal control and the COSO cube, including the five components of internal control: Control Environment, Risk Assessment, Control Activities, Information and Communication, and Monitoring Activities. The most significant change made in the 2013 Framework is the codification

---

of findings and recommendations in October 1987, the *Report of the National Commission on Fraudulent Financial Reporting*. As a result of this initial report, the Committee of Sponsoring Organizations (COSO) was formed and retained Coopers & Lybrand, a major CPA firm, to study the issues and author a report on an integrated framework of internal control. The original chairman of the Treadway Commission was James C. Treadway, Jr. (source: www.coso.org).

2. Original text Sarbanes-Oxley Act on https://www.gpo.gov/fdsys/pkg/PLAW-107publ204/pdf/PLAW-107publ204.pdf

of the 17 principles that support the five components. The 17 principles were fundamental concepts implicit in the 1992 Framework.[3]

In 2016 COSO published its new ERM Framework.[4] This update to the 2004 publication addresses the evolution of enterprise risk management and its new title 'Enterprise Risk Management – Aligning Risk with Strategy and Performance' recognizes the increasing importance of the connection between strategy and entity performance. As a result of not using the 'cube' as a model for ERM it becomes clearer that ERM is connected and that IC is part of ERM.

9.2 WHY MONITORING

By means of monitoring, an organization can consider how well the enterprise risk management components and related internal controls are functioning over time and in light of substantial changes. Monitoring is therefore related to the organization's risk management for objectives with regard to strategy, operations, (financial) reporting and compliance. The emphasis of monitoring is on the effectiveness (and efficiency) of internal controls.

In the IC 'cube' of COSO as shown in the previous paragraph you can see that monitoring is the fifth component of the framework and safeguards the effectiveness of the 'cube' as a whole.

According to COSO's Monitoring Guidance,[5] monitoring builds on two fundamental principles:

- ongoing and/or separate evaluations enable management to determine whether the other components of internal control continue to function over time; and
- internal control deficiencies are identified and communicated in a timely manner to those parties responsible for taking corrective action and to management and the board as appropriate.

In order to have effective and efficient monitoring, personnel with appropriate skills, authority and resources should be charged by management with addressing four fundamental questions:[6]

1. Have we *identified the meaningful risks to our objectives*, for example the risks related to producing accurate, timely and complete financial statements?

---

3. Internal Control – Integrated Framework (2013) was released by COSO on May 14, 2013. The 140-page 2013 Framework includes the following appendices: Glossary; Roles and Responsibilities; Considerations for Smaller Entities; Methodology for Revising the Framework; Public Comment Letters; Summary of Changes to the COSO Internal Control – Integrated Framework (1992); and Comparison with COSO Enterprise Risk Management – Integrated Framework. For more information see the press release and executive summary at www.coso.org.
4. Committee of Sponsoring Organizations of the Treadway Commission (COSO), Risk Management – Aligning Risk with Strategy and Performance, Public Exposure, June 2016.
5. COSO's 2006 Guidance on Monitoring Internal Control Systems: 2.
6. COSO – Guidance on Monitoring Internal Control Systems – Introduction (2009).

2. Which controls are *key controls* that will best support a conclusion regarding the effectiveness of internal control in those risk areas?
3. What *information* will be persuasive in telling us whether the controls are continuing to operate effectively?
4. Are we presently performing effective monitoring that is not well utilized in the evaluation of internal control, resulting in *unnecessary and costly further testing*?

These four questions are the basis for reports on the outcome of monitoring in terms of Key Risk Indicators (KRIs), related Key Controls and underlying evidence for the controls. These reports are also the basis for setting scenarios to trigger discussions among managers and staff about the risks the organization faces and the possible responses.

9.3 MONITORING AS A PROCESS ('HOW AND WHAT')

COSO provides guidance on the application of monitoring of internal control systems.[7] Figure 3 shows the various steps of a solid monitoring process. This is the kind of process we will generally find explicit or implicit in monitoring programs of officers who deal with so-called 'fresh-look monitoring'. The idea is that 'fresh-look monitoring' is applied by second line of defense officers in alignment with 'day-to-day ongoing monitoring' by first line officers and 'audits' by third line officers. In chapter 3 *supra* the various roles within the three lines of defense were described in more detail.

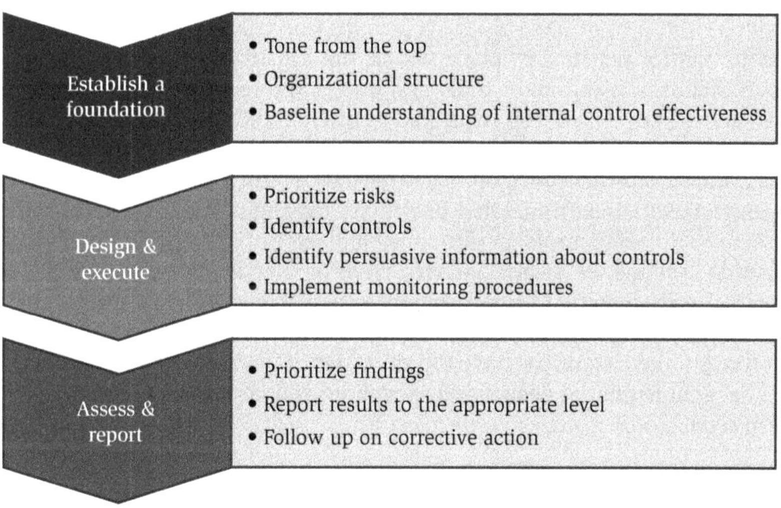

Figure 2: Monitoring process according to COSO

7. Internal Control – Integrated Framework; Guidance on Monitoring Internal Control Systems (Volume III – Application Techniques); the pictures in this section are derived from this source.

9.3.1 Establish a foundation

In order to achieve an effective and efficient monitoring process the organization establishes a foundation by means of 'tone from the top'; board and senior management advocate the need for and execution of a monitoring process. The organization establishes alignment within the three lines of defense in the organizational structure, in terms of both mandate and dynamic interaction. Management makes sure that all staff involved have a baseline understanding of internal control effectiveness, given the nature, structure and size of the organization. This is done through training and frequent communication, including access to policies, control standards and related procedures.

9.3.2 Design & execute

The actual design and execution comprises four phases:

Prioritize Risks – understand and prioritize risks to organizational objectives, taking into account events that may influence the achievement of organizational goals in terms of strategy (new products and markets), operations (efficiency), reporting (relevant and reliable) and compliance (meeting internal and external rules and codes). Therefore, design and execution of monitoring do not start by taking the internal control measures that are in place and 'checking' them as such, but with a risk-based approach.

Identify (Key) Controls – identify key controls across the internal control system that address those prioritized risks. In practice this will be done by using the 'risk and (key) control register' in place within the organization. Due to a traditional focus on accounting and audit trails and due to the requirements of laws such as the Sarbanes-Oxley Act, these registers are often well organized in relation to the 'reporting' objective.

As stated *supra*, examples of (internal) control activities are analytical top-level reviews, direct functional or activity oversight, management information processing, physical controls, performance indicators and segregation of duties. For information systems we distinguish two types of specific internal controls: general controls (IT management, IT infrastructure, security management, development and maintenance) and application controls (e.g. check digits, reasonableness tests). All the aforementioned examples have the character of 'hard controls'. Soft controls are also to be included in the design and execution; soft controls are described in more detail in section 10.4 *infra*.

Identify Information – identify information that will persuasively indicate whether the internal control system is operating effectively. In order to monitor the design, existence and effectiveness of internal controls, underlying information is needed; information that demonstrates who performed which internal control at what time (sequentially with other controls) and under what circumstances (e.g. segregation of duties). This information can be obtained through internal or external documents. In general external documents are considered to be more weighty as 'proof'.

Implement Monitoring - develop and implement cost-effective procedures (monitoring programs and test scripts) to gather and evaluate the identified persuasive information. This phase is about the actual testing by means of desktop review, data analysis, direct own observations, obtaining external information and interviews with staff involved. Cost-effectiveness can be achieved by focusing on alignment and integration of risks and controls. For example, some controls can be important for objective compliance and for objective reporting and are at least parts of the same primary business process. Nowadays the term 'embedded testing' is quite popular. It refers to the coming together of ongoing monitoring and fresh-look monitoring by having fresh-look monitoring make use of tests performed in the same manner (test procedure and related documentation) and with the same timing within the day-to-day monitoring.

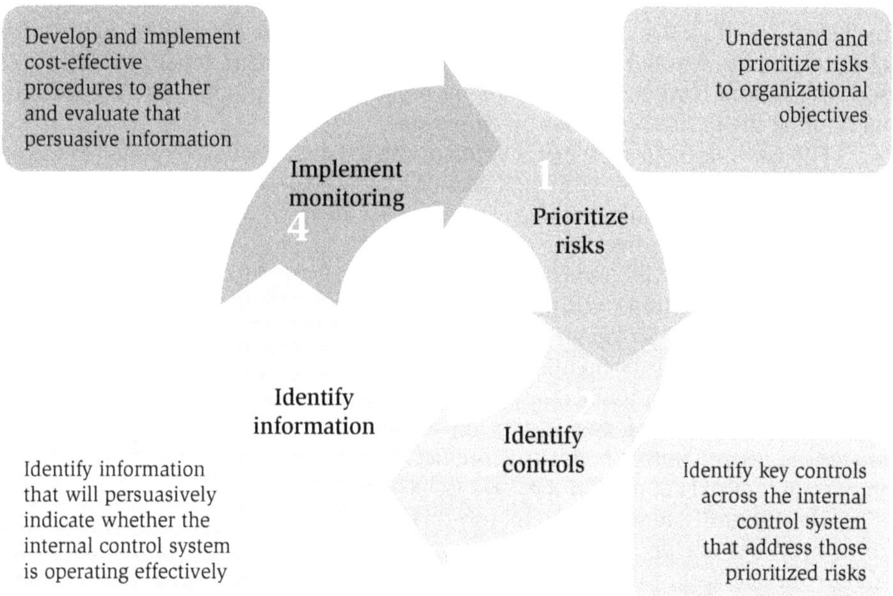

Figure 3: The four phases visualized

9.3.4 Assess & report

The final step of monitoring is about prioritizing findings, reporting results to the appropriate level and following up on corrective action. Prioritizing findings can be done in various ways: using a scale of high, medium and low impact of findings in relation to the importance and strength of the key controls; or using a scale that is related to net and desired risk; or using a scale from a managerial or stakeholder perspective. An attractive approach can be to use scoring scales that are used in major project and IT implementations, such as the 'COBIT maturity scale: non-existent, initial/ad hoc, repeatable but intuitive, defined, managed and measurable and optimized'.[8]

Always keep in mind that prioritization is first and foremost a professional judgment-driven process and that the findings only become effective when shared and accepted by the appropriate managerial level within the organization. The appropriate level is the level that is able to oversee the objectives of risk management and internal control of the organization and that is able and mandated to decide upon and implement a risk and control response. External regulators, shareholders and business partners are also important groups to keep in mind, although there will always be room for discussion on the level of transparency an organization will strive for with regard to internal controls.

9.4 MONITORING YOUR BUSINESS

In section 2.2 *supra* the soft and hard controls were discussed in relation to the three elements of the Fraud Triangle: opportunity, pressure and rationalization. In this section soft and hard controls will be discussed as ways to open the path towards monitoring the desired behavior by employees.

Soft controls focus on the promotion of desired integrity based on shared values and norms by management and employees. With the aid of soft controls, organizations try to create an environment where employees are aware of the desired behavior and act accordingly by self-imposing the desired norms in all their activities. These soft controls are carefully and consistently applied in the organization through a clear vision and mission; tone at the top, codes of conduct, training and employment conditions such as employment contracts, education, training, promotion, bonuses or penalties. Soft controls try to influence the behavior of employees, thereby ensuring compliant behavior through motivation and stimulation. The problem lies in the need for a continuous focus on the importance of acting in accordance with the shared values and norms of desired conduct. 'Soft controls' were first introduced as important internal controls in the 1992 COSO framework.

Hard controls, however, do not rely on the intrinsic motivation of the employee to comply, but are imposed on the employee by means of procedures, protocols, authorizations, segregation of duties, mandates, planning, etc. These hard controls are compulsory and are part of the routine requirements of the employees.

Hard controls can be automated or semi-automated and are hence easier to monitor. Soft controls are closely linked to what was described in sections 1.1 and 3.6 *supra* as *personal* integrity, making them more difficult to monitor. The monitoring of behavior needs a sharp eye and focused attention, and the bigger the organization, the more difficult it becomes.

As discussed in section 2.2 *supra*, the vast majority of all existing controls are aimed at the element of opportunity, preventing the misuse of means, funds or information, generally through hard controls and – in large organizations – where possible automated hard controls. Where pressure is concerned both hard controls and soft controls are applied. With regard to rationalization, soft controls are self-evident.

8. https://www.isaca.org/COBIT.

Both the hard and soft controls help control the equilibrium between opportunity, pressure and rationalization.

Monitoring soft controls is not easy. As a result, organizations must try carefully to lay down these soft controls in procedures and where possible 'harden' them with the aid of mandatory training and sign-off and through the use of computerized management systems. Monitoring is no longer an internal issue. External supervisory authorities stress the importance of (constant and consistent) monitoring. Particularly since the financial crisis of 2008, stringent laws and regulations and strict monitoring requirements concerning business processes (e.g. 'Segregation of Duties' is one of the key outcomes of the Sarbanes-Oxley Act) and employees' conduct have significantly 'hardened' the soft controls. To comply with these monitoring requirements, computerized management systems have become key. Not only in financial institutions, but also in other sectors, corporate governance and risk management requirements demand close monitoring of the important and vulnerable business processes. Tech companies offer specific management systems to monitor the most vulnerable processes such as third-party due diligence or export controls and/or sanctions. Existing management systems offer additional modules to assist in monitoring these vulnerable processes with the aid of inputting of the information the organization has already accumulated through the main management systems. However, using a new system or applying an extra module on the existing management system is just the beginning of a long journey leading to more compliant behavior through effective monitoring of processes. In fact, organizations are often quite disappointed because they do not have a working system but merely a license to use a platform that offers possibilities for using special fields within the platform that still have to be filled with compliance rules. All too often, the tool is not a monitoring tool but merely a platform that enables the organization to build a monitoring environment. A long and winding path will finally lead to such an environment. Organizations find this quite disappointing. Another problem the organization encounters on this path is the limited scope to connect the platform to the numerous other tools existing within the organization. An endless range of adaptors have to be knitted together in order to be able to assess the information that lies scattered within numerous departments and other platforms. Times are changing and vendors need to realize that they must assist the organization in devising manageable products that communicate easily with products from different vendors and offer safe and secure solutions to clients. Another option would be to introduce a new industry standard enabling communication between the different platforms.

Monitoring requires accurate data, while keeping in mind the many threats that surround the platform such as limitations due to privacy rules and regulations, 'identity and access management', attacks by hackers, power cuts etc. It is possible, but it will need a different mindset within the tech companies.

Another problem that occurs with computerized management systems is the user-friendliness of the system. The systems (platforms) are built by highly qualified engineers who develop state of the art solutions. However, these systems have to be used by average employees. The lack of ready usability and user-friendliness are in fact compliance risks. When systems are difficult to use and the employee needs to gather information from different sources, the temptation to circumvent the system will increase, thus increasing the possibility of non-compliance. For example, if in the case of third-party due diligence an employee has to fill out a computerized form with information on the third party and possibly its ultimate beneficial owner from far and near, the employee will be tempted to circumvent the system and engage directly in a deal with the third party.

The manufacturers of the (financial) systems should develop systems that are easy to use and safeguard compliance at the same time.

What if the ultimate beneficial owner turns out to be a sanctioned party? Generating information from different sources that are but a click away is possible and user-friendly. Also, the look and feel should be user-friendly; no unnecessary information, just letting the employee go through the motions, while also generating information for others such as compliance officers. Finally, the proverbial 'stop' button is necessary in vulnerable processes to prevent wrong deals being done.

The issue of user-friendliness brings us to increasing the possibility of compliance with the softer shared values and norms through the use of an intranet, which would bring great benefits for the monitoring of soft controls. Even in organizations with several hundred employees it is worthwhile setting up a compliance intranet site that contains all the necessary information such as the training the employee still has to undergo, the compliance procedures applicable to his position, frequently asked questions, etc. Also, tooling can be linked to the intranet site offering direct access to a whistleblower tool or a tool to claim expenses such as travel costs and entertainment. All these tools offer monitoring possibilities. However, when creating such an intranet site, it is important to bear in mind that the employee's attention has to be drawn to the intranet site. This can be achieved by linking tools to the intranet and – why not – a little fun factor.

The importance of compliance has increased dramatically since the beginning of this century, and so, therefore, has the significance of monitoring of both soft and hard controls. Many of the soft controls are rapidly 'hardening', but the human factor remains the most important – and also difficult – element to control.

10. Stakeholder and Reputation Management

F.R.P.M. van der Grint[1]

10.1 INTRODUCTION

The worldwide flow of scandals related to fraud, bribery, mismanagement, personal gain, boardroom fights, etc., have put compliance in the spotlight in almost all self-respecting organizations. In some cases this has been demanded by regulators (e.g. banking after Libor), whereas in others it is a demonstration of good behavior and/or change towards shareholders and (legal) authorities. As a result, the increase in the importance of compliance leads to an increase in expectations. This triggers a new challenge for organizations. Their stakeholders all have different ideas about what compliance is, what they can expect and what it can do (not what it cannot do ...).

Traditionally, the compliance function looks at laws, rules and regulations enacted by lawmakers and regulators, and at rules and bylaws set out by companies in integrity management guidelines and regulations. It is quite a judicial function, where the rules of the game are available in writing, there for everyone to read and to interpret and discuss. But societal developments have added new rules which are not so clear and certainly not written down. Companies and organizations have increasingly become actors in the court of public opinion. And public opinion does not judge according to formalistic rules; it judges according to which corporate behavior society finds acceptable or unacceptable at any given time. And what is acceptable today may not be acceptable tomorrow.

In the same vein, it is important to understand that we live not only in a democracy with its known rules, but at the same time in a 'mediacracy'. The power of (social) media in the process of forming society's ideas of what it expects from organizations and corporations has become much greater over the past decade or so. Organizations therefore also have to play by the rules of this mediacracy. And those rules change all the time and are not in any way formalized. It makes the job of assessing compliance and managing risks exponentially more difficult. It also makes the job of the compliance

1. With thanks to Ingo Heijnen for his contribution to this chapter.

manager much more complex: it requires an ability to judge behavior not only on the basis of the formal rules, but also on what is socially acceptable.

One can argue that it is not the job of a compliance function to assess an organization's compliance with society's definition of acceptable behavior. Reputation managers are expected to do this and to advise senior management on how to adjust behavior in order to maintain and strengthen the organization's reputation as an actor in society – and with that its license to operate. And while this is indeed the traditional segregation of functions, today's reality requires a different approach. It is in the best interest of organizations to broaden the (perceived and formalized) responsibility for managing risks for the said license to operate. Compliance managers are naturally well placed to play a role in this development. Their formalized involvement in (re)defining corporate behavior gives them a natural position in assessing how an organization is coping with the informal rules of being a good, and therefore acceptable, citizen. Under this premise, it makes sense for anyone in a compliance function to understand how an organization makes an impact on its surroundings, on the ecosystem in which it operates. Understanding who your stakeholders are, how they relate to you as an organization and to each other, what their evoked set of norms and values is, how they are being influenced and how they can be influenced – having knowledge as well as an operational understanding of these aspects – makes the compliance manager infinitely more effective in his role.

In this chapter, we will therefore cover the following aspects of managing reputation and risk, with a focus on what is known as stakeholder and issue management:

1. How reputations are formed and why it pays off to build and defend them.
2. Reputation management in a mediocracy.
3. The role of leadership behavior.
4. The importance of trust and credibility.
5. Stakeholders: analysis.
6. Managing your stakeholders to manage risks.

10.2 HOW REPUTATIONS ARE FORMED AND WHY IT PAYS OFF TO BUILD AND DEFEND THEM

Back in 2002, the IKEA retail chain and the Van der Valk hotel chain faced a very similar problem in the Netherlands. They were confronted with collapsing rooftops at one of their sites. These situations occurred more or less at the same time. IKEA's rooftop at its Utrecht site gave way because of a surplus of rainwater – suggesting faulty construction. Van der Valk's parking deck roof in Tiel collapsed spontaneously – the result of a 'stupid mistake' when the deck was constructed. Public reaction to the occurrences, however similar they seem technically, were strikingly different. IKEA was off the hook very quickly – it was not their fault that such heavy rains fell that summer. Van der Valk's management, however, came under heavy scrutiny. Whereas the IKEA store was allowed to reopen only one week after the accident, Van der Valk's motel had to remain closed for two months, with strict government inspections at all of the company's sites.

A study of both cases demonstrates different reactions among similar stakeholder groups. The media criticized the Van der Valk management, but not IKEA's. The media also reported on the danger to customers at the Van der Valk site; it was not even mentioned in the IKEA reports. Local government reacted strongly against Van der Valk, but were invisible in the case of IKEA. The responsible ministry started a 'thorough investigation' of all Van der Valk outlets, but nothing of the kind for IKEA.

What caused this difference in stakeholder reactions? The overriding dominant factor is reputation. IKEA's reputation as a socially responsible, employee- and customer-friendly company meant that media and politics were restrained. But Van der Valk's reputation as a more closed business played against them.

While reputation is a widely and often used term in boards and, especially at times of crisis, is seen as the most important company asset to manage, today it is still not the best understood management aspect. People use reputation as a generic word, but what it really is and how it should be managed is often poorly developed within entities. The most frequently used description of reputation is that of Fombrun.[2] Together with a team of communications scientists he developed six reputation drivers, each of which can be managed and therefore influenced.

Fombrun's reputation drivers are:

- emotional appeal (from stakeholders to a company);
- vision & leadership (of the company management and board);
- financial performance (often the main measure of success);
- workplace environment (as experienced by employees and perceived by external audiences);
- social responsibility (in relation to the 'license to operate');
- products & services (why do we have this company in the first place).

Although the words that describe the drivers may differ (other words used are innovation, governance and citizenship), the advantage of using a set of drivers to determine reputation is that drivers can measured. By doing so, reputation becomes more than just a gut feeling, a temporary suggestion based on unfavorable press cuttings, or reactions in the CEO's peer group.

The importance of managing one's reputation is now beyond discussion. Fombrun & Low[3] wrote in their 'The Real Value of Reputation': 'Global forces are causing shifts in public perceptions of companies that in turn drive changes in regulatory, political and financial structures around the world. Companies that enjoy strong and favorable reputations have a competitive advantage in these global markets. Iconic brands and exemplary reputations help companies "translate" their offering to new customers, because the values they embody provide a shorthand interpretation of what they have to offer.'

While Fombrun's drivers are mostly used by communications professionals, we believe the drivers in the model of Brammer & Pavelin[4] are equally interesting. They have found that reputation is determined by:

- social performance;
- financial performance;

2. Van Riel & Fombrun 2007.
3. Fombrun & Low 2011.
4. Brammer & Pavelin 2006, pp. 435–455.

- market risk;
- long-term ownership;
- business activities.

Although one could argue that this is just another mix of words for the same principles, the interesting part of Brammer & Pavelin's view is that they herald the need for a 'fit' between a company's social performance and the expectations among stakeholders.

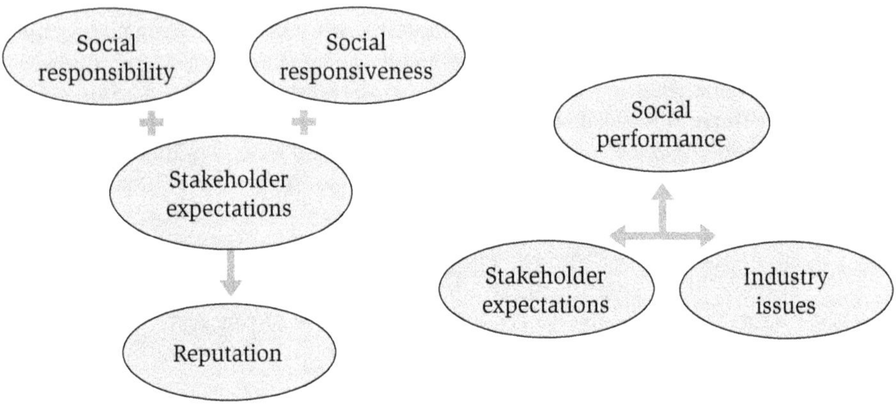

Figures 1 and 2: Models according to Fobrum and Brammer & Pavelin

If corporate social performance could be split between social responsibility (driven by the company and sector) and social responsiveness (driven by society), both should be linked and related to the stakeholder expectations. If not, social responsibility can be an expensive but inefficient, if not counterproductive, exercise. As such, reputation management is the management of the 'fit' between the company's social performance, the issues related to the industry in which it is operating and the expectations of stakeholders surrounding the company.

So why is it important to build and defend a reputation? One could argue, and many people have, that damage to reputation is only temporary and that in any event it will not harm or affect the core of the organization. There are enough companies and organizations out there with a bad or damaged reputation but with a thriving business. Think of large oil companies, think of pharmaceuticals, to name just two. There is, however, enough scientific evidence that suggests that companies with a good reputation perform better on the stock exchange, will attract better talent and will have better business deals. But, most of all, a sound reputation provides a buffer for when things do go wrong. The court of public opinion will be more lenient on those who have earned their trust previously and have been able to create a positive, reliable, trustworthy perception.

What does this mean for a compliance manager?

Clearly, compliance experts have to deal with laws, rules, company values and culture and in some sectors also an 'oath'. But, in relation to reputation management, the compliance function should also be aware of the relationship between the company's social performance, industry issues and stakeholder expectations and how these influence the risk of a company losing its license to operate.

10.3 REPUTATION MANAGEMENT IN A MEDIACRACY

In matters of compliance and integrity, the legal and financial contexts are not the only aspects to take into account. The social context in which an organization operates is equally important. This context today is largely based on the fact that we live in a mediacracy. And this has an effect on how stakeholders interact with organizations, since stakeholders base their judgment of a reputation in part on information they receive from these parties, including media. A compliance manager needs to anticipate this reality, which is hard and becoming harder every day.

One definition of the concept of 'mediacracy', or media-democracy, is an expression of the idea that (democratic) countries are mainly ruled by those who have the power to influence public opinion through the media. Often this concept is also applicable to the media themselves, who are a steering power in a country. The concept is a mix of Greek and Latin, meaning 'ruling through media'.

A mediacracy has four characteristics:

- *A focus on people and what they are doing wrong.* The best stories are about people, not about companies. What goes wrong is news; was goes well is not.
- *Fierce competition between media.* Media are in a constant rat race. And they have to cope with 'public journalists' who broadcast constantly on social media.
- *Extreme populism.* What is seen in politics throughout the world is also seen in the media. Populism leads the editorial agenda. On this, we should stress that because of Brexit and the US elections there is a renewed debate on the value of truth. Whether this will reduce populism in media remains to be seen.
- *Image is everything.* People share photos and video. Those with the best image win the media battle.

Whoever is involved in the science of reputation management and managing the license to operate for an organization will have to understand how media need to be managed. Not only traditional, journalistic media, but also social media. There is a school that says that directing the dynamics in these media nowadays is impossible. The speed at which news and stories are disseminated is seen as just too high - an organization cannot keep up. We tend to disagree. The management of stories, how they are delivered and by whom has never been so important.

There are certain truths and rules to be taken into account. Here are the top five truths when dealing with the mediacracy:

1. *Speed is of the essence* - when dealing with issues, incidents and/or crises, communicate - fast. There is no time for long deliberations. Because while you are still thinking, there are people out there who will not wait to express their opinions or reveal new facts, thereby upping the pressure. An organization can gain speed by preparing for the worst case.

2. *Think in scenarios* – and by doing so, be prepared for what else could come your way. It will make your response time much shorter and your impact a lot greater.
3. *Communicate with facts* – and make sure the media possess the correct facts. Fight 'untruths' or 'alternative truths'.
4. *Create visible leadership* – be seen and be heard at times when it matters, show you take the lead and create new perspectives for stakeholders involved. To avoid misunderstanding, demonstrating leadership does not necessarily mean your leaders should always be the visible communicators themselves.
5. *Calibrate your moral compass* – and make sure that what you find morally acceptable is echoed by your stakeholders. Show responsibility and show that you care about your surroundings and the world at large.

Finally there is one other important truth to consider: in crises, reputational damage always occurs first, often long before financial and/or legal damage. Today there are still legal battles about companies that no longer even exist (e.g. World Online), while the reputational damage was there immediately and at least contributed to the downfall of these companies. Similarly, Volkswagen's reputation was already heavily damaged by the Dieselgate scandal, long before the financial settlements were reached.

10.4 THE ROLE OF LEADERSHIP BEHAVIOR

Leaders and executives play a crucial role when an organization is being judged on its social performance, intentions and credibility. More than ever before, we live in an era when an organization is measured by the behavior of its leaders. There is an enormous focus on 'people' when the media and politicians set out to judge. This is true of all types of corporations, whether they are for profit or not for profit.

A general sense of distrust towards corporate executives and politicians has emerged from the scandals that kicked off the 2008 crisis, and even before that, when Enron in the United States collapsed. Time and again, some bad examples among executives and politicians have shown behavior that was seen as egocentric, greedy, snobbish, elitist and other similar traits. This (perceived) behavior by executives, influences more than before the overall perception and reputation of an organization. When a board member shows conduct that does not comply with what stakeholders expect, the whole company will come under fire.

Today, therefore, when an organization is in crisis, a high-ranking scapegoat is rarely far away and will be sacrificed to defend the corporate reputation. At Rabobank, there were two board members who did not survive the Libor scandal. Tony Hayward had to resign as CEO of BP after the Deepwater Horizon disaster and in 2016 Saatchi & Saatchi CEO Kevin Roberts was sacked after denying gender bias in the advertising world. Those board members were not necessarily the ones who created the problems. But they were held accountable for the culture they allowed to develop within their organizations. In the case of Hayward, it did not help that at some time during the crisis when the oil had destroyed a lot of natural resources around Florida's coastline and fishermen could not go out and earn their wages, he complained that he 'wanted his life back'. These examples show that leaders are judged on a wide range of behavior, not only related to financial aspects or technical dramas, but increasingly also based on aspects that 'society deems unacceptable'. Sometimes, as in Kevin Roberts' case, it is the CEO's own behavior or utterances that lead to his downfall, whereas in other cases a leader is simply held accountable for failures in his organization that just should not have occurred, irrespective of the fact that the leadership itself was not directly responsible.

In this age of mediacracy, socially unacceptable behavior will not only be scrutinized but will lead to public defamation of individuals. In those cases, as so often, a picture says more than a thousand words. We have seen once respected leaders literally being depicted as criminals, including with black bars over their eyes in newspaper pictures, following revelations of behavior that was certainly unacceptable but not necessarily criminal. Actors on social media are ruthless in this respect – individuals' sound reputations can be destroyed in a matter of hours on Facebook and Twitter.

This insight should lead, and indeed does lead, to a culture of more scrutiny within organizations. Behavior that was once accepted or ignored will no longer be tolerated. It is just too costly from a trust and therefore reputation point of view. Leading by example has taken on a new dimension and is absolutely essential when it comes to displaying the right behavior. But since leaders too are only human, it requires an open, honest and bold corporate staff to help them display this and not go astray. It is typically the reputation and compliance managers who can play this role, supported by the corporate legal function.

10.5 THE IMPORTANCE OF TRUST AND CREDIBILITY

There is also another way of looking at the interaction between reputation and stakeholders. Especially at times of incidents and crises, companies start to communicate about 'restoring trust'. Whether this a smart way of communicating is a separate discussion, but let us look at 'trust' a little more closely.

$$\text{Trust} = \text{intention} \times \text{result}$$

Our definition of trust is straightforward: trust is built upon the intention of a company in relation to the results the company is achieving. And results here can be seen as results within the range of drivers as described by either Fombrun or Brammer & Pavelin.

The aggregate of a company's intentions forms the basis of its existence. It is the DNA of the organization. Sometimes it is called 'mission'; a more modern term is 'purpose'. Companies that have an ill developed intention and/or a poorly communicated intention have a more difficult task in establishing trust. They have to rely on the much used goals-strategy-results approach, which will only establish a temporary and – what we call – 'minor trust'. This is the type of trust that can easily disappear with an incident or several quarters of disappointing financial results.

To gain major trust, companies must not only have a clear and communicated intention, they also have to have a well described perspective for all their stakeholders. Intention and perspective are by their nature long-term, and therefore much more suitable for establishing sustainable trust – the kind of trust that helps a company to protect its reputation, even in difficult times.

Credibility

So trust is an operative word for reputation managers, and of course also for compliance managers. The same goes for the word credibility. Both functions in an organization, reputation management and compliance management, thrive by establishing and safeguarding the credibility of their employers. In communication campaigns, credibility is the springboard towards an authoritative position, which is a position that provides the highest reputational resilience.

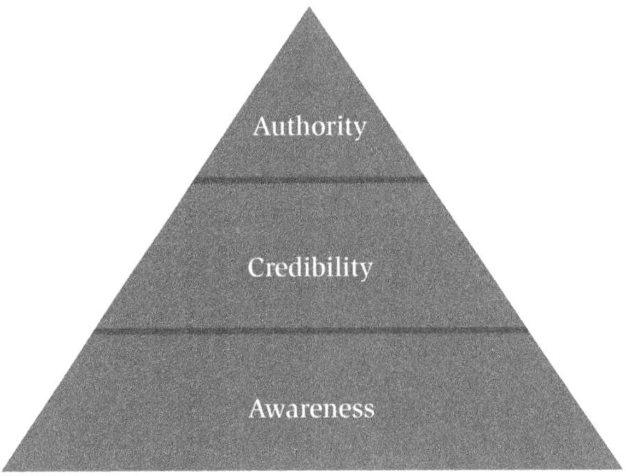

Figure 3: Credibility is the springboard towards authority

Many leaders of organizations strive for positions of authority. We have often seen company position papers or communication briefings that either try to achieve it or pretend they are already there and want to build upon it. What is often forgotten is the fact that a position of authority is impossible without an established position of credibility. While everybody understands that the statement 'I am credible' does not have any power and even comes across as pretty silly, there are still enough managers to be found who believe 'I am an authority' is less silly. Just look at the websites where the corporate description contains the words 'we are an authority in …'

There is no authority without credibility and there is no credibility without awareness. Yet awareness can be bought. High advertising budgets spent in print and online media can bring products and companies the awareness they strive for. For the most part they are also easy to measure. Credibility, however, cannot be bought, for the simple reason that you can only earn it.

$$\text{Credibility} = \text{trust} \times \text{recognition}$$

We have described *supra* how sustainable trust relies on an organization's intentions. Since credibility relies on trust, it is clear that there is also a tangible relationship between credibility and intentions.

Trust and recognition are both to be provided by third parties – try to sell 'I trust myself' or 'I give myself recognition'. Yet trust can be steered by means of intentions, and intentions can be clearly communicated, demonstrated and proved. Furthermore, trust can be steered by means of results, and results can also be communicated, demonstrated and proved.

Given the importance of recognition in gaining credibility, one has to look at stakeholders to gain recognition. Third parties – spread across all relevant stakeholder groups – can provide recognition, but must have a reason to do so. That makes credibility dependent on the interaction with stakeholders. And stakeholders mostly rely on information provided by third parties if they judge companies.[5] In the next section the most important aspects of stakeholder management are reviewed.

10.6 STAKEHOLDERS: ANALYSIS

'Make your friends before you need them.'

Stakeholders are not necessarily your friends. But they can certainly be friends, if managed well. First and foremost, stakeholders are those groups of individuals who have a vested interest in an organization. So stakeholders are those people who will have exposure to the organization in some shape or form and who will have a view on the acceptability of that organization. In that capacity, stakeholders can determine whether or not an organization has a sustainable future. Because, with enough negative pressure from stakeholders, organizations can be in very dire straits and ultimately they may collapse. The Medici Bank experienced this already back in 1494, when the excessive lifestyle of the owners caused stakeholders to lose their trust in the bank.

Communicating with stakeholders is often seen as the playground for communications departments. This is an enormous misunderstanding of what stakeholder management is, what it entails and whose responsibility it is. Ultimately, stakeholder management is the responsibility of the board(s). But only in few instances do boards discuss their full stakeholder field, let alone have awareness of who the key players are in each of the relevant groups.

As we have said before, compliance managers need to be aware of stakeholder expectations. They should see them as one of the drivers for compliance and integrity in their understanding of a company. This means a compliance manager cannot have the luxury of looking into only one stakeholder group (e.g. solely regulatory stakeholders). In today's society a variety of audiences form opinions on issues related to compliance and integrity.

Infra we describe some fundamental aspects of stakeholder management, all of which can be helpful in determining key players surrounding your own company.

Inventory

The inventory of relevant stakeholders can best be drawn up per group:

- shareholders (founders, family owners, stock owners);
- financial community (investors, analysts, banks, insurers);
- customers (end users of products and/or services);

---

5. Mahon & Wartick 2003, pp. 19–35.

- trade parties (e.g. wholesale, retail);
- suppliers (producers, OEMs);
- boards (management, supervisory board);
- employees (in various layers);
- works council(s);
- unions;
- pension funds;
- government (national, regional, local);
- politicians;
- EU and EC;
- regulators;
- supervisors;
- consumer organizations;
- NGOs;
- universities;
- sector organizations;
- competition (peers);
- media;
- opinion leaders;
- the public.

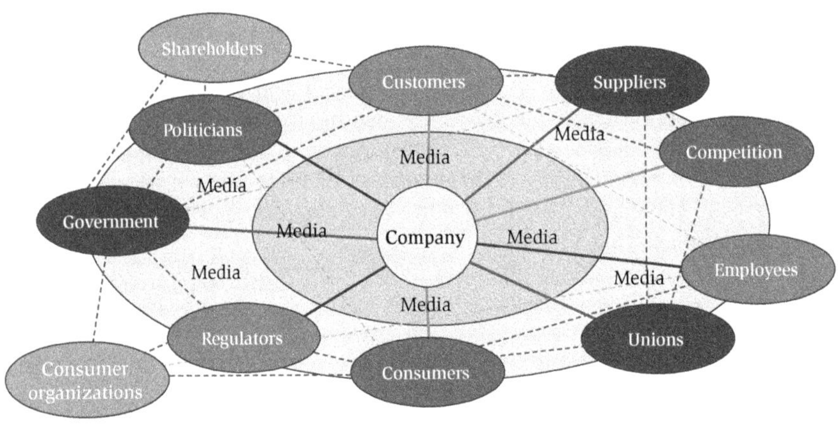

Figure 4: Stakeholders' model

In order to make stakeholder management effective, specific names of persons for each stakeholder group need to be mentioned. This is a critical and ongoing effort – every company must be aware of the key influencers. But being aware is not enough, nor is it enough to simply keep a list of people. A relationship needs to be established. This relationship is key for the organization to ensure support and even endorsement from third parties in cases when it really matters. Corporations under scrutiny will always be looking for third parties, for their stakeholders, to provide them with support, verbally or actively, to help them out. If and when such third-party endorsement is required – and in today's environment this may be the case every single day of the week – the third parties of choice need to know the company, its intentions, results and perspective. Only then can stakeholders put an organization's or executive's behavior into perspective and provide a new angle for bystanders watching and judging.

As it is impossible to establish a meaningful relationship in one day, ongoing investment in stakeholder relations is an important requirement. Especially in times of crisis, third-party support is vital. Therefore we very much believe that 'making friends before you need them' is a truth that should not be underestimated.

Mapping

Knowing who your stakeholders are is one thing. Knowing what their position is in relation to important subjects for the organization is quite another. While stakeholder inventory is an ongoing exercise, stakeholder mapping is even more an activity that requires continuous contacts and monitoring. Several mapping tools are available and which one is best depends on the situation and issues at hand. Here we present a number of these tools, as a reference.

Circle of Influence

This tool is used to determine which stakeholders around your organization are in favor or against certain positions/viewpoints/products (themes and/or issues). It shows the level of support and opposition at various tier levels.

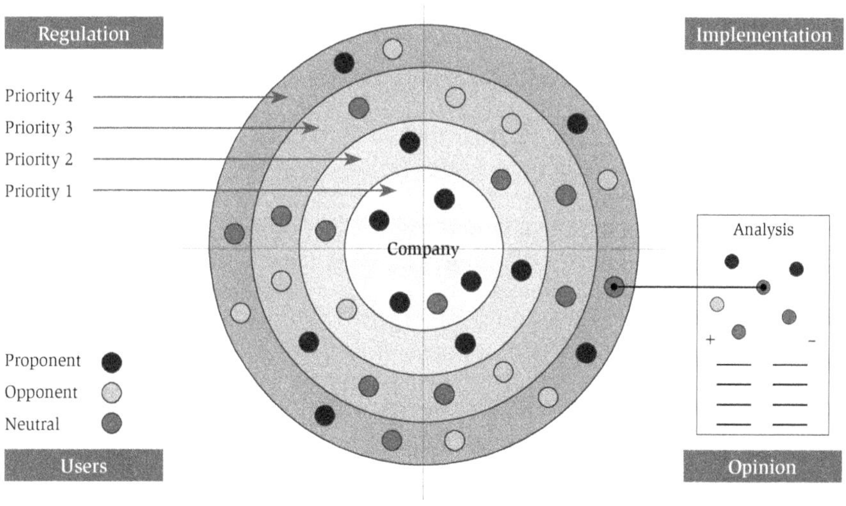

Figure 5: Circle of Influence

Stakeholder Position

Another much used tool is the Stakeholder Position quadrant, in which supporters and opposition are mapped against two (related) topics. It shows immediately where you have enough third-party endorsement and where you still have some work to do. With regular updates, it can also track changes of positions.

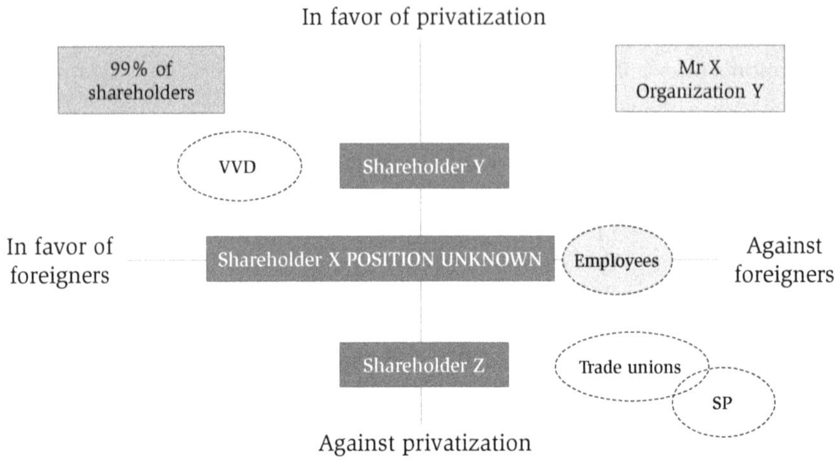

Figure 6: Stakeholder Position quadrant

Stakeholder Network Analysis

A more sophisticated but also more expensive tool is the Stakeholder Network Analysis. It shows which influencers are influencing others. By making the right combinations, approaching stakeholders can be much more effective.

10.7 MANAGING STAKEHOLDERS TO MANAGE RISK

Establishing a relationship with stakeholders so that you can call upon them in times of need is not the only objective of active stakeholder management. Having ongoing conversations and interactions will also allow you to gain insights into the stakeholder's own agenda, themes, and focus areas.

For instance, interacting with trade unions on a regular basis provides you with insights into their areas of interest – and therefore provides the organization with intelligence concerning the potential impact that actions by the unions may have on the credibility, trust and/or reputation of the organization and its leadership. Engaging with customers on top of the normal business course of action also provides important intelligence that allows a company, for instance, to manage expectations or provide an early warning for potential publicly voiced dissatisfaction.

Active stakeholder management is the action of *listening* to stakeholders, *engaging* with them in conversations and *influencing* their perception and acceptance of the organization. By doing so, an organization can generate intelligence, prevent damage and therefore manage risks. Stakeholder management may not be the first task of the compliance manager, as other functions will be better suited to it. But the compliance manager needs to understand if and how a company is actively managing these parties – because this provides a level of prediction for the company's ability to prevent damage and to contain issues.

BIBLIOGRAPHY

Brammer & Pavelin 2006
S. Brammer & S. Pavelin, 'Corporate reputation and social performance: the importance of fit', *Journal of Management Studies*, 43(3), 2006, pp. 435–455.

Fombrun & Low 2011
C.J. Fombrun & J. Low, 'The Real Value of Reputation', *Communication World*, 28(6), 2011, pp. 18–22.

Mahon & Wartick 2003
J.F. Mahon & S.L. Wartick, *'Dealing with stakeholders: how reputation, credibility and framing influence the game'*, *Corporate Reputation Review*, vol.6, 2003, pp. 19–35.

Van Riel & Fombrun 2007
C.B.M. van Riel & C. J. Fombrun, *Essentials of corporate communication- Implementing practices for effective reputation management*, London: Routledge 2007.

PART III – REGULATION, SUPERVISION AND ENFORCEMENT

'Just ten commandments, proclaimed by Moses, held the entire Jewish people in fear of God, in the exercise of virtue, justice and patriotism, for hundreds of years. To expand their republic and protect the entire empire, the Romans needed just 12 extremely short tables. We have 60 shelves full of laws and every day we produce new regulations.'

(After the Florentine architect Leon Baptista Alberti, 15th century)[1]

1. Gestel and Hertogh 2006, p. 27, note 28; found and translated from the German in P. Noll, 'Der Mensch und die Gesetze', from: P. Noll, *Gedanken über Unruhe und Ordnung*, Zürich 1985, p. 166.

11. Regulation and Supervision on Financial Markets[1]

R.A.M. Houben

11.1 INTRODUCTION

Regulation and supervision of the private (and semi-public) sector including the financial markets is not new and has existed since the dawn of time.[2] In the 1980s and 1990s there was a trend towards liberalization, privatization and deregulation. This was based on the economic insight that – with sufficient competition – the private sector produces goods and services more cheaply than the government, private production better meets the wishes of customers and there is greater innovation in the private sector.[3] Central to these objectives is the creation and maintenance of market forces. There must be sufficient competition, few barriers if any to market entry and sufficient incentives for technological renewal. Perfectly operating markets (100% efficient market forces) with sufficient competition, no barriers to entry and sufficient incentives for technological renewal plainly do not exist.[4] This is considered to be market failure and is viewed as socially undesirable.

In other words, companies' behavior jeopardizes desirable or economically efficient wealth distribution. Market regulations are required as well as supervisors who monitor compliance with these rules to ensure that companies comply with

1. Some passages in this chapter have been drawn from the article by R.A.M. Houben previously published in the *Jaarboek Compliance 2013*, or an edited version of it, see Houben 2013. This will be stated in this chapter.
2. There have been thinkers who have tried to explain society on the basis that people once lived without rules and with unlimited freedom, but for various reasons (such as safety) entered into a societal (or social) contract with each other whereby they surrendered certain freedoms. Important founders of this social contract are Thomas Hobbes, John Locke, Jean-Jacques Rousseau, Immanuel Kant and John Rawls.
3. SEO 2005, p. 1.
4. Ibid. In the case of market forces, for example, there is always a trend towards the formation of monopolies.

them.[5] The common factor here is that this supervision promotes a public interest (including an economic interest). Market regulations protect consumers and other participants against market failure.[6]

The dividing line between regulation and supervision is thin and these terms are sometimes confused. There are many supervisors in the Netherlands. Supervision can be divided into state supervision, market supervision and supervision in the semi-public and private sector.[7] Some sources even state that the Netherlands has become a country of supervision.[8] Primacy in regulation, however, rests in principle with the legislator. Supervisors in the financial and other markets only have limited scope to set rules themselves within a specific mandate.[9]

The financial crisis in 2008 clearly showed that supervision of financial markets had failed worldwide. As a result, not only have a large number of new, complex laws and regulations been introduced at national, European and global level for (mostly financial) companies, but supervision has also been reformed in such a way as to avoid another crisis.[10] In this regard people also speak of a 'regulation, supervision and enforcement reflex'.[11] Although it can be argued that there is a need for this, it can also be observed that legal certainty and legal protection have come under pressure. There is no or hardly any deregulation with regard to laws and regulations in the financial sector. Furthermore, the effectiveness of these measures is difficult to ascertain. Self-regulation could be an (additional) alternative, but this has proven to be difficult to put into practice.[12]

In this chapter the focus is on regulation and supervision of the financial markets and on the financial undertakings operating in those markets. Supervision refers to market supervision by the market supervisors with a focus on financial supervisors.[13] The chapter does not go into the specifics of supervision by the government, as in the case of government inspections.[14] It does, however, draw on insights from

---

5. Baarsma 2010, pp. 3–4; Aelen 2014, pp. 3, 7 and 97–109; Raaijmakers 2013a, pp. 19 and 23; Schleifer 2005, p. 440.
6. Aelen 2014, p. 3.
7. The latter refers to self-regulation and self-supervision. *See* section 11.2.5 *infra*.
8. Baarsma 2010, p. 3.
9. *See* section 11.2.4 and notes 69 and 70 *infra* concerning Art. 1:29 of the Wft.
10. *See also* the De Wit Committee 2010 and the De Wit Committee 2012.
11. That means that after every (societal) incident, whether major or minor, new rules are introduced (or existing rules tightened) in order to prevent any recurrence in the future. Compliance with new rules must be supervised and supervisory bodies must be capable of enforcement in the event of non-compliance.
12. *See* section 12.2.5 *infra*.
13. Market supervisors can be deemed to include the AFM, DNB, the Authority for Consumers & Markets (ACM), the Dutch Data Protection Authority (AP), the Netherlands Gaming Authority (Ksa) and the Dutch Healthcare Authority (NZa). Financial supervisors are the AFM and DNB.
14. Examples of government supervision are the Employment Inspectorate, the Health Care Inspectorate, the Inspectorate of Education and the Netherlands Food and Consumer Product Safety Authority. Examples of self-supervision are the Royal Netherlands Institute of Registered Accountants (NIVRA) and the Dutch Bar Association.

research into regulation and supervision in general, i.e. including supervision by the government.[15]

Section 11.2 deals with regulation of the financial markets and the most common theories from an economic perspective. It also deals with subjects such as market failure, deregulation and self-regulation, as well as the advantages and disadvantages of open and closed standards. As an interlude, section 11.3 includes a brief digression on financial supervision regulations and the consequences resulting from the financial crisis. Section 11.4 deals with supervision of the financial markets and the financial undertakings operating in it from the perspective of the government, the supervisor and academia. This chapter comes to a close with section 11.5, which deals with a number of theories relating to the actual or desired effectiveness of regulation and supervision of financial markets and financial undertakings.

11.2 REGULATION OF THE FINANCIAL MARKETS

11.2.1 Theories of regulation

11.2.1.1 Introduction

The term financial markets covers more than just the capital markets, encompassing all the parties involved in the financial sector.[16] It is also possible to speak of economic markets, although this term is broader.[17]

According to Aelen,[18] supervision is seen from the perspective of economic theory as one of the instruments of government intervention intended to counter and resolve market failure. She states that this idea results from the welfare theory and is also referred to in the context of market regulation and supervision as the public interest theory.[19] An environment in which more market forces, market regulation and supervision are introduced is also referred to as a regulatory state.[20] The idea behind the regulatory state is that companies (markets) can be better regulated and supervised than if states offer citizens certain goods or services themselves through state enterprises. The regulatory state contrasts with the welfare state in which the government sees itself as the principal actor in the creation of prosperity for its citizens. In the regulatory state, however, companies have more room to maneuver and a supervisor is given responsibility for correcting market failure – on the basis of laws and regulations. It does this mainly by enforcing regulations or setting and refining rules itself.

15. For example, insights from the reports of the WRR. For more on this *see* for example section 12.4.3 *infra*.
16. *See also* Raaijmakers 2013a, p. 19. Financial markets include every form of financial service, such as savings, investment, loans, insurance, intermediation and advice.
17. Aelen 2014, p. 95.
18. Ibid., p. 97.
19. Ibid. She refers to Ogus 2004, p. 29.
20. Aelen 2014, p. 97. Aelen borrowed the term from Gilardi & Maggetti 2011, p. 201.

11.2.1.2 The welfare theory and Pareto efficiency

On the basis of the welfare theory it is assumed that competition between companies in markets provides a better distribution of wealth. In economic terms this involves efficient distribution of wealth, according to Aelen.[21] An important theory associated with thinking on efficiency and market efficiency concerns Pareto efficiency and the Pareto optimum.[22] Pareto efficiency is the use of resources in such a way that no one in a group can advance without someone else retreating (an optimum market outcome). In the strong form the group increases its welfare if at least one individual is better off and no single individual is worse off; in the weak form everyone must be better off. This is achieved in a perfect market in which prices are such that all products produced are also consumed. If the optimum is not obtained and the situation is not Pareto efficient, that means the situation is below the Pareto limit. A change can then be made so that at least one individual wins, without any of the others losing.[23]

According to Aelen[24] the assumptions on which Pareto efficiency would arise in a free-market economy, have been disproved in economic theory and on the basis of experience. Although many economists still refer to the invisible hand theory of the economist Adam Smith, market forces without regulation and supervision are now inconceivable. This is based on various arguments. Reference is usually made to the information asymmetry between the consumer and the market. Another cause lies in the situation whereby consumers simply have no need to make an extensive comparison between products.

11.2.1.3 The public-interest theory

In addition, according to Aelen[25] there is a frequently heard objection that a free-market economy does not necessarily lead to full competition. On the contrary, markets (or market participants) could sometimes have monopolistic inclinations. The conditions on the basis of which an efficient distribution of wealth would arise are not easy to achieve. The result is that markets fail and so there is no efficient distribution of wealth, unless the market failure is corrected. In the regulatory state the supervisor assumes a central responsibility in this regard. The independent supervisor must be an expert in countering and resolving market failure. This idea is central to the public-interest theory. Market failure is countered through regulation of the market by regulators and supervision by (independent) supervisors.

---

21. Ibid., pp. 97–98.
22. Named after the Italian economist Vifredo Pareto (1848–1923). *See also* Aelen 2014, p. 98 and Raaijmakers 2013a, p. 23.
23. Aelen 2014, p. 98 and Raaijmakers 2013a p. 23. Aelen also considers another theory, namely Kaldor-Hicks efficiency. The main point is that the highest degree of efficiency is when supply and demand are matched so there is no overproduction and consumers can satisfy their needs. It should also be mentioned that Kenneth Arrow and Gérard Debreu won the Nobel Prize in Economics for their general equilibrium theory in 1972 and 1983 respectively. Their theory is an argument against government intervention. *See also* Raaijmakers 2013a, p. 23.
24. Aelen 2014, pp. 99–100.
25. Ibid., p. 100.

Shleifer[26] also thinks along the same lines. He believes that the standard 'public interest' or 'helping hand' theory of regulation is based on two assumptions. First, unhindered markets often fail because of the problems of monopoly or externalities. Secondly, governments are benign and capable of correcting these market failures through regulation. This theory of regulation has been used both as a prescription of what governments should do, and as a description of what they actually do, at least in democratic countries. According to Shleifer, the public interest theory of regulation has become the cornerstone of modern public economics, as well as the bible of socialist and other left-leaning politicians. It has been used to justify much of the growth of public ownership and regulation over the twentieth century.

11.2.2 Market failure

On the basis of the foregoing, it is clear that in contrast to neoclassical economic thought, financial markets do not operate efficiently (enough) or optimally and market failure exists. There are various examples of market failure and a great deal of literature has been published on the subject.[27] Five forms of market failure are briefly outlined below.

11.2.2.1 Information asymmetry

Information asymmetry or 'information skewing' is deemed to mean that parties do not have equivalent, sufficient or high-quality information to compare a product or service in terms of quality and price.[28] For the legislator and – by way of extension – a supervisor such as the AFM, this is the primary reason for intervening. Consumers such as savers or mortgage lenders do not have access to the information that is available to a provider such as a bank or insurer. This is a familiar problem in agent-principal theory.[29] The consumer (the principal) must be able to have confidence in the provider (the agent). This is also why the AFM, which advocates the promotion of transparent markets, obliges providers to give consumers as much information as possible so that they can better assess the products.[30]

26. Shleifer 2005, pp. 440–441. According to Shleifer this theory has been criticized, principally by the Chicago School of Law and Economics. This criticism is essentially that government intervention is not necessary; the market will solve its own problems (competition). If this does not hold true completely, the market will provide its own solution by means of 'private litigation' (Contracting Theory, Coase 1960). Even if the above does not hold true, governments are still unable to resolve the market failure because they are incompetent, corrupt and excessively 'captured' (the Capture Theory, *see* Stigler 1971). *See also* Sparrow 2000, p. 35 which points to the danger of capture.
27. Aelen 2014, p. 100. She refers to various sources in note 27 of her thesis.
28. Ibid., p. 101. Reference is made here to various sources such as Ogus 2004, p. 24. *See also* Raaijmakers 2013a, p. 29.
29. Unequal information can also lead to conflicts of interest because the agent does not necessarily promote the interests of the principal in the correct way and, for example, allows other interests (such as a personal interest) to play a role. *See* chapter 6 *supra*.
30. A familiar example is the financial information leaflet.

There are various reasons for the information skewing. Providing sufficient information can be expensive or too complex.[31] Another reason is that there are incentives for the market to deliberately provide consumers with insufficient or inaccurate information.[32] Information skewing generally has two consequences, namely moral hazard and adverse selection.[33] Moral hazard means that a party deliberately takes a risk at the expense of another person. An example of this in the financial sector is the deposit guarantee system. A bank customer is generally unable to determine how solvent or liquid a bank is. As a result of 'guaranteeing' a deposit held at the bank concerned, the customer can assume a form of laziness, as a result of which he worries less about the quality of the service provided by the bank.[34] 'Adverse selection' can include making insufficient choices because parties deliberately withhold information.[35]

11.2.2.2 Externalities

Externalities, also referred to as external effects or external costs, are non-compensated costs incurred by third parties or damage suffered as a result of an economic activity such as production. These effects have among other things the (negative) characteristic that they are not included in the market (or production) price and therefore can constitute a form of market failure. An example of a negative external effect is the use of public highways and associated traffic congestion. Everyone who goes on to the public highway (ultimately) causes a traffic jam and consequently (indirect) costs for other road users. These costs are not included, for example, in the building of roads or in the transport of goods. The costs of transporting goods are then (finally) passed on to the consumer. This will result in product prices being

31. Interest rate derivatives or investment mortgages are complex products and it may be too expensive to explain these or provide advice to the average consumer. The legislator has now intervened in the provision of these products by banning or 'simplifying' them.
32. Aelen 2014, p. 101, in which she refers to Baldwin, Cave & Lodge 2012, p. 18. A familiar example of this is the erstwhile practice of paying commissions to insurance and other intermediaries, for example by an insurer, as a result of which the intermediary tended to prioritize the products of this company above other equivalent (or perhaps even better) products from other providers. *See also* the references to conflicts of interest in chapter 6 *supra*.
33. Aelen 2014, p. 101.
34. *See also* Raaijmakers 2013a, p. 30. Fully comprehensive insurance on a car can also have such an effect. The policyholder may be tempted to take more risks on the road because everything is 'insured'.
35. An example is the second-hand car market. Akerlof (1970) shows that as a result of the information gap a potential buyer of a second-hand car (a 'lemon') will be inclined to pay as little as possible because he cannot precisely estimate the quality (and hence the value) of the car. As a result, too low a price is offered for cars that are of high quality and above average, which in turn means that suppliers of such cars no longer enter the second-hand market and the only cars left are of lower quality. This also applies to financial products if consumers, for example, cannot recognize the quality improvement. If this is the case, they are not prepared to pay the higher price, which again has an adverse selection effect with regard to those products. *See also* Aelen 2014, p. 102 and Raaijmakers 2013a, pp. 30–31.

too low, strictly speaking.[36] This in turn leads to inefficient market operation because overproduction can arise due to an excessively low price.[37]

Another example is the financial crisis. As a result of the securitization of mortgages and the associated excessively low cost, overproduction arose in the granting of mortgages because the loans were granted to unsuitable borrowers.[38] An example of a positive external effect is a company that establishes itself in an area where previously established companies already provided a good infrastructure, to take advantage of a trained workforce, etc., without having to pay for it.

11.2.2.3 Bounded rationality

Bounded rationality means that people do not act rationally on the basis of the available information when it comes to maximizing their wealth. Bounded rationality is seen as a form of market failure because, for example, it leads to consumers taking suboptimal decisions which lead to inefficient market outcomes.[39] Insights into bounded rationality received a huge impetus from the prospect theory of Kahneman and Tversky in 1979[40] and provided new insights on decisions taken by people in uncertain situations from the perspective of behavioral economics.[41]

11.2.2.4 Market power

If a company has (excessive) market power or a monopoly position (being the only one in the market), this is also considered to be market failure. After all, the company can then charge its own price that is higher than the marginal cost or an efficient price. This then results in higher prices and lower and more inefficient production and inefficient wealth distribution.[42] It erects a barrier for other businesses seeking to enter the market. This does not benefit the Pareto optimum. Aelen notes that this also applies to an oligopoly (the situation in which a limited number of companies can determine the market prices) and cartel formation. These are also considered to be market failure.[43]

---

36. After all, the costs of a delayed delivery (loss of income for the transport company, products that have become perishable or of which more could have been sold in a shorter time) as a result of the congestion are not taken into account.
37. If the costs had been passed on, in order to maintain the Pareto optimum, less would be produced.
38. The example is taken from Raaijmakers 2013a, p. 24.
39. *See also* Raaijmakers 2013a, p. 34.
40. Kahneman & Trevesky 1979.
41. *See also* chapter 7 *supra*, where the themes of Behavioral Finance and Economics arise again.
42. Aelen 2014, pp. 100–101.
43. Ibid., p. 101. The ACM is the authority that supervises and counters undesirable cartel formation or monopoly positions.

11.2.2.5 Collective or public goods

A characteristic of these goods is that persons who do not pay for them cannot be excluded from them. A second characteristic is that these goods are not in competition, which means that consumption by one is not at the expense of the other.[44] Collective or public goods include, for example, dykes, the military or street lighting.[45] The dyke holds the water back for everyone, including the people who do not contribute to the cost. The military defends an area and that also means people who do not pay for it. Street lighting is there for everyone. The collective or public nature of the good is normally used as an argument to have the government bear responsibility for it (rather than the consumer). The government then ensures that everyone contributes to the cost through general taxation, i.e. indirectly. This avoids the problem whereby the good is not offered because one party hopes that the other will pay for it. It also avoids the free-rider problem. Since it is not possible to provide public goods only for consumers who pay for them, consumers will not be prepared voluntarily to pay for the use of the good. After all, they can take advantage of these goods without paying.[46]

11.2.3 Regulatory burden and deregulation

> 'There is a strong social need for rules. People need rules to maintain order in society, to counter injustice, undesirable inequality or distortion of competition and to discourage free-rider behavior. The need for legal protection and legal fairness has increased rather than decreased. But the main question is who should make the rules. Society often assigns that responsibility to the government, but the downside to government rules is that they are perceived as regulatory burden.'[47]

Business in the Netherlands, including in the financial sector, generally perceives the regulatory burden to be high.[48] The legislator has taken extensive measures, however, in order to reduce this.[49] In addition to the complaints on excessive rules, there are simultaneous calls for more rules. This is the so-called regulation paradox. The result may be that in practice little or too little comes of any reduction in the regulatory burden.

A common definition of regulatory burden is:

---

44. Raaijmakers 2013a, p. 26 who refers *inter alia* to Samuelson 1957.
45. In addition to collective goods a distinction is also made in terms of quasi- or semi-collective goods. The government thus creates a 'pseudo-market' by means of a contribution system, in which the users nevertheless pay a certain contribution towards the financing of the collective provision concerned. Financing nevertheless continues to rely in principle on general taxation. Examples are university education (in the Netherlands) and highways.
46. Raaijmakers 2013a, p. 26 who refers *inter alia* to Samuelson 1957.
47. Notitie regeldruk 2006, p. 3.
48. *Compliance officers denounce multiplicity of new rules. 78% believe higher regulatory pressure since crisis misses target*, Financieel Dagblad December 3, 2015.
49. It is striking in this regard that deregulation initiatives never genuinely affect the financial sector. This is partly because of the sector's current negative image. *See also* Houben 2013.

> 'the investment and effort which citizens, companies and institutions have to make in order to adhere to the rules and the restriction of freedom which they consequently undergo. This concerns the scope which rules leave for alternative conduct (freedom of choice), the recognizability and transparency of rules, consistency with other rules, the way in which rules are implemented and compliance is assured, the way in which rules are enforced and violations are punished and the administrative burdens.'[50]

One can distinguish six causes of regulatory burden:[51]

1. *The question of control or more control.* The underlying causes of this are a breach of trust between the government and the citizen, a juridification of society and risk aversion on the part of the government (cover against future accusations of maladministration).
2. *Increasing bureaucratization.*[52] The underlying causes of this are the (increasing) administrative burden, specialization and compartmentalization of functions and organizations that work alongside each other and finally 'bureaucratism'.[53]
3. *The need for rules and equality in rules.* The underlying causes of this are the incorporation of equality theory into rules, fear of discrimination, difficult cultural and political choices, tension between centralization and decentralization and complex or excessively complex systems against which rules must be tested.
4. *The search for support.* The underlying causes of this are consensus democracy, the Dutch 'polder model' and lobby formation, as a result of which the decision-making process can be drawn out over a very long time.
5. *Handling or panicked handling of incidents.* The underlying causes of this are an excessive political focus on incidents and their prevention,[54] media democracy,[55] too much emphasis on risk minimization and extensive lobbying by interested organizations with regard to incidents.[56]
6. *Internationalization.* The underlying causes of this are a negative image of the government or European authorities,[57] too great a distance between the

50. Notitie regeldruk 2006, p. 4.
51. Ibid, pp. 7–29. Reference is also made to Gestel and Hertogh 2006, pp. 17–18, which lists a number of the investigations into deregulation being conducted at the time.
52. *See also* De Jong 2011.
53. Rosenthal et al. 1996. When bureaucratization is driven to an extreme, bureaucracy degenerates into bureaucratism: strict categorization of duties, tight hierarchical lines and highly objectified competence criteria then rapidly turn into formalism, red tape and almost coercively equal treatment of unequal cases.
54. That means that politics (the minister and MPs) want to show their concern for the fate of those they represent. It should come as no surprise that there have been many examples of this over the past ten years in the financial sector.
55. That means the role of the public media has become so important that politicians want to see immediate results on the basis of public statements. There are countless examples of this. In the case of consumer protection, for example, there is the TROS Radar program.
56. The familiar call for more rules ('Where was the government?').
57. As a result of excessive interference by European legislators at micro level (for example a directive on the percentage bending of bananas).

regulator and the recipient of the rules, a poor European and international focus, decision-making geared excessively to compromises and no alignment with national legal and cultural traditions.

The Dutch government has been engaged for a long time in programs aimed at permanently reducing the regulatory burden. Mention could be made in this regard of deregulation as a separate trend in contrast to regulation. On the one hand, therefore, many rules are drawn up and introduced, and on the other hand methods are devised in order to reduce these, i.e. to introduce rules as efficiently as possible. The government-wide approach to the regulatory burden essentially comprises the following activities:[58]

- less regulatory burden by improving the quality of legislation;
- structural reduction in the regulatory burden by EUR 2.5 billion in the period 2012–2017 for citizens, businesses and professionals;
- marked reduction in the regulatory burden in highly regulated fields;
- less accumulation of rules and smarter supervision;
- less regulatory burden through administrative collaboration;
- better digital and other services.

Actal has also launched various initiatives to reduce the regulatory burden. Actal is the Dutch advisory board on regulatory burden.[59] It advises the government and the States General on ways of lowering the regulatory burden for businesses, citizens and professionals in healthcare, education, security and social security as much as possible. It aims to contribute to a society in which the government fulfills its objectives and at the same time people are hindered as little as possible by rules. It looks for new ways of limiting the regulatory burden in the Netherlands and challenges regulators to make use of these. The advisory board works with organizations in the Netherlands and abroad, including sister organizations in other European Member States. With its future vision it has launched a program aimed at reducing the regulatory burden.[60] It also draws attention to this in its annual report for 2015.[61]

---

58. *Parliamentary papers II* 2007/16, 29362 including the reports on the regulatory burden and its reduction. Another notable fact is that the Ministry of Security and Justice established the Legislation and Legal Affairs Knowledge Centre a number of years ago. This center is aimed at future-proof (and hence more efficient) laws and regulations. *See* the website https://www.kcwj.nl.
59. www.actal.nl. As of June 1, 2017 the successor to Actal will be the Aviescollege toetsing regeldruk (ATR).
60. Actal 2016.
61. Actal 2015. Actal also conducts audits of the regulatory burden, Actal April 2015. The regulatory burden audit in 2015 revealed a varied picture among ministries (including the Ministry of Finance). Only laws and significant orders in council are subjected to an independent, external assessment of regulatory burden. This assessment does not cover ministerial regulations and minor orders in council. It is therefore unclear to what extent their consequences in terms of the regulatory burden have been adequately assessed and what scope they have.

11.2.4 Open and closed standards[62]

In the regulation of financial markets, it is important to consider the terms 'open' and 'closed' standards. In parallel there is a discussion regarding rules-based versus principles-based standards. In the cases of closed or rules-based standards the issue is that the legislator gives the financial undertaking little or no scope to interpret the rules in question. In this case it would be possible to speak of direct transparent rules which create a kind of 'black-and-white' certainty among the parties to which the standards apply. In the case of open or principles-based standards, the financial undertaking is given more scope for interpretation (only frameworks and principles are formulated) and in day-to-day practical implementation it must look at the objectives of the specific rule. The disadvantage is that this approach offers less legal certainty.

It has been noted that the main change in the development of financial supervision regulations over the past two to three decades appears to have been the transition from rules-based to principles-based standards.[63] Laws and rules are becoming more general and formulated more in line with objectives, with the financial undertakings to which the regulations apply being able to determine themselves how they should act in order to fulfill the specified principles (to a certain extent). According to the De Wit I Committee[64] this creates more flexibility and decision-making scope for these undertakings. It believes that rational agents (i.e. the financial undertaking) in efficient markets must not be excessively constricted by laws and regulations. According to the Committee, the main question in this regard is whether principles-based financial supervision regulations are able to secure these objectives. Such regulations are based on *a priori* trust in the disciplined nature of financial undertakings – either on the basis of their own interest or on the basis of their enforceability through competitive and/or pseudocompetitive pressure.

According to Kockelkoren,[65] an open standard approach supports the supervision strategy of the AFM, although he himself takes a nuanced position. The advantage on the one hand is the flexible applicability to wide-ranging situations that leads to lower compliance costs and fewer conflicts, but the disadvantage on the other hand is the increased uncertainty with regard to legal compliance. The latter regularly leads to a more detailed interpretation, which in turn leads to more rules but which are possibly less visible. In this regard he acknowledges the criticism that open standards actually do not remain open, because the AFM publishes guidelines with more detailed indications of how it interprets the open standards.[66] He nevertheless believes that the guidelines state that it is not about obligations, but about examples of how the open standard can be applied. He observes the legitimate fear among financial undertakings that neither the AFM nor the courts will go along with the undertaking's own interpretation but will adhere to the published guideline. In his

62. Parts of the text have been drawn from Houben 2013.
63. *Parliamentary papers II* 2009/10, 31980, 6, p. 175.
64. De Wit Committee 2010.
65. Kockelkoren 2011; Veerman & Mulder 2010, p. 61.
66. An example cited by Kockelkoren himself is the *AFM Leidraad tweede pijler pensioenadvisering* (2009). There are various other examples, for example in the field of investment services.

opinion this criticism will always be able to be leveled at open standards, however, because if the AFM does not publish guidelines, the court will publish judgments. Open standards do, however, offer flexibility for both the financial undertaking and the government.

A follow-up question is when it is sensible to use open standards. Favorable factors for this include, for example, different circumstances in which the laws and regulations must be applied, the existence of less specific performance requirements, implementation by professionals and discretionary supervision by professionals.[67] The duty of care is referred to as an example of this.

A further follow-up question is when the government would be well advised to give direction itself in an open standard and when it would be better to do this through the courts.[68] The AFM does not seek to flesh out all open standards in the Financial Supervision Act (Wft) with guidelines, for example. The AFM opts to publish a guideline if: a) it has the impression that many financial undertakings are finding it difficult to determine how they should interpret the open standard; b) little direction and guidance is given by publications of market organizations (such as quality marks or interest groups); c) there is little or no case law; and d) the combined struggle by the companies leads to substantial problems in the market.

Kockelkoren rejects the criticism that the democratic content of such direction-giving information is insufficient. He considers that the legislator can always flesh out the open standard later if it finds that a supervisor is deviating too far from its intentions in interpreting an open standard. This is despite the fact that there is a separation in principle between the legislator, who passes the law, and the supervisor, who interprets the published law. Here, however, Kockelkoren partly refutes the objective behind the open standard. Although the AFM has the power to set generally binding requirements, it must adhere to the frameworks set in the Wft.[69] One of those is an unreasonable burden on the financial markets.[70] The objective of an open standard is precisely to leave the financial undertaking with the responsibility of fleshing out the standard and not (increasingly) to strip it of this responsibility. Striking a balance in practice is difficult, however.

11.2.5 Self-regulation

11.2.5.1 Introduction

Proper market forces make regulation superfluous in principle; if they fail, regulation is second best. Self-regulation is actually a self-correcting, self-cleansing mechanism for a sector. There is self-regulation if rules are drawn up by a particular sector or

67. Veerman & Mulder 2010, p. 111.
68. Kockelkoren 2011.
69. Arts 1:28 and 1:29 of the Wft.
70. Art. 1:29 paragraph 2 of the Wft states that if the generally binding regulations adopted by the regulator place an unreasonable burden on the financial markets and the supervisor fails to eliminate the imperfections observed after consultation, the Minister of Finance can issue a ministerial regulation setting rules on the matter concerned, simultaneously withdrawing the generally binding regulations adopted by the supervisor on the matter.

professional group and implemented in relation to their own action and if these rules are enforced by that sector or group by means of discipline. There are various examples of this, such as the VvV and the Financial Services Disciplinary Board (Insurance), the NVB and the Foundation for Banking Ethics Enforcement[71] and the codes of conduct or disciplinary law governing law firms, accountants, medical specialists and notaries. Self-regulation can be a supplement or alternative to regulation by the government. There is conditioned self-regulation when the government deliberately permits forms of self-regulation, or encourages them, but at the same time attaches certain conditions to them.[72] The biggest disadvantage of self-regulation is that it can impede competition.[73]

SEO Amsterdam Economics states that a solution to the moral hazard problem may be more market forces.[74] By this it means that supervision at government level should be scaled back and transferred to the private sector. That can be achieved, for example, by producing fewer rules as a result of which less supervision is also necessary. According to SEO, self-regulation is a feasible option in such a case if:[75]

1. The problem is not serious enough to warrant intervention and sufficient time can be gained with self-regulation for businesses, citizens and organizations.
2. The problem is serious enough for intervention but no permanent power of intervention is required and conditioned self-regulation is used as well as outsourcing of supervision to the market sector.
3. Seven preconditions for self-management have been sufficiently fulfilled, namely:
   (a) There must be sufficient detailed knowledge available concerning the problem and the possible solutions.
   (b) The must be sufficient knowledge of the costs of self-regulation.
   (c) There must be a positive attitude among the stakeholders with regard to self-regulation and there must be a readiness to devote sufficient time and money to it.
   (d) There must be a sufficient degree of organization in the sector so that self-regulation can take place.
   (e) There must be sufficient social pressure in the solving of the problem.
   (f) There must be a legal framework within which enforcement of self-regulation can be carried out.
   (g) Finally, there must be a good basis of trust between the various parties involved in the self-regulation.
4. There is no lack of competition.
5. There is a social (economic) problem that does not fall within the category of unfair wealth distribution and/or a social imbalance.

71. *See* VvV 2013 and NVB 2013.
72. For example in the case of certification.
73. SEO 2005, p. 27. For example in the case of high fixed prices or goodwill.
74. Ibid., p. 26.
75. Ibid., pp. 27–28.

11.2.5.2 Self-regulation in the financial sector[76]

In self-regulation in the financial sector the responsibility for drawing up and complying with rules rests, as stated above, entirely with the financial undertakings themselves. As a result of the financial crisis, the Ministry of Finance and the House of Representatives made clear that codes of conduct were necessary in order to counter the observed irregularities. This was confirmed by the sector itself.[77]

One may question, however, whether self-regulation works in extreme circumstances such as those of a crisis. A follow-up question is whether the legislator came to a different view under political pressure and is imposing regulations which go beyond or actually replace self-regulation. As a result of the previously observed increase in the volume of laws and regulations in the financial sector and the associated political pressure, there appears to be little room for self-regulation.[78]

The AFM appears not to be a real advocate of self-regulation in the financial sector. Kockelkoren notes, for example, that research has been conducted into the possibilities of self-regulation and other self-correcting mechanisms.[79] He states that this correctly notes the assumption that society itself is in a position to identify its problems, set priorities and work resolutely towards a solution. This free approach can only work, however, if the parties (i.e. financial undertakings and customers) with conflicting interests are more or less equally powerful. He believes that in the financial markets in particular that is often not the case. This does not mean, incidentally, that the corrective mechanisms can play no role. The AFM does appear to be an advocate of the so-called enforceable self-regulation as an effective self-correcting mechanism. This means creating scope for the financial sector to devise its own solutions to problems that arise, but with the government in the background being able if necessary to enforce an appropriate solution.

Kockelkoren also believes[80] that enforceable self-regulation combines obvious advantages of enforceability with the advantages of stimulating individual responsibility in the market and retaining flexibility to respond to changing circumstances. For this reason, an arrangement comparable to that of the 2010 Banking Code, for example, should be seriously considered. Once again, a principle in the law, such as making the customer interest central and the compulsory application of a product approval process, would make enforceability of self-regulation possible, while the banks are allowed the scope to specify their own intentions in a code which can be adapted where necessary to the changing circumstances.

---

76. Drawn in part from Houben 2013.
77. Reference is made to the recommendations of the Maas Committee.
78. For example to make the customer's interest first and continue to counter 'perverse' pay incentives. An illustrative source in this connection is a report by Nauta Dutilh in which the principles of the 2010 Banking Code were compared to the financial supervision regulations applicable to Dutch banks (analysis of differences carried out by Nauta Dutilh for the Banking Monitoring Committee, presented on April 27, 2012). It is not surprising that a considerable part of the then current and forthcoming (and now current) provisions of the financial supervision regulations applying to banks corresponded to or even went beyond the principles of the 2010 Banking Code.
79. Kockelkoren, 2011.
80. Ibid.

Such ideas could be said to be outdated, however. Over the past few years regulations have been drawn up which cover or exceed a large part of the 2010 Banking Code.[81] There is no longer any scope for banks' own solutions (and those of other financial undertakings), except the freedom to interpret the 'open' standards themselves. It would nevertheless be worth undertaking further work on self-regulation. The NVB, for example, points out that legislation works differently than self-regulation. Self-regulation requires reflection and invites a debate on how the aim behind the rules can best be achieved. Laws and regulations (legislation), by contrast, invite a box-ticking mentality and discussion of how to avoid 'hassle' with the supervisor.[82] The VvV also points to the positive sides of self-regulation.[83] At present, however, the trend of regulation by the legislator appears to be continuing in place of self-regulation.[84]

11.3 FINANCIAL SUPERVISORY REGULATIONS[85]

The financial sector fulfills an important function in the economy. Banks, for example, are an important hub between those who save and borrow and thereby ensure that credit is provided for businesses, institutions and consumers. They also handle day-to-day payments. Insurers are an important link in the transmission or coverage of risks and also have a role as an institutional investor. These important functions mean that the existence or continued existence of a financial undertaking is often of great importance for the continued proper operation of all or part of the economy.[86] In politics there has been broad consensus since the 1930s that public interests are bound up with the proper operation of the financial system and that those public interests must be safeguarded in some way by the government. The government has therefore always intervened in the financial sector. This has led to specific laws and regulations for, and government supervision of, the financial sector, which have a long history and on various occasions have been enacted in response to a preceding crisis or war.[87]

11.3.1 General trends

The 2010 De Wit Committee notes that a retreating government sought to leave control of financial markets in the pre-crisis years to market processes as much as possible,

81. The 2010 Banking Code has now been replaced by the 2014 Banking Code, which among other things firmly establishes the so-called banker's oath. The bankers oath is, however, also legally provided for in the Financial Sector (Oath or Solemn Affirmation) Regulation 2015. Hence there is no longer any self-regulation.
82. Buijink 2014.
83. De Boer & Martius 2014.
84. Partly as a result of the numerous laws and regulations at European level. *See* section 11.3 *infra*.
85. Drawn in part from Houben 2013.
86. *See also Parliamentary papers II* 2009/10, 31980, no. 6, p. 101.
87. Ibid.

and geared the laws and regulations accordingly.[88] The leeway for operators in the financial services market outside the Netherlands has also increased in the past few years. In 1999 the European market for financial services made a strong start when the (European) Action Plan for Financial Services was published. The aim was to remove practical impediments to financial services transactions caused by differences in financial and other regulations between the European Member States. In the next ten years the Action Plan would lead to a large number of directives with which these regulations were harmonized.[89]

Despite this liberalization of financial markets, it is noted that new regulations, particularly from the European Union (EU), actually led to new impediments and bureaucracy (not a level playing field and high administrative costs). For example, the Lamfalussy structure,[90] which was introduced at European level in 2001 to ensure that the European Parliament and Council of Ministers set out only a general framework in Directives,[91] did not have the intended effect. The views of the financial sector were not taken into account sufficiently in the designing of new regulations. In addition, the European Commission did not sufficiently ensure uniform implementation by the Member States and the avoidance of 'gold-plating' (supplementing European regulations with national policy).

The 2010 De Wit Committee concludes in this respect[92] that on the one hand there is a trend towards deregulation and decentralization, out of a desire to define only the framework at European level and to leave the details to the Member States (in accordance with the subsidiarity principle) or to the supervisors and the sector itself. But on the other hand there is also an inclination to define more matters centrally. For example, Member States are pressing for a 'level playing field' throughout the EU, because businesses in one Member State suffer a competitive disadvantage if regulations in other EU states differ from those of their own. There is also a widely perceived need to safeguard the quality of regulations and supervision in other EU Member States by laying down rules and requirements at European level. That gives rise to a development of 'minimum harmonization' in which European rules set minimum requirements which Member States can exceed under a 'national heading', to 'maximum harmonization', in which the directives explicitly exclude the addition of a national heading.

In the field of conduct supervision too, the De Wit Committee notes that there has been an increase in regulation in the past few years, particularly in the Netherlands. Up to 2002, the year in which the AFM was established, this hardly ever

88. *Parliamentary papers II* 2009/10, 31980, nos. 3–4, p. 101. *See also* section 11.1 *supra*.
89. Ibid. Important milestones included, for example, the revised Banking Directive 2006, in which the 'European passport' for banks was given a more solid basis, and the Markets in Financial Instruments Directive (MiFID) from 2004 (which will be replaced in 2018 by MiFID II).
90. The aim of the Lamfalussy structure is to simplify and accelerate the legislative process in the EU for the financial services sector by means of a four-stage plan. In this process the European institutions, led by the Commission, provide only the political framework. The technical content and detailed implementation provisions, by contrast, are provided by the Commission, with the support of four technical committees.
91. As was the case at the time of MiFID.
92. *Parliamentary Papers II* 2009/10, 31980, nos. 3–4, p. 104.

occurred in the Netherlands.[93] According to Kockelkoren, however, the deregulation (liberalization) did not mean there was no conduct regulation. Starting in 1980, scandal after scandal stimulated the growth of conduct rules to increase the equity of the financial markets.[94]

The supervision of the financial sector therefore internationalized much less rapidly than the sector itself. That gave rise in the EU to a common market for financial services which remained dependent on a patchwork of national supervisors in terms of supervision and crisis response, based on the assumption that conflicts of interest, interpretation and cultural differences posed no significant impediment to appropriate collaboration and exchange of information between the various national supervisors and governments.

According to the 2010 De Wit Committee, the question of whether the changes in the past few years in the field of financial regulation in the Netherlands and Europe should be characterized as 'deregulation' or 'liberalization' ultimately produces a nuanced response.[95] The harmonization of financial regulations in Europe also meant that the focus of regulation shifted from the national to the European level. Without there necessarily being an increase in the volume of regulation which companies had to fulfill, this did mean, however, that over the past few years a great deal of new laws and regulations have been written, negotiated and in turn implemented at national level.

11.3.2 Regulation of the financial sector as a result of the financial crisis

As a result of the financial crisis, the volume and complexity of financial supervision regulations on a global, European and national level has increased (greatly) in comparison with the preceding period. There are no precise figures for the financial sector as a whole, however, and the statistical evidence for this statement requires a further comparative and historical study of national and international financial supervision regulations.[96] As stated above, this 'upturn' is not the first of its kind, however. A normal reflex in a democracy with checks and balances is that the legislator and politicians wish to tackle (evident) social abuses by means of regulations.[97] At national level, incidentally, it is necessary to look at more than just the crisis. Before the crisis and even after it various scandals led, for example, to a big increase in conduct supervision (by the AFM) with regard to consumer protection.[98] The crisis merely strengthened this trend. A factor which makes the whole situation even less

93. Ibid. *See also* section 11.1 *supra*.
94. Kockelkoren 2011 section 36.
95. *Parliamentary papers II* 2009/10, 31980, nos. 3–4, p. 131.
96. The VvV made an attempt, however. In the brochure entitled 'Factsheets Tweede Kamerverkiezingen 2012' (May 2012, p. 9) it is noted that in the case of insurers more than 100 Dutch bills and 31 European initiatives for directives and regulations are of direct or indirect significance. The survey dates from November 2011. In addition, not all bills have been introduced as a result of the financial crisis.
97. *See* section 12.1 *supra*.
98. Notable examples are the Legiolease affair and the settlements with regard to endowment insurances with an investment component known popularly as the 'profiteering policies affair' ('woekerpolis' affaire).

transparent concerns all the existing, mainly European, legislative initiatives resulting from the aforementioned Lamfalussy Action Plan.[99]

The connecting elements of many legislative initiatives as a result of the financial crisis can be traced back to: a) a solid financial sector; b) strengthening of the position of the consumer and conduct and cultural changes in the financial sector; and c) strengthening of the institutional or supervisory framework.[100]

11.4 SUPERVISION OF THE FINANCIAL MARKETS

11.4.1 Supervision in general

> 'Supervision is everywhere. In society there is a prevailing view that without supervision we run all kinds of risks.'[101]

One cannot escape the impression that the Netherlands is a country of supervision.[102] After all, the Netherlands has supervisors at government level, at decentralized level and in the semi-public and private sectors. They all represent a public interest, including the economic interest. This section elaborates further on supervisors which promote economic interests, the so-called market supervisors, with a focus on the financial markets. The supervisors have been appointed to correct[103] or counter market failure.[104]

When referring to supervision (and enforcement) in the broad sense, different terms are applied in the literature.[105] According to SEO the terms supervision and enforcement concern efforts intended particularly to ensure (better) compliance with laws and/or rules. It considers supervision to be: 'gathering information on whether organizations, policy or facilities meet the specified requirements and then forming a judgment and possibly intervening in response'. A supervisor is: 'an organization that acts on behalf of the government as a market superintendent, referee or watchdog and has the purpose of monitoring competition and/or promoting market forces'.[106]

According to SEO, the enforcement of a standard is central.[107] That standard can be imposed by the government in a law or rule. Every new standard requires supervision to determine whether it is being complied with. With every new law or regulation, a supervisory relationship is therefore created. The accumulation of

99. MiFID and MiFID II, the MiFIR, MAD and MAD II, the MAR and the Alternative Investment Fund Managers Directive (AIFMD) are good examples of this.
100. In the booklet entitled '*Aanpak financiële sector*' of April 13, 2012 the Ministry of Finance set out 40 legislative initiatives relating to the financial sector. These have all been implemented.
101. Aelen 2014, p. 3.
102. Baarsma 2010, p. 3.
103. Aelen 2014, p. 3.
104. For the term market failure *see* section 11.2.2 *supra*.
105. *See also* Brenninkmeijer 2010.
106. SEO 2005, p. 5.
107. Ibid., p. 3. SEO then quotes a dictionary definition. The definition of supervision is: 'ensuring that something happens or that someone behaves in accordance with a particular standard'.

supervision (multiple supervision) is an accumulation of laws and regulations. There is multiple supervision if multiple supervisors focus on the same entity from the perspective of different supervisory frameworks.[108]

Another more or less equivalent definition of the term supervision comes from the Holtslag Committee,[109] which describes supervision as gathering information to determine whether an action or case fulfills the specified requirements, subsequently forming a judgment on it and possibly intervening on the basis of that judgment. The SER applies a broader definition of supervision and distinguishes three elements:[110]

1. *Vertical supervision*: the formal hierarchical accountability structure running from the politically responsible body (often the Minister) to the executive body.
2. *Internal supervision*: accountability and control within the institution itself, the relationship between the board and the supervisory bodies.
3. *Horizontal supervision*: participation of and information provision for third parties such as users and social organizations.[111]

The program 'Andere overheid'[112] adds an element to the definition of supervision and sees it as not only a means of enforcing compliance with rules and improving the quality of policy but also as a means of limiting risks. The supervisor therefore also has the task of reducing risks. There are two types of supervision with regard to risks: a) supervision focused on reducing quantifiable risks; and b) supervision aimed at reducing anxiety, in which the perception of risks is central. The public must be protected against basic anxieties. With regard to security and order, these fears have increased since September 11, 2001.[113] Supervision therefore has many facets. For example, there is internal and external supervision, ex post (repressive) and ex ante (preventive) supervision, sector-specific and generic supervision, statutory (public) and self-regulating (private) supervision, horizontal and vertical supervision and supervision by local, regional and central government.[114]

Furthermore, it is possible to distinguish various perspectives on market and other supervision. First, the legal perspective that relates to guaranteeing compliance with laws and regulations, safeguards the principles of a democratic state under the rule of law and ensures that the general principles of sound administration are complied with. Supervision can also be seen from the economic perspective, i.e. limiting market failure.[115] There is also a political-administrative perspective relating to the democratic legitimacy of the supervisor.[116] Finally, reference can be made to

---

108. SEO 2005, p. 3. Various examples can be given. This also covers the financial sector. An average financial (insurance) group, for example, will have to deal with DNB, the AFM, the NZA and the ACM.
109. Holtslag Committee, p. 4.
110. SER 2005, section 4.5.
111. SEO 2005, p. 4
112. *See* http://www.andereoverheid.nl/ and https://www.rijksoverheid.nl. The program has now been discontinued. *See also Parliamentary papers II* 2007/16, 29362.
113. SEO 2005, p. 5. The MH17 disaster can also be placed in this category.
114. Ibid.
115. For the term market failure *see* section 11.2.2 *supra*.
116. Aelen 2014, pp. 6–8.

the psychological perspective that concerns influencing culture and behavior.[117] Llewellyn draws a distinction between regulation (the establishment of specific rules of behavior), monitoring (observing whether the rules are obeyed) and supervision (the more general observation of the behavior of financial firms).[118]

11.4.2 Structure of supervision of the financial sector

In the Netherlands two supervisors have been designated to supervise financial undertakings[119] and the financial markets.[120] This supervision is organized on a functional basis[121] using the 'Twin Peaks' model.[122] The functional model structures the supervision on the basis of the three functions of financial supervision: system supervision,[123] economic (or prudential) supervision and conduct supervision. The Financial Supervision Act (Wft) should be seen in this framework as the final piece of the functional model and logically is also organized on a functional basis. At European level there are no plans to introduce functional or non-sector-based supervision laws and regulations. All laws and regulations remain sector-based. In the Netherlands this poses problems because the bulk of these laws and regulations are now European.[124]

---

117. *See* chapter 13 *infra* for detailed consideration of the supervision of conduct and culture by DNB and the AFM.
118. Llewellyn 1999, p. 6.
119. For the definition of financial undertaking, *see* Art. 1:1 of the Wft. Currently 18 types of company fall within the definition of financial undertaking. Pension funds are covered by the Pensions Act and trust companies are covered by the Trust Office Supervision Act (Wtt).
120. Also referred to as 'the financial supervisors'.
121. *Parliamentary Papers II* 2001/02, 28122, 2, p. 2.
122. Grundman-van de Krol 2010, p. 50. She refers to M. Taylor, *Twin Peaks: A regulatory Structure for the New Century*, London: Centre for the Study of Financial Innovation 1995. The twin-peaks model is a supervision model with two peaks, one comprising supervision of the soundness of financial undertakings and the other comprising supervision of the way in which parties should conduct themselves in the financial markets. Other supervision models are the (old) sector-based model (a supervisor for each type of undertaking, such as DNB for banks, the erstwhile Pension and Insurance Chamber for pension funds and insurers and the Securities Transactions Supervisory Board for securities institutions), and the concentration model (all supervisory duties in a single organization). A residual question is what should be understood by integrity supervision in this regard. DNB is also the monetary authority under the Banking Act 1998. Following the report of the Scheltema Committee (established as a result of the DSB affair) a separation of responsibilities was introduced at DNB into monetary and prudential supervision. Reference is made to the Wet versterking governance van DNB en de AFM (the Improved Governance (DNB and AFM) Act), which came into force on February 16, 2012 (*Parliamentary papers II*, 32782, 2011/12).
123. The system supervision is exercised by DNB on the basis of the Banking Act 1998. *See* note 122 *supra*.
124. Grundman-van de Krol 2010, p. 87. She was already considering this because European laws and regulations are now and will remain sector-based. This gave rise to a large-scale review of the Wft but not the supervision model.

Under Article 1:24 of the Wft, DNB is the prudential supervisor. It supervises the soundness of financial undertakings and the stability of the financial system. Under Article 1:25 of the Wft the AFM[125] is the conduct supervisor. It supervises orderly and transparent financial market processes, pure relationships between market participants and careful treatment of customers. It also contributes to the stability of the financial system. Separate supervisors were designated for the two types of supervision on the basis that prudential supervision and conduct supervision are equally important and each would benefit if the two areas of supervision were not in the hands of the same supervisor, thereby avoiding the risk of one area of supervision gaining the upper hand over the other in a particular situation.[126]

The ACM, the competition authority,[127] conducts supervision on the basis of its own mandate. It supervises access to payment systems on the basis of Article 1:25a of the Wft. Mention should also be made of the NZA which also has its own mandate.[128]

As a result of the financial crisis in 2008, the SSM was formed.[129] It is one of the pillars of the European Banking Union.[130] The SSM came into force on November 4, 2013 and relates to the law of banking supervision. Since November 4, 2014 all banks established in a European Member State having the euro as its official currency have had to deal with a new prudential supervisor, the European Central Bank (ECB). The SSM applies to all (at that time around 4,900) banks established in the participating Member States. The ECB conducts prudential supervision of 'significant' banks in the Netherlands in place of DNB.[131] The ECB also exercises major influence indirectly over the other Dutch banks – through DNB.

125. AFM is an independent conduct supervisor in the savings, loans, investment and insurance markets. It promotes honest and diligent provision of financial services for consumers, private investors, professionals and semi-professional customers and supervises honest and efficient operation of capital markets. Its aim is to strengthen the trust of consumers and companies in the financial markets, nationally as well as internationally. In this way AFM contributes to the stability of the financial system, to the operation of the economy and to the reputation and prosperity of the Netherlands. That is the stated mission of AFM.
126. Grundman-van de Krol 2010, p. 50.
127. Under Art. 2 of the Mw.
128. As provided for in Art. 3 of the Healthcare (Market Regulation) Act (Wmg). It should be noted that health insurers are also covered by the Wft and therefore have to deal with three supervisors, namely DNB, the AFM and the NZA.
129. Van der Eerden & Silverentand 2015, pp. 32–38. The duties of the SSM are laid down in the SSM Regulation and the SSM Framework Regulation. They have direct effect in the Netherlands. Efforts were made in the Implementing Law on the Regulation of Banking Supervision to make the ECB's supervision consistent with the Wft as far as possible.
130. Established as a result of the financial crisis.
131. *See* Art. 6 paragraph 4 of the SSM Regulation and Art. 53 paragraph 1 of the SSM Framework Regulation for the definition of 'significant bank'. At the inception of the SSM 120 banking groups (comprising approximately 1,200 supervised banks) were designated as significant. As of November 15, 2016 there were 126. In the Netherlands the following are designated as significant (as of November 15, 2016): ABN AMRO Group N.V., ING Groep N.V., Coöperatieve Rabobank U.A., SNS Holding B.V., Bank Nederlandse Gemeenten N.V., Nederlandse Waterschapsbank N.V.

11.4.3 The changing role of supervision and the supervisors

In recent years, particularly after the financial crisis, the supervision and role of supervisors (particularly financial supervisors) has changed considerably. A great deal of research has been and is being carried out into supervision and the role of market and other supervisors. People even speak of the science of supervision.[132] This is considered further below from various perspectives.

11.4.3.1 From the perspective of the government

An authoritative piece of research is that carried out by the WRR in 2013 into supervision in the Netherlands.[133] The central question in this research is what changes are necessary in the policy and practice of supervision in order to increase social added value of state supervision.[134] State supervision is deemed to mean supervision carried out by or for the state, in particular state inspectorates and market supervisors.[135] The WRR concludes in its report that there are a substantial number of deficiencies. One of these is that the three core values of the supervision need to be guaranteed or guaranteed more effectively, namely: a) an impartial attitude; b) independent positioning; and c) public, multiple accountability.[136]

The WRR has issued the following recommendations.[137] The first recommendation is that the government's view of supervision needs to be reassessed. The guiding principle is the social function of supervision and the added value which state supervision can offer in safeguarding public interests. A second recommendation concerns the promotion of a yield-oriented culture and improvements to the infrastructure for a stronger scientific underpinning of evaluation and supervision. A third recommendation is the promotion of the use of sphere-of-influence analyses in issues relating to the establishment, design and implementation of state supervision. From this perspective agreements should be entered into with the supervisors on the strengthening of the information, monitoring and knowledge function in their organizations. All supervisors should state in their annual plans how they use existing checks and balances and counterforces and how they use and contribute to other forms of supervision. A fourth important recommendation is that the reflective function of the state supervisors should be strengthened. On the basis of the WRR idea this means a strengthening of the feedback role which supervisors play in the agenda-setting, preparation and evaluation of their policy.

As already stated above, a fifth recommendation concerns stronger safeguards for impartial fulfillment of functions and associated independent positioning of supervisors.[138] The WRR calls for the proposal of the collaborating inspectorates for an

---

132. Aelen 2016, p. 3.
133. WRR 2013. *See also* Knottnerus 2012, who announced the report at the time. A (brief) synopsis of the report was also published.
134. WRR 2013, pp. 28–29.
135. Ibid., p. 30. *See* section 11.4.1 *supra* for the definition of market supervisor.
136. WRR 2013, p. 13 (summary) and p. 151.
137. Ibid., pp. 152–158.
138. *See* further in this section.

'independence protocol' to be included with safeguards for independent risk analyses and consistent publication of reports. A sixth recommendation relates to adequate public accountability of supervisors on deployed capacity, instruments and results achieved and for an appropriate accountability relationship with Parliament. WRR believes that the government should call on supervisors to strengthen their public information and accountability on the way in which they perform their supervision.[139]

The seventh and final call from the WRR is for a real relationship between the benefits expected from the supervision and the available capacity, both quantitatively and qualitatively. There should be a reconsideration of the principle of paying for supervision in principle entirely from taxation with an assessment of how this partial recharging of the costs of supervision could provide incentives for supervised parties to assume more responsibility themselves.[140]

11.4.3.2 From the perspective of the supervisor

A vision document by the market supervisors provided the impetus to define criteria for good market supervision.[141] The document builds on various earlier initiatives developed in order to produce an overview of the elements which make up good supervision. Instead of setting up a new survey, it was decided to review earlier findings. The selected elements in this document which define good supervision therefore result from these earlier surveys, or are a reworking of them.[142] The intention of the document is to provide supervisors with solid guidelines for good supervision in practice.

In summary this means that a good supervisor: 1) is effective (i.e. mission-driven, effect-oriented, accountability-oriented and change-oriented; 2) is efficient (i.e. empowering, collaborative and efficiently organized; and 3) has a professional attitude (which means independent, transparent[143] and made up of professionals).

139. This may be at odds with the confidentiality provisions for the AFM and DNB as set out in the Wft.
140. This idea has evidently been abandoned in the financial sector. Under the Financial Supervision (Financing) Act all supervised undertakings in the financial sector pay DNB and the AFM for the supervision they carry out. This raises the question of how objective this supervision can be because it potentially involves a conflict of interest. Although it is of course an attractive idea that ultimately, with perfect compliance with rules, less supervision is necessary, the question nevertheless arises of whether supervision could develop as a 'self-fulfilling prophecy'. In addition, there are plans for the supervision carried out by the ECB also to be paid for entirely by the institutions themselves.
141. Markttoezichthoudersberaad 2014. The Markttoezichthoudersberaad consists of the ACM, the AFM, the AP, DNB, the KSA and the NZA.
142. This looked particularly at: a) Kaderstellende visie op toezicht – 2005, 'Minder last, meer effect', *Parliamentary Papers II* 2005/06, 27 831, 15; b) 'Effectief Markttoezicht' inbreng van Markttoezichthoudersberaad voor de herziening van de Kaderstellende Visie op Toezicht (2011); and c) Viñals, Fiechter, 'The Making of Good Supervision: Learning to Say "No"', IMF paper, (May 18, 2010), SPN/10/08 and d) previous evaluations of supervisors. *See* Markttoezichthoudersberaad 2014, p. 2.
143. In this connection it is interesting to note that a 2016 bill on transparent supervision in the financial markets was drawn up by the Ministry of Finance. The objectives of the bill are: a) to expand the possibilities for supervisors to issue a public warning; b) a power

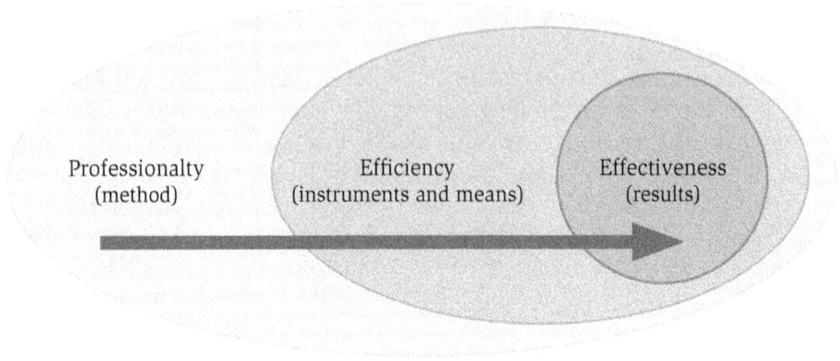

Figure 1: Criteria for good market supervision 2014

11.4.3.3 From the perspective of academia

In her dissertation Aelen investigated the question of what the principles of good market supervision were and how they should be developed for evolving supervision in the financial markets.[144] She identifies three categories of principles. First, there are principles which flesh out the effectiveness of the supervision (effective supervision). Secondly, principles are identified which flesh out the (democratic) legitimacy of the supervision (legitimized supervision). Finally, there are principles which flesh out the fairness of the supervisor's actions (proper supervision). According to Aelen these principles jointly make up the principles of good supervision.[145]

Aelen further notes in this regard that:

> 'a clear connection can be outlined here with what Hessel refers to as the three-track approach. The three-track approach represents the necessary multidisciplinary approach of government intervention in the market. Within

for the AFM and DNB to name names of individual institutions when they announce results of thematic investigations into the degree of compliance and risks to compliance; c) a possibility for the supervisors to react to disclosures by institutions concerning supervision; and d) a basis for DNB to publish key figures of banks as designated in an order in council. It is intended also to include powers b) and c) in the Accounting Organizations (Supervision) Act, the Pensions Act and the Occupational Pension Schemes (Compulsory Membership) Act, to the extent that these have not yet been included. The bill gives the supervisors new powers to publish information. This makes the supervision more transparent. These new powers are in line with existing practices. The powers will be applied to information already held by the supervisor so that the use of the new powers does not lead to new costs. The proposal has drawn strong criticism from the sector and parts of it have now been amended and sent to the Council of State. It is not yet clear when the bill will come into force.

144. Aelen 2014, p. 5.

145. Ibid., pp. 8–9 and 431–432. For the elaboration of these principles, *see* part 3 of her dissertation.

this multidisciplinary approach, legal, economic and sociological aspects must come together in the organization of government action. The first track is the ends-and-means track, centered on elements of effectiveness and efficiency. The second track is the legal track, which relates to procedural legitimacy and material justice. The third track is the influence track, which relates to the "democratic content of government intervention". The three tracks must be combined to optimize government intervention. Combining these elements is not always simple, however. The principles of good supervision should play a leading role in this.'[146]

11.4.3.4 Supervision dilemmas

Aelen[147] distinguishes five dilemmas in the supervision of the financial markets that are characteristic of the field of tension between the instrumental function of public economic law[148] on the one hand and the safeguard function of public economic law on the other.

a) *Institutional independence versus the importance of legitimacy*: the independence requirement[149] is at odds with the legitimacy requirement that is aimed at guaranteeing a connection between the will of the people and government intervention. The legitimacy requirement after all requires a direct connection between the supervisor and the electorate. The independence principle, on the other hand, demands an independent role of the supervisor in which a conflict of interest must be avoided.
b) *Operational independence versus standards of proper conduct:* according to Aelen the operational independence of the supervisor is at odds with the legal guarantees for various reasons. That is because this independence means that the supervisor must have a degree of discretion (for example with open standards). If this means that in certain circumstances the supervisor takes politically sensitive or policy decisions, the primacy of the legislator (which results from the legality principle) impedes it. The primacy of the legislator means after all that the legislator is responsible for determining public interests and not the supervisor (the latter having limited democratic legitimacy). The legality principle furthermore specifies that a legal basis is required for all the actions of the supervisor. Effective supervision approaches that require the supervisor to focus on countering harmful behavior, irrespective of whether this conduct is illegal, is at odds with the legality principle. If these theories also require the supervisor to take no action against conduct which has been qualified by the legislator as illegal (because according to the supervisor it is not harmful), tension also arises with principle of the duty of enforcement.[150]

146. Aelen 2014, p. 9. The reference to Hessel concerns: B.E. Hessel, *Overheidsoptreden in de relationistische rechtsstaat*, Zwolle: W.E.J. Tjeenk Willink 1988.
147. Aelen 2014, pp. 439-442 and 18-19. *See also* Raaijmakers 2013b, pp. 98-103.
148. In this instance, public law refers *inter alia* to the Wft.
149. Which means that the supervisor must be physically remote from the political sphere.
150. Aelen 2014, pp. 191-203.

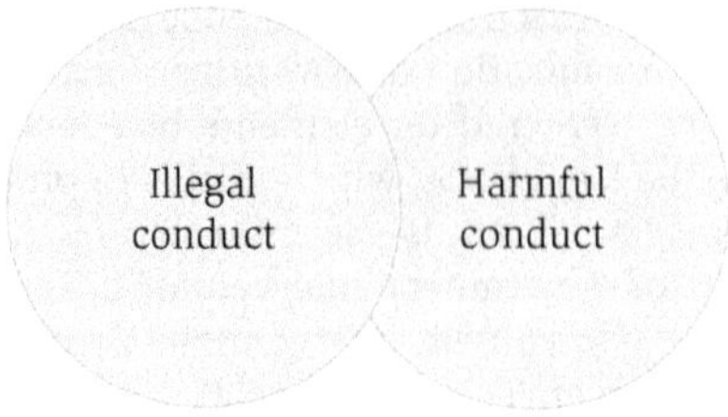

Figure 2: The strategy of the AFM

With regard to the foregoing it is interesting to refer to the work of the American professor Malcolm Sparrow. The issue of supervisors' approach to harmful conduct is central in his work.[151] AFM's supervision is based on his theories.[152] Sparrow's message can be summarized as: 'pick the important problems and fix them; and be transparent about it.'[153] The latter is necessary to ensure that the measures taken have the biggest possible impact so that market participants see that the supervisor is taking enforcement action. The approach from Sparrow's perspective amounts to a problem- and risk-oriented approach to enforcement issues, in which the problem requiring solution is paramount. A financial supervisor (such as the AFM and DNB) must promptly flag, tackle and publicize externally any harmful practices which could damage trust in and the stability of the financial markets. The problem lies in the fact that harmful conduct does not necessarily have to be illegal, i.e. prohibited by law. Certain practices may therefore be harmful but not prohibited.[154] On the other hand there may be illegal practices which are not necessarily harmful. This poses a dilemma for the supervisor because in performing his duties he is bound by the general principles of sound administration.[155] Maatman & Azahaf wonder in this regard where the boundary should be and call for the liability of financial supervisors to

151. Sparrow 2000. *See also* Sparrow 2008.
152. DNB and other supervisors are interested in his theories as well.
153. Sparrow 2000, p. 132.
154. The AFM cites *inter alia* the example of commission paid to insurance and other intermediaries. The (past) practice of paying commissions to insurance and other intermediaries impedes objective provision of service for the customer. After all, it is likely that the intermediary will offer the products of the organization which pays the most commission, which are not necessarily in the interests of the customer. As a result of the ban on commissions (since January 1, 2013) this problem has been solved. *See also* chapter 6 *supra* on conflicts of interest.
155. For example the legality principle as set out above by Aelen. The main principles are the legality principle, the speciality principle, the legal certainty principle, the proportionality principle and the prohibition of *détournement de pouvoir*. Reference is also made to the terms of Art. 3:1 of the Awb, which states that the general principles of sound administration also apply to acts by administrative bodies other than decisions.

be limited. In their opinion supervisors have only limited potential to tackle harmful (but nevertheless legal) conduct.[156]

c) *Principles-based supervision versus legitimacy, appropriateness and legal certainty*: according to Aelen[157] the intention of principles-based regulation is to assign responsibility to supervised institutions and introduce flexibility in the supervision. She believes, however, that principles-based supervision gives rise to questions relating to the appropriateness, legitimacy and legal certainty of the acts of supervision. In the first place principles-based supervision makes the powers of the supervisor so broad that tension arises with the demands of legitimacy and legality. Secondly, the requirements of care and motivation are strict, so the intended flexibility is soon called into question. Far-reaching requirements for motivation and care could undermine the intended effectiveness of the principles-based supervision. Thirdly, the principle of legality (resulting from the principle of legal certainty) requires that all parties must be able to determine clearly which conduct may lead to their prosecution. This requires the supervisor to make known clearly in advance how the (principles-based) standard must be interpreted. This is a complex process, because the principles-based supervision must allow room to maneuver for the institutions being supervised. The supervisor should therefore flesh out the standards in detail, but should make them known sufficiently before enforcing them.[158]

   Finally, according to Aelen,[159] actions by the supervisor are tested thoroughly, because the margin of appreciation in principles-based supervision belongs not to the supervisor but to the institutions being supervised. This constrains the flexibility of the supervision. The dilemmas concerning the effectiveness of the principles-based supervision versus the legal guarantees involved are interesting, because they clearly show not only the dilemma but also the tension between attempts to broaden the effectiveness of the supervision and the legal guarantees. In the case of principles-based supervision, an overly strict interpretation of the legal guarantees (in this case comprising the legality principle, the principles of sound supervision and the principle of legal certainty) seriously undermine the intended effectiveness of the principles-based supervision. After all, if the legal guarantees are applied in a very strict sense, there is still little in the way of own responsibility for the market participants and flexibility of supervision.

156. Maatman & Azahaf 2010. Art. 1:25d of the Wft limits the liability of supervisors. This was in response to the DSB affair, in which supervisors were accused of (alleged) improper supervision. The article specifies that DNB, the management and the supervisory board and its employees are not liable for damage caused by actions or omissions in the exercise of a task assigned or a power granted on the basis of a legal provision, unless such damage largely results from intentional improper performance of the task or intentional improper exercise of powers or is largely attributable to gross negligence. The same applies to the AFM.
157. Aelen 2014, p. 440.
158. In the law of financial supervision this remains the eternal dilemma. *See* section 11.2.4 *supra* for the discussion on open versus closed standards.
159. Aelen 2014, pp. 440–441.

d) *Confidentiality versus transparency*[160] *and accountability*: according to Aelen[161] there is a restrained approach in financial supervision to the publication of information because information on the stability of financial undertakings, for example, could lead to a bank run. On the other hand, the transparency of the supervisor is seen as essential within the framework of (political and public) accountability.[162] Openness on the part of the supervisor means that the supervisor can be monitored. Transparency also has an instrumental function. The publication of supervision information helps propagate standards and also has a warning effect. A dilemma thus arises between confidentiality in the framework of the effectiveness of the supervision and transparency in the framework of the accountability on the one hand and the effectiveness (instrumentality) of the supervision on the other hand. Transparency of supervision information is of great importance, but must be responsible.

e) *Naming and shaming versus legal guarantees*: finally Aelen[163] notes the dilemma between openness of supervision in the framework of enforcement[164] and various legal guarantees intended to protect the position of the supervised institution vis-à-vis the supervisor. Within the framework of the transparency principle, the supervisor has various powers or an obligation to make fining decisions public.[165] Public disclosure of fining decisions has the effect of propagating standards and also acts as a warning. The public disclosure of a fining decision can, however, also have an enforcing effect due to the likely reputational damage resulting from disclosure. This reputational damage may prove problematic if it subsequently emerges that the penalty should not have been imposed. In that case there is a tension with legal guarantees that require the penalty to be applied only once it has been established in law that a violation has been committed. With regard to the foregoing, Aelen sees the express embedding of the independence of financial supervisors as a challenge together with the strengthening of the accountability mechanism of the financial supervisors.[166]

---

160. *See also* section 11.4.3 *supra* concerning the bill on transparent supervision of financial markets. *See also* De Vries 2016. In her inaugural speech she deals with the question of whether transparency leads to more trust in the supervisor. She concludes among other things that there are opportunities for fruitful cooperation between supervision and academia.
161. Aelen 2014, p. 441.
162. *See* note 160. *See also* section 11.4.3 *supra*.
163. Aelen 2014, p. 441.
164. The Enforcement Policy document of the AFM and DNB (*Government gazette* 2008, 132, p. 30) and the further clarification by the AFM and DNB (of May 17, 2011) formulated the guiding principles for the (joint) enforcement by the AFM and DNB. The main formal means of enforcement are: issuing an instruction to adopt a particular course of action (Art. 1:75 of the Wft), imposing an incremental penalty (Art. 1:79 of the Wft), imposing an administrative fine (Art. 1:80 of the Wft), issuing a public warning (Art. 1:94 of the Wft), appointing a custodian (Art. 1:76 of the Wft), dismissing a policymaker (Art. 1:87 of the Wft) and withdrawing the license (Art. 1:104 Wft).
165. Set out in Art. 1:97 of the Wft, also referred to as 'naming and shaming'.
166. Aelen 2014, pp. 458–459. She calls for a so-called transparency officer.

11.4.3.5 Supervisory failure

The previously cited investigation by SEO examined what supervisory failure was in a more general sense. According to SEO, supervisory failure occurs if the creation of a supervisor gives rise to regulatory failure that is greater than the market failure which the supervisor is endeavoring to correct.[167] SEO identifies various forms of supervisory failure, a number of examples of which are highlighted here that are of importance to supervision in the financial markets.

- There may be excessive supervision: this is unnecessary and excessive supervision for matters which could be resolved better or more efficiently without the supervisor. Excessive supervision removes responsibility from the supervised party, which may consequently display moral hazard behavior. He is no longer held to account with regard to his own responsibility, but expects all risks to be covered by supervision and enforcement.[168]
- There may be multiple supervision (accumulation): this can lead to high administrative expenses and the risk of conflicting rules if institutions or persons have to deal with multiple supervisors.[169]
- There may be improper supervision: as a result of an information gap the government may take measures that are no longer necessary.
- Another form of supervisory failure occurs if the supervisor itself does not adhere to the rules or sets the wrong example by its conduct.[170]
- The supervisor is not always independent.[171] This has to do, for example, with what is also known as 'regulatory capture'. This means a supervisor is inclined to focus less on protecting the general interest and more on protecting the interests of the institution or group being supervised.[172]
- There is too much supervision driven by incidents. This applies particularly to members of the Lower House of the Dutch Parliament who as a result of a

167. SEO 2005, p. 16.
168. This problem arises in healthcare. If it is no longer deductible, average citizens would possibly lead (even) unhealthier lives. In private life, car insurance can serve as an example. Because 'everything is insured' it is possible that the driver will take more risks on the road.
169. There are countless examples of this. See the various investigations and reports in the bibliography.
170. One of the more recent examples is the NZA. In April 2014, whistleblower Arthur Gotlieb's report was made public (in the NRC newspaper). He believed patients' details and confidential documents were not secure within the NZA. The management was also concealing the poor financial situation of the NZA, and there were disputed travel and other expenses claims by the Board of Directors. The scandal led to the establishment of a committee chaired by Hans Borstlap. The committee's conclusion was devastating and it proposed a large number of improvement measures. The Board of Directors had by then already resigned. The AFM also regularly came under fire due to a lack of good exemplary conduct.
171. *See* previous comments *supra* on supervision dilemmas.
172. *See* Stigler 1971 and Stigler 1974. The supervisor apparently identified too much with the supervised institutions. This could also reflect the paradox that the sector creates the supervisor's right to exist, as they pay for the supervision. *See also* section 11.2.1 *supra*.

focus on incidents become involved in supervision of local or regional issues or matters which have nothing to do with the government. This attitude means that more supervision takes place than is necessary. This also leads to cost increases. In order to make the supervised institutions aware that firm action will be taken against unauthorized conduct, the supervisor may also overreact.

11.5 EFFECTIVENESS OF REGULATION AND MARKET SUPERVISION[173]

As argued above, various factors including the financial crisis, but also other large-scale incidents, have meant that (many) more laws and regulations have been introduced into sectors, including the financial sector. Supervision of compliance with these rules has also increased concomitantly. The first question is whether the rules themselves are achieving the intended effect and the second question is whether their supervision is also intended to have an effect. After all, supervisors too are required to be accountable.[174] It is stated in the literature that effect measurement must therefore form an integral part of the supervision process.[175] One may also wonder whether regulation itself has an effect in the first place. Since laws and regulations in the financial sector (financial supervision regulations) have expanded enormously in the years since the crisis, this is considered in more detail below.

11.5.1 Effectiveness of regulation

In general it can be stated that the main objectives pursued in financial supervision regulations are promoting the stability of the financial market, promoting trust in the financial market and, thirdly, protecting non-professional parties in the financial market.[176] As a result of these objectives, measuring the effectiveness of these regulations is a complex matter. This is made clear by the following examples:

- Does requiring an oath or solemn affirmation from everyone working in the financial sector actually contribute to the desired cultural change in the financial sector? And if so, how can that be measured?
- How, for example, should the objective of 'treatment of customers with due care' be measured objectively?
- How can the sound operational management of a financial undertaking be objectively measured? Is an undertaking more sound if (on paper) it has introduced all the required regulations?
- Does the 'pure market model'[177] manage to put the customer's interest first and how do you measure that?
- Does the comprehensive and enforceable moderation or prohibition of pay and bonuses really guarantee a less 'perverse incentive' in the financial undertaking?

173. Drawn from Houben 2013.
174. With regard to the transparency of the supervisor, *see* section 11.4.3 *supra*.
175. Hilbers et al. 2012, p. 38.
176. *See also Parliamentary Papers II* 2001/02, 28122, 2, p. 10.
177. For the term '*het zuivere marktmodel*' *see inter alia* section 6.7 *supra*. The point is that the customer interest is served professionally and as objectively as possible.

A follow-up question is, if effectiveness can be measured, what should be done with the results. Will this improve the legislative process? Or is it justified to conclude that self-regulation works better and that less regulation should take place?

A starting point in determining effectiveness is the definition of the concept of effectiveness.[178] A useful definition of the effect of legislation (and hence effectiveness) is: 'The social changes that take place after a law comes into force, as a result of the adjustment in the conduct of actors, with the changed activities resulting from legislation that has made this conduct possible or compulsory.'[179]

According to Veerman & Mulder, the changed activities concern various actors. For example, there are parties subject to the standards who wish to act within the framework of the law, but also various government bodies which carry out activities based on delegated powers. In the definition the 'effect' is linked to the influence on society, which also includes the influence on social institutions. For them it is a question of the social effect. The fact that a law has come into force legally through publication in the *Bulletin of Acts and Decrees* does not automatically mean that it also operates in a social sense. If a law does not work, it exists but it does nothing in or to society.[180]

Veerman & Mulder also include the process of preparing regulations in their research. A law is intended to tackle a social problem (that problem is usually the starting point). The solution to that problem is the ultimate objective, the criterion for success. What is important, therefore, is whether the law corresponds to the identified problem. The cause and preparation may be of importance to and have an influence on the subsequent effect. There is also a difference between the two processes. The process of the law in gestation does not fall within the effect of the law itself. In the gestation stage of a law different actors and interests play a role than when the law is in force; the contexts differ. The law marks the end of the preparation process; it also marks the start of a - new - process.[181] In summary it can therefore be stated that to determine the effectiveness of financial supervision regulations (such as the Wft) it is first necessary to look at the definition of effectiveness, the creation process and the objectives of regulations.

Kockelkoren distinguishes three approaches to the measurement of effectiveness of financial supervision regulations such as the Wft.[182] The Law and Economics approach (cost-benefit analysis) looks first at whether it is sensible to introduce financial supervision regulations. After they come into force an assessment is made as to whether the regulations are efficient and effective at an acceptable cost. According to Kockelkoren, such an analysis often produces unclear conclusions. And even more often it is not possible to implement these on a solid basis. The problem

178. Various terms such as efficiency and efficacy are assimilated to effectiveness for the sake of convenience in this chapter.
179. Veerman & Mulder 2010, p. 13. At the beginning of their study, when describing the research question, they considered the definition of terms such as effect, efficiency and effectiveness.
180. Veerman & Mulder 2010, p. 13.
181. Veerman & Mulder 2010, p. 14.
182. Kockelkoren 2011. The types of approach referred to in the speech are drawn from the research and from literature published on it. References to the sources can be found in the speech.

is that the level of direct costs of legislation and the causality between an increase in costs and the introduction of legislation often cannot be determined effectively. The indirect costs, such as losses of growth and the prevention of innovation, can scarcely be measured objectively. Furthermore, the causality is difficult to determine with legislation.[183]

Problems are also encountered in the determination of the benefits. How, for example, should the effectiveness of the Wft with regard to the 'treatment of clients with due care'[184] be measured objectively? One way in his view would be to measure the damage avoided as a result of the introduction of the Wft. However, measuring the quantity of damage which has not arisen is already difficult in and of itself, but measuring which part of that avoided damage is attributable to the Wft is many times more difficult. Kockelkoren concludes that the cost-benefit analysis must only be used to a limited extent. He believes that these analyses are useful, provided they are used in subareas where good research is possible.[185]

In the Behavioral Economics approach Kockelkoren states that the aim is to quantify the 'bounded rationality' of customers.[186] Such analysis can be based on 'laboratory' research and objective facts concerning the volume of the various submarkets. The extent to which the Wft protects customers against limited rationality should then be determined. He believes that here too there are grounds for objection. The main objection is perhaps that insight into the 'bounded rationality' of customers is still limited. There is even less understanding of how this bounded rationality impacts the many types of decisions on products and services that customers have to make. It is also not easy to determine what effect the Wft will then have on people's decision-making behavior.[187]

Finally in the Sociology of Law approach qualitative consideration is given to the effectiveness of legislation. This approach states that it is necessary to look not only at the act itself, but also at the actors around it, after which a statement will be made on the overall effectiveness. Institutes are deemed to be not only the supervisors, but also the legislator, interest groups, self-regulating organizations, the judicial authority, the supervised institutions and consumers and investors. This approach looks critically not only at the means, but also at the objectives in the judgment about effectiveness. Kockelkoren uses an example from this approach in which the effectiveness is assessed on the basis of three layers. First an assessment is made as to whether the combined body of law and institutes is internally consistent. Then an assessment is made of whether the law and institutes are able to solve the specified social problem. And finally an assessment is made of whether there is another body of law and institutes that is clearly better able to solve the social problems.[188] He concludes that the latter approach appears to be the most usable in

183. Kockelkoren refers to Stewart 1981.
184. Art. 4:25 paragraph 1 of the Wft.
185. On Actal *see* section 11.2.3 *supra*. New regulation always includes an Actal calculation. It is striking that there are sometimes major differences in calculations of administrative costs and compliance expenses by Actal and the financial sector itself when establishing and complying with the Wft.
186. For an explanation of this term *see* section 11.2.2 *supra*.
187. Kockelkoren refers here to Veerman & Mulder 2010, p. 29.
188. Kockelkoren, 2011. The example cited is drawn from Teubner 1983, p. 252.

determining the effectiveness of the Wft. Due to the many problems encountered in measuring or quantifying costs or benefits of financial supervision regulations, a qualitative approach appears better. Moreover, the initial objectives and the process of creating the regulations, for example, can be analyzed in greater detail, giving more coherent insight.

11.5.2 Effectiveness of supervision

Hilbers et al. deal with the measurement of the effect of supervision. They draw a distinction between the strategic, tactical and operational levels. This theory proves difficult to put into practice, however. Measurements mostly take place on the tactical or operational level.[189] They distinguish four challenges in the proper measurement of effects.[190]

The first challenge concerns the use of the research method. In financial supervision it is not easy to separate effectively the experimental group from the control group. This is necessary, however, because otherwise it would not be possible to obtain an accurate answer to the question of what would have happened if there had been no supervision or if the supervisor had taken no action.[191] An additional problem is the fact that selecting supervised entities for a control group can pose a problem. This can raise questions because the selection may result in a deliberate decision to ignore undesirable practices of the control group. This impairs the level playing field and may be in conflict with the principle of equality.

The second challenge with regard to measuring effect is the situation in which supervision interventions have both short- and long-term effects, which in some cases may also be opposed.[192]

The third challenge is making the effect clear to the outside world.[193] The confidentiality obligation of financial supervisors in many cases impedes communication on interventions in individual companies. For example, DNB and the AFM are only permitted to use information on individual companies to the extent necessary to perform their duties. In principle this does not include measuring effect. This forces

189. Hilbers et al. 2012, p. 39.
190. Ibid., pp. 40–41.
191. The example is cited of the situation in which the supervisor aims to raise the level of financial services by talking to intermediaries about their controlled and sound business operation. It is very likely that companies or individuals in the control group will learn of the supervision intervention through the media, the Internet, an industry organization or their network.
192. The example is cited of the situation in which a financial supervisor, for example, can force a financial company to sell complex investments when there is insufficient balance between the complexity of the investment policy and the level of the risk control in the fund. These interventions can then be accompanied in the short term by additional costs and therefore have a negative effect on the company's financial position, but in the longer term have the aim of strengthening the financial position or reducing the risks to which this company is exposed. If the financial position is used as an indicator of effect, the effect may initially be negative, but ultimately – if the company is adequately able to control its risks – may become positive.
193. Hilbers et al. 2012, p. 41.

supervisors in some cases to report generically on the effects achieved, whereas they would actually prefer to do this specifically in order to highlight the achieved effect clearly. It is also conceivable that reporting on effect as a whole is undesirable in light of the objectives pursued by a supervisor. This arises for example in the case of near misses. In the case of a near miss when the disaster has been averted through the intervention of the supervisor, it is plausible that its action had an effect.[194]

The final challenge is that measuring effect requires time and capacity.[195] In order to carry out a reliable measurement, a good research method must be developed and data must be gathered. The supervisor must also guarantee that sufficient expertise is available internally or externally (for example through a link with academia). Since supervisors always have to make choices due to scarce resources, this means that investing in the measurement of effect results in a number of other supervisory activities being unable to be tackled. The measurement of effect must therefore form an explicit part of the prioritization of supervisory work.

Hilbers et al. do, however, see possibilities for a solution to the challenges outlined above, asserting that the more concrete the effect to be measured is, the simpler it is to measure this effect. Hence there are also calls to select good indicators that fit in with the concrete objective for the measurement of an effect.[196] It is also necessary to seek out ways to increase the plausibility of the causal relationship. Measuring the effect would be particularly promising on a tactical level. The supervisor then measures whether a specific intervention has led to a change of behavior. If the interventions have been carefully selected, they will also contribute to achieving the higher social objective.[197]

Welp finally calls for a more responsive approach in the evaluation of the results of supervision. That means that the set-up and implementation of impact evaluations match unique elements in the supervision and the specific characteristics of various supervisors and areas of supervision. In 'responsive evaluation' it is not the policy goals and associated performance indicators that are central in assessing the supervision carried out, but much more the involvement of all the stakeholders around the supervision and (the effectiveness of) the action taken by each of them.[198]

194. The example is cited of the averting of an impending bankruptcy of a financial undertaking through the intervention of the supervisor. By intervening the supervisor contributed to the soundness of the financial undertaking, the public's trust in this undertaking and presumably in the financial sector as a whole. Communication on it, however, could immediately destroy that effect if the public consequently lost confidence in the sector to which the company belongs. 'There's no smoke without fire', would then be the public's reaction. If one company was in difficulty, that could also apply to other similar companies. Communication on a near miss could thus have a negative effect on the public's trust in the financial sector.
195. Hilbers et al. 2012, p. 41.
196. Ibid., p. 45. A distinction is made here between hard and soft indicators.
197. Ibid., p. 49. The term higher objective refers to the public interest. *See also* section 11.1 *supra*.
198. Welp 2012, p. 22. The writer himself states that the focus in his article is on the external 'vertical' supervision which the central government carries out through state inspectorates and authorities, but that this may also be of interest for supervision on other levels (such as market supervision).

BIBLIOGRAPHY

Articles and books

Aelen 2014
M. Aelen, *Beginselen van goed marktoezicht. Gedefinieerd, verklaard en uitgewerkt voor het toezicht op financiële markten*, (diss. Utrecht), The Hague: Boom Juridische uitgevers 2014.

Aelen 2016
M. Aelen, 'Toezichtwetenschap', *TvT* 2016-2, pp. 3-7.

Akerlof 1970
G. Akerlof, 'The Market for Lemons', *The Quarterly Journal of Economics*, Vol. 84, No. 3, 1970, pp. 488-500.

Baarsma 2010
B.E. Baarsma, 'Nederland Toezichtland', *TvT* 2010-2, pp. 3-5.

De Boer & Martius 2014
H.L. de Boer & R.M.L.A. Martius, 'Zelfregulering: een goed betrouwbaar alternatief voor publieke regulering', *FR* 2014, no. 6, pp. 232-235.

Brenninkmeijer 2010
A.F.M. Brenninkmeijer, 'Wat is toezicht', *TvT* 2010-3, pp. 71-73.

Buijnk 2014
C.P. Buijink, 'Bancaire zelfregulering in roerige tijden', *FR* 2014, no. 6, p. 231.

Coase 1960
R. Coase, 'The problem of social cost', *Journal of Law and Economics*, Vol. 3, 1960, pp. 1-44.

Gilardi & Maggetti 2011
F. Gilardi & M. Maggetti, 'The independence of regulatory authorities', in: D. Levi-Faur (ed.), *Handbook on the Politics of Regulation*, Cheltenham: Edward Elgar Publishing Limited 2011, pp. 201-215.

Grundmann-van de Krol 2010
C.M. Grundmann-van de Krol, *Koersen door de mist: op weg naar transparante wetgeving?* (oratie Nijmegen), Den Haag: Boom Juridische Uitgevers 2010.

Hilbers et al. 2012
P.L.C. Hilbers, D.R., Rijsbergen, K. Raaijmakers & F. de Vries, 'Effectmeting in het toezicht op de financiële sector: "If your business is harm-control, show me the harms you have controlled!"', *TvT* 2012-2, pp. 38-49.

Houben 2013
R.A.M. Houben, 'Regulering of overregulering? Zoektocht naar de effectiviteit van financiële toezichtregelgeving', in: C.A. Wielenga et al. (ed.), *Jaarboek Compliance 2013*, Capelle aan den IJssel: Nederlands Compliance Instituut 2012, pp. 15-33.

Kahneman & Tversky 1979
D. Kahneman & A. Tversky, 'Prospect Theory: An Analysis of Decision under Risk', *Econometrica*, vol. 47(2), 1979, pp. 263-291.

Kockelkoren 2016
Th.F. Kockelkoren, *Toezicht als beroep*, Gentian Publishing 2016.

Llewellyn 1999
D. Llewellyn, 'The Economic Rationale for Financial Regulation', *Financial Services Authority Occasional Paper*, April 1999.

Maatman & Azahaf 2010
R.H. Maatman & S. Azahaf, 'Financieel toezicht en schadelijk gedrag', *Ondernemingsrecht* 2010-7, pp. 296–302.

Ogus 2004
A. Ogus, *Regulation: Legal Form and Economic Theory*, Oxford: Hart publishing 2004.

Raaijmakers 2013a
K. Raaijmakers, 'De economische theorie achter de werking van financiële markten', in J.B.S. Hijink, K. Raaijmakers & K.A. Kralj (eds.), *Tien jaar financieel recht in Rotterdam. Lustrumbundel Master Financieel Recht*, Rotterdam: Erasmus Universiteit Rotterdam 2013, pp. 19–38.

Raaijmakers 2013b
K. Raaijmakers, 'Oplossingen voor marktfalen, de rationale en aard van regulering en toezicht', in J.B.S. Hijink, K. Raaijmakers & K.A. Kralj (eds.), *Tien jaar financieel recht in Rotterdam. Lustrumbundel Master Financieel Recht*, Rotterdam: Erasmus Universiteit Rotterdam 2013, pp. 87–112.

Rosenthal et al. 1996
U. Rosenthal, A.B. Ringeling, M.A.P. Bovens, M.A.P., P. 't Hart, & M.J.W. van Twist, *Openbaar bestuur, beleid, organisatie, politiek*, Alphen aan den Rijn: Samson H.D. Tjeenk Willink, 1996.

Samuelson 1957
P.A. Samuelson, 'Pitfals in the analysis of public goods', *Journal of Law and Economics*, Vol. 19, 1957, pp. 199–204.

Schleifer 2005
A. Shleifer, 'Understanding Regulation', *European Financial Management*, Vol. 11, No.4, 2005.

Schram & Van Twist 2016
J. Schram & M. van Twist, 'Toekomst voor toezicht: open samenleving, open toezicht?', *TvT* 2016-3, pp. 56–72.

Sparrow 2000
M.K. Sparrow, *The Regulatory Craft. Controlling risks, solving problems, and managing compliance*, Washington: Brookings Institution Press 2000.

Sparrow 2008
M.K. Sparrow, *The character of Harms. Operational Challenges in Control*, New York: Cambridge University Press 2008.

Stewart 1981
R.B. Stewart, *Regulation, innovation, and administrative law: A conceptual framework*, 69 California Law Review, 1259 (1981).

Stigler 1971
G.J. Stigler, 'The theory of economic regulation', *The Bell Journal of Economics and Management Science,* Vol. 2, 1971, pp. 3-21.

Stigler 1974
G.J. Stigler, 'Free riders and collective action: an appendix to theories of economic regulation', *The Bell Journal of Economics and Management Science,* Vol. 5, 1974, pp. 359-365.

Stiglitz 2010
J.E. Stiglitz, 'Government Failure vs. Market Failure', in: E.J. Balleisen & D.A. Moss (eds.), *Government and Markets. Toward a New Theory of Regulation,* Cambridge: Cambridge University Press 2010, pp. 13-51.

Terlouw 2009
A.B. Terlouw, *Angst en regelgeving; onderscheid door de overheid op grond van nationaliteit, afkomst en religie* (oratie Nijmegen), Nijmegen: Wolf Legal Publishers, 2009.

Teubner 1983
G. Teubner, 'Substantive and Reflexive Elements in Modern Law', *Law & Society Review,* Vol. 17, no. 2, 1983, pp. 239-285.

Van der Eerden & Silverentand 2015
F.W.J. van der Eerden & L.J. Silverentand (eds.), *Hoofdlijnen Wft,* Deventer: Wolters Kluwer 2015.

Veerman & Mulder 2010
Gert-Jan Veerman & Robin Mulder, *Wetgeving met beleid, bouwstenen voor een bruikbare wetgevingstheorie,* The Hague: Boom Juridische Uitgevers 2010.

De Vries 2015
F. de Vries, *Leidt transparantie tot meer vertrouwen in de toezichthouder* (oratie Groningen), Groningen: Rijksuniversiteit Groningen 2015.

Welp 2012
P. Welp, 'Effectiviteit van het toezicht: tijd voor '*responsive evaluation*'', *TvT* 2012-2, pp. 7-22.

Reports

Actal 2015
The Dutch Advisory Board on Regulatory Burden (Actal), *Jaarverslag 2015. Van minder regeldruk naar meer ruimte voor vernieuwing.*

Actal April 2015
The Dutch Advisory Board on Regulatory Burden (Actal), *Scherp op regeldruk. Aanbevelingen op basis van de tweede regeldrukaudit,* April 2015.

Actal 2016
The Dutch Advisory Board on Regulatory Burden (Actal), *Visie toekomstig regeldrukbeleid. Van regeldrukbeleid naar betere regels,* 2016.

Bovenberg, Van Dalen & Teulings 2003
A.L. Bovenberg, H.P. van Dalen & C.N. Teulings, *De Calculus van het publieke belang*, report on behalf of the Ministry of Economic Affairs and the Ministry of Finance, June 2003.

Holtslag Committee
De ministeriële verantwoordelijkheid ondersteund. Een checklist voor een systematische beschrijving en analyse van toezichtsarrangementen. Report of the Holtslag Committee to the Minister of the Interior, The Hague, July 1998.

Maas Committee
Report of the Advisory Committee on the Future of the Banking Industry (Commissie Maas), *Naar herstel van vertrouwen*, April 2009.

Rapport Regeldruk 2011
J. Arnoldussen & M. Pijzel, *Regeldruk; Een kwalitatief onderzoek naar de perceptie van overheid en regeldruk vanuit de overheid*, research report by Motivaction on behalf of the Ministry of the Interior and Kingdom Relations, July 2011.

RMO 2014
The Netherlands Council for Social Development (RMO), *De verleiding weerstaan. Grenzen aan beïnvloeding van gedrag door de overheid*, opinion number 55 on behalf of the government and the parliament, The Hague, March 2014.

SEO 2005
B.E. Baarsma, *Nederland Toezichtland – een economisch perspectief*, Research on behalf of the 'Programma Andere Overheid'/Committee 'Marktordening en economische sectoren' by SEO Amsterdam Economics (SEO) of the University of Amsterdam, April 2005.

SER 2005
The Social and Economic Council of the Netherlands (SER), *Ondernemerschap voor de publieke zaak*, Draft opinion of the Committee on Entrepreneurship in Public Service, The Hague, 2005.

Van Gestel & Hertogh 2006
R.A.J. van Gestel & M.L.M. Hertogh, *Wat is regeldruk? Een verkennende internationale literatuurstudie*, research on behalf of The Research and Documentation Centre (WODC), The Hague: Ministry of Justice 2006.

De Wit Committee 2010
Report of the Parliamentary Commission of Inquiry into the Financial System, *Verloren Krediet, Parliamentary papers II* 2009/10, 31980, 4.

De Wit Committee 2012
Report of the Parliamentary Commission of Inquiry into the Financial System, *Verloren Krediet II – De balans opgemaakt, Parliamentary papers II* 2011/12, 31980, 61.

WRR 2013
Toezien op publieke belangen. Naar een verruimd perspectief op rijkstoezicht, The Scientific Council for Government Policy (WRR) report number 89, Amsterdam: Amsterdam University Press 2013 (a synopsis of the report was also published).

WRR 2014
Met kennis van gedrag beleid maken, The Scientific Council for Government Policy (WRR) report number 92, Amsterdam: Amsterdam University Press 2014.

Other references

27831 | Kaderstellende visie op toezicht
Parliamentary papers II 2005/06, 27831, 15 (inclusief bijlage 1: de Toezichtvisie 'Minder last, meer effect. Zes principes van goed toezicht').

28122 | Hervorming van het toezicht op de financiële marktsector
Parliamentary papers II 2001/02, 28122, 2.

29362 | Modernisering van de overheid
Parliamentary papers II 2007/16, 29362.

31731 | Integraal wetgevingsbeleid
Parliamentary papers II 2008/15, 31731.

31980 | Commissie de Wit
Parliamentary papers II 2009/10, 31980, 6.
Parliamentary papers II 2011/12, 31908, 61.

32782 | Wet versterking governance van De Nederlandsche Bank en de Autoriteit Financiële Markten
Kamerstukken II 2011/12, 32782.

Financial Sector (Oath or Solemn Affirmation) Regulation 2015
Regulation of the Minister of Finance of December 12, 2014, reference: FM 2014/1237 M, Financial Markets directorate, including rules with regard to the oath or solemn affirmation required of persons referred to in articles 3:8, paragraph 1, 3:17b, paragraphs 1 and 2, 4:9, paragraph 1, and 4:15a, paragraph 1, of the Financial Supervision Act (Financial Sector (Oath or Solemn Affirmation) Regulation 2015), *Government Gazette. 2014*, 37261.

De Jong 2011
J. de Jong, *De diagnose en behandeling van overbodige bureaucratie. Pleidooi voor een klinische benadering van een hardnekkig probleem*, (essay written on behalf of the Ministry of the Interior and Kingdom Relations, Programma Regeldruk), 2011.

Knottnerus 2012
A. Knottnerus, *Regels, compliance en toezicht*, lecture October 4, 2012.

Kockelkoren 2011
Th.F. Kockelkoren, *Effectiviteit van de Wft* (address at the symposium 'De effectiviteit van het financieel toezichtrecht' organized by the Institute for Financial Law of Radboud University Nijmegen on February 17, 2011).

Markttoezichthoudersberaad 2011
Effectief markttoezicht. Inbreng van Markttoezichthoudersberaad AFM, Consumentenautoriteit, CBP, DNB, NMa, NZa en OPTA voor de herziening van de Kaderstellende Visie op Toezicht, September 2011.

Markttoezichthoudersberaad 2014
Criteria voor goed toezicht. Visie Markttoezichthoudersberaad, February 2014.

Notitie regeldruk 2006
'*In regels gevangen?*' Een verkenning van mogelijke oorzaken van regeldruk', essay written by a working group of the ministries of Justice, Finance, Economic Affairs, and the Interior and Kingdom Relations, February 2006.

NVB 2013
Zelfregulering, brochure of the NVB, March 2013.

VvV 2013
In eigen hand. Organisatie en controle op zelfregulering in de verzekeringsbranche, brochure of the VvV, April 2013.

12. Regulatory Compliance and Enforcement

Prof. W. Huisman

12.1 INTRODUCTION

The word compliance derives from the verb 'to comply', which means to conform in the fulfillment of official requirements. The requirements may be laid down in laws and regulations. While the word compliance refers to acting in accordance to these rules, in the world of business 'compliance' is usually used for the activities and processes that aim to guarantee such norm-conforming behavior. For this, 'compliance programs' are set up, 'compliance management systems' are implemented and monitored by 'compliance officers'. These aim to ensure that the organization as such as well as its employees act in compliance with governmental regulation as well as internal standards and guidelines.

Regulation is the pre-condition of both compliance as well as enforcement. Enforcement refers to the process of making sure people obey a law. As regards content, compliance and enforcement seem to have the same meaning. However, compliance refers to the process within business organizations, while enforcement refers to the same process executed by governmental agencies responsible for law enforcement. Compliance management and enforcement share the reason of being that compliance with business regulation is neither automatic nor self-evident. (New) norms may not correspond to business practices, management and employees might not be aware of regulations and compliance with such regulations costs time and money. Social and economic regulation of business therefore has an intrinsic compliance problem. External incentives by regulatory enforcement is seen to be needed.

Effective enforcement makes people comply with regulation. A condition for effective enforcement – as well as compliance management – is knowing what makes people comply with the law. And perhaps even more important: what makes them not comply. Several academic disciplines provide knowledge on the roots of compliance. Understanding why people obey the law is the domain of social psychology,[1] understanding why (people working within) business organizations obey the law is the domain of both management and regulation studies[2] and understanding why people and organizations do not comply with the law is the domain of criminology.[3] This chapter will draw upon all these disciplines, with a focus on criminology.

Criminologists label business non-compliance as 'white collar crime'. Since the introduction of this term by the criminologist Edwin Sutherland at his presidential address for the American Sociological Association in 1939, criminologists have been arguing over the proper definition of this concept. For the purpose of this paper, white collar crime is defined as 'illegal acts proscribed by law, committed by legitimate organizations and respectable individuals, aimed at illicit advantage while giving the appearance of legitimacy in the context of business transactions in an organizational/ professional setting'.[4] The ultimate non-compliance so to say.

This chapter will look at the relations between compliance and enforcement. First, enforcement strategies will be discussed, including a model for enforcement that includes motivations for compliance and non-compliance. Secondly, results of studies on causes of compliance and non-compliance from various academic disciplines will be studied. This chapter will conclude with the relevance of these results for better law enforcement and compliance.

12.2 REGULATORY ENFORCEMENT

Empirical research on the way regulatory agencies enforce business regulations reveals two types of enforcement styles: a deterrence strategy and a compliance strategy. Alternative models develop integrative strategies, based on assumptions about the causes of compliance and non-compliance. All three perspectives on enforcement will be elaborated below.[5]

12.2.1 Deterrent enforcement

The deterrence style is also referred to as 'command and control': regulations are drafted by government agencies and imposed on business, and compliance is strictly monitored. Regulatory enforcement is concentrated on detecting and sanctioning violations. The deterrence style is mostly associated with criminal justice. However, the application of civil or administrative law for regulatory enforcement can also have punitive or even incapacitating effects on business, for instance, issuing administrative fines or revoking licenses.

The deterrence style is based on the assumption that compliance and violation are led by economic motives. Companies are seen as rational actors calculating the costs and benefits of compliance and non-compliance. A deterrence strategy assumes that offenders will refrain from future offending, if detection and punishment occur

1. Tyler 1990.
2. Parker & Nielsen 2011.
3. Simpson & Weisburd 2009.
4. Simpson 2013.
5. Huisman 2014.

with sufficient frequency and severity. However, the strategy is counterproductive when it takes away the voluntary motivation to comply.

Research is skeptical about the effectiveness of deterrent enforcement in improving business compliance. In a first systemic review on corporate deterrence, Simpson et al. found hardly any significant effects. Sanctioning had minimal to no deterrent impact at the individual and company levels.[6] Further, Thornton et al. and Van Wingerde examined whether companies learn about cases of severe penalties in the same industry, and whether this knowledge changes the firms' compliance-related behavior.[7] They found that less than half of the companies could identify the 'signal cases' of severe legal penalties. They concluded that explicit deterrence does not enhance the perceived threat of legal punishment, but it may serve as a reminder to check on reliability of internal compliance routines and as a reassurance that compliance is not injudicious.

Due to the difficulties of directly influencing compliance-related behavior by legal penalties, contemporary regulators have set their hopes on reputational damage as a result of the 'naming and shaming' effect of publicly sanctioning companies. Substantial reputational damage might result from publicly shaming corporate misconduct, even though there is not much knowledge about the impact in terms of financial and social reputation damage for business.[8] Research by Karpoff et al. showed that such market sanctioning differs from one type of corporate misconduct to another: reputational damage is the 'big hammer' in companies losing value in cases of accounting fraud, while reputational damage was non-existent in cases of environmental pollution and bribing of foreign officials.[9]

12.2.2 Compliance assistance

Perhaps due to the 2008 economic crisis and recent scandals of business fraud and corruption, current official rhetoric is tough on tackling corporate crime and non-compliance. However, empirical studies show that most regulatory agencies apply enforcement styles that rely on cooperation rather than confrontation; they use advice and negotiation rather than coercion and formal legal action. 'Compliance assistance' is the preferred official enforcement strategy of several regulatory agencies.[10]

Where violation results from organizational shortcomings, negotiation and consultancy as an enforcement style can be used to teach a corporation how to comply with regulations. Cooperative regulation is used to stimulate companies to maintain internal compliance management systems. Compliance management systems are viewed as important tools for companies to organize and monitor regulatory compliance.

The rise of compliance-oriented enforcement styles also results from shifts in the regulation of business. Instead of a traditional 'rule-based' approach with detailed prescriptions for business operations, governments shifted to 'principle-based'

6. Simpson et al. 2014.
7. Thornton et al. 2005; Van Wingerde 2012.
8. Van Erp 2013.
9. Karpoff & Lott 1993; Karpoff et al. 2005.
10. Van de Bunt & W. Huisman 2007.

regulation, containing broad duty-of-care provisions and the obligation for businesses to maintain compliance management systems. For example, this is the case when regulation no longer dictates what kind of equipment should be used to reduce a certain level of emission but prescribes a compliance system that ensures a sustainable business operation. Enforcement is then based on reports provided by the companies themselves and it is aimed at ascertaining whether compliance mechanisms are working effectively. However, such an approach may prove counterproductive in the case of intentional violation. Regulatory capture is the pitfall of cooperative enforcement.[11]

Whether compliance management systems have had a positive impact on non-compliance has to date received little attention in empirical research. Compliance programs create awareness and give instructions on how to comply. Kaptein found a positive effect of ethical codes of conduct on compliance.[12] It was observed, however, that the effectiveness of corporate compliance officers could be compromised when they report to the business line management, rather than the corporate board. Compliance programs could even be considered to be more cosmetic than real, largely serving a PR function. In some cases, they may actually increase or facilitate corporate offenses, by regulatory capture or keeping up appearances.[13]

12.3 RESPONSIVE REGULATION

The downsides of both styles of regulation and enforcement led to the propagation of integrative models. Academics who suggest these models try to find an optimal mix of compliance and deterrence. A widely adopted model is that of 'responsive regulation'.[14] The central notion of 'responsive regulation' is that enforcement styles should be tuned to the motives and competences of individual companies laid down in an 'enforcement pyramid'. Regulators should start at the bottom of the pyramid, assuming that a company is willing to comply voluntarily. When this is shown not to work, regulators should escalate up to deterrence-oriented strategies. The regulatory pyramid has become the paradigm for a 'sequential' combination of compliance and deterrence styles of enforcement. It has been adopted by regulatory and enforcement agencies worldwide.

In academic debate, the model has had a mixed reception. Empirical studies on its use show that it is very difficult to apply the entire pyramid in practice. It is hard to assess the actual motives of companies, it is difficult to shift between enforcement styles, and it ignores other environmental influences on compliance than state regulation. Also, its main premise, that strong sanctions and eventually incapacitation are available as a last resort against recurrent offenders, is often not met in practice.[15]

As a result of the above insights, new and more sophisticated models have evolved such as 'smart regulation', adopting the principles of responsive regulation,

11. Gunningham 2011.
12. Kaptein 2011.
13. Friedrichs 2010.
14. Ayres & Braithwaite 1992.
15. Mascini 2012.

but expanding regulation to third parties as surrogate regulators.[16] In the field of compliance management in contemporary business, private market regulators and professional auditors, such as rating agencies and accounting firms, seem to fit this role. As for all modern regulatory theories, smart regulation advocates government to facilitate and mobilize other network members rather than direct intervention. Smart regulation has to organize public enforcement so that it can reinforce third parties to help with regulating.

12.4 CAUSES OF (NON-)COMPLIANCE

A main premise of responsive regulation and other contemporary models of effective enforcement is that interventions should be targeted at the root causes of (non-) compliance. Factors influencing compliance behavior of companies and their representatives are found on several aggregate levels: the instructional level of economic markets and governmental regulation, the organizational level of companies and their characteristics and the individual level of personal norms and traits of corporate executives, managers and employees.

12.5 INSTITUTIONAL LEVEL

According to some criminologists, white collar crime is inherently related to the capitalist economic system that has become the dominant worldwide model, especially after the collapse or erosion of communist economic systems. These scholars try to expose how capitalist economy leads to the commission of crime as well how ideologies of neo-liberal economy lead to redefining crime as acceptable costs of capitalist production. Social harms are not unfortunate side effects of, but intrinsic to the logic of neo-liberal economic theory.[17]

According to other criminologists, it is not so much the economy in general, but it is the condition of the economy that creates the problem of financial and economic crime. However, empirical research is scarce, and criminogenic effects have been attributed to both economic downturns and economic booms. Fraud increases during economic contractions as well as during economic booms, but for different reasons. Booms provide booty: during booms, investors become irrationally exuberant and expect better earnings and are less likely to monitor firms who put out positive information. Recessions produce more fraud and non-compliance by companies due to scarcity. During recessions there is a strong pressure to achieve financial goals and generally, external monitoring of firms is laxer, due to concerns about the economy and cuts in the budgets of monitoring agencies.[18]

At the institutional level, regulation itself has been associated with compliance and non-compliance. The recent 2008 financial crisis is often used as a case in point. In the United States of America, federal policies encouraging homeownership and deregulation created a subprime mortgage loan market while taking away the

16. Gunningham & Grabosky 1998.
17. Ruggiero 2013.
18. Simpson & Rorie 2016.

Chinese walls between retail and investment banking. This created the incentives and opportunities that sparked off the subprime mortgage frauds and the large scale high-risk trade in collateralized debt obligations that caused the crisis. Deregulation and too much trust in 'principle-based' regulation and self-regulation in the financial industry are generally seen as causes of the misconduct that led to financial crisis. The government that bailed out corporations considered too economically important to fail, also negotiated settlements permitting giant firms to avoid the consequences of criminal convictions. Hence banks being perceived to be 'too big to fail, too powerful to jail'.[19] Presenting detailed data from more than a decade of federal cases, Garrett reveals a pattern of negotiation and settlement between prosecutors and corporations, leading to vaguely defined reforms and high-level employees tending to get off scot-free.[20] Yet, the crisis has led to calls for more and more stringent regulation. However, research also shows that regulation can reduce moral norm-internalization (compliance as 'tick-the-box').[21] The paradox is that both deregulation and overregulation of markets appear to have criminogenic effects.

12.6 ORGANIZATIONAL LEVEL

At the firm level, three types of motives for compliance and non-compliance are distinguished: economic, social and normative motives.[22] Economic motives refer to the extent to which the firm is committed to maximizing its own economic or material utility, such as increasing turnover and profit. Social motives refer to the extent to which a firm is committed to earning the approval and respect of significant people with whom an actor interacts including other businesses, trading partners, employees, customers, local communities and the wider public. Normative motives refer to the extent to which the firm is committed to obeying the regulation for its own sake because of a sense of moral agreement with the specific regulation or a generalized sense of moral duty to comply. Empirical research has made it clear that there are a wide range of relevant motives and they interact with each other in reciprocal ways: personal motives of managers are extrapolated to the motivations of the organization as a whole, and in turn, these shape the motivations of individual managers.

While the general perception of non-compliance sees it in the light of intention and economic motives, empirical studies have identified less rational causes such as widespread routine and other types of organizational shortcomings.[23] Motivation to comply is of secondary importance if a firm does not possess the capacity to comply. In view of this, corporate rule breaking is the outcome of bounded rationality. Managers do not possess all the relevant information on the cost and benefits of options for action and organizational procedures lead to suboptimal outcomes. Landmark cases of organizational deviance - such as the Ford Pinto and the NASA Challenger - have falsified the initial explanation of these cases as being the result of rational and

19. Pontell et al. 2013.
20. Garrett 2014.
21. Parker & Nielsen 2011.
22. Ibid., pp. 10–14.
23. Vaughan 1999.

amoral calculation on the basis of cost-benefit assessments. Instead, the accidents were framed as being the result of organizational failure.[24]

This dichotomy of ends and means varies with the amount of autonomy of departments. However, lack of internal control shows up in diverse organizational structures: in highly bureaucratic structures managerial responsibility for shop-floor level misconduct tends to be diffused over several hierarchical layers, while in decentralized – loosely coupled – organizational structures, more autonomous subsidiaries might escape the monitoring of the parent company.[25]

Organizational culture has been especially identified as a factor influencing regulatory compliance by or within the firm. Ethical business culture is found to have a strong influence on managers and employee conduct.[26] Also in criminology, much explanatory power is attributed to criminogenic corporate cultures in the causation of white collar and corporate crime.[27] Organizational cultures may transmit rule transgression by 'normalizing' lawbreaking by neutralization and rationalization.[28] After the financial crisis, the business culture of the financial industry has been criticized as being immoral and unethical. In the journal *Nature*, Cohn et al. show that employees of a large, international bank behave, on average, honestly in controlled conditions.[29] However, when their professional identity as bank employees is rendered salient, a significant proportion of them become dishonest. This effect is specific to bank employees because control experiments with employees from other industries and with students show that they do not become more dishonest when their professional identity or bank-related items are rendered salient. These results thus suggest that the prevailing business culture in the banking industry weakens and undermines the honesty norm, implying that measures to re-establish an honest culture are very important.

12.7 INDIVIDUAL LEVEL

For decades, the individual characteristics of corporate executives and managers have not been seen as relevant variables in regulating and stimulating corporate compliance. White collar crime is typically understood to be a result of criminogenic work-related environments in which individual differences have little importance or relevance. White collar offenders themselves are typically assumed to be socially and psychologically normal, conventional and law-abiding members of society, who lack traits or predispositions that are generally associated with criminals. Most research in white collar criminology has focused on how criminogenic contextual factors turn these 'normally good people into bad'.[30] What's more, '[a] bad apple explanation for

24. Cullen et al. 1997; Vaughan 1996.
25. Keane 1995.
26. Kaptein 2008; Kaptein 2010.
27. Huisman 2016.
28. Shover & Hochstetler 2002.
29. Cohn et al. 2014.
30. Apel & Paternoster 2009.

white collar crime tends to deflect attention away from the structural and institutional conditions that give rise to systematic white collar and corporate offending'.[31]

The financial crisis and large accounting fraud cases have renewed the attention for personality traits that influence individuals' motives for corporate crime. Large financial accounting fraud such as Enron has been related to the personality traits of corporate executives. Public, political as well as academic debate on the causes of the financial crisis of 2008, have indicated the roots of the current credit crunch to be the result of excessive risk taking, moralistically referring to 'greed'.[32] As a result, (Dutch) financial market regulators are now attempting to assess the individual integrity of corporate executives.

While in the strict neo-liberal model, the personal characteristics of managers do not matter for corporate decision-making, an emerging stream of work in accounting and finance recognizes that financial reporting practices vary predictably with specific individual traits of executives.[33] Even (adapted) applications of rational theories (in which cost and benefits are shaped by situational conditions) demonstrate that individual norms, attitudes, and values play an important role in non-compliance decisions.[34] Several studies show that the likelihood of offending is reduced if a manager perceives the act as being immoral or socially harmful, or carrying negative social and reputational consequences for himself or the firm.[35] For example, a self-report survey on bribery among Dutch public officials and business people showed that besides social norms and opportunity to comply with integrity standards, individual norms – measured as feelings of moral obligation to refrain from corruption strongly contributed to the explanation of proneness to corruption.[36]

In recent studies several personality traits are related to white collar crime, such as the need for control, bullying, charisma, fear of falling or failing, ambition, lack of integrity, and a lack of social conscience.[37] Particularly elevated levels of narcissism are found in white collar offenders.[38]

Psychopathy is a psychological construct that incorporates various traits, including narcissism, arrogance, intelligence and extraversion. These are many of the traits and characteristics that white collar offenders seem to possess, but combined with an inability to feel empathy. Psychopaths have no conscience and are incapable of empathy, guilt, or loyalty to anyone but themselves. Babiak & Hare found relatively high levels of psychopathy among CEOs of large corporations.[39] Some of the characteristics of psychopathy (e.g., charm, grandiosity) emulate those features that make a successful business person. However, managers with psychopathic traits can also harm the corporation. In a British self-completion management survey, Boddy found that 'corporate psychopaths' have a large and significant impact on conflict and bullying, and employee affective well-being; these have a large and significant impact

31. *See* note 1 *supra* of this chapter.
32. Huisman 2011.
33. Davidson et al. 3013; Schrand & Zechman 2012.
34. Paternoster & Simpson 1996.
35. *See* note 1 *supra*, p. 317.
36. Gorsira et al. 2016.
37. Benson & Manchak 2014.
38. Blickleet al. 2006; Rijsenbilt et al. 2013.
39. Babiak & Hare 2006.

on counterproductive work behavior.[40] And while such 'functional' psychopathy might not always lead to fraud, the question remains as to how psychopathy is related to corporate compliance.

Researchers interested in financial decision-making have used biological measures of neuro-physical factors to help explain (economic) behavior. So far, these measures have not been used to explain regulatory compliance. Neuroscientist Coates (a former trader at Goldman Sachs, Merrill Lynch and Deutsche Bank), studied the biology of risk taking and stress by monitoring steroid hormones and their cognitive effects, and examined potential links to trader performance in the financial markets. The findings suggest that cortisol codes for risk and testosterone for reward. A key finding of this endocrine research is the different cognitive effects of acute versus chronic exposure to hormones: acutely elevated steroids may optimize performance on a range of tasks; but chronically elevated steroids may promote irrational risk-reward choices. Coates suggests that the irrational exuberance and pessimism observed during market bubbles and crashes may be mediated by steroid hormones. This finding is interesting in the light of various cases in which (formerly) successful traders committed fraud in trying to cover up losses, such as Nick Leeson of Barings Bank, Jerome Kerviel of Societé Generale and Kweku Adoboli of USB.

A recent line of biological research associates an individual's facial structure with 'masculine' behavior such as aggression, egocentrism, risk seeking, and a desire to maintain social status. In this research, testosterone is thought to influence behavior because it shapes an individual's neural circuitry early in life and because the brain responds to changes in current testosterone levels. Testosterone not only affects brain development but is also associated with face shape. This means that an individual's facial features can be used as a biological marker of masculine behavior. Jia et al. have taken this to the world of corporate compliance.[41] They argue that facial structures meaningfully capture variation in those CEO personal characteristics that are associated with financial reporting. They focus on the risk of materially misstated financial statements and test the hypothesis that it varies systematically with the degree to which the CEO is disposed to show masculine behavior. They examined the relation between a measure of male CEOs' facial masculinity and financial misreporting. One possible mechanism for this relation is that the hormone testosterone influences both behavior and the development of the face shape. They used a sample of pictures of 1,136 CEOs from S&P1500 companies in 2009 and computed a facial structure metric, the facial width-to-height ratio, by measuring the distance between cheekbones and the height of the upper face of each CEO from his picture. They then traced the full employment history of each CEO to construct a panel data set of 3,909 firm years during the 1996–2010 period. They controlled for firm-fixed effects. Jia et al. found a strong positive association between CEO facial masculinity and various misreporting proxies. They complement this evidence by documenting that a CEO's facial masculinity predicts his firm's likelihood of being subject to an enforcement action. They also show that an executive's facial masculinity is associated with the likelihood of the US Securities and Exchange Commission naming him as a perpetrator. The point here is that the masculine qualities of the CEOs are not

40. Boddy 2011.
41. Jia et al. 2014.

so much - or not only - associated with their own compliance behavior, but with the masculinity of the corporate culture they create and the incentives this culture provides for corporate fraud in attaining goals.

The research on the effect of testosterone brings us to the much debated issue of the relation between gender and regulatory compliance. This issue is often framed by quoting Christine Lagarde of the IMF: what if the Lehman Brothers had been the Lehman Sisters? There would have been no crisis. To prevent excessive risk taking and to change 'masculine' corporate cultures, several European countries have introduced laws demanding a quota of female members on corporate boards: Norway, Finland, France, Spain, and Italy. At least 30% women would be needed to change the masculine corporate culture that is associated with too much risk taking and too much competition.

Would such a gender quota also have a positive effect on compliance? From criminological theory, we can deduct two hypotheses. First, the dominant criminological explanation of white collar crime is situational: it's the economy and organizational criminogenics. Men are more exposed to risk factors for committing white collar crime as these are connected to the professional and managerial positions in business and organizations that are mostly occupied by men. Less female white collar crime is then simply explained by the gender gap in upper management levels. Successful female managers may be socialized into the ethos of commercial interests and market dominance at all costs, or they will be selected for their masculine traits and qualities.[42]

Secondly, from research on gender differences in crime, we can argue that women are less vulnerable to such criminogenic factors and are less inclined to commit white collar crime than their male colleagues.[43] Research into gender differences in white collar offenders is too scarce to draw conclusions on differences in the propensity to commit economic and financial crimes between men and women.

12.8 CONCLUSION

This chapter has explored relations between compliance and enforcement. Empirical research has shown that the way law enforcement agencies and officers operate is strongly influenced by perceptions of company attitudes towards regulation and motivations for compliance and non-compliance. Popular models prescribe that law enforcement is tuned to actual motivation for compliance. Compliance management has made a similar development, moving away from formalistic and legalistic approaches to compliance management and towards a behavioral approach. 'Soft' controls are now in fashion. This requires true insights in underlying causes and reasons why companies and their managers obey the law, and why they do not. This chapter has discussed these factors by looking at the institutional, organizational and individual level. Institutional and organizational factors are most commonly associated with business compliance levels. Yet, in the end it is the behavior of individuals (acting on their own behalf or on behalf of the organization) that is in compliance with regulatory requirements, or not. These individuals are not

42. Steffensmeier et al. 2013.
43. Piquero et al. 2013.

automated robots programmed by economic incentives and organizational cultures and structures. They are however restrained by their psychological and biological traits and competences. Studies on individual factors such as personality traits and biological factors are therefore very relevant for understanding regulatory compliance. Studies discussed above show how psychological and biological factors can steer behavior and especially in the case of executives – 'tone at the top' – the corporate culture. Integrative approaches to understanding compliance crime are necessary. Explaining compliance and non-compliance ultimately has to do with understanding the interplay between individual and environmental factors.

BIBLIOGRAPHY

Apel & Paternoster 2009
R. Apel & R. Paternoster, 'Understanding "Criminogenic" Corporate Culture: What White-Collar Crime Researchers Can Learn from Studies of the Adolescent Employment–Crime Relationship', in: S.S. Simpson & D. Weisburd (eds.), *The Criminology of White-Collar Crime*, New York: Springer 2009, pp. 15–33.

Ayres & Braithwaite 1992
I. Ayres & J. Braithwaite, *Responsive Regulation: Transcending the Deregulation Debate*, Oxford: Oxford University Press 1992.

Babiak & Hare 2006
P. Babiak, P. & R. Hare, *Snakes in Suits: When Psychopaths Go to Work*, New York: HarperCollins Publishers 2006.

Benson & Manchak 2014
M.L. Benson & S.M. Manchak, *The Psychology of White collar Offending*, Oxford Handbooks Online 2014.

Blickle et al. 2006
G. Blickle, A. Schlegel, P. Fassbender, & U. Klein, 'Some Personality Correlates of Business White-Collar Crime', *Applied Psychology*: An International Review 55, 2006, pp. 220–233.

Boddy 2011
C.R. Boddy, 'Corporate Psychopaths, Bullying and Unfair Supervision in the Workplace', *Journal of Business Ethics*, 100(3), 2011, pp. 367–379.

Cohn et al. 2014
A. Cohn, E. Fehr, & M.A. Maréchal, 'Business culture and dishonesty in the banking industry', *Nature*, 516(7529), 2014, pp. 86–89.

Cullen et al. 1997
F.T. Cullen, W.J. Maakestad W.J. & G. Cavender, *Corporate crime under attack: The Ford Pinto case and beyond*, Cincinnati, Ohio: Anderson, 1997.

Davidson et al. 2013
R. Davidson, A. Dey & A. Smith, 'Executives 'Off-the-Job' Behavior, Corporate Culture, and Financial Reporting Risk', *Journal of Financial Economics*, 117(1), 2013, pp. 5–28.

Friedrichs 2010
D.O. Friedrichs, *Trusted criminals: white collar crime in contemporary society*, Belmont, Calif.: Wadsworth Cengage Learning 2010.

Garret 2014
B.L. Garrett, *Too Big to Jail. How Prosecutors Compromise with Corporations*, Harvard University Press 2014.

Gorsira et al. 2016
M. Gorsira, A.J.M. Denkers & W. Huisman, 'Both Sides of the Coin - Motives for Corruption among Public Officials and Business Employees', *Journal of Business Ethics* 2016.

Gunningham & Gabrosky 1998
N. Gunningham & P. Grabosky, *Smart regulation: Designing environmental policy*, Oxford: Oxford University Press 1998.

Gunningham 2011
N. Gunningham, 'Strategizing compliance and enforcement: responsive regulation and beyond', in: C. Parker & V. Nielsen, *Explaining Compliance: Business Responses to Regulation*, Cheltenham: Edward Elgar Publications 2011, pp. 199-221.

Huisman 2011
W. Huisman, 'Corporate crime and crisis: Causation scenarios', *Sociology of Crime, Law and Deviance* 16, 2011, pp. 107-125.

Huisman 2014
W. Huisman, 'Compliance and corporate crime control', in: D. Weisburd & G.J.N. Bruinsma (eds.), *The Encyclopedia of Criminology and Criminal Justice*, New York: Springer 2014, pp. 489-496.

Huisman 2016
W. Huisman, 'Criminogenic Organizational Properties and Dynamics', in: S.R. van Slyke, M.L. Benson & F.T. Cullen (eds.), *The Oxford Handbook of White-Collar Crime*, New York: Oxford University Press, 2016, pp. 435-462.

Jia et al. 2014
Y. Jia, L. van Lent & Y. Zeng, 'Masculinity, Testosterone, and Financial Misreporting', *Journal of Accounting Research*, (52)5, 2014, pp. 1195-1246.

Kaptein 2008
S.P. Kaptein, 'Developing a Measure of Unethical Behavior in the Workplace: A Stakeholder Perspective', *Journal of Management*, 34, 2008, pp. 978-1008.

Kaptein 2010
S.P. Kaptein, 'The Ethics of Organizations: A Longitudinal Study of the U.S. Working Population', *Journal of Business Ethics*, 92, 2010, pp. 601-618.

Kaptein 2011
S.P. Kaptein, 'Towards Effective Codes: Testing the relationship with unethical behavior', *Journal of Business Ethics*, 99(2), 2011, pp. 233-251

Karpoff & Lott 1993
J.M. Karpoff & J.R. Lott Jr., 'The Reputational Penalty Firms Bear from Committing Criminal Fraud', *The Journal of Law and Economics*, 36(2), 1993, pp. 757-802.

Karpoff et al. 2005
J.M. Karpoff, J.R. Lott Jr. & E.W. Wehrly, 'The Reputational Damage for Environmental Violations: Empirical Evidence', *The Journal of Law and Economics*, 48(2), 2005, pp. 653-675.

Keane 1995
C. Keane, 'Loosely Coupled Systems and Unlawful Behaviour: Organization Theory and Corporate Crime', in: F. Pearce & L. Snider (eds.), *Corporate crime; contemporary debates*, Toronto: University of Toronto Press 1995, pp. 168-181.

Mascini 2012
P. Mascini, 'Why was the enforcement pyramid so influential? And what price was paid?', *Regulation & Governance*, 6, 2012, pp. 1-13.

Parker & Nielsen 2011
C. Parker & V. Nielsen, *Explaining Compliance: Business Responses to Regulation*, Cheltenham: Edward Elgar Publications 2011.

Paternoster and Simpson 1996
R. Paternoster & S.S. Simpson, 'Sanction Threats and Appeals to Morality: Testing a Rational Choice Model of Corporate Crime', *Law and Society Review*, 30, 1996, pp. 549–83.

Piquero et al. 2013
N.L. Piquero, L.M. Vieraitis, A.R. Piquero, S.G. Tibbetts & M. Blankenship, 'The Interplay of Gender and Ethics in Corporate Offending Decision-Making', *Journal of Contemporary Criminal Justice*, 29(3), 2013, pp. 385–98.

Pontell et al. 2013
H.N. Pontell, W.K. Black & G. Geis, 'Too Big to Fail, Too Powerful to Jail? On the Absence of Criminal Prosecutions Following the 2008 Financial Meltdown', *Journal of Crime, Law and Social Change*, vol. 61:1, 2013, pp. 1–13.

Ruggiero 2013
V. Ruggiero, *The Crimes of the Economy: A Criminological Analysis of Economic Thought*, Oxford: Routledge 2013.

Rijsenbilt et al. 2013
J.A. Rijsenbilt, H.R. Commandeur & A.G.Z. Kemna, 'Narcissus enters the courtroom: CEO Narcissism and fraud', *Journal of Business Ethics*, 117(2), 2013, pp. 413–429.

Schrand & Zechman 2012
C.M. Schrand & S.L.C. Zechman, 'Executive Overconfidence and the Slippery Slope to Financial Misreporting', *Journal of Accounting and Economics*, 53, 2012, pp. 311–29.

Shover & Hochstetler 2002
N. Shover & A. Hochstetler, 'Cultural explanation and organizational crime', *Journal of Crime, Law & Social Change*, vol. 37, 2002, pp. 1–18.

Simpson & Weisburd 2009
S.S. Simpson & D. Weisburd, *The Criminology of White-Collar Crime*, New York: Springer 2009.

Simpson 2013
S.S. Simpson, 'White collar Crime: A Review of Recent Developments and Promising Directions for Future Research', *Annual Review of Sociology*, 39, 2013, pp. 309–31.

Simpson et al. 2014
S.S. Simpson, M. Rorie, M.E. Alper, N. Schell-Busey, W. Laufer, N. Craig Smith, *Corporate Crime Deterrence: A Systematic Review*, Oslo, Norway: Campbell Collaboration 2014.

Simpson et al. 2016
S. S. Simpson & M. Rorie, 'Economic Fluctuations and Crises', in: S. van Slyke, M. Benson and F.T. Cullen (eds), *Oxford Handbook of White-Collar Crime*, Oxford: Oxford University Press 2016, pp. 326–44.

Steffensmeier et al. 2013
D. J. Steffensmeier, J. Schwartz & M. Roche, 'Gender and Twenty-First-Century Corporate Crime: Female Involvement and the Gender Gap in Enron-Era Corporate Frauds', *American Sociological Review*, 78, 2013, pp. 448-476.

Thornton et al. 2005
D. Thornton, N. Gunningham & R. Kagan, 'General Deterrence and Corporate Environmental Behavior', *Law & Policy*, 27, 2005, pp. 262-288.

Tyler 1990
T.R. Tyler, *Why People Obey the Law*, New Haven: Yale University Press, 1990.

Van de Bunt & Huisman 2007
H.G. van de Bunt & W. Huisman, 'Organizational crime in the Netherlands', *Crime & Justice. A Review of Research*, vol. 35, 2007, pp. 217-260.

Van Erp 2013
J.G. van Erp, 'Naming and shaming', in: G. Bruinsma & D. Weisburd (Eds), *Encyclopedia of Criminology and Criminal Justice*, New York: Springer 2013, pp. 3209-3217.

Van Wingerde 2012
C.G. van Wingerde, *De afschrikking voorbij. Een empirische studie naar afschrikking, generale preventie en regelnaleving in de Nederlandse afvalbranche* (diss. Nijmegen), Oisterwijk: Wolf Legal Publishers 2012.

Vaughan 1996
D. Vaughan, *The Challenger Launch Decision. Risky technology, culture, and deviance at Nasa*, Chicago: Chicago University Press 1996.

Vaughan 1999
D. Vaughan, 'The dark side of organizations: Mistake, misconduct, and disaster', *Annual Review for Sociology*, 25, 1999, pp. 271-305.

13. Supervision of Conduct and Culture[1]

R.A.M. Houben

13.1 INTRODUCTION

One of the main lessons of the financial crisis is that supervision relates to more than just the solvency, liquidity and profitability of financial undertakings. There is a danger that the risks resulting from the corporate culture of a financial undertaking and the conduct of persons working in it will be neglected.[2]

DNB notes in this regard:

> 'Undesirable conduct in financial institutions today causes the solvency and liquidity problems of tomorrow. That is now also generally acknowledged, as is evidenced by the attention devoted to the matter in international regulations. ... DNB uses various methods to assess the culture of an institution. ... Often, the results are far from satisfactory. Directors do not yet always have sufficient concern for the conduct and culture in their organization and their own role within it. We also regularly see financial institutions in which the risk culture does not match the nature of the institution. The question is what should be done. What works less well in this case is imposing and enforcing rules. There is no single correct culture or set of conduct rules. DNB is not a culture police but wants to hold a mirror up to directors: we present our observations and ask whether they recognize themselves in it. We also convey the importance of culture by means of speeches, publications and seminars and we show the key role that the board can play. In the assessment of directors, there is thus also the question of the extent to which a new director strengthens the composition of

1. This chapter is an adaptation of previous articles by R.A.M. Houben concerning the supervision of conduct and culture (Houben 2014 and Houben 2015).
2. Nuijts & de Haan 2013. This conclusion is also broadly supported by the De Wit Committees I and II; see the reports 'Verloren krediet' and 'Verloren krediet II – de balans opgemaakt' ('Lost credit' and 'Lost credit II – assessment made'). According to DNB, subsequent incidents such as the manipulation of the London Interbank Offered Rate (Libor) also confirm that this form of supervision is necessary.

> the board. Changing it can considerably affect the dynamics around the board table. Culture change is a long-term process. It begins by raising awareness of the problem among directors, followed by readiness to take action and a sometimes long process to change the culture of the organization. That requires stamina on the part of the institution and the supervisor.'[3]

DNB therefore introduced a new form of supervision in 2009, the supervision of conduct and culture. This form of supervision is complementary to traditional prudential supervision.[4] The fundamental idea behind this supervision is that there is a relationship or correlation between the conduct and culture of a financial undertaking and (the effect of) sometimes risky decisions or conduct in that undertaking. By means of this supervision DNB aims to focus more on conduct and culture so as to prevent, or at any rate try to prevent, future (major) incidents, such as the financial crisis. Over the years, the AFM has also begun to focus (more) on conduct and culture with an emphasis on consumer protection (the customers' interests first).[5]

The (academic) question of whether there is a relationship or correlation between certain forms of conduct and/or culture and the return or (the effects of) prudent risk management of a financial undertaking is difficult to answer.[6] According to DNB, conduct and culture can have a predictive value with regard to (risky) decisions of a financial undertaking.[7] In short, a particular culture could have a predictive value for future conduct.[8] A culture driven (only) by revenues could result, for example, in a management style that leads to taking more than average risks.[9] In this connection one would logically expect there to be a certain 'ideal' management style. However, this has not been demonstrated as such.[10]

Such (new) supervision of course gives rise to various questions and criticism based on practice.[11] On the other hand there is no doubt that a culture change was necessary in the financial sector.[12] A focus on ethics, integrity, culture and conduct in the financial sector is not new. The problem encountered sometimes, however, is that in practice DNB does not, or does not sufficiently, tackle the question of the form this should take. In addition, the question of whether such supervision is effective or whether the desired objectives have been or are being achieved remains

3. DNB Bulletin 2014.
4. DNB booklet 2009.
5. *See* section 13.2 *infra*.
6. It would be more logical to reverse the order because conduct is an expression of culture. 'Supervision of conduct and culture', however, has become a common expression in practice. This article has been written on the basis that conduct is an expression of culture.
7. Nuijts & De Haan 2013.
8. *Also* according to Van Beusekom & Raaijmakers 2010, p. 167. Moreover, DNB answers this question positively on the basis of extensive research particularly in (organizational) psychology. *See also* chapters 1 and 2 *supra*, which deal extensively with the fact that the culture of the undertaking greatly influences the conduct of the individual.
9. A dominant or excessively dominant management style, for example.
10. With regard to management styles see *inter alia* chapter 4 *supra* on Managing Organizational Integrity & Leadership.
11. Houben 2015.
12. *See also* Karssing 2013.

unanswered. Important aspects, after all, are what kind of culture has to be aimed for and what type of conduct or management style; in short, what is the 'right culture'?

Given the lack of clear and concrete 'benchmarks', there is a chance that, on the basis of research, DNB will advocate a certain model that is propagated as 'best market practice'. Here, there is a danger that it will take over too much of the role of the director of the supervised undertaking.[13] On the other hand, a great deal of research has been conducted into culture and conduct in undertakings and a certain relationship with 'performance' has been demonstrated.[14] It has yet to be seen, however, whether the course embarked on will actually deliver the desired end results and whether the 'desired' culture is the answer to the financial crisis.[15]

This chapter gives further consideration to the development of supervision of conduct and culture in section 13.2, the rationale and legal basis for such supervision in sections 13.3 and 13.4, and supervision and enforcement from the perspective of supervision law in section 13.5. The chapter is then concluded with some considerations in section 13.6.

13.2 DEVELOPMENT OF SUPERVISION OF CONDUCT AND CULTURE

Following the financial crisis, DNB produced a policy vision in November 2009 on the conduct and culture of financial undertakings and the related supervision.[16] This document formed the basis for the further development and adaptation of the supervision of conduct and culture over the years.[17] This expansion and refinement came about as a result of research among dozens of financial undertakings, first into 'governance' and decision-making and subsequently also into 'board effectiveness'.[18] The central aspects here include management, decision-making, communication and group dynamics. DNB also considered aspects such as group dynamics, behavior patterns and 'mindset'.[19] By means of workshops, publications, lectures and 'round tables', DNB also devoted increasing attention to conduct and culture aspects in its

13. Houben 2015.
14. *See also* chapter 4 *supra* on Managing organizational integrity & leadership.
15. It is noted here that DNB states that it expressly seeks dialogue with the financial sector.
16. DNB booklet 2009. The idea of such an approach is not new, however, cf. Kaptein & Dunning 2010.
17. The original concept of 'The seven elements of a sound culture' is still usable but compared to the current state of affairs this was the beginning. Reference is made to De Haan & Gorter 2015. This book, intended in the first place only for supervisors, contains twelve sections dealing with all the ins and outs of the supervision of conduct and culture. The book was published following a conference on September 24, 2015 ('Looking forward: effective supervision of behaviour and culture at financial institutions'), organized by DNB for over 100 other prudential supervisors worldwide.
18. DNB booklet 2011, DNB report 2011, DNB booklet 2012, DNB booklet March 2013, DNB booklet August 2013, DNB and AFM booklet 2014 and DNB booklet 2015 were published in connection with this research. These booklets included anonymized results of the various investigations, including 'good practices' and 'bad practices'.
19. *See* DNB booklet August 2013 and DNB booklet 2015.

supervision.[20] This ultimately resulted in supervision with a risk-oriented approach with regard to conduct, culture and integrity.[21]

Figure 1: The seven elements of a sound culture

In politics, with the legislator, the media and other stakeholders, a great deal of attention has also been devoted to the existence (or lack) of integrity, the 'right' culture and the 'right' conduct in the financial sector, whether driven by the financial crisis or other factors, leading to countless investigations, committees, codes of conduct, laws and regulations.[22]

Supervision of conduct and culture does not feature specifically[23] in DNB's more recent vision documents,[24] but the emphasis is more on supervision of integrity,[25] restoration of trust, capacity for change and strategic decision-making. This is due among other things to the course charted for a European Banking Union and the SSM, in which the emphasis is on prudent risk management. The most recent developments

20. Examples of articles are: Bökkerink & Veldhuis 2010, De Haan & Jansen 2011, Nuijts 2012, Piena & Christensen 2013, Nuijts & De Haan 2013, Raaijmakers & Scholten 2014. *See also* Karssing & Wirtz 2011.
21. Also included in FOCUS!, the successor to *Financiële Instellingen Risicoanalyse Methode* (Financial Institutions Risk Analysis Method – FIRM). This system has in turn been replaced by the Risk Assessment System (RAS) in connection with the introduction of the European Single Supervisory Mechanism.
22. Commonly discussed subjects include pay, bonuses, suitability and the banker's oath. Reference is made to the extensive literature on this subject, ranging from academic to more popular. The results of the (parliamentary) inquiries by the De Wit Committees and the Wijffels Committee, *inter alia*, provide good overviews. *See also* the interview with Jeroen Dijsselbloem in het Financieele Dagblad of December 10, 2016 in which he blames the banks (and the financial crisis) for the populism that is emerging in the Netherlands.
23. In contrast to what is stated in DNB booklet 2010, p. 22.
24. DNB booklet March 2014 and DNB booklet 2016.
25. Such as combating money laundering and corruption.

in the field of supervision of conduct and culture concern 'error management',[26] concurrence with the 'governance' of a financial undertaking[27] and the influence of (external) supervisors on internal supervision.[28]

As stated in section 13.1 *supra*, the AFM has also begun to focus more on conduct and culture over the years. To this end, it has developed a vision with DNB which can be characterized as 'Capacity for change'.[29] In developing and applying this vision, the AFM has been guided among other things by the philosopher Ken Wilber's AQAL model.[30]

13.3 THE RATIONALE FOR SUPERVISION OF CONDUCT AND CULTURE

DNB has basically questioned what influence human action and group-dynamic processes have on financial performance, integrity and the risk profile of a financial undertaking. The follow-up question is what facilitating or inhibiting role the culture of the undertaking plays in this regard. This then gives rise to the question of what measures are necessary in order to eliminate the risks of human conduct as far as possible. DNB states that supervision of conduct and culture is based on the following (scientifically substantiated) principles:[31]

1. Preventing another crisis requires more than just tightening up rules and laws.
2. There is a connection between public trust in financial undertakings and financial stability.
3. The culture and performance of the financial undertaking is largely determined by the conduct of directors, including with regard to the decisions they take.
4. Financial undertakings are responsible for conduct and culture: in this regard too, DNB is not going to take the place of the director.
5. Conduct and culture are an integral part of operational management: effective management is only possible if structure and culture go hand in hand.

---

26. De Haan & Gorter 2015, pp. 281–300. 'Errors' in this connection means 'unintended mistakes'. In short, how a financial undertaking deals with the mistakes it makes. Fraud, for example, is excluded from this definition.
27. Van Dijk & Nuijts 2015, Van de Loo & Winter 2016 and Mikulski 2016. In the new Corporate Governance Code of December 8, 2016 Principle 2.5 is devoted entirely to culture.
28. De Haan & Gorter 2015, pp. 305–319.
29. Although this supervision is often lumped together with that of DNB, it essentially involves an entirely different form of supervision. The vision and approach are described in the DNB and AFM booklet 2014. Attention is also devoted to this in the DNB booklet 2016 and the AFM's 2015 annual report. *See also* Van Beusekom & Raaijmakers 2010 for an approach to conduct and culture adopted by the AFM.
30. K.E. Wilber devised among other things the idea of the 'Integral Approach'. AQAL references the 'Integral Model' and stands for 'All quadrants, all levels, all lines, all states, all types'. This is not pursued further. Reference is made to the works of Ken Wilber on his website, www.kenwilber.com.
31. DNB booklet 2015, p. 7, de Haan & Gorter 2015, pp. 28–31. The views formulated in these principles are those of DNB.

6. There is no blueprint for an 'ideal' culture. A culture can nevertheless entail risks. The supervision is about identifying and controlling these risks.
7. The supervision of conduct and culture can be applied to all groups within a financial undertaking (i.e. not only at the top).

More (or more extensive) laws and regulations alone are therefore not sufficient to prevent another crisis or major incidents. The fall of Lehman Brothers in 2008, which is often seen as the trigger for the financial crisis, was followed by a slew of new laws and regulations.[32] Although this was necessary, it actually creates a false sense of security or a feeling of being in control. The conduct of particular persons (at the top), however, is perhaps still more important despite all the control measures. According to the Group of Thirty: 'Supervisors must focus on the demonstration of effective behaviors, not just on structural matters such as board composition and mandate'.[33] People (and hence their conduct) play a part in determining the performance of an undertaking.

> 'There is strong relation between the perceived behavior and culture of financial organizations, and the public trust in the financial sector. Trust is the foundation on which the financial system is built.'[34] This means that financial undertakings must (continue to) work on a culture of integrity which includes, for example, a controlled remuneration policy and sustainable enterprise. Supervision of conduct and culture helps in this regard. As an extension of this, a financial company must make conduct and culture part of its operational management.

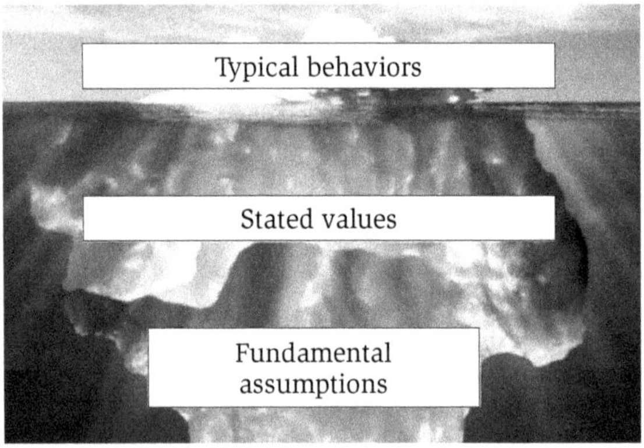

Figure 2: Model based on Schein 1985

On the basis of extensive (psychological) scientific research into culture and performance, it is generally assumed that there is a relationship between culture and the

32. See *inter alia* the reports of the De Wit Committees referred to in note 2.
33. Group of Thirty 2012.
34. De Haan & Gorter 2015, p. 30.

performance of the organization and that this is therefore influenced by culture.[35] DNB makes a case for the more psychological approach of the 'homo economicus' model accepted at that time.[36] Patterns of conduct in an undertaking – in which culture expresses itself in conduct that can be observed – have an influence on the 'performance' of the undertaking.

13.4. LEGAL BASIS

The basis of the prudential supervision by DNB of financial undertakings is set out in Article 1:24 of the Wft. Prudential supervision is deemed to mean supervision focused on the solidity of financial undertakings and the stability of the financial system. This is important, because it sets the direction of DNB's supervision strategy, namely the solidity of the financial undertaking. At first sight, one would not associate supervision of conduct and culture with the solidity of the undertaking. The AFM exercises so-called conduct supervision, whereas it might rather be said to concern conduct and culture.[37] As noted earlier, the AFM and DNB have been working together for a number of years on the supervision of conduct and culture.[38]

Article 3:10 of the Wft forms the legal basis for controlled and sound business operations of (*inter alia*) banks and insurers.[39] The obligation to set up business operations in such a way as to guarantee controlled and sound operation by the company is set out in Article 3:17, paragraph 1 of the Wft.[40] The question that arises, however, is to what extent the supervision of conduct and culture fits in with this. In its 2009 policy vision, DNB assumes that this supervision is consistent with the sound operation of a financial undertaking and hence also with the supervision thereof.[41]

In one of its legislative letters DNB requested the Minister of Finance to: 'make explicit in article 17, paragraph 1 of the Decree on Prudential Rules under the Wft that the undertaking is responsible for standards of conduct within the corporate culture aimed at honest conduct and appropriate risk control. These conduct standards must be integrated into the business processes.'[42] The Minister stated that he was amenable to exploring this request but did not say what form he wished it to take.[43]

DNB stated this desire because it believes controlled and sound business operations are an important element in its supervision for the financial solidity of

35. In the supervision of conduct and culture DNB uses models developed by Edgar Schein and Alex Straathof.
36. De Haan & Gorter 2015, pp. 35–40. This section (2.5 The psychological paradigm) cites a great deal of scientific literature substantiating the relationship in more detail. For further study purposes, reference is made to the summary of this literature on De Haan & Gorter 2015, p. 40.
37. Pursuant to Art. 1:25 of the Wft.
38. See note 29 *supra*.
39. Elaborated in greater detail in secondary legislation such as the Bpr.
40. So-called controlled operational management. The AFM's supervision of investment undertakings, among others, is based on Art. 4:11 and 4:14 of the Wft.
41. DNB booklet 2009, pp. 3–5.
42. Legislative letter 2014 from DNB of July 4, 2014, p. 7.
43. Letter from the Minister of Finance to the president of the Second Chamber of the States-General of July 15, 2014 (FM/2014/1131M), p. 4. No further action was taken.

an institution. It stated that it was currently looking among other things at conduct and culture within a financial undertaking. It believes supervision of conduct and culture is not an unequivocal standard or a legal objective in itself, but a means of supporting controlled and sound business operations. It believes it is desirable, however, to refer explicitly to supervision of these aspects in secondary legislation, hence its wish to include it in the above-mentioned decree.[44]

In view of the above, the basic proposition is that the 'right' culture and the 'right' conduct should lead to sound business operations and that - according to DNB - the legal basis for supervision of conduct and culture is evidently embedded in the aforementioned articles of the Wft. Moreover, the provisions of these articles predate the Wft.[45] The text has never been fundamentally amended and serves as a 'legal hook' for integrity aspects for which there is no concrete legal basis. It is clear in any event that DNB classifies supervision of conduct and culture within the controlled and sound business operations of a financial undertaking.

European regulations such as CRD IV and CRR[46] also include culture and conduct aspects for banks and investment companies. For example in the following article: 'Each member of the management body will act fairly, honestly and with independence of mind in order to effectively assess the decisions of the management and to contest them if necessary and in order to exercise effective supervision and control.'[47] On October 28, 2016, the EBA issued a consultation on guidelines for the terms fairness, honesty and independence.[48]

It can be concluded that there may well be a legal basis for supervision of honest and controlled business operations incorporating culture and conduct aspects, but that there is no 'real' legal basis for 'supervision of conduct and culture'. 'Catch-all articles' are used, which are developed into secondary legislation or policy rules on each subject.[49] Grundmann-van de Krol notes in this regard that in the formulation of these articles deliberate use was made of 'principles-based' legislation whereby this (existing) standard could be interpreted in greater detail as a result of changes in circumstances and/or social views.[50]

A point of criticism is that the above leaves room for interpretation of these 'open standards'. Instead of 'supervision of conduct and culture', it is better to speak of supervision of sound business operations in which culture and conduct aspects play a role. Culture and conduct themes are also covered by various parts of the Wft and European regulations and hence not consistently under a single heading

44. Legislative letter 2014 from DNB of July 4, 2014, p. 7.
45. For example in the Regulation on Organization and Control (incorporated in the Wft), *Government Gazette* 2001, 65, p. 23.
46. CRD IV came into force on January 1, 2014. The same applies to the associated CRR. In the Netherlands, the act introducing CRD IV did not come into force until August 1, 2014.
47. Recitals 53, 54, 57 and 60 and Art. 91 paragraph 8 of CRD IV. Art. 91, paragraph 8 has been incorporated in Art. 3:8, paragraph 3 and 4 of the Wft.
48. Under Art. 91 paragraph 12 of CRD IV; see the Consultation Paper on the Joint ESMA and EBA Guidelines on the assessment of the suitability of members of the management body and key function holders under Directive 2013/36/EU and Directive 2014/65/EU of October 28, 2016, p. 34.
49. Which must also comply, however, with the obligations in Arts 1:28–1:29a of the Wft.
50. Grundmann-van de Krol 2010, p. 72.

of supervision of conduct and culture.[51] In addition, supervision of conduct and culture sounds rather loaded and may conjure up a picture of DNB having a matrix of culture and conduct risks and wanting to impose the 'ideal' management model on the financial sector and then acting as a kind of 'culture police'.[52]

13.5 SUPERVISION AND ENFORCEMENT

Prudential supervision is aimed, among other things, at gaining information on financial undertakings, so that DNB can fulfill its duties in respect of Article 1:24 of the Wft. There does not have to be any violation or reasonable suspicion of a violation. To supervise compliance with the Wft, DNB has the power to demand information from any party.[53] The proportionality principle as laid down in Article 5:13 of the Awb does apply, however.[54] DNB is therefore only permitted to demand information to the extent reasonably necessary for the fulfillment of its duties. DNB may also face an enhanced justification requirement when requesting information if a criminal investigation is also ongoing.[55] Under Article 5:20 of the Awb, every party is obliged to cooperate fully with DNB's reasonable information requests within the (reasonable) time allowed by DNB.[56] Requesting information from a third party must not, however, have the character of a 'fishing expedition'.[57] In addition to the power based on Article 1:74 of the Wft, the DNB supervisors have the power to demand information on the basis of Article 5:16 of the Awb. If, on the basis of the obtained information, DNB identifies an actual or impending violation of the standards set out in the Wft, it may enforce the breached standards or endeavor to prevent the impending violation.[58]

The investigations conducted by DNB as part of its supervision of conduct and culture[59] involved the use of 'boardroom observations', and personal interviews were conducted with members of boards of directors of financial undertakings. When conducting such investigations it would have been – and still would be – advisable to give legal or other guarantees with regard to privacy and secrecy.[60] For example,

51. For example suitability and reliability requirements, pay, bonuses, the oath or promise and disciplinary law for bank employees.
52. DNB itself states that it does not wish to act as a 'culture police', *see* section 13.1 and note 3 *supra*.
53. Art. 1:74 paragraph 1 of the Wft.
54. Art. 1:74 paragraph 2 of the Wft.
55. Van der Eerden & Silverentand 2015, p. 425. Reference is made to the summary judgment of the court of Rotterdam of November 5, 2012.
56. Art. 1:74 paragraph 2 of the Wft.
57. Van der Eerden & Silverentand 2015, p. 426.
58. Ibid.
59. This concerns the investigations referred to in the DNB booklets cited in this chapter.
60. DNB must of course adhere to the confidentiality provisions set out in Art. 1:89 paragraph 1 of the Wft. Under Art. 1:89 paragraph 2 of the Wft DNB does, however, have the authority to discuss certain matters if these cannot be traced back to individual persons. DNB still might face considerable dilemmas in certain cases, because for well-established insiders it may be fairly easy to trace certain data back to specific undertakings or persons.

DNB can derogate from secrecy provisions under certain circumstances.[61] This means that if DNB has obtained certain information in the research, it would be able to share this information both internally and externally if it had grounds to do so. This could conflict with the right to privacy of the persons concerned.[62]

When enforcement action is taken it is assumed that the provisions of the Wft have been violated. DNB has various enforcement tools at its disposal, such as giving an instruction or imposing a penalty or an administrative fine.[63] Enforcement is also regulated in different ways, i.e. through administrative law, criminal law and also disciplinary law.[64] The question therefore arises of how DNB wishes to enforce supervision of culture and conduct. Although it states that this supervision is complementary to prudential supervision, that it aims to promote dialogue and raise awareness, it appears that the (heavy) instrument of suitability assessment will be used for this in the first place.[65]

DNB states that it wishes to have no or at any rate less of a regulatory and supervisory role.[66] It is noted, however, that the legislator clearly wishes to enshrine suitability (including management styles) as well as other conduct aspects in law and thereby have the ability to enforce them. However, the 'desired' culture and the resulting 'desired' conduct is difficult to encapsulate in rules.

13.6 CONSIDERATIONS

The answer to the question of whether a heavy emphasis on supervision of culture and conduct aspects in financial undertakings will be of benefit to the financial sector requires further analysis. In view of the enormous amount of attention paid to the subject in the media and elsewhere and the resulting actions and regulations, it can be concluded in any event that a great deal of work has been done.[67] However, their effectiveness can only be judged retrospectively. The path embarked on also gives no guarantee as yet of preventing a new financial crisis.[68] The fact that there

61. Arts 1:90–1:93e of the Wft.
62. The relevant questions here are how requesting personal data relates to the PDP Act and how efficient (and open) an interview is if the answers to such questions are not clear in advance. Such research can also have a psychological character due to the highly personal nature of the questions asked. Therefore, the chosen methodology could be at odds with the very strict confidentiality provisions in section III.3.3 of the 'Beroepscode voor psychologen' (Professional Code for Psychologists) of July 2007 of the Dutch Association of Psychologists (NIP).
63. Arts 1:75, 1:79 and 1:80 of the Wft.
64. With regard to disciplinary law *see also* Soeharno 2014.
65. An interesting question is whether DNB can be held liable for an erroneous decision if it emerges (possibly with hindsight), for example, that a financial undertaking has encountered problems despite the fact that DNB has 'made an adjustment' during a suitability assessment by means of an instruction under Art. 1:75 of the Wft. In this connection see also Art. 1:25d of the Wft on the exclusion of liability of DNB and the AFM.
66. *See inter alia* the cited text of DNB in section 13.1 *supra*.
67. *See inter alia* DNB Bulletin 2015.
68. According to the President of DNB, Klaas Knot, in an interview with RTL Z on July 16, 2014.

is a social interest in cultural change in the financial sector is not up for discussion, but the method is.

The legislator's guiding principle is the ability to adjust socially inappropriate conduct by means of standards.[69] It is striking, however, that the legislator appears to want to link the 'desired conduct' of directors to the 'performance' of a financial undertaking by creating a legal basis and powers for supervision. The will to 'intervene' in the culture of a financial undertaking and the conduct of persons that manage it raises questions, however, with regard to supervisory powers, enforcement, secrecy, protection of rights and privacy. In a democratic state based on the rule of law, with checks and balances, people expect regulation to involve legally prudent assessment.[70] The will to raise awareness and enter into dialogue with regard to conduct and culture is a good aim but must not give rise to a culture of fear of sanctions or a 'wrong management style' and mutual mistrust.

There is a legal basis for supervision of sound and controlled business operations of a financial undertaking in which culture and conduct aspects can be incorporated, but this is not a solid basis for supervision of 'conduct and culture'. It is better to speak of supervision of honest and controlled business operations in which culture and conduct aspects play a role.[71] An important point here is that in practice functions such as Compliance and HRM are often called upon. The discussion of culture or conduct aspects and their supervision, however, is something that must take place in the 'business' of the undertaking and at the senior level. (Internal) supervision of culture and conduct cannot be simply assigned to the compliance function.[72]

Culture and conduct (aspects) should not be further or excessively 'juridified', nor should their supervision. Self-regulation would be more appropriate. In one article, for example, the NvB points out that legislation works differently than self-regulation. Self-regulation requires reflection and invites a debate on how the aim behind the rules can best be achieved. Legislation (regulation), by contrast, invites a tick-the-boxes mentality and discussion of how to avoid 'hassle' with the supervisor.[73] The VvV also points to the positive sides of self-regulation.[74]

DNB could do even more with regard to the transparency of this supervision. It is sometimes assumed too readily that there is a relationship between certain management styles or a particular culture and poor or less good results of a financial undertaking. On the other hand, it is also striking in practice that DNB is also 'searching' at times.[75] DNB could also be even more transparent with regard to the results of this supervision. In short: it should demonstrate that this supervision has the desired effect and how it is achieved.[76]

69. *See also* Veerman & Mulder 2010, pp. 12–14.
70. A worrying factor in this regard, for example, is that opinions of the Council of State are very easily set aside by the Minister of Finance when it comes to regulation of the financial sector.
71. The legal embedding of supervision of integrity was also a matter discussed in the introduction of the Wft (and prior to that).
72. Houben 2012. For a different opinion, *see* Wielenga & Van den Hout 2013.
73. Buijink 2014. *See also* Houben 2013.
74. De Boer & Martius 2014.
75. Even more research could be conducted into culture as a 'governance' component.
76. Understandably, the limit here lies in its confidentiality obligation.

Despite the points and objections specified earlier, the concept of supervision of conduct and culture could be important for the non-financial sector (such as the semi-public sector, and the construction, energy and telecom sectors) and for undertakings supervised by the AFM and DNB that are not included in the investigations (such as payment institutions and intermediaries). After all, the points set out above are universal.[77] The financial sector is leading the way in this regard.

77. The investigation referred to is, after all, wide-ranging, i.e. covering undertakings in various sectors. *See* note 36 *supra*.

BIBLIOGRAPHY

Bökkerink & Veldhuis 2010
M.J. Bökkerink and I. Veldhuis, 'Toezicht op gedrag en cultuur', in: C.A. Wielenga et al. (ed.), *Jaarboek Compliance* 2011, Cappelle aan den IJssel: Nederlands Compliance Instituut 2010, pp. 151-164.

Buijnk 2014
Chr.P. Buijink, 'Bancaire zelfregulering in roerige tijden', *FR* 2014, no. 6, p. 231.

De Boer & Martius 2014
H.L. de Boer & R.M.L.A. Martius, 'Zelfregulering: een goed betrouwbaar alternatief voor publieke regulering', *FR* 2014, no. 6, pp. 232-235.

De Haan & Gorter 2015
J. de Haan & J. Gorter (eds.), *Supervision of Behaviour and Culture. Foundations, practice & future developments*, Amsterdam: De Nederlandsche Bank N.V. 2015.

De Haan & Jansen 2011
J. de Haan & D. Jansen, *Corporate Culture and behaviour: A survey* (DNB Working Paper, no. 334, December 2011.

Grundmann-van de Krol 2010
C.M. Grundmann-van de Krol, *Koersen in de mist: op weg naar transparante wetgeving?* (oratie Nijmegen), The Hague: Boom Juridische Uitgevers 2010.

Houben 2012
R.A.M. Houben, 'Overschatting van de compliancefunctie leidt tot morele luiheid', *TvCO* 2012, no. 4, pp. 259-261.

Houben 2013
R.A.M. Houben, 'Regulering of overregulering? Zoektocht naar de effectiviteit van financiële toezichtregelgeving', in: C.A. Wielenga et al. (ed.), *Jaarboek Compliance 2013*, Capelle aan den IJssel: Nederlands Compliance Instituut 2012, pp. 15-33.

Houben 2014
R.A.M. Houben, 'Toezicht op gedrag en cultuur; op de grens van het toezicht?', *FR* 2014, no. 9, pp. 360-365.

Houben 2015
R.A.M. Houben, 'Toezicht op gedrag en cultuur; op de grens van het toezicht?', in: C.A. Wielenga et al. (ed.), *Jaarboek Compliance* 2015, Capelle aan den IJssel: Nederlands Compliance Instituut 2015, pp. 75-87.

Kaptein & Dunning 2010
M. Kaptein & F.B. Dunning, 'Zeven principes voor een goed ingebedde bedrijfscode. De code als fundament voor een effectief complianceprogramma', in: C.A. Wielenga et al. (ed.), *Jaarboek Compliance 2010*, Capelle aan den IJssel: Nederlands Compliance Instituut 2009, pp. 201-216.

Karssing 2013
E.D. Karssing, 'Moet de wolf vegetariër worden', in: C.A. Wielenga et al. (ed.), *Jaarboek Compliance 2013*, Capelle aan den IJssel: Nederlands Compliance Instituut 2013, pp. 233-249.

Karssing & Wirtz 2010
E.D. Karssing & R. Wirtz, 'Veranderen van Cultuur', in: C.A. Wielenga et al. (ed.), *Jaarboek Compliance* 2011, Capelle aan den IJssel: Nederlands Compliance Instituut 2010, pp. 177-192.

Mikulski 2016
R.E.W. Mikulski, 'Gedrag en cultuur in governance regelingen voor banken', *FR* 2016, no. 3, pp. 91-97.

Nuijts 2012
W.H.J.M. Nuijts, 'Hoe gaat dat eigenlijk: toezicht houden op gedrag en cultuur? Uitkomsten van het DNB thema-onderzoek Besluitvorming', *TvCO* 2012, no. 1, pp. 41-46.

Nuijts & de Haan 2013
W.H.J.M. Nuijts & J. de Haan, 'DNB Supervision of Conduct and Culture', in: A.J. Kellerman, J. de Haan & F. de Vries (eds.), *Financial Supervision in the 21st Century*, Berlin, Heidelberg: Springer-Verlag 2013, pp. 151-164.

Piena & Christensen 2013
J. Piena & C. Christensen, 'Gedrag & Cultuurtoezicht. DNB en AFM boeken resultaat met toezicht op Gedrag & Cultuur', in: C.A. Wielenga et al. (ed.), *Jaarboek Compliance 2013*, Capelle aan den IJssel: Nederlands Compliance Instituut 2013, pp. 251-265.

Raaijmakers & Scholten 2014
M. Raaijmakers & W. Scholten, 'Ervaringen van twee psychologen als toezichthouder bij De Nederlandsche Bank; reflectie in de bestuurskamer', *De psycholoog*, October 2014, pp. 46-54.

Schein 1985
E.H. Schein, *Organizational Culture and Leadership*, San Francisco: Jossey-Bass 1985.

Soeharno 2014
J.E. Soeharno, 'Tuchtrecht en de wens tot integere bankiers. Een kritische beschouwing', *FR* 2014, no. 6, pp. 243-251.

Straathof 2009
A.J.M. Straathof, *Zoeken naar de kern van cultuurverandering; Inzicht, meten, sturen*, (diss. Rotterdam), Delft: Eburon 2009.

Van Beusekom & Raaijmakers 2010
H. van Beusekom & K. Raaijmakers, 'Grip op cultuur in het toezicht', in: C.A. Wielenga et al. (ed.), *Jaarboek Compliance 2011*, Capelle aan den IJssel: Nederlands Compliance Instituut 2010, pp. 165-175.

Van de Loo & Winter 2016
E. van de Loo & J. Winter, 'Cultuur en gedrag volgens de nieuwe corporate governance code', *Ondernemingsrecht* 2016/72, pp. 338-347.

Van Dijk & Nuijts 2015
A.G. van Dijk & W.H.J.M. Nuijts, 'Gedrag & cultuur toezicht en de samenhang met de 'governance' van een financiële instelling', *Ondernemingsrecht* 2015/114, pp. 588-597.

Van der Eerden & Silverentand 2015
F.W.J. van der Eerden & L.J. Silverentand (eds.), *Hoofdlijnen Wft*, Deventer: Wolters Kluwer 2015.

Veerman & Mulder 2010
G.J. Veerman & R. Mulder, *Wetgeving met beleid. Bouwstenen voor een bruikbare wetgevingstheorie*, The Hague; Boom Juridische uitgevers 2010.

Wielenga & Van den Hout 2013
C.A. Wielenga & H.T.J.M. van den Hout, 'Borging van cultuur in het compliancesysteem', in: C.A. Wielenga et al. (ed.), *Jaarboek Compliance 2013*, Capelle aan den IJssel: Nederlands Compliance Instituut 2013, pp. 267-279.

Other references

AFM annual report 2015
Annual report of the AFM for 2015, published on April 7, 2016.

DNB booklet 2009
DNB booklet, 'De 7 elementen van een Integere Cultuur (The seven elements of a sound culture); Beleidsvisie en aanpak gedrag en cultuur bij financiële ondernemingen 2010-2014', November 2009.

DNB booklet 2010
DNB booklet, 'Visie DNB toezicht 2010-2014', March 2010.

DNB booklet 2011
DNB booklet, 'Thema's DNB toezicht 2011', January 2011.

DNB booklet 2012
DNB booklet, 'Onderzoek naar Leiderschap, besluitvorming en communicatie', 2012.

DNB booklet March 2013
DNB booklet, 'Leading by example', March 2013.

DNB booklet August 2013
DNB booklet, 'Toezichtmethodieken gedrag en cultuur', August 2013.

DNB booklet March 2014
DNB booklet, 'Visie DNB toezicht 2014-2018', March 2014.

DNB and AFM booklet 2014
DNB and AFM booklet, 'Verandervermogen in de financiële sector', October 2014

DNB booklet 2015
DNB booklet, 'Gedrag en Cultuur in de Nederlandsche financiële sector', October 2015.

DNB booklet 2016
DNB booklet, 'Vooruitblik Toezicht 2017', November 2016.

DNB Bulletin 2014
DNB Bulletin of June 12, 2014: 'Goed toezicht houden is vooruitkijken'.

DNB Bulletin 2015
DNB Bulletin of September 24, 2015: 'Aandacht voor gedrag & cultuur in bestuurskamer werpt vrucht af'.

DNB report 2011
DNB interim report of December 6, 2011 on supervision of conduct and culture.

Group of Thirty 2012
Report of the Group of Thirty April 2012, '*Toward effective governance of financial institutions*'.

14. Financial Markets and Compliance

T.A.H.M. van de Laar EMoC

14.1 INTRODUCTION

Financial market regulation governs the most important system in the economy, the financial system. This regulatory landscape is a fast-growing and ever-changing environment. Anyone working in compliance will confirm that there is a huge body of legislation to keep abreast of, let alone to comply with. It often seems that as soon as one set of rules is complied with, new sets of rules will quickly spring up. As an illustration, by 2007 the Basel Committee on Banking Supervision had published 37 regulatory standards since its establishment in 1974. From January 2008 to February 2017 this number increased massively with the publication of 101 new regulatory standards.[1] This exponential growth of regulation is also related to the enduring effects of the global financial crisis.

Today, the financial industry is still plagued by a 'silo' approach to financial market regulation. Compliance professionals have an important task in coping with these never-ending changes, getting a grip on financial market regulation and in the meantime also maintaining awareness of regulatory fatigue. If this is performed inadequately, it can have a detrimental impact on the organization's viability.

This chapter will focus on the goals of financial market regulation through the rules of economics (section 14.2), the strategies financial regulation employs to achieve these goals (section 14.3) and the insights this provides for the compliance profession (section 14.4). For an overview of the goals and strategies of financial regulation this chapter will draw on the noteworthy work of John Armour et al.[2]

In doing so, this chapter makes several important contributions. First, characterizing the goals of financial market regulation through the rules of economics will help compliance professionals to develop focused principles and criteria for assessing the merits of financial market regulation in order to develop a compliance

1. The list of publications can be found on the BCBS website: http://www.bis.org/bcbs/publications.htm by selecting the publication type 'Standards'.
2. Armour et al. 2016.

framework. These principles and criteria are connected to the underlying functioning of the financial system which the regulation is seeking to improve. Secondly, these principles and criteria can be used to assess and gain a deeper understanding of any financial regulation in any jurisdiction and could be used as heuristics. Thirdly, this will enable compliance professionals to think about the interrelationships of the goals with each other and with the financial system. This will help compliance professionals to escape from the 'silo' approach that disrupts the treatment of financial market regulation.

14.2 GOALS OF FINANCIAL MARKET REGULATION THROUGH THE RULES OF ECONOMICS

John Armour et al. have described the goals and strategies of financial market regulation through the rules of economics.[3] They explain that 'the primary purpose of financial market regulation is to improve the functioning of that system':[4]

> 'The design of financial regulation is thus ultimately an exercise in economics – applying the analytic tools of economics to determine the legal regulatory framework best suited to correcting the failures of a financial system.'[5]

14.2.1 The rules of economics

The starting point of economics for regulation is the concept of the 'invisible hand' first introduced by Adam Smith in *The Theory of Moral Sentiments*.[6]

> 'The proud and unfeeling landlord views his extensive fields, and without a thought for the wants of his brethren, in imagination consumes himself the whole harvest … [Yet] the capacity of his stomach bears no proportion to the immensity of his desires … the rest he will be obliged to distribute among those, who prepare, in the nicest manner, that little which he himself makes use of, among those who fit up the palace in which this little is to be consumed, among those who provide and keep in order all the different baubles and trinkets which are employed in the economy of greatness; all of whom thus derive from his luxury and caprice, that share of the necessaries of life, which they would in vain have expected from his humanity or his justice … The rich … are led by an invisible hand to make nearly the same distribution of the necessaries of life, which would have been made, had the earth been divided into equal portions among all its inhabitants, and thus without intending it, without knowing it, advance the interest of the society …'

Adam Smith describes the unintended social benefits of individual action and captures his notion that individuals' efforts to pursue their own interest may frequently benefit society more than if their actions were directly intending to benefit society. There has

3. Ibid., chapter 3: The Goals and Strategies of Financial Regulation.
4. Ibid., p. 51.
5. Ibid., p. 51.
6. Smith 2009, Introduction, pp. vii–xxix. The exact phrase is used just three times in Smith's writings, *see also* Smith 1980, p. 49; Smith 1976, p. 184.

been criticism of his theory, among others from the Nobel Prize-winning economist Joseph E. Stiglitz. Stiglitz explains that the invisible hand is not always there, due to the market failures as described in chapter 12.[7] Powers that were emerging during Adam Smith's life, such as large-scale industry, finance and advertising, diminish its effectiveness. Thus, in addition to the rules of economics for regulation, there is a need to interfere in order to prevent the failure of the financial market.

There are particular features of financial markets that make them especially prone to malfunctioning. As long as consequences of individual purchases and sales are immediate and freely observable, it is relatively easy to safeguard the smooth working of markets. If you are selling rotten apples, by experience and word of mouth you will soon have no customers left. But in the financial market, the consequence of actions may not be discovered for lengthy periods of time, perhaps years or decades. In that case the possible market failure and the complexities of fixing it are much greater. Examples include pension plans or home mortgages. These types of large transactions involve substantial borrowing and investment decisions over long periods of time. Consequently, even fairly small mistakes can accumulate into large losses by the time the product matures. These problems of uncertainty are even aggravated by the fact that consumers of such products are less well informed than the sellers. This gives rise to market failures and then there is a *prima facie* case to correct these failures with financial market regulations.

Chapter 11 explained the common market failures that can arise in financial markets, namely asymmetries of information, negative externalities, behavioral biases in consumer decision-taking (bounded rationalities), imperfect competition and public goods. As explained, these market failures can arise in financial markets and therefore justify regulation to correct them. Regulation can then be 'understood as the means of rectifying relevant market failures'.[8]

14.2.2 Review of the goals of financial market regulation

This section will discuss the goals of financial market regulation in light of the common market failures that are described in chapter 11. These market failures explain the economic rationale for these rules and regulations. Financial market regulation refers to specific goals that could be understood as responding to a particular type of market failure. There are six underlying goals of financial market regulation:[9] (1) the protection of investors, (2) the protection of customers, (3) financial stability, (4) market efficiency, (5) competition, (6) preventing financial crime.

14.2.2.1 The protection of investors

In security legislation such as MiFID II, the Transparency Directive and the Prospectus Directive, investor protection is mentioned as an important goal of the regulation.[10]

7. Altman 2006.
8. Armour et al. 2016, p. 61.
9. Ibid., section 3.4: The Goals of Financial Regulation.
10. *See* for example the Prospectus Directive, recitals 10, 12 and 16; MiFID II, recitals 3, 7, 39, 45, 57, 58, 97 and 133; the Transparency Directive, recitals 1, 5 and 7.

In relation to the issuance of securities, this must be understood as requiring the disclosure of relevant information. Without this information potential investors would not be able to make an assessment of the risks they are taking on. Consequently, they will be reluctant to advance funds. If we relate this back to the underlying market failure, the concern is asymmetries of information which could lead to an adverse selection problem.[11]

Investor protection is also articulated as 'client protection' or 'customer protection', when the investor needs to rely on a financial firm for decisions about investment choices or the execution of trades and/or for safe custody of assets.[12] The risks of poor investment choices or misappropriation or failure to segregate assets are risks that are caused by asymmetries of information. These risks lead to agency problems and costs such as license requirements, custodial requirements, measures to control conflicts of interest and the enhancement of competences.[13]

Agency problems also arise when bank depositors, mutual fund investors and insurance policy holders transfer funds to financial intermediaries in return for claims against the intermediary's balance sheet. The value of these claims depends on the investments of the intermediary. In order to control the agency costs related to the difficulty of monitoring the intermediary's behavior, regulations are described in terms of 'investor protection',[14] 'policy holder protection'[15] and 'depositor protection'.[16]

John Armour et al. state that these information asymmetries in the financial market should lead to regulation because *'the business model of financial firms is unusually opaque'*, explaining that rating agencies disagree much more about the credit rating of bonds issued by financial institutions than in the case of non-financial firms.[17] Furthermore, they state that since the industry is all about money, it is particularly prone to abuse. In that regard they refer to well-known Ponzi frauds such as the case of Bernie Madoff.[18]

14.2.2.2 The protection of customers

Especially in relation to retail banking when consumers act outside the course of their business, consumer protection is described explicitly as an express goal.[19] Just as in the case of investor protection, in the case of consumers the concern for

11. Armour et al. 2016, p. 62.
12. See for example MiFID II, note 10 *supra*, recitals 5 and 80; the Investment Advisers Act of 1940 (US), § 201(1).
13. Armour et al. 2016, p. 62.
14. *See* for example Investment Company Act of 1940 (US), § 1; the UCITS V Directive, recitals 8 and 10.
15. *See* for example the Solvency II Directive, recital 16 and Art. 27.
16. *See* for example CRD IV, recital 47; Federal Deposit Insurance Act (US) §3(I), 12 USC §1813(I).
17. Armour et al. 2016, p. 63.
18. Armour et al. 2016, pp. 63–64.
19. *See* for example Directive 2011/83/EU on Consumer Rights 'Consumer Rights Directive'), OJ L 304/64, 2011; Directive 2008/48/EC on Credit Agreements for Consumers ('Consumer Credit Directive') OJ L133/66, 2008; the Dodd-Frank Act of 2010 (US), §1001 (the short title of Title X is 'Consumer Financial Protection Act of 2010').

asymmetries of information is applicable. In addition, and particularly in the case of consumers, behavioral bias in consumer decision-taking is an important economic rationale to broaden the scope of the legislation. This regulation is meant to protect consumers from the abuse of their biases and erroneous decisions. Consequently, the type of regulation aimed at intervening in market failures related to customers' protection is different from the legislation aimed at protecting professional or more sophisticated users. In both the European Union and the United States the legislation identifies designated categories of investors that manifest certain qualities, particularly wealth, which consider them to be sophisticated.[20] If companies are offering securities exclusively to these types of investors, they do not have to fulfill all the disclosure rules to which they would otherwise be subject.

14.2.2.3 Financial stability

The global financial crisis has emphasized the importance of the stability of the financial system as a whole. Clearly this is also a goal of financial market regulation. Financial institutions and markets are interconnected and consequently the actions of one (group of) actor(s) can have an adverse impact on other actors. This is the so-called 'domino effect'. The domino effect can have a prevailing detrimental impact on the economy as a whole. After the fall of Lehman Brothers, for example, banks panicked. Lenders withdrew their funds by declining to roll over their loan agreements. Banks stopped lending to other banks and decided to hoard liquid buffers because they had concerns about the solvency of their counterparties in interbank operations, the increased risk in their asset portfolio and potential liquidity risk resulting from drawdowns of committed lines of credit. Liabilities on the balance sheet of one bank impacted the balance sheet of other banks, transmitting a shock following its failure. The failure of one or more important banks in which depositors or other creditors suffer losses may lead to cash hoarding by other financial firms and 'runs' on other banks. This will also reduce the flow of credit to non-financial firms. Consequently, a financial sector crisis can quickly become a general global economic crisis. This resulted in new 'macroprudential' legislation focusing on the stability of the financial system as a whole.[21]

In terms of market failure, we can comprehend these effects as negative externalities.[22] Externalities arise when a person or institution takes actions that impose costs, but that person or institution is not charged (fully) in the event of negative externalities on other parties (conversely, externalities could also lead to benefits to other persons or institutions for which that person is not fully compensated). Externalities occur when incentives and prices are not fully aligned with the consequences of actions taken. A deviation may arise when the interests of those who own and operate financial institutions diverge from the interests of society at large. This occurs particularly in the case of financial markets, since the consequences of

20. *See* for example Prospectus Directive, note 10 *supra*; Regulation D Offerings under the Securities Act of 1933, Rule 501.
21. Armour et al. 2016, chapter 19: The Macroprudential approach.
22. *See also* section 11.2.2 *supra*.

failure are distributed widely. Consequently, shareholders of financial institutions bear only a fraction of the overall loss to society connected to failure.

In order to control financial stability, measures such as capital adequacy requirements and deposit insurance schemes are enforced.

14.2.2.4 Market efficiency

The term 'market efficiency' is somewhat confusing. It can be understood with two different meanings.[23] First, it could be understood in the sense that efficiency relates to the efficiency with which the economy produces and allocates resources. This could be subdivided into allocative efficiency (scarce resources should be allocated to those activities and individuals that value them the most), productive efficiency (resources should yield as much output as possible from the given set of scarce resources) and dynamic efficiency (resources should be allocated as efficiently as possible between different points of time – between generations or between this year and next year, as well as within years and generations). Secondly, it could be understood as how efficiently the market incorporates new information in the market price, which John Armour et al. call 'informationally efficient' markets.[24]

In financial market regulation, market efficiency is mostly explained in the sense of 'informationally efficient'. Capital markets serve to allocate funds to projects that organizations wish to pursue. The greater the liquidity, the better investors are able to participate in the market. Informationally efficient markets stimulate liquidity and therefore help to mobilize investors to participate in the market. If the market is informationally inefficient, some parties may assume that their counterparty is acting on the basis of superior information. Consequently, the market price will be shaded. Other parties might postpone trading, because they believe that not all relevant information is incorporated into the market price. These scenarios will limit the parties prepared to trade and will lead to a decline in liquidity.

Regulation can help in expediting the production of information. Empirical research suggests that increasing the scope of mandatory disclosure of information will lead to accurate pricing of securities in public equity markets.[25] Organizations might have an incentive not to disclose certain information without such regulation. This is socially undesirable, because the public at large has an interest in fully informed stock prices. In terms of market failure, corporate information is to be understood as a public good.[26]

Better dissemination of information of course promotes the efficiency with which the economy produces and allocates resources (the other meaning of efficiency).

23. Armour et al. 2016, sections 3.2. and 3.4.4: The Efficiency of Markets *and* Market efficiency.
24. Ibid., p. 67.
25. Fox et al. 2003, pp. 331–386.
26. *See also* section 11.2.2 *supra*.

14.2.2.5 Competition

Financial regulation is also concerned with promoting competition.[27] The most notable example is of course the European Union, whose primary purpose is to have pan-European markets where organizations can compete with each other. The European Union adopted minimum standards that are harmonized in the European Union by European legislation. Consequently, Member States have to drop restrictions on other financial service firms and let them operate on the basis of a 'passport' to market their services throughout the European Union.

Competition can also be promoted in different ways than cross-border markets by eliminating anticompetitive practices. John Armour et al. among others refer to the 'Big Bang' in the United Kingdom in 1986, which among other things removed the prohibitions on the free entry of new participants, and the removal by the SEC of the market rule that confined the trading of securities listed on the New York Stock Exchange (NYSE) to the NYSE itself.[28] Competition in terms of market failure is evidently connected to imperfect competition.

14.2.2.6 Prevention of financial crime

The prevention of financial crime is also a primary goal of financial market regulation, in the sense that financial institutions should have effective measures in place to prevent the financial system being used for socially harmful behavior. This includes (i) the use of the financial system for terrorist financing, (ii) the use of the financial system for money laundering purposes, (iii) the making of payments to improperly influence decision-makers (bribery and corruption), (iv) the making of payments in relation to prohibited goods, services (such as slavery and weapons), (v) the making of payments in relation to sanctioned countries, organizations, persons and services, (vi) the use of the financial system for tax evasion.[29]

Financial institutions operate in that sense as gatekeepers and this can be understood in economic terms as negative externalities that are socially harmful.

14.2.2.7 Other goals

Sometimes financial regulation uses other terms such as 'lowering the costs of capital' or promoting 'capital formation'.[30] These goals could be understood as

27. *See* for example the Prospectus Directive, note 10 *supra*, recital 41; the Transparency Directive, note 10 *supra*, recital 36; the UCITS V Directive, note 14 *supra*, recital 3; National Securities Market Improvement Act 1996 (US) §106.
28. Armour et al. 2016, p. 68–69.
29. *See* the Anti-Money Laundering Directive; Bank Secrecy Act (Currency and Foreign Transactions Reporting Act of 1970; Patriot Act of 2001 (US); Common Reporting Standards (OECD); Foreign Account Tax Compliance Act 2010 (US).
30. *See* for example the Prospectus Directive, note 10 *supra*, recital 41; the Transparency Directive, note 10 *supra*, recital 36; National Securities Market improvement Act 1996 (US) § 106.

being primarily connected to the goals of investor/customer protection and market efficiency already described.

Another goal that is sometimes mentioned is the need to 'encourage innovation in financial markets'.[31] These goals could be understood as being primarily connected to the goals of investor/customer protection and competition.

14.3 REGULATORY STRATEGIES TO ACHIEVE GOALS

John Armour et al. identified a number of strategies that financial regulation around the world employs to achieve the goals outlined in the previous paragraph.[32] These strategies represent techniques that are used in financial market regulation to achieve the goals. They identified the following seven strategies: (1) entry regulation, (2) conduct regulation, (3) information regulation, (4) prudential regulation, (5) governance regulation, (6) insurance regulation and (7) resolution regulation.

14.3.1 Entry regulation

First, entry regulation relates to the ability of potential participants in the financial system to participate in the financial transaction with other participants.[33] The example provided is the security and investment product that may only be provided for certain investors, the so-called 'qualified investors' or 'accredited investors'.[34] Consequently, the not so sophisticated investor may not participate in securities of this type. This could be regarded as a participation restriction. Secondly, entry regulation relates to the ability of organizations to participate in the financial business through licensing requirements. Before the financial institution is allowed to participate to open its doors for business, the regulator must grant that organization a license. Part of the license requirement is that this license can be withdrawn in the event of non-compliance with the financial market regulation. Thirdly, before granting the license the regulator will set qualification requirements especially for the owners and managers of the financial institution in order to clear out those who have committed a serious violation of financial regulations or are unsuitable for that position. Fourthly, financial regulation also formulates so-called 'product regulation' as a means of entry regulation. This regulation affects the ability of financial institutions to offer particular types of products to particular types of investors.[35] Fifthly, entry regulation relates to structural restrictions. Structural restrictions could relate to the nature and scope of the services that may be carried out by certain financial institutions or could have the intention of segmenting the financial sector in order to reduce systemic risk, conflicts of interest or both. An example of structural restriction is the Volcker Rule preventing banks engaging in proprietary trading or the separation between

31. See sources cited in footnote 25 *supra*.
32. Armour et al. 2016, section 3.5: The Strategies of Financial Regulation.
33. Ibid., section 3.5.1: Entry.
34. Ibid., p. 169.
35. *See* for example, MiFID II, Art. 69 paragraph 2(s); MiFIR, Art. 40 paragraph 2.

commercial and investment banking in the United States.[36] Sixthly and finally, there is also entry legislation fostering competition, i.e. the opposite of restricting entry.

14.3.2 Conduct regulation

Conduct regulation prescribes appropriate standards of conduct for participants in the financial system. First, conduct regulation covers trading restrictions. Trading restrictions affect the way in which trades may be performed. An example is market manipulation. Market manipulation covers actions aimed at causing an artificial movement in the market price, so as to make a profit or avoid a loss (for example by releasing false information into the market in order to raise the price of the securities and let the manipulator profit from the price change).[37]

Secondly, conduct regulation affects conduct of business rules, which describe the way business is required to carry out business. These conduct of business rules could be divided into (1) the way in which financial institutions deal with clients/ customers (these rules focus on marketing, advertising and sales technique), (2) the handling of client assets (focusing on custody and segregation requirements) and (3) the management of conflicts of interest.[38]

14.3.3 Information regulation

Information regulation focuses on two techniques. The first technique is education as an ostensibly straightforward response to prevent 'bad' choices and to facilitate the consumer's own achievement of good (or at least better) choices. An example is the Dodd-Frank Act that specifies that the Consumer Financial Protection Bureau must conduct financial education programs for the public.[39]

The second technique is disclosure regulation that mandates the disclosure of relevant information in relation to particular transactions. These information regulations require information about financial products and firms' investment strategies to be supplied to customers, investors and regulators.[40] They relate to (1) disclosure of pre-contractual information to investors and consumers as a means of informing them about financial products and securities, (2) the obligation to provide initial, periodic and event-driven disclosure of information by issuers of securities in order to prevent information asymmetries of security markets, and (3) reporting obligations on financial institutions to regulators regarding their balance sheets and investment strategies, so that these regulators can maintain an overview of risk in the financial system as a whole.

---

36. Included in the Dodd-Frank Act of 2010 (US) which became effective on April 1, 2014.
37. The MAR. *See also* section 21.6 *infra*.
38. Armour et al. 2016, section 3.5.2: Conduct.
39. Dodd-Frank Act of 2010 (US), §1021(c)(1). See also, European Commission Communication on Financial Education, COM 808 final, 2007, p. 8 (pressing Member States to ensure financial education is actively promoted).
40. Armour et al. 2016, section 3.5.3: Information.

14.3.4 Prudential regulation

Prudential regulation relates to the way in which financial institutions manage their assets and liabilities. It encompasses rules on (1) capital adequacy (banks and other financial institutions are required to maintain a minimum level of net assets to ensure that a certain proportion of their liabilities are subordinated), (2) rules on assets demanding that a certain proportion of asset holdings be of a liquid character (rules relating to the capacity of banks and other financial institutions to respond to a sudden withdrawal of short-term funds without having to sell illiquid assets), and (3) 'rules restricting the riskiness of investment and insurance firms' asset portfolios, including prohibitions on the purchase of particular asset classes and procedural obligations regarding portfolio management and risk allocation'.[41]

Finally, the global financial crisis demonstrated how financial institutions and markets are interconnected, resulting in new 'macroprudential' legislation that focuses on the stability of the financial system as a whole.[42]

14.3.5 Governance regulation

Rules relating to governance relate to the way organizations are organized and managed, such as executive compensation and board structure.[43] These governance rules could be understood in economic terms as being related to the protection of investors and customers. However, given the negative externalities related to risk-taking by financial institutions and the effects they may have on the financial system as a whole, these governance rules could also be understood in economic terms as financial stability measures.[44] Furthermore, these rules may also be explained in the sense of being 'informationally efficient'.[45] Take the example of remuneration. Remuneration affects managers' incentives with regard to trading behavior, which may have implications for the effectiveness of financial markets in aggregating new information (in the event that these trading platforms are dominated by managers driven by perverse incentives).

14.3.6 Insurance regulation

The previous five strategies operate *ex ante*, meaning that the relationship between the investor or consumer and the financial institution is already shaped by regulation. Insurance regulation, however, operates *ex post*, because the regulation is triggered by the failure of a financial institution. This type of legislation provides a safety net (liquidity) if the financial institution is in financial distress. Examples are deposit insurance schemes, the lender of last resort function played by the central bank and state bail-outs.[46] These techniques may nevertheless lead to moral hazard and are

41. Ibid., p. 76.
42. Ibid., chapter 19: The Macroprudential Approach.
43. Ibid., section 3.5.5: Governance.
44. Ibid.
45. Ibid.
46. Ibid., section 3.5.6: Insurance.

therefore 'only justified by reference to the adverse impact of failure of financial firms on the economy at large'.[47]

14.3.7 Resolution regulation

Resolution regulation, just like insurance regulation, is also to be understood as *ex post* legislation. If possible, a bank resolution procedure achieves the objective of minimizing the negative externalities of bank failure. Ideally it allocates the costs primarily to the bank's shareholders and bondholders and only thereafter, if at all, to the taxpayer. Two principal resolution mechanisms can be distinguished. The first involves the swift transfer to a solvent acquirer of the bank's insured deposits and possibly other viable businesses of the bank, with the liquidation of the residual part of the bank which is not transferred. The second procedure is commonly referred to as 'bail-in'. It involves reorganizing the failing bank so that it develops as a restored, viable entity. Consequently, the restored entity does not have to be put into standard bankruptcy and no transferee has to be found for its viable businesses.[48] This can be accomplished through voluntary agreement among the banks' creditors and shareholders, but a statutory procedure will impose it in the absence of agreement. The losses will then be inflicted on long-term creditors, without the company being put into bankruptcy.

14.4 THE ROLE OF COMPLIANCE

The previous sections explained the anatomy of financial market regulation. This provides a better understanding of financial market failures, its regulation to overcome such failures and the strategies of regulatory techniques that regulators employ in order to attain their goals. For compliance officers operating across international markets it is a tremendous challenge to comply with the range of international requirements that they have to be aware of. The rules-of-economics approach helps compliance professionals to navigate in this increasingly demanding regulatory environment and move away from 'tick-the-box' thinking. In other words, it helps to understand the 'why' and 'how' of financial market regulation. In this section we will build upon this approach and discuss the role of compliance.

14.4.1 Compliance should adopt a *why*-based mindset

The objectives and *why* of financial market regulation are explained in the previous sections. There is, however, a broader goal in financial market regulation, namely (public) trust. The increase in regulation and regulatory scrutiny is a consequence of the pressure governments and regulators face as a result of events that undermine confidence in the financial system as a whole. The public consensus in the wake of the financial crisis that began in 2007 is that we created a financial system that privatized the benefits of banking for a few, while at the same time attributing the

47. Ibid., p. 78.
48. Ibid., section 3.5.7 and chapter 16: Resolution *and* Bank Resolution.

risks and associated costs to society at large. Regulators are accused of being too close to banks. Banks, regulators and governments became trust-violators. Consequently, public trust in banks, regulators and governments has faded, causing the pendulum of regulation to swing too far the other way with an intent to restore that trust.

Consequently, financial institutions, especially those operating on the global stage, are confronted with a huge set of regulations to comply with. This immense body of legislation unfortunately encourages a 'box-ticking' approach. The vast set of rules leaves professionals with little or no time to consider the spirit of the law. Although it is important to comply with the letter of the law, compliance should abandon this box-ticking approach and look for the underlying thinking and the spirit of the law. A spirit which should be linked to the *why* guiding both the financial institutions and their regulators. Only then will financial institutions be capable of making courageous decisions redirecting the financial industry towards a sustainable business model with a focus on socially responsible banking. This requires thinking 'outside the box'. The emphasis should be on 'why' and 'how' a business should be conducted, beyond just the 'what'. Hence there should be an increased focus on corporate culture and behavior, the role of leadership and standards of corporate governance beyond the so-called 'hard controls'.[49]

14.4.2 Compliance should act as a countervailing power

We now understand the detrimental impact if trust in the financial market is lost. One way to prevent that from happening again is to neutralize the power vested in the hands of a few, by having a countervailing power that acts when it really matters.

The concept of 'countervailing power' is introduced by Galbraith in the context of the power play between businesses and their customers.[50] Galbraith states that 'unrestrained economic power is still an enemy of the good society'.[51] He also states that unrestrained economic power cannot be totally mitigated by law alone:

> 'Economic power in the economy is pervasive. It goes far beyond the limits set by the classical concepts of monopoly. It is an attribute of large-scale enterprise, the most striking characteristic of the American economy. Are we, by legislative and judicial action, going to work a revolution in the American economy? The answer is no.'

Galbraith states that 'private economic power is held in check by the countervailing power of those who are subject to it'.[52] 'The large corporation can have significant power over the prices it charges, over the prices it pays, even on the mind of the consumer ...'.[53]

He refers to the power play within the market economy, arguing that if the economic power lies in the hands of a relatively small number of businesses creating

49. *See* chapter 4 on Managing organizational integrity & leadership.
50. Galbraith 1952, pp. 118–119.
51. Ibid., p. 6.
52. Ibid., p. 118
53. Ibid., p. 7.

strong suppliers, it ultimately also leads to stronger customers. After all, they interact with each other. Galbraith argues quite boldly that the suppliers or consumers will be encouraged 'to defend themselves against exploitation'.[54] He continues by stating that 'the existence of ... power creates an incentive to the organization of another position of power to neutralize it'.[55] Galbraith states that 'the core thesis that an established answer to economic power is the building of a countervailing power is, indeed, still valid'.[56]

The possibility of external checks is increased due to the Internet and social media.[57] The Internet and social media encourage a participatory culture by enhancing the input of individuals and communities. Due to this connectivity it has become even more vital for financial institutions to understand the relationship with the society they serve in order to have a basis for a meaningful dialogue. If Galbraith were still alive, he would most probably have given social media a prominent place in his thinking (apart from the self-regulating effect of competition).[58]

The compliance officer is ideally suited to fulfilling the role of countervailing power in the organization. However, in order to fulfill the role of countervailing power, the compliance officer must have a certain degree of independence. Therefore this should be taken into account when positioning the (chief) compliance officer in the organizational structure.

14.4.3 Compliance as a strategic advisor

The foregoing should also lead to a rethinking of the role of compliance within financial institutions.[59] The primary task of compliance is advising the business, instead of spending the whole time performing tasks associated with the implementation of laws and regulations. Compliance has become top-heavy in many financial institutions, becoming an alien body in the second line of defense and putting all its effort into converting infinite requirements into official policy so that all the right boxes are kept formally ticked. With the increased focus on behavior, the role of compliance is now gradually starting to change into the field of business consultancy as direct advisors of the business. This should be increased even further, so that they become true influencers. It is important to build these trusted relationships across the business. This will determine whether compliance is positioned as a key asset to the business and an enabler of growth rather than a blocker. This will also help to integrate corporate values and desired behavior. Compliance should, however, integrate even more beyond just operations, covering matters such as strategy, human resources, risk management and internal audit. In that way, compliance will also become a more strategic advisor. Finally, compliance should be a strategic advisor to senior management, for example advising the board on the inherent risk a product might

54. Ibid., p. 119.
55. Ibid., p. 119.
56. Ibid., p. 7
57. Bleker-van Eyk 2013, paragraph 3.2.
58. Ibid.
59. *See* section 1.6 *supra*.

bring. Arguably, this should elevate the role of compliance to a more strategic place from its current position. It is important for compliance to work with leadership to understand *how* compliance is able to support business operations to deliver long-term sustainable growth. This will impact the type of skills, expertise and competences required by the compliance professionals.

14.4.4 Managing conflicting interests

There is often tension and conflict between the goals of financial regulation. They therefore need to be balanced against each other. For example, financial stability regulation has a moderating effect on diversity and may thus cause tension or conflict with investor and consumer protection. On the other hand there may also be a tension or conflict between the promotion of competition and investor or consumer protection and financial stability. In the case of excessive competition, financial institutions will most probably be inclined to engage in riskier activity as a result of lower profitability.

It is important to understand how the goals may be in conflict or subject to tension so as to be able to resolve these issues and prioritize certain goals without destabilizing them. It is therefore important for compliance to maintain oversight of all the applicable interests at stake and to think about the corpus of financial market regulation in the round, instead of taking a 'silo' approach to financial market regulation. This is the reality: compliance should be the strategic advisor providing independent advice to balance regulatory requirements on the one hand, while pragmatically advising the business on balancing conflicting interests and preventing inadvertent regulatory breaches. Compliance should advise on shaping the culture and conduct of the organization.

As explained in chapter 4, it is of key importance to understand that we are still driven by the weaknesses and strengths that are inextricably linked to our human nature. We constantly juggle our own interests with those of the organization or society at large. A divergence of this kind may arise especially in financial markets. In the event of a failure of the financial institution, the shareholders of that financial institution will suffer to some extent. The issue with financial markets, however, is that those losses are distributed so far and wide that shareholders bear only a small part of the overall loss to society due to failure.

Financial institutions are paid to take on risk. The profit of risk-taking can be paid out to shareholders as dividends during times of prosperity, but it is not repayable by them should the financial institution fail. Shareholders thus take the profit of risk-taking, but the associated costs in the event of failure with systemic consequences are borne by society at large. The risk here is that shareholders may push financial institutions to take on more risk than is appropriate having regard to the interest of society as a whole.

Risk, however, can also be taken for reward, preferably while achieving and maintaining public trust in the financial system as a whole. Risk governance and value creation are inseparable and should therefore not be seen as opposed or mutually exclusive. Every decision, activity and initiative that aims to create or protect value involves some degree of risk. The primary objective of appropriate risk-taking should therefore be the safeguarding of all stakeholders' interests, i.e. in conformity with the interest of society as a whole, on a sustainable basis, and to discourage an excessive focus on short-term financial targets. As Larry Rittenberg puts it:[60]

> 'To be successful, risk management has to be a core process of managing the enterprise, not merely a project. A lot of directors seem to think that because they devise a "strategy" to deal with known risk, they've got a good handle on risk. My perception is that they don't. Too often, all they want to do is identify the top 10 risks based on what people know. It's a project approach – and that's not what's really needed. A systemized approach of understanding the most basic business assumptions has more long-lasting potential'.

Funston and Wagner refer to this as the 'risk intelligent enterprise'.[61] They define risk intelligence as 'a way to make better decisions amid uncertainty and under turbulent conditions'.[62] Risk intelligence is then not an end-status which can then be enjoyed even more, but is rather a continuum of doing business, a 'deliberate and sustainable enterprise process, and not a project'.[63]

As discussed in chapter 4 *supra*, Paine explains that organizations should provide their members with a 'common frame of reference' that can 'serve as a unifying force across different functions, lines of business, and employee groups'.[64] It defines what the organization stands for and gives life to a shared set of values and guiding principles that are deeply entrenched throughout the organization. This should enable everyone in the organization to engage in responsible conduct, by cutting to the ethos and operating systems of the organization.

In order to create such a deliberate and sustainable enterprise process, organizations should develop and apply the required supporting guidance, skills, systems, tools and processes in place. To be effective, this must be common and deployed throughout the organization and applied with discipline. All managers, at all levels and across all business lines, are responsible for managing this responsible risk-taking by focusing on what value they are going to bring to the customer.

As Funston and Wagner state:[65]

> 'At its best, risk intelligence informs every area of the business at every level such that the practices become part of every function, strategy, initiative, decision, activity and job. This entails making risk intelligence an organizational value on the order of practicing true customer focus or achieving high quality through zero effects. Such values do not come about themselves or by executive decree or through a one-shot training initiative, a short-term project, or a "check-the-box" approach. They come about, because the board and management views them as worthwhile, practices them publicly, recognizes them in compensation programs, and embeds them in core processes and systems.'

---

60. Larry Rittenberg, Professor and Chairman Emeritus, Committee of Sponsoring Organizations of the Treadway Commission (COSO), as quoted by: Funston and Wagner 2010, p. 298.
61. Funston & Wagner 2010, p. 298.
62. Ibid.
63. Ibid.
64. Paine 1994, p. 111.
65. Funston & Wagner 2010, p. 299.

Risk governance and value creation should go hand-in-hand, and should be disseminated throughout the organization: any part of the whole should embody the material goods and values of the whole. Compliance should be the strategic and independent advisor of the whole.

14.4.5 Behavioral biases and customer and investor welfare

Customers and investors may be biased in decision-making. Cognitive bias can be described as a mental shortcut or heuristics, which glitch our thinking and cause us to make questionable decisions and make us reach erroneous conclusions. It is a subconscious process that has to do with our limitations in mental processing. Examples are anchoring (the tendency to rely too heavily, or 'anchor', on one trait or piece of information when making decisions), availability bias (the tendency to overestimate the likelihood of events with greater 'availability' in memory, which can be influenced by how recent the memories are or how unusual or emotionally charged they may be), representativeness (judging probabilities on the basis of resemblance), status quo bias (the tendency to like things to stay relatively the same), and optimism and overconfidence (the tendency to be overoptimistic, overestimating favorable and pleasing outcomes).[66]

Although we cannot be sure about where the consumer's or investor's subjective best interests lie, it is undesirable for financial institutions to seek to trigger or enlarge these biases in the decision-making process. In competitive markets such as the financial market today, financial institutions might be inclined to design products that consumers or investors find attractive due to these biases. An example is offering products with low upfront fees and hidden high costs. It is therefore important for compliance officers to have an understanding of these biases and how to mitigate them.

In economic theory we like to think that people are rational beings, but people are not completely rational. Research has demonstrated that individuals, for example, exhibit a strong preference for 'instantaneous gratification'.[67] This seems to have neurological foundations. Different parts of the brain are activated for decisions with short-term rewards than for longer-term options.[68] When making decisions about the present moment, it seems credible that a fast and intuitive process is deployed, most probably because such decisions need to be made very quickly.[69] The concept of 'instantaneous gratification' can also explain the phenomena of inertia and procrastination (avoidance of doing a task that needs to be accomplished) in individual choice:

> 'Where doing something – including making a decision – involves an investment in time, individuals put off the cost of doing so until "later" because they perceive a cost that must be paid today as much greater than one payable tomorrow. When tomorrow comes, the same process is repeated to delay the cost for another

66. Thaler & Sunstein 2008, p. 33–48.
67. Harris & Laibson 2013, pp. 205–248.
68. McClure et al. 2004, pp. 503–507; McClure et al. 2007, pp. 5796–5804.
69. Kahneman 2011.

> day. Consequently, complexity in problems tends to delay choice, because of the upfront costs. This tends to push individuals towards procrastination and the selection of default options.'[70] This aspect of decision-making is most probably aggravated for those who are less well-educated or older, because they most probably have to take more time to understand a new financial product.[71]

Another consequence of economizing the human brain is that we discard objective sensory data, which also has a neurological underpinning.[72] A famous example is how we sense temperature. If you put one hand into a bowl of cold water and the other hand into a bowl of hot water for a period of one minute, and then put both hands into a bowl of luke warm water, you would probably feel 'that the same bowl of water is simultaneously hot (via the hand that was in cold water) and cold (via the hand that was in hot water)'.[73] This mismatch is caused by the somatosensory cortex, which causes a reference-dependence on sensory data.[74] The somatosensory cortex sits just below where your headsets rest on your head and is responsible for processing all of the sensory information. The point is that most of the objective sensory data are in fact discarded, and that human beings principally rely upon 'evidence of changes, rather than objective values'.[75] The brain only makes use of a (small) part of the information it is served and draws cues from limited information. It uses heuristics that require less processing power. This is simply because human beings face constraints on their information-processing capacity. Viewed in evolutionary terms, human beings apparently sacrificed a little accuracy for speed since there are limits to our mental processing capacity.

The question is whether the decision-making can be modified so as to ameliorate these problems. You may wonder, for example, whether you need to give consumers and investors a little 'nudge', an extra push, so that they make the most advantageous choice for themselves. Thaler & Sunstein call this 'libertarian paternalism'.[76] In libertarian paternalism a nudge is defined as an aspect of choice-making architecture which affects the behavior of individuals without limiting freedom of choice or changing economic incentives. A familiar example of nudging is distributing products on the shelves in the supermarket. The sales of any product can be significantly increased by placing them at eye level on the shelves. Placing fruit and vegetables at eye level in all supermarkets is therefore a nudge, as opposed to larger operations such as banning junk food.

Thaler & Sunstein state that we like to think of ourselves as homo economicus: the notion that each of us always thinks carefully and chooses rationally. The foregoing has already demonstrated that we do not act as econs ('homo economicus'). Thaler & Sunstein summarized that this was caused by two types of systems on the basis of which we act: (1) an automatic and intuitive system, and (2) a reflective rational

70. Armour et al. 2016, p. 210.
71. Ibid., p. 210.
72. Ibid., p. 211.
73. Ibid.
74. *See* for more information about this experiment: https://www.thenakedscientists.com/get-naked/experiments/how-we-sense-temperature.
75. Armour et al. 2016, p. 211.
76. Thaler & Sunstein 2008, p. 13.

system.[77] As the use of the reflective rational system requires higher energy costs and there are limits to our mental processing capacity, a nudge could ensure that humans are better able to rely on their automated intuitive system, making it easier to make the right choices.

Thaler & Sunstein provide six principles of choice-making architecture: (1) providing sensible default options, (2) avoiding human errors, (3) giving feedback when things go wrong or well, (4) comparing options by mapping them, (5) where there are a large number of (complex) choices, structuring them, and finally (6) using incentives for sensible choices.[78] These six principles can encourage people in a relatively inexpensive and easy way to make choices in their best interest. When designed well, it may work even better than law, because humans are then helped to make better decisions themselves instead of being forced by law. Behavioral bias-sensitive defaults are a beneficial intervention 'where the only impediment to the consumer making a "rational" choice concerns overweighting the immediate value of the time spent in researching, or signing up for a program. A well-known example concerns voluntary contributions to tax-subsidized occupational pension schemes. Many employees do not sign up for these even where they represent exceptionally good opportunities or even "free money"'.[79]

Nudging, however, is very delicate. The more persistent the nudge is, the less likely it is that consumers or investors will respond to it. There might be other reasons for those consumers or investors to be unwilling to participate or for it not being in their best interest to participate.[80] The more persistent a nudge is, the more it will have the power of a mandatory rule. The conditions for a nudge value depend on the context, 'meaning that intervention should be preceded by a careful program of evidence-gathering'.[81]

A way to prevent practices of unwanted biased decision-making is to have a proper product approval process in place to test whether the product meets the standards of good conduct. This product approval process should encompass the full life cycle of the product, including the design, testing and marketing.[82] In the United Kingdom, the FCA developed a conduct-based intervention strategy known as 'product governance'.[83] This initiative was subsequently adopted by EU-level authorities.[84] The rationale behind this legislation is to keep regulatory oversight

77. Ibid., p. 29 et seq.
78. Ibid., pp. 97–116.
79. Armour et al. 2016, pp. 220–221; Bernartzi & Thaler 2007. *See also* S. Benartzi & R.H. Thaler, pp. 81–104.
80. Mitchell 2005, pp. 1245–1277; Hausmann & Welch 2010, p. 123; Sunstein & Thaler 2003, pp. 1159–1202.
81. Armour et al. 2016, p. 221.
82. Ibid., pp. 265–266.
83. *See* the FSA, 'Treating Customers Fairly (TCF) in product design', 2007; FSA, 'Retail Product Development and Governance – Structured Products Review', finalized guidance, 2012.
84. This will be applicable to all investment firms in the EU through MiFID II. *See* MiFID II, Arts 16 paragraph 3 and 24 paragraph 2; The EU sectoral authorities have consulted on product governance frameworks to be implemented under corporate governance rules. *See* ESMA, 'Structured Retail Products – Good Practices for Product Governance Arrangements', March 2014; EIOPA, 'Consulting Paper on the Proposal for Guidelines on Product

of the systems and processes in place with regard to product quality throughout the lifecycle of the product.[85] For each new product, a business case needs to be developed that identifies the target market. Furthermore, in the product governance steps also have to be taken in the design and marketing of the product to ensure that the products match the identified target group. Senior management needs to identify this target group at the outset of the product design, and it will be tested against this target market in each subsequent phase in the product development and distribution strategy. The design process includes stress testing of the product, to ensure that the product will add value to the target market. Furthermore, the uptake of the products needs to be monitored to ensure that they reach the target market and are not sold inappropriately (for example due to incorrect compensation techniques).

Designing good products that do not exploit the biases of consumers and investors and truly add value to the target group is the most advantageous path to foster the welfare of customers and investors.[86] Compliance should advise on setting up a proper product approval process and act as a countervailing power in the role of the ethical conscience of the financial institution.

Oversight and Governance Arrangements by insurance undertakings', October 2014; EBA, 'Draft Guidelines on Product Oversight and Governance Arrangements for Retail Banking Products', November 2014.

85. See the principles expressed in FCA, 'Structured Products: Thematic Review of Product Development and Governance', March 2015.

86. Armour et al. 2016, p. 233.

BIBLIOGRAPHY

Altman 2006
D. Altman, 'Managing Globalization: Q&A with Joseph E. Stiglitz', The Economist's View 2006-October. To be consulted on: http://economistsview.typepad.com/economistsview/2006/10/joseph_stiglitz.html

Armour et al. 2016
J. Armour, D. Awrey, P. Davies, L. Enriques, J.N. Gordon, C. Mayer & J. Payne, *The Principles of Financial Regulation,* Oxford: Oxford University Press 2016.

Bernartzi & Thaler 2007
S. Bernartzi & R.H. Thaler, 'Heuristics and Biases in Retirement Savings Behavior', *Journal of Economic Perspectives,* 2007, Vol. 21, Issue 3.

Bleker-van Eyk 2013
S.C. Bleker-van Eyk, Compliance officer 2.0 (on file with the author).

Fox et al. 2003
M.B. Fox, R. Morck, B. Yeung & A. Durney, 'Law, Share Price Accuracy and Economic Performance: The New Evidence', *Michigan Law Review,* 2003, Vol. 102, Issue 3.

Funston & Wagner 2010
F. Funston & S. Wagner, *Surviving and Thriving in Uncertainty: Creating the Risk Intelligent Enterprise,* New Jersey: John Wiley & Sons Inc. 2010.

Galbraith 1952
J.K. Galbraith, *American Capitalism: The concept of countervailing power,* New Jersey: Transaction Publishers 1952.

Harris & Laibson 2013
C. Harris & D. Laibson, 'Instantaneous Gratification', *Quarterly Journals of Economics,* 2013, Vol. 129, Issue 1.

Hausmann & Welch 2010
D.M. Hausmann & B. Welch, 'Debate: To nudge or Not to Nudge', *Journal of Political Philosophy,* 2010, Vol. 18.

Kahneman 2011
D. Kahneman, *Thinking, Fast and Slow,* New York: Farrar, Strauss and Giroux 2011.

McClure et al. 2004
S.M. McClure, D.I. Laibson, G. Loewenstein & J.D. Cohen, 'Separate Neural Systems Value Immediate and Delayed Monetary Rewards', *Science,* 2004, Vol. 306, Issue 5695.

McClure et al. 2007
S.M. McClure, K.M. Ericson, D.I. Laibson, G. Loewenstein & J.D. Cohen, 'Time discounting for Primary Rewards', *Journal of Neuroscience,* 2007, Vol. 27, Issue 21.

Mitchell 2005
G. Mitchell, 'Libertarian Paternalism is an *Oxymoron*', *Northwestern University Law Review,* 2005, Vol. 99, Issue 3.

Paine 1994
L.S. Paine, 'Managing for Organizational Integrity', *Harvard Business Review*, 1994, March/April.

Smith 1976
A. Smith, *The Theory of Moral Sentiments, vol. 1, The Glasgow Edition of the Works and Correspondence of Adam Smith, vol. 7*, Oxford: Oxford University Press, 1976.

Smith 1980
A. Smith, *Volume III: The Glasgow Edition of the Works and Correspondence of Adam Smith, vol. 7*, Oxford: Oxford University Press, 1980.

Smith 2009
A. Smith, *The Theory of Moral Sentiments (reprint of the 6th ed. 1790)*, London: Penguin Books 2009.

Sunstein & Thaler 2003
C.R. Sunstein & R.H. Thaler, 'Libertarian paternalism is nog an oxymoron', *University Chicago Law Review*, 2003, Vol. 70, Issue 4.

Thaler & Sunstein 2008
R. Thaler & C. Sunstein, *Nudge: Improving Decisions about Health, Wealth and Happiness (Dutch translation)*, Amsterdam/Antwerp: Business Contact 2008.

Other references

Commission of the European Communities 2007
Communication from the Commission - Financial Education, COM 808 final, 2007.

EIOPA 2004
EIOPA, 'Consulting Paper on the Proposal for Guidelines on Product Oversight and Governance Arrangements by Insurance Undertakings', 2004, October.

ESMA 2014
ESMA, 'Structured Retail Products - Good Practices for Product Governance Arrangements', 2014, March.

European Banking Authority (EBA) 2014
EBA, 'Draft Guidelines on Product Oversight and Governance Arrangements for Retail Banking Products', 2014, November.

FSA 2007
FSA, 'Treating Customers Fairly (TCF) in product design', 2007.

FSA 2012
FSA, 'Retail Product Development and Governance - structured Products Review', finalized guidance, 2012.

FCA 2015
FCA, 'Structured Products: Thematic Review of Product Development and Governance', 2015, March.

Sensory data experiment
See for more information about this experiment: https://www.thenakedscientists.com/get-naked/experiments/how-we-sense-temperature.

PART IV – CAPITA SELECTA

15. Fraud and Internal Investigations

Prof. S.C. Bleker-van Eyk

15.1 INTRODUCTION

According to *Black's Law Dictionary*, the definition of fraud is

> 'an intentional perversion of truth for the purpose of inducing another in reliance upon it to part with some valuable thing belonging to him or to surrender a legal right. A false representation of a matter of fact, whether by words or by conduct, by false or misleading allegations, or by concealment of that which should have been disclosed, which deceives and is intended to deceive another so that he shall act upon it to his legal injury. Anything calculated to deceive, whether by a single act or combination, or by suppression of truth, or suggestion of what is false, whether it be by direct falsehood or innuendo, by speech or silence, word or mouth, or look or gesture.'[1]

Fraud is a (legal) concept and consists of a wide variety of offenses, such as collusion, deceit, forgery, theft, corruption, bribery, extortion, concealment, and false reporting or misappropriation of assets. It can involve defrauding the company or a third party, and it can be carried out by an organization, by an employee of an organization, or by a third party.

Management responsibilities, in matters of fraud and other acts of non-compliance, extend to understanding the fraud risks that can undermine their business objectives. Management is responsible for implementing systems and controls, which are capable of minimizing the risk of fraud or other non-compliant acts occurring, through prevention, detection and deterrence of fraudulent behavior and to monitor these controls on an on-going basis to ensure that they are operating effectively. Leadership is responsible for the management and resourcing of the internal investigation and the implementation of a response plan.

1. *Delahanty v. First Pennsylvania Bank N.A.*, as cited in *Black's Law Dictionary*, sixth edition, St. Paul Minn. West Publishing co., 1990, p. 660.

Not all acts of non-compliance are fraudulent. It is the will and intent to deceive that draws the fine line between fraud and other instances of non-compliance. However, instances of fraud or other forms of non-compliance need to be addressed properly, due to the impact they can have on the organization.

In chapters 17–19 *infra* of this book, enforcement of certain unlawful acts, such as bribery or dealing with sanctioned states of private parties, will be discussed in more detail. The current chapter mainly serves as an introduction to the first steps to be taken from the moment of detection of an alleged fraud or non-compliance issue, in order for the company to respond adequately and prevent a wide variety of – sometimes irreparable – damage.

The consequences of fraud and other kinds of non-compliance can be massive. From a financial point of view, the consequences of fraud may affect the covenants with banks and other investors and may influence the stock market value. Fraud and other non-compliant behavior may give rise to extensive costs due to matters such as:

- direct damages;
- discharges;
- internal investigation;
- legal fees;
- settlements/penalties;
- debarment.

Also, fraud and non-compliance will entail non-financial consequences, such as loss of trust, reputational damage, loss of management time, uncertainty among employees, and even the possibility of loss of employees who prefer to work for a more trustworthy organization.

More than one in three organizations experiences economic crime. Both developed and emerging markets are affected, and the internal detection methods cannot keep pace. Almost half of the fraudsters are an organization's own employees. More than half of internal perpetrators originate from middle and senior management. The most likely characteristics of the internal fraudster are:[2]

- male;
- university/college graduate;
- 31–40 years old;
- 3–5 years of service.

15.2 DETECTION OF FRAUD AND OTHER INSTANCES OF NON-COMPLIANCE

When an organization is confronted with evidence or allegations of potential wrongdoing, it should act quickly and should also assure that it understands all the facts and responds promptly with appropriate discipline, remediation, and (in certain cases) perhaps even discussions with the government.[3]

2. PwC 2016, p. 12.
3. GIR 2016, introduction p. 3,

With regard to detection of fraudulent or other non-compliant behavior, national as well as international (European) authorities emphasize the need for a compliant culture where reporting deviations to line management is part of usual business conduct. However, organizations should have a whistleblower policy to assure that employees can report issues without any fear of retribution.[4]

An effective method to prevent fraud and non-compliance is through early warning detection by means of periodic analysis of the clusters of data, with the help of data analytics, which the organization possesses. Organizations save enormous amounts of data with backups of their computer systems. Data analytics offers the possibility to search for abnormalities. These abnormalities may be red flags that point to possible undetected fraud or non-compliance. By regularly applying data analytics as a sanity check within the organization's processes, fraud and other sorts of non-compliance can be detected, thereby opening the possibility for immediate response and remediation as well as preventing - or at least controlling - possible damage. A fortuitous fact is that supervisory authorities and/or enforcement agencies - especially in the US - will react favorably to early warning systems.[5]

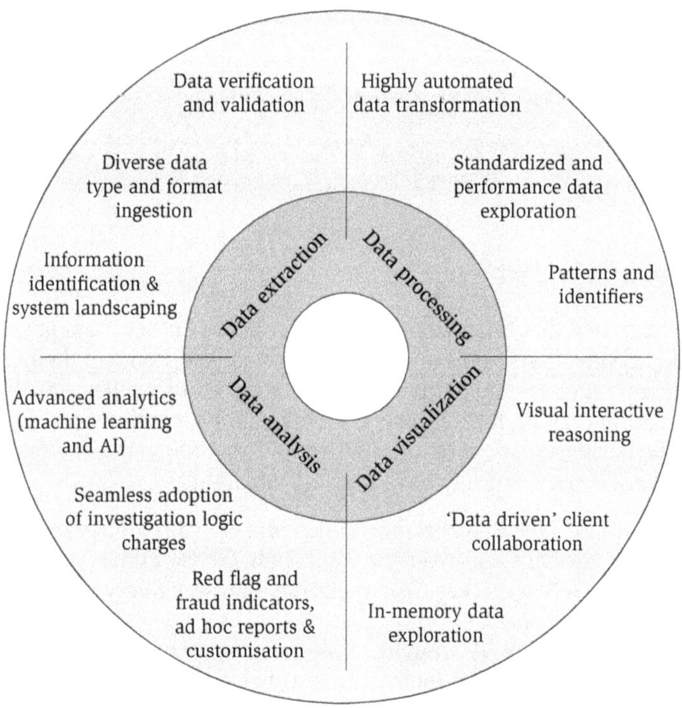

Figure 1: PwC Forensic Data Analytics[6]

4. *Supra* chapter 3.
5. *Infra* chapters 17–19.
6. PwC, Forenic Technology Solutions, 2017-04-25.

Adversary	Motives	Targets	Impact
Nation state	• Economic, political, and/or military advantage	• Trade secrets • Sensitive business information • Emerging technologies • Critical infrastructure	• Loss of competitive advantage • Disruption to critical infrastructure
Organized crime	• Immediate financial gain • Collect information for future financial gains	• Financial/payment systems • Personally identifiable information • Payment card information • Protected health information	• Costly regulatory enquiries and penalties • Consumer and shareholder lawsuits • Loss of consumer confidence
Hacktivists	• Influenced political and/or social change • Pressure business to change their practices	• Corporate secrets • Sensitive business information • Information related to key executives, employees, customers and business partners	• Disruption of business activities • Brand and reputation • Loss of consumer confidence
and even ...			
Cyber terrorists	• Political and/or ideological change • Create fear, uncertainty, and doubt	• Critical infrastructure • Operational technologies • Highly visible venues	• Destabilise, disrupt, and to destroy physical and logical assets

Figure 2: PwC Cyber threats[7]

It is a digital paradox that organizations today are able to cover more ground, thanks to new digital connections, tools and platforms which can connect them in real time with customers, suppliers and partners. Yet, at the same time, cybercrime has become a powerful countervailing force which is limiting that potential.[8]

Over the last few years, economic cybercrime has evolved to a point where two distinct categories of cybercrime have become apparent:

- Cyber fraud. This is cybercrime which aims to gain money by means of, for example, identity and payment card theft. These crimes are the ones first thought of when discussing cybercrime, but they rarely pose an existential threat to companies.
- Transfer-of-wealth/IP attacks. The more critical economic crime facing organizations is that of international cyber espionage – the theft of critical IP (trade secrets, product information, negotiating strategies, and the like). Cyber professionals call such breaches 'extinction-level events' and for good reason: the damage could extend to the billions of dollars, and include

7. PwC, Forensic Data Analytics, 2016-04-20.
8. PwC 2016, p. 13.

destruction of a line of business or even a company. Not only are these kinds of attacks difficult to detect. They may not even be on a company's threat radar.[9]

In general the fraud policy of an organization should contain a provision stating that every employee is required to internally report a (suspected) fraud or form of non-complaint behavior. Different kinds of notification are possible, for example:

- direct contact with the line manager or senior management;
- direct contact with the compliance officer or internal auditor;
- direct contact with the internal and/or external contact point (whistleblower procedure);
- web-based solutions.[10]

Web-based solutions hold several advantages. A web-based tool can be tailored to be user-friendly; to be contacted anonymously; to offer direct insight to the compliance officer; to offer possibility for the employee access through use a private computer; and to offer - even anonymously - possibilities to remain in contact with the employee through a separate numbered and encrypted mailbox (in case of anonymous reporting), which is essential for communication with the reporter and possibility to upload evidence. Last, but not least, the same web-based tool may be used for other compliance solutions, such as a system of reporting and granting permission for travel, gifts and entertainment. The latter offers the compliance officer to screen requests and generate reports at the push of a button.

15.3 INTERNAL INVESTIGATION AND SCOPING

> 'Under the right circumstances, conducting an effective corporate internal investigation [if necessary protected by the attorney-client privilege] - can benefit the company in a number of ways:
> - Revealing all of the relevant facts so that management and/or the board can make a fully informed decision as to how best to proceed;
> - Stopping the conduct to prevent further violations;
> - Memorializing the company's good-faith response to the facts as they become known;
> - Insulating management and/or the board against allegations of complicity; and
> - Promoting a culture of transparency and compliance throughout the organization.'[11]

The organization must decide on how fraud and other non-compliant behavior should be tackled. In those instances where the organization recently had an encounter with enforcement agencies, the management will often decide to uphold a *zero-tolerance* policy. This entails the obligation to assess every single report, however minor. When proclaiming zero-tolerance and not investigating minor incidents, the credibility of

9. Ibid., p. 19.
10. *Supra* chapter 10.
11. GIR 2016, introduction p. 3.

the organization's fraud prevention system is at risk and compliance culture may become a slippery slope, where some employees may be encouraged to try out the limits of compliance.

One of the first difficulties with starting an investigation is to understand the alleged crime that was committed and who the possible perpetrator(s) might be. As depicted in Figure 3, the crime can be committed within the company or outside the company. The question of whether the alleged fraud was committed *intra muros* or *extra muros* is of great importance to the possibilities and also to the limits set to the investigation of the alleged fraud. The investigation may be seriously hampered if fraud is committed by outsiders or by the organization's own employee(s) in collusion with a third party. The organization will need formal approval and authorization by the third-party management to carry on the investigation *extra muros*, in order to assess data belonging to the third party and when interviewing their employees. It's at the discretion of the third party to cooperate with the investigation. It is advisable that organizations include their code of conduct and a special clause on cooperation, in case of an investigation into their contracts with third parties. However, such a clause will only improve cooperation during investigations, but will not remove all limitations regarding third-party collaboration.

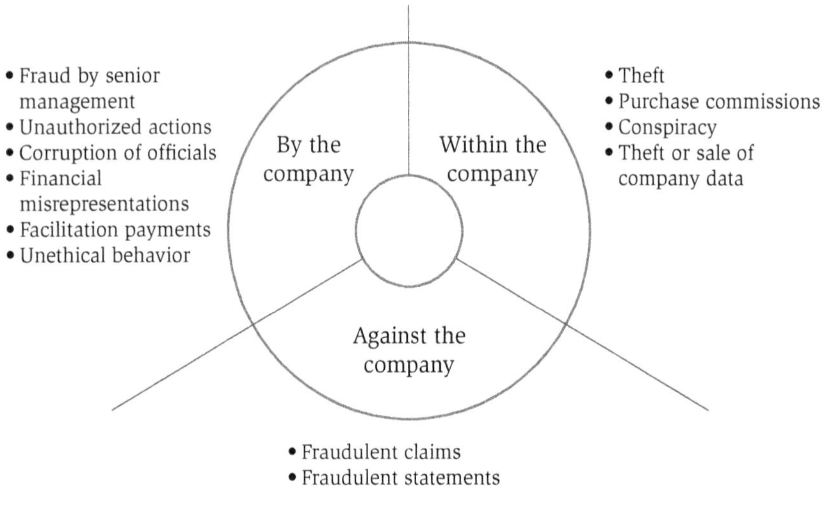

Figure 3: Fraud environment[12]

On the presumption that the organization has a sound fraud policy, which explicitly deals with the rights and duties of the organization as well as the employees based on an interview protocol and an investigation protocol, the organization has prepared itself and its employees in the event of a fraud investigation. The policies should at least state that employees are obligated to cooperate with fraud investigations and to promptly deliver all requested information and, where necessary, to hand over

12. Figure retrieved from lecture by Prof. S.C. Bleker-van Eyk.

their devices. Privacy laws differ per country and may hamper the investigative rights of the organization. In order for investigations to be effective and to be carried out swiftly, policies should already be in place.

At the earliest stage of the internal investigation, the investigators should commence with 'scoping' interviews with witnesses who have little, if any, personal knowledge of the conduct in question, but who can provide an overview of relevant corporate processes, practices and/or personnel.[13]

Regarding the investigation of employees and the methods that can be applied during such an investigation, it is important that the fraud policy clearly states the definition of the concept 'employee'. The definition of 'employee' should aim at all persons - whether or not on the basis of a contract - who are functioning within the organization and acting on behalf of representing the organization, as well as other persons hired by the organization and employees who are employed by another employer but who are hired by and functioning within the organization. It is critical to have all those persons who are included in the definition of 'employee' sign the code of conduct as well as the fraud policy.

Finally, if the alleged fraud may be material to financial position of the organization, the fraud investigator should immediately inform the Chief Financial Officer.

15.3.1 Securing evidence

As soon as an alleged fraud or other non-compliant behavior is detected, a freeze on all relevant data and the collection of relevant hard-copy documentation should be made. Most organizations have a backup system where all information is secured. An image should be made of all (possibly) involved data. In practice, this will not be as easy as it sounds. The first problem is that many (mostly smaller) organizations do not have a backup system or only have a backup for parts of their systems. As a result, laptops and desktops need to be secured to image the information. Another problem is that most organizations use a variety of management systems and often these systems are not aligned. As a result, data may be scattered all over the different systems and with no - or just slight - interconnection between systems, thereby severely hampering data collection and interpretation.[14]

During the initial phase of the investigation, it is vital to secure all data - soft copy and hard copy - as soon as possible, preventing the possibility of destruction of data by the alleged fraudsters. The Enron investigation was renowned for the use of shredders during the initial phase of the investigation. 'Enron employees were shredding documents at the company's Houston offices as recently as last week, a former executive said yesterday. Her statement was the first indication that documents were destroyed at Enron amid investigations of the company's collapse

13. GIR 2016, p. 4.
14. During an export control violation investigation the author was confronted with a medium-sized company (5000 employees) where every subsidiary used its own systems. In total there were 36 different systems including three different versions of BAAN, an old version of SAP and a 'selfmade' management system. None of the systems were interconnected.

by Congress and the Justice Department and followed reports of document shredding by accountants at Enron's auditor, Arthur Andersen.'[15]

Next to hard copy data, as well as desktops and laptops, important data can also be found on communication systems, such as mobile phones, Lync, Skype for Business, or WhatsApp.[16] Retention and investigation of these data may conflict with data privacy legislation. Confiscating the desktop and/or laptop provided by the organization is no problem. However, reading private messages may be forbidden. Lync is a typically made to prevent large amounts of email by enabling quick questions and answers between employees. Although often used as 'chat', such systems are made for business communication and work via intranet, thereby easing the burden of proof that the information is not deemed to be private information that it may be investigated. Most systems back up Lync automatically, but the Lync messages can be deleted. Confiscating a mobile phone may be more difficult because of privacy laws. In order to investigate data, it is important that organizations include statements in fraud policy or IT policy that all devices provided for by the employer may only be used for business purposes and that the employee agrees with the terms that, in case of an investigation, all data may be retained and read.[17]

All data - hard copy and soft copy - must be recorded and stored in a secure (virtual) environment. Only the investigation team members must have access to the data on a 'need to know' basis.

Finally, if necessary, while taking into account the interests of the organization, its employees and third parties, the organization may temporarily prevent employees from accessing their workplace, PC, mobile phone, iPad, network, assets and premises.

15.3.2 Pre-investigative communication

At the beginning of the investigation, communication should be strictly limited and on a 'need to know' basis. However, sooner or later, the moment will arrive where a better overview will be acquired as to the facts. As soon as perpetrators can be singled out, they will have to be informed that they are under investigation. If the investigation is instigated by enforcement authorities, local laws and regulations will guide the information to the subject of investigation.

At the beginning of the investigation, especially when the scope and group of possible suspects is not yet determined, communication should be kept to an absolute minimum, thus preventing the destruction of evidence. However, as discussed in chapter 11 *supra*, communication may be necessary, either directly to affected employees, to prevent the spread of rumor and to avoid uncertainty among employees, or to external stakeholders that may be affected by the investigations (e.g., authorities, lenders, or clients). Here external legal counsel should be sought to assure that the national laws and regulations on the information of public authorities are met.

15. *New York Times*, January 22, 2002.
16. During an investigation by the author, all fraudulent acts had taken place through use of WhatsApp messaging.
17. *Infra* chapter 20.

15.3.3 Investigation of documentation

A thorough investigation of data is necessary to piece together all significant information and also to refresh the memories of the witnesses during interviews. All the applicable laws and regulations, as well as the organization's policies, company bylaws, contractual provisions, or statutes define the scope and the framework of the investigation. In the more complex investigations and/or investigations, where the outcome needs to be reported outside the organization, an independent forensic accountant can examine the organization's books and records, together with bank records, to help unravel complex payments and money transfers – thereby tracing the money to further an investigation of fraud or malfeasance.[18]

The services of an expert in computer forensics can also be exceptionally useful when the investigation is beginning. With so much company data and communication stored electronically, a computer forensic expert is usually the most proficient at quickly finding information critical to the investigation and scoping a work plan for the collection of electronically stored information that will be credible upon review by third parties. Such an expert can also help shape the investigation by working with the legal team, to develop the best search terms, interview questions and overall investigative strategy.[19]

There are two different types of data: structured data (such as the data in a financial database) and unstructured data (such as emails, office documents and photographs). A forensic data analytics expert can analyze both types of data swiftly and expertly.[20]

15.3.4 Interviews

Interviews are a valuable source of information and are necessary to corroborate data and activities. The fraud investigator can interview employees, as well as former employees, third parties, or other witnesses, in order to corroborate the facts. Depending on national privacy laws and regulations, interview hearings can be recorded using a recording device to facilitate reporting of interview. The interview reports are sent to the respondents for review with the request to check, comment and sign off. The most accurate – and therefore most useful – interview report is one that is prepared very soon after the interview and based on the recollections and copious notes of the participants.[21]

It is imperative for interviewers to clearly set the ground rules for the interview at the very outset, before substantive questioning begins – including, where appropriate, straightforward warnings (in case the interviewee is the subject of investigation).

Witness interviews are a critical part of an internal corporate investigation. Witnesses have the facts: the 'who, what, where, when, and why'. 'From this perspective, a good interview is, fundamentally, one that enables: (i) the discovery

18. GIR 2016, p. 35.
19. Ibid., pp. 35–36.
20. PWC, E-disclosure and data analysis, 2017.
21. GIR 2016, p. 8.

of as many relevant facts (or sources of such facts) from the witness as possible; and (ii) an accurate assessment of the witness's credibility.'[22]

Before the interview, the investigators should determine whether any company policies, company bylaws, contractual provisions, or statutes would afford the witness the right to counsel or other representation at the interview.[23] It is advisable for the organization to draw up a list of law firms, independent from the organization and its (outside) legal counsel, from which the employees may choose their representative counsel. The organization compensates the legal costs up to a reasonably agreed upon maximum. However, the organization should preserve the right to terminate this fee - in case the employee appears to be guilty of fraud or other non-compliant behavior and agrees on the allocation of the legal fees in a settlement. The benefit of providing independent legal counsel by preapproved law firms is based on the possible lack of knowledge and experience with challenging business matters by legal counsels hired by employees and the harmful consequences that unknowledgeable actions can have for the organization as such.

15.3.5 Reporting, management decisions and remediation

At the end of the investigation, the management has to take an informed decision on how to move on. The decision must be based on accurate facts, and the board needs be assured that no uninvestigated threads are left over, in order to prevent future unraveling of the investigated incident. All data needs to be corroborated and a thorough argumentation is necessary - in order to prove why further investigation of potential open ends will not lead to a different set of facts or may even be impossible.

In case of an infraction, the board may decide to press charges against the perpetrators. Also, the board can decide to disclose the infraction to the appropriate, applicable national supervisory authorities and/or enforcement agencies. In chapter 18 *infra*, the procedure on Voluntary Self-Disclosure to the US Department of Justice will be discussed in more detail.

If the investigation indicates that an employee is guilty of fraud or other non-compliant behavior, management has to take appropriate action to remediate the existing infractions. Also, management will have to decide on possible disciplinary measures with regard to perpetrators, such as an official warning, suspension, or dismissal. Enforcement authorities may decide to prosecute the perpetrators, the responsible management and/or the organization itself. In the chapters 18 and 19 *infra*, ample attention will be given to enforcement of bribery & corruption (18) and export controls & sanctions (19). In practice, the enforcement agencies attach special attention to disciplinary measures, and the absence of such measures taken by the organization may encourage these agencies to prosecute the individual employees, alongside the prosecution of the organization.[24]

22. Ibid., p. 1.
23. Ibid., p. 5.
24. For example, as discussed in chapter 17 *infra*, the Yates Memorandum.

15.3.6 Communication

In this chapter and chapter 11 *supra*, the importance of timely communication has been dealt with substantively. Often medium and larger organizations have a communication department assisting management in dealing with press and other – both internal and external – communication. However, when dealing with significant investigations of fraud or other non-compliant behavior, it may be advisable to involve external specialized communication experts and outside legal counsel to assist with all outside communication. Keeping the organization out of harm's way may require expert knowledge and experience.

15.4 CONCLUSION

Investigating possible incidents of fraud or other non-compliant behavior is not only a matter of organizational hygiene, it is imperative to prevent the creation of an organizational culture where non-compliance is an option merely due to the fact that the organization does not respond adequately to incidents. Responsive measures are necessary in order to maintain a hale and hearty organization. However, response, which refers to infraction and prevention, as well as to early detection, is preferable to a responsive incident-driven management style.

Alongside all the commercial benefits, modern technology also enables organizations to remain in constant control, untangling deviant patterns, and thereby avoiding fraud and acts of non-compliance. However, as discussed in chapter 2 *supra*, fraud and other non-compliance remains an issue of human behavior. The one thing that technology can't bring about is *compliant* human behavior. As a result, prevention requires a culture of compliance.

16. Extraterritorial Jurisdiction[1]

Prof. S.C. Bleker-van Eyk

16.1 INTRODUCTION

In this chapter the concept of extraterritorial jurisdiction will be discussed, due to the enormous importance of this issue to both national and international companies, their executive officers and their employees. The dangers of extraterritoriality of foreign legislation are highly underrated, however, and the consequences can be enormous. Companies are only slowly beginning to realize that there really is an issue. The word 'extraterritoriality' is now used more frequently in day-to-day practice, but many company lawyers do not genuinely understand what it means for them and for their company and – even worse – compliance officers are held responsible for not having tackled such issues. It already seems enough of a challenge to ensure compliance with laws and regulations in one's home jurisdiction and those relating to one's subsidiaries and activities abroad, but the task becomes three-dimensional when the extraterritorial laws of foreign countries also impact activities in all other locations.

This extraterritorial reach, brought into being by foreign countries, is an increasingly important phenomenon that affects not only natural persons that are suspected of having committed criminal offenses, but also corporate enterprises. Such enterprises are often unwillingly or unknowingly involved in illegal activities; sometimes companies are entirely unaware that they have crossed a line that should not have been crossed. It is therefore high time to consider the subject of 'extraterritoriality' in greater depth, because companies are increasingly encountering the long, extraterritorial arm of, for example, the United States of America.

1. Parts of this chapter were previously published in Bleker-van Eyk 2013, pp. 53–61 and Bleker-van Eyk 2012.

16.2 EXTRATERRITORIAL JURISDICTION AS A DRIVING FORCE OF COMPLIANCE

In recent years we have seen increasing attention being paid to compliance in non-financial companies, owing to growing awareness of the extraterritorial application of anti-corruption legislation. Since 1997 the OECD Anti-Bribery Convention has enabled the US to enforce its legislation more effectively in other countries, as the States Parties to it – not only the OECD Member States – meet the requirement of dual criminality once they have ratified it. Real awareness in boardrooms of the extraterritorial application of foreign legislation only seems to have developed after the passing of the United Kingdom Bribery Act (UKBA), however.[2] No doubt Great Britain is not so far away that European directors can sleep at night. Most of them slept fine with the Foreign Corrupt Practices Act (FCPA), which presented – and still presents – a far greater danger. Competition cases have also created a good deal of turmoil in recent years, though they are rarely regarded as compliance matters, usually still being dealt with by legal departments. The question is whether this is correct. Competition cases fall under national and international legislation and can entail substantial risks. As stated earlier in this book, the purpose of compliance is to promote the observance of national and international laws and regulations, as well as internal rules and standards, to protect the integrity of the organization and its directors and staff. The aim is to control the risks of non-compliance with laws, regulations and standards and to prevent the damage that could result. However, the compliance function often does not realize that it may also have to take into account foreign legislation, even when the company has no subsidiary in that foreign country. During the past twenty-odd years compliance has slowly become aware of the extraterritorial ramifications of anti-bribery, export control or sanctions legislation. As soon as the executives within a company start feeling the hot breath of foreign enforcement agencies, the compliance departments grow rapidly. The extraterritorial application of American export rules is still the driving force behind the creation of many compliance roles in the industrial world.[3] This does not apply by definition to all laws and regulations, but particularly to those related to achieving the company's key objectives. It is fair to say that compliance derives its *raison d'être* from a company's license to operate. Compliance risks are risks that can pull the proverbial rug from under the company, or at least cause major material and reputational damage.

The extraterritorial effect of legislation is being experienced worldwide by an increasing number of companies because American anti-terrorism legislation regularly exceeds the territorial boundaries of the United States. Various companies (mostly financial institutions and large industrial conglomerates) headquartered outside the United States have felt the painful effects of this phenomenon in recent years. This began with the FCPA, particularly after the ratification of the OECD Anti-Corruption

2. Bleker-van Eyk 2012.
3. Cf. the United States: Directorate of Defense and Trade Controls (DDTC) http://www.pmddtc.state.gov/compliance/index.html; Bureau of Industry and Security (BIS) http://www.bis.doc.gov/complianceandenforcement/emcp.htm; Office of Foreign Assets Control (OFAC) http://www.treasury.gov/about/organizational-structure/offices/Pages/Office-of-Foreign-Assets-Control.aspx.

Convention (ACC) and later on the UKBA. This will be discussed in chapter 17 on Anti-Bribery & Corruption *infra*. Like the US legislator, the British legislator - and in its wake the British judiciary - is also moving beyond its territorial boundaries. However, the most dangerous exponents of 'extraterritorialism' are the so-called 'export controls' and 'sanctions' provisions in the US. This will be discussed later in more detail in the chapter 18 on Export Controls & Sanctions *infra*.

16.3 THE DEFINITION OF EXTRATERRITORIALITY

Extraterritorial jurisdiction is the extension of jurisdiction over offenses that have been committed outside the territory of a country. States are sovereign and independent. In principle a state determines the scope of its legal system, and as such, the use of extraterritorial jurisdiction is an extremely controversial subject. It is contrary to the territorial sovereignty of the state when another foreign state claims extraterritorial jurisdiction over its subjects.

The starting point is and remains that every state should decide on its own laws and regulations, and on how compliance with these rules is to be enforced. Nowadays the world has become a global village where cross-border economic activities create new challenges for states in their attempt to control the activities of their own (corporate) citizens. States also want to control the activities of foreign persons within their territorial borders and, finally, to protect their own interests and those of their citizens. Sometimes the level of control requires a state to take actions beyond its territorial limits. All these cross-border activities create overlapping jurisdictional claims.

There are countless international treaties that obligate states to establish jurisdiction in a certain way in respect of offenses committed not on their own territory but elsewhere in the world. The extraterritorial jurisdiction can be divided into various core principles:[4]

- The *active personality principle*, which means that jurisdiction can be claimed for acts committed by the country's own citizens.
- The *passive personality principle*, in which jurisdiction is claimed in respect of offenses committed against a country's own citizens.[5]
- The *universality principle*, which claims jurisdiction on the basis of the seriousness of the existing offenses.
- *Derivative or subsidiary jurisdiction*, in which a country also acquires jurisdiction over the offense by means of a transfer of criminal proceedings. The basis for this lies in the various treaties in which one party requests the other party to take over the criminal proceedings. That state then actually takes over the original jurisdiction of the requesting state.[6]

4. Klip & Massa 2010, p. 506.
5. Sjöcrona & Orie 2002, p. 72.
6. In the Netherlands the legal basis is incorporated in Art. 522hh paragraph 2 of the Code of Criminal Procedure and in the European Convention on the Transfer of Proceedings in Criminal Matters of the Council of Europe.

- The *principle of protection*, protecting specific interests of the state justifying extraterritorial intervention, for example in the case of counterfeiting.
- The *subjective territoriality principle*, in which the extraterritorial jurisdiction is claimed because, for example, an act committed abroad has an effect within the state claiming jurisdiction. Conversely, it is also possible that the offense was started in the state claiming jurisdiction, but its effect is generated primarily outside the boundaries of that state.[7]

16.4 PRINCIPLES OF EXTRATERRITORIALITY

16.4.1 The active personality principle

Jurisdiction can be claimed for offenses that have been committed by the claimant country's own nationals. The nationality of the offender is the basis on which extraterritorial jurisdiction is claimed. Countries may refuse to extradite their own nationals; for instance, the Netherlands does not extradite its own nationals without a bilateral or multilateral extradition agreement. An example of extradition in the Netherlands is the approval by the Dutch Supreme Court of the extradition of a Dutch CEO to the US on a charge relating to the violation of the FCPA.[8] Despite this, due to political pressure, the CEO has not been extradited to the US.

16.4.2 The passive personality principle

Here jurisdiction is claimed on the basis of the nationality of the victims of a crime. This principle is rarely applied, although it may arise, for example, in the aftermath of wars.

16.4.3 The principle of universality

Under this principle countries can claim jurisdiction based on the severity of the crime. Extraterritoriality is part of the international agreements among countries. Best known are international crimes such as war crimes, crimes against humanity, genocide, piracy, aircraft hijacking and international drug trafficking. Today these are considered international crimes and jurisdiction may be claimed on the basis of the principle of universality.

In the case of piracy there has long been a difference of opinion as to whether universal jurisdiction applies. The crime of piracy can take place on ships and in aircraft. Maritime law has described the question of extraterritoriality in such a way that the state which liberates the ship can claim jurisdiction.[9] Over time a large number of states have accepted the *universality principle* for piracy. That means that within certain limits (figuratively speaking) states consider that they have jurisdiction over

7. Council of Europe, Convention on the Prevention of Terrorism, Art. 14(2); UN Convention Against Transnational Organized Crime, Art. 15(2).
8. Dutch Supreme Court, Case 01631/024, July 8, 2003.
9. Art. 19 of the Convention on the High Seas 1958.

offenses committed by foreigners having regard to the nature of the offense and the circumstances under which it was committed. Legislations do not all claim universal jurisdiction to the same extent. In the case of piracy, hijackings and international drugs trade, war crimes, crimes against humanity and genocide, a claim for jurisdiction can reasonably be made on the basis of the universality principle.[10]

On the basis of the universality principle, all countries have the right (or perhaps even the *duty*) to penalize certain serious crimes, regardless of where the crime took place or the nationality of the perpetrator or the victim. In international law the *Lotus* case is the basis for the principle of universality. The Permanent Court of International Justice of the League of Nations[11] reasoned at the time that any country is entitled to adopt legislation that allows the country to prosecute crimes committed abroad. In his dissenting opinion in the *Lotus* case[12] Judge Moore suggested that piracy allows for universal jurisdiction. Nowadays it is accepted that a jurisdictional claim may be based on the principle of universality in cases of piracy, hijacking and international drug trafficking, war crimes, crimes against humanity and genocide.

Article 5 of the Statute of the International Criminal Court states that the jurisdiction of the Court shall be limited to the most serious crimes of concern to the international community as a whole. The Court has jurisdiction in accordance with this Statute with respect to the following crimes:

- the crime of genocide;
- crimes against humanity;
- war crimes;
- the crime of aggression.

This leaves us with the question of whether terrorism can be regarded as an act to which the principle of universality applies. Terrorists are not ordinary criminals; they act out of political and often also religious motives. They use terror to achieve their objectives. Their status may change from that of a terrorist to that of a recognized representative of a state.[13] International law has a different regime with regard to the legal position of revolutionaries. Terrorists form a separate category with which the world is still struggling, both literally and figuratively. But countless regional and international treaties have been concluded to establish jurisdiction over terrorists. Many national legislators have also established jurisdiction over terrorists in their national legislation.

Extraterritoriality is part of the international agreements which states have entered into for many years. Well-known examples are international crimes such as war crimes, crimes against humanity, including genocide,[14] piracy, aircraft hijacking

10. Brownlie 1990, pp. 304–305.
11. This was the predecessor of the International Court of Justice of the United Nations.
12. PCIJ, Series A, no. 10, 1927, p. 70. www.invispress.com/law/international/lotus.html.
13. Yasser Arafat, the leader of Al Fatah is a good example. He was regarded as one of the first terrorist leaders in the 1970s. Finally, he became one of the peace negotiators together with Israel and Egypt in the White House in Washington DC as official leader of the Palestinian People.
14. The list of crimes are to be found in Art. 5 of the Statute of the International Criminal Court.

and the international drugs trade, in which the universality principle is nowadays accepted. Here we encounter the second core principle referred to above: the *universality principle.*

On the basis of the universality principle, all states have the right (and perhaps also the duty) to penalize certain serious crimes, regardless of the location in which the crime took place or the nationality of the offender or the victim.[15] In terms of international law the question of extraterritoriality of jurisdiction arose in the *Lotus* case. It concerned a question relating to piracy. The Permanent Court of International Justice of the League of Nations ruled at the time that every state was entitled to adopt legislation allowing the state to prosecute offenses committed abroad. In his dissenting opinion in the *Lotus* case Judge Moore stated that piracy created the possibility of universal jurisdiction. This means that any state in which the pirate is located at a particular time may prosecute the piracy.

The principles relating to *derivative or subsidiary jurisdiction*, i.e. the protection of specific interests of the state, and the *subjective territoriality principle* will not be discussed in greater detail here, because they are of less significance in the context of the extraterritorial effect of foreign legislation on Dutch business – as articulated in the central question of this chapter.

16.5 THE LINK BETWEEN JURISDICTION AND THE STATE

The sovereign state sets the groundwork for the extraterritorial enforcement of jurisdiction. Legislators increasingly focus on the relationship between the 'fact', the 'offender' and the 'victim' of the offense or on the extraterritorial scope of the jurisdiction. A crime committed by a (corporate) citizen of country X in country Y may be considered so important to country X that it will want to claim extraterritorial jurisdiction. In 2004 the Dutch law 'Wet Terroristische Misdrijven' (Terrorist Crimes Act) came into force. This law is an amendment to the (Dutch) Criminal Code. Article 4 concerns the extraterritorial effect of Dutch jurisdiction, stating that Dutch criminal law is applicable to terrorist acts committed outside the Netherlands if the terrorist is a Dutch citizen or if he is currently staying in the Netherlands and, as a consequence, such persons can be prosecuted in a Dutch court.[16] Many may feel that the search for a link between the territory, the offender and the victim is too 'far-stretched'. Consider this example: the Prosecutor in Rotterdam wants to prosecute a Nigerian human rights and environmental activist for complicity in plotting a terrorist attack in the Niger Delta. Terrorism researcher Quirine Eijkman expresses her concern that there may be an ulterior political motive, because she can see no direct link with Dutch interests.[17] However, a clear link with the Netherlands exists, because five years earlier the man was granted asylum and still resides in the Netherlands. The territorial link is even more abstract when it concerns the use of modern means of communication. In the US the FCPA opens the possibility of claiming jurisdiction in cases where a crime is committed by

15. Van den Wyngaert 2009, p. 157.
16. Art. 4 paragraphs 13 and 14 of the Criminal Code.
17. NRC (Dutch Newspaper) 09-03-2011.

means of an email sent abroad as long as it can be proven that the email passed through a server within US territory.

However, extraterritoriality may also arise in a more abstract form if a country wishes to protect its interests abroad. The use of the US dollar most frequently requires passage through the US-based clearing system as banks make transfers between them. The use of US clearing through New York or elsewhere in the USA must not facilitate the financing of terrorism. As world trade mostly takes place in US dollars, the territorial jurisdictional claim of the US concerning any wrongdoing within global trading activities involving the US dollar is greatly expanded. Also, certain products and know-how may trigger the application of extraterritorial jurisdiction, as will be discussed later in chapter 18 on Export Controls and Sanctions.

At a very practical level, even in transactions that only involve non-US legal entities, companies with international staff might be subject to US law due to the mere fact that one of the employees negotiating the contract is a US passport or Green Card holder. Further down the line, employees with American citizenship or a Green Card may be compelled to inform the US authorities of their knowledge of possible infringements of US laws and regulations on issues such as anti-trust, anti-bribery and corruption, export controls or sanctions.

16.6 EXTRADITION RISK

Extradition is mostly based on bilateral or multilateral treaties. Where corruption is concerned the ACC plays a dominant role. Article 10 'Extradition', makes clear that any 'Bribery of a foreign public official shall be deemed to be included as an extraditable offence under the laws of the Parties and the extradition treaties between them' and that 'if a Party which makes extradition conditional on the existence of an extradition treaty receives a request for extradition from another Party with which it has no extradition treaty, it may consider this Convention to be the legal basis for extradition in respect of the offence of bribery of a foreign public official', adding that jurisdiction should be 'interpreted broadly so that an extensive physical connection to the bribery act is not required'. Such a broad risk of extradition for the violation of laws of which employees may not have been made aware must present a major surprise when applied.

Ultimately it is up to the state to decide to what extent it will cooperate on its own territory with the exercise of extraterritorial authority by another state. Most forms have been established through bilateral and multilateral treaties, usually concerning extradition. In the Netherlands, for example, we have the case against a Dutch CEO with regard to a request from the United States to extradite the director of a Dutch multinational for an offense under the FCPA. It is not intended in this article to examine the subject of extradition and the double criminality requirement in detail. However, due to the specific importance of the FCPA for business in the Netherlands, it is sensible to devote attention to this specific point.

On February 1, 2001 the Dutch Criminal Code was amended with regard to the provisions of the ACC. The 'small print' in the Convention turns out in practice to have major consequences for Dutch business. These concern particularly relationships with the United States and their consequences on the basis of the FCPA. The FCPA dates from 1977 and has a limitation period of 12 years. As a result of the ratification of the ACC[18] and the changes in the Dutch Criminal Code, *double criminality* has existed since February 1, 2001. The double criminality requirement is fulfilled in the extradition law between the Netherlands and the United States. In other words, the offense for which extradition is sought must be punishable in both states. This has applied since February 1, 2001. Extradition[19] is set out in Article 10 of the ACC.

Notably, this meant that up to 2013 Dutch businesses could still be prosecuted for corrupt acts committed with foreign public servants in the Netherlands or elsewhere and that the US could claim jurisdiction through a connection with the US. Surrender is possible, including with retrospective criminalization, because the prohibition of retroactive effect has expressly not been included in Dutch extradition law. This is understandable in itself, for example from the perspective of prosecuting war crimes in World War II. After all, the treaties that make war crimes punishable (the four Geneva Conventions) only came into being after the Second World War. Finally, if we look at the link between the corrupt act and the jurisdiction of the US, the OECD ACC states that 'the territorial basis for jurisdiction should be interpreted broadly so that an extensive physical connection to the bribery act is not required'.[20]

With regard to fines there is a long list, but recently, especially after the Yates Memorandum, attention is also given to the individual perpetrators.[21]

The following (incomplete) list gives an impression of the fines imposed in recent years as a result of a violation of the FCPA above USD 250 million:

- Siemens: USD 800 million (2008) (total of USD 1.6 billion in several related fines in this case);
- KBR/Halliburton: USD 579 million (2009);
- BAE: USD 400 million (2010);
- Snamprogetti/ENI: USD 338 million (2010);
- Technip SA: USD 338 million (2010);
- Daimler AG: USD 185 million (2010);
- Alcoa: USD 384 million (2014);
- Teva Pharmaceutical: USD 519 million (2016);
- Braskem S.A.: USD 957 million (2016);
- JPMorgan: USD 264 million (2016);
- VimpelCom: USD 795 million (2016).

Fines related to sanctions can exceed billions of US dollars.

In May 2013 the French energy giant Total SA, a huge multinational with significant legal resources, agreed to a USD 245 million settlement for breaches under US criminal law related to the payment of bribes to secure oil and gas contracts in Iran. Total's Chief Financial Officer seemed to stress the challenge to global companies of

18. Art. 9 (Mutual Legal Assistance) states: 'Where a Party makes mutual legal assistance conditional upon the existence of dual criminality, dual criminality shall be deemed to exist if the offence for which the assistance is sought is within the scope of this Convention.'
19. In principle, the Netherlands does not extradite its own nationals. The Dutch do not refer to the term 'extradition' but 'transfer' the suspect to be tried abroad.
20. Note 25 to the Convention. The notes are officially part of the Convention.
21. https://www.justice.gov/dag/file/769036/download.

monitoring such extra-jurisdictional risks when in the context of the fine he stated that the company had 'not committed any offence under applicable French law'.[22]

16.7 DRASTIC INCREASE IN EXTRATERRITORIAL RISK

Following the US example, the UK has significantly strengthened its territorial claim through the enforcement of the UKBA. The scope of the UKBA is wider than that of the FCPA. The UKBA prohibits not only the bribery of foreign public officials but *any* kind of bribery, including low-level 'facilitation payments' and intra-business bribery. To top it all off, the UKBA makes the absence of an effective anti-bribery compliance program a criminal offense. Breach of the law can lead to a prison sentence of up to ten years and an unlimited fine, and penalties can be imposed on both individuals and companies. It is not surprising that UK boards of directors are concerned – but to what extent are boards of non-UK firms aware of the risks they are running?

What is the effect of the UKBA on foreign companies? The UK courts clearly have jurisdiction over foreign companies if the crime took place within the territory of the UK, but they are also able to claim jurisdiction over foreign companies for crimes committed outside the UK in a number of situations. It is possible for a foreign company to be prosecuted for a failure to have adequate systems and controls in place to prevent bribery as long as the foreign company carries on a business, or part of a business, in any part of the UK. This can mean that having a subsidiary in the UK can trigger a UK prosecution for a non-UK company involved in corruption, even if the UK subsidiary was not involved in the act of bribery itself. In chapter 17 on Anti-Bribery and Corruption, the UKBA will be discussed in more detail.

16.8 DUAL-USE GOODS: THE SINK-HOLE IN THE COMPLIANCE STRUCTURE

In order to prevent the export of what might be termed strategic goods to countries at war, to unstable regions, to countries where human rights are violated, or to embargoed countries, the Member States of the EU and a number of other countries – the US among them – have signed a treaty, the so-called Wassenaar Arrangement, which places restrictions and license requirements on the trade in strategic goods, including clearly military and less obvious dual-use goods (for example chemicals used in the production of a detergent which can also be used for the production of chemical weapons – or metal tubes that can be used for civil engineering projects but also for gun turrets). The export control legislation of both the EU and Member States does not control the export of commercial (or civil) goods, however. Whether or not an item is an unrestricted commercial or civil product will depend on whether it is present on official Military or Dual Use Lists. The definition is further impacted by the nature of the purchasing party, such as military or government-owned customers, or so-called 'suspect' customers that might be considered dangerous

22. 'Total agrees penalty to settle US bribes charge over Iran deal' Financial Times May 29, 2013.

in countries that feature on various and differentiated United Nations, US, EU or related country embargo lists.

16.9 A TIME FOR COMPLIANCE TO LOOK OVER ITS SHOULDER

It would seem that a significant proportion of the international business community is blissfully unaware of the extraterritorial effect of American export control legislation. And not just US legislation, but also European and national export laws! There is no easy rule of thumb to guide companies on the risks they run in terms of the anti-corruption, anti-terror or export control legislation that carries extraterritorial risk; indeed the list of legislation that needs to be reviewed is ever-expanding. However, ignorance is no defense in the face of the law, and companies need to evaluate the extent to which their operations expose them to such risks. Screening for extraterritorial risk typically requires close collaboration between legal, compliance and front office departments to identify exposed business practices and export goods. Asking the question of whether your organization has potential concerns in this area is a price worth paying to avoid a surprising prosecution or extradition request from a third country in relation to a business activity commonly considered to be outside the scope of its jurisdictional reach. Compliance needs to be aware of the extraterritorial trap and an even more difficult task: compliance needs to sharply raise awareness among the executives of the organization while training its legal colleagues. In 2016 a company was fined due to the fact that the legal officer had never heard of extraterritorial jurisdiction and told compliance that it was sheer rubbish. Times are changing and compliance officers may well be held criminally responsible for non-compliance; the same fate awaits the executive officer. In January 2017 the executive officer in charge of Regulatory Compliance at Volkswagen in the US was arrested by the FBI.[23] This action is fully in accordance with the so-called Yates Memorandum, in which the Deputy Attorney General of the US, Sally Q. Yates, announced that alongside fines and other penalties, the responsible employees of companies should also be held criminally accountable for wrongdoings of the company. According to Mrs. Yates:

> 'the Department [of Justice of the US] fully leverages its resources to identify culpable individuals at all levels in corporate cases. To address these challenges, the Department convened a working group of senior attorneys from Department components and the United States Attorney community with significant experience in this area. The working group examined how the Department approaches corporate investigations, and identified areas in which it can amend its policies and practices in order to most effectively pursue the individuals responsible for corporate wrongs.'[24]

23. http://money.cnn.com/2017/01/09/news/companies/volkswagen-emissions-scandal-arrest.
24. Deputy Attorney Department of Justice, Yates Memorandum, https://www.justice.gov/dag/file/769036/download, p. 2.

BIBLIOGRAPHY

Bleker 2012
Dr. S.C. Bleker-van Eyk, 'Extraterritorialiteit: het meest onderschatte thema', in: C.A. Wielenga et al. (ed.), *Jaarboek Compliance* 2012, Capelle aan den IJssel: Nederlands Compliance Instituut 2012, pp. 51-67.

Bleker 2013
Dr. S.C. Bleker-van Eyk, 'The Extraterritorial Web', *Business Compliance*, 05/2013, pp. 53-61.

Brownlie 1990
I. Brownlie, *Principles of Public International Law*, New York: Oxford University Press 1990.

Klip & Massa 2010
A.H. Klip & A.S. Massa, *Communicerende grondslagen van extaterritoriale rechtsmacht*, Maastricht: Maastricht University 2010.

Sjöcrona & Orie 2002
J.M. Sjöcrona & A.M.M. Orie, *Internationaal strafrecht vanuit Nederlands perspectief*, Deventer: Kluwer 2002.

Van den Wyngaert 2009
C. van den Wyngaert, *Strafrecht & Strafprocesrecht in Hoofdlijnen*, Apeldoorn: Malku 2009.

Other references

Chazan 2013
G. Chazan, 'Total agrees penalty to settle US bribes charge over Iran deal', *Financial Times* May 29, 2013.

Smith & Perez 2017
A. Smith & E. Perez, 'Volkswagen executive arrested in emissions scandal', *CNN* 9 January 2017.

U.S. Department of Justice 2015
U.S. Department of Justice, Individual Accountability for Corporate Wrongdoing, September 9, 2015.

17. Anti-Bribery & Corruption

Prof. S.C. Bleker-van Eyk[1]

17.1 INTRODUCTION

At the heart of corruption lies what is natural to all men: reciprocity. Ever since the time of the cavemen, mankind has survived on 'returning a favor'. It lies at the core of survival within the tribe. It was the means of exchange before currency took over that task. The caveman who was good at hunting exchanged meat for bread. When a member of the tribe was unfit to hunt, he would still get the meat in order to get his strength back, which was a way of ensuring the survival of the tribe, for he would hunt when fit again and give meat to the ones who were then unfit to hunt but graciously gave him meat during his illness.

Reciprocity can easily slide towards corruption. The hunter promises extra meat to his fellow tribe member without exposing him to the danger of the hunt in return for allegiance when the time comes to select a leader. Because of the slippery slope into the gray zone, corruption has been persistent within all civilizations and throughout the centuries. The use of currency assists in setting a fair price for services rendered. However, currency is an asset that enables man to obtain all kind of goods and can enhance his welfare and hence his wellbeing and man is often inclined to pursue more welfare and as a result be more open to corruption. Evolution has shown that corruption cannot be erased from society. In fact, corruption is the cancer that constantly lurks within society and it is very difficult or almost impossible to eradicate it. Corruption is a threat to society. Corruption can kill, not only through the criminal act of killing, keeping dictators in power, but also through discarding safety measures when building, etc.

In our modern civilization, currency opens the possibility for better estimating the value of services and goods. Also, the media can easily reveal corruption. The cancer can only be treated through extraction. As a result, the effort is globally focused

1. The author would like to express her gratitude to Margriet De Smaele, who screened this publication against the latest laws and regulations. Margriet De Smaele taught me almost everything I know about US Export Controls.

on prohibiting corruption and only allowing 'facilitation payments' under stringent conditions. A worldwide quest to eradicate corruption is now well on its way, using enforcement with large penalties and incarceration as a deterrent.

17.2 BRIBERY, CORRUPTION AND DEFINITIONS

The first question to be dealt with when discussing corruption concerns the definitions of corruption and bribery. Bribery is 'the crime of giving money or other valuable things or rights to another as an inducement to him to act in a certain way, or to reward him for having so done. It is penalized by statute in various contexts, such as bribing judges, voters, members of local authorities or public officers'.[2] Corruption is 'the perversion of anything from its original pure state, used particularly of accepting money or other benefit in consideration of showing favor to or benefiting the donor'.[3] With regard to the efforts made by the OECD to combat corruption, the most effective definition is that given by Senturia: 'corruption is the *misuse* of *public* power for *private* profit.'[4] Corruption is on the 'receiving' side, whereas bribery is linked to the act of offering, giving or promising. However, much more is at stake. The actual acceptance is forbidden, but also the solicitation and the promise of a bribe. Also, the term 'bribe' is not as restricted as it may seem. Article 1(1) of the OECD Anti-Corruption Convention (ACC) defines corruption as follows: 'it is a criminal offence … for any person intentionally to offer, promise or give any undue pecuniary or other advantage, whether directly or through intermediaries, to a foreign public official, for that official or for a third party, in order that the official act or refrain from acting in relation to the performance of official duties, in order to obtain or retain business or other improper advantage in the conduct of international business.'[5] The ACC has been ratified by 41 states, six of which are not OECD Member States.[6]

Corruption has become a widespread disease affecting international business transactions. Bribery is one of the most common and troubling problems faced by international managers. They often deeply resent giving bribes and yet in some countries bribery appears to be a condition under which business transactions take place. It has become 'usual practice' in many countries and is a secondary source of illegal income for many a foreign public officer. Worse, in some less-developed countries, bribery or 'grease money' is the official's primary source of income. As President Clinton stated, corruption is 'inconsistent with democratic values, such as good governance and the rule of law. It is also contrary to the basic principles of fair competition and harmful to efforts to promote economic development'.[7]

2. Walker et al. 1980.
3. Walker et al. 1980.
4. Senturia 1993. *See also* Svensson, 2005, p. 20.
5. http://www.oecd.org/daf/anti-bribery/ConvCombatBribery_ENG.pdf.
6. Argentina, Australia, Austria, Belgium, Brazil, Bulgaria, Canada, Chile, Colombia, Czech Republic, Denmark, Estonia, Finland, France, Denmark, Germany, Greece, Hungary, Iceland, Ireland, Italy, Israel, Japan, Korea, Latvia, Luxembourg, Mexico, Netherlands, New Zealand, Norway, Poland, Portugal, Russian Federation, Slovak Republic, Slovenia, South Africa, Spain, Sweden, Switzerland, Turkey, United Kingdom, United States.
7. W.J. Clinton, Statement by the President, November 10, 1998.

Even where law exists, managers face dilemmas as they try to do business abroad. Competitive pressures, the perception that 'everybody's doing it' and the idea that a practice may not be wrong because it is firmly rooted in local cultural values complicate moral decision-making. Where the latter is concerned, it is necessary to stress that there are limits to the respect for localized values.[8] Also, we have to keep in mind that the local custom can be in contradiction with the local values. The fact that in some parts of Eastern Europe or Africa corruption has become a fact of life does not imply that corruption is an Eastern European or African cultural value.

17.3 THE ACC

The FCPA will be discussed in the following section. However, it is important to refer to the FCPA at the beginning of the current section, because it became the impetus of US striving towards a more global approach to combating bribery and corruption. In 1977 the US was by far the most important Member State within the OECD and it still is. The US used its influence within the OECD to encourage its trading partners to prohibit bribery in international business transactions and to enact legislation similar to the US FCPA. Within the framework of the OECD, the concept of combating bribery began to take root. The Committee on International Investment and Multinational Enterprises (CIME) began to discuss the issue of bribery in international business transactions. This discussion was not new to CIME, because in the 1976 OECD Guidelines on Multinational Enterprises, a reference to the corruption of foreign officials and political parties was already discussed. The OECD Guidelines on Multinational Enterprises state that organizations should not render any bribe to a public officer or give (unless legally permissible) any contribution to political candidates, and should abstain from improper involvement in local political activities. It is obvious that organizations should not bribe any public servant or holder of public office. The Lockheed affair is a well-known example of bribery of national authorities of host states by Lockheed, in order to convince the holders of important public offices to recommend Lockheed aircraft to the national governments.

The illegitimate sphere surrounding the subject of bribery is obvious. Less apparent, but just as conspicuous, are the contributions paid to local political parties. It is evident that if organizations contribute considerable funds to local political parties, the parties may well become dependent on the organization's contributions and the party may be willing to render special services to the organization in order to obtain more funds.

It should be noted that these discussions stemmed from the fear of political involvement of large multinational organizations in the national political affairs of foreign states, which increased at the end of the 1960s and peaked in the 1970s. From the 1980s and 1990s the discussion focused on the prevention of corruption and the time was right to take important measures within the Western world, especially within the OECD. In 1994, the OECD Council adopted a general Recommendation on this issue and as a result the Working Group on Bribery in International Business Transactions was established. The main purpose of this Working Group is to develop a program of systematic follow-up to the 1994 Recommendation. In 1997 the 1994

8. Green 1994, p. 292.

Recommendation was reviewed.[9] This Recommendation reflects the broad approach the OECD has taken on the issue of combating corruption in international business transactions. As a result, an important step in the joining of forces against corruption was taken through the adoption of the ACC. That was in 1997, exactly twenty years after the FCPA.

The ACC focuses on the corruption of foreign officials. Article 4(1) a) gives the definition: 'foreign public official' as 'any person holding a legislative, administrative or judicial office of a foreign country, whether appointed or elected; any person exercising a public function for a foreign country, including for a public agency or public enterprise; and any official or agent of a public international organization'. An official does not have to be elected or be officially appointed. The crux lies in a person who legitimately represents the (national, municipal or other) governmental organizations. For instance, an architect representing the municipal authorities while negotiating building requirements with developers, construction or infrastructure companies is to be regarded as a public official. This brings us to quite an interesting reflection: what if the architect pretends to hold the required powers, but in fact is cunningly placing himself in the midst of the building process? Can a contractor be held responsible in case of bribery even though the architect has no official status? Legally this becomes an interesting question, because courts tend to grant him public stature, due to the fact that the municipality has not taken sufficient action against the architect by failing to state his lack of official capacity. The contractor can be prosecuted, but in this case there is also a civil claim on the part of the contractor against the municipality. The previous example shows that before doing business, due diligence is necessary. Below, in chapter 18 on Export Controls and Sanctions, attention will be devoted to the importance of third-party due diligence, which is equally important with regard to anti-bribery and corruption!

With regard to the prosecution of corruption, Article 4(3) of the ACC states: 'When more than one Party has jurisdiction over an alleged offence described in this Convention, the Parties involved shall, at the request of one of them, consult with a view to determining the most appropriate jurisdiction for prosecution.' That is understandable because every state in the world has some kind of anti-corruption legislation and the crime of corruption will almost always be punishable in the state of the public official as well as the state of the organization or individual carrying out the act of bribery. Hence, the question of extradition may arise. Article 10(1) of the ACC states: 'The bribery of a foreign public official shall be deemed to be included as an extraditable offence under the laws of the Parties and the extradition treaties between them.' Article 10(2) follows by declaring that 'If a Party which makes extradition conditional on the existence of an extradition treaty receives a request for extradition from another Party with which it has no extradition treaty, it may consider this Convention to be the legal basis for extradition in respect of the offence of bribery of a foreign public official.'

9. The text of the 1997 Recommendation of the Council on Combating Bribery in International Business Transactions has been inserted in section 10a.

17.4 THE FCPA

In the aftermath of the Watergate affair, the military coup in Chile[10] at the request of ITT, the Lockheed bribery scandal involving payments by US companies to public officials including in the Netherlands and Japan, there were political repercussions within those countries and the reputation of American companies was sullied throughout the world. In response, in 1977 under President Jimmy Carter, Congress passed the Foreign Corruptive Practices Act. Through this Act, the United States declared its policy that American companies should act ethically when bidding for foreign contracts and should act in accordance with the US policy of encouraging the development of democratic institutions and honest, transparent business practices.

The importance of the issue of corrupting foreign public officials has increased considerably since governmental influence and hence the impact of public officials on economic transactions has grown. The risk of corrupting a foreign official has become an issue of daily relevance on the grounds of:

- the globalization of the world economy resulting in transnational business; and
- the commercialization of public services, changing the role of public officials from mere bureaucrats to entrepreneurs.

Since the passage of the FCPA, US businesses have operated at a disadvantage relative to foreign competitors who have continued to pay bribes without fear of penalty. In his statement of November 10, 1998 accompanying the signature of the International Anti-Bribery and Fair Competition Act (S. 2375), President Clinton stated that ever since the 1977 FCPA:

> 'US businesses have faced criminal penalties if they engaged in business-related bribery of foreign public officials. Foreign competitors, however, did not have similar restrictions and could engage in this corrupt activity without fear of penalty. Moreover, some of our major trading partners have subsidized such activities by permitting tax deductions for bribes paid to foreign public officials. As a result, US companies have had to compete on an uneven playing field, resulting in losses of international contracts estimated at USD 30 billion per year.'
>
> After the approval of the FCPA, amending chapter *2b* Securities Exchanges of Title 15 Commerce and Trade of the United States Code, the US began to lobby with a view to convincing its major trading competitors to pass similar national laws, leading to the ACC as mentioned in the previous paragraph.
>
> 15 US Code § 78dd-1 states as follows 'to make use of the mails or any means or instrumentality of interstate commerce corruptly in furtherance of an offer, payment, promise to pay, or authorization of the payment of any money, or offer, gift, promise to give, or authorization of the giving of anything of value to –

10. United States House of Representatives, United States and Chile During the Allende Years, 1970–1973, Hearings before the Subcommittee on Foreign Affairs of the House of Representatives, US Government Printing Office, Washington 1975, pp. 405 *et seq.*

(1) any foreign official for purposes of –

(A)

(i) influencing any act or decision of such foreign official in his official capacity,

(ii) inducing such foreign official to do or omit to do any act in violation of the lawful duty of such official, or

(iii) securing any improper advantage; or

(B) inducing such foreign official to use his influence with a foreign government or instrumentality thereof to affect or influence any act or decision of such government or instrumentality,

in order to assist such issuer in obtaining or retaining business for or with, or directing business to, any person;

(2) any foreign political party or official thereof or any candidate for foreign political office for purposes of –

(A)

(i) influencing any act or decision of such party, official, or candidate in its or his official capacity,

(ii) inducing such party, official, or candidate to do or omit to do an act in violation of the lawful duty of such party, official, or candidate, or

(iii) securing any improper advantage; or

(B) inducing such party, official, or candidate to use its or his influence with a foreign government or instrumentality thereof to affect or influence any act or decision of such government or instrumentality,

in order to assist such issuer in obtaining or retaining business for or with, or directing business to, any person; or

(3) any person, while knowing that all or a portion of such money or thing of value will be offered, given, or promised, directly or indirectly, to any foreign official, to any foreign political party or official thereof, or to any candidate for foreign political office, for purposes of –

(A)

(i) influencing any act or decision of such foreign official, political party, party official, or candidate in his or its official capacity,

(ii) inducing such foreign official, political party, party official, or candidate to do or omit to do any act in violation of the lawful duty of such foreign official, political party, party official, or candidate, or

(iii) securing any improper advantage; or

(B) inducing such foreign official, political party, party official, or candidate to use his or its influence with a foreign government or instrumentality thereof to affect or influence any act or decision of such government or instrumentality,

in order to assist such issuer in obtaining or retaining business for or with, or directing business to, any person.'

Finally, the FCPA provides an exception related to offers or payments to foreign officials (facilitation payments) provided in exchange for routine government action. The FCPA states that its anti-bribery prohibition 'shall not apply to any facilitating or expediting payment to a foreign official, political party, or party official the purpose of which is to expedite or secure the performance of a routine governmental action'. According to the FCPA a 'routine governmental action' is:

'an action which is ordinarily and commonly performed by a foreign official in – (i) obtaining permits, licenses, or other official documents to qualify a person to do business in a foreign country; (ii) processing governmental papers, such as visas and work orders; (iii) providing police protection, mail pick-up and delivery, or scheduling inspections associated with contract performance or inspections related to transit of goods across country; (iv) providing phone service, power and water supply, loading and unloading cargo, or protecting perishable products or commodities from deterioration; or (v) actions of a similar nature'.

17.5 FCPA PROSECUTION AND COMPLIANCE

The FCPA enforcement lies with both the Department of Justice (DOJ) and the Securities and Exchange Commission (SEC): the SEC has authority for civil enforcement of the FCPA over issuers and their officers, directors, employees, agents, and stockholders acting on the issuer's behalf. The SEC has a specialized FCPA unit with attorneys in Washington, D.C., and in regional offices.

In order for an action to constitute a violation of the FCPA, a payment must be made 'corruptly'. The perpetrator must have the intent to wrongfully influence the recipient. As a result, a violation may be possible even if no bribe was actually paid. Even if the identity of the recipient is unknown, or even if the company does not ultimately receive a benefit as a result of the payment, a violation takes place through the simple intent to commit an act of bribery. Also, the act must have been done 'willfully', which means that the person must act with a 'bad purpose' or knowledge that the conduct is unlawful, although this requirement is not so rigid that the person should know exactly which act he has violated. Note, however, that proof of willfulness is relevant only to violations by individuals; willfulness is not required to establish corporate criminal or civil liability!

According to Chapter Eight of the US Federal Sentencing Guidelines (USFSG),[11] 'the fine range for any other organization should be based on the seriousness of the offense and the culpability of the organization. The seriousness of the offense generally will be reflected by the greatest of the pecuniary gain, the pecuniary loss, or the amount in a guideline offense level fine table. Culpability generally will be determined by six factors that the sentencing court must consider. The four factors that increase the ultimate punishment of an organization are:

(i) the involvement in or tolerance of criminal activity;
(ii) the prior history of the organization;
(iii) the violation of an order; and
(iv) the obstruction of justice.

The two factors that mitigate the ultimate punishment of an organization are:

(i) the existence of an effective compliance and ethics program; and

11. United States Sentencing Commission, 2014 Federal Sentencing Guidelines Manual, the 2014 Guidelines Manual (effective November 1, 2014), Chapter Eight, Introductory Commentary, Principle III.

(ii) self-reporting, cooperation, or acceptance of responsibility.'

A Voluntary Self-Disclosure (VSD) can mitigate the harshness of possible penalties. In general, it is said that a VSD will reduce the penalty by 50%. However, it should be noted that this cannot be proved in practice. In most cases the negotiations end with the penalty reflecting the seriousness of the infraction and it is influenced by the maturity of the organization's compliance, the cooperation throughout the negotiations, the disciplinary actions taken against the violators within the organizations, criminal prosecution of individuals and, last but not least, the financial resources of the organization. This subject will also be touched on in the next chapter on export controls and sanctions.

As already discussed above in the introductory chapter on extraterritorial jurisdiction, since the Yates -Memorandum[12] it has become obvious that the penalties applied when sentencing are strongly influenced by the sanctions applied to the individual violators as well as the strong wish not only to inflict financial penalties, but also to prosecute individuals on all levels, including the executive level.

It is of importance that an organization also focuses on preventing measures. However, it should be kept in mind that where preventive measures combating bribery within an organization are concerned, the system can never be watertight. It is impossible to fully prevent such a crime. For instance, if an employee is very eager to obtain a promotion, he may be tempted to promise, offer or give a bribe with a view to obtaining a commission and hence impressing his superiors. A system must be developed to achieve the highest possible level of protection against corruptible practices. Through such a system, instances of bribery can be prevented or the system can be used in court as proof that the enterprise exercised due diligence in seeking to prevent and detect criminal conduct by its employees and other agents.

In Chapter Eight, §8B2.1 of the USFSG deals with the requirements of an effective compliance and ethics program, also described in the 2012 *Resource Guide* to the US Foreign Corrupt Practices Act.[13] According to the *Resource Guide* 'DOJ and SEC will give meaningful credit to a company that implements in good faith a comprehensive, risk-based compliance program, even if that program does not prevent an infraction in a low risk area because greater attention and resources had been devoted to a higher risk area.'

Due to the importance of Article §8B2.1 of the USFSG on an 'effective compliance and ethics program' was also inserted in full *supra* in chapter 3.

In conclusion, the USFSG is looking for an effective program to prevent and detect violations of law. In the event of a violation, the organization should be able to redress it swiftly and effectively. This program must be reasonably designed, implemented, and enforced so that it generally will be effective in preventing and detecting criminal conduct. Effectiveness should be seen in connection with the principle of due diligence.

A good compliance system can prevent instances of bribery. However, if bribery does occur, it can be detected by and mitigated through compliance structures. In

12. https://www.justice.gov/dag/file/769036/download.
13. Criminal Division of the U.S. Department of Justice and the Enforcement Division of the U.S. Securities and Exchange Commission, A Resource Guide to the U.S. Foreign Corrupt Practices Act, 2012.

the worst-case scenario, the act of bribery may be prosecuted. In the latter case, the existence of an effective compliance system can serve as mitigating circumstances to the defense leading to a reduction of sentence. With regard to affirmative defenses, the FCPA only offers two distinct defenses:

- if the organizations can provide proof that the act is a lawful payment under local written laws; or
- if the organization can prove that the money spent was reasonable, *bona fide*, and directly related to the performance of a contract, or marketing, promotion, or product demonstration.

Finally, in the 'Principles of Federal Prosecution of Business Organizations'[14] the *US Attorney's Manual* reflects upon the

> 'Duties of Federal Prosecutors and Duties of Corporate Leaders. Corporate directors and officers owe a fiduciary duty to a corporation's shareholders (the corporation's true owners) and they owe duties of honest dealing to the investing public and consumers in connection with the corporation's regulatory filings and public statements. A prosecutor's duty to enforce the law requires the investigation and prosecution of criminal wrongdoing if it is discovered. In carrying out this mission with the diligence and resolve necessary to vindicate the important public interests discussed above, prosecutors should be mindful of the common cause we share with responsible corporate leaders who seek to promote trust and confidence. Indicting corporations for wrongdoing enables the government to be a force for positive change of corporate culture, and a force to prevent, discover, and punish serious crimes.'

New in November 2015 is Chapter 9-28.010 stating that 'the prosecution of corporate crime is a high priority for the Department of Justice. By investigating allegations of wrongdoing and bringing charges where appropriate for criminal misconduct, the Department promotes critical public interests. These interests include, among other things: (1) protecting the integrity of our economic and capital markets by enforcing the rule of law; (2) protecting consumers, investors, and business entities against competitors who gain unfair advantage by violating the law; (3) preventing violations of environmental laws; and (4) discouraging business practices that would permit or promote unlawful conduct at the expense of the public interest.' According to the *US Attorney's Manual*

> 'one of the most effective ways to combat corporate misconduct is by holding accountable all individuals who engage in wrongdoing. Such accountability deters future illegal activity, incentivizes changes in corporate behavior, ensures that the proper parties are held responsible for their actions, and promotes the public's confidence in our justice system. Prosecutors should focus on wrongdoing by individuals from the very beginning of any investigation of corporate misconduct. By focusing on building cases against individual wrongdoers, we accomplish multiple goals. First, we increase our ability to identify the full extent

14. United States Department of Justice, Offices of the United States Attorneys, *US Attorney's Manual*, Title 9, Chapter 9-28.000 'Principles of Federal Prosecution of Business Organizations', revised November 2015.

> of corporate misconduct. Because a corporation only acts through individuals, investigating the conduct of individuals is the most efficient and effective way to determine the facts and the extent of any corporate misconduct. Secondly, a focus on individuals increases the likelihood that those with knowledge of the corporate misconduct will be identified and provide information about the individuals involved, at any level of an organization. Thirdly, we maximize the likelihood that the final resolution will include charges against culpable individuals and not just the corporation.'

In Chapter 9-28.210 the focus is once again on the individual wrongdoers. It states that the

> 'prosecution of a corporation is not a substitute for the prosecution of criminally culpable individuals within or without the corporation. Because a corporation can act only through individuals, imposition of individual criminal liability may provide the strongest deterrent against future corporate wrongdoing. Provable individual culpability should be pursued, particularly if it relates to high-level corporate officers, even in the face of an offer of a corporate guilty plea or some other disposition of the charges against the corporation, including a deferred prosecution or non-prosecution agreement, or a civil resolution. In other words, regardless of the ultimate corporate disposition, a separate evaluation must be made with respect to potentially liable individuals. Prosecutors should not allow delays in the corporate investigation to undermine the Department's ability to pursue potentially culpable individuals.'

The latter will happen when a foreign company is negotiating a plea bargain with the DOJ, while in the meantime trying to dismiss personnel that committed the violations and hence losing their ability to force employees to cooperate with the company during the investigation.

The addition and revision of the US Attorney's Manual in 2015 are the precursors of the 2016 Yates Memorandum emphasizing the importance of prosecuting individuals.

17.6 THE UKBA

The UKBA is a pivotal point in the effort to combat bribery and corruption. Not only because the United Kingdom has decided to follow the example of the US in claiming extraterritorial jurisdiction, but because it goes far beyond the corruption of foreign officials. The UKBA forbids any kind of corruption, be it the corruption of officials (foreign or national) or intra-business bribery. The scope of the UKBA is much wider than that of the FCPA and in addition to the bribery of a public official it also contains the following offenses:

- Section 1: offering, giving or promising to give a 'financial or other advantage' to another individual in exchange for 'improperly' performing a 'relevant function or activity' (active);
- Section 2: being bribed: requesting, accepting or agreeing to accept such an advantage, in exchange for improperly performing such a function or activity (passive);

- Section 6: promising, offering or giving a financial or other advantage to a foreign public official, either directly or through a third party, where such an advantage is not legitimately due;
- Section 7: the broad and innovatory offense of the failure of commercial organizations to prevent bribery on their behalf;
- Section 14: criminalizing those senior officers of the organization with whose 'consent or connivance' the bribery was committed (although where the bribery takes place overseas, they must have a 'close connection with the UK').

Also, so-called 'facilitation payments' are fully banned. The FCPA leaves room for small facilitation payments. By contrast, the UKBA allows no such payments, however small they may be.

Section 7 is quite remarkable, because unlike the US legislation it does not offer a reduction of penalties in the case of an effective compliance and ethics program; the mere absence of an effective compliance program is a criminal offense.

The penalties are harsh and bribery can lead to a sentence of up to ten years and an unlimited fine, both for the individual and the company.

The UK court claims jurisdiction when bribery has taken place within the territory of the United Kingdom, but also if the offense was committed outside the UK. The offense can be prosecuted within the UK in the case of a foreign company having:

- a subsidiary or a representative in the UK;
- a British citizen as an employee who is involved in an act of bribery or a British citizen in a management position who knows or should have known about the fact;
- a listing on the London Stock Exchange;
- an organization with agents/representatives in the UK;
- (important) activities in the field of sales & marketing in the UK.

The effect of the UKBA on foreign organizations is not yet fully clear. The Serious Fraud Office (SFO) has only recently started prosecutions and the British courts still have to start creating case-law further explaining the international realm of the UKBA. The requirements for a good defense under the UKBA still have to be set in practice. The minimum requirements for an effective compliance program under the UKBA will at least encompass elements such as:[15]

- risk assessment;
- top level commitment;
- due diligence;
- clear, practical & accessible policies & procedures;
- effective implementation;
- monitoring and review.

15. Jonathan Cotton, partner at Slaughter & May, during a corruption seminar at De Brauw Blackstone Westbroek, Amsterdam, January 25, 2011.

In the 'Guidance about procedures which relevant commercial organisations can put into place to prevent persons associated with them from bribing', the SFO states six Principles regarding procedures that organizations should have in place:[16]

> '1. A commercial organisation's procedures to prevent bribery by persons associated with it are proportionate to the bribery risks it faces and to the nature, scale and complexity of the commercial organisation's activities. They are also clear, practical, accessible, effectively implemented and enforced.
>
> 2. The top-level management of a commercial organisation (be it a board of directors, the owners or any other equivalent body or person) are committed to preventing bribery by persons associated with it. They foster a culture within the organisation in which bribery is never acceptable.
>
> 3. The commercial organisation assesses the nature and extent of its exposure to potential external and internal risks of bribery on its behalf by persons associated with it. The assessment is periodic, informed and documented.
>
> 4. The commercial organisation applies due diligence procedures, taking a proportionate and risk based approach, in respect of persons who perform or will perform services for or on behalf of the organisation, in order to mitigate identified bribery risks.
>
> 5. The commercial organisation seeks to ensure that its bribery prevention policies and procedures are embedded and understood throughout the organisation through internal and external communication, including training that is proportionate to the risks it faces.
>
> 6. The commercial organisation monitors and reviews procedures designed to prevent bribery by persons associated with it and makes improvements where necessary.'

Regarding Principle 1, the SFO gives an indication of possible procedures that organizations should have in place in order to prevent bribery:

'- The involvement of the organisation's top-level management (see Principle 2).
- Risk assessment procedures (see Principle 3).
- Due diligence of existing or prospective associated persons (see Principle 4).
- The provision of gifts, hospitality and promotional expenditure; charitable and political donations; or demands for facilitation payments.
- Direct and indirect employment, including recruitment, terms and conditions, disciplinary action and remuneration.
- Governance of business relationships with all other associated persons including pre and post contractual agreements.
- Financial and commercial controls such as adequate bookkeeping, auditing and approval of expenditure.
- Transparency of transactions and disclosure of information.

16. Ministry of Justice, The Bribery Act 2010, Guidance about procedures which relevant commercial organizations can put into place to prevent persons associated with them from bribing, March 2011.

- Decision-making, such as delegation of authority procedures, separation of functions and the avoidance of conflicts of interest.
- Enforcement, detailing discipline processes and sanctions for breaches of the organisation's anti-bribery rules.
- The reporting of bribery including "speak up" or "whistle blowing" procedures.
- The detail of the process by which the organisation plans to implement its bribery prevention procedures, for example, how its policy will be applied to individual projects and to different parts of the organisation.
- The communication of the organisation's policies and procedures, and training in their application (see Principle 5).
- The monitoring, review and evaluation of bribery prevention procedures (see Principle 6).'

Is it an offence?	**FCPA**	**UK Bribery Act**
Bribery of FPOs	Yes	Yes
Domestic bribery	No	Yes
Private sector bribery	No	Yes
Facilitation payments	No	Yes
Strict liability	No	Yes
Failure to keep accurate records	Yes	No
Liability for acts of third parties	Yes	Yes

Figure 1: showing the offenses under the FCPA and the UKBA

17.7 CONCLUSION

In conclusion we can safely state that the UKBA has taken combating bribery and corruption to a new level. Only time will tell what the impact of the UK's extraterritorial jurisdiction will be. Time has already taught us that the extraterritorial claim made by the US has been very successful and the financial penalties for foreign companies have been enormous. Many companies have paid hundreds of millions of US dollars in fines.

BIBLIOGRAPHY

Green 1994
R.M. Green, *The Ethical Manager: A New Method for Business Ethics*, London: Maxwell Macmillan International 1994.

Senturia 1993
J.J. Senturia, *Encyclopedia of Social Sciences*, Volume VI, 1993.

Svensson 2005
J. Svensson, 'Eight Questions about Corruption', *Journal of Economic Perspectives* 2005, 19, 2005, no. 3.

Walker 1980
D.M. Walker et al., *The Oxford Companion to Law*, Oxford: Clarendon Press 1980.

18. Export Controls & Sanctions

Prof. S.C. Bleker-van Eyk[1]

18.1 EXTRATERRITORIALITY OF AMERICAN EXPORT CONTROLS AND SANCTIONS

To prevent the export of strategic goods to countries at war, to unstable regions, to countries where human rights are violated, or to embargoed countries, the Member States of the European Union and a number of other countries – among others the US – have signed a treaty, the so-called Wassenaar Arrangement,[2] to place restrictions and license requirements on the trade in strategic goods (military goods and dual-use goods). The export control legislation of both the EU and Member States does not control the export of 'commercial' (or civil) goods. Commercial goods are goods that are not mentioned on the Military List or Dual Use List. However, if commercial goods are exported to military customers, government-owned customers or so-called 'suspect' customers in countries subject to United Nations sanctions, restrictions may be imposed by the EU or unilaterally by a country. The US has its own system of export controls and sanctions. Although some of these may be similar to those of the EU where commercial goods are concerned, some export control measures do exist. BIS describes its goals as follows:

> 'The mission of the Office of Export Enforcement (OEE) at BIS is to enforce the provisions of the Export Administration Regulations (EAR), secure America's trade, and preserve America's technological advantage by detecting, investigating, preventing, and deterring the unauthorized export and re-export of US-origin items to parties involved with: (1) weapons of mass destruction programs; (2) threats to national security or regional stability; (3) terrorism; or (4) human

---

1. Part of this chapter was published previously, *see* Bleker-van Eyk 2013. The author would like to express her gratitude to Margriet De Smaele, who screened this publication against the latest laws and regulations. Margriet De Smaele taught me almost everything I know about US Export Controls.
2. Accessible by: http://www.wassenaar.org

> rights abuses. Export Enforcement at BIS is the only federal law enforcement agency exclusively dedicated to the enforcement of export control laws and the only agency constituted to do so with both administrative and criminal export enforcement authorities.'[3]

By far the largest portion of the European business world is *unconsciously incompetent* with regard to the extraterritorial effect of the US export control and sanctions legislation. And not just US legislation, but also European and national export laws. To be quite honest, US-based companies are often also unaware of – at least – their national export controls legislation. Where parties subject to sanctions are concerned, the 'War on Terrorism' seems to have created some level of awareness.

The US tends to reinforce the extraterritorial jurisdiction of its export legislation as soon as there is a US nexus. Extraterritorial jurisdiction based on the illegal (illegality from the perspective of US law) use of the US dollar has already led to large fines for financial institutions. And not just fines; often the cure is more painful than the disease. Companies often pay hundreds of millions in fines and spend several hundred millions more on compliance programs, lawyers and forensic researchers. However, it is worth spending such amounts, because if companies do not invest in internal investigations and compliance, the fines would far exceed the amount invested in improvements, and recidivism may even lead to incalculable fines, debarment, blacklisting or revocation of the license to operate in the US. Compliance pays off not only through a reduction of the fine, but also in enhanced compliance alertness to prevent future mistakes.

In this chapter it is only possible to highlight a small part of the export controls and sanctions issue. The legislation is bulky and highly complicated. The goal of this chapter is merely to create awareness with regard to the dangers of US export controls and their extraterritorial ramifications. Further in-depth reading of literature and legislation is described on the governmental website.[4]

The US has a comprehensive system of sanctions, as well as export and import control measures. Reference was made above to the use of US dollars. The US also upholds sanctions to certain countries such as Iran and Cuba.[5] It is all about the American nexus.

Export controls are aimed at the export of raw materials, semi-finished and finished products, as well as information and technology. Exports from the US to other countries may be restricted and licenses may be required, not only for high-risk countries, but all kinds of restrictions exist on products and data for numerous countries. A number of products or technologies require a US export license. The use of the product, technology or data must be identified as well as the destination, both the transitional and the final destination. The request for an export license from

3. Export Administration Regulation(s).
4. Accessible by: https://www.treasury.gov/resource-center.
5. The US is the only country with sanctions in place against Cuba. By contrast, for instance, when a Dutch company deals with Muslim countries and the company is asked whether or not it also deals with Israel, this is forbidden by US law on grounds of discrimination against Israel. If the company is also active on US territory, it should notify the US State Department. There must of course be an American nexus. That is understandable, but still a clear case of double standards.

the competent authorities must always be submitted in advance. The exporting of controlled goods without a license may lead to prosecution. Exports to an intermediary country where the controlled goods, technology or data will be processed must have a permit for re-export when exported to another country. Note, however, that there may be a *de minimis* rule for processing certain US technology or materials such as 10% or 25%, depending on the classification of goods and technology.

18.2 EXPORT

Finally, what is the definition of export?

- The *export* of goods, services, information, software or technical data from the US to another country. Note that a telephone call from New York to Amsterdam is therefore a form of export of information! The question is whether the export of information is permitted or if it is controlled information that needs a license.
- A *re-export* occurs when the software of goods, services, information, software or technical data exported from the US to country X is then exported from country X to country Y. For example, a Frenchman in Paris receives a call from the US to explain how a system works (export) and the Frenchman calls a colleague in Germany to explain the system to him (re-export).
- The so-called *deemed export* is equally a hazardous activity. Deemed export concerns the exchange of information or technical data within the boundaries of a country, between a national of that country and a national of another country. For example, an American and a Frenchman exchange controlled information during a meeting in San Francisco. A license must be obtained before exchanging the information.
- A *transfer* takes place when goods, services, information, software or technical data are sent from the US to another country, for example to Berlin in Germany, and then sent from Berlin to a subcontractor in Munich. The transfer occurs in the same country but may require an export license.

Export controls are complicated. It is imperative to analyze the classification of the goods, services, information, software, or technical data to decide whether a license is required.[6] Additional complications may arise, for instance, with regard to the license requirements in the case of dual nationality employees. For example, an Iranian refugee having acquired the right to asylum may be excluded from working with goods or technology containing US-controlled military technology. Employees with, for instance, Chinese nationality may encounter the same problems. Often, companies do not realize that they have to build internal Chinese walls to ensure

6. First, it should be determined if there is a US nexus. If so, what percentage of American content does the product/information or data contain? For instance strategic goods or nuclear goods may be under a very strict regime. Sometimes no permit is necessary below 10%. Sometimes 25%. Some products may not be exported unless a permit is granted. Export controls are a maze of requirements. And then there is the question of how the exact percentage of US content can be established.

that only authorized employees are in contact with controlled goods, otherwise prosecution by US authorities may follow.

Another problem concerns imports of goods to the US. Here is a simple example to demonstrate the complexity of US export and import regulations. A company in Europe has a warehouse facility that imports and exports items. The US does not allow imports from certain countries. If a product originates in Iran or has been on Iranian territory through transfer or temporary possession by Iranian (corporate) citizens, it cannot be imported into the US. Therefore, the company must keep an accurate, updated curriculum vitae of each item to ensure that no prohibited goods enter US territory.

The above is only a brief glimpse of the complicated world of export controls. The question is how companies can protect themselves against involuntary infringements of such complex regulations.

18.3 DIRECTORATE OF DEFENSE TRADE CONTROLS (DDTC)

DDTC is the supervisory authority with regard to the export of ammunition, military technology and equipment. The legislation has been laid down in the International Traffic in Arms Regulations (ITAR)[7] with the corresponding United States Munitions List (USML).[8] DDTC handles the administration and license requirements of military items.

According to ITAR § 127.1 the following violations are described:

> '(a) Without first obtaining the required license or other written approval from the Directorate of Defense Trade Controls, it is unlawful:
> (1) To export or attempt to export from the United States any defense article or technical data or to furnish or attempt to furnish any defense service for which a license or written approval is required by this subchapter;
> (2) To re-export or retransfer or attempt to re-export or retransfer any defense article, technical data, or defense service from one foreign end-user, end-use, or destination to another foreign end-user, end-use, or destination for which a license or written approval is required by this subchapter, including, as specified in § 126.16(h) and § 126.17(h) of this subchapter, any defense article, technical data, or defense service that was exported from the United States without a license pursuant to any exemption under this subchapter;
> (3) To import or attempt to import any defense article whenever a license is required by this subchapter; or
> (4) To conspire to export, import, re-export, retransfer, furnish or cause to be exported, imported, re-exported, retransferred or furnished, any defense article, technical data, or defense service for which a license or written approval is required by this subchapter.
>
> (b) It is unlawful:
> (1) To violate any of the terms or conditions of a license or approval granted pursuant to this subchapter, any exemption contained in this subchapter, or any rule or regulation contained in this subchapter;

7. Accessible by: https://www.pmddtc.state.gov/regulations_laws/itar.html.
8. Accessible by http://www.fas.org/spp/starwars/offdocs/itar/p121.htm.

(2) To engage in the business of brokering activities for which registration and a license or written approval is required by this subchapter without first registering or obtaining the required license or written approval from the Directorate of Defense Trade Controls. For the purposes of this subchapter, engaging in the business of brokering activities requires only one occasion of engaging in an activity as reflected in § 129.2(b) of this subchapter.

(3) To engage in the United States in the business of either manufacturing or exporting defense articles or furnishing defense services without complying with the registration requirements. For the purposes of this subchapter, engaging in the business of manufacturing or exporting defense articles or furnishing defense services requires only one occasion of manufacturing or exporting a defense article or furnishing a defense service.

(c) Any person who is granted a license or other approval or who acts pursuant to an exemption under this subchapter is responsible for the acts of employees, agents, and all authorized persons to whom possession of the defense article or technical data has been entrusted regarding the operation, use, possession, transportation, and handling of such defense article or technical data abroad. All persons abroad subject to US jurisdiction who obtain temporary or permanent custody of a defense article exported from the United States or produced under an agreement described in part 124 of this subchapter, and irrespective of the number of intermediate transfers, are bound by the regulations of this subchapter in the same manner and to the same extent as the original owner or transferor.

(d) A person with knowledge that another person is then ineligible pursuant to §§ 120.1(c) or 126.7 of this subchapter may not, directly or indirectly, in any manner or capacity, without prior disclosure of the facts to, and written authorization from, the Directorate of Defense Trade Controls:

(1) Apply for, obtain, or use any export control document as defined in § 127.2(b) of this subchapter for such ineligible person; or

(2) Order, buy, receive, use, sell, deliver, store, dispose of, forward, transport, finance, or otherwise service or participate in any transaction which may involve any defense article or the furnishing of any defense service for which a license or approval is required by this subchapter or an exemption is available under this subchapter for export, where such ineligible person may obtain any benefit therefrom or have any direct or indirect interest therein.

(e) No person may knowingly or willfully cause, or aid, abet, counsel, demand, induce, procure, or permit the commission of, any act prohibited by, or the omission of any act required by, 22 U.S.C. 2778 and 2779, or any regulation, license, approval, or order issued thereunder.'[9]

Since July 1, 2016 the Department of State applies the following penalties in case of an ITAR infraction:[10]

1. For each violation of 22 U.S.C. 2778, an amount not to exceed USD 1,094,010;

9. 39316, Federal Register 1993, Vol. 58, No. 139 and Code of Federal Regulations, Title 22, Part 127, 26-04-01, https://www.gpo.gov/fdsys/pkg/CFR-2016-title22-vol1/xml/CFR-2016-title22-vol1-part127.xml.
10. Civil Penalty Inflation Adjustments, OMB Memorandum M-16-06, dated February 24, 2016.

2. For each violation of 22 U.S.C. 2779a, an amount not to exceed USD 795,445; and
3. For each violation of 22 U.S.C. 2780, an amount not to exceed USD 946,805.

18.4 MILITARY, DUAL-USE ITEMS, EXPORT RESTRICTIONS AND SANCTIONS

For a clear understanding it is important to understand that international export regulations are divided into export controls and sanctions. While export controls are based on the nature of the products, technologies and services to be exported, sanctions are based on the individuals, companies or countries to whom the products, technologies and services are to be provided.

The fact that a company does not produce 'military' items is no reason to assume that it will not face US export controls. Many companies manufacture parts which could also be processed in military goods, such as a simple screw. If this screw can resist 3G forces, it will be a dual-use item. Often products such as paints, glues and such certain substances are of such a quality that they also fit the requirements for military use and as a result those products will become controlled and hence fall within the export controls regime.

If a company produces military goods, it may be a little simpler. All military goods and all the technology necessary for the development, production, or use of goods referred to in the common military list of the European Union or the USML are subject to licensing if they are exported from one country to another.

Potentially, the danger lies in the OFAC sanctions particularly the export of goods to US-blacklisted countries, organizations, companies or individuals. Here is a simple example: a ship transporting grain from Brazil to the United Arab Emirates may pose considerable difficulties. If 20% of the bulk grain originates from the US and the only known destination is a port in the UAE, it must be clear that the final destination must not be Iran. The Iranian Republican Guard is blacklisted and in Iran the higher members of the Republican Guard are offered lucrative side jobs, such as harbormaster. This delivery is a flagrant violation of US export control legislation and will have serious consequences.

18.5 OFFICE OF FOREIGN ASSETS CONTROL (OFAC)

According to OFAC's Economic Sanctions Enforcement Guidelines effective from November 9, 2009:

> 'the primary mission of OFAC is to administer and enforce economic sanctions against targeted foreign countries and regimes, terrorists and terrorist organizations, weapons of mass destruction proliferators, narcotic traffickers, and others, in furtherance of U.S. national security, foreign policy, and economic objectives. OFAC acts under Presidential national emergency powers, as well as specific legislation, to prohibit transactions and block (or "freeze") assets subject to U.S. jurisdiction. Economic sanctions are designed to deprive the target of the use of its assets and to deny it access to the U.S. financial system and the benefits of trade, transactions, and services involving U.S. markets,

businesses, and individuals. These same authorities have also been used to protect certain assets subject to U.S. jurisdiction and to further important U.S. non-proliferation goals.'[11]

OFAC is no stranger within financial institutions. All financial institutions are aware of the OFAC sanctions program and the so-called 'Specially Designated Nationals'[12] and the countries that are on the US financial sanctions list. OFAC is a regulator within the Department of Finance of the US and oversees the implementation of economic and trade sanctions against certain countries and regimes, terrorists, international drug traffickers and individuals or organizations who possess or sell weapons of mass destruction. The sanctions arise from foreign policy and national security goals.[13]

OFAC is a supervisor that comes under the US Treasury Department and supervises the implementation of economic and trade sanctions resulting from foreign policy and national security objectives against certain states and regimes, terrorists, international drug dealers and persons or organizations possessing or selling weapons of mass destruction.[14] A good example is the dollar. The dollar belongs to the United States, as do the clearing banks. The US therefore claims jurisdiction over those who finance prohibited transactions in dollars, as well as jurisdiction over the transactions themselves. For example, OFAC can demand to inspect transactions and freeze funds which fall under the jurisdiction of the United States. OFAC sanctions may require the prohibition of financial transactions and the freezing of assets that fall under the jurisdiction of the US. Transactions or assets in US dollars will lead to the US claiming jurisdiction over those who enable the prohibited financial transactions, as well as jurisdiction over the transactions themselves.

Examples of OFAC sanctions in recent years:

- ABN AMRO: USD 80 million (2005);
- Chiquita: USD 25 million (2007);
- Lloyds Bank USD 350 million (2009);
- DHL: USD 9,4 million (2009);
- Barclays: USD 298 million (2010);
- Credit Suisse AG: USD 536 million (2010);
- Balli Aviation: USD 17 million (2010);
- BNP Paribas: USD 963,619,900 (2014);
- Crédit Agricole: USD 329,593,585 (2015);
- Commerzbank: USD 574,801,770 (2015).

The list shows that not only are financial institutions targeted by OFAC, but other industries are also arousing the attention of OFAC.

11. 57593, Federal Register, Vol. 74, No. 215.
12. Specially Designated National and Blocked Persons List (SND), Accessible by: http://www.treasury.gov/resource-center/sanctions/SDN-List/Pages/default.aspx
13. Terrorism and Financial Intelligence, Office of Foreign Assets Control (OFAC) accessible by: http://www.treasury.gov/about/organizational-structure/offices/Pages/Office-of-Foreign-Assets-Control.aspx
14. Terrorism and Financial Intelligence, Office of Foreign Assets Control accessible by: http://www.treasury.gov/about/organizational-structure/offices/Pages/Office-of-Foreign-Assets-Control.aspx

18.6 BUREAU OF INDUSTRY AND SECURITY (BIS)

The BIS controls commercial semi-finished products, products and technologies that could have a military application (dual-use). The regulations which apply to these dual-use items are the EAR.[15] Part of the EAR is a list of items that are controlled, the Export Control Legislation of the United States of America Commerce Control List, or CCL.[16] The US CCL is the equivalent of the European Dual Use List[17] and contains basically the same items, and the same Export Control Classification Numbers (ECCN). These numbers identify the level of export controls and thus provide insight into the prohibitions as well as the necessary license requirements. However, the US has unilaterally imposed export restrictions on certain 'sensitive' civil items, such as civil aircraft parts and civil navigation instruments. Under US regulations these products have ECCN classifications containing '99'. US export license requirements for dual-use items are quite complicated and depend on the ECCN classification and the country of destination/end-use. ECCNs containing '99' only require an export license when exported or re-exported to countries or entities that are embargoed by the US.

According to the Enforcement Guidelines the

> 'OEE's [Office of Export Enforcement] criminal investigators and analysts leverage their subject-matter expertise, unique and complementary administrative enforcement tools, and relationships with other federal agencies and industry to protect our national security and promote our foreign policy interests. OEE protects legitimate exporters from being put at a competitive disadvantage by those who do not comply with the law. It works to educate parties to export transactions on how to improve export compliance practices, supporting American companies' efforts to be reliable trading partners and reputable stewards of U.S. national and economic security. BIS also discourages, and in some circumstances prohibits, U.S. companies from furthering or supporting any unsanctioned foreign boycott (including the Arab League boycott of Israel).'

For violations of the Export Administration Act of 1979, the International Emergency Economic Powers Act, the EAR, other statutes administered or enforced by BIS, as well as executive orders, regulations, orders, directives, or licenses issued pursuant thereto, the following penalties may be applied:

1. USD 1,000 with respect to a transaction valued at less than USD 1,000;
2. USD 10,000 with respect to a transaction valued at USD 1,000 or more but less than USD 10,000;
3. USD 25,000 with respect to a transaction valued at USD 10,000 or more but less than USD 25,000;
4. USD 50,000 with respect to a transaction valued at USD 25,000 or more but less than USD 50,000;

---

15. Export Administration Regulation(s), accessible by http://www.bis.doc.gov/index.php/regulations/export-administration-regulations-ear.
16. Commerce Control List (CCL), accessible by http://www.bis.doc.gov/index.php/regulations/commerce-control-list-ccl.
17. European Commission, Dual-use export controls, accessible by http://ec.europa.eu/trade/import-and-export-rules/export-from-eu/dual-use-controls.

5. USD 100,000 with respect to a transaction valued at USD 50,000 or more but less than USD 100,000;
6. USD 170,000 with respect to a transaction valued at USD 100,000 or more but less than USD 170,000;
7. USD 250,000 with respect to a transaction valued at USD 170,000 or more.

The Enforcement Guidelines include some interesting features. One renowned feature concerns VSDs. When companies find that they have infringed US laws and regulations (export controls, sanctions, bribery), they decide to make a VSD to the US authorities. EAR § 764.5 deals with VSD. According to this paragraph:

> '(a) *General policy.* BIS strongly encourages disclosure to OEE if you believe that you may have violated the EAR, or any order, license or authorization issued thereunder. Voluntary self-disclosure is a mitigating factor in determining what administrative sanctions, if any, will be sought by OEE.
>
> (b) *Limitations.*
>
> (1) The provisions of this section do not apply to disclosures of violations relating to part 760 of the EAR.
>
> (2) The provisions of this section apply only when information is provided to OEE for its review in determining whether to take administrative action under part 766 of the EAR for violations of the export control provisions of the EAR.
>
> (3) The provisions of this section apply only when information is received by OEE for review prior to the time that OEE, or any other agency of the US Government, has learned the same or substantially similar information from another source and has commenced an investigation or inquiry in connection with that information.
>
> (4) While voluntary self-disclosure is a mitigating factor in determining what administrative sanctions, if any, will be sought by OEE, it is a factor that is considered together with all other factors in a case. The weight given to voluntary self-disclosure is solely within the discretion of OEE, and the mitigating effect of voluntary self-disclosure may be outweighed by aggravating factors. Voluntary self-disclosure does not prevent transactions from being referred to the Department of Justice for criminal prosecution. In such a case, OEE would notify the Department of Justice of the voluntary self-disclosure, but the consideration of that factor is within the discretion of the Department of Justice.
>
> (5) A firm will not be deemed to have made a disclosure under this section unless the individual making the disclosure did so with the full knowledge and authorization of the firm's senior management. ...'

As discussed in the chapter on Bribery & Corruption *supra* VSDs can mitigate the harshness of possible penalties.

A significant change in the proposed rule was the introduction of the concept of base penalty amounts for egregious and non-egregious apparent violations and the principle of reducing the base penalty amount by one-half if the case is based on a VSD. Base penalty amounts could then be adjusted based on aggravating, mitigating and general factors (which could be either aggravating or mitigating). The existing guidelines treat a VSD as a mitigating factor of 'great weight'. Several commentators expressed concern over the rule's treatment of VSDs, stating that it would reduce the incentive for voluntary disclosure and that it seemed to diminish the importance of VSDs.[18]

18.7 THE ROLE OF COMPLIANCE IN PROTECTING AGAINST 'EXPORT CONTROL' INFRINGEMENTS

The compliance officer is the key to efficient and secure business operations. Besides the 'normal' compliance topics, the compliance officer must ascertain that all necessary export controls are implemented and monitored in a manageable way.

With regard to the compliance environment of military goods, the ITAR regulations provide sufficient guidance on the requirements for compliance.

BIS operates on the basis of the nine so-called BIS principles:[19] According to these principles an organization should:

- perform a meaningful risk analysis;
- have a formal written compliance program;
- appoint senior officials of a high level who are responsible for overseeing the compliance program;
- provide adequate, ongoing training to its employees and keep records of such trainings;
- adequately screen customers and transactions;
- have adequate record-keeping;
- have an active internal system for reporting export violations;
- periodically hold internal/external reviews or audits (and modifications reflecting the reviews and changes in the law and in business practice); and
- take effective remedial action in response to export violations, including disciplining employees who violate export compliance.

This program does not differ much from the requirements set under the USFSG concerning the FCPA.[20]

18.8 THIRD-PARTY SCREENING

It is of particular importance for all organizations to be aware of the party with whom they do business, especially with regard to export controls and sanctions, but also with regard to the prevention of bribery and corruption. You are affected by those you choose to do business with. For instance, politically exposed persons (PEPs) may pose a threat with regard to bribery and corruption, but also with regard to circumventing export controls or gaining assets for denied persons or entities. The UFSG address the issue of third-party due diligence. Organizations should be diligent not only with regard to countries in which they operate but also with regard to the

18. 40499 Federal Register, Vol. 81, No. 120.
19. Darryl Jackson, Assistant Secretary for Export Enforcement: keynote address at the BIS Export Control Forum in Newport Beach, California on March 17, 2008.
20. Bleker 2009, p. 184.

persons and organizations they do business with or those they choose to officially represent them as agents.

According to the DOJ and the SEC, third parties, including agents, consultants, and distributors, are commonly used to conceal the payment of bribes to foreign officials in international business transactions. Risk-based due diligence is particularly important with third parties and will also be considered by the DOJ and the SEC in assessing the effectiveness of a company's compliance program.

Although the degree of appropriate due diligence may vary based on the industry, country, size and nature of the transaction, and the historical relationship with the third party, some guiding principles always apply.[21]

> '*First*, as part of risk-based due diligence, companies should understand the qualifications and associations of its third-party partners, including its business reputation, and relationship, if any, with foreign officials. The degree of scrutiny should increase as red flags surface.
>
> *Second*, companies should have an understanding of the business rationale for including the third party in the transaction. Among other things, the company should understand the role of and need for the third party and ensure that the contract terms specifically describe the services to be performed. Additional considerations include payment terms and how those payment terms compare to typical terms in that industry and country, as well as the timing of the third party's introduction to the business. Moreover, companies may want to confirm and document that the third party is actually performing the work for which it is being paid and that its compensation is commensurate with the work being provided.
>
> *Third*, companies should undertake some form of ongoing monitoring of third-party relationships. Where appropriate, this may include updating due diligence periodically, exercising audit rights, providing periodic training, and requesting annual compliance certifications by the third party. In addition to considering a company's due diligence on third parties, the DOJ and the SEC also assess whether the company has informed third parties of the company's compliance program and commitment to ethical and lawful business practices and, where appropriate, whether it has sought assurances from third parties, through certifications and otherwise, of reciprocal commitments. These can be meaningful ways to mitigate third-party risk.'

This quotation comes from the FCPA *Resource Guide*, but it is equally applicable to export controls and sanctions. Denied parties will try to find ways to circumvent embargoes. Also, organizations may themselves look for escapes via third parties to circumvent embargoes that prevent them from doing business with embargoed parties that will pay high prices to acquire goods, technology or assets.

In manufacturing companies or high-tech knowledge organizations, as well as banks, it is advisable to organize automated third-party screening based due diligence through management systems connecting the different systems and tools that includes

21. A Resource Guide to the U.S. Foreign Corrupt Practices Act, by the Criminal Division of the U.S. Department of Justice and the Enforcement Division of the U.S. Securities and Exchange Commission, November 2012, pp. 61–62.

the entire supply chain, from the moment a potential supplier or a customer is defined through to delivery, including where necessary an automated system where ECCNs can be attached to the product, a license repository and a license request procedure up to the time of payment of the invoice. Unfortunately, as discussed above in the paragraphs on OFAC, DDTC and BIS, the system must be 'foolproof' due to the enormous ramifications of non-compliance. As the saying goes: 'Rome wasn't built in a day', but an organization could well be ruined in less than a day.

18.9 CONCLUSION

The increase in extraterritorial jurisdictional claims by the US (and probably by the UK in the future) may be a threat to the organizations and natural persons when they are thoroughly unaware that they may infringe foreign laws. It may be seen as unjust or even illegal, but when extraterritorial jurisdictional claims from country X are not precluded by the judicial system of country Y, the (corporate) citizens of Y will have to submit to it. It is not always understandable and may not seem to be justifiable, but 'law' and 'justice' are not synonymous. The legal system may not always be regarded as 'just' and extraterritorial jurisdiction is a fact of life. Organizations have to protect themselves as best they can against intricate (foreign) legislation such as export controls. The compliance officer plays a significant part in the protection of the organization. It is his task to identify the risks and to see how the business operations can be optimally adjusted so as to ensure compliance with domestic and foreign laws and regulations.

BIBLIOGRAPHY

Bleker 2009
S.C. Bleker-van Eyk, 'Compliance als bescherming tegen corruptie', in: C.A. Wielenga et al. (ed.), *Jaarboek Compliance* 2009, Nieuwerkerk aan den IJssel en Waddinxveen: Gelling Publishing en Nederlands Compliance Instituut 2009, pp. 173–192.

Bleker 2013
S.C. Bleker-van Eyk, 'The extraterritorial web: Tracking the ever expanding reach of extraterritorial jurisdiction Part II', *Business Compliance* 06/2013, pp. 75–84.

Other references

A Recourse Guide to the U.S. Foreign Corrupt Practices Act
A Resource Guide to the U.S. Foreign Corrupt Practices Act, by the Criminal Division of the U.S. Department of Justice and the Enforcement Division of the U.S. Securities and Exchange Commission, November 2012.

European Commission
European Commission, Dual-use export controls.

Jackson 2008
D. Jackson, Assistant Secretary for Export Enforcement: keynote address at the BIS Export Control Forum in Newport Beach, California on March 17, 2008.

Memorandum for the heads of executive departments and agencies 2016
S. Donovan, Implementation of the Federal Civil Penalties Inflation Adjustment Act Improvements Act of 2015, February 24, 2016.

U.S. Department of the Treasury
U.S. Department of the Treasury, Civil Penalties and Enforcement Information, Resource center.

U.S. Department of the Treasury
U.S. Department of the Treasury, Terrorism and Financial Intelligence, Office of Foreign Assets Control (OFAC).

U.S. Department of the Treasury
U.S. Department of the Treasury, Specially Designated Nationals and Blocked Persons List (SDN), Recourse Center.

U.S. Department of Commerce
U.S. Department of Commerce, Bureau of Industry and Security, Commerce Control List (CCL).

19. Information Management and Privacy

W. Seinen

19.1 INTRODUCTION

Information Management typically refers to the activities that take place within an organization with respect to information used and generated by it. Information Management is considered a cycle of activity, starting with the collection of information from available sources, the custodianship or archiving of that information and the sharing of it with others. The cycle is completed with the deletion of information, when further use or storage is no longer needed or appropriate.

Information Management is a key element of almost every compliance function. Compliance with a rule, law or policy can only be organized and demonstrated on the basis on evidence and other information. Compliance with tax laws requires robust management of the organization's financial information. Compliance with anti bribery and corruption requires information on the employee's behavior and compliance with export control regulations requires insight into information on the organization's customers (Know Your Customer, KYC).

Collecting, organizing, disseminating, securing and deleting information are key elements of modern Information Management that have become a compliance domain in its own right. Protecting information against unauthorized access, loss and corruption - the domain of *information security* - is caught by quality norms such as the ISO/IEC 27001 standard and industry-specific requirements and standards such as PCI-DSS for the payment industry.

Another area of Information Management compliance concerns the requirements governing the processing of 'personal data', which is the subject of a collection of specific laws and regulations that has expanded rapidly in recent years.

Many requirements of data protection law do not apply to other types of information, but those who are familiar with the underlying principles of modern data protection law will find themselves better equipped to deal with Information Management challenges in general. For this reason, and against the background of the increasing impact of data protection laws, the latter will be the focus of this chapter.

19.2 INFORMATION SECURITY

Information security is an aspect of information management that relates to any kind of information that is processed in an organization: financial data, know-how, personal data, system-generated data, etc.

The most commonly used standard for information security is the ISO/IEC 27001:2013 standard. This builds on the User Code of Practice standard, published by the UK Department of Trade and Industry in 1989.[1] This standard was superseded by the British Standard 7799 (BS 7799). Part 2 of BS 7799 was published in 1998. In 2005 it was revised by the International Organization for Standardization (ISO) and the International Electrotechnical Commission (IEC).

ISO/IEC 27001:2013 specifies 114 controls in 14 groups:

Information security policies	*Operational security*
How information security is organized	Secure communications and data transfer
Human resources security – controls that are applied before, during, or after employment.	Secure acquisition, development, and support of information systems
Asset management	Security for suppliers and third parties
Access controls and managing user access	Incident management
Cryptographic technology	Business continuity/disaster recovery (to the extent that it affects information security)
Physical security of the organization's sites and equipment	Compliance – with internal requirements, such as policies, and with external requirements, such as laws.

In Europe, there is no comprehensive legal framework for information security. Rather, there is a patchwork of various European directives that address specific elements of information security.[2] This is in sharp contrast to the field of European data protection law – which is characterized by omnibus style laws, covering the processing of personal data by private companies, governmental bodies and individuals.

As a result there is no clear minimum norm or baseline for data security which can be used across the board to verify whether an organization's information security controls are compliant with the law.

Compliance with information security is hence by and large a matter of observance of norms established by an organization for a variety of reasons that often go beyond what is prescribed by law.

1. S.T. Arnason & K.D. Willett, 'Introduction to ISO Security Standards', http://www.infosectoday.com/Articles/27001.htm.
2. See for a more detailed overview of the data security policy framework in the EU: A.M. Arnbak, *Securing private communications: Protecting private communications security in EU law: fundamental rights, functional value chains and market incentives* (diss. Amsterdam UvA), Amsterdam: UvA 2015, pp. 32–64.

19.3 DATA PROTECTION LAWS

Data protection laws in Europe are embedded in Europe's system of fundamental rights – more specifically the right to respect of private life, home and communications (Article 7 of the EU Charter of Fundamental Rights) and the right to protection of one's privacy, family life and communication (Article 12 of the Universal Declaration of Human Rights).

The cultural background was a collective sense that the creation of vast collections of personal data about individual citizens – most notably in the hands of governmental bodies – created a significant risk of improper use and damage to society. The Second World War was a clear example of the consequences of having comprehensive registrations and insufficient controls to ensure these cannot be used for the wrong purposes.

We are entering the third cycle of data protection laws:

The first cycle started in 1980, when the OECD issued its 'Recommendations of the Council Concerning Guidelines Governing the Protection of Privacy and Trans-Border Flows of Personal Data'.[3] This was a set of non-binding requirements, organized around seven data protection principles.

Some 15 years later the seven OECD principles were used as the basis for the EU Data Protection Directive of 1995 (DPD).[4] The DPD has been implemented in all EU Member States. In the Netherlands, the local implementation was via the DPD Act (PDPA).

The system of national data protection laws did introduce binding norms, but in most Member States these were not enforced very rigorously (for example, between 2000 and 2016 the maximum fine under the PDPA was EUR 4,500, whereas fines for other types of breaches often amount to hundreds of thousands of euros, if not millions).

Moreover, international companies struggled to comply with national data protection laws throughout Europe because of the number of different interpretations and incompatible requirements.

Nowadays there is a common understanding that the use of personal data has risen spectacularly, and that the existing regulations were not sufficient to ensure a fair balance between the privacy interests of citizens and the interests of the private and public sectors. A robust data protection framework was considered critical to retaining the consumer's trust in the digital ecosystem – a cornerstone of Europe's economic policymaking. Governments and private companies would have to be subject to stricter and more harmonized rules. In 2016, after years of intense lobbying, a regulation on the protection of personal data was enacted: the General Data Protection Regulation (GDPR).[5] The GDPR replaces the DPD and was designed to

3. The OECD '*Guidelines on the Protection of Privacy and Transborder Flows of Personal Data*', 1st edition, 1980.
4. Directive 95/46/EC on the protection of individuals with regard to the processing of personal data and on the free movement of such data.
5. Regulation (EU) 2016/679 of the European Parliament and of the Council of April 27, 2016 on the protection of natural persons with regard to the processing of personal data and on the free movement of such data, and repealing Directive 95/46/EC.

harmonize data privacy laws across Europe, to protect and empower all EU citizens' data privacy and to reshape the way organizations across the region approach data privacy. The GDPR is also based on the OECD privacy principles referred to above, and many of its requirements are in line with the current DPD. However, on top of the existing requirements, a couple of new concepts were introduced. The most important aspect of the GDPR is, however, not the new requirements, but the new enforcement regime: violations of the GDPR can trigger fines, amounting to as much as 4% of a company's turnover or EUR 20,000,000.

The GDPR will overhaul the current landscape of 28 different state laws; those laws will be repealed by the national governments as of May 25, 2018.

The GDPR has a significant impact on the risks for organizations associated with their processing of personal data. In order to address these new risks, data protection compliance has become a priority for many organizations worldwide.

Most organizations that prepare for the GDPR start by assessing to what extent their processes are compliant with current data protection requirements. When that is done, the additional requirements and refinements can be translated into the measures and controls that form the organization's data protection framework.

19.4 SOURCES OF DATA PROTECTION LAWS

In the Netherlands, the main source of data protection law is the PDPA of July 6, 2000, which implements the DPD. The PDPA came into effect on January 1, 2016, when a general data breach notification obligation was introduced and the maximum fines were increased significantly.

Various delegated laws and regulations have been enacted under the PDPA, the most important of which is the Notification Exemption Decree ('*Vrijstellingsbesluit Wbp*') of May 7, 2001, as last amended on December 9, 2014 (effective date January 1, 2015), which exempts certain processing activities from the general data processing notification obligation.

Moreover, the AP has issued various guidelines and policy rules, which include:

- policy on fines and penalties (2016);
- active publication policy (2016);
- policy on data breach notification (2016);
- guidelines on data security (2013);
- enforcement activity policy (2011);
- policy on DPA opinions on request (2009).

19.4.1 Key actors and concepts

The following actors and concepts play a central role in the PDPA.

19.4.1.1 Personal data

The PDPA applies to the processing of 'personal data', which means any information relating to an identified or identifiable individual/natural person ('Data Subject'). Data regarding a legal entity of a person who is deceased does not fall within the scope of the definition of personal data. On the other hand, information relating to an individual in his capacity of representative of a legal entity or owner of a company does qualify as personal data.

Moreover, the Dutch Data Protection Authority holds the view that information that may be used to single out individuals - such as telephone numbers, license plate numbers and IP addresses - should be treated as personal data.

Finally, data collected using cookies and similar techniques is considered personal data unless proven otherwise.

19.4.1.2 Data processing

The concept of 'processing' is extremely broadly defined and covers any operation or set of operations performed on personal data including its collection, recording, organization, and even its deletion. The PDPA applies to automated data processing as well as to manual processing of personal data that is entered or intended to be entered in a file.

19.4.1.3 Data Subject, Data Controller and Data Processor

The individuals to whom certain personal data relates is the 'Data Subject'. As the purpose of the PDPA is to protect the individual's privacy rights, the PDPA grants certain rights and powers to the Data Subject, such as the right to demand information on the handling of his personal data and the right to demand correction or removal of personal data processed in breach of the PDPA.

The key subjects of the PDPA are those persons or entities that, alone or in conjunction with others, determine the purpose and means of processing of personal data. They are the 'Data Controllers' and the majority of the norms of the PDPA directly address the Data Controller.

The third actor in the data processing scheme is the 'Data Processor'. This is the individual or organization that collects or otherwise processes personal data for and on behalf of a Data Controller. The PDPA imposes certain obligations on the Data Processor that processes personal data for a Data Controller, mainly the obligation of secrecy and restrictions on the transfer of personal data to countries outside the European Economic Area.

Under the PDPA, the carrying out of processing activities by a Data Processor must be governed by a (written) agreement ('Data Processing Agreement') or another legal act whereby an engagement is created between the Data Processor and the Data Controller. In several instances, the Dutch DPA has issued guidance as to the requirements of a Data Processing Agreement and the level of detail required by the Dutch DPA.

19.4.2 Jurisdiction/territoriality

The PDPA applies to:

- the processing of personal data carried out in the context of the activities of an establishment of a Data Controller in the Netherlands; or

- the processing of personal data by or for Data Controllers that are not established in the EEA, involving the use of automated or non-automated means situated in the Netherlands (unless these means are used only for forwarding/transporting personal data).

The latter criterion is interpreted rather broadly: in 2016, the court in The Hague decided that the Canadian company WhatsApp, Inc. was caught by this provision since, for the provision of its services, it was using the smartphones of end-users in the Netherlands.[6]

In summary, the PDPA is likely to apply if personal data of individuals in the Netherlands is processed by a Data Controller that is (i) established in the Netherlands, or (ii) is established in another country, but uses a branch office in the Netherlands, or (iii) established in a country outside the EU. If the Data Controller is located in another EU Member State, the data protection laws of that Member State will apply, in lieu of the PDPA.

As indicated above, this will all change on May 25, 2018, as from that date there will just be one European data protection law, the GDPR.

19.4.3 Key principles of personal data processing

19.4.3.1 Purpose limitation

Personal data may only be processed on the basis of one of the following six processing grounds provided for by the law:

a. the Data Subject has unambiguously given its consent for the processing;
b. the processing is necessary for the performance of a contract to which the Data Subject is party, or for actions to be carried out at the request of the Data Subject and which are necessary for the conclusion of a contract;
c. the processing is necessary in order to comply with a legal obligation to which the Data Controller is subject;
d. the processing is necessary in order to protect a vital interest of the Data Subject;
e. the processing is necessary for the proper performance of a public law duty by the administrative body concerned or by the administrative body to which the data is supplied; or
f. the processing is necessary to uphold the legitimate interests of the Data Controller or of a third party to whom the data is supplied, except where the interests or fundamental rights and freedoms of the Data Subject, in particular the right to protection of individual privacy, prevail (the 'legitimate interest condition').

For most of the personal data processing in the private sector, the grounds listed under c., d. and e. are not available due to their specific nature. In practice most of

6. http://www.cecileparkmedia.com/leading-internet-case-law/article_template.asp?Contents = Yes&from = eclr&ID = 1155

the personal data processing takes place in the provision of services and goods for the Data Subject or the organization of which the Data Subject is part (e.g. its employer).

The second most popular ground for processing is the 'legitimate interest' condition. In many cases, a company would collect more information than is strictly required for the service provision, but does not consider this to be an infringement of the Data Subjects' privacy interests. This could be the case, for example, if publicly available information is used or when personal data is used for analytics and other statistical research to improve the Data Controller's services.

If these two grounds cannot be relied upon, the Data Controller could seek the Data Subjects' consent. Consent is considered as the 'last resort', as it often complicates the data processing policies and administration.

Consent can only be obtained lawfully if: (i) the Data Subject gave its permission of its free will, (ii) it was provided with proper information on the processing for which the consent is sought and (iii) the Data Subject was given the right to withdraw its consent at any time.

Consent can be express or implied, but the appropriate form of consent will depend on the circumstances, the expectations of the Data Subject and the sensitivity of the personal data involved. When the Data Subject gives consent, it is understood to cover only the purpose(s) identified by the Data Controller when fulfilling its information requirements. 'Fresh' consent is required for data processing activities for other purposes that have not been previously identified and consented to.

It is not necessary for a consent to be set out in writing, but if consent is relied upon, the Data Controller must be able to demonstrate that consent was indeed given (unambiguously and/or explicitly). The PDPA does not contain any specific requirements regarding the language of the consent. However, to satisfy the information requirement which applies to the consent ground, the Data Subject should be informed in a language that he is able to understand. Otherwise, the consent may be deemed invalid.

19.4.3.2 Proportionality principle and data minimization

Whilst the proportionality principle is not specifically mentioned in the provisions of the PDPA and the DPD, it is a fundamental principle of European data protection law that is often considered by the courts when applying the law. Reference to the proportionality principle can be found in many provisions of the PDPA, in particular whenever the word 'necessary' is mentioned.

The proportionality principle is applied whenever the processing ground for a given personal data processing operation is assessed. If a Data Controller claims that processing is necessary for the performance of its contractual obligations, it will have to demonstrate that this purpose cannot be achieved by using less personal data or choosing a set-up that is less intrusive. Even if consent is provided, a Data Controller should, in each specific situation, verify that reliance on that consent and the impact of the processing are proportionate to the objective of the processing.[7]

---

7. Supreme Court September 9, 2011 (*X (verweerder) v. Santander*) http://deeplink.rechtspraak.nl/uitspraak?id=ECLI:NL:HR:2011:BQ8097.

Data minimization and data deletion requirements are features of the proportionality principle. When collecting personal data, the Data Controller should consider whether its purposes can be achieved using less personal data. For instance, if data is used for statistical analysis, the Data Subject's name is typically not needed. In that case, copying the name and contact fields to the data analytics dataset may be disproportionate. Similarly, if retention of the personal data that was collected is no longer necessary, the Data Controller should delete the data.

19.4.4 Sensitive Personal Data

Specifically, more extensive restrictions apply to the processing of 'special categories' of personal data. Such 'Special Personal Data' largely corresponds to 'Sensitive Personal Data', but it is important to note that the two are not the same. Special Personal Data is defined as personal data relating to racial or ethnic origin, political opinions, trade union membership, religious or philosophical beliefs, unlawful or objectionable conduct, criminal conduct, and data concerning health or sexual life.

The PDPA generally prohibits the processing of Special Personal Data and subsequently provides for one generic and various specific exceptions.

Notwithstanding the specific exemptions for the processing of Sensitive Personal Data, in general, the prohibition of processing Special Personal Data does not apply where:

- the processing is carried out with the express consent of the Data Subject;
- the personal data has been made public by the Data Subject itself;
- the processing is necessary for the establishment, exercise, or defense of a right in law;
- the processing is necessary to comply with an obligation of international public law; or
- the processing is necessary with a view to an important public interest, where appropriate guarantees have been put in place to protect individual privacy and this is provided for by law or else the Dutch Data Protection Authority has granted an exemption. When granting an exemption, the Data Protection Authority can impose rules and restrictions. The processing of Sensitive Personal Data on this basis must be notified to the European Commission.

Further exemptions may apply to the processing of Sensitive Personal Data that is carried out for the purpose of scientific research or statistics (if certain conditions are met).

The category-specific exceptions are set forth in detail in the PDPA. For example, political personal data may be processed by political parties; medical data may be processed by healthcare providers in the course of their treatment and data relating to union membership may be processed by the trade union concerned or the trade union federation to which this trade union belongs, provided that this is necessary for the aims of the trade union or trade union federation.

Moreover, a person's personal identification number (PIN), which is created on the basis of specific legal requirements for the purposes of identifying a person (e.g. a social security number), may only be used for the processing of personal data in execution of the said law or for purposes stipulated by the law. Even with the consent of the Data Subject, the processing of such PINs is prohibited.

19.4.5 Information duties (information on request, privacy policies and notification)

Aside from ensuring that personal data is obtained lawfully, the Data Controller is also required to ensure that the Data Subjects are properly informed of the fact that their personal data is being processed and by whom.

19.4.5.1 Notifications

Organizations that process personal data must notify the Data Protection Authority. In some EU Member States there is only a general obligation for Data Controllers to register with the Data Protection Authority, but in the Netherlands notifications must be filed for each individual data processing operation. In order to avoid unnecessary administration, an exemption was introduced to the notification duty for 42 data processing operations that are considered most common. They include processing of employee data for payrolling and basic HR administration, processing of membership data by associations, processing of customer data for financial administration and so forth.

Please note that strict conditions apply to each exemption. If those conditions cannot be met, the processing is not automatically unlawful. The consequence is simply that a notification must be filed with the Dutch DPA for this processing operation.

As of January 2016 failure to notify is no longer subject to a fine, which means that the only theoretical means of enforcement available to the Dutch DPA is an order to file a notification.

19.4.5.2 Notice requirements when collecting data from the Data Subjects

On collection of personal data directly from the individual concerned, Data Controllers must provide information on who they are, what information they collect and for what purpose, in an intelligible form. When collecting data online, this is often achieved by referring to a privacy policy. If the data concerns employees, there is often a general data processing notice which explains what type of employee data processing takes place within the company.

Failure to notify does not render the data unlawful, but a Data Controller may be instructed to inform the Data Subjects to remedy the failure. This is not always possible and may sometimes even adversely impact the Data Subject's privacy. How information is to be provided is hence something to assess on a case by case basis. For example, Google was ordered to provide information on the data it collected in its StreetView project, but was allowed to do so via website and newspaper advertisements, rather than having to visit or send letters to all addresses in the area that was photographed.

19.4.5.3 *Notice requirements when collecting data from the Data Subjects*

If personal data is obtained indirectly, i.e. from another Data Controller, two notification requirements are triggered: the Data Controller who provides the personal data must check whether this activity is caught by the existing privacy notices given to the Data Subject. In other words, he must check whether the Data Subject could reasonably have expected him to supply their data to the recipient. The privacy policy may be an important indicator here. If it says: 'we may also share your personal data with business partners', an additional notice may not be required. If it says: 'we may share your personal data with other companies in our Group' and the recipient is not an affiliate, then an additional notice is probably required. NB: If the privacy policy says: 'we only use your personal data in the context of our service to you and do not share it with others', there is probably no processing ground available and the data cannot be transferred in the first place.

The recipient of the data must in turn also inform the Data Subject. This must be done upon receipt of the data or else no later than when actively using the data for the first time.

19.4.6 Data Subjects' rights (including 'right to be forgotten')

Data Subjects not only have the right to know who processes their personal data, but they can also request copies of the personal data that is being processed, including information on to whom information on them was supplied.[8]

If personal data is incorrect, the Data Subject may require that corrections are made, and if there is no right to continue using certain personal data, the Data Subject can demand its deletion. The latter has drawn much attention since the Google Spain decision of the European Court of Justice, pursuant to which Google was forced to remove search results relating to a 15-year-old press article containing information on a Data Subject. Since this decision, thousands of deletion requests have been issued to Internet service providers. However, around 75% of these requests have been refused as the rights of the Data Subject in question did not outweigh the rights to have the specific content searchable.[9]

19.4.7 International data transfers

A particularly thorny aspect of Dutch and European data protection law is the restriction on 'transferring' personal data to countries that are considered not to offer an 'adequate level of protection' of individuals' privacy rights.

The background to this concept is that the DPD aims for harmonized data protection laws in order to create a single 'level playing field' and ensure the free flow of information within the EU. For this reason, transferring data from one Member State to another is *not* an issue under data protection law. The idea is that the level

8. Rijkeboer vs. Rotterdam Municipality: http://eur-lex.europa.eu/legal-content/EN/TXT/HTML/?uri=CELEX:62007CJ0553&from=EN
9. See for a recent report on the Google RtbF statistics: http://searchengineland.com/report-2-years-75-percent-right-forgotten-asks-denied-google-249424.

of protection is similar and hence it does not really matter whether information on a Data Subject in Amsterdam is processed in Rotterdam, Athens, Helsinki or Lisbon.

However, as mentioned above, many countries outside the European Union have different types of data protection laws, which often do not apply to all types of personal data but only to specific industries or sectors. The European legislator considers the protection offered by such laws 'inadequate' and as a consequence personal data should not be transferred to such countries unless a specific exception can be relied on.

The following countries are considered to have an 'adequate level of protection' and hence transferring data to recipients in these countries is *not* an issue:

Andorra; Argentina; Canada; Switzerland; Faroe Islands; Guernsey; State of Israel; Isle of Man; Jersey; New Zealand; Uruguay.[10] Moreover, a specific arrangement was created for the United States – the so called EU-US Privacy Shield.[11]

Transfer of personal data to a country that is not on this 'white list' is prohibited, unless:

i. the Data Subject has given specific consent for the transfer – after being informed that the data protection laws in the recipient country are considered 'inadequate';
ii. the transfer is necessary for the performance of a contract between the Data Subject and the responsible parties, or for actions to be carried out at the request of the Data Subject and which are necessary for the conclusion of a contract;
iii. the transfer is necessary for the conclusion or performance of a contract concluded or to be concluded between responsible parties and third parties in the interests of the Data Subject;
iv. the transfer is necessary on account of an important public interest, or for the establishment, exercise or defense in law of any right;
v. the transfer is necessary to protect a vital interest of the Data Subject; or
vi. the transfer is carried out from a public register set up by law or from a register which can be consulted by anyone or by any persons who can invoke a legitimate interest, provided that in the case concerned the legal requirements for consultation are met.

In most cases, only exceptions ii. and iii. can help overcome transfer restrictions. Consent is often not an option, as the Data Controller would need to document consent of all Data Subjects. Often a data set also contains data pertaining to employees of customers, suppliers and their staff and others with whom the Data Controller does not have a direct contractual relationship.

In particular the use of cloud services and other Internet-based IT services involves data processing outside the US. For these situations the above exceptions would not suffice.

10. http://ec.europa.eu/justice/data-protection/international-transfers/adequacy/index_en.htm.
11. http://ec.europa.eu/justice/data-protection/international-transfers/eu-us-privacy-shield/index_en.htm.

Additional means to ensure that an international transfer of personal data is compliant are the use of EU Model Clauses or approved Binding Corporate Rules. Model Clauses are designed by the European Commission for incorporation in an agreement between the Data Controller in the EU and a data recipient in a foreign country. They by and large impose the main data protection requirements and obligations by means of contract on the foreign data recipient and provide for third-party covenants on which the Data Subject can directly rely.

Binding Corporate Rules are a more sophisticated international data protection instrument that is only used by a fraction of the companies involved in international data transfers. Those who have implemented Binding Corporate Rules and had them approved by the Data Protection Authority are exempt from the data transfer ban.

19.4.8 Data breach notification duty

On January 1, 2016, a new 'data breach notification' provision was added to the PDPA. Under this provision, Data Controllers are generally obligated to report data security incidents to the DPA in the event that such data breach will (likely) have an adverse effect on the protection of the personal data at issue.

Furthermore, if the data breach is likely to adversely affect the privacy of the relevant Data Subjects, these Data Subjects must also be notified of the data breach.

19.4.9 Enforcement & demonstrability

Failure to comply with data privacy laws can result in complaints, Data Protection Authority investigations and audits, Data Protection Authority orders, administrative fines, penalties or other sanctions, seizure of equipment or data, civil actions, criminal proceedings and/or private rights of action.

As mentioned above, the fines for failure to comply with the PDPA have been raised dramatically. The maximum amount of penalties for violations of the PDPA has been increased to EUR 820,000, or 10% of annual turnover, for failure to comply with the rules of the PDPA. The actual amount of a penalty that can be imposed in the case of a violation of the PDPA depends on the nature of the violation. The increased maximum penalty of EUR 820,000 also applies to the new data breach notification obligations.

In the Netherlands fines are not imposed very often. The PDPA typically first investigates and grants the Data Controller the option to remedy any issues found. If the Data Controller refuses or fails, the typical next step is a specific performance order, enforced by a penalty for each day the order is not complied with (*'last onder dwangsom'*).

As many breaches are not black and white in nature, one of the key instruments for Data Controllers to reduce their risks is to make sure their choices are well documented. If the DPA investigates a matter and finds that personal data is stored for too long, or is not really necessary, it will help a great deal if the Data Controller has a record to demonstrate that he did consider this, but came to a different conclusion. Without such historical file, the DPA will have an easier case arguing that the Data Controller did not (demonstrably) consider its data protection obligations and hence breached the PDPA.

19.4.10 Future law (GDPR)

With effect from May 25, 2018, the GDPR will replace the DPD and be directly applicable in all EU Member States without any need to implement national laws. As stated above, the GDPR is based on the same principles as the DPD, but it provides more detailed rules, has a broader geographic scope and streamlines certain international aspects. The newly introduced concepts and key changes as compared to existing data protection laws can be categorized in the following thirteen 'game changers'.

19.4.10.1 Expanded scope and one-stop-shop

The GDPR applies to:

- the processing of personal data by Data Controllers and Processors established in the EU, as well as
- by Data Controllers and Processors outside the EU where their processing activities relate to:
  - the offering of goods or services (even for free) to Data Subjects within the EU, or
  - the monitoring of the behavior of Data Subjects within the EU.

  This second element of (Article 3 paragraph 2 of) the GDPR is particularly relevant to all providers of online services who are established outside the EU but who render their services to Data Subjects in the European Union. Electronic marketplaces, app developers, social media platform operators and many other online service providers will be subject to the GDPR to the extent they service individuals in the EU. Another example concerns non-European businesses that offer service platforms to personnel, distributors and customers in countries within the EU. They will often be caught by the 'monitoring of behavior' element.

Companies that are active in more than one Member State should have some benefit from the GDPR as well. They will no longer have to deal with data protection authorities in each and every Member State where they have a presence. Under the 'one-stop-shop' principle, the supervisory authority in the jurisdiction of the main or sole establishment of the Data Controller/Processor will be the lead authority for cross-border processing. Please note that there are quite a number of derogations, so for certain activities and requirements national DPAs may still have to be considered.

The GDPR contains a much discussed 'consistency mechanism'[12] intended to ensure consistent application of the GDPR across the EU (one of the major downfalls of the current regime under the Directive). The European Data Protection Board (EDPB), which will replace the Article 29 Working Party,[13] will play an important role in this regard by issuing opinions and guidance, reporting to the EU Commission and resolving disputes between national Data Protection Authorities.

12. Arts 63–67 GDPR.
13. The EDPB will comprise the European Data Protection Supervisor and the heads of the national Data Protection Authorities.

19.4.10.2 Enhanced rights of Data Subjects

The rights for Data Subjects were given a more prominent place in the GDPR than was the case under the DPD. The existing rights include the right to demand erasure of one's data ('right to be forgotten'), the right to claim restriction of processing, the right to object to the use of one's personal data for profiling and the right to object against automated processing decisions.

A newly introduced right for the Data Subject is the right to 'data portability': the right to obtain a copy of one's personal data from the Controller and/or have it transferred to another Controller.

Moreover, Controllers will be required to supply significantly more information to Data Subjects about their processing activities than is the case under the DPD.

19.4.10.3 Profiling restrictions

Data Subjects will have the right not to be subject to a decision based solely on automated processing, including profiling, which produces legal effects concerning them or similarly significantly affects them. Individuals will also have an express right to 'opt out' of profiling and automated processing in a wide range of situations.

19.4.10.4 Consent

Consent is retained as a processing condition but the GDPR is more prescriptive than the Directive when it comes to the conditions for obtaining valid consent. The key change is that consent will require a statement or clear affirmative action of the Data Subject. Silence, pre-ticked boxes and inactivity will not be sufficient.

The GDPR clarifies cases where consent will not be freely given (e.g. no genuine choice to refuse, clear imbalance between the Data Subject and Controller). Data Subjects must be informed of their right to withdraw consent.

19.4.10.5 Data Processors

The GDPR imposes compliance obligations directly on Data Processors, such as implementing security measures, notifying the Data Controller of data breaches, appointing a DPO (if applicable), maintaining records of processing activities, etc.

Data Controllers and Processors will be required to enter into detailed processing agreements or renegotiate existing ones.

The GDPR has significant impact on (IT) service providers and other parties that act as 'Processors'. A major change is the obligation on Processors to disclose the identity of the sub-Processors they are using for their service provision and seek the Ccontroller's consent prior to engaging such sub-Processors (Article 28 paragraph 2). Another fundamental change for Processors is that they will be directly liable in case of non-compliance and may be subject to direct enforcement action.

19.4.10.6 Data Mapping

Data Controllers and Processors will have to maintain records of processing activities. Detailed information must be kept and supplied to supervisory authorities upon request.

Data Mapping is the process of identifying, understanding and mapping out the data flows of an organization. A good Data Map (also referred to as a 'record of processing activities'[14] or Data Inventory) will provide a comprehensive overview of the data flows within, to and from an organization.

A Data Map should provide information on the identity of the Data Controller, the various categories of data held and processed by the various entities/business units in a company, the associated processing purposes, the data transfers and disclosures within the group of companies to which the Controller belongs and with service providers and other third parties. Where possible the Data Map should also give insight into applicable data retention and data deletion policies and the technical and organizational security measures applicable to the personal data in question.

This is a new requirement and complex organizations often struggle to implement it. The GDPR does not give specific guidance as to the level of detail and, for example, the question of whether visual representation of the data flows is required. Many companies do, however, try to realize certain basic visual representations of their main flows of personal data.

19.4.10.7 Data protection by design and by default

These concepts are codified in the GDPR and require Controllers to ensure that individuals' privacy is considered from the outset of each new processing, product, service or application, and that, by default, only minimum amounts of personal data as necessary for specific purposes are collected and processed.

Data minimization has already been a requirement for years, as an implicit element of the proportionality principle and purpose limitation concept, but the GDPR clearly requires Controllers to consider whether and how they can design and configure new information systems in such a manner that no more personal data is collected in the first place than is necessary for the processing purposes as identified by the Controller.

The *data protection by design* provision provides that Controllers should implement appropriate measures: (i) having regard to the state of the art and the cost of implementation and (ii) taking account of the nature, scope, context and purposes of the processing as well as the risks of varying likelihood and severity for rights and freedoms of individuals posed by the processing (the so-called 'risk-based approach').

In other words, what measures will be appropriate in each case will depend on the state of the art and the cost of implementation as well as the risks to the rights and freedoms of natural persons resulting from a processing activity. This is very similar to the existing obligations regarding data security under Article 17 of the DPD.

The *data protection by default* requirement obliges Controllers to configure systems in such a manner that the default setting presented to Data Subjects leads

14. Art. 30 GDPR.

to a minimum of personal data collection, effectively forcing the Data Subject to actively choose to apply settings that cause more personal data to be processed.

19.4.10.8 Data Protection Impact Assessments (DPIAs)

Controllers will be required to perform a DPIA where the processing of personal data (particularly when using new technologies) is likely to result in a high risk to the rights and freedoms of individuals. DPIAs will be required particularly in cases of (i) an evaluation of personal aspects based on automated data processing including profiling, (ii) processing on a large scale of special categories of data, or (iii) systematic monitoring of a publicly accessible area.

Where a type of data processing is likely to result in a high risk for the rights and freedoms of individuals, Controllers must carry out a DPIA *prior to the processing* to assess the impact of the envisaged processing operations on the protection of personal data.

The GDPR text itself does not provide much guidance as to what would be considered a 'high risk' for the rights and freedoms of individuals, but it does provide a non-exhaustive list of examples as to when DPIAs will be required. Moreover, further guidance from Data Protection Authorities can be expected.

The GDPR does not prescribe the process for undertaking DPIAs. Further guidance on conducting DPIAs of data protection authorities and the EDPB should be used to assess what methodology to apply best in a given situation.

If a DPIA carried out by a Controller indicates that envisaged processing would result in a high risk in the absence of risk-mitigating measures taken by the Controller, the Controller must consult its Data Protection Authority prior to the processing.

The obligations to carry out DPIAs and consult with Data Protection Authorities in relation to high-risk processing operations apply directly to Controllers only. Processors will be required to assist Controllers, where necessary and upon request.

19.4.10.9 Accountability

Businesses will have to ensure compliance with the requirements of the GDPR through appropriate technical and organizational measures and be able to objectively *demonstrate* such compliance.

The GDPR text provides very little guidance as to what measures Controllers will need to implement to discharge their accountability obligations. Further guidance in the form of codes of conduct, certification mechanisms and clarifications from the Article 29 Working Party/EDPB can be expected.

A best-practice approach for organizations to satisfy their accountability obligations would be to build and implement a structured privacy management program, but less comprehensive approaches may be appropriate as well, depending on the level of risk posed by the data processing.

The 'demonstrability test' is an important instrument for Controllers to assess and mitigate their risks of enforcement. The GDPR contains many open norms, and it will be significantly harder to rebut an allegation that the GDPR requirements were not satisfied if there is no record at all to demonstrate what factors were considered when deciding on a particular data processing operation or policy. Similarly, those companies which have better documentation to demonstrate that they considered the GDPR and why they considered their choices compatible with the GDPR requirements will have an easier job whenever they have to defend their choices.

19.4.10.10 Data Protection Officers (DPOs)

Certain private and most public sector organizations will be required to appoint a DPO to oversee their data processing operations.

A DPO will be required where (i) the processing is carried out by a public authority or body, (ii) the core activities of the Data Controller or Processor consist of processing which requires regular and systematic monitoring of Data Subjects on a large scale, (iii) the core activities consist of processing special categories of data on a large scale, or (iv) the processing is required by Member State law.

Even when the GDPR does not specifically require the appointment of a DPO, organizations may sometimes find it useful to designate a DPO on a voluntary basis. The Article 29 Data Protection Working Party has published an opinion on the DPO requirement and has clearly indicated that it encourages these voluntary efforts.[15]

DPOs are not personally responsible in case of non-compliance with the GDPR. The GDPR makes it clear that it is the Controller or the Processor who is required to ensure and to be able to demonstrate that the processing is performed in accordance with its provisions.[16] Data protection compliance is a responsibility of the Controller or the Processor.

Organizations are free to choose whether to appoint an internal or external DPO. Furthermore, DPOs do not have to work exclusively in their DPO capacity. Rather, they may also perform other tasks as long as that does not result in a conflict of interest and provided that the other tasks (even if not conflicting) leave the DPO enough time to perform the obligations as DPO. An affiliated group of Controllers may appoint a single DPO provided that such DPO can effectively be approached from each group entity.

The GDPR only broadly requires DPOs to possess the professional qualities and expert knowledge of data protection law and practice enabling them to fulfill their role. No more details are prescribed by the GDPR.

Tasks of the DPO: As a minimum, and having regard to the risks associated with the processing operations, the DPO must (i) inform and advise the Controller (or Processor as the case may be) and its employees involved in data processing of their obligations under the GDPR and other data protection laws and (ii) monitor compliance with the GDPR, other applicable data protection laws and internal data protection policies.

The DPO would typically also be involved in assigning internal data protection responsibilities, training staff and conducting a compliance audit. Moreover, it would provide advice in relation to data protection impact assessments.

Finally the DPO is obliged to cooperate with, act as point of contact for and, as appropriate, consult with the Data Protection Authorities.

---

15. Guidelines on Data Protection Officers (DPOs), Adopted on December 13, 2016, last Revised and Adopted on April 5, 2017, Art. 29 data protection working party, Brussels, 2017.
16. Art. 24 paragraph 1 GDPR.

The Controller/Processor must (i) ensure that the DPO is involved in all data protection issues properly and in a timely manner, (ii) provide the resources necessary for the DPO to maintain the necessary knowledge and perform its tasks, (iii) ensure that the DPO can independently perform its tasks and report to the highest level of management and (iv) refrain from retaliation against the DPO for performing its tasks.

19.4.10.11 Overhauled data transfer rules

The GDPR retains the cross-border data transfer rules of the Directive, but adds new ones such as certification mechanisms and codes of conduct, as well as a new very limited derogation for occasional transfers based on legitimate interest. Country-specific authorization processes will no longer be needed (with some exceptions). BCRs are formally recognized in the GDPR.

In principle, data may be transferred out of the EU/EEA only to countries which have been recognized as providing an adequate level of data protection, unless the transferor can rely on specific derogations or adduces specific additional safeguards ensuring an adequate level of data protection.

Subject to the changes listed below, the list of available derogations and options for adducing additional adequate safeguards will remain the same.

Adequacy decisions and standard contractual clauses issued by the Commission under the Directive as well as BCRs and contractual clauses approved by national supervisory authorities under the Directive will remain valid unless and until formally amended, replaced or repealed.

Noteworthy changes to the cross-border data transfer rules include the following:

- transfers will no longer be subject to country-specific authorization processes, except that transfers based on contractual clauses which have not been adopted or approved by the Commission will require specific supervisory authority approval;
- adequacy decisions will be subject to clearer and more prescriptive standards as well as regular review and may be made in relation to territories and industry sectors within a country;
- the GDPR offers certification mechanisms and codes of conduct as additional options for adducing appropriate safeguards;
- BCRs will be formally recognized as measures adducing appropriate safeguards and will be subject to uniform rules when it comes to their adoption;
- approved standard contractual clauses may be supplemented with additional clauses or safeguards subject to certain conditions;
- transferors wanting to rely on consent as a derogation will need to inform the Data Subject about the risks resulting from the transfer before obtaining its explicit consent;
- the GDPR will introduce one new but very limited derogation which may help legitimize occasional transfers which are small in scope and would otherwise be prohibited.

19.4.10.12 Data breach notification

Controllers will have to report data breaches to the relevant supervisory authority without undue delay and, where feasible, within 72 hours of becoming aware of the breach (unless the breach is unlikely to result in a risk for Data Subjects' rights and freedoms).

A proper justification must accompany the notification if it is not made within 72 hours. Affected Data Subjects must be notified of a breach without undue delay if the breach is likely to result in a 'high risk' for their rights or freedoms.

A 'personal data breach' is defined as a breach of security leading to the accidental or unlawful destruction, loss, alteration, unauthorized disclosure of, or access to, personal data transmitted, stored or otherwise processed.

Notification to Data Protection Authority: Controllers must notify a personal data breach to the competent supervisory authority, unless the breach is unlikely to result in a risk to the rights and freedoms of individuals. Importantly, those breaches that are unlikely to result in a risk to the rights and freedoms of individuals are exempt from the notification obligation, providing some discretion for Controllers to assess whether or not a breach must be reported.

However, this exemption should be interpreted narrowly and would require the Controller to demonstrate - in accordance with the accountability principle - that the breach is unlikely to result in a risk to the rights and freedoms of individuals.

Notifications to Data Subjects: Data breaches must also be communicated to affected Data Subjects if they are likely to result in a high risk to their rights and freedoms.

Exceptions to the notification requirement apply where:

- the Controller adequately secured the relevant data by implementing appropriate technical and organizational protection measures (such as encryption) in relation to it;
- following the breach, the Controller has taken measures to ensure that the high risk to the rights and freedoms of Data Subjects is no longer likely to materialize; or
- the notification of individual Data Subjects would require disproportionate effort - in this case a public communication of the breach would be required, however.

Timing: Organizations must notify data breaches to the SA without undue delay and, where feasible, not later than 72 hours after becoming aware of it; affected Data Subjects must be notified without undue delay. This means that affected individuals should be notified as soon as reasonably feasible and in line with any guidance provided by the notified DPA.

The DPA also has the power to order Controllers to communicate a personal data breach to Data Subjects.

19.4.10.13 Enforcement & sanctions

The GDPR will harmonize the tasks and powers of supervisory authorities and significantly increase fines. For major infringements (such as failure to comply with cross-border transfer rules or to obtain adequate consents), fines can be up to EUR 20,000,000 or, in the case of an undertaking, up to 4% of the total worldwide annual turnover of the preceding financial year (whichever is higher).

Each Member State is required to establish one or more independent public authorities responsible for monitoring compliance with, and enforcing the provisions of, the GDPR. The GDPR goes further than that and clarifies that each such supervisory authority should be provided with the financial, human and technical resources, premises and infrastructure necessary for the effective performance of their tasks. Importantly, those supervisory authorities which previously relied on notification fees as a resource will no longer have this income stream available. It remains to be seen whether the GDPR will result in better equipped and more active regulators.

The GDPR expressly states that, in order to ensure consistent monitoring and enforcement, DPAs should have the same tasks and effective powers across Member States. From an enforcement perspective, these powers include investigative powers, corrective powers and sanctions, as well as powers to bring infringements of the GDPR to the attention of judicial authorities and/or engage in legal proceedings to enforce the provisions of the GDPR.

As a general rule, enforcement measures must be appropriate, necessary and proportionate having regard to each individual case. DPAs have less discretion about enforcement rules, but critically they retain discretion about the application of the provisions.

The GDPR expressly states that as a general rule (in order to strengthen enforcement of the GDPR rules), penalties and administrative fines should be imposed for any infringement of the GDPR in addition to, or instead of, appropriate measures imposed by the SA. The exceptions are minor infringements and cases in which a fine would constitute a disproportionate burden on a natural person. In those cases, a reprimand may be issued instead of a fine. Therefore, the imposition of fines is likely to become the norm.

The following rules for determining the scope of administrative fines to be imposed:

- The imposition of administrative fines must in each case be effective, proportionate and dissuasive.
- Depending on the circumstances of each individual case, administrative fines should be imposed in addition to, or instead of, other corrective measures.
- Various factors need to be considered when determining whether to impose a fine and of what amount, including in particular:
  - the nature, gravity and duration of the infringement;
  - the intentional or negligent character of the infringement;
  - actions taken to mitigate damage suffered;
  - the degree of responsibility or any relevant previous infringements;
  - the manner in which the infringement became known to the DPA;
  - the degree of cooperation with the DPA in order to remedy the infringement and mitigate the adverse effects;
  - compliance with measures previously ordered against the Data Controller/Processor;
  - adherence to a code of conduct; and

  - any other aggravating or mitigating factors (such as financial benefits gained).
- If a Controller or Processor violates several provisions of the GDPR in relation to the same or linked processing operations, the total amount of the fine may not exceed the amount specified for the gravest violation.

The GDPR differentiates between two categories of infringements. Tier-one infringements are subject to administrative fines of up to EUR 10,000,000 or, in the case of an undertaking, up to 2% of the worldwide annual turnover of the preceding financial year (whichever is higher). Tier-two infringements are subject to administrative fines of up to EUR 20,000,000 or, in the case of an undertaking, up to 4% of the worldwide annual turnover of the preceding financial year (whichever is higher).

20. Duty of Care

R.A.M. Houben

20.1 INTRODUCTION

The AFM considers that the question of how far the duty of care extends and how the responsibility should be fulfilled is one of the most important issues the financial sector will have to contend with in the years ahead. The AFM believes the attendant risks cannot be totally eliminated. The primary task of supporting consumers rests with the financial sector itself. The responsibility for the duty of care rests with the financial sector, with the AFM acting as supervisor. The AFM also considers that consumers themselves must assume their responsibility, even though it is often difficult for them, because they must be genuinely in a position to take decisions.[1]

The above points demonstrate the importance of the duty of care in the financial sector. The term 'duty of care' comes from private law and has become a catch-all term over the years.[2] Aspects such as diligence, including at corporate level, play a role in every contractual or non-contractual relationship between persons or legal entities.[3] The term 'civil-law duty of care' is also used in this context. For financial

1. According to Merel van Vroonhoven, chairman of the AFM, who said that the AFM was not meant to act as a consumer association. See www.amweb.nl (March 23, 2016).
2. According to the Van Dale dictionary, duty of care means the duty to look after or take care of something. In the financial sector many elements, such as 'the customer's interest first', are lumped under the heading of duty of care without any precise definition of the specific (legal) frameworks. It is perhaps better to speak of provision of services with due care, as advocated by Grundmann-van de Kroll. This notion is much broader, however, than the notion of duty of care; the duty to exercise care is part of provision of services with due care. A detailed description of provision of services with due care for investment undertakings can be found in Grundmann-van de Kroll 2012, pp. 605–634. *See also* Broekhuizen 2016, pp. 133–134 for a more detailed consideration of the term duty of care as a 'catch-all' term.
3. An example is the (normal) fulfillment of obligations in a contract concluded between two persons as set out in the BW. If there is no contractual legal relationship, the doctrine of

undertakings operating in the Netherlands, the so-called 'public-law duty of care'[4] as set out in financial supervision law[5] has started to play an increasingly important role over the years.

In general terms, private law covers the relationship between citizens and/or businesses, while public law covers the relationship between citizens and/or businesses and the government.[6] Financial undertakings have to deal with duties of care in both private and public law.

This section outlines the duty/duties of care for financial undertakings.[7] Section 20.2 deals with the duty of care in private law and section 20.3 deals with the duty/duties of care in public law. Section 20.4 deals with the interaction between private law and public law and section 20.5 deals with the generic (public-law) duty of care for financial service providers. Finally, this chapter draws to a close in section 20.6 with a number of observations.

20.2 THE DUTY OF CARE FOR FINANCIAL UNDERTAKINGS UNDER PRIVATE LAW[8]

Private law contains various (open) standards with regard to the duty of care. Article 7:401 of the BW specifies, for example, that in performing his work the contractor must exercise the care of a good contractor.[9] In the case of a bank this means that in providing its services it must exercise the necessary care and take account of the customer's interests to the best of its ability.[10] Since the 1990s the Supreme Court has applied the 'good contractor criterion' in assessing whether the contractor has behaved in a way that may be expected of a reasonably competent and reasonably acting peer or fellow professional. It assesses the degree of professionalism. The more professional the service provider claims to be, the greater is the duty of care.[11]

In the event of a dispute concerning the execution of the contract between a financial undertaking and the customer, the civil court will apply a different assessment framework than the supervisor or the administrative court. The latter are bound, after all, by public law.[12] A civil court will have to assess interests which may

---

the unlawful act applies as set out in 6:162 of the BW. Laws such as the BW, but also the Wft and corporate due diligence, can be seen as sources for the duty of care.

4. A distinction can be drawn between the duty of care specific to the securities industry and the generic duty of care. More information on this can be found in sections 20.2 and 20.3 *infra*.
5. For example the Wft.
6. A familiar example is criminal law.
7. Specifically with regard to banks, insurers, financial service providers and investment undertakings as described in Art. 1:1 of the Wft.
8. *See also* Tjong Tjin Tai 2012, pp. 37–42.
9. The legal relationship between a financial undertaking and customers usually qualifies as a commission contract as referred to in Art. 7:400 of the BW. *See also* Van der Eerden & Silverentand 2015, pp. 25–26.
10. As set out in Art. 2 of the General Banking Conditions, *see* www.nvb.nl
11. Schotsman 2013, p. 272.
12. Such as the Wft and the Awb.

include reasonableness and fairness.[13] Due to the requirements of reasonableness and fairness, certain obligations may arise for the financial undertaking (as a service provider), such as duties to provide information and warnings.

In short, the court will generally apply the principle that financial undertakings, due to their nature and role in society, have a special duty of care which extends to protecting consumers against their own rashness and lack of insight when providing financial services. The fulfillment and scope of such duty depends partly on the specific circumstances of each individual case. Factors that play a role are the nature and complexity of the product, the nature of the service, and the customer's circumstances and background (expertise and experience). Two pillars of the duty of care are that information supplied to the customer must be complete, accurate and not misleading and that in this connection the undertaking must conduct a sufficient analysis of the financial position, investment objectives and investment wishes so as to provide appropriate service.[14]

A breach of the duty of care as described above may lead to compensation for error,[15] non-performance or an unlawful act.[16] A claim for non-performance will be based on the fact that the financial undertaking failed to fulfill its obligations towards the customer, for example because it did not act in accordance with the civil-law duty of care. In the case of a claim for an unlawful act, the customer must be able to argue that the undertaking acted contrary to the principles of corporate integrity or diligence as a result of breaching the duty of care incumbent on it or acted contrary to legal obligations.[17] In the case of both non-performance and unlawful acts, a requirement is that there is a causal connection between the failure and the damage. This does not mean, however, that the entire cost of the damage suffered by the customer must be borne by the financial undertaking. If the customer himself is to blame, he may be required to bear part of the cost himself.[18] This will depend on the specific circumstances of the case.[19] The civil-law duty of care for banks applies not only to customers, incidentally, but also to third parties.[20]

20.3 DUTIES OF CARE FOR FINANCIAL UNDERTAKINGS UNDER PUBLIC LAW

In addition to the aforementioned duty of care under private law, financial undertakings also have to deal with duties of care under public law as set out in European

13. As referred to in Art. 6:248 of the BW.
14. Van der Eerden & Silverentand, p. 25 and Schotsman 2013, p. 272 which refers to the LJN judgment: BH2822 recital 3.5.
15. In the pre-contract phase, *see* Art 6:228 of the BW.
16. Arts 6:74 paragraph 1 and 6:162 of the BW.
17. Van der Eerden & Silverentand, p. 25–26, for example acting contrary to the Wft.
18. Pursuant to Art. 6:101 of the BW.
19. Van der Eerden & Silverentand, p. 26. A further analysis of civil-law remedies in the event of a breach of the Wft by financial undertakings can be found in Grundmann-van de Krol 2012, pp. 814–835.
20. *See* Safe Haven judgment (HR December 23, 2005 NJ 2006, 289). *See also* Van der Eerden & Silverentand 2015 p. 26; Schotsman 2013, p. 272.

directives and regulations, the Wft and derivative regulations.[21] These are also referred to as rules of conduct, because most of them are included in part 4 of the Wft (and derivative regulations), which includes supervision of the conduct of financial undertakings. A distinction must be drawn here between the type of customer,[22] the type of product or form of service,[23] and the type of financial undertaking.[24] In short, the rules of conduct depend on which financial product or financial service is being supplied, by which undertaking and to whom.

An example is a bank that also provides investment services. Then there is a combination of a bank and investment undertaking,[25] a so-called bank investment undertaking. Different duties of care then apply under the applicable laws and regulations.[26] With regard to the provisions of service with due care in the case of investment undertakings, these duties of care can be classified as rules relating to:

1. The general requirement to act in an honest, fair and professional manner on behalf of the interests of actual and potential customers.[27]

---

21. Grundmann-van de Krol notes in this regard that in public securities law the free-market principle has been restricted by the transparency principle (in order to eliminate the information inequality between customers and financial undertakings as far as possible) and the care principle (so that a fair transaction takes place). *See* Grundmann-van de Krol 2010, pp. 9–10.
22. Such as private customers (consumers), business customers (professional customers) and (third-party) beneficiaries.
23. The product may be 'simple', such as a savings account, but also complex, particularly if it contains an asset-accumulation or investment component and becomes a combined product such as an investment or savings mortgage or an insurance investment product (a so-called complex product). In the case of providers with asset-accumulation products, the boundaries in terms of legal regimes between financial services and investment services have also faded over the years. Different rules of conduct apply to a greater or lesser extent to every type of product. This also applies to different types of service, such as advice (or intermediation only), execution only or asset management (for private customers).
24. Art. 1:1 of the Wft lists 18 types of institution covered by the term 'financial undertaking'. As stated in note 7, this chapter deals only with banks, insurers, investment undertakings and financial service providers. The definitions of these undertakings can be found in Art. 1:1 of the Wft.
25. A bank is an institution which (in principle) accepts cash or savings and provides credit. An investment undertaking is an undertaking that provides investment services or conducts investment activities. The provision of investment services includes: receiving and transmitting orders from customers with regard to financial instruments (the remisier), executing customers' orders in relation to financial instruments on behalf of customers, managing individual and other assets (asset management), and advising on financial instruments (investment advice), see Art. 1:1 of the Wft.
26. The bank must then comply not only with rules of conduct with regard to lending, but also with the rules of conduct as set out in part 4 of the Wft (provision of services with due care). Art. 2:13 of the Wft states that a bank can apply for a license as a bank investment undertaking.
27. Art. 4:90 of the Wft, which states: 'When providing investment or ancillary services, an investment undertaking will act in an honest, fair and professional manner in the interest of its clients. It will also act honestly, fairly and professionally in the performance of investment activities and refrain from practices that are harmful to the integrity of the market.'

2. The classification of customers.[28]
3. Information obligations towards actual or potential counterparties and the method of advertising.[29]
4. The information which must be obtained before and after entering into a service contract.[30]
5. Specific rules of conduct.[31]
6. Rules on remuneration or commission.[32]

According to Grundmann-van de Krol, there are specific rules covering the pre-contractual and contractual relationship between the investment undertaking and the investor, including under written or unwritten private law. The reason for also including private-law standards in the rules set in or by virtue of the Wft is twofold: 1) the private-law standard is not sufficiently clear in the opinion of the Wft legislator, and 2) private law is insufficiently effective. A double (private-law and public-law) setting of standards combined with public-law enforcement could lead, however, to moral risk[33] for the investor, problems with the supervision of compliance with standards relating to the closed contractual relationship between the investment undertaking and the investor (increased risk of civil-law liability due to failure of supervision), and divergent or even conflicting case law in the administrative, criminal and civil courts.[34]

Another example – distinct from the investment undertaking – is the financial service provider. A financial service provider is a party that provides a financial product other than a financial instrument, advises on a financial product other than a financial instrument, or intermediates, acts as a reinsurance intermediary or acts as an authorized agent or sub-agent.[35] Amongst others, a financial service is deemed to be: offering, advising on financial products other than financial instruments (for example a mortgage or insurance) and intermediating (including reinsurance intermediation).[36] The largest group falling within this definition is the (insurance) intermediary. This group is also subject to various (and in some cases the same) duties of care. Banks

28. Arts 4:18a-4:18c of the Wft.
29. Arts 4:19–4:22 of the Wft.
30. Arts 4:23–4:24 of the Wft, also known as know your customer (not to be confused with know your customer or customer due diligence in the combating of money-laundering and the financing of terrorist activities).
31. Such as the prohibition of cold calling (Arts 81–82 of the Bgfo) and churning (Art. 84 of the Bgfo).
32. Art. 4:90 paragraph 2 of the Wft in conjunction with Arts 168a-168aa. For financial service providers, *see* Art. 4:25a of the Wft in conjunction with Arts 86a-ea of the Bgfo. See also Grundmann-van de Krol 2012, p. 605 et seq. The rules on professional competence and the Product Approval & Review Process (PARP) could be added here, but these have more to do with the (correct) set-up of business operations and product integrity. These rules are important, however, for provision of services with due care. A detailed explanation of these rules can be found in Grundmann-van de Krol 2012, pp. 607–634.
33. This includes the investor's inclination to take additional risks, assuming that any financial problems can be passed onto others.
34. Grundmann van de Krol 2012, pp. 605–606.
35. Art. 1:1 of the Wft.
36. Ibid.

and insurance companies can also act as intermediaries, but since they already need a license to operate, they have an exemption.[37]

To give more concrete meaning to the term duty or duties of care, it is better to speak of provision of services with due care as part of the supervision of conduct of financial undertakings.[38] The term 'duty of care' does not arise explicitly in the Wft or the Bgfo. With the inclusion of the so-called generic duty of care for financial service providers, this term was, however, referred to specifically in the parliamentary documents.[39]

The duties of care thus cover a broad and complex area because they constitute a set of obligations under private law, public law and case law. Broekhuizen summarizes this as follows:[40]

> 'Depending on the circumstances, the precise import of the duty of care may differ from case to case depending on the type of customer and the specific interests which merit legal protection. Comparable cases may nevertheless be regulated or assessed in similar ways. For example, legislation and case law formulate more or less concrete duties of care with regard to particular financial products or financial services ...[41] The setting of open ("vague") standards for due diligence may thus become specific in concrete situations, both temporarily (on one particular matter) and permanently (on comparable matters). This is a process of legal development. A distinction can therefore be drawn between duties of care set out ("elaborated") in more or less specific rules of conduct (the term *care obligations* is then used) and the general duty of care, which prescribes unspecified diligent conduct as an overarching open standard.'

In addition to the aforementioned rules of conduct specific to products, services, customers and companies, financial undertakings are also subject to general rules of conduct. These include rules with regard to information provision[42] and the requirement to exercise care. The latter is enshrined in Article 4:25 of the Wft, which states as follows:[43]

> 'In its treatment of the participant, consumer or, in the case of a financial instrument or insurance, the client, a financial undertaking must comply with

37. The definition of financial service provider, as currently included in the Wft, has its origins in the (no longer applicable) Financial Services Act, which, after existing for barely a year, was incorporated in the Wft on January 1, 2007.
38. The domain of the AFM. Schotsman has spoken of the duty of care section of the Wft, Schotsman 2013, p. 266. See Art. 4:18 et seq. of the Wft, Section 4.2.3. Provision of services with due care. These rules have been further elaborated *inter alia* in section 8 of the Bgfo and the Nrgfo. Reference is also made to the numerous European regulations (such as MiFID II and MiFIR for investment undertakings), which may or may not have been included in the Wft or have direct effect.
39. *See* section 20.5 *infra*.
40. Broekhuizen 2016, p. 137.
41. For example the advisory rules under the Wft.
42. Arts 4:19–4:22 of the Wft. Art. 4:19 paragraph 2 of the Wft obliges financial undertakings, for example, to provide information for customers that is correct, clear and not misleading.
43. This is in fact a general provision with regard to due diligence. *See also* section 20.5 *infra*. The article has been further elaborated for financial service providers in the Bgfo (for example in Art. 81), as well as for investment undertakings (*see* note 32 *supra*).

more detailed rules laid down in or by virtue of an order in council with regard to the care to be exercised. More detailed rules with regard to the care to be exercised are deemed to include rules relating to the costs charged by the financial undertaking if the participant, consumer or client terminates a contract for a financial service or financial product and enters into a contract relating to that financial service or that financial product with another financial undertaking.'

In recent years further rules have been introduced with regard to provision of services with due care and these have been tightened up. Further details of the introduction of a so-called generic duty of care for financial service providers can be found in section 20.5 *infra*. In addition, there is an obligation to draw up and issue a service document (plus a cost-price model)[44] and an obligation with regard to the so-called 'financial driving license'. The latter means that if a customer is offered a product without advice (also known as 'execution only') other than an investment product (such as a mortgage), the undertaking must conduct a basic assessment to determine whether the product is appropriate for the customer concerned.[45] The undertaking is also then obliged to warn the customer if the product is not appropriate for him.[46] If the customer provides no or insufficient information concerning his knowledge and experience, the financial service provider must warn the customer that it will consequently be unable to examine whether the financial service or product is suitable for him. The service provider must then indicate to the customer that it is advisable to seek advice.[47]

20.4 INTERACTION BETWEEN PRIVATE LAW AND PUBLIC LAW

The obligations included in the Wft are a matter of a public law (also referred to as administrative law or supervision law) and are aimed at financial undertakings. As stated above, these obligations have an impact on the relationship between the undertaking and the customer. The question then arises as to what the consequences are of a violation of obligations under the Wft in the relationship between the financial undertaking and the customer.

Before the Wft came into force on January 1, 2007 it was unclear whether such a violation could lead to the nullity or voidability of the respective legal act by virtue of Article 3:40 of the BW.[48] This led to great legal uncertainty. After all, if a legal act is null or voidable, the entire performance up to that time must be undone.[49] This is complex in financial supervision law due to the often fluctuating values of financial

44. With effect from January 1, 2013, *see* Art. 4:25b of the Wft in conjunction with Arts 86f-86g of the Bgfo.
45. With effect from January 1, 2013, *see* Art. 4:24 paragraph 1 of the Wft in conjunction with Art. 80e of the Bgfo. In the case of investment services such an obligation already existed under Art. 4:24 paragraph 1 of the Wft. *See also* Van der Eerden & Silverentand 2015, pp. 338–339.
46. Art. 4:24 paragraph 2 of the Wft in conjunction with Art. 80e of the Bgfo. The product can still be offered, however.
47. Art. 4:24 paragraph 3 Wft in conjunction with Art. 80e of the Bgfo.
48. For example on the basis of error: Arts 6:228–230 of the BW.
49. *See* Arts 3:49–3:58 and 6:265–6:279 of the BW.

products, the long period for which contracts are concluded and the large number of interrelated transactions.[50] The introduction of the Wft created more clarity with regard to the foregoing in Article 1:23 of the Wft. This states: 'The legal validity of a private-law legal act performed contrary to the rules stated in or by virtue of this Act cannot be thereby impaired unless specified otherwise in this Act.'

Hence, if a legal act has been performed contrary to the Wft or derived regulations (such as the Bgfo), this does not mean in principle that such legal act is null or voidable. An exception to this principle only applies if the Wft explicitly states that a legal act can be affected – if it has been entered into contrary to the Wft.[51] This means that in the case of most violations of the Wft any legal acts performed contrary to the Wft will not be null and voidable. Rules under supervision law may play an important role, however, in the civil-law relationship between the financial undertaking and the customer.

Cherednychenko refers in this context to 'financial supervision private law'.[52] She states that from a legal-technical point of view conduct rules in the Wft concern the relationship between the undertaking and the supervisor and hence form part of administrative law. At the same time, however, they regulate the conduct of the financial undertaking in the relationship with the actual or potential customer and are intended partly to protect the latter. Conduct rules can therefore actually be classified as semi-private-law standards which influence the contract-law relationship between the financial undertaking and its actual or potential customer. Whereas standards under contract law are normally set *ex post* by the court, in the case of a duty of care under administrative law the standards are set *ex ante*. Another difference is that unlike a breach of a private-law standard, a breach of an administrative-law standard does not lead to reparatory sanctions in the form of compensation, but to a sanction to be determined by the supervisor – usually of a punitive nature. She states that this creates a field of tension.

20.5 THE GENERIC DUTY OF CARE FOR FINANCIAL SERVICE PROVIDERS[53]

With effect from January 1, 2014, Article 4:24a of the Wft has included the following obligation on financial service providers:[54]

---

50. Van der Eerden & Silverentand 2015, p. 23. *See also Parliamentary documents II* 2005/06, 29708, 19, p. 391.
51. In practice, however, there are only a few such explicit provisions, such as Art. 4:74 of the Wft which prohibits an intermediary from receiving commission from any party other than the provider. *See also* Van der Eerden & Silverentand 2015, p. 24 and for a further analysis Grundmann-van de Krol 2012, pp. 802–806.
52. Also referred to as regulatory private law, Cherednychenko 2012, pp. 86 and 88.
53. On September 21, 2012 the UvA Amsterdam Centre for Insurance Studies (ACIS) held a symposium on the generic duty of care featuring speeches by various specialists in the field of the duty of care. A summary can be found in De Jong 2012, pp. 425–428. A more in-depth analysis can be found in the collection of all lectures given, *see* Hendrikse & Rinkes 2012.
54. In the law of November 25, 2013 amending the Financial Supervision Act and a number of other acts (Financial Markets Amending Act 2014), *Bulletin of Acts and Decrees* 2013,

> '1. A financial service provider shall diligently take into account the legitimate interests of the consumer or beneficiary.
>
> 2. A financial service provider that provides advice shall act in the interest of the consumer or beneficiary.
>
> 3. With regard to the first and second paragraphs the Netherlands Authority for the Financial Markets only applies article 1:75 in the case of manifest abuses which may harm trust in the financial service provider or in the financial markets.
>
> 4. No later than three years after this article comes into force Our Minister shall send to the States General a report on the efficiency and effects of this article in practice.'

The wording of the original bill was:[55]

> '1. A financial service provider shall diligently take into account the legitimate interests of the consumer or beneficiary.
>
> 2. A financial service provider that provides advice shall act in the interest of the consumer or beneficiary.'

When the bill was introduced there was criticism from both the financial sector and from academia. An argument[56] against the bill was that the AFM would assess the duty of care on the basis of different standards than the Financial Services Complaints Board (Kifid) or the court. For example the court carefully weighs up all the interests involved and the interests of all stakeholders (including the entire customer population), whereas the AFM has a different focus. In practice this will result in customers, providers and intermediaries not knowing where they stand, leading to legal uncertainty. Assessment of conduct on the basis of purely civil-law standards is not the responsibility of the AFM and is the exclusive domain of the civil courts.

A second argument was that with such an open standard the AFM is actually seen as a type of pseudo-regulator, since it will fulfill this standard on the basis of its own insights (within its assigned mandate). Any act at variance with the AFM's interpretation will then be pursued as action contrary to the Wft. This not only results in a lack of clarity, but in practice also leads to a shift of regulatory authority to the AFM outside its assigned mandate.

A third argument was that the proposed open standard does not lend itself to the imposition of fines or pecuniary penalties. That is contrary to the principle of legality, namely the *nulla poena* principle. According to this principle a penalty may only be imposed for conduct if there was a law (or rule) in force when it took place

487. In the bill this obligation was referred to as a generic duty of care, i.e. in addition to the existing specific duties of care for financial undertakings.

55. *Parliamentary papers II* 2012/13, 33632, 2, p. 19. Subsequently, by means of a (modified) amendment, the current paragraphs 3 and 4 were added, *see Parliamentary documents II* 2012/13, 33632, 9 and *Parliamentary documents* II 2013/14, 33632, 14. The consultation text even included a third paragraph, which stated: 'A financial service provider shall in any case refrain from any acts or omissions which clearly have or could have detrimental consequences for the consumer, client or beneficiary.'

56. The stated arguments have been drawn among other things from the letter of the VvV and the NVB of October 18, 2012 in response to the proposal of the Financial Markets Amendment Act 2014.

that made the specific conduct a criminal offense. In other words, if a standard is not specific and it is therefore unclear when it has been violated, no penalties can be imposed.

A fourth argument was that as a result of the generic duty of care the AFM could theoretically almost be given *carte blanche* to act against actual or alleged careless acts. Consumers may soon start to feel that they do not need to be so critical, giving rise to a problem of moral hazard.

Finally, it was argued that insurers and banks from another EU Member State operating (with a European passport) in the Netherlands would not be (legally) bound by the generic duty of care. That would lead to unfair competition and a distortion of the level playing field.

The Council of State also issued a negative opinion on the bill.[57] An additional argument was that the duty (or duties) of care was/were already provided for in the BW[58] and the Wft[59] and the AFM had sufficient potential to play an enforcing role.[60] The general feeling was that such an article had only been included to provide the AFM with (new) guidelines for enforcement in the event of actual or alleged breaches of duties of care in the Wft.[61] The proposed article was ultimately approved, but with the aforementioned additions. In the explanatory notes to the latter amendment the following observations were made in this regard:[62]

'The proposed article 4:24a of the Wft provides for a generic duty of care for financial service providers so that the Netherlands Authority for the Financial Markets (AFM) can intervene in the event of a violation of the duty of care falling outside the scope of the Wft. After all, if article 4:24a of the Wft is not complied with, the AFM may impose a fine or incremental penalty (if a previous instruction has not been complied with). This article potentially leaves a great deal of leeway for the AFM. The AFM can fulfil the duty of care according to its own insight by enforcing this generic duty of care. Such fulfilment is not subject to any parliamentary scrutiny. The purpose of this amendment is to establish that interventions by the AFM based on

57. *Parliamentary papers II* 2012/13, 33632, 4. *See* also the *Financieele Dagblad* of June 8, 2013 in which T. Loonen considers the negative opinion of the Council of State and calls for the consumer to assume responsibility rather than relying on the legal article on duty of care included in the Wft.
58. *See* section 20.2 *supra*. Going to court is an option.
59. For a number of financial undertakings. *See* Arts 4:25 and 4:90 of the Wft, section 20.3 *supra*. *See also* Art. 4:59b of the Wft, which states that the manager of a UCITS must act in an honest, fair and professional manner for the UCITS which he manages and the participants in the UCITS which he manages and must refrain from conduct harmful to the integrity of the market (further elaborated in Art. 83 of the Bgfo). Art. 17 of the new directive on insurance distribution (*OJEU* 2015, L 26/19) also includes an obligation on Member States to ensure that when insurance distributors carry out insurance distribution, they always seek to protect their customers' interests in a loyal, fair and professional manner. The definition of insurance distributor is deemed to include an insurance intermediary, an ancillary insurance intermediary or an insurance undertaking.
60. *See inter alia* Arts 1:75, 1:79, 1:80 and 1:97 of the Wft.
61. Tjon Tjin Tai wondered in this regard whether a generic duty of care was a pleonasm (Tjon Tjin Tai 2012, p. 37). On the other hand, there were also a number of supporters, *see* De Jong 2012 and Hendrikse & Rinkes 2012.
62. *Parliamentary papers II* 2013/14, 33632, 14.

the violation of the generic duty of care can only take place in the event of manifest errors. The guiding principle must be that the care standard should preferably be fulfilled through generally binding rules. The AFM can only carry out enforcement on the basis of the generic duty of law if the serious nature of the violation and the urgency of enforcement means it is not possible to wait for generally binding rules to be established or amended. In addition, this amendment provides for the effect of the general duty of care to be evaluated. The general duty of care will be evaluated no later than three years after it comes into force.'

A (mandatory) evaluation of the generic duty of care was conducted by the Minister of Finance in accordance with Article 4:24a paragraph 4 of the Wft at the end of 2016. This provided no grounds for him to amend it. He stated as follows:[63]

'In summary the evaluation gives me no grounds to take measures. The embedding of the general duty of care in administrative law was introduced to supplement the consumer protection system (standard-setting effect) and as a safety net on the basis of which the AFM can conduct enforcement if there are no specific rules in the Wft (sanctioning effect). The arrangement is operating well in that regard. The parties did raise a number of points during the evaluation. However, these do not appear to result so much from the introduction of the general duty of care in the Wft, but seem to relate (more) to critical voices on the lack of sufficient legal protection in a general sense. In this letter I endorse the importance of transparency and openness (as far as possible) in the conduct of financial supervision and the use of legal remedies by the sector where necessary. There are disadvantages associated with the amendments to the legal system suggested by the consulted parties and it was not sufficiently shown that these proposals would or could sufficiently address the points made or that they would be necessary. In view of the lack of formal enforcement and administrative case law, I do see grounds, however, for a new evaluation of the general duty of care. By 1 January 2022 at the latest the States General will receive a report with the findings of this evaluation.'

20.6 CONCLUSION

In conclusion it can be stated that the duty of care has become a sensitive matter for financial undertakings. On the other hand, this area is of course nothing new. The De Ruiter Committee, for example, stated in its final report in 2006 that the provisions of the Wft with regard to investment institutions[64] should in its opinion also be declared applicable to funds in which an insurer is the sole participant and other forms of collective investment by insurers on behalf of their customers (known as unit-linked insurances or unit-linked investment funds).[65] In 2005 the AFM concluded

63. *Parliamentary papers I* 2016/17, 33632, E, p. 2.
64. Investment institutions are either an investment company (a legal entity which requests or obtains monies or other assets for collective investment to enable participants to share in the income) or an investment fund (assets not placed in an investment company including monies requested or obtained for collective investment to enable participants to share in the income from the investments). *See* Art. 1:1 of the Wft.
65. Recommendation 6 in the opinion of December 20, 2006 issued by the Committee on Transparency of Investment Insurances to the VvV. This committee conducted research

that the process relating to product development in financial undertakings was not well organized and that the same applied to the surveying of product risks and transparent communication on these risks with customers.[66]

In the field of consumer protection (and hence also the duty of care), regular modifications are made to European[67] and national laws and regulations and to the supervisors' agendas.[68] There is also progressive insight, driven in some cases by incidents but also by new case law. An example is whether consumer protection should also apply to small and medium-sized businesses (partly in response to the interest-rate derivatives scandal).[69] Another example is the introduction of a general ban on advertising of harmful financial products[70] and the guaranteeing of competence in the case of automated advice.[71]

Having regard to the above, it is expected that there will be more rules relating to the duty of care and that it will therefore be expanded. This will have an impact on the earnings model of financial undertakings.[72]

---

into the 'profiteering policy affair' ('woekerpolis affaire'). Unit-linked (UL) insurances are not investment institutions within the meaning of the Wft. However, if the regime that applied at that time to investment institutions had also applied to UL insurances, such an affair would probably have been less likely to occur. With the introduction of the Alternative Investment Fund Manager Directive on July 22, 2013, the requirements with regard to investment funds and investment companies were tightened up.

66. *See* the AFM booklet of October 2005 concerning 'Ongoing duty of care. Generic reporting of the investigation into the Duty of Care in the development and sale of products'. This booklet is still valid.
67. Such as the Insurance Mediation Directive II (IMD II), the MIFID II and the Packaged Investment Products (PRIPS) Regulation.
68. *See* the AFM Agenda 2017 and the AFM Activities Calendar 2017, www.afm.nl. This could also include the AFM's plans with regard to cost transparency and cost efficiency in investment services (also referred to as Total Costs of Ownership, TCO).
69. See the consultation document of the Ministry of Finance of September 1, 2016 on the 'Effectiveness and desired degree of protection for self-employed persons and SMEs in financial services and products. This introduced a new term, *beschermingsbehoeftigheid* ('protection neediness'). The purpose of the consultation was to gather information from stakeholders and experts on the effectiveness and desired degree of protection of self-employed persons and SMEs in financial services. With this consultation the Ministry of Finance gives stakeholders and experts an opportunity to contribute from their various perspectives. It is not certain at the outset that there will be an adjustment or expansion of legal protection of small business customers. The result of this consultation could also be that the current legal protection is sufficient. In the consultations on any additional protection, the advantages and disadvantages of additional protection will have to be weighed up. Following the end of the consultation period (which has now elapsed) the ministry is organizing meetings with stakeholders and experts to consult them on specific subjects in the consultation document. On the basis of these results, the current legal protection of small business customers will be assessed and consideration will be given to the desirability of any amendments or expansions.
70. AFM consultation of February 20, 2017 on a ban on advertising of harmful financial products. This ban is intended to come into force on July 1, 2017.
71. AFM Legislative letter of March 6, 2017.
72. A vision for 2020 can be found in the NautaDutilh booklet: '2020: Banks' Duty of Care'. https://www.nautadutilh.com/nl/information-centre/nieuws/2013/6/nautadutilh-publishes-

BIBLIOGRAPHY

Broekhuizen 2016
K.W.H. Broekhuizen, *Klantbelang, belangenconflict en zorgplicht* (diss. Amsterdam UvA), The Hague: Boom juridisch 2016.

Cherednychenko 2012
O.O. Cherednychenko, 'Naar een generieke zorgplicht voor verzekeraars en verzekeringstussenpersonen bij 'verzekeringsbeleggingsproducten' in de Wft?', in: M.L. Hendrikse & J.G.J. Rinkes (eds.), *Naar een (doorlopende) generieke zorgplicht voor verzekeraars en verzekeringstussenpersonen?*, Zutphen: Paris 2012, pp. 83–103.

Grundmann-van de Krol 2010
C.M. Grundmann-van de Krol, *Koersen in de mist: op weg naar transparante wetgeving?* (oratie Nijmegen), The Hague: Boom Juridische Uitgevers 2010.

Grundmann-van de Krol 2012
C.M. Grundmann-van de Krol with assistance from J.B.S. Hijink, 'Koersen door de Wet op het financieel toezicht', The Hague: Boom Juridische Uitgevers 2012.

't Hart 2012
F.M.A. 't Hart, 'De impact van het klantbelang op het verdienmodel', in: E.M. Dieben & F.M.A. 't Hart (eds.), *Klantbelang Centraal*, Amsterdam: NIBE-SVV 2012, pp. 27–69.

Hendrikse & Rinkes 2012
M.L. Hendrikse & J.G.J. Rinkes (eds.), *Naar een (doorlopende) generieke zorgplicht voor verzekeraars en verzekeringstussenpersonen?*, Zutphen: Paris 2012.

De Jong 2012
C.J. de Jong, 'Naar een (doorlopende) generieke zorgplicht voor verzekeraars en verzekeringstussenpersonen?', *FR* 2012, no. 11, pp. 425–428.

Schotsman 2013
R.J. Schotsman, 'Praktijkgids Wft. Financiële markten en ondernemingen onder toezicht', Amsterdam: NIBE-SVV 2013.

Tjong Tjin Tai 2012
T.F.E. Tjong Tjin Tai, 'Generieke zorgplicht in theorie en praktijk', in: M.L. Hendrikse & J.G.J. Rinkes (eds.), *Naar een (doorlopende) generieke zorgplicht voor verzekeraars en verzekeringstussenpersonen?*, Zutphen: Paris 2012, pp. 37–49.

Van der Eerden & Silverentand 2015
F.W.J. van der Eerden & L.J. Silverentand (eds.), *Hoofdlijnen Wft*, Deventer: Wolters Kluwer 2015.

report-2020-banks-duty-of-care. *See also* 't Hart 2012 for the influence of the customer's interest on the earnings model of financial undertakings.

21. Market Abuse

R.A.M. Houben

21.1 INTRODUCTION

Compliance officers of companies which have issued shares or bonds[1] and/or are listed on a (licensed) securities exchange or compliance officers who work for investment companies (including asset managers) have to deal with the supervision of compliance with rules on market abuse in and by their company.

The Ministry of Finance has concisely summarized the importance of rules to combat market abuse as follows:[2]

> 'Insider dealing and market manipulation, both covered by the expression market abuse, are serious offences which harm the integrity of the financial markets and hence undermine the public's trust in these markets. Market integrity is essential for the proper operation of the financial markets. If markets are no longer sound, investors lose trust, with the possible result that investors and companies seeking capital are no longer prepared to participate in the financial markets. In view of the important economic function which the financial markets fulfil, namely bringing together providers and seekers of capital, a lack of market integrity and trust may therefore have serious consequences. It is therefore essential to provide adequate rules to prevent market abuse and ensure that investors are provided with complete, accurate and accessible information, so that every investor can make investment decisions based on the same information.'

The legal framework with regard to market abuse was amended and expanded in 2016 by the MAR and MAD II, which became applicable to all Member States on July 3,

1. The 'issuer'; *see* Art. 3 paragraph 1(21) of the MAR for the definition of issuer.
2. *Parliamentary Papers II* 2015/16, 34455, 3, pp. 1–2.

2016. The MAR[3] and MAD II[4] replaced the 2003 MAD.[5] The MAR, like all European regulations, has direct effect in the Netherlands and has largely replaced the relevant provisions of the Financial Supervision Act and laws and regulations derived from it.[6] MAD II includes criminal sanctions for breach of market abuse provisions and, to the extent necessary, has been implemented in the Wft and the Wed.[7] Although the scope of the MAR has been expanded in various subareas compared to MAD, its impact is limited because the Dutch legislator had already anticipated a number of matters. The same applies to the provisions of criminal law.[8] In addition to the MAR and MAD II, there are various implementing regulations and delegated regulations issued by the EC which jointly make up the European legal framework.[9]

The legal provisions on market abuse are extensive, have a broad scope[10] and are difficult to comprehend.[11] In addition, in the event of non-compliance, they give rise to major risks to employees and directors in the form of penalties, liability and criminal law enforcement.[12]

In general the following can be considered the most important elements in the market abuse regime:

- the prohibition of insider dealing;
- the prohibition of communicating inside information unlawfully to others;
- the obligation on issuers to disclose inside information relating to themselves; and
- the prohibition of manipulation of the market.

Under the (new) regime of the MAR these elements have remained in place with a number of additions, amendments and enhancements.[13]

3. The MAR came into force on July 2, 2014 and became applicable to all Member States on July 3, 2016. Reference is made to Art. 39 paragraph 2 of the MAR.
4. MAD II came into force on July 2, 2014 and became applicable to all Member States on July 3, 2016. Reference is made to Art. 13 of the MAD II.
5. MAD came into force on April 12, 2003 and became applicable to all Member States on October 12, 2004.
6. Section 5.4 of the Wft, entitled 'Rules to prevent market abuse and governing operations in markets in financial instruments', has ceased to apply completely, with the exception of the (amended) Arts 5:68–5:69. Art. 5:25i of the Wft has also ceased to apply; *see* section 21.3 *infra*. The Market Abuse Decree Wft will also largely cease to apply as the (draft) Decree on the Implementation of the MAR is introduced.
7. By means of the MAR and MAD II Implementation Act and the (draft) Decree on the Implementation of the MAR.
8. Van Straaten & Schouten 2016, p. 483.
9. The annex to this chapter contains a full overview of the applicable legal framework.
10. The prohibition of insider dealing in securities, for example, applies to everyone in the Netherlands.
11. Partly because the legal framework has become (more) European.
12. Insider dealing and market manipulation are criminal offenses and are deemed to be offenses under Arts 1 and 2 of the Wed. *See also* Doorenbos 2016 for an explanation of the consequences of the market abuse regime in economic criminal law.
13. Van Straaten & Schouten 2016, p. 480; Dinant 2017, pp. 343–344.

This chapter outlines a number of elements of the market abuse regime.[14] Section 21.2 deals with the prohibition of insider dealing, including the prohibition of communicating inside information unlawfully to others. Section 21.3 deals with the obligation on issuers to disclose inside information. Section 21.4 deals with the duty to investigate and report market abuse. Section 21.5 deals with the obligation to draw up 'insider lists' and finally section 21.6 deals with market manipulation.

21.2 INSIDER DEALING[15]

21.2.1 Introduction

Insider dealing is an offense and is prohibited for everyone. A person who has inside information has certain confidential, non-public information. This information may relate, for example, to a forthcoming acquisition or an issuer's payment problems. A person may have inside information due to his employment, profession or duties as an issuer (as a member of the Executive Board, a legal or financial adviser, or an employee). It is also possible that a person may 'unintentionally' have inside information. For example, because he hears his neighbor or acquaintance, who is a member of the Executive Board of an issuer, talking in the garden or in the train. Once disclosed, inside information can affect the price of the issuer's shares, for example. The issuer is required to disclose information relating directly to it as soon as possible, so that all investors are aware of this information and all investors have an equal opportunity to obtain a good investment return.[16]

The importance of the prohibition of insider dealing is described by the EC as follows:[17]

> 'The essential characteristic of insider dealing consists in an unfair advantage being obtained from inside information to the detriment of third parties who are unaware of such information and, consequently, the undermining of the integrity of financial markets and investor confidence. Consequently, the prohibition against insider dealing should apply where a person who is in possession of inside information takes unfair advantage of the benefit gained from that information by entering into market transactions in accordance with that information by acquiring or disposing of, by attempting to acquire or dispose of, by cancelling or amending, or by attempting to cancel or amend, an order to acquire or dispose of, for his own account or for the account of a third party,

14. A lot of literature has been published on market abuse with regard to the regime both before and after the MAR. This area is also very extensive and there is a substantial amount of case law. This chapter provides a brief introduction. More in-depth analysis can be found in the bibliography.
15. This section deals only with the main points of the prohibition of insider dealing. For more literature on this area or subject, *see* Italianer 2008; Van der Eerden & Silverentand 2015, pp. 399–403; Van Straaten & Schouten 2016; Langendijk & Wilmink 2016; AFM booklets 2016/1 and 2016/6. If literature refers to the (no longer valid) articles of the Wft, these must be seen in the light of the current regime of the MAR and MAD II.
16. According to the AFM in its booklet 2016/1, p. 4.
17. Recital 23 of the MAR.

directly or indirectly, financial instruments to which that information relates. Use of inside information can also consist of trading in emission allowances and derivatives thereof and of bidding in the auctions of emission allowances or other auctioned products based thereon that are held.'

The MAR includes three prohibitions,[18] namely the prohibition to:

- engage or attempt to engage in insider dealing;[19]
- recommend that another person engage in insider dealing or induce another person to engage in insider dealing;[20] or
- unlawfully disclose inside information.[21]

Inside information is deemed to mean:[22] 'Information of a precise nature, which has not been made public, relating, directly or indirectly, to one or more issuers or to one or more financial instruments, and which, if it were made public, would be likely to have a significant effect on the prices of those financial instruments or on the price of related derivative financial instruments.'

In addition, for commodity derivatives and emission allowances or associated auctioned products there is an independent definition of the term inside information.[23] In the case of persons charged with the execution of orders for financial instruments, inside information also means information conveyed by a client and relating to the client's pending orders in financial instruments, which is of a precise nature, relating, directly or indirectly, to one or more issuers or to one or more financial instruments, and which, if it were made public, would be likely to have a significant effect on the prices of those financial instruments, the price of related spot commodity contracts, or the price of related derivative financial instruments.[24]

Information shall be deemed to be of a precise nature[25] if it indicates:

- a set of circumstances which exists or which may reasonably be expected to come into existence; and
- an event which has occurred or which may reasonably be expected to occur, where it is specific enough to enable a conclusion to be drawn as to the possible effect of that set of circumstances or event on the prices of the financial instruments or the related derivative financial instrument, the related spot commodity contracts, or the auctioned products based on the emission allowances.

---

18. Art. 14 MAR. Before July 3, 2016 these prohibitions were included (among others) in Arts 5:56–5:57 of the Wft.
19. Further elaborated in Art. 7 and 8 paragraph 1 of the MAR. Exceptions to the prohibition are included in Arts 5, 6 and 9 of the MAR.
20. Further elaborated in Arts 7 and 8 paragraphs 2 and 3 of the MAR.
21. Further elaborated in Arts 7 and 10 of the MAR.
22. Art. 7 paragraph 1(a) of the MAR.
23. Art. 7 paragraph 1(b) and (c) of the MAR.
24. Inside information relating to trading, see Art. 7 paragraph 1(d) of the MAR. *See* AFM booklet 2016/1, p. 7. For the subject of 'market surveys' (introduced as a new subject by the MAR), reference is made to Jennen 2016; Dinant 2017, pp. 358–362; Langendijk & Wilmink 2016, pp. 206–211.
25. As referred to in Art. 7 paragraph 1 of the MAR.

In this respect in the case of a protracted process that is intended to bring about, or that results in, particular circumstances or a particular event, those future circumstances or that future event, and also the intermediate steps of that process which are connected with bringing about or resulting in those future circumstances or that future event, may be deemed to be precise information.[26] An intermediate step in a protracted process shall be deemed to be inside information if, by itself, it satisfies the criteria of inside information as referred to in the MAR.[27]

It must concern information which, if it were made public, would be likely to have a significant effect on the price of financial instruments, associated derivative financial instruments, related commodity spot contracts or auctioned products based on emission allowances. The foregoing refers to information which an investor, acting reasonably, will probably use in part as basis for his investment decisions.[28]

Insider dealing is deemed to have taken place if a person who has inside information uses it to purchase or sell, directly or indirectly, financial instruments to which such information relates for his own account or for the account of third parties. The use of inside information by canceling or amending an order[29] relating to a financial instrument to which the inside information relates whereas the order was placed before the person concerned had access to the inside information is also deemed to be insider dealing.[30]

Inside information is deemed to have been disclosed unlawfully if a person possesses inside information and discloses it to any other person, except where the disclosure is made in the normal exercise of an employment, a profession or duties.[31] An associated condition, however, is that the person who receives the information has a duty of confidentiality.[32] Unlawful disclosure of inside information is also deemed to include the onward disclosure of recommendations or inducements as referred to in the MAR[33] if the person making such recommendation or inducement knew or ought to have known that such onward disclosure was based on inside information.[34]

21.2.2 Scope of prohibition

The prohibition of insider dealing applies to financial instruments:[35]

- admitted to trading on a regulated market or for which a request for admission to trading on a regulated market has been made;

26. Art. 7 paragraph 2 of the MAR.
27. Art. 7 paragraph 3 of the MAR.
28. Art. 7 paragraph 4 of the MAR.
29. Or a bid in an auction of emission allowances or other auctioned products based on emission allowances.
30. Art. 8 paragraph 1 of the MAR.
31. Art. 10 paragraph 1 of the MAR.
32. Following from the final sentence of Art. 17 paragraph 8 of the MAR. *See also* AFM booklet 2016/3.
33. *See* Art. 8 paragraph 2 of the MAR.
34. Art. 10 paragraph 2 of the MAR.
35. Art. 2 paragraph 1 of the MAR.

- traded on a Multilateral Trading Facility (MTF), admitted to trading on an MTF or for which a request for admission to trading on an MTF has been made;
- traded on an Organized Trading Facility (OTF);[36]
- not covered by the previous definitions and the price or value of which depends on or has an effect on the price or value of a financial instrument referred to in those points, including, but not limited to, credit default swaps and contracts for difference.

The prohibition also applies to behavior or transactions, including bids, relating to the auctioning on an auction platform authorized as a regulated market of emission allowances or other auctioned products based thereon, including when auctioned products are not financial instruments, pursuant to Regulation (EU) No. 1031/2010.[37]

The AFM supervises compliance with rules relating to inside information.[38] It takes its duties as supervisor of the prohibition of insider dealing very seriously.[39] In so doing it actively monitors the conduct, orders and transactions of investors in the market. If particular acts breach the prohibition, a sanction is imposed under administrative or criminal law.[40]

The AFM states that it is responsible for compliance with the prohibition of insider dealing relating to:[41]

- all acts performed in the territory of the Netherlands; and
- acts performed abroad relating to instruments which have been admitted to trading on a regulated market, for which a request for admission to trading on such a market has been filed, which are auctioned in an auction or which are traded on an MTF or OTF, or for which a request has been filed for admission to trading on an MTF operating in the territory of the Netherlands.

Whether such a transaction has actually taken place through the systems of the market in financial instruments in question is irrelevant. Transactions in bonds admitted to trading on Euronext Amsterdam, for example, also fall within the scope of the prohibition if a transaction in these financial instruments takes place in over-the-counter (OTC) trading or, for example, through the systems of another platform. Insider dealing in or from the Netherlands is therefore prohibited. It is also prohibited if it relates to financial instruments which, although not admitted to trading on a Dutch regulated market, are admitted to trading on a European regulated market. A transaction is deemed to be conducted in the Netherlands if the person who conducts

36. The terms MTF and OTF have been taken from MiFID II and MiFIR.
37. Commission Regulation (EU) No. 1031/2010 of November 12, 2010 on the timing, administration and other aspects of auctioning of greenhouse gas emission allowances pursuant to Directive 2003/87/EC of the European Parliament and of the Council establishing arrangements for greenhouse gas emission allowances trading within the Community, *OJEU* 2010, L 302/1.
38. It has this mandate on the basis of Art. 1:25 paragraph 2 of the Wft.
39. *See* AFM booklet 2016/1, pp. 4–5.
40. That means it can impose an administrative fine or file a report with the Public Prosecution Department.
41. AFM booklet 2016/1, p. 8.

or effects it is located in the Netherlands or abroad, whereas the transaction takes place through the systems of a market in financial instruments in the Netherlands. A transaction is also deemed to be conducted in the Netherlands if the counterparty (in the case of a private transaction) is located in the Netherlands.

A transaction is deemed to be conducted from the Netherlands if the person is located in the Netherlands when the transaction is conducted or effected. In this case, the transaction takes place through the systems of a market in financial instruments established abroad, or with a counterparty abroad (if it concerns a transaction under a contract, for example). The location of the company which performs the transaction is irrelevant, particularly because the prohibition relates to the person who conducts the transaction and not that company. It can be seen from its scope that the prohibition of insider dealing also applies to financial instruments traded on an MTF or OTF.[42]

21.2.3 Applicability of the prohibition

The prohibition of insider dealing applies to every person or legal entity having inside information. A distinction is drawn between two categories of persons who may have inside information, namely 'primary' and 'secondary insiders'.[43] Primary insiders are persons having a particular relationship with the issuer, such as members of the executive and supervisory boards of an issuer or participants in trading in emission allowances or persons participating in the capital of the issuer. Persons who have access to inside information as a result of their profession, business or duties also qualify as primary insiders, as do persons who have inside information as a result of participation in criminal activities.

It is therefore irrelevant whether the persons deemed to be primary insiders know or should know that they have inside information. On the basis of the fact that they occupy a particular position or have a particular relationship with the issuer, they are (always) assumed to know when the information which they hold qualifies as inside information.

Secondary insiders are all persons other than primary insiders. In the case of secondary insiders, however, it must be demonstrated that they know or should know that the information they hold is inside information. Secondary insiders are less likely to be aware that they have inside information.[44]

42. AFM booklet 2016/1, p. 9.
43. Art. 8 paragraph 4 of the MAR. In the case of a legal entity, the foregoing also applies to the natural persons who under national law were involved in the decision to acquire or dispose of or to cancel or amend an order for the account of the legal entity in question, *see* Art. 8 paragraph 5 of the MAR.
44. The distinction between 'primary' and secondary' insiders was already known and applicable before the MAR came into force. An observation regarding insiders can be found in 't Hart 2016. *See also* section 21.5 *infra*.

21.3 PUBLIC DISCLOSURE OF INSIDE INFORMATION[45]

21.3.1 Introduction

Another important element in the market abuse regime is the immediate disclosure of inside information by issuers with regard to information that relates to themselves.[46] A transparent market in which companies inform the investors fully, correctly and promptly is a market that maximizes the trust of market participants. This minimizes risks, thereby helping to keep the costs of capital as low as possible, which is in the interests of both companies and the investing public. In addition, the fastest possible publication ensures that insider dealing is prevented as far as possible.[47]

The issuer discloses the inside information in such a way that it is rapidly accessible and complete, can be assessed accurately and promptly by the public and if applicable is added to the AFM register. This inside information is distributed:[48]

- among the widest possible public in a non-discriminatory manner;
- free of charge;
- simultaneously throughout the EU.

Inside information can be issued to media directly or through a third party so that the public can have confidence in efficient distribution. The inside information is issued using electronic resources that ensure that the completeness, integrity and confidentiality of the information are maintained during the transmission, and will clearly state:[49]

- that the issued information is inside information;
- the identity of the issuer or participant in the emission allowances market;
- the identity of the person making the disclosure;
- the subject of the inside information; and
- the date and time of the disclosure to the media.

The content of the press release must be clear and not misleading. A specific headline, to which reference can be made and including a clear summary of the report, is recommended. The press release must not be combined with advertising for the company's activities. The information must be posted on the issuer's website and remain accessible there for at least five years.

45. For literature on this area or subject *see* the very extensive (legal comparison) study by G.T.J. Hoff concerning the disclosure of price-sensitive information (Hoff 2011). *See also* Hoff 2016 for a consideration of the disclosure of price-sensitive information in the new MAR regime, as well as Dinant 2017, pp. 435–348 and Langendijk & Wilmink 2016, pp. 200–205. For a practical translation *see* AFM booklet 2016/3.
46. Art. 17 paragraph 1 of the MAR. Before the MAR came into force, this obligation was in Art. 5:25i paragraph 2 of the Wft. Under Art. 17 paragraph 2 of the MAR this obligation also applies to participants in the emission allowances market.
47. AFM booklet 2016/3, p. 4.
48. Art. 2 of the Implementing Regulation for article 17 of the MAR.
49. Art. 3 of the Implementing Regulation for article 17 of the MAR.

21.3.2 Definition of inside information

Which information is inside information differs depending on the company and sector and also depends on market sentiment and recent developments. That also depends on questions such as how up to date the information is, to what extent such information adds to existing information on the same subject and to what extent it is new information. The extent to which the disclosure of information could have a significant effect on the price is also determined by the nature of the financial instruments concerned. Information that has a significant effect on the price of one specific financial instrument (for example a share) does not necessarily have to have a significant effect on the prices of other types of financial instrument (such as bonds). There is no hard, uniform formula for determining when there is a significant effect on the price. An issuer itself is responsible for assessing whether there is inside information. It knows what is important for the institution and hence for actual or potential investors in the company.[50]

The AFM gives the following examples of possible inside information:

- important facts concerning the financial position and/or results, such as announcements of periodic financial results;
- important facts concerning the strategy of the company, such as the purchase or sale of important participating interests and/or business units;
- important facts concerning capital/control/governance, such as the consolidation or division of shares.[51]

The AFM also gives examples of situations which must be avoided in this regard, such as:

- deferring publication merely because it is not yet possible to provide complete clarity;
- deferment merely to protect the image of the company or of the members of the Executive Board;
- waiting until the next regular report before disclosing inside information;
- in the case of bad news, postponing until the situation or event has been rectified.[52]

Finally, the AFM provides examples of situations in which the issuer must in any event divulge information, such as:

- disclosing both good and bad news as soon as possible;
- disclosing deviations from previously published forecasts or targets as soon as possible;

50. AFM booklet 2016/3, p. 9. The AFM recommends disclosure of the information if there is doubt as to whether the information held by the issuer can be considered inside information that relates directly to the issuer.
51. Further examples can be found in AFM booklet 2016/3, pp. 9–11.
52. Ibid.

- considering the publication of a press release if there is an inaccurate rumor in the market if the company's response could cause a significant price or volume movement;
- arranging for a press release to be published if inside information has accidentally been distributed in an interview or presentation;
- issuing clear and unambiguous forecasts or refraining from giving any forecasts.[53]

21.3.3 Delay of disclosure of inside information

Situations may arise in which an issuer or a participant in the emission allowances market can decide to defer the disclosure of inside information.[54] There are three cumulative conditions in which deferment is permitted:

- immediate disclosure is likely to prejudice the legitimate interests of the issuer or emission allowance market participant;[55]
- delay of disclosure is not likely to mislead the public; and
- the issuer or emission allowance market participant is able to ensure the confidentiality of that information.
- As soon as any of the above conditions cease to be fulfilled, the respective inside information must be disclosed as rapidly as possible.

Immediately after the disclosure of deferred inside information, the issuer or emission allowance market participant must inform the AFM that the obligation to disclose inside information as soon as possible was deferred.[56] If an issuer defers the disclosure of inside information, he must state in writing how the deferment conditions were fulfilled. The minimum details which the issuer must maintain in order to continue to fulfill the deferment conditions are:[57]

- the dates and times when: a) the inside information first existed within the issuer or the emission allowance market participant, b) the decision to delay the disclosure of inside information was made, c) the issuer or emission allowance market participant is likely to disclose the inside information;

---

53. Ibid. Although such guidance is useful for everyday practice, it does not constitute the issuing of any legal qualification. There is a considerable amount of case law in this area and much depends on the specific circumstances of the case. Nevertheless there is a tendency whereby such booklets are elevated to the status of 'pseudo-legislation', which does nothing to promote legal certainty (*lex certa*).
54. Art. 17 paragraph 4 of the MAR. See also AFM booklet 2016/3, pp. 12–15 and in the literature referred to at the beginning of this section *supra* for more detailed consideration of these conditions.
55. According to Dinant the first condition appears to differ from the condition set by the legislation prior to July 3, 2016. Under previous legislation the issuer could defer in order to protect his legitimate interests, while the MAR sets the condition that damage is likely to be caused to these interests as a result of the disclosure (Dinant 2017, p. 347). See also the lapsed Art. 5:25i paragraph 3(a) of the Wft.
56. Art. 17 paragraph 4, final sentence, of the MAR.
57. Art. 4 of the implementing regulation for article 17 of the MAR.

- the identity of the persons within the issuer or emission allowance market participant responsible for: a) making the decision to delay disclosure and deciding on the start of the delay and its likely end, b) ensuring the ongoing monitoring of the conditions for the delay, c) making the decision to publicly disclose the inside information, d) providing the requested information about the delay and the written explanation to the competent authority;
- evidence of the initial fulfillment of the conditions and of any change of this fulfillment during the delay period, including: a) the information barriers which have been put in place internally and with regard to third parties to prevent access to inside information by persons other than those who require it for the normal exercise of their employment, profession or duties within the issuer or emission allowance market participant, b) the arrangements put in place to disclose the relevant inside information as soon as possible where the confidentiality is no longer ensured.

21.4 PREVENTION AND DETECTION OF MARKET ABUSE[58]

21.4.1 Introduction

The MAR includes the obligation that if a person or legal entity reasonably suspects that the prohibition of insider dealing or market manipulation has been breached, or an attempted breach has taken place, he/it is obliged to report such suspicion to the competent authority without delay. In addition, the MAR has introduced a duty to investigate market abuse. This means that arrangements, systems and procedures must be established and maintained in companies with the aim of preventing and investigating actual or attempted market abuse.[59]

The persons or legal entities referred to in the MAR are: (i) market operators of regulated markets, (ii) investment companies operating a trading platform and (iii) any person or legal entity arranging or executing transactions professionally in relation to financial instruments. The third category is deemed to include any person professionally engaged in the receipt and onward transmission of orders or the execution of transactions in financial instruments.[60] This therefore includes own-account traders who may have been excluded from a licensing obligation before the MAR came into force.

58. For specific literature on this subject *see* AFM booklet 2016/2; Dinant 2017, pp. 349–353; Uitermark & Wilmink 2016; Langendijk & Wilmink 2016, pp. 189–198.
59. Art. 16 paragraphs 1 and 2 of the MAR, further elaborated in Delegated Regulation concerning Article 16 of the MAR. An attempt is deemed to mean, for example, a cancelation or amendment of an order or transaction. The AFM is the competent authority in the Netherlands. Before the MAR came into force such a reporting duty existed for investment companies in the Netherlands (also referred to as '*klikplicht*' or 'obligation to snitch') and was included in Arts 5:62–5:63 of the Wft. *See also* 't Hart 2008.
60. Art. 3 paragraph 1(28) of the MAR.

The disclosure required to the competent authority (the AFM) is made by means of a Suspicious Transaction and Order Report (STOR).[61] The MAR requires that all suspicious orders are reported, regardless of whether they have been executed (for example if a broker has refused to place an order for a client), as well as all transactions which may constitute actual or attempted market abuse. Attempts may consist of, but are not limited to, situations in which the activity was started but not completed. For example as a result of interim intervention, a technical problem or a non-executed order. The obligation to submit STORs also applies to OTC derivatives trading in which the underlying instrument is traded on a regulated market, a multilateral trading facility or an organized trading facility. The obligation applies regardless of the capacity in which the order was entered, whether the transaction has been executed (i.e. for own account or for the account of a client) and regardless of the nature of the clients concerned.[62]

According to the AFM the notifying persons[63] are not always in a position to determine whether transactions and/or orders are suspicious. For example, if they know they are only one of the brokers (intermediaries) used by the client, as a result of which they do not have a complete picture of the trading. Companies must therefore take into account all information which they have available, such as other transactions and/or orders. There may also be cases in which there are good reasons or particular indications on which to base a suspicion of market abuse, but of which the company is not certain. Such uncertainty must not be a reason for non-disclosure, but that must be clearly stated in the STOR. In a situation in which a chain of market participants is involved in executing an order and/or effecting a transaction, each person or legal entity subject to the MAR has an obligation to report suspicions of market abuse. Reporting by one company in the chain does not discharge another company of its duty to report its own suspicions of market abuse with regard to the same or related transactions and/orders.[64]

21.4.2 Active investigation[65]

The MAR obliges companies to establish and maintain arrangements, systems and procedures to investigate suspicious orders and transactions. This means that a company must continually analyze and evaluate its operations (including the organization, customer base, asset classes and markets) in the light of the handling of risks of market abuse. In connection with the investigation of actual or attempted market abuse, companies must therefore have a system that is able to analyze each order and transaction, individually and on a comparative basis, and that issues warnings for further analysis. In the vast majority of cases a highly or fully automated monitoring system will therefore be necessary. After all, as soon as a company is to perform trading activities – particularly if there is little or no contact with a front

61. A template for the STOR can be found in the annex to the Delegated Regulation for Article 16 of the MAR.
62. These may therefore be institutional, professional or retail clients.
63. For example the compliance officer.
64. According to the AFM. *See also* AFM brochure 2016/2 and the website www.AFM.nl.
65. Arts 2–3 of the Delegated Regulation for Article 16 of the MAR.

office that could flag suspicious orders and transactions – it will be very difficult to investigate suspicious orders and transactions continuously and effectively without an automated system.

It is important that the monitoring system used is actually effective and among other things able to assess each order and transaction individually and in comparison with each other. A company fulfills the MAR if the inspection level is effective and appropriate in relation to the extent and nature of the business activities which the company performs. In this connection the company will not readily be able to escape a degree of automation of its monitoring system. In assessing the extent to which the automation of the system must be carried out, companies must take account of the type and number of transactions and orders that must be monitored. This could include:

- the type of financial instruments traded and the markets on which they are traded;
- the frequency and volume of the orders and transactions;
- the scale, complexity and/or nature of the company.

For a company of limited size it may be sufficient to use a relatively simple automated system, whereas for more complex and advanced companies an extensive, tailor-made system is required in order to effectively monitor the order and transaction flow. In any case the monitoring system, whether automated or otherwise, must relate to all trading activities.

The company must be able to explain on request to the AFM how the alerts are generated by the system and why the chosen level of automation is appropriate. Furthermore, there must always be human interpretation in the investigation of market abuse. This plays an important role. After all, the most effective form of monitoring is a mix of automated and human interpretation. The systems which trading platforms use to investigate market abuse must include software that is able to read, reconstruct, replay and analyze order book data retrospectively. This allows proper analysis of the activity and dynamics of a trading activity.[66]

21.5 INSIDER LISTS[67]

Issuers or any person acting on their behalf or on their account, shall draw up a list of all persons who have access to inside information and who are working for them under a contract of employment, or otherwise performing tasks through which they have access to inside information, such as advisers, accountants or credit rating

66. AFM booklet 2016/2, pp. 8–9.
67. For specific literature on this area or subject see AFM booklet 2016/1, pp. 25–26; Dinant 2017, pp. 354–355; Italianer & Dorant 2013, p. 205; 't Hart 2016; Langendijk & Wilmink 2016, pp. 211–214. The MAR also includes extensive provisions for the reporting of transactions in own shares by persons with managerial responsibility. Before the MAR came into force, such provisions were found in Art. 5:60 of the Wft. *See also* Art. 19 of the MAR and the Implementing Regulation for Article 19 of the MAR and AFM booklet 2016/1, pp. 18–22. For more in-depth information on this subject *see* Schutte 2008; Dinant 2017, pp. 355–358; Langendijk & Wilmink 2016, pp. 215–221.

agencies.[68] This list must be constantly updated and if requested must be made available as soon as possible to the competent authority.[69] The list must be drawn up in accordance with the template of the EC.[70]

Issuers or persons who act on their behalf must also take all reasonable measures to ensure that the persons on the insider list declare in writing that they are aware of the legal and regulatory duties entailed by their activities, as well as the penalties that apply to insider dealing and unlawful disclosure of inside information. If another person draws up and amends this list on behalf of the issuer, the issuer remains responsible for compliance with the obligation to draw up an insider list.[71]

The list must in any case contain the following information:

- the identity of all persons who have access to inside information;
- the reason for inclusion in the insider list;
- the date and time at which those persons gained access to the inside information;
- the date on which the list was drawn up.[72]

The list must be continuously updated, for example if a new person has access to inside information or a person no longer has inside information. The list must be kept for five years after it has been drawn up or updated.[73]

Issuers whose instruments are traded on an SME growth market are exempt from drawing up the insider list if they fulfill the following two conditions:

- The issuer concerned takes all reasonable steps to ensure that everyone who has access to inside information is aware of the associated legal and regulatory obligations and of the sanctions associated with insider dealing and unlawful disclosure of inside information.
- The issuer concerned is able to issue an insider list to the competent authority on request.[74]

The obligation to draw up and maintain an insider list applies to:

- issuers who have requested or approved admission of their financial instruments to trading on a regulated market in a Member State, or whose instruments are traded on the basis of their request or with approval on an MTF or OTF;[75]

68. It should be noted that there is a difference between primary insiders and secondary insiders. See section 21.2 *supra*. *See also* 't Hart 2016, pp. 484–487. He distinguishes three regimes of insiders.
69. Art. 18 paragraph 1 of the MAR. The AFM is the competent authority in the Netherlands.
70. Art. 2 paragraph 3 and Annex I of the Implementing Regulation for Article 18 of the MAR.
71. Art. 18 paragraph 2 of the MAR.
72. Art. 18 paragraph 3 of the MAR.
73. Art. 18 paragraphs 4 and 5 of the MAR. On its website the AFM provides a number of further guidelines on dealing with insider lists and non-disclosed inside information, *see* https://www.afm.nl/nl-nl/professionals/onderwerpen/marktmisbruik/openbaarmaking-voorwetenschap.
74. Art. 18 paragraph 6 of the MAR.
75. *See* note 36 *supra*.

- emission allowance market participants if the information concerns their activities;
- any auction platform, auctioneer and auction monitor in relation to auctions of emission allowances or other auctioned products based thereon that are held.[76]

21.6 MARKET MANIPULATION[77]

21.6.1 Prohibition of market manipulation

A person shall not engage in or attempt to engage in market manipulation.[78] For the purposes of the MAR, market manipulation shall comprise the following activities:[79]

- entering into a transaction, placing an order to trade or any other behavior which: (i) gives, or is likely to give, false or misleading signals as to the supply of, demand for, or price of, a financial instrument, a related spot commodity contract or an auctioned product based on emission allowances; or (ii) secures, or is likely to secure, the price of one or several financial instruments, a related spot commodity contract or an auctioned product based on emission allowances at an abnormal or artificial level; unless the person entering into a transaction, placing an order to trade or engaging in any other behavior establishes that such transaction, order or behavior have been carried out for legitimate reasons, and conform with an accepted market practice;[80]
- entering into a transaction, placing an order to trade or any other activity or behavior which affects or is likely to affect the price of one or several financial instruments, a related spot commodity contract or an auctioned product based on emission allowances, which employs a fictitious device or any other form of deception or contrivance;
- disseminating information through the media, including the Internet, or by any other means, which gives, or is likely to give, false or misleading signals as to the supply of, demand for, or price of, a financial instrument, a related spot commodity contract or an auctioned product based on emission allowances or secures, or is likely to secure, the price of one or several financial instruments, a related spot commodity contract or an auctioned product based on emission allowances at an abnormal or artificial level, including the dissemination of rumors, where the person who made the

76. Art. 18 paragraphs 7 and 8 of the MAR.
77. For specific literature on this area or subject *see* Raas 2008 (the situation before the entry into force of the MAR). For a practical description *see* AFM booklet 2016/4.
78. Art. 15 of the MAR. Before the MAR came into force the prohibition of market manipulation was included in Art. 5:58 paragraph 1 of the Wft.
79. Art. 12 of the MAR.
80. As laid down in accordance with Art. 13 of the MAR. This article concerns market practices that are accepted and therefore not seen as market manipulation.

dissemination knew, or ought to have known, that the information was false or misleading;[81]

- transmitting false or misleading information or providing false or misleading inputs in relation to a benchmark where the person who made the transmission or provided the input knew or ought to have known that it was false or misleading, or any other behavior which manipulates the calculation of a benchmark.[82]

21.6.2 Scope of the prohibition of market manipulation and exceptions

The prohibition of market manipulation applies to the same financial instruments as the prohibition of insider dealing[83] and in addition to:

- spot commodity contracts, which are not wholesale energy products, where the transaction, order or behavior has an effect on the price or value of a financial instrument;[84]
- types of financial instruments, including derivative contracts or derivative instruments for the transfer of credit risk, where the transaction, order, bid or behavior has or is likely to have an effect on the price or value of a spot commodity contract where the price or value depends on the price or value of those financial instruments; and
- behavior in relation to benchmarks.[85]

The AFM is the competent authority for ensuring compliance with the prohibition of market manipulation.[86] It has issued various interpretations of what is meant by market abuse.[87] There are two exceptions to the prohibition of market manipulation. The first exception relates to trading in own shares in a buy-back program and financial instrument stabilization measures.[88] Exemptions apply to transactions in a buy-back program or financial instrument stabilization measures provided the trading

81. In practice also referred to as information manipulation. Before the MAR came into force, this was prohibited under Art. 5:58 paragraph 1(d) of the Wft.
82. Under Art. 5:58a the AFM was already able to intervene from January 1, 2015 in the event of manipulation of benchmarks. More or less identical text was already included in this article, which has since lapsed. The article was included in the Wft in response to the Libor and Euribor scandals involving the (large-scale) manipulation of these benchmarks.
83. Art. 2 paragraph 1 of the MAR.
84. As referred to in Art. 2 paragraph 1 of the MAR.
85. Art. 2 paragraph 2 of the MAR.
86. *See* AFM booklet 2016/4, pp. 6–7. The same applies as to the prohibition of insider dealing, *see* section 21.2.2 *supra*.
87. For practical examples *see* AFM booklet 2016/5 and *see also* AFM booklet 2006/4 pp. 10–13. In the field of market manipulation, the AFM has published four interpretations (www.afm.nl) namely: 1) manipulation by transactions aimed at influencing price, 2) manipulation by misleading orders and/or transactions, 3) market manipulation in trading on the basis of market orders, and 4) manipulation by means of wash trades. A more detailed specification of market manipulation indicators can be found in Commission Delegated Regulation (EU) 2016/522, *OJEU* 2016, L 88/1.
88. Art. 5 of the MAR.

takes place in accordance with the specified conditions, including with regard to transparency. In addition to the conditions, the MAR sets the objectives which the buy-back programs must fulfill. If these objectives and conditions are not fulfilled, it is not possible to make use of the exception. The second exemption category concerns transactions as part of monetary and public debt management activities.[89]

89. Art. 6 of the MAR.

BIBLIOGRAPHY

Busch 2016
D. Busch, 'Het civiel effect van de Marktmisbruikverordening', *FR* 2016, no. 12, pp. 525-537.

Dinant 2017
J. Dinant, 'De Europese Verordening Marktmisbruik. *Een overzicht van de belangrijkste wijzigingen per 3 juli 2016*', in: C.A. Wielenga et al. (ed.), *Jaarboek Compliance* 2017, Capelle aan den IJssel: Nederlands Compliance Instituut 2017, pp. 341-362.

Doorenbos 2016
D.R. Doorenbos, 'De Verordening marktmisbruik in het economisch strafrecht', *FR* 2016, no. 12, pp. 538-544.

't Hart 2008
F.M.A. 't Hart, 'De klikplicht', in: D.R. Doorenbos, S.C.J.J. Kortmann & M.P. Nieuwe Weme (eds.), *Handboek Marktmisbruik* (Serie Onderneming en Recht, deel 34, tweede druk), Deventer: Kluwer 2008, pp. 299-339.

't Hart 2016
F.M.A. 't Hart, 'Insiders', *FR* 2016, no. 12, pp. 484-492.

Hoff 2011
G.T.J. Hoff, *Openbaarmaking van koersgevoelige informatie* (diss. Nijmegen), Deventer: Kluwer 2011.

Hoff 2016
G.T.J. Hoff, 'Openbaarmaking van voorwetenschap volgens het nieuwe regime van de Verordening marktmisbruik', *FR* 2016, no. 12, pp. 507-524.

Honig 2016
S.L. Honig, 'De Verordening Marktmisbruik: veranderingen per 3 juli 2016', *BB* 2016/60.

Italianer 2008
J. Italianer, 'Gebruik van voorwetenschap', in: D.R. Doorenbos, S.C.J.J. Kortmann & M.P. Nieuwe Weme (eds.), *Handboek Marktmisbruik* (Serie Onderneming en Recht, deel 34, tweede druk), Deventer: Kluwer 2008, pp. 71-98.

Italianer & Dorant 2013
J. Italianer & J.B.S. Dorant, 'Compliance en marktmisbruik', *TvCo* 2013, no. 3, pp. 199-207.

Jennen 2016
B.C.G. Jennen, 'Mededelingsverbod en marktpeilingen', *FR* 2016, no. 12, pp. 493-500.

Langendijk & Wilmink 2016
C.J. Langendijk & A.L. Wilmink, 'Opgelet: nieuwe, verscherpte regels over marktmisbruik. *Vijf belangrijke verplichtingen uit de Verordening marktmisbruik* toegelicht', in: C.A. Wielenga et al. (ed.), *Jaarboek Compliance* 2016, Capelle aan den IJssel: Nederlands Compliance Instituut 2016, pp. 187-222.

Nieuwe Weme & Stevens 2008
M.P. Nieuwe Weme & T.M. Hoff, 'Openbaarmaking van koersgevoelige informatie', in: D.R. Doorenbos, S.C.J.J. Kortmann & M.P. Nieuwe Weme (eds.), *Handboek Marktmisbruik* (Serie Onderneming en Recht series, deel 34, tweede druk), Deventer: Kluwer 2008, pp. 175-275.

Raas 2008
R.P. Raas, 'Marktmanipulatie', in: D.R. Doorenbos, S.C.J.J. Kortmann & M.P. Nieuwe Weme (eds.), *Handboek Marktmisbruik* (Serie Onderneming en Recht, deel 34, tweede druk), Deventer: Kluwer 2008, pp. 141-173.

Schutte 2008
J.J.J. Schutte, 'Meldingsverplichtingen', in: D.R. Doorenbos, S.C.J.J. Kortmann & M.P. Nieuwe Weme (eds.), *Handboek Marktmisbruik* (Serie Onderneming en Recht, deel 34, tweede druk), Deventer: Kluwer 2008, pp. 277-298.

Van der Eerden & Silverentand 2015
F.W.J. van der Eerden & L.J. Silverentand (eds.), *Hoofdlijnen Wft*, Deventer: Wolters Kluwer 2015, pp. 381-418.

Van Straaten & Schouten 2016
M. van Straaten & A. Schouten, 'De reikwijdte van verordening en richtlijn marktmisbruik', *FR* 2016, no. 12, pp. 480-483.

Uitermark & Wilmink 2016
E.M.M. Uitermark & A.L. Wilmink, 'Market Abuse Regulation: de opsporings- en meldingsplicht', *FR* 2016, no. 12, pp. 501-506.

Other references

AFM booklet 2016/1
AFM booklet 'Handel met voorwetenschap', July 2016.

AFM booklet 2016/2
AFM booklet 'Meldingsplicht marktmisbruik', June 2016.

AFM booklet 2016/3
AFM booklet 'Openbaarmaking van voorwetenschap', June 2016.

AFM booklet 2016/4
AFM booklet 'Marktmanipulatie', June 2016.

AFM booklet 2016/5
AFM booklet 'Interpretaties marktmanipulatie. *Enkele praktijkvoorbeelden*', June 2016.

AFM booklet 2016/6
AFM booklet 'Leidraad voor Uitgevende instellingen, bestuurders en commissarissen', June 2016.

AFM booklet 2016/7
AFM booklet 'Marktmisbruikregels gelden ook voor (medewerkers van) instanties in het publieke domein', June 2016.

APPENDIX: LEGAL FRAMEWORK[90]

European

Delegated Regulation for various articles of the MAR

Commission delegated Regulation (EU) 2016/522 of December 17, 2015 supplementing Regulation (EU) No. 596/2014 of the European Parliament and of the Council as regards an exemption for certain third countries public bodies and central banks, the indicators of market manipulation, the disclosure thresholds, the competent authority for notifications of delays, the permission for trading during closed periods and types of notifiable managers' transactions, *OJEU* 2016, L 88/1.

Delegated Regulation for Article 5 of the MAR

Commission delegated Regulation (EU) 2016/1052 of March 8, 2016 supplementing Regulation (EU) No. 596/2014 of the European Parliament and of the Council with regard to regulatory technical standards for the conditions applicable to buy-back programs and stabilization measures, *OJEU* 2016, L 173/34.

Delegated Regulation for Article 11 of the MAR

Commission delegated Regulation (EU) 2016/960 of May 17, 2016 supplementing Regulation (EU) No. 596/2014 of the European Parliament and of the Council with regard to regulatory technical standards for the appropriate arrangements, systems and procedures for disclosing market participants conducting market soundings, *OJEU* 2016, L 160/29.

Delegated Regulation for Article 13 of the MAR

Commission delegated Regulation (EU) 2016/908 of February 26, 2016 supplementing Regulation (EU) No. 596/2014 of the European Parliament and of the Council laying down regulatory technical standards on the criteria, the procedure and the requirements for establishing an accepted market practice and the requirements for maintaining it, terminating it or modifying the conditions for its acceptance, *OJEU* 2016, L 153/3.

Delegated Regulation for Article 16 of the MAR

Commission delegated Regulation (EU) 2016/957 of March 9, 2016 supplementing Regulation (EU) No. 596/2014 of the European Parliament and of the Council with regard to regulatory technical standards for the appropriate arrangements, systems and procedures as well as notification templates to be used for preventing, detecting and reporting abusive practices or suspicious orders or transactions, *OJEU* 2016, L 160/1.

Delegated Regulation for Article 20 of the MAR

Commission delegated Regulation (EU) 2016/958 of March 9, 2016 supplementing Regulation (EU) No. 596/2014 of the European Parliament and of the Council with regard to regulatory technical standards for the technical arrangements for objective presentation of investment recommendations or other information recommending or suggesting an investment strategy and for disclosure of particular interests or indications of conflicts of interest, *OJEU* 2016, L 160/15.

90. According to the state of affairs as at March 12, 2017.

Implementing Regulation for Article 4 of the MAR

Commission implementing Regulation (EU) 2016/378 of March 11, 2016 laying down implementing technical standards with regard to the timing, format and template of the submission of notifications to competent authorities according to Regulation (EU) No. 596/2014 of the European Parliament and of the Council, *OJEU* 2016, L 72/1.

Implementing Regulation for Article 11 of the MAR

Commission implementing Regulation (EU) 2016/959 of May 17, 2016 laying down implementing technical standards for market soundings with regard to the systems and notification templates to be used by disclosing market participants and the format of the records in accordance with Regulation (EU) No. 596/2014 of the European Parliament and of the Council, *OJEU* 2016, L 160/23.

Implementing Regulation for Article 17 of the MAR

Commission implementing Regulation (EU) 2016/1055 of June 29, 2016 laying down implementing technical standards with regard to the technical means for appropriate public disclosure of inside information and for delaying the public disclosure of inside information in accordance with Regulation (EU) No. 596/2014 of the European Parliament and of the Council, *OJEU* 2016, L 173/47.

Implementing Regulation for Article 18 of the MAR

Commission implementing Regulation (EU) 2016/347 of March 10, 2016 laying down implementing technical standards with regard to the precise format of insider lists and for updating insider lists in accordance with Regulation (EU) No. 596/2014 of the European Parliament and of the Council, *OJEU* 2016, L 65/49.

Implementing Regulation for Article 19 of the MAR

Commission implementing Regulation (EU) 2016/523 of March 10, 2016 laying down implementing technical standards with regard to the format and template for notification and public disclosure of managers' transactions in accordance with Regulation (EU) No. 596/2014 of the European Parliament and of the Council, *OJEU* 2016, L 88/19.

MAR

Regulation (EU) No. 596/2014 of the European Parliament and the Council of April 16, 2014 on market abuse (market abuse regulation) and repealing Directive 2003/6/EC of the European Parliament and of the Council and Commission Directives 2003/124/EC, 2003/125/EC and 2004/72/EC, *OJEU* 2014, L 173/1.

MAD

Directive 2003/6/EC of the European Parliament and of the Council of January 28, 2003 on insider dealing and market manipulation (market abuse), *OJEU* 2003, L 96/16.

MAD II

Directive 2014/57/EU of the European Parliament and of the Council of April 16, 2014 on criminal sanctions for market abuse (market abuse directive), *OJEU* 2014, L 173/179.

The Netherlands[91]

Decree on the Implementation of the Market Abuse Regulation (draft)[92]
Decree of ... implementing regulation (EU) No. 596/2014 of the European Parliament and of the Council of the European Union of April 16, 2014 on market abuse (OJEU 2014, L 173) (Decree on the Implementation of the Market Abuse Regulation), *Bulletin of Acts and Decrees* 2017, ...

Decree on the Implementation of EU Regulations
Decree of June 23, 2016 regulating the amendment of the Decree on the Implementation of EU Regulations to implement Regulation (EU) No. 596/2014 of the European Parliament and of the Council of April 16, 2014 on market abuse (Market Abuse Regulation) and repealing Directive 2003/6/EC of the European Parliament and of the Council and Directives 2003/124, 2003/125/EC and 2004/72/EC of the Commission, *Bulletin of Acts and Decrees* 2016, 247.

Market Abuse Regulation and Directive Implementation Act
Act of July 15, 2016 amending the Financial Supervision Act, the Consumer Protection Enforcement Act, the Economic Offences Act and the Code of Criminal Procedure in connection with the implementation of Regulation (EU) No. 596/2014 of the European Parliament and of the Council of the European Union of April 16, 2014 on market abuse (OJ 2014, L 173) and Directive No. 2014/57/EU of the European Parliament and of the Council of the European Union of April 16, 2014 on criminal sanctions for market abuse (OJ 2014, L 173) (Market Abuse Regulation and Directive Implementation Act), *Bulletin of Acts and Decrees* 2016, 297.

91. The remaining provisions of the Wft and the Decree on Market Abuse as promulgated in the Wft are not included in this list. Reference is made to the statements concerning the legal framework in section 21.1 *supra*.
92. The Decree on the Implementation of the Market Abuse Regulation was still going through Parliament at the time of writing this chapter. In order to guarantee (continued) consistent introduction of the MAR and MAD II, however, this decree is expected to be published shortly.

22. Competition

M.J. Osse

22.1 WHAT IS COMPETITION LAW AND WHY IS IT RELEVANT FOR COMPLIANCE OFFICERS?

Generally speaking, the main purpose of competition law systems is 'to maximize welfare'. Whether this should be 'total welfare' or 'consumer welfare' remains a subject of extensive discussions.[1] Often, the underlying idea is that in more competitive markets, prices for products and services are lower, quality is relatively higher and there is more choice and more innovation than in less competitive markets. It may seem contradictory, but competition rules actually interfere in the market to help the market function properly by overcoming market imperfections and failures. As a result, competition law should help to maintain or restore the level playing field and ensure effective and fair competition on the market.

The definition of 'compliance' used by the postgraduate program in Compliance and Integrity Management at VU University Amsterdam is: 'Observance of external (international and national) laws and regulations, as well as internal norms and procedures, to protect the integrity of the organization, its management and employees with the aim of preventing and controlling risks and the possible damage resulting from these compliance and integrity risks.' Where does competition law fit in this definition? Competition laws are external, national and international laws and regulations that encompass a very high-risk level for the organization in the case of non-compliance. Non-compliance may not only result in extremely high fines for the organization, but may also lead to personal fines for employees or even jail sentences in some jurisdictions. Moreover, even the investigation of a potential infringement of competition law in itself can be disruptive for the organization. These investigations often run for long periods, sometimes in multiple jurisdictions, creating legal and financial uncertainty and requiring substantial manpower, financial

1. For the economics of competition law, *see* various economic theories and possible goals of competition law in: A. Jones & B. Sufrin (eds), *EU Competition Law – Text, Cases, and Materials* (sixth edition), Oxford: Oxford University Press 2016, pp. 1–90.

input and control, effort and attention within the organization. This can also easily lead to an internal conflict of interest between the organization and specific (often high-ranking) individuals within the organization. Further on in this chapter, the potential sanctions and risks will be discussed in more detail.

Given this high risk level, it is very important that a compliance officer has competition law on his radar. However, in practice, the application of competition laws is often regarded as complicated. The legal assessment depends to a large extent on the market power of the organization involved, which requires a proper assessment of the product/service markets and geographical markets in which the specific organization is active. In other words, the actual risk level and specific risks involved are, to a large extent, dependent on the organization itself. In-depth knowledge of the activities of the organization, its suppliers, customers, competitors and memberships of trade associations or groupings in the market is required. This will automatically require a 'translation' of the applicable external competition laws into more condensed and practical guidance within the organization. In general, this does not mean that the compliance officer needs to know all the ins and outs of the applicable competition laws, but it does mean that the compliance officer has the obligation to create a certain amount of trust and awareness within the organization. The focus should be on the managerial level, in particular the sales and procurement managers, to identify the potential risks at the earliest stage possible and react appropriately to signals from all levels within the organization. However, signals from outside the organization should also not be ignored.

22.2 COMPETITION LAW IN THE EU – AN OUTLINE

Worldwide, competition law is enforced in many jurisdictions, usually with their own set of competition rules. In this section, we will take a closer look at the EU, where competition law has a 'supranational' status. We will review the interaction between the Commission and national competition authorities within the EU, in particular in the Netherlands.

The entity we today call the EU was originally founded by the Treaty of Rome in 1957.[2] Today, the treaties governing the EU are the Treaty on the European Union (TEU),[3] the Treaty on the Functioning of the European Union (TFEU)[4] and the Charter of Fundamental Rights of the European Union (Charter).[5] Competition policy is part of the '*acquis communautaire*': the accumulated legislation, legal acts and case law of the Court of Justice, which constitute the body of EU law. The *acquis* has supranational power, which means that Member States are obliged to comply with the *acquis* and it overrules national laws that conflict with the *acquis*.

2. Treaty of Rome, officially the Treaty establishing the European Economic Community (TEEC), signed on March 25, 1957, effective on January 1, 1958.
3. Treaty on the European Union, February 7, 1992, consolidated version 2016, *OJEU* C 202, 2016; 12016M/TXT.
4. Treaty on the Functioning of the European Union, March 25, 1957, Consolidated version 2016, *OJEU* C 202, 2016; 12016E/TXT.
5. Charter of Fundamental Rights of the European Union, *OJEU* C 202, 2016, pp. 391–407, 12016P/TXT.

In the EU, competition law is considered a vital part of the internal market. The internal market is based on the 'four freedoms', which are the free movement of persons, goods, services and capital. The internal market creates a single economic area establishing free competition between undertakings.

In principle, competition law is enforced and developed by the European Commission, which has the power to investigate potential infringements and take binding decisions vis-à-vis undertakings. The Commission's powers are embedded in public laws. In the European Commission, one Commissioner is assigned responsibility for the policy area of competition in the form of the Directorate-General Competition (DG COMP), which is managed by a Director-General. The DG COMP policy areas are cartels, abuse of dominance, mergers and state aid. Articles 101 and 102 TFEU contain the substantive laws on competition. These articles are directly applicable in the Member States and must be applied by the national courts. In addition to the provisions in the TFEU, a number of regulations are relevant for competition law. Important regulations are the Merger Regulation[6] and Regulation 1/2003. Other regulations deal with particular types of conduct, with specific sectors or are of a procedural nature. There are also numerous relevant non-regulatory documents, such as guidelines and notices. In these non-regulatory documents, the Commission often provides an insight into the way in which it assesses certain types of conduct and into procedural matters.

Regulation 1/2003 decentralizes the enforcement of EU competition laws related to cartels (Article 101 TFEU) and abuse of dominance (Article 102 TFEU). As a result, both the European Commission and national competition authorities can enforce Articles 101 and 102 TFEU. They work together in the European Competition Network (ECN).[7] Often national competition authorities will impose fines based on both their national competition laws and European competition laws, if the alleged infringement may influence the national market or parts of it.

For example, in the Netherlands the national competition authority, the ACM, imposed a fine totaling EUR 65.9 million on several Dutch, Belgian and German flour producers in 2010.[8] According to the ACM, they infringed both the Dutch[9] and the European cartel prohibition[10] by entering into several anti-competitive agreements. They allocated customers to each other and as a result were able to maintain higher prices. In addition, a competitor that did not take part in the cartel was acquired by the other flour producers and taken out of the market to reduce capacity. Their cartel had a share of approximately 90 per cent of the Dutch flour market. The highest

6. Council Regulation (EC) No. 139/2004 of January 20, 2004 on the control of concentrations between undertakings (the EC Merger Regulation), *OJEU* 2004, L 24, pp. 1–22.
7. http://ec.europa.eu/competition/ecn/index_en.html.
8. ACM Case 6306/Meel, December 16, 2010. The fines were lowered in the ACM decision of March 14, 2012, after objections were raised. In subsequent cases the ACM fined private equity companies, marking the first time that antitrust liability was extended to companies investing in one of the cartel partners. The District Court in Rotterdam recently confirmed the parent-liability assessment of the ACM (Case ROT 15/6572, January 26, 2017, ECLI:NL:RBROT:2017:588).
9. Art. 6 Mw.
10. Art. 101 TFEU.

Dutch administrative court (the Trade and Industry Appeals Tribunal) recently upheld most of the decisions.[11]

A compliance officer should have at least a basic knowledge of anti-competitive conduct, in order to recognize when action or further assessment is required. The following non-exhaustive sections on cartels, abuse of dominance and merger filings explain some basic features of these infringements.

22.3 CARTELS

In principle, under Article 101(1) TFEU, all agreements and concerted practices between undertakings and associations of undertakings which have as their object or effect the prevention, restriction and distortion of competition within the internal market are prohibited. The system operates on the basis that this type of conduct is prohibited, unless an exemption applies. Put simply: 'prohibited, unless'. First, I will explain some basic concepts that a practitioner needs to understand to appreciate the broad application of the competition rules. I will then dig deeper into the type of conduct which is prohibited under the cartel prohibition, before taking a closer look at the main exemptions.

Under competition law the concept of an 'undertaking' is different from the concept of legal personality under corporate law. Undertaking is much broader, as it 'encompasses every entity engaged in an economic activity, regardless of the legal status of the entity and the way it is financed'.[12] An economic activity is regarded as the offering of goods and services on the market, which could (at least in theory) make a profit. Tasks of purely public interest are excluded. The formal purpose of the entity or whether profit is actually made is not relevant. This means that a private practitioner, a public institution and a commercial entity may all fall within the concept of 'undertaking', depending on the nature of their activities. Employees are considered to be not directly engaged in an economic activity, as they perform labor and are therefore not included in the concept of an undertaking.

Furthermore, it is important to understand that the 'undertaking' can encompass more than one entity (legal persons, natural persons, agents, etc.) that is considered one 'single economic unit'. Basically, the 'undertaking' entails every economic activity under the same 'decisive influence'. The relevant question to determine the size of the undertaking is which 'entity' has decisive influence over the commercial policy of other 'entities' and is therefore able to determine the market behavior of the others. For a group of undertakings with one parent company and only 100% subsidiaries, the presumption[13] automatically applies that this whole group, as a single economic unit, is one 'undertaking'. Supposed that in such a group one subsidiary is involved in a cartel infringement, the parent company can then be held jointly and severally liable for the infringement. However, with joint ventures the assessment may become more complex and may even have an unexpected outcome, if one is not fully aware

---

11. *See* CBb case 14/581, July 14, 2016, ECLI:NL:CBB:2016:185.
12. Case C-41/90 *Höfner and Elser v. Macroton GmbH*, April 23, 1991; European Court Reports 1991 I-01979, paragraph 21.
13. Case C-97/08 *Akzo Nobel v. Commission*, September 10, 2009; European Court Reports I-8237, paragraphs 59–63.

that the decisive influence is not equal to the shareholding percentage. In practice, a 20% shareholder in a joint venture may have decisive influence if it has certain veto rights determining the commercial policy of the joint venture.

In line with the concept of 'undertaking', the concept of 'association of undertakings' relates to several 'single undertakings' that are active in an association. A clear example is a trade association.

Another concept that is important for an understanding of cartel infringements is the concept of an 'agreement'. This concept is much broader than a valid and binding contract between two or more parties. In the case *Bayer AG v. Commission* the court stated: 'It follows that the concept of an agreement within the meaning of Article 85(1) of the Treaty [currently 101 TFEU], as interpreted by the case-law, centres around the existence of a concurrence of wills between at least two parties, the form in which it is manifested being unimportant so long as it constitutes the faithful expression of the parties' intention.'[14] The court clarified that it is sufficient that the undertakings in question should have expressed their joint intention to conduct themselves on the market in a specific way.[15] This includes written and oral agreements, whether or not legally binding, like gentlemen's agreements. However, when an undertaking has adopted a genuinely unilateral measure, it falls outside the scope of Article 101 TFEU. But if there is coordinated behavior that does not fall within the category of an 'agreement' it may still be considered a 'concerted practice', to which Article 101 TFEU equally applies. According to established case-law, a concerted practice constitutes a form of coordination between undertakings that knowingly substitutes practical cooperation for the risks of competition.

The *T-Mobile* case shows that a concerted practice can be established if only one single meeting between competitors takes place.[16] The European Court of Justice ruled: 'An exchange of information between competitors is tainted with an anti-competitive object if the exchange is capable of removing uncertainties concerning the intended conduct of the participating undertakings.' Depending on the subject-matter of the concerted action and the particular market conditions, a single meeting may be sufficient to induce an anti-competitive object and infringe competition law.

What happened? On June 13, 2001, the only five operators in the Netherlands with their own mobile telephone network at that time held a meeting. Access to the market for mobile telecommunication services was possible only through the conclusion of an agreement with one or more of the five existing operators. At that meeting one of the participants unilaterally informed its competitors of its intended reduction of standard dealer remunerations for postpaid subscriptions on or about September 1, 2001. Afterwards, on or about September 1, 2001, an adjustment to standard dealer remuneration by the operators actually took place. The ACM's predecessor, and later the European Court of Justice, applied a presumption that the other operators had taken account of the confidential information exchanged and that there was a causal connection between the concerted practice and the conduct

14. Case T-41/96, *Bayer AG v. Commission*, October 26, 2000, European Court Reports II-3383, paragraph 69.
15. Ibid., paragraph 67.
16. Case C-8/08, *T-Mobile Netherlands BV v. Raad van bestuur van de Nederlandse Mededingingsautoriteit*, June 4, 2009, European Court Reports I-4529.

of the undertaking on that market, even though the concerted action was the result of one single meeting.

More guidance can be obtained from the Advocate-General in this case, who stated that:

> 'each economic operator must determine independently the policy which he intends to adopt on the common market. That requirement of independence precludes any direct or indirect contact between economic operators by which an undertaking influences the conduct on the market of its competitors or discloses to them its decisions or deliberations concerning its own conduct on the market, if as a result conditions of competition may apply which do not correspond to the normal conditions of the market in question. ... That applies a fortiori when the exchange of information concerns a highly concentrated oligopolistic market. ... It is irrelevant in that connection whether only one undertaking unilaterally informs its competitors of its intended market behaviour or whether all participating undertakings inform each other of their respective deliberations and intentions. Simply when one undertaking alone breaks cover and reveals to its competitors confidential information concerning its future commercial policy, that reduces for all participants uncertainty as to the future operation of the market and introduces the risk of a diminution in competition and of collusive behaviour between them.'[17]

Cartels with an anti-competitive object are considered graver and are more easily proven by a competition authority than cartels with an anti-competitive effect. In the 'by object' situation, the authority can apply the assumption that the anti-competitive conduct is harmful for competition and prohibited, whereas in the 'by effect' situation the authority has to prove the actual harmful effect before it can decide that an infringement took place. This makes a huge difference for the defense.

Prohibited and never exempted, for example, are agreements or concerted practices between competitors that contain or result in:

- price-fixing (this includes all elements of pricing, such as fixing surcharges, fixing rebates etc.);
- allocation of markets or customers;
- production limitation;
- collusive tendering or bid-rigging (coordination on pricing or conditions in relation to (public) tenders).

Prohibited and almost never exempted are agreements or concerted practices between undertakings that, although not competitors, are active at different levels of the production or distribution chain (e.g. supplier-buyer) and agree on resale-price maintenance. However, maximum or recommended resale prices are permitted, provided they do not result in a fixed or minimum resale price.

The types of conduct mentioned here are considered 'hardcore' infringements and are always prohibited. There are, however, many types of conduct which may – in

17. Opinion of Advocate General Kokott, delivered on February 19, 2009, Case C-8/08, *T-Mobile Netherlands BV and Others*, reference for a preliminary ruling from the College van Beroep voor het bedrijfsleven (Netherlands), ECLI:EU:C:2009:110.

principle – be anti-competitive, but which may be exempted from the cartel prohibition. Most important is Article 101(3) TFEU, which provides a general exemption if four criteria are met. These criteria are such that ultimately the pro-competitive effects overrule the anti-competitive effects, such that the anti-competitive conduct can be justified. In short, i) the conduct must result in an improvement of production or distribution or technical or economic progress; ii) consumers must obtain a fair share of the benefits; iii) the anticompetitive impact must be limited to what is indispensable to achieve the benefits; and iv) competition may not be eliminated. In order to rely on this general exemption, the undertaking has the burden of proof that the agreement fulfills the criteria of Article 101(3) during the full term of the agreement. In practice, this is an important downside having regard to the legal uncertainty and the high risks involved.

Legal certainty can be obtained by relying on 'block exemptions'. The European Commission created 'safe harbors' where the assumption applies that the conduct complies with the exemption of Article 101(3) TFEU. Block exemptions exist, for example, on technology transfer agreements, specialization agreements, R&D agreements and vertical agreements. The agreement must fully comply with the scope and criteria of the block exemption; otherwise the assumption of the safe harbor does not apply. Often the market shares of the parties are important in establishing whether the agreement can fall within the scope of the block exemption. For example, the vertical block exemption can only be applied 'on condition that the market share held by the supplier does not exceed 30% of the relevant market on which it sells the contract goods or services and the market share held by the buyer does not exceed 30% of the relevant market on which it purchases the contract goods or services'.[18] If the market shares are below the threshold and the criteria of the block exemption are met, it is assumed that the agreement will not harm competition and Article 101(1) does not apply.

Compliance officers should be vigilant that cartels can exist in a wide variety of markets and can be active and unnoticed for a long period of time. Only recently, the European Commission imposed a record fine of EUR 2.9 billion on truck manufacturers. The Commission found that several truck makers had colluded for 14 years on truck pricing and on passing on the costs of compliance with stricter emission rules.

22.4 ABUSE OF A DOMINANT POSITION

Under Article 102 TFEU 'any abuse by one or more undertakings of a dominant position within the internal market or in a substantial part of it shall be prohibited as incompatible with the internal market in so far as it may affect trade between Member States.'

Article 102 TFEU only applies to undertakings with a dominant position. If no dominance exists, the prohibition does not apply. Dominance exists if an undertaking has the ability to prevent effective competition on the relevant market through its economic strengths, as it can behave, to an appreciable extent, independently of its

18. Art. 3 paragraph 1 of the Commission Regulation (EU) No. 330/2010 of April 20, 2010 on the application of Article 101(3) of the Treaty on the Functioning of the European Union to categories of vertical agreements and concerted practices, *OJEU* 2010, L 102/1.

competitors, customers and ultimately its consumers.[19] Dominance is presumed to exist when an undertaking has a market share of 50% or more. However, even with lower market shares dominance may still exist, especially if there are barriers to market entry, such as access to essential facilities (networks), financial resources or particular intellectual property rights. On the other hand, market shares of over 50% dominance may not exist, if, for example, sufficient countervailing buyer power exists. In the latter case, the undertaking cannot act independently of its customers. Determination of the market share is therefore very important. However, in practice it is not that easy to establish an exact market share and the outcome from economic reports may differ greatly. This makes the assessment under Article 102 TFEU a protracted affair.

A compliance officer should be aware that if the undertaking he is working for has a dominant position, a more severe regime of compliance should be applied. Dominant parties have a special responsibility to maintain competition. Being dominant is not prohibited, but abuse of the dominance is. Market conduct that is acceptable in the case of an ordinary undertaking in the market may not be permitted in the case of an undertaking with dominance. Such conduct may be considered 'abuse' within the meaning of Article 102 TFEU. The concept of 'abuse' covers a wide range of conduct.

Abuse may occur, for example, if excessive prices are charged; if prices are (temporarily) set at a loss-making level to prevent market entrance; or if one refuses to supply input that is indispensable for competition in an ancillary market. Also, the tying of one product to another product, although it has objectively no connection to the contract product and is actually tied to foreclose that market, is considered abuse. This played a part in one of the Microsoft cases, where Windows Media Player[20] was preinstalled with the purchase of the Windows operating system.

22.5 MERGERS AND ACQUISITIONS

In many jurisdictions, merger filings are required *before* an acquisition, merger or the establishment of a joint venture may take place, if certain thresholds are met. Often, these thresholds are related to the turnovers of the companies involved. In the Netherlands, notification to the ACM is required if the combined worldwide turnovers of the undertakings[21] concerned are EUR 150 million or more *and* at least two undertakings concerned have turnover of at least EUR 30 million in the Netherlands. At the EU level, notification must be made to the European Commission, which applies much higher thresholds. In some jurisdictions, market share thresholds apply instead of turnover thresholds.

Compliance requires an adequate assessment – at an early stage – of the notification requirements in the relevant jurisdictions. Timing is of the essence, as in general

19. Case 27/76, *United Brands Company and United Brands Continentaal BV v. Commission of the European Communities*, Judgment of the Court of February 14, 1978, European Court Reports 1978-00207, paragraphs 64–66, ECLI:EU:C:1978:22.
20. Case T-201/04, *Microsoft v. Commission*, September 17, 2007, European Court Reports 2007 II-03601, ECLI:EU:T:2007:289.
21. The concept of undertaking applies, so – as explained above – the turnover of each business group must be taken into account.

the desired transaction cannot be enforced until approval of all the relevant competition authorities has been obtained. Not acting in accordance with this requirement is called 'gun-jumping' and can result in severe consequences such as a high fine.

22.6 SANCTIONS AND RISKS

Competition law is a subject of compliance because the risks involved are high.

First, high fines may be imposed by competition authorities. Often, the maximum fine for an undertaking amounts to 10% of the net turnover of the business group in the preceding financial year. For trade associations, 10% of the joint turnover of the members may be taken into account as a maximum fine. In several jurisdictions, such as the Netherlands, personal fines may be imposed up to EUR 900,000. In some jurisdictions, jail sentences may be imposed.

Secondly, an agreement that is not in compliance with competition law may be fully or partially null and void. This may have serious consequences for the business. For example, if similar arrangements were made with several distributors. In the case of gun-jumping, an authority may order the parties to unwind the illegal transaction.

Thirdly, more and more victims of cartels are initiating civil damages claim actions, and victims are invited to assign their debt to a claims vehicle. A Directive on antitrust damage actions[22] is implemented in national legislations and enforced to facilitate claims for compensation. In the past, it was often difficult for victims to bring a successful claim for damages, as there were many obstacles, such as the burden of proof that the harm and the damage was caused by the cartel infringement. The Directive establishes the rebuttable presumption that cartels cause harm and a final decision by a national competition authority constitutes full proof before a civil court in the same jurisdiction that the infringement occurred. Victims can claim full compensation for the harm suffered, which includes actual loss, loss of profit and interest. Victims have at least one year from the final infringement decision to bring damage actions. Furthermore, any participant in an infringement is in principle jointly and severally liable to the victims for the whole harm caused by the infringement. However, this will not apply to infringers who obtained immunity under a leniency program. These parties (who obtained immunity) will only be required to compensate their own customers. Needless to say, this may result in high civil damages claims, while it also prolongs the negative impact of the cartel on the undertaking.

Fourthly, in external relations the impact of an infringement of competition law may also be high. In some industries, the reputational damage may harm business considerably, over a long period of time. Sometimes, parties are not allowed to take part in tenders or are excluded from certain contracts. In many competition law infringements, a leniency applicant triggers the competition authority's investigation. A first leniency applicant is often granted immunity from fines. While immunity is clearly advantageous for the leniency applicant, it will also potentially harm its relationships with others on the market.

22. Directive 2014/104/EU of the European Parliament and of the Council of November 26, 2014 on certain rules governing actions for damages under national law for infringements of the competition law provisions of the Member States and of the European Union (Text with EEA relevance), *OJEU* 2014, L 349, pp. 1-19.

22.7 HOW TO LIMIT RISKS – COMPLIANCE TIPS

How can risks be limited, considering that resources and time are often limited? Some guidance is provided below.

Tip 1. Start with an inventory of the real risks related to the business activities[23] and the markets in which the activities take place. Relevant questions are: in which product/service markets and which geographical markets is the business active? How many competitors, customers and suppliers are there? Does the company have any cooperation agreements with other parties, and is there a need to cooperate? What is the level of market regulation? Have there been prior investigations or infringement decisions by competition authorities? In addition, the position of certain employees within the business may encompass more risks (e.g. sales managers, procurement managers and employees who attend meetings of trade associations).

Tip 2. It is better to be informed and to be informed at an early stage. It is essential to create a climate of trust within the undertaking, and to be clear about the 'hotline' in case of issues or concerns regarding competition law. Preferably, the hotline should be the compliance officer. The compliance officer must make sure that the information is protected as from the first moment, as it may contain incriminating information. Furthermore, a speedy follow-up of hotline information is essential.

Tip 3. Compliance should be carried out from the top. As always, the higher the rank the better the example should be. The persons in the positions with the highest risk should be trained in competition compliance and should be encouraged to apply this training in their daily business within their teams. After awareness has been created within the undertaking, it should be clear that sanctions may be imposed in the case of non-compliance. However, dismissal should not be the first step, as the interests of individuals and the undertaking may need to be kept in line.

Tip 4. Set up a tailor-made competition compliance program. Apart from appointing a compliance officer, the compliance program should at least entail permanent education, e.g. an annual competition compliance course related to day-to-day business issues for employees in high-risk positions. This annual occasion can be used to create a trusted environment, in small groups, to discuss issues encountered in the business. Also, create a compliance policy, internal and external rules of conduct that are carried from the top and applied by the top. In addition, a competition compliance manual can help to inform employees what behavior is acceptable or unacceptable under competition law. Be transparent within the undertaking about sanctions in the case of non-compliance. Draw up dawn raid instructions for the reception, containing contact persons with contact details, and a script for the relevant persons, including the line of responsibilities and required actions.

It is a cliché, but when it comes to compliance with competition laws, it is actually better to be safe than sorry.

23. Keep in mind that the wide concept of 'undertaking' applies, as explained earlier in this chapter.

Index

D